ENVIRONMENTAL LIABILITIES

Environmental Liabilities

by

Brian Jones
Consultant, Herbert Smith, London

and

Neil Parpworth
De Montfort University, Leicester

Shaw & Sons

Shaw's
Since 1750

Published by
Shaw & Sons Limited
Shaway House
21 Bourne Park
Bourne Road
Crayford
Kent DA1 4BZ

www.shaws.co.uk

© Shaw & Sons Limited 2004

Published February 2004

ISBN 0 7219 1640 6

A CIP catalogue record for this book is available from the
British Library

Printed and bound in Great Britain by
Antony Rowe Limited, Chippenham

SUMMARY OF CONTENTS

CONTENTS

Chapter 10 – OFFENCES IN THE CONTEXT OF WASTE

Part III: Administrative Liabilities

Chapter 11 – STATUTORY NUISANCE: THE SUBSTANTIVE LAW

Chapter 12 – STATUTORY NUISANCE: PROCEDURAL MATTERS

PREFACE

The title of this book should be reasonably self-explanatory. The focus is on various forms of "liability" which may arise under English law in the context of environmental harm.

The notion of "liability" is quite broadly construed, covering liability to civil remedy by way of damages or an injunction (Part 1 – Civil Liability), liability to criminal prosecution (Part 2 – Criminal Liability), and liability to administrative direction to take action (or to pay costs incurred by a public body in taking such action) (Part 3 – Administrative Liabilities). It is hoped that by its exclusive focus on these issues the book will be distinctive in its contribution to the literature on Environmental Law.

The emphasis of the book is very much upon the law as it presently exists in England and Wales. Nevertheless, it has been felt appropriate to include (in the final chapter) an account of progress at EU level towards a framework Directive on liability for damage to the environment. It remains too early to know whether, when, or in what precise form such a Directive may be adopted. However, at the time of writing there is good reason to think that agreement on the Commission's proposal of early 2002 may be reached in the first half of 2004; and also that such agreement will be to a text not differing markedly from the mid-2003 Common Position of the Council (upon which text our chapter has been written).

The chapters which follow represent our understanding of the law at the start of November 2003. The subsequent decision of the House of Lords in *Transco plc* v *Stockport Metropolitan Borough Council* is, however, referred to briefly in Chapter 6. To our great relief the general tenor of the Law Lords' statements about the scope of liability under the rule in *Rylands* v *Fletcher* proved, upon examination, to be quite consistent with the text, which at that stage was at page proof stage. The decision of the House of Lords in *Marcic* v *Thames Water* (4th December 2003), overturning the Court of Appeal's ruling in favour of the claimant, came however too late for proper treatment in the main text. We set out overleaf a summary of the House of Lords' decision, and have provided appropriate cross-references to that summary within the main text. We have also been able to include two further recent developments. First, on page xx, is a summary of the report *Trends in Environmental Sentencing in England & Wales* which is relevant to material covered in Chapter 7 and, secondly, a brief note on the European Parliament's Second Reading vote on 17th December 2003 appears on page xxii, updating Chapter 15 and confirming expectations suggested therein.

The authors wish to put on record their thanks to Shaw & Sons for the very efficient way in which the text has been prepared for publication; and, in particular, to Crispin Williams for his patience and understanding: the book having been written at a time when he believed both authors to have been focusing on other projects for Shaws.

Brian Jones and Neil Parpworth

Update on *Marcic* v *Thames Water Utilities Ltd*
[2003] UKHL 66; [2003] All ER (D) 89 Dec *(see below, pp. 102-107)*

On 4th December 2003 the House of Lords unanimously allowed Thames Water's appeal, finding against the claimant as regards both his common law cause of action and also his action based on the Human Rights Act 1998.

Their Lordships emphasised that, in order to understand the scope of Thames' obligations and liabilities, it was essential to consider the statutory context within which it exercised its water and sewerage functions.

A fundamentally important feature of the current legislation[1] was that the exercise of water and sewerage functions by the privatised water and sewerage undertakers is subject to supervision and control by the Director General of Water Services, the water industry "regulator". A notable aspect of such supervision and control is the Act's provision for the making of enforcement orders.[2] These provide a means by which the DGWS may enforce the obligations of sewerage companies. Indeed, the matter is one of "duty":[3] where the DGWS considers a water company to be contravening statutory obligations,[4] he or she must make an enforcement order, which the company must obey.[5] Furthermore, this obligation to obey the enforcement order is expressly stated to be a "duty owed to any person who may be affected by contravention of the order".[6] Accordingly, a breach of the duty to obey an enforcement notice will give rise to a civil action on the part of any persons who suffer loss or damage thereby.[7] By way of *quid pro quo* for this action for breach of the duty to comply with an enforcement notice, the Act provides that, in situations where the enforcement order is applicable, the availability of other remedies is limited. Section 18(8) provides that in such a situation:

> "... the only [other] remedy ... shall be those for which express provision is made by or under any enactment and those that are available in respect of that act or omission otherwise than by virtue of its constituting such a contravention."

Turning to the substantive obligations imposed on sewerage undertakings, their Lordships noted that section 94 imposes substantial duties to provide and maintain public sewers so as to ensure that land is effectively drained. Section 94(4) provides for this obligation to be enforceable by the DGWS by the contravention notice procedure. In consequence, in the words of Lord Nicholls, who gave the leading speech:

> "A person who sustains loss or damage as a result of a sewerage

---

[1] The Water Industry Act 1991, consolidating earlier legislation.
[2] Sections 18-22.
[3] Subject to the exceptions within section 19; e.g. trivial contraventions, cases where the company is already putting matters right, cases where compliance would put at risk "return on capital".
[4] Under section 18.
[5] Section 18(5).
[6] Section 22.
[7] The action is subject to a "due diligence" defence on the part of the company.

undertaker's contravention of [section 94] has no direct remedy in respect of the contravention."[8]

Such a person may bring an action for damages only where (i) an enforcement order has been made by the DGWS,[9] (ii) that order has not been complied with, and (iii) that non-compliance has caused the individual loss or damage.

In the case under appeal no such enforcement order had been made by the DGWS in relation to the inadequate drainage of the claimant's property. It followed, according to Lord Nicholls, that:

> "in advancing claims based on common law nuisance and under the Human Rights Act 1998 Mr Marcic [was seeking] to sidestep the statutory enforcement code."[10]

Marcic was asserting a right to do so by reference to the wording of the final part of section 18(8), under which the enforcement order procedure was not to be an exclusive remedy where the claimant's cause of action exists separately (i.e. in tort and under the HRA 1998) from the contravention of the statutory requirement to which the enforcement notice procedure applied.

On the basis that Marcic's claim was not defeated by the *express* language of the Act, their Lordships considered whether the Act should be regarded as *implicitly* limiting the field of operation of common law actions.

Lord Nicholls noted a clear line of authority which, in his view, suggested that such implication was proper. Reference was made, for example, to Lord Esher's statement in *Robinson v Workington Corporation*.[11]

> "[I]f a duty is imposed by statute which but for the statute would not exist, and a remedy for default or breach of that duty is provided by the statute which creates the duty, that is the only remedy."[12]

But for Lord Nicholls the implications properly to be drawn from the statutory scheme involved rather more than this. In his view it was a proper inference from the statutory scheme that the court should define the very ambit of common law liability so that the rules of nuisance should not be regarded as providing a remedy which could, in turn, be argued to be actionable notwithstanding section 18(8) or the principle laid down by Lord Esher.

Lord Nicholls explained:

> "Since sewerage undertakers have no control over the volume of water

---

[8] At para. 21 of the judgment.

[9] Lord Nicholls adverted to the possibility that an individual frustrated by the unwillingness of the DGWS to make a contravention order might in an appropriate case bring judicial review proceedings in respect of that decision.

[10] At para. 22.

[11] [1897] 1 QB 619. Note that this statement represents no broader an implied exclusion than that contained in section 18(8) of the 1991 Act. It applies in relation to duties which apart from the statute do not exist. Marcic's claim was that the breach of section 94 was also, and separately, a breach of his common law and HRA 1998 rights.

[12] At 621.

entering their sewerage systems it would be surprising if Parliament intended that whenever sewer flooding occurs, every householder whose property was affected can sue ... On the contrary it is abundantly clear that one important purpose of the enforcement scheme in the 1991 Act is that individual householders should not be able to launch proceedings in respect of failure to build sewers. When flooding occurs the first enforcement step under the statute is that the Director ... will consider whether to make an enforcement order. He will look at the position of the individual householder, but in the context of the wider considerations spelled out in the statute ... The existence of a parallel common law right ... would set at nought the statutory scheme. It would effectively supplant the regulatory role the Director was intended to discharge ..."[13]

Accordingly, it was held that the cause of action at common law having been impliedly excluded by the 1991 Act, there was therefore no cause of action separate from the alleged breaches of section 94 which the claimant could pursue outside the enforcement notice procedure.

Very much the same approach was adopted to the claim under the Human Rights Act 1998 (relating to Art 8 of the Convention, and Art 1 of the First Protocol). The House noted that, in view of its understanding of the statutory scheme, the question to be answered was not whether Thames Water had as a public authority conducted itself so as to have invaded the claimant's Convention rights, but whether the statutory scheme (described above) met the requirements of Art 8 and Art 1 Protocol 1.

For Lord Nicholls the key to the scheme's conformity with the Convention was that it struck what was to him a "reasonable balance". It imposed broad duties on undertakers, but left enforcement to a regulator entrusted with exercising his or her functions with a view to balancing the interests of customers as a whole (those affected by flooding who would benefit from enforcement, and those not so affected who would face potentially higher water charges without securing personal benefit). As such the scheme established was Convention-compliant.

It was certainly the case that the claimant had in a number of respects been ill-served by Thames Water. Lord Nicholls commented, for example, that:

"At times Thames Water handled Mr Marcic's complaint in a tardy and insensitive fashion."[14]

However, it could not be said that it was the *statutory scheme* which had caused the claimant his problems with Thames Water. Indeed, the claimant had failed to take advantage of that scheme by his very choice of seeking to sidestep it by seeking a separate civil law remedy.

Lord Hoffmann's approach on this point is illuminating. He commented:

"The Convention does not accord absolute protection to property or even

---

[13] At para. 35.

[14] At para. 43.

to residential premises. It requires a fair balance to be struck between the interests of persons whose homes and properties are affected and the interests of other people, such as customers and the general public. National institutions, and particularly the national legislature, are accorded a broad discretion in choosing the solution appropriate to their own society or creating the machinery for doing so. There is no reason why Parliament should not entrust such decisions to an independent regulator such as the Director. He is a public authority within the meaning of the 1998 Act and has a duty to act in accordance with Convention rights. If (which there is no reason to suppose) he has exceeded the broad margin of discretion allowed by the Convention, Mr Marcic will have his remedy under … the 1998 Act. But that question is not before your Lordships. His case is that he has a Convention right to have the decision as to whether new sewers should be constructed made by a court in a private action rather than by the Director in the exercise of his powers under the 1991 Act. In my opinion there is no such right."[15]

In conclusion, we would draw attention to certain comments made by Lord Nicholls towards the end of his speech. Having noted that there exist certain statutory compensation schemes for those who suffer flooding pending the carrying out of flood alleviation schemes, his Lordship noted that the schemes applied only to internal flooding and not to flooding of (e.g.) gardens. This he regarded as inappropriately limited. His Lordship explained this on the basis of the following principle of fairness between individuals:

"It seems to me that, in principle, if it is not practicable for reasons of expense to carry out remedial works for the time being, those who enjoy the benefit of effective drainage should bear the cost of paying some compensation to those whose properties are situated lower down … The minority who suffer damage and disturbance as a consequence of the inadequacy of the sewerage system ought not to be required to bear an unreasonable burden."[16]

It is hard to resist the following suggestion: was this not essentially the thrust of Mr Marcic's arguments throughout the litigation; and was not "subsidy" of victims of flooding by those whose actions have indirectly been the root cause of the flooding a result that was fully within the gift of their Lordships in this case?

---

[15] At para. 71.
[16] At para. 45.

Update on Chapter 7: sentencing for environmental offences

At the end of 2003, Claire Du Pont and Dr Paul Zakkour of Environmental Resources Management Ltd (ERM) concluded their DEFRA commissioned research into *Trends in Environmental Sentencing in England & Wales*. The catalyst for the study was the concerns which have been expressed in a number of quarters (and which are referred to in Chapter 7) at the low levels of fines which have been imposed by the courts in respect of environmental offences.

A number of interesting and important findings emerge from the study. In common with previous studies, the authors of the report draw attention to issues relating to the completeness and availability of information in the public domain relating to environmental sentencing. The absence of centralised data meant that the authors had to rely on a number of different data sources in the form of governmental and non-governmental agencies. In this context it should be noted that the authors experienced particular difficulties in obtaining detailed information from large numbers of local authorities who were either not actively pursuing environmental prosecutions, or not keeping detailed records of those which they did bring.[17]

The research has revealed a distinct lack of consistency in environmental sentencing. Thus there are significant regional variations[18] in the number of offences which are prosecuted and the level of penalties which are imposed. Interestingly, the report identified a correlation between the two so that the regions with the highest number of prosecutions were also the ones with the lowest average penalties. Thus during the course of the last four years (1999-2002), London Magistrates' and Crown Courts heard 235 offences as compared with 1,089 in Wales.[19] However, in the London region the average fine for all environmental offences was £4,812, whereas in Wales it was £1,650. The authors of the report note that the trend was similar when the data was split between Magistrates' and Crown Courts.

Perhaps one of the most interesting points to emerge from the research is the distinction which can be made between Magistrates' Courts and Crown Courts with regard to the use of their sentencing powers. Concerns about the perceived failure of magistrates to use the full range of their sentencing powers when dealing with environmental offenders have been voiced in the past with the result that various initiatives have either been taken or suggested in order to try to encourage a more robust approach by the magistracy in this connection.[20] However, the ERM research seems to suggest that either the focus of the attention might previously have been misplaced, or that it has perhaps started to have a positive effect since of the two courts, it is in the Magistrates' Courts that the picture is more encouraging. Between 1999 and

---

[17] *Trends in Environmental Sentencing in England & Wales* (2003) DEFRA, at p. 7.
[18] ERM opted to divide England and Wales into nine regions based on county boundaries as follows: London; South East; Eastern; South West; East Midlands; West Midlands; North West; North East; and Wales.
[19] Since a lot of the information which ERM received was logged in terms of individual offences rather than cases, it opted to structure its database using the same format.
[20] For a discussion of some of these initiatives, see Chapter 7.

2002, there was a general increase in the average size of fines (£1,979 to £2,730[21]) and in the length of custodial sentences[22] imposed by magistrates (1.8 to 3.2 months) for environmental offences. In the Crown Courts, however, the trend has been in the opposite direction. The research has found, for example, that whereas the average Crown Court fine for an environmental offence was approximately £8,600 between 1999-2000, that average fell to about £4,600 for the following two years. Disparities between the Magistrates' and Crown Courts also occurred in relation to the award of costs. Whilst the percentage of cases in which costs were awarded in the Magistrates' Courts remained fairly constant between 1999-2002 (72-74 per cent), it fell sharply in the Crown Courts from 81 to 42 per cent during the same period.

---

[21] It should be noted, however, that since magistrates have the power to impose a fine of up to £20,000 for most environmental offences, this figure still falls a long way short of the statutory maximum.

[22] Not surprisingly, however, the report identifies a consistently low level use of custodial sentences across the various regions of England and Wales. The range throughout the regions was 0-3.8 per cent of cases resulting in a term of imprisonment being imposed, and the average for England and Wales was 1.2 per cent.

Update on Chapter 15: proposal for a Directive on environmental liability

On 17th December 2003 the European Parliament adopted just four amendments at its second reading vote, none of them expected to prove controversial so as to require formal conciliation procedures to be set in train (see below, pp. 627-8). This suggests that a final text may very likely be agreed quite early in 2004, so bringing the provisions of the Directive into operation (prospectively) from 2007.

The four amendments provide:

(i)   That Common Position Art 4(3) should be deleted. This stated that the Directive should be "without prejudice to the right of the operator to limit his liability in accordance with national legislation implementing the Convention on Limitation of Liability for Maritime Claims (LLMC), 1976, ... or the Strasbourg Convention on Limitation of Liability in Inland Navigation (CLNI), 1988 ...".

(ii)   That the power of competent authorities within Common Position Art 6(2)(e) "itself to take the necessary remedial measures" where environmental damage has occurred is specifically to be a power "of last resort", limited one presumes to cases where the powers within Art 6(2)(a) to (d) will not suffice to produce the necessary remedy. However, no amendment has been proposed in relation to the parallel provision (Art 5(3)(d)), which is applicable where harm is imminent (see below, p. 640).

(iii) That Common Position Art 14(2) shall be replaced by three clauses providing as follows. Within five years after entry into force of the Directive (i.e. 2009) the Commission shall report to the Parliament on the measures adopted by Member States under Art 14(1) (see below, p. 651). If no appropriate instruments or markets for insurance or other forms of financial security have been established by that time the Commission shall, in the light of that report, submit proposals for a "harmonised compulsory financial guarantee for water and soil damage based on a gradual approach". The amendment then states that "after a two year assessment period this provision shall apply to the remediation of damages (*sic*) caused to species and natural habitats." The amendment then provides that a ceiling may be established for the financial guarantee "by case and by location", to be determined in accordance with a sliding scale drawn up by Member States "taking into account in particular the risks of the activities carried out and the annual turnover". Finally, the amendment permits Member States to decide not to apply this provision to "low risk activities"; and Member States may also "consider establishing thresholds in relation to any insurance requirements under these provisions".

(iv)   That Common Position Art 18(3) – under which Member State reports on experience gained in the application of the Directive must review the application of Art 4(2) (Directive not to apply to environmental damage arising from an incident covered by the international conventions listed in Annex IV; e.g. the oil pollution and carriage of hazardous and noxious substances conventions) – shall include an additional requirement to consider "the relationship between shipowners' liability and oil receivers' contributions".

THE AUTHORS

Brian Jones currently works as a consultant in Environmental and Planning Law to the international law firm, Herbert Smith. Prior to that, he was Professor of Environmental Liability at De Montfort University in Leicester, having previously taught at the University of Nottingham, as well in Australia for two short periods.

He is co-author of *Countryside Law* (for Shaw & Sons) and has also written textbooks and casebooks on *Administrative Law* and *Civil Liberties*. Since 1992 he has edited the bi-monthly journal *Environmental Liability* (published by Lawtext Publishing Ltd).

He is married, with two children, and lives (happily, but for reasons he cannot now quite recall) on the borders of Shropshire.

Neil Parpworth works in the Department of Law, De Montfort University, Leicester. Previously he was employed as a research assistant to the Parliamentary Counsel at the Law Commission. His teaching and writing interests lie in the fields of Constitutional and Administrative Law, Environmental Law and Civil Liberties.

He is a co-author of *Environmental Law* (Butterworths) and has also authored *Constitutional and Administrative Law* (Butterworths) and co-authored *Introduction to Administrative Law* (Cavendish), *Constitutional & Administrative Law: Text with Materials* (Butterworths) and *Air Pollution: Law and Regulation* (Jordans). He has been the Assistant Editor of the *Encyclopedia of Environmental Health Law and Practice* (Sweet & Maxwell) since 1993 and was, until recently, an editor of the *Environmental Health Law Reports* (Sweet & Maxwell).

He lives in Leicester with his partner, Katharine Thompson (also a Shaw's author) and their two children, Catriona and Calum.

TABLE OF STATUTES

TABLE OF STATUTORY INSTRUMENTS

References to footnotes are shown by 'n' after the page number

TABLE OF EUROPEAN LEGISLATION

References to footnotes are shown by 'n' after the page number

Conventions

Directives

Treaties

TABLE OF CASES

Part I

CIVIL LIABILITY

Chapter 1

THE ROLE OF CIVIL LIABILITY IN THE CONTEXT OF ENVIRONMENTAL DAMAGE

INTRODUCTION

The chapters which immediately follow in Part I of this book describe in some detail the ambit of civil liability for environmental damage. The purpose of this first chapter is, however, rather different. Its aim is to offer some initial thoughts as to the most appropriate scope of such civil liability rules.

GUIDING PRINCIPLES

Let us begin by suggesting two general principles which may provide a helpful starting-point. These can be set out, in quite dogmatic form, as follows:

Principle one

The rules which a legal system develops on the matter of *civil liability for environmental damage* should integrate in a way which is rationally justifiable within that legal system's *general body of civil liability rules.*

Principle two

In considering the appropriate scope and nature of tortious civil liability for environmental damage it should be kept in mind that such civil liability rules are but one aspect of a rather broader collection of legal rules which, when taken together, may be described as *environmental liability law*. Environmental liability law may be argued to comprise rules of civil liability, rules of criminal law and liabilities to administrative direction (or cost recoupment in respect of administrative action), each in the context of actual or threatened environmental harm. Ultimately, what matters is that the combined and collective operation of these several facets of environmental liability should deliver desired environmental benefits: benefits which, no doubt should involve both:

- the deterrence of environmentally hazardous activity; and
- the repair of environmental damage where such harm has occurred.

In our commendable environmental zeal there is an ever-present danger that we may lose sight of the fact that the rules of tortious civil liability – with which we are in this Part presently concerned – constitute just one of the several liability tools available to achieve those objectives. No doubt tortious civil liability may prove a valuable legal instrument in this context and be found to have a significant part to play. However, it is by remaining mindful of the contributions which may be expected from the other principal legal instruments falling within the broad field of environmental liability law that we may best avoid the temptation of pressing for reform of civil liability rules, so as to require them to perform functions for which they may not readily be suited and, in consequence, producing unjustifiable irrationalities between civil liability in the environmental damage context and in other contexts.

EXPLANATION OF TERMS: TORTIOUS CIVIL LIABILITY AND LIABILITY FOR ENVIRONMENTAL DAMAGE

As this chapter proceeds, the significance and the implications of these two basic principles should emerge. However, for the moment we need to remind ourselves of certain basic notions of tortious civil liability and also to explore what range of meanings may lie behind the apparently simple concept of liability for environmental damage.

Tortious civil liability

When ordinarily we use the expression "tortious civil liability" we have in mind the body of legal rules which define the circumstances when (independently of breach of contract, breach of trust and so on) one person may be obliged to compensate another for harm which has been done by the former to the latter. Ordinarily we will be thinking about compensation for harm falling within quite a limited range of legal categories: for example, bodily injury or illness, harm to land or to movable property, harm to the plaintiff's enjoyment of his or her property. In some situations, but generally somewhat cautiously, conduct by a defendant which "merely" affects a plaintiff's financial well-being may be countenanced as giving rise to tort liability: liability for "pure economic loss".

If these statements properly describe our conventional understanding of the ambit of rules of tortious civil liability, the question that arises is how readily can the notion "civil liability for environmental damage" be fitted within this basic scheme of ideas? However, before we can address this issue we need to identify more clearly what we mean when we refer to *environmental damage*. More than one answer may be offered to this important question.

"Environmental damage": a first meaning

At first sight it may seem, when reference is made to civil liability for environmental damage, that what is meant is civil liability for having caused harm to the natural and, in many instances, the "unowned" environment. In other words, liability to pay compensation for having, for example, polluted the air, polluted water resources or for having harmed wildlife.

This first notion of liability for environmental damage presents some immediate difficulties in terms of the ready applicability of civil liability rules. It raises, in particular, in the typical situation where harm has been done to the unowned environment, the fundamental question: who should qualify to be a plaintiff in such an action?

Civil liability rules do not, ordinarily, confer upon individuals a right to sue for compensation except in relation to harm done to *themselves*, or to their *property*, or to their *enjoyment of their property*. Now, in so far as some incident which has given rise to harm to the unowned environment may at the same time have interfered with a plaintiff's enjoyment of his or her own property, a "private nuisance" or "neighbour" action may quite readily be envisaged. Equally, we may readily see scope for a civil claim arising out of a pollution-related *public nuisance* in a case where an individual plaintiff is able to demonstrate harm suffered which is over and above, or different from, that suffered by members of the pubic generally.[1]

However, rather more conceptual difficulty arises, in determining who may be an appropriate plaintiff to maintain a claim for compensation, in cases where the only harm in issue is what may be called harm to the (unowned) environment *per se* (that is, harm which is unrelated to, or independent of, any consequences personal to the plaintiff or to any asset owned or possessed by the plaintiff).

Of course, legal concepts are infinitely malleable. It is perfectly possible to provide for such an action in defined circumstances and for the benefit of defined persons. For example, it is perfectly feasible for a legislature to decide that where harm has been done to the unowned environment a civil claim should be afforded, in effect, to the community as a whole: perhaps on the rationale that what is owned by no individual may equally be considered to be owned by all. It may, according to this logic, be felt appropriate for a legal system to confer rights upon governmental (or similar) agencies to recover, on behalf of the community at large, compensation for harm done to natural resources. The natural resource damage recovery actions conferred in the United States under, for example, the Comprehensive Environmental Response, Compensation and Liability Act (CERCLA) and the Oil Pollution Act, are quite well-known illustrations of this technique.

Such legal mechanisms may seem attractive in terms of the utilisation of the law to the achievement of environmental ends. However, the point we should note – in keeping with one of the principal themes of this chapter – is that these aims may just as well be satisfied by a combination of (i) *criminal* liability in respect of conduct causing defined categories of environmental damage (perhaps linked to penalties in the form of requirements to engage in restorative actions – in addition to the more usual penalties); and (ii) liability to *administrative* directions and *administrative* cost recoupment.

The question of the most appropriate legal instruments to be utilised against those who may have harmed unowned environmental assets,

---

[1] For private nuisance and actions for damages arising out of public nuisance, see below, Chapters 2-4 and 5.

demonstrates well the choices which exist as regards the legal instruments to be deployed. Moreover, there may be very good reasons why one legal system may place more emphasis on one mechanism than does another: why the emphasis may differ as between legal systems. One system may place relatively strong reliance on the potentiality of civil law redress; another may focus more on criminal liability; and a third may have conferred relatively stringent powers upon administrative/governmental agencies to require environmental repair (and to reimburse public sector costs so incurred). Such differences may seem important when each legal mechanism is considered and compared in isolation from the others; but the differences may matter little when attention remains focused on the important broader picture – that of the combined impact of the several forms of environmental liability laws. Provided each legal system works in its own way to maximise the achievement of commonly sought objectives – to prevent, and to secure the restoration and repair of, environmental damage – it should matter little that the package of measures deployed may differ, a little or a lot, between one system and another.

Particular features of a legal or administrative system may make the solution which is most attractive in that system different from the optimum combination of measures to be favoured elsewhere. One must, therefore, be ever-careful about advocating the transplantation of legal solutions from one jurisdiction to another. An awareness of what may work well in other jurisdictions may provide a fruitful source of ideas as regards reform of the law "back home". But the efficacy at home of a solution which may be seen to work well abroad should be a matter of judgment, not ever a matter of assumption.

We have digressed a little from the particular point under consideration: that the use of civil actions for damages in relation to harm to the unowned environment is to put rules of tortious civil liability to a use which is rather different from that which is usually made of those rules. Good reason may exist for such imaginative manipulation or development of this particular liability mechanism. However, if the objectives sought may be perfectly well achieved by the provision and use of liability rules *other* than those relating to civil liability, the use of those other rules may be likely to be the more appropriate solution. Ultimately, perhaps what it comes down to is that we should regard the onus as being firmly upon those who seek to do the unusual with civil liability rules to explain and to demonstrate why this is necessary.

Moreover, we should expect the reasons which may be offered to support such change to be cogent and particular – the mere incantation of general slogans of environmental policy really should not suffice. Few – and certainly not the present writers – would wish to argue against the fundamentals underlying and supporting the "polluter pays principle" of environmental policy; nor against stringent rules of environmental liability. But more particular and more sophisticated argumentation is necessary when it comes to determining what should be the *detail* of particular liability rules and what should be the balance to be struck between environmental liabilities of the various different kinds which we have outlined. In such discussions references to such quite general notions as the "polluter pays principle" are unlikely to move discussion forward; and its inarticulate major remise – "all environmental liability is good liability" – should at all costs be eschewed.

On the basis of such assumptions we can return to the general questions: What is sought to be achieved by means of a "community" civil tort action for natural resource damages? And cannot those aims equally be achieved by some other legal (liability) technique?

It may help here to broaden our focus and to think beyond the particular sphere of damage to the environment. Persons who have engaged in conduct which has caused damage to the unowned environment may be characterised, more broadly, as having harmed, or threatened harm, to the interests of the community generally, rather than specifically, to the interests of particular identifiable individuals. Generally speaking, persons who have caused or threatened such harm are regarded more naturally as being the focus of the attention of rules of criminal law than of modified civil liability rules.

On this basis we might think that the true challenge, in such situations, is not to fashion new causes of civil law redress, but rather to devise criminal laws and criminal penalties which may serve to secure valuable environmental benefits (involving, for example, obligations to remove the threat to, or to remedy, environmental damage) in addition to the more usual features of such liability, such as the objectives of punishment and deterrence. Moreover, handling this matter by way of the criminal rather than the civil law may seem to have several other advantages. Criminal proceedings may be regarded as involving more by way of stigma than is associated with a "mere" civil claim; and may give rise to more rationally acceptable results in terms of the consequences which may be faced by a guilty party. As will appear, it is a significant problem of civil liability rules that the loser in a tort action will usually be ordered, upon having been found liable, to pay full compensation to the successful plaintiff. A convicted defendant in a criminal case, on the other hand, will have his or her penalty assessed on the basis of what the convicting court thinks appropriate in the light of all the circumstances of the case. The magnitude of the damage which has been caused will be important amongst the circumstances to be taken into account but it will be just one amongst several important considerations.[2] In other words the more sophisticated nature of criminal penalty assessment, as compared with the more crude and typically "all or nothing", "full compensation or no compensation at all" approach of the civil law, should make recourse to the criminal law the more readily favoured approach. Moreover, one should not assume that the broader range of factors likely to be taken into account in assessing criminal penalties will always, or even generally, favour defendants in

---

[2] See further on this matter, see below, p. 244.

comparison with principles of civil liability. So, for example, a substantial criminal penalty might be considered to be appropriate in relation to conduct which may have grossly endangered but, perhaps by good fortune only, not actually damaged the environment.[3] Whereas civil law would tend to say "no harm – no damages", a criminal court would likely feel perfectly at ease in imposing what might be a substantial penalty in relation to the conduct which led to such endangerment.

"Environmental damage": a second meaning

It is time to note a second meaning which may be attributed to the ambiguous expression *environmental damage*. In addition to the meaning already considered – liability for damage to environmental assets – the expression is used also to refer to something quite different. The use of this single expression to describe two quite different concepts has served on occasions to obscure rather important points of distinction.

What then is this second meaning? Very commonly, when civil liability for environmental damage is under discussion, the issue is not one of seeking to bring within the ambit of civil liability a right to compensation in respect of a new or different kind of damage (i.e. damage *to* the environment). Rather, what is under discussion is whether special rules of tortious civil liability should be made applicable in situations where quite standard kinds of damage (for example, personal injury/illness or property damage) have been caused to plaintiffs *by means of* environmental pollution. What is distinctive here is not the *kind* of damage in issue (as the phrase "civil liability for environmental damage" might suggest would be the case) but rather the *manner* in which some quite conventional category of legal damage may have been caused.

In a number of parts of the world there is a discernible trend towards civil liability regimes which single out this means of causing harm for special legal treatment as regards the applicable civil liability rules. To take examples close to home, legislation has been enacted in relatively recent years in Sweden, Norway, Denmark, Finland and Germany; and legislative proposals exist in Austria and Spain. In each case it has been felt appropriate to establish a special set of principles to operate in cases where such conventionally compensable damage has been caused by the mechanism of what we may loosely describe as "pollution". A clear head of steam appears to have developed in favour of separating out for distinctive civil liability treatment this particular *means* of having inflicted harm; and for a feature of such distinctive treatment to be that liability for the damage caused by such environmental means should be "strict" rather than dependent upon proof of fault.

---

[3] In its advice to the Court of Appeal on sentencing for environmental offences, the Sentencing Advisory Panel made a similar point, i.e. that the level of fine imposed should be high where the defendant's culpability was high, "even if a smaller amount of environmental damage has resulted from the defendant's actions than might have been expected" (1st March 2000, para.17).

Now, convincing reasons may very well exist which may lend support to this clear trend. It may be that these reasons should lead us to conclude that such distinctive and onerous civil liability rules should typically be a feature of a legal system's rules on environmental liability: that over and above what may be achieved by way of criminal law and administrative liability, it is appropriate for individuals who have suffered in their persons or to their property by way of environmental pollution should be specially favoured plaintiffs in civil liability claims.

But the question should be asked – one is inevitably curious – what justifications have been proffered to support this departure from the application of more conventional, fault-based, principles of tort liability? Why precisely should special rules of civil liability apply for the benefit of plaintiffs who have suffered quite ordinary kinds of compensable harm simply because that harm has been suffered by means of the environmentally polluting conduct of the defendant? Is there a rational justification, or is it just that the environmental lobby has shouted the loudest?

A discussion of justifications for such departure from the more conventional principles of tortious civil liability requires, however, that we should first describe, in broad outline, those conventional bases of tortious civil liability. It is these principles which are, it appears, increasingly coming to be considered to be inappropriate for the purpose of dealing with civil claims in respect of harm caused by pollution.

How should we describe the most basic principles underlying English tort liability? This question is very much easier to ask than to answer. In particular, it would be wrong for any suggestions offered to give an impression that the English law of tort is notably characterised by intellectual coherence or logical consistency. As with much of English law, solutions have been dictated more by considerations of pragmatism than by the application of *a priori* principles of tortious civil liability. The tendency has been for judicial elaboration of principles from, and in order to explain, decisions reached in earlier cases, as distinct from general theories of liability dictating decisions. Of course, the matter is not really so simple and the differences presented are not really so stark. A group of "pragmatic" decisions may engender a principle of liability – and then that principle will serve to prescribe the decisions to be reached in substantially similar cases. Nevertheless, and subject to these reservations about the unsystematic and unprincipled nature of English tort law, it is possible to offer a few basic suggestions as regards such fundamental principles.

We should start with a feature which appears all too easily forgotten. This is that English tort liability does not proceed from any *a priori* assumption that, whenever it can be shown that one person has caused harm to another, the former should be required to compensate the latter for that damage or loss. It is a dangerous trap into which the unwary may fall, to assume that once causality has been demonstrated – between the conduct of the defendant and the harm to the plaintiff – liability will follow.

Of course, in very many situations those who may be shown by evidence to have caused harm to others may bear liability in tort: the scope of modern tort liability is, indeed, quite broad. However, such liability is far from all-embracing. There are many contexts in which the judges have been, and remain, quite prepared to hold that no duty to pay compensation arises even though it may be indisputable, even undisputed, that a plaintiff's damage has been a direct consequence of the defendant's actions. Indeed, the whole purpose of the law of tort is to identify contexts where one person is liable for the harm caused to another, and to distinguish those situations from situations where harm may have been caused *without* incurring tort liability.

Let us accept, nevertheless, that modern tort liability is quite extensive in scope. There *are* many situations in which the law of tort *does* recognise a cause of action for the benefit of a person who has been harmed by a defendant. We may even say that where one person may be shown *deliberately* to have caused harm to another there will quite commonly be a liability in tort to pay compensation. However, even here it is important to note that this is only "quite commonly" the case: it is not the case invariably. There exist a number of contexts in which the courts have held that one may deliberately and without impunity act so as to cause damage (particularly in the form of purely financial disadvantage) to another person. So not only can we not say that the law of tort provides compensation for all those who can show that they have been harmed by others, we cannot even say that the law of tort provides compensation for those who have been deliberately so harmed. Often it *will* do so, but not always.

We may go a little further in our generalisations. Very commonly those who have acted *carelessly* and have caused otherwise avoidable harm to others will bear liability to compensate those persons for the harm which they have caused. In the modern law there is extensive liability in the law of negligence. But note again the use of the guarded expression "very commonly". Liability for harm caused by negligence is by no means all-embracing. The courts have taken pains to mark out contexts or circumstances in which, notwithstanding that it might be demonstrable that a defendant has caused the plaintiff harm by behaviour which falls below a standard involving reasonable care in respect of the plaintiff's interests, nevertheless good reasons may exist for denying (or limiting) liability to pay compensation. Here we refer to the contexts in which the courts have held no duty of care in the law of negligence to exist; and, also, where the courts may hold that notwithstanding the existence of a duty of care the harm suffered by the plaintiff must be regarded as too remote a consequence of the defendant's negligence for that harm to be compensable.

So we may say that very commonly tort liability arises in instances of deliberately caused harm; and quite commonly tort liability arises in instances of harm caused by negligence. What about situations where harm has been caused *unintentionally* and without any demonstrable departure from a standard of reasonably careful behaviour which the law may, in the law of negligence, prescribe? What generalisation may one make about the scope of liability where one person *without fault* may have caused harm to another?

The answer must be this: in cases where a defendant neither intended the harm which has resulted, nor failed to take reasonable care to prevent such harm occurring, the tendency has been for the courts to hold that no obligation to pay compensation arises. Liability in tort is fundamentally and ordinarily fault-based. Although, as we have noted, proof of fault will not inevitably suffice to secure liability, it is usually the case that in the absence of some species of fault on the part of the defendant – or some person for whom the defendant bears legal responsibility – tort liability will not ensue.

Once again, however, it is important to note the limiting word "usually", included in this broad generalisation. Although liability in tort without demonstration of fault is not the typical case, it is not unknown. In certain exceptional situations the English law of tort has seen fit to recognise *strict liability*. For example, in relation to harm done by animals for which one may have responsibility, in relation to defective products, and under the *Rule in Rylands* v *Fletcher*.[4]

What conclusion may be drawn from this very general discussion? Perhaps it should be this. Given the fact that the judges have tended to be cautious as regards the contexts and circumstances in which those who have caused harm should be required to pay compensation – and that, in the main, the legislature has not intervened to substitute a different approach in place of such judicial reticence – it would seem legitimate that cogent justification should be sought from those who may advocate, in relation to any particular type of case, an extension of tort liability – be it to introduce liability where none previously existed, or to make liability strict where liability has hitherto been founded only upon a judicial finding of fault. The plain fact should be acknowledged that the spectre of the uncompensated victim of another person's activities is one with which the judges seem less uncomfortable than do some others.

Applying this to our principal subject – the scope of civil liability for environmental damage (in each of the earlier discussed senses of that expression) – we may say the onus would seem to be upon those who may favour extension of the scope of ordinary tort liability, or the substitution of strict liability for liability hitherto founded upon fault, to explain convincingly why this context of damage warrants such special treatment.

Cogent reasoning to support any such change is particularly important for the following reason. Before adopting such a special liability regime we should be confident that we may explain to those who may suffer harm

---

[4] See further, below, p. 191.

outside the "environmental" context, and who may for that reason remain outside the enhanced protection afforded, what it is that is so special about environmental damage cases and, accordingly, why their own cases should, in contrast, not qualify for such special treatment. Any special rules which we may choose to develop in this particular context should integrate in a rationally justifiable way into the more general body of civil liability rules. This may seem unexceptionable but it is something which can all too easily be forgotten in the mustering of all potential legal weapons to protect the environment.

RATIONALES BEHIND EXTENSION OF LIABILITY

What reasons are typically offered for the introduction of a special strict liability regime in respect of harm caused by pollution of the environment?

It is often stated that such imposition of tort liability, or the imposition of *strict* tort liability where liability may presently be founded upon *fault*, is justified on the basis of this being an application of the "polluter pays principle" of environmental policy. Certainly, so to enlarge tort liability would seem to involve an application and implementation of that important principle. However, as a justification of such extensive civil liability this reasoning is, by itself, quite inadequate. There are, as this chapter has been at pains to stress, a variety of legal mechanisms by which the polluter may be made to pay in respect of pollution caused: civil liability for environmental damage is just one amongst several possibilities.

This is not to say that the "polluter pays principle" has not much to recommend it. Its essence involves a desire for the internalisation of environmental costs into the operating costs of environmentally burdensome activity. As a general policy goal this objective should be strongly supported. Nevertheless, such general support does not mean that all the possible implications, and all the possible ramifications, of the policy need to be accepted without question. In particular it should be noted that when its requirements are applied to matters of civil liability it may easily seem to call for an approach which is fundamentally at odds with the basic notions of conventional tort liability which we considered earlier. The "polluter pays principle" might seem, crudely, to support the touchstone of civil liability as being simply the demonstration of harm and the proof of causality. It fails to contain within itself any appreciation or acknowledgment of the more sophisticated issues which judges in tort cases have regarded as significant before determining whether or not any person who has caused harm should be required to pay compensation.

A second reason sometimes offered for the imposition of strict liability relates to the "deterrence" which is said to result from the establishment of such a liability regime. The argument asserts that benefits may be secured by the imposition of strict liability in terms of discouraging activities which present risk of harm, and also in encouraging the taking of special and exceptional care in the avoidance of harm in relation to those activities.

Now, whether, and if so to what degree, the imposition of strict liability may influence the conduct of potential defendants in these ways is very much a matter of speculation. Such influence seems to be rather more an article of faith than a matter which is readily demonstrable; and the faith is not one which is shared by all. To the sceptical in outlook it may seem that any correlation between (i) fault as compared with strict liability and (ii) the conduct of potential defendants is at best to be regarded as unproven; at worst, it may be thought implausible.

No pretence is made here to empirical knowledge of the impact that strict (rather than fault-based) liability may have on potential defendants – either in this "environmental" context or in others. Indeed, research into this matter would seem rather difficult. To relate the motivation for any identified change of attitude or conduct to an appreciation of the potential for civil liability, as distinct from any of the very many other influences which may influence modern business operations, would seem likely to be impossible. In the context of environmental harm there would seem to be very many good reasons why a business may make strides to seek to avoid its operations causing such damage; and many of these may be quite unrelated to concern as regards legal liability.[5]

It may seem strange to be doubting the influence that rules about legal liability may have on the conduct of those to whom they apply. Surely, it may be asked, one of the essential functions of legal rules is to regulate conduct: to deter persons from certain activities or ways of behaving and, perhaps, to steer them towards more positively ordained behaviour. That this is a function of legal rules need not, however, be doubted. And it is entirely plausible that rules of *criminal* liability may influence behaviour. It is also entirely plausible that rules about *administrative* liability may have such an effect. What one may legitimately be less easily persuaded about is the degree of influence upon conduct possessed by rules of *civil* liability and, in particular, the extent to which conduct may be more greatly influenced by civil liability being strict as compared with being founded upon a judicial finding of fault.

A third rationale sometimes put forward in purported justification of strict civil liability is that it is necessary in order to ease practical difficulties confronting plaintiffs in succeeding in the civil actions which they may seek to bring. This suggestion seems, however, only to beg further, more specific, questions. In particular, we need to ask: what difficulties have

---

[5] In a criminal liability context, "bad publicity" resulting from a prosecution or conviction has been recognised by the Sentencing Advisory Panel as a form of "non-tangible" damage. However, it did not consider that it should affect the penalty imposed by a court for the commission of an environmental offence (1st March 2000, para.20). In a study carried out to determine how effectively the integrated pollution control system was operating under Part I of the Environmental Protection Act 1990, the authors, Mehta and Hawkins, found, inter alia, that small firms were concerned about the financial costs of a prosecution whereas larger firms were more concerned about the attendant bad publicity and its effect on their corporate image. It would appear that the regulators took advantage of this fear of bad publicity in order to secure compliance with the legislative provisions: see "Integrated Pollution Control and its Impact: Perspective from Industry" (1998) JEL 61.

confronted plaintiffs, which a move towards strict civil liability may overcome?

This question is sometimes answered in the following way. It is said that in environmental damage cases there are commonly experienced considerable and special difficulties in demonstrating fault on the part of the defendant. The argument is that whereas in other contexts it may not impose undue burdens to require a plaintiff to prove fault before civil liability will attach to a defendant, there is something about environmental damage cases which presents particular difficulties to plaintiffs as regards this basic task.

Let us assume for the moment that this contention is one with which we may agree.[6] The issue then becomes whether the difficulties of proof which we are acknowledging are indeed difficulties which should lead us to a conclusion that a regime of strict civil liability is appropriate. There must be some doubt whether this is the case.

When reference is made to problems of proof in environmental damage cases it is important to be clear about precisely what issues of proof are referred to. In particular it seems important to stress that we are not here concerned with the special difficulties said to exist, at least with regard to certain situations of environmental damage, as regards *proof of causality*. Rather we are assuming that a court is prepared to hold that there exists a sufficient causal linkage between the actions of the defendant and the harm which is the basis of the claim. Our focus here is simply with the contention that there is something about environmental damage cases which presents special difficulties for plaintiffs when it comes to the demonstration that the conduct of the defendant should be characterised as having involved "fault". Our "problem case" is where a defendant who has been at fault may not be demonstrably so, with the result that a defendant who should have borne responsibility is in practice all too often able to avoid judgment to that effect.

Now, if the problem is that those who may in fact have been at fault may escape liability because plaintiffs have special difficulties, in this kind of case, in demonstrating fault, it would seem that the most appropriate response to the problem should not be to make all those who have caused such harm liable to pay compensation regardless of the matter of fault, but rather to see whether some modification or manipulation of the ordinary rules of civil procedure or civil evidence may suffice to overcome, or at least ease, the difficulties of proof of fault faced by plaintiffs.

If there is, indeed, something about environmental damage cases which makes it particularly problematic for plaintiffs to demonstrate fault, there may well be a good case for modifying in such cases the ordinarily applicable rules of civil procedure or civil evidence: for example, rules in

---

[6] In fact the proposition very probably overstates difficulties of evidence and proof in environmental damage cases. In this, as in all categories of civil claim, there are cases where proof is simple and cases where proof is problematic. It is doubtful whether there are particular or more frequent difficulties in environmental damage cases.

relation to the onus or burden of proof on this particular matter. Indeed, it may very well be the case that where the facts are peculiarly within the realm of the defendant or because of the highly technical or scientific nature of the necessary evidence, it is appropriate to require that the defendant should *disprove* fault in order to avoid liability, rather than that the plaintiff should have to prove fault in order for liability to attach. As will be seen later, this is a device which is sometimes utilised in tort law and has the merit of remaining consistent with the basic principle that civil liability be founded upon a judicial finding of fault, merely adjusting the ordinary rules as regards the party upon whom the onus or burden of proof or disproof, shall lie.

However, such modification of rules of civil procedure or civil evidence is something quite different from the imposition of strict liability. The changes to which we have referred do certainly impose burdens upon defendants but the burden is not the same as that imposed by a shift to a regime of civil liability based upon strict liability. A defendant who is able to meet the requirements imposed as regards proof that he or she was *not* at fault – who can demonstrate that the harm was caused notwithstanding that he or she had taken all due care to avoid such damage – will, where all that has been done is to shift the burden of proof, avoid liability. Where there has been introduced a change to a regime of strict liability a defendant who can demonstrate absence of fault on his or her part will, nevertheless, likely be held liable to pay compensation.[7]

This discussion of the supposed rationales for the imposition of strict civil liability in the context of environmental damage indicates some scepticism as regards the justifications put forward. This should not be taken to suggest that there is no proper place for regimes of strict liability within a coherent general system of tort liability. Strict liability principles do commonly operate within certain limited contexts and we shall, in due course, indicate the typical scope of, and the plausible justifications for, such liability.

PROBLEMS OF INTEGRATION

Before so doing we should focus upon certain problems which may be encountered in any attempt to integrate a regime of strict liability for environmental damage into an otherwise fundamentally fault-based system of tort liability. At root our concern will be to seek a credible answer to the following question: why should plaintiffs in environmental damage cases be afforded advantages in litigation which are denied other plaintiffs in non-environmental damage cases? Are there good reasons of policy which may justify the distinctions and differentiations which will result from the carving out of this new field of strict liability?

---

[7] The word "likely" reflects the fact that regimes of strict liability often admit limited defences to liability.

The crux of this matter may be described quite vividly. Assume that civil liability for personal injuries caused by road traffic accidents remains fault-based. How are we to explain the lack of a civil compensation remedy available to an injured person who is unable to prove fault on the part of a driver of a vehicle which has caused him or her injury in a road accident; in comparison with the strict liability claim which, it is posited, should be available for the benefit of a plaintiff who has been injured or made ill not in a road accident but as a consequence of an incident of environmental pollution? It is important that where stark contrasts such as these may arise as regards the way in which the law of tort treats different kinds of case some rational justification for the distinction should be evident.

Let us take another simple example illustrating, quite pointedly, the problems of differential treatment which may arise from the introduction of a strict liability regime defined by reference to the mechanism by which harm has been caused (i.e. by, or following, pollution of the environment). An explosion occurs at a chemical factory. Let us assume that the explosion has occurred notwithstanding that all due care has been exercised by those charged with operating the factory. Two people who have suffered harm seek your advice. One has become ill following inhalation of chemical vapours released into the atmosphere by the explosion. The other suffers no such illness, but was seriously injured by pieces of flying glass and masonry: by the very force of the explosion itself. What advice should each of these victims receive as regards their claims for compensation?

Let us take first the person made ill. This person might seem to be a likely beneficiary of any special regime to be introduced providing for strict civil liability in relation to environmental damage. We noted earlier, when we reviewed the meaning of the expression "civil liability for environmental damage",[8] that the typical situations covered by such liability regimes were those where perfectly conventionally compensated kinds of harm (i.e. personal injury, illness, property damage) were caused by, or as a consequence of, the defendant having polluted an environmental medium (air, water or land). This would seem to meet the basic facts of our first hypothetical client: the explosion at the defendant's factory has polluted the air with harmful chemical vapours and those vapours have resulted in illness being suffered by our client. This client should be advised to proceed with his or her claim.

What, however, of our other client? Having learned that his or her fellow sufferer should gain compensation, he or she asks us about his or her own prospects. Remember: that person suffered personal injuries, having been struck by glass and masonry which was propelled through the air by the force of the explosion. It is difficult to see how this person would qualify for beneficial treatment under our hypothetical environmental damage regime. This person has not suffered environmental damage, nor suffered from environmental damage. The injured person is not, let us assume, "the

---

[8] See above, p. 8.

environment"; nor have his or her injuries been sustained by means of any damaged environmental medium. Rather, the case is a perfectly standard personal injury, accident, claim. As such it is a typical instance of a case where liability ordinarily depends upon the court being satisfied that the injuries flowed from behaviour of the defendant which it is prepared to characterise as falling within the notion of fault.

Now, this basic principle of civil liability – that liability depends upon demonstration of fault – is one which may quite readily be explained to clients, and most clients will accept the principle as, ostensibly, a reasonably sensible first criterion for delimiting the scope of legal liability to pay compensation. It is a proposition which most will accept as seemingly reasonable, that a person who behaves with all due care but causes harm may not bear liability; whereas a person whose behaviour has fallen below a standard of care expected by the law should be required to pay. As such our injured victim, if responding solely to the advice offered to him or her, might be reasonably easily consoled in his or her disappointment. The principle by virtue of which this injured party (who it will be remembered cannot demonstrate fault) cannot recover is one which has seemed reasonable to many systems of civil compensations for many years. What our injured client may be less able to understand is why quite different advice has been given to our other client, who has (merely) been made ill. Even unconnected and impartial observers may regard the contrast between the two cases as somewhat grotesque.

An even starker example might have been offered. This time let us compare the claim of our physically injured victim with the claim which might be presented by an owner of land in the vicinity of the factory, whose trees have been harmed by the chemical vapours which drifted over his land following the explosion. This neighbouring landowner may, one presumes, be advised that his claim seems to involve either damage *to the environment* (be it described as the trees themselves, or the habitat which they may provide), or harm caused *by the damaged environment* (by the polluted air). In either case it would seem that his claim would fall within the hypothetical strict liability environmental damage regime which we have in mind. If this is the case this plaintiff will succeed in a claim for compensation notwithstanding, let us remember, that no evidence of fault on the part of the operator of the chemical plant can be adduced. The contrast so produced between the civil liability protection afforded to the trees adversely affected in this way, and the absence of compensation for the person physically injured should give cause for concern. Environmental lawyers (and others) are properly fond of trees and the habitat they may provide; but they should also have due regard for people and be prepared to explain the basis upon which their favoured proposals may seem to treat the latter less generously than the former.

It would seem difficult to imagine any explanations of the contrasts depicted above which would suffice to calm the disquiet of the less advantaged parties. Perhaps, however, we may avoid these problems by modifying the ambit of the strict liability regime so that it will apply more broadly, so as to confer its benefits upon all of the above parties?

A POSSIBLE SOLUTION?

A way of achieving such a result may be suggested. A strict liability environmental damage regime is likely to be designed not as being applicable to *all* acts or activities which may give rise to environmental damage, but as applicable to environmental damage caused by particular categories of plant and installation, or particular categories of conduct only. In other words, certain installations only, broadly or more narrowly defined, will be subject to the strict liability regime. Installations falling outside the categories defined will remain subject only to liability on a more conventional basis. Might we not take advantage of this focusing of strict liability for environmental damage on selected categories of operations, and provide that those operations should also bear strict liability, more generally, in relation to all personal injuries (and perhaps other damage also) suffered as a consequence of any event or occurrence in the operation of that plant? In other words if we have singled out certain categories of operation as appropriate to bear strict liability for environmental damage, might we not be willing to go a step further and impose strict liability more broadly still? If we are prepared to go so far we would seem to have achieved a solution to our problem as regards the apparent inequity in the contrasting advice which earlier we were required to offer our sick and injured accident victims. Under our broadened strict liability regime – no longer tied to the constraints of "environmental damage" – we would be able to offer both victims the prospect of a successful claim. Both have suffered a compensable kind of harm (illness or personal injury). It now matters not that one has suffered via a polluted environmental medium (poisonous vapours in the air) while the other suffered more directly the impact of the explosive blast. We have simply categorised the installation in question as – for some reason which may itself require some justification – one which should operate at greater risk of having to compensate those harmed by its operations than is ordinarily the case.

The support which we may feel able to give to this proposed solution will ultimately depend very much on the reasons which may support the inclusion of any particular category of operations within this new legal regime. More on this later. The point to be noted more immediately is that although the solution achieves a more readily acceptable solution to the particular problem of the two victims who have suffered as a result of our imaginary explosion, it is only necessary to alter the facts of that example slightly to produce a further, and still unresolved, apparent anomaly.

Imagine that two quite separate and unrelated factory explosions were to occur in the same town and on the same day. A passer-by at one is made ill by the inhalation of vapours; a passer-by at the other is physically injured by the blast. The former factory is one which is engaged in operations which render it within the scope of our imaginary strict liability regime. The operators of this factory must bear strict liability for environmental and other kinds of harm. By contrast, the other factory is engaged in more seemingly benign operations. It does not fall within any of the categories defining the ambit of our strict liability regime. Let us assume, further, that in neither case is any evidence available which would tend to show that the explosion which caused the harm was a consequence of any want of due care on the part of the operators of the factories. So, if liability is dependent on a judicial finding of fault the plaintiff will fail. If liability is, however, strict the plaintiff will win.

Each of the victims seeks your advice. Presumably, the advice to be given is that – for reasons given earlier – the party made ill by the "scheduled" factory will succeed; whereas the party bodily injured by the blast at the "non-scheduled" factory will recover nothing. It is a salutary exercise to consider how one might seek to explain this distinction in the scope of civil liability to the disappointed party.

We might begin by asking the basis upon which installations or processes have been selected for inclusion within such a regime of strict liability? The most probable answer is that the list of operations subject to the strict liability regime was devised on the basis of the propensity for harm to be associated with those operations. Relatively benign operations might likely be excluded; potentially hazardous activities included. The thinking behind this policy may well be founded upon the assumption, referred to earlier, that the imposition of strict liability may lead to the targeted activities being conducted all the more carefully as a consequence of the increased likelihood of successful claims for compensation should any damage ensue from those operations. If such a consequence be demonstrable, or even simply be believed to be the case, it may provide a rationally defensible justification for the differing civil liability regimes applicable as between certain kinds of activities and others. The rationale would involve the notion that there are good reasons to seek to secure that the very highest degree of care be taken in relation to activities which pose special hazards; whereas in relation to other operations, presenting only ordinary risks, it may suffice for operators to feel they need only take such care as may, with hindsight, be considered to have been reasonable.

This may be thought to provide a reasonably credible ground for differentiation between the legal regimes applicable to our two factories, and even as regards the advice proffered to each victim. Those who are engaged in activities with a relatively high propensity to do harm, or a propensity to do harm of a relatively serious nature, should be expected (and should expect) to do more to minimise the risk of such harm than is to be expected of those who are engaged in activities which give rise to substantially lesser worries.

This differentiation in our expectations is indeed quite warranted. The point to be noted, however, is that this sensible differentiation is one which will be found, upon examination, already to exist within the practical workings of systems of fault-based liability. In other words, it is not necessary to impose a regime of strict liability in order to secure this differentiation in the amount of care which the law may require should be taken: judgments as to what degree of care will be regarded as reasonable are, already within fault-based liability, made in the light of an assessment of the risk (magnitude and likelihood of harm) associated with the activity in question.

Indeed, to impose strict liability is actually to go rather further and to impose a more extreme differentiation than that described earlier. It is to go beyond imposing expectations that a higher degree of care be taken in the one context compared to the other. It is to impose liability even upon those who may have been exemplary in the care that they had taken, guarding against even the least likely foreseen risks. It is to impose not a high standard of care to be complied with: it is to impose a guarantor's liability – a liability which will attach equally to those who are blameworthy and to those whose conduct might, notwithstanding that harm has resulted, nevertheless quite properly be characterised as exemplary. In consequence we may wonder whether the imposition of strict liability is an appropriate device for seeking, by way of the civil law, to promote higher standards of care within certain categories of operation. Incentives and inducements towards the use of a substantial degree of care seem already to be a component of the operation of ordinary fault-based liability. Perhaps the issue may reduce to this: does the imposition of a *guarantor's* liability achieve something substantially greater in terms of the securement of precautions against risk than does the operation, as just described, of fault-based principles?

An answer to this question may not easily be given. It was suggested earlier that statements about the empirical impact of civil liability rules tend to be supported more by mere assertion than by demonstration. As such our conclusions may depend much on the sheer plausibility (or otherwise) of assertions which are made. Whilst it may seem plausible that the imposition of fault-based liability, as compared with a situation of immunity from negligence liability, may have an impact on conduct, there would seem to be room for rather less ready acceptance of contentions that a move from fault-based liability (exacting as this may be in contexts of high risk) to strict liability will give rise to similar empirical consequences.

If this suggestion be accepted it means that our first explanation as regards to why some categories of activity should be subject to strict liability rather than (just) fault-based liability would seem to flounder. We therefore need to look to other possible rationales to see whether any may be more persuasive.

Two possibilities may be offered. Both are founded upon the idea that strict liability is a guarantor liability. In neither case is any claim made that the imposition of strict liability will reduce the prospects of harm occurring: the arguments relate simply to why it may be appropriate that, atypically, a person who has caused harm should pay compensation regardless of whether his or her conduct has fallen short of any standard of care which ordinarily the law expects to be achieved.

A first context in which such strict liability may seem justifiable may be explained in the following way. Let us begin with the broad proposition, albeit one not likely to be universally accepted, that as well as securing some regulation of the way in which activities are conducted, it may be proper for civil liability rules to reflect also a policy judgment as regards whether the activity to which the liability regime applies is one which it is sought to encourage or to discourage. There are many activities to which our hypothetical strict liability regime might very likely be applied (e.g. chemical installations) which provide us, individually and collectively, with very substantial benefits. It is important that we do not slip into thinking of such activities as these as intrinsically objectionable: as existing only on sufferance. Quite the opposite. The general consensus should surely be that it is in the common or public interest that such activities should flourish. The purpose of strict liability cannot, therefore, in this situation be to seek to discourage such activity.

Let us turn, though, to other activities in respect of which the policy of the law may quite legitimately be that if the impact of applicable civil liability rules should go beyond merely regulating the conduct of the activity in question, so as also to secure some discouragement as regards engagement in that activity, then such a secondary consequence may be no bad thing. Consider, for a moment, the approach of the law to the liability of keepers of animals for the harm which those animals may do. The Animals Act 1971, modernising but not radically altering earlier rules, imposes two broad schemes of liability. A broad distinction is drawn between dangerous and non-dangerous species of animal. Although strict liability is imposed in relation to *both* categories, there is a substantial difference in the scope of application of that strict liability as between the two categories. To put the matter rather crudely, and inevitably without full accuracy, strict liability is imposed in relation to all damage done by a dangerous species of animal. However, in relation to damage done by non-dangerous species, strict liability only attaches where the keeper knew, or ought to have known, about the propensity of the particular animal to do harm. This may look like fault-based liability; but note that in the situation described the keeper will be liable for damage done even though he or she may have exhibited all reasonable care (judged in the light of those known propensities) to prevent such harm as has occurred. By way of contrast, the keeper of an animal of a non-dangerous species, and which as an individual has no known propensity to do harm, will only be liable if a court is satisfied that the keeper failed to exhibit reasonable care in his or her custody and control of the animal.

Perhaps we may explain the policy behind the incidence of strict and fault-based liability in respect of harm done by animals in the following way. There seems to be, within the civil liability regime, some implicit discouragement of the keeping of dangerous species of animal; and also some implicit discouragement of the continued keeping of other animals which may have demonstrated their harmful individual characteristics. This may be a situation in which by the laws we have fashioned we seem to be saying: "We may not have gone so far as to have rendered your keeping a certain animal unlawful. But we do not support what you are doing. Should the animal in question do harm the victim should have a right to compensation without the need to prove fault. If this principle of liability should discourage you and others from keeping – or continuing to keep – such animals, so much the better." One may see a marked contrast here with any equivalent policy statement which might have been formulated as regards our earlier example of a chemical factory producing much-valued products.

A suggestion may, therefore, be offered that strict liability may be justified in relation to "dangerous" activities possessing relatively little social merit or community value. What, though, of justifications for strict liability in relation to activities where, in principle, the activities are ones in respect of which it should be no policy of the law to provide discouragement? This brings us to a second broad justification which we may offer for the imposition of a regime of strict liability rules.

Let us consider this in relation to the well known strict liability *Rule in Rylands* v *Fletcher*, and what may be thought to be the underlying rationale of that principle. A more detailed explanation of this principle must await a later chapter. For the moment it will suffice to explain that the strict liability imposed under the principle seeks to provide advantages in civil litigation for the benefit of persons whose properties lie within the risk of harm in the event that matter accumulated on the neighbouring land should escape and do harm. To draw an example from recent litigation: if I bring onto my land, for storage prior to industrial use, quantities of chemicals (of a kind which are likely to do harm if they should escape) I will bear liability without need for proof of fault should such an escape occur and harm be done to the property of my neighbour.[9]

Certain limits to this principle of strict liability need immediately to be stressed. Assume that the escape has occurred as a consequence of an accident on the site where the chemicals are stored. A person who has been injured on-site by the chemicals will have no strict liability claim: such a person will only succeed upon proof of fault.[10] So, probably, must a mere passer-by who may have been injured off-site by escaping material: the benefit of this strict liability rule (probably) being restricted to neighbours and the property damage which those persons may suffer.[11] The rationale supporting the principle would appear to be this: a person whose neighbour engages in activities which pose a continuing special risk of harm should accumulated matter escape is offered solace, for the ongoing risk to which

---

[9] *Cambridge Water Company Ltd* v *Eastern Counties Leather* [1994] 1 All ER 53. See below, Chapter 6.
[10] See, for example, *Read* v *Lyons* [1947] AC 156 (see below, at p. 193).
[11] See, below, p. 191.

he or she is subjected, by being afforded an action for compensation without need to prove fault should that omni-present risk materialise. The apparent limitation of the principle to property damage is an implication of the tort now being regarded by the judges as a species of liability in nuisance.[12] The non-applicability of the principle for the benefit of the mere passer-by seems explicable in terms of the basic rationale explained above: such a person has not been exposed through time to the brooding menace presented by the matter which has escaped – such a person therefore should not qualify for this special legal benevolence.

REPRISE AND SUMMARY

Let us retrace our steps and think again of our second pair of hypothetical victims: two persons, each harmed following explosions at factories; one factory operating within, and the other outside the ambit of an imagined strict liability regime. We have been exploring justifications which may satisfactorily explain why we might wish to provide compensation to one victim irrespective of fault, whilst leaving recovery of any compensation by the other victim dependent on a finding of fault. We noted that we could not explain this differentiation by reference to the *kind* of harm suffered by the victim (both have suffered similarly); nor to the *means* by which such harm has been caused. The distinction must relate, we have suggested, to either the nature of the activity in question (warranting it being subject to a more stringent liability regime than is normal), or to the relationship which the plaintiff may have with that activity (for example, those whose property lies within the omnipresent "shadow of risk" seeming to be favoured). In the former case strict liability may be the price exacted by the law for its toleration of the activity in question (short of outright prohibition); in the latter case, strict liability may be justified as providing some reassurance to those most prone to harm, should such harm occur.

Conclusions

When considering such justifications for strict liability we should note how far our discussion has moved from its starting point. We began this chapter by focusing on the notion of a strict liability regime imposed in respect of damage to the environment. We then felt disposed to enlarge the strict liability regime so that it would encompass notions of harm construed more broadly than may be regarded purely as environmental damage. But then, in order that we did not simply replace fault-based liability for strict liability "across the board" we noted the necessity to impose limits on the kinds of operations to which this broad strict liability regime would apply. No longer would it seem appropriate to define such "included" operations by reference to their potential for damage to the environment. Rather different considerations might, however, justify the selection of activities upon which to impose such unusually onerous liabilities.

---

[12] For which, see below, Chapter 2.

All this has, of course, moved us fundamentally away from our original inquiry – the appropriateness of special rules of strict liability, confined to the specific context of civil liability for environmental damage. As should have become evident, substantial misgivings may be voiced as regards both the *need* for any such liability regime and the problem of rational integration of any such liability scheme into the main corpus of tort liability principles. But such misgivings as regards regimes of strict liability tailored to the context of environmental damage should not be thought to be misgivings about strict liability generally. As has been explained, there would seem to exist contexts, within a rationally defensible system of tort liability, in which the departure from the fault-principle may be perfectly explicable. Such acceptable departures from the fault principle may, in some cases, operate for the benefit of plaintiffs in cases where their harm has in fact been caused via pollution of the environment. But here the benefit will be coincidental: neither the kind of harm which has been suffered, nor the mechanism by which it has been suffered should, of itself, provide the justification for the strict liability which may, for other reasons which have been explained, seem appropriate.

Chapter 2

PRIVATE NUISANCE: SUBSTANCE OF LIABILITY

INTRODUCTION

Certain short statements defining the ambit of tort of private nuisance have gained common currency. For example, W*infield and Rogers* states that private nuisance involves:

> "an unlawful interference with a person's use or enjoyment of land, or some right over, or in connection with it."[1]

In similar vein *Clerk and Lindsell* states that:

> "the essence of nuisance is a condition or activity which unduly interferes with the use or enjoyment of land."[2]

These statements are helpful in so far as they provide a reasonable indication of the essential nature of this branch of liability in tort. However, care must be taken not to subject such brief phrases to over-exacting examination. They make no pretence to encapsulate the field of liability with precision and, when subjected to close examination, they will inevitably be found wanting. For example, and to take just one inadequacy in the definitions, it seems clear that the tort of private nuisance is concerned both with harm to land itself[3] as well as harm to the use and enjoyment of that land, and yet it is only the latter of these two kinds of harm which is referred to in the definitions given as the subject of this tort's protection.

POTENTIAL (AND LIMITATIONS) OF PRIVATE NUISANCE AS AN ENVIRONMENTAL TORT

Nevertheless, definitions such as these do suffice to make evident that this tort, essentially a tort aimed at the protection of interests in land (i.e. in the value of that property and in the value of the enjoyment of that property),[4] may at the same time afford a private law remedy to stop (by injunction) or provide compensation (in the form of damages) for polluting or otherwise environmentally harmful conduct on the part of a defendant.

It is, however, important to stress certain limitations of the tort in this context. First, as already noted, the courts have stressed that the tort is one fashioned for the purpose of protecting property and the interests of

---

[1] See, for example, Lord Wright in *Sedleigh-Denfield* v *O'Callaghan* [1940] AC 880; [1940] 3 All ER 349.
[2] Eighteenth edition (2000), para.19-01, p. 973.
[3] See below, p. 27.
[4] For this distinction, see further below p. 153.

"owners" of property. It is not a tort which we may properly describe as "first and foremost" an "environmental tort", and the courts have, as will be seen,[5] drawn back from any temptation to refocus its ambit. Second, and fairly obviously, a tort which purports to do no more than protect certain private law property interests cannot be expected to provide any comprehensive and adequate overall regulation of activities which may present threats to the environmental media. It is clear that alongside this branch of the civil law there must exist other environmental laws and, in particular, systems of administrative regulation (permitting schemes) and liabilities under the criminal law.

There has sometimes been a tendency to suggest that because the private law of nuisance cannot alone be regarded as a sufficient and adequate corpus of rules of environmental law, it should be regarded as of no very great modern significance. This is an inappropriate over-reaction. Within its own particular sphere – with its own aims and objectives – the law of private nuisance remains an important body of rules of civil law, setting the boundaries of legally acceptable and unacceptable behaviour between, typically, persons who are neighbours.[6] The common law rules of private nuisance can be traced back a good few centuries and indeed sometimes this is in itself taken as an indication that the principles cannot be adequate in relation to modern conceptions of environmental protection. But antiquity alone is no ground for criticism. Provisions of law may well have survived for the very reason that they continue to meet ongoing requirements which in essence may change only little with the passage of time. As we shall see, the older cases rather belie their antiquity, demonstrating that there is really little which is new in the fields of anti-social and un-neighbourly behaviour.

MATTERS FOR DISCUSSION

The substance of the tort of private nuisance is described in this chapter. Defences to liability in private nuisance are discussed in Chapter 3; and certain issues relating to remedies are dealt with in Chapter 4.

The discussion in this chapter focuses principally on the following matters:

- the categories of interests protected by private nuisance: harm to land and harm to the use and enjoyment of land
- the standard(s) of liability: strict liability, and the notion of reasonable user
- who may sue?
- who may be sued?

---

[5] See below, at p. 34.
[6] Note, however, that it is not *essential* for the defendant to be a neighbour of the plaintiff. See, below, at p. 85.

CATEGORIES OF PRIVATE NUISANCE
Significance of the nature of harm

The judges have consistently indicated that the principles which govern the incidence of liability in private nuisance differ somewhat depending on the nature of the harm which forms the basis of a plaintiff's action.

The critical distinction was explained, back in 1865, by Lord Westbury in *St Helen's Smelting Co* v *Tipping*,[7] in language which has been much quoted:

> " ... it is a very desirable thing to mark the difference between an action brought for a nuisance upon the ground that the alleged nuisance produces *material injury to the property*, and an action brought for a nuisance on the ground that the thing alleged to be a nuisance is productive of *sensible personal discomfort*."[8]

Then, proceeding to explain in broad terms the reason why this distinction was of importance, Lord Westbury noted:

> "With regard to ... personal inconvenience and interference with one's enjoyment, one's quiet, ... whether that may be denominated a nuisance, must undoubtedly depend greatly on the circumstances of the place where the thing complained of actually occurs. If a man lives in a town, it is necessary that he should subject himself to the consequences of those operations of trade which may be carried on in his immediate locality, which are ... necessary for trade and commerce, and also for the enjoyment of property, and for the benefit of the inhabitants of the town and of the public at large. If a man lives in a street where there are numerous shops, and a shop is opened next door to him, which is carried on in a fair and reasonable way, he has no ground for complaint, because to himself individually there may arise much discomfort from the trade carried on in that shop. But when an occupation is carried on by one person in the neighbourhood of another, and the result of that trade ... is a material injury to property, then there unquestionably arises a very different consideration. ...[T]he submission which is required from persons living in society to that amount of discomfort which may be necessary for the legitimate and free exercise of the trade of their neighbours, would not apply to circumstances the immediate result of which is sensible injury to the value of the property."[9]

---

[7] (1865) 11 HL 642

[8] At 650. Emphasis added.

[9] In *St Helen's* the House of Lords found in favour of the plaintiff, who had bought an estate in an area containing many factories, amongst which was the defendant's copper smelting works. The claim related not to mere discomfort in the plaintiff's use and enjoyment of his property (a claim which might not have succeeded in view of the nature of the locality), but to material damage in the form of harm done, by gases emitted by the defendant's plant, to the plaintiff's trees and to his cattle.

This distinction, and also its implications, were well explained also by Veale J, in *Halsey* v *Esso Petroleum Co Ltd*:[10]

> "So far as the present case is concerned, liability for nuisance by harmful deposits could be established by proving damage by the deposits to the property in question, provided, of course, that the injury was not merely trivial. Negligence is not an ingredient of the cause of action, and the character of the neighbourhood is not a matter to be taken into consideration. On the other hand nuisance by smell or noise is something to which no absolute standard can be applied. It is always a question of degree whether the interference with comfort or convenience is sufficiently serious to constitute a nuisance. The character of the neighbourhood is very relevant and all the relevant circumstances have to be taken into account. What might be a nuisance in one area is by no means necessarily so in another. In an urban area, everyone must put up with a certain amount of discomfort and annoyance from the activities of neighbours, and the law must strike a fair and reasonable balance between the right of the plaintiff on the one hand to the undisturbed enjoyment of his property, and the right of the defendant on the other hand to use his property for his own lawful enjoyment."[11]

In differentiating the approaches of the courts in the contexts of (i) physical damage to land, and (ii) to harm as regards the use or enjoyment which may be made of land, a word of caution is necessary. The statements describing the approach taken in relation to non-physical harm suggest that those who live in certain kinds of locality may reasonably be expected to tolerate certain inconveniences or discomforts which others, living elsewhere, might make the subject of legitimate complaint. As one judge put it, in memorable terms:

> "… what would be a nuisance in Belgrave Square would not necessarily be so in Bermondsey."[12]

This may well be true. However, such a statement should not suggest that such differentiations as regards "localities" should deprive residents of such less projected locations of *all* protection. As Cozens-Hardy LJ noted in *Rushmer* v *Polsue and Alfieri*:[13]

> "It does not follow that because I live, say, in the manufacturing part of Sheffield that I cannot complain if a steam hammer is introduced next door, and so worked as to render sleep at night impossible …"[14]

---

[10] [1961] 2 All ER 145. For the facts, see below, p. 164.
[11] At 151.
[12] Per Thesiger LJ in *Sturges* v *Bridgman* (1879) 11 Ch D 852 at 865.
[13] [1906] 1 Ch 234.
[14] At 250-1.

STANDARDS OF LIABILITY: THE CONCEPT OF REASONABLE USER

We have noted the quite starkly differing approach of the law of private nuisance to instances of each of the two broad categories of harm which have been described. In the one category liability is not based upon demonstration of fault ("negligence is not an ingredient of the action"), although the scope of liability may, as we shall see, be tempered by the operation of rules of remoteness of damage.[15] In the other, where damage is non-physical and relates to the amenity value of the land, liability depends upon the outcome of a judicial balancing of the respective interests of the plaintiff and the defendant. This involves a form of liability, where the defendant has upset such reasonable balance,[16] which may perfectly properly be regarded as a species of "fault-based" liability; albeit one in which "fault" is assessed rather differently than in the case of the fault liability to be found in the tort of negligence.

This point was graphically explained by Sir George Jessel MR in *Broder* v *Saillard*,[17] referring to a claim of nuisance arising out of noise from horses in a stable:

> "It is very hard on the defendant, who is a gentleman with three horses in his stable, and whose horses do not appear to make more than the ordinary noise that horses do, if he is not to be allowed to keep his horses in his stable. On the other hand, it is very hard on the plaintiffs if they cannot sleep at night, and cannot enjoy their house, because the noise from the stables is so great as seriously to interfere with their words and comfort. The question is, on which side the law inclines. ... I take it the law is this, that a man is entitled to the comfortable enjoyment of his dwelling-house. If his neighbour makes such noise as to interfere with the ordinary use of his dwelling-house, so as to cause serious annoyance and disturbance, the occupier of the dwelling-house is entitled to be protected from it. It is no answer to say that the defendant is only making a reasonable use of his property, because there are many trades and many occupations which are not only reasonable, but necessary to be followed, and which still cannot be allowed to be followed in the proximity of dwelling-houses, so as to interfere with the comfort of their inhabitants ... If a stable is built, as this stable is, not as stables usually are, at some distance from dwelling houses, but next to the wall of the plaintiff's dwelling-house, in such position that the noise would actually prevent the neighbours sleeping, and would frighten them out of their sleep, and would prevent their ordinary and comfortable enjoyment of their

---

[15] See below, p. 94.

[16] Most particularly so where the defendant continues such "unreasonable" conduct after having been made aware of its impact on the plaintiff.

[17] (1876) 2 Ch D 692.

dwelling-house, all I can say is, that is not a proper place to keep horses in, although the horses may be ordinarily quiet."[18]

It will be seen that where the harm of which the plaintiff complains in non-material in nature liability will depend on the outcome of a judicial balancing of the interests of the plaintiff and the defendant. Taking all the circumstances of the case into account the task for the court may be said to be to make an assessment of, and balance:

(i)   the reasonableness of the conduct of the defendant *in the light of its impact on the plaintiff*, and

(ii) the reasonableness of the complaint of the plaintiff that he or she should not have to suffer such interference with the quiet enjoyment of his or her property.

A flexible test

Inevitably, a test of liability of this nature will involve an element of uncertainty as regards the ambit of the tort. However, to adopt the words of Lord Halsbury in *Colls* v *Home and Colonial Stores Ltd*,[19] we may say that "what may be called the uncertainty of the test may also be described as its elasticity". Moreover, it is the very "elasticity" of the test for liability in this aspect of private nuisance which has permitted the tort to be applied in a very broad range of contexts of interference with the use and enjoyment of land: the reported cases offering testimony to the myriad ways in which one person's activities may interfere with the use and enjoyment of land by another. In this respect the tort is comparable with the tort of negligence and, just as with the tort of negligence, care must be taken to remember that a decision of a court that conduct in a particular case amounted to an actionable nuisance must never be taken as a ruling on a matter of law. The decision of the court, the outcome of the balancing process described above, must be considered simply as a conclusion of mixed law and fact, to which the court has come following its assessment of the broad range of evidence presented in the particular case. Cases will be described shortly which shed valuable light on the reasoning processes of the judges as they proceed towards conclusions on the issue of the reasonableness of "actions", and of the "reactions" of others. The cases should not, however, be pushed further. Similar behaviour on the part of a different defendant and in different circumstances might quite possibly be adjudged differently. Furthermore, just as texts on the law of negligence tell us that no list can be drawn up of what conduct may be regarded as negligent, so it is not possible to formulate a list which would state definitively what behaviour falls within, and what falls outside, the bounds of liability in nuisance.

---

[18] At 700-702. For the position where planning permission has been afforded as regards the siting of a building to be used for a particular purpose, and with inevitable impact on neighbours, see below at pp. 54-58.

[19] [1904] AC 179

Some illustrations: a short survey

The applicability of the law of private nuisance to a very broad variety of forms of conduct causing interference with the amenity value of adjacent property may readily be demonstrated. The cases serve also to demonstrate how little is new in neighbour disputes. We may take examples from odour nuisances, the causing of noise and vibrations, dust nuisance, nuisance by glare of the sun, by the conduct of immoral activities and by interference with television reception.

A good example of nuisance by smell is provided by *Bone* v *Seal*.[20] Here, the defendant ran a pig farm from which smells emanated as a consequence of the storage of pig manure and the boiling of pig swill. The two plaintiffs were the owners of neighbouring properties. They brought an action for an injunction in 1958 to restrain the defendant from committing a nuisance. Despite the fact that the defendant undertook steps to minimise the discharge of smells from the farm as part of the settlement in those proceedings, the nuisance continued. In part, this was attributable to an intensification of pig farming in the intervening years evidenced by an increase in the pig herd from 300 to over 700. Accordingly, in 1968, the plaintiffs sought injunctive relief once again. At first instance, Walton J granted the injunction and ordered that the defendant pay each of the plaintiffs the sum of £6,324.66 damages. The defendant appealed on three grounds, one of which was that the finding that there had been a nuisance by smell over the years was not supported by the evidence. This ground of appeal was rejected by the Court of Appeal. In the words of Stephenson LJ with which Scarman and Ormrod LJJ agreed:

> "There was a considerable weight of evidence, making allowance for hypersensitivity and making every allowance for exaggeration, that these two sources, boiling swill and the accumulation of pig manure, were so offensive as to constitute an intolerable nuisance over the years. It was an intermittent nuisance; it was a nuisance which no doubt those who had to live with it tended to exaggerate. But it was a nuisance; it was a serious nuisance, coming and going by day and by night, over a period of something like 12½ years."[21]

However, in relation to the question of the *quantum of damages* awarded for interference with the plaintiffs' enjoyment of their property, the Court of Appeal took a different view to that of the trial judge. On the basis that there was an analogy between the present case and personal injury cases involving loss of amenity, the Court concluded that the sum of damages awarded was much too high. In the words of Stephenson LJ, it was "the kind of figure that would only be given for a serious and permanent loss of amenity as the result of a very serious injury, perhaps in the case of a young person."[22] Accordingly, in the circumstances of the case, the Court

---

[20] [1975] 1 All ER 787.
[21] At 792.
[22] At 793.

considered that £1,000 was a reasonable sum to award to each of the plaintiffs.[23]

Leeman v *Montagu*[24] was a case of noise nuisance caused by the crowing of cockerels in an orchard on the defendant's farm approximately 100 yards from the plaintiff's house. The noise was of such a level that both the plaintiff and his wife had to sleep with cotton wool in their ears and with all the windows in the house firmly closed. An injunction was therefore granted, although it was suspended for a month to allow the defendant to take steps to reduce the nuisance. In *Tetley* v *Chitty*,[25] McNeill J held, "making all due allowance for the subjective nature of this evidence, and for the fact that residents have an axe to grind"[26] that the operation of a Go-Kart track on land belonging to a local authority amounted to an actionable noise nuisance.[27]

Dust as well as noise nuisance was the issue in *Matania* v *National Provincial Bank*.[28] Here the plaintiff, a music teacher, claimed amongst other things that he was seriously injured in his profession as a result of extensive alterations being made to the first floor of a building in which he occupied a number of rooms on the second and third floors. The Court of Appeal concluded on this point that the evidence supported the contention that the plaintiff had been prevented from carrying on his lawful business by means of the noise and the dust. Moreover, the evidence also supported the view that the effect of the noise and dust could have been avoided by: (i) refraining from carrying out the noisiest renovation work when the plaintiff was teaching, and (ii) putting sheets down.

A case illustrating the protean[29] nature of the tort of private nuisance – extending its applicability to nuisance in the form of a somewhat novel complaint – may be found in *Bank of New Zealand* v *Greenwood*.[30]

The plaintiff complained of dazzling glare which he experienced as sunlight reflected from the glass roof of a verandah on the defendant's building. The evidence indicated that the effect of the glass on the verandah was not simply to reflect the sunlight, but to concentrate the reflected light so as to produce a glare too bright for the eye to bear: the light was diffused as if from a multitude of mirrors. It was held by the New Zealand court that the construction of a building which caused such

---

[23] In *Hunter* v *Canary Wharf Ltd* [1997] 2 All ER 426, Lord Lloyd noted that the decision in *Bone* "illustrates and confirms that the right to sue in private nuisance is linked to the correct measure of damages" (at 444). The right to sue in private nuisance is discussed below, see p. 71.

[24] [1936] 2 All ER 1677. See also, *Halsey* v *Esso Petroleum* (below, p. 164), *Christie* v *Davey* (below, p. 63) and the *Hollywood Silver Fox Farm* case (below p. 64).

[25] [1986] 1 All ER 663.

[26] At 667.

[27] This case is returned to later in this chapter when the issue of who may be liable for a nuisance is considered, see below, p. 112.

[28] [1936] 2 All ER 633.

[29] See Lord Wright in *Sedleigh-Denfield* v *O'Callaghan* [1940] AC 880 at 903.

[30] [1994] 1 NZLR 525.

intensity of glare to a neighbour, or to allow such a state of affairs to continue, could be considered an actionable nuisance.

In accepting that nuisance could extend to this situation Hardy Boys J commented:

> "The dearth of authority should ... present no obstacle, for nuisance is one of those areas of the law where the courts have long been engaged in the application of certain legal concepts to a never-ending variety of circumstances."[31]

Immoral activities formed the bases of the complaints in *Thompson-Schwab* v *Costaki*[32] and in *Laws* v *Florinplace*.[33] The facts of the former case are considered in some detail below.[34] For present purposes it need only be noted that the plaintiffs brought an action to restrain the defendants from continuing to use a house in a residential street for the purposes of prostitution. They were duly granted an interlocutory injunction pending trial of the action. The defendants appealed. In giving judgment in the Court of Appeal, Lord Evershed MR noted that the question raised by the appeal was a matter of "some public interest, and, I do not doubt, some public importance too".[35] On the defendants' behalf, it was argued that the action amounted to a novel claim in that the law of nuisance had never comprehended activities of this kind which, although possibly shocking, did not physically interfere with the plaintiff's land or their use of it. In response to this argument, Lord Evershed MR noted that the different types of conduct which may amount to an actionable nuisance were "exceedingly varied" and "that they are not capable of precise or close definition". Therefore, the test to be adopted was:

> "... whether what is being done interferes with the plaintiff in the comfortable and convenient enjoyment of his land, regard being had ... to the usages in this matter of civilised society, and regard being also had to the character, as proved, of the neighbourhood."[36]

Applying this test to the facts before him, Lord Evershed concluded (and Romer LJ agreed) that using the house for the purposes of prostitution did amount to an actionable nuisance.

The decision in *Thompson-Schwab* v *Costaki* was applied in *Laws* v *Florinplace Ltd*. Here, the plaintiffs were successful in persuading Vinelott J to grant an interim injunction to restrain a proposed sex centre and cinema club from selling pornographic magazines, books and video films on the corner of a residential street in a commercially developed area. Although the nature of the proceedings meant that it would have been both

---

[31] At 530.
[32] [1956] 1 All ER 652.
[33] [1981] 1 All ER 659.
[34] See p. 49.
[35] [1956] 1 All ER 652 at 652.
[36] At 654.

unnecessary and wrong for Vinelott J to express an opinion as to whether the existence of the business constituted an actionable nuisance, he did observe that:

> "... it is impossible to say that there is not at least a triable issue whether the existence of a business of this kind, conducted in the way in which it was initially conducted, so that the nature of the business is evident to residents of, and visitors to, Longmore Street, is not a nuisance independently of any risk of attracting any undesirable and potentially dangerous customers, and of any risk that the shop may in the future prove a plague spot which will be a source of infection in the neighbourhood."[37]

We may conclude this brief demonstration of the breadth of applicability of the law of private nuisance by discussion of the decision of the House of Lords in *Hunter* v *Canary Wharf Ltd*.[38]

The substantive issue raised in this appeal concerned "harm" caused to the plaintiffs by way of interference with their reception of television signals.[39] The plaintiffs lived mostly in the Poplar/Isle of Dogs District of London and claimed that on the construction of Canary Wharf Tower – over 800 feet in height and clad in stainless steel – their homes fell within the electromagnetic shadow of that building as regards reception of television signals from the Crystal Palace transmitter. In due course a relay transmitter (and adjustment to aerials) resolved the problem; but the plaintiffs claimed compensation in private nuisance for the harm to their use and enjoyment of their homes for the period of interference – some two to three years. The claim raised important issues as regards (i) whether receipt of television signals was an interest in the use and enjoyment of property which should receive protection in the law of private nuisance,[40] and (ii) whether, assuming an affirmative answer to this first issue, the manner in which the interference had been caused by the defendant (the construction of a building, leading to an electromagnetic shadow) was such as should trigger such liability?

In the House of Lords their Lordships were unanimous that the second question should be answered negatively; but a majority of their Lordships indicated a willingness, in other circumstances, to countenance the receipt of television signals as an interest which might warrant the protection of the modern law of private nuisance.

Their Lordships took note that this issue had been previously considered in a case in 1965: *Bridlington Relay Ltd* v *Yorkshire Electricity Board*.[41] In

---

[37] [1981] 1 All ER 659 at 666.

[38] [1997] 2 All ER 426; [1997] Env LR 488.

[39] For the other main issue – that of *standing* to maintain an action in private nuisance – see below, p. 71.

[40] East Enders being unable to watch "EastEnders"?

[41] [1965] Ch 436.

that case, involving alleged interference by electromagnetic radiation from high-tension electric cables, Buckley J had offered the following comment:

"... I do not think it can at present be said that the ability to receive television free from occasional, even recurrent and severe, electrical interference is so important a part of the ordinary householder's enjoyment of his property that such interference should be regarded as a legal nuisance ..."[42]

In *Hunter*, Lord Goff noted that Buckley J had not ruled out the possibility that ability to receive television signals free from interference might one day be recognised as a sufficiently important aspect of enjoyment of property to fall within the protection of this branch of the law. Lord Hoffmann described Buckley J's statements as made "tentatively", and commented that:

"the judge was plainly not laying down a general rule that interference with television can never be an actionable nuisance."[43]

On the basis, then, that the tentative statements in *Bridlington* might be ripe for review, what views were expressed by their Lordships on this general question?

Lord Goff seemed sympathetic to the law of nuisance having some potential for operation in this context, explaining the modern significance of television reception in the following terms:

" ... the average weekly hours for television viewing ... which your Lordships were told were 24 hours per week, show that many people · devote much of their time to watching television ... Certainly it can be asserted with force that for many people television transcends the function of mere entertainment, and in particular that for the aged, the lonely and the bedridden it must provide a great distraction and relief from the circumscribed nature of their lives."[44]

Lord Hoffmann was prepared to go so far as to express the view that in an appropriate case in which conduct such as that in *Bridlington* occurred an action might lie.[45]

Lord Cooke expressed a similar general view. Following the lead taken by courts in Canada,[46] he stated that:

"in appropriate cases, television and radio reception can and should be protected by the law of nuisance."[47]

---

[42] At 447.
[43] [1997] 2 All ER 426 at 453.
[44] At 431.
[45] At 453.
[46] See the reasoning of Robins J in *Nor-Video Services Ltd* v *Ontario Hydro* (1978) 84 DLR (3d) 221.

Lords Lloyd and Hope focused their speeches upon the reasons, accepted by all their Lordships, why the particular claim presented by the plaintiffs should not succeed: as described below. Their speeches do contain certain statements which might seem, however, more generally, to deny *any* applicability of private nuisance to the reception of television signals. For example, Lord Lloyd commented:

> " ... I agree ... that interference with television reception is not capable of constituting an actionable nuisance ... ... I would not want it to be thought that I regard television reception as being of little or no moment. The annoyance caused by the erection of Canary Wharf and the consequential interference with television reception must have been very considerable. But unfortunately the law does not always afford a remedy for every annoyance, however great ..."[48]

It is tempting to seek to confine the breadth of this statement by relating it to the facts of the particular case (nuisance by the mere interposition of a structure between the signal and the would-be recipient) and to suggest that it was not intended to refer also to cases of the *Bridlington* variety (cases where signals are interrupted by some interfering active conduct on the part of the defendant, for example the emission via high-tension cables of electromagnetic radiation). However Lord Lloyd seems not to have intended this restricted interpretation. Later in his speech he explained:

> "Another argument which [counsel for the defendants] put forward ... is that interference with television reception was not due to any *activity* on the part of the defendants ... It was due solely to the existence of the building itself. However ... nuisance does not depend in every case on an activity ... It may arise from a mere state of affairs on a man's land which he allows to continue ... So I would not decide the case on the ground that interference with the plaintiff's television reception did not involve any activity on the defendant's part."[49]

It would seem to follow that Lord Lloyd considered the plaintiff's claim to fail because of the quality or nature of what was being interfered with rather than because of the particular way in which that interest was adversely affected.

Lord Hope's speech confined itself to the specific reasons for denying the particular claim under consideration, without offering speculation more broadly. Overall, therefore, three of their Lordships chose to express opinions, *obiter*, in favour of a potential protective role being played by the law of nuisance in relation to television reception, with only Lord Lloyd seeming positively to discount that possibility.

---

[47] At 463.

[48] At 445.

[49] *ibid* (emphasis added).

Turning from that general issue to the more specific question which was raised by the case – was it an actionable nuisance to have interfered with television reception in the particular way alleged? – their Lordships were unanimous that, on the facts, presented no private nuisance claim could succeed.

Lord Goff explained that whereas in *Bridlington* the interference with reception resulted from the activities of the defendant Electricity Board (the transmission of high voltages and the emission of electromagnetic radiation), in *Hunter* the interference was a result of the mere presence of the structure at its particular location; and that this raised for consideration the approach long-adopted by the common law as regards a landowner's entitlement at common law to build on his or her land, notwithstanding some adverse consequences which might thereby ensue for neighbours.

On this matter Lord Goff commented:

> "... as a general rule, a man's right to build on his land is not restricted by the fact that the presence of the building may of itself interfere with his neighbour's enjoyment of his land. The building may spoil his neighbour's view, ... it may restrict the flow of air onto his neighbour's land ... and, ... it may take away light from his neighbour's windows ...: nevertheless, his neighbour generally cannot complain of the presence of the building, though this may seriously detract from the enjoyment of his land."[50]

And later Lord Goff summarised the position as follows:

> "..the mere fact that a building on the defendant's land gets in the way and so prevents something from reaching the plaintiff's land is generally speaking not enough [to amount to a private nuisance]."[51]

Lord Lloyd explained similarly:

> "The house-owner who has a fine view of the South Downs may find that his neighbour has built so as to obscure his view. But there is no redress, unless, perchance, his neighbour's land was subject to a restrictive covenant in the house-owner's favour."[52]

Moreover, to Lord Lloyd:

---

[50] At 432. Lord Goff noted that rights to air and to light might arise as easements by the process of grant or by prescription.

[51] At 433.

[52] At 445. Note that property law does not recognise an easement in the form of the right to a view. See *Aldred's* case (1610) 9 Co Rep 576; *Dalton v Angus* (1881) 6 App Cas 740. Nor, per Lord Hoffmann (at 521) could there be an easement of TV reception.

"The analogy between a building which interferes with a view and a building which interferes with television reception seems to me ... to be very close."[53]

Lord Hope noted:

"There is no reported case where an easement against the interruption of the receipt of radio or television signals has yet been recognised. The closest analogy is with uninterrupted prospect, which cannot be acquired by prescription, but only by agreement or express grant. Unless restricted by covenant the owner is entitled to put up whatever he chooses on his own land, even though his neighbour's view is interrupted. The interruption of view will carry with it various consequences. It may reduce amenity generally, or it may impede more particular things such as the transmission of visual signals to the land from other parties. That may be highly inconvenient and it may even diminish the value of the land which is affected. But the proprietor of the affected land has nevertheless no actionable ground of complaint."[54]

Lord Cooke reached a similar conclusion via a rather different process of reasoning. Rather than reach his conclusion on the basis of analogy with traditional principles as regards rights of property ownership, His Lordship preferred to base himself upon application of the ordinary "principle of reasonable user, of give and take". In other words, for Lord Cooke, it was a sufficient answer to the plaintiff's claim that the erection of the building in question could be regarded as a reasonable use of the defendant's land. In coming to this conclusion his Lordship noted that Canary Wharf Tower was built in an "enterprise zone" in an "urban development area" and had been authorised under special statutory procedure intended to encourage regeneration. In this situation it was proper to conclude that:

"although it did interfere with television reception the Canary Wharf Tower must ... be accepted as a reasonable development in all the circumstances."[55]

Moreover,

"The tower is clad in stainless steel and the windows are metallised but it would seem hopeless to contend that the use of these material and the design of the tower constituted any unreasonable or unexpected mode of constructing a building of this height."[56]

In other words this was the very kind of building which the system of development control chosen for this area of London seemed to countenance. It was, in Lord Cooke's opinion, appropriate for the court to

---

[53] *ibid.*
[54] At 470.
[55] At 466.
[56] *ibid.*

have regard to this consideration in judging whether what had been done by the defendant was, or was not, a reasonable user of the land.[57] Or to put the matter another way, the statutory process adopted for redevelopment of this area of London might be considered as "denoting a standard of what is acceptable in the community".[58]

It is clear from *Hunter*, therefore, that the mere fact of the interposition of a building between the signal source and the receptor so as to block signal reception will not involve the commission of a nuisance. For the majority of their Lordships this conclusion followed from their understanding of the common law right to build; for Lord Cooke there was no nuisance because the building could be characterised in the circumstances as a reasonable construction. Now, in *Hunter* itself there was, as Lord Cooke indicated, no allegation that the construction of the tower was either intended to have had such a consequence, or that the defendants were aware of the likely effect of the structure as regards lee-ward reception. What difference might such knowledge or such intention have made? We need to consider how the differing approaches of their Lordships might apply in such circumstances.

For Lord Cooke, it seems, such alteration of the facts might have some significance. Mindful of earlier case law on the significance of malice as regards the characterisation of actions as amounting to a nuisance, he stated:

> "in the light of the versatility of human malevolence and ingenuity, it is well to add ... a qualification. The malicious erection of a structure for the purpose of interfering with television reception should be actionable in nuisance on the principle of ... *Christie* v *Davey* ... and *Hollywood Silver Fox Farm Ltd* v *Emmett*..."[59]

Such liability in relation to the erection of a structure seems limited, however, according to Lord Cooke's approach to situations where a defendant not only is aware of the consequences of his actions in terms of interference with reception, but also can be shown to have acted not for legitimate benefit to himself or herself, but rather in order to have caused harm or disadvantage to the plaintiff. This quite narrow approach to liability follows from an example given by Lord Cooke, based upon the facts of a Canadian decision.[60] The example given involved the construction by a farmer on his land of a steel tower 74 feet high and serving no agricultural purpose. The tower was directly in line with the runway of an adjoining airport, and was erected with the sole purpose of

---

[57] Lord Cooke expressly stated that this was not at all the same as making compliance with planning control *ipso facto* a defence to a nuisance action. So, for example, in a case of "an injudicious grant of planning permission", such as in *Wheeler* v *JJ Saunders* [1995] 2 All ER 697 (and see below p. 52), it was proper for a court to characterise lawful development as unreasonable user of land.

[58] *ibid.*

[59] At 465. For these cases and this principle, see below at p. 60.

[60] *Manitoba* v *Campbell* (1983) 26 CCLT 168.

damaging the interests of the airport owners. In such circumstances a liability in nuisance arose. Had, however, the tower been built in order to achieve a legitimate agricultural purpose, and the effect on the neighbouring airport been merely a known incidental consequence, the matter would it seems have been different.

For Lord Cooke a distinction seemed to apply between (i) user of land which is unreasonable because it is motivated by malice; and (ii) user of land which is reasonable because it serves to achieve a reasonable benefit in connection with the defendant's land, even if the defendant well knows that this benefit may be attained only at some disadvantage to his or her neighbour.

This distinction may, however, present the issues too simply. In particular it fails to take account of the likely situation in which a defendant may have acted out of "mixed motives" or for a "plurality of reasons". It may well be the case – indeed it seems not an unlikely scenario – that a defendant may have acted both to benefit him/herself in what may in principle be regarded as the reasonable use of his or her land, as well as also having taken pleasure in securing an additional objective as regards the adverse impact upon his or her neighbour. Perhaps we really need to formulate Lord Cooke's principle, in such cases, in terms of *predominant* motive.

Alternatively, perhaps a more adequate analysis should include some recognition that where an ostensibly reasonable construction on land is known to be likely to give rise to harm to a neighbour, that user will forfeit its claim to being reasonable if it can be shown that some reasonable alternative course of action would have sufficiently served the interests of the defendant without having caused the harm in question to the plaintiff. To refer back to the Canadian example used by Lord Cooke: if the steel tower served no purpose other than to deliberately harm the neighbour, it would involve the commission of a nuisance. If it served an agricultural purpose, but the motivating reason for its construction was to harm the neighbour, the tower would be a nuisance under the principle in *Christie*. If the motivating reason for the construction of the tower was genuinely agricultural, albeit that the effect on the neighbour was known, an issue would arise whether the agricultural purpose could have been reasonably achieved without such adverse effects (e.g. by construction of the tower elsewhere on the defendant's land). If the benefit to the defendant (in gaining reasonable benefit from his land) could reasonably have been achieved without giving rise to the known adverse effects on the plaintiff's use and enjoyment of his land, that use of land might well forfeit the appellation "reasonable user". Ultimately, however, we should note that (according to Lord Cooke's analysis of "reasonable user") if the adverse consequence for the plaintiff is one which is unavoidable, or has already been kept to a minimum by the defendant's choice of action, then the intrinsic reasonableness of the benefit sought by the defendant as regards his or her use of land will render that conduct not a nuisance notwithstanding its known consequences for the plaintiff.

The minority approach adopted by Lord Cooke would seem, therefore, to admit of some flexibility as regards its handling of the various situations – more complex than in *Hunter* itself – which may in due course arise for decision. What, however, of the "common law right to build" approach favoured by the majority? For the majority the defendants in *Hunter* could not be regarded as liable in nuisance because they were exercising their common law right to build on their land notwithstanding the effect of any such building on neighbouring amenity. The issue arises, therefore, whether this right extends to building for a malicious rather than for a self-serving purpose?

A definite answer to this question cannot, it seems, be given. We are in the realms of the perennially difficult issue of how far common law rights may be tempered by notions of "abuse of rights". None of their Lordships, who adopted this general approach, adverted to this issue. This may very well have been simply because there was no need, on the facts of the case, to have explored the matter. However, an equal possibility is that, properly understood, the common law right to build exists irrespective of the motivation of the defendant.

Had their Lordships addressed the issue they might well have followed the approach to common law rights adopted and applied in the well-known case of *Bradford Corporation* v *Pickles.*[61] In that case the House of Lords resisted the idea that the common law right of an owner of land to abstract water from his land should be forfeited because the motive for such abstraction was to have caused harm to the defendant. If the *Bradford* principle remains in favour it would seem that quite different conclusions will follow, in the sort of examples considered earlier, depending upon whether the approach of Lord Cooke or of the majority is followed. For the moment it would seem that the latter, more simple but less sophisticated, approach commands wider judicial support.

FACTORS RELEVANT TO THE ASSESSMENT OF REASONABLE USER AND REASONABLE REACTION

In the process of coming to a conclusion as regards the reasonableness of a defendant's conduct the courts have made clear that certain factors, without ever individually being decisive, may be influential as regards the final conclusion reached.

The most significant of these factors may be listed and described as follows.

---

[61] [1895] AC 587. See further, below, p. 66.

Locality

Reference has already been made to the statements of Lord Westbury in *St Helen's Smelting Co* v *Tipping*,[62] in which his Lordship seemed to provide some degree of reassurance to operators of industrial processes in urban-industrial areas. Operations in such places might constitute reasonable user of land which neighbours might reasonably be expected to tolerate, even though such operations in other kinds of locality might be viewed rather differently. It was also explained that this approach, reflecting as it does differing ordinary expectations as regards "give and take" in areas of differing character, should not be regarded as giving *carte blanche* as regards intrusive activities even in areas of already dense and intense industrial activity. As we noted, there must come a point where a plaintiff is entitled reasonably to take the view that "enough is enough".

A question which may then arise is whether a person may move to a property in full knowledge of the nuisance to which it is exposed and then, notwithstanding such witting purchase, commence proceedings in respect of that nuisance?

The issue arose quite starkly in *Miller* v *Jackson*.[63] For a period of more than 70 years the defendant cricket club had played cricket on a small ground: so small that the ball had been hit out of the ground with some frequency. This caused no substantial concern until the early 1960s when houses were built close to the edge of the ground. A small fence provided little protection against the risk of property damage or personal injury, and in 1975 the height of this protection was raised to fourteen feet and nine inches, the maximum practicable given the potential impact of wind. Notwithstanding this quite high fence, cricket balls continued to be hit into the new neighbouring gardens on a number of occasions each season. The owners of one of the new houses brought proceedings in, *inter alia*, nuisance seeking damages and an injunction. The principal issue raised was well explained by Geoffrey Lane LJ:

> "Can someone, by building a house on the edge of the field in circumstances where it must have been obvious that balls might be hit over the fence, effectively stop cricket being played? Precedent apart, justice would seem to demand that the plaintiffs should be left to make the most of the site they have selected to occupy with all its obvious advantages and all its equally obvious disadvantages ... If the matter were *res integra*, I confess, I should be inclined to find for the defendants. It does not seem just that a long-established activity – in itself innocuous – should be brought to an end because someone chooses to build a house nearby and so turn an innocent pastime into an actionable nuisance. Unfortunately, however the question is not open."[64]

---

[62] (1865) 11 HL 642. See above, p. 27.
[63] [1977] 3 All ER 338.
[64] At 348-349.

His Lordship continued, explaining that:

> "In *Sturges* v *Bridgman*,[65] this very problem arose ... That decision involved the assumption ... that it is no answer to a claim in nuisance for the defendant to show that the plaintiff brought the trouble on his own head by building or coming to live in a house so close to the defendant's premises that he would inevitably be affected by the defendant's activities, where no one had been affected previously..."[66]

Geoffrey Lane LJ therefore felt constrained to acknowledge this principle; and both he and Cumming-Bruce LJ concluded that the facts demonstrated an actionable nuisance. By contrast, Lord Denning MR, dissenting on this point, regarded *Sturges* as turning on different issues and considered that no actionable nuisance had been demonstrated by the plaintiffs. However, notwithstanding that the majority regarded an actionable nuisance to have been demonstrated, a (different) majority of the Court of Appeal (Cumming-Bruce LJ and Lord Denning MR) held that no injunction should issue: the defendants should be content with their remedy in damages only. Accordingly, although the stated implication of Geoffrey Lane LJ's judgment – that a finding of nuisance would "effectively stop cricket being played" on the ground – was a feature of his Lordship's own judgment, the overall decision of the Court of Appeal produced a rather different result.

The reasoning which lay behind the exercise of discretion, on the part of Cumming-Bruce LJ and Lord Denning MR, not to award injunctive relief is important. Both of their Lordships took into account, at the stage relating to availability of the discretionary remedy by way of injunction, certain facets of the *public interest*: the public interest of the local community in playing fields being preserved for recreational activities and, more specifically, the public interest that the village should not lose a valuable location at which its team might play cricket. These concerns as regards the interests of the public were regarded by the majority as relevant to the question whether the successful plaintiff should be awarded both of the forms of relief sought, or should be awarded damages only. This is a matter to which we shall return later, in our discussion of the availability of injunctive relief.[67]

A final twist in the *Miller* tale brings us full circle. Cumming-Bruce LJ considered there to be a further reason also for denying injunctive relief. Although he had agreed that the fact that the plaintiffs had "come to the nuisance" did not prevent the nuisance from being *actionable* at their suit, he took the view that this was a factor which was relevant to the question of the availability of *injunctive* relief.

---

[65] (1879) 11 Ch D 852.
[66] [1977] 3 All ER 338 at 349.
[67] See, below, Chapter 4.

A reason which might seem to support the approach of Cumming-Bruce LJ is that the award of an injunction in addition to damages may, overall, result in what might be regarded as the over-compensation of the plaintiff. This may be explained as follows. A person who has moved to a nuisance may be expected to have paid a purchase (or rental) price for that property which reflects the nuisance which that property experiences. Having paid such an attenuated price for the property it may well be that any claim for damages for compensation in respect of the nuisance will not be a substantial one: the difference between the price paid and market value of the property in the light of the nuisance may well be nil. Damages to be awarded would reflect, rather, the amenity value loss[68] – a sum to reflect the spoiled enjoyment of the property, compensated as a form of non-material loss. In short we will be thinking in terms of an award of damages of a rather lower order than may be awarded where property, not previously exposed to a nuisance, loses market value.

If next we consider the consequences of granting an injunction to restrain the nuisance to which the plaintiff has, voluntarily and at fair market price, "come" we may, perhaps, feel some disquiet by the fact that to impose restraint upon the continuing conduct of the defendant may leave the plaintiff "in profit" in financial terms. A consequence of the injunction would be to raise the capital (or rental) value of the formerly adversely affected property. On this basis the plaintiff, awarded damages and an injunction, may be regarded as having been rather amply – perhaps too amply – rewarded for having brought the nuisance proceedings.

The question arises whether this benefit to the plaintiff – which may seem to go beyond the compensation-only objectives of the law of tort – should be welcomed or should be regarded truly as anomalous. Tort lawyers may perhaps instinctively consider the latter to be the case. However, certain factors which may favour the former view may be noted. To begin with, we could regard such benefit as legitimate reward – and some incentive – for a plaintiff having gone to the trouble and expense, and subjected himself or herself to the risks involved, of obtaining the court order prohibiting continuance of the nuisance. Of course, this is an aspect of all successful tort actions – and is not generally considered to be a justification for remedies which cumulatively do more than provide "mere" compensation. Nevertheless, it may still be that, where we find a rule which incidentally provides some further such benefit to a plaintiff, we should not for this reason feel ill-disposed to that rule. Secondly, we may note that the beneficial consequences which we have noted for our hypothetical plaintiff may result even on the basis of a principle, as suggested by Cumming-Bruce LJ, that injunctive relief should *not* favour those who have come to a nuisance. This may be simply explained. Suppose that the nuisance in question is one which has affected not just the plaintiff's property, but also that of his, let us imagine, rather longer-resident neighbours. There may, in such a situation, be little difficulty in those neighbours taking proceedings to obtain both damages and an

---

[68] For this distinction, see below, p. 153.

injunction.[69] As will be seen when we look more closely at remedies, in the context of nuisance the courts have been generous in their willingness to award injunctive relief. Any limitation in the context of those who may have "come to the nuisance" with eyes open is, as we shall note, something rather exceptional. Given that injunctive relief obtained by these neighbours will serve to benefit the (on the view of Cumming-Bruce LJ, disentitled) person who has come to the nuisance, the resulting position would seem anomalous. Whilst Cumming-Bruce LJ's approach would deny such benefit to a new resident who has gone to the trouble of commencing his or her own proceedings, such a new resident would benefit financially should proceedings brought by his or her neighbours secure an injunction to put an end to the nuisance, so benefiting them all.

These arguments may be thought, on balance, to undermine support for Cumming-Bruce LJ's approach. It may, or may not be, that general public interest considerations should be taken into account when a court has to decide whether to grant injunctive relief in a private nuisance action. This view of the majority in *Miller* will be returned to later. What seems not appropriate, as argued above, is to discriminate in this respect against a plaintiff simply on the basis that he or she may have "come to" the nuisance.

Whilst we are considering the general issue of how the law should treat those who may be said to have come to a nuisance one further thought may be ventured. We began with a quotation from Geoffrey Lane LJ suggesting considerable sympathy for defendants in such situations. His Lordship seemed to have felt constrained by authority to reach a conclusion on liability (and in his judgment, on remedy) contrary to his view of the true merits of the case.

On reflection, however, the arguments on the merits may have been quite finely balanced. Certainly it is not inaccurate to describe the facts of *Miller* in terms of it having been a case where a cricket club had played cricket for some 70 years, prior to the adjacent homes being built, without complaint and without thereby causing an actionable nuisance. An equally accurate description, however, would be to regard the club as having been no more than fortunate in that matter. It had good fortune throughout that period of time in that, owing to the neighbouring land not having been developed, the club could continue to benefit from playing cricket on an evidently undersized ground.

---

[69] Given that the injunction should restore the market value of the property the quantum of damages will in principle reflect the amenity loss during the period during which the nuisance was experienced. See further, below, p. 153. More substantial "loss of market value" damages may be available to any who may have sold at a lower market value during the period of the nuisance. Provided they commence their claim within the period of limitation they should be able to claim damages to compensate them for the effect the nuisance had on the sale price of their property. Although not an owner of land at the time of the action such a plaintiff would have the requisite property interest at the time the tort was committed, and this should suffice to give standing in a nuisance claim. See further on this requirement, below, p. 71.

On what basis should we seek to argue that a club which has benefited in the past from the undeveloped nature of its neighbour's property should have a claim thereby to disentitle that neighbour from subsequently making such ordinary use of that land? One such argument might be that a prescriptive right to commit the nuisance may have been acquired.[70] However, for this to be the case an actionable nuisance must have been acquiesced in for the requisite prescription period. This was not, of course, the situation in *Miller*. That was not a case where it was sought by action to put an end to a nuisance which a neighbour had "consented" to for a long period: it was, rather, a case where the consequences for the neighbouring land had only recently (upon the arrival there of the plaintiff) had the quality of being a nuisance in relation to that land. When prescriptive right is discounted as a ground for thinking the merits may lie with the defendant cricket club, it is hard to see any other basis upon which a past history of extending the effects of its activities beyond the confines of its property should serve to justify continuance of such behaviour. Indeed, in terms generally of the relative equities, it may be fair to say that far from it having been in some way an inappropriate user for the developer of the neighbouring land to have built homes on that land so close to where the cricket was played, the less meritorious claim was that of the club to be permitted with impunity to continue to play cricket on land inadequate in area for that purpose.

Such an approach to the relative merits as between adjacent owners may, indeed, be noted in the decision in *Sturges* v *Bridgman*.[71] For a period of at least 26 years the defendant had, as a part of his confectionery business, operated two large pestles and mortars. These large machines emitted some substantial amount of noise and vibrations, but for most of the period in which they had operated they caused no nuisance. The land immediately bordering formed the end of the plaintiff's garden and his use and enjoyment of his property was, therefore, not adversely affected. Things changed, however, when the plaintiff, a doctor, built a consulting-room in that part of his garden, close to the defendant's machinery. The plaintiff experienced some difficulty examining patients; the noise and vibrations from the defendants property affecting his ability properly to listen to his patients' chests. For reasons which will be considered later,[72] the Court of Appeal held that – just as in *Miller* – no right to commit a nuisance could be contended to have been acquired by prescription. On the issue of whether the plaintiff should be denied a remedy because he had "come to the nuisance"[73] Thesiger LJ commented that a rule denying an action to those who had come to property knowing of nuisances to which it was exposed, or who had developed land in a way which rendered previously unobjectionable activities a nuisance would "produce a prejudicial effect upon the development of land". Rather, in his Lordship's view, the law

---

[70] For this, see below, p. 132.

[71] (1879) 11 Ch D 852.

[72] See below, p. 133.

[73] The plaintiff had (i) purchased his property only eight years earlier, and (ii) built in a position affected by the noise and vibrations.

should adopt the policy that those who wished to conduct activities which might subject neighbours to discomforts or inconveniences beyond what was acceptable in that locality[74] did so precariously. If they wished greater security as regards their continuance of activities they should enlarge the area of their property – so that the effects of their activities would not extend (or would not extend so strongly) to that of their neighbours. Thesiger LJ used the example of a blacksmith:

> "the smith in the case supposed might protect himself by taking a sufficient curtilage to ensure what he does from being at any time an annoyance to his neighbour."[75]

Changes in the nature of localities

Before we conclude our discussion of "locality" – as one amongst several significant factors in the judicial estimation of reasonable user and reasonably to be expected tolerance – one further matter should be considered. It is a matter of common knowledge that over periods of time the nature of localities may change. Maybe Belgrave Square remains true to its former character, but all will be aware of districts formerly genteel which have more recently developed a more "cosmopolitan" atmosphere, of rural areas now developed for residential or even industrial use, or areas where once practically "anything went" in terms of acceptable and accepted conduct which have more recently become "gentrified", its new residents ever alert to activities which might seem not now fitting to the locality. All this is commonplace. The matter to consider is whether and how the law of nuisance may recognise and take account of such changes.

Let us begin with an example. Take an urban area in which there have existed for many years a number of manufacturing companies. These businesses have for a substantial period of time engaged in manufacturing operations throughout the night and day, and there has been a steady flow of delivery vehicles to and from each of the premises. The district is associated in people's minds strongly with these activities. It has little in the way of residential accommodation. Any who do live in the vicinity have fully accepted the sounds from the factories and vehicles as very much an aspect of the character of life in the area. Let us assume also that none of the factories is impinging upon quietude excessively, or more than is necessary in order to undertake its operations.

In such circumstances we might well conclude that it is very likely that no private nuisance is being committed by any of the factories: either one to

---

[74] Note Thesiger LJ's example: "It is said that if this principle is applied ... it would [mean that] a man might go – say into the midst of the tanneries of Bermondsey ... and, by building a private residence upon a vacant piece of land, put a stop to such trade and manufacture altogether ... It may be answered that whether anything is a nuisance or not is a question to be determined, not merely by an abstract consideration of the thing itself, but in reference to circumstances ... and where a locality is devoted to a particular trade ... in a ... manner not constituting a public nuisance, judges ... may be trusted to find, that the trade ... so carried on in that locality is not a private or actionable wrong ..." (1879) 11 Ch D 852 at 865.
[75] *ibid.*

another, or to any local resident. We are within the stock situation epitomised by the "Belgrave Square-Bermondsey" dichotomy. Those residing within the district will be expected, as reasonable persons, to tolerate a level of intrusion into their "quiet enjoyment" which might go beyond that which they might be expected to accept in rather different localities.

All this is simply to reassert, and to apply, to a simple example the basic principle which was outlined earlier. Let us, then, vary the example a little. Suppose that business has not been good and that many of the businesses in the district have failed. The formerly busy and tolerably noisy industrial premises have largely become silent. At the same time, developers have been purchasing those properties, converting them into luxury residential accommodation and then selling or letting the new residential units to persons in search of inner-city convenience combined with a reasonable degree of residential quiet. It would appear that the character of the area is changing – and one would expect that the courts, in their estimates of reasonable user and reasonable tolerance, would take the change into account in their overall assessment of whether activities continuing in the area have overstepped the mark. Certainly, if a factory, unused for some time and now surrounded closely by such converted premises housing new residents, were to recommence operations of a kind formerly commonplace in the area, it might legitimately be met with the protest that what may once have been acceptable in the locality no longer is so.

Let us vary the example again. The locality continues the change we have described, to such an extent that now just one factory continues to operate. This factory operates in a way unchanged from previous decades. However, what was typical and accepted then in terms of environmental impact is now exceptional and has given rise to complaints from the new residents, who complain that the noise (etc.) is out of keeping in what has become a generally quiet residential urban district. What approach would or should the judges take? Should they conclude that at some point, as the character of the locality changes, activities which were once "part and parcel" of the character of the area should now be regarded as illegitimate, being beyond that which the new residents should reasonably be expected to bear? The answer would seem to be that they should. Assuming that the nature of localities may change it would seem, indeed, to follow that what may formerly have been permissible may become impermissible. What, though, of the possibility that the defendant to such an action may have acquired by prescription the right to commit such a nuisance? Such hopes will founder on the simple ground that since the activity has only quite recently become an actionable nuisance the requirement that the nuisance should have been acquiesced in for the substantial prescription period will not have been satisfied.[76]

We may continue with our illustration a stage further. Our district has changed from an industrial area to one characterised by quiet residential

---

[76] See further, below, p. 132.

activity. But local entrepreneurs have now discovered that money is to be made in this quite centrally located district by keeping public houses open late and by using the remaining vacant warehouse premises as late-night dance clubs. The consequence is a substantial volume of late-night noise from these premises and from movement in the streets: levels of intrusion though, which, let us add, are no more than is inevitably associated with such activities, and which in districts which have the character of areas of late-night entertainment would be quite unexceptionable.

What, however, of such activities in *this* locality? One would imagine that as such clubs begin to operate, it would be possible to advise adversely affected residents that the kinds of activity involved are not appropriate for this, now predominantly residential, district and that proceedings for an injunction to prohibit or to regulate such activity might well be successful. If we assume that such advice is correct and that steps are taken, instance by instance, to prevent such nuisances occurring, the result is that the reasonably peaceful character of the locality will be preserved.

What, however, we might ask, would be the position if neighbours, although adversely affected, have – for whatever reason – failed to have taken such action to assert their rights. As a consequence the first club continues to operate. Then a second opens, followed by a third, a fourth, and so on. The district becomes well-known as a part of town where late-night entertainment flourishes. It would seem that by having allowed such activity to have gained a foothold a point may occur at which unlawful nuisances may, through toleration, begin to represent the modified character of a locality; and that what might not so long ago have been subject to an injunction on the part of affected neighbours, may now fall within the ambit of what may be considered to be reasonable activity. It should be noted that we are not talking here of any defendant having acquired by some means a right to commit a nuisance; we are simply opting no longer to characterise an activity as a nuisance because, given the changed nature of the locality, it no longer falls into a category we may condemn as inappropriate.

An illustration of this process may be found in a case which has already been mentioned, *Thompson-Schwab* v *Costaki*.[77] The plaintiff was a residential occupier of a house in the West End of London. He lived there with his family (including a young son) and three young girls who were employed as domestic servants. Until the time of the events which formed the dispute, the street upon which they lived had the character of a good class residential street, albeit that it was not far distant from other streets with a very much more unsavoury reputation. The activities of which the plaintiff made complaint related to the use of the house immediately next to his own for the purpose of prostitution, seriously depreciating the value of his own house and seriously interfering with his comfortable and convenient enjoyment of his house as a residence. The evidence against the defendant occupiers was that they had been using the house next to the

---

[77] [1956] 1 All ER 652. See above, p. 33.

plaintiff's as a "resort" while carrying on their "practices" as prostitutes. They would leave the premises, walk the local streets and return with men they had solicited. Then the men would leave and the women return to the street: activity which, Lord Evershed MR, explained "needs ... no further exposition to anyone who is at all acquainted with the ways of the world".

The defendants appealed against the grant to the plaintiff of an interlocutory injunction restraining them from using the premises in question for the purposes of prostitution pending trial of the action. Lord Evershed MR noted:

> "... the forms which activities constituting actionable nuisances may take are exceedingly varied, and there is the highest authority for saying that they are not capable of precise or close definition."[78]

Turning to the activities of the defendants his Lordship explained:

> " ... it does not follow at all that their activities should ... be regarded as free from the risk or possibility that they cause a nuisance ... to a neighbour merely because they do not impinge on the senses – for example, the nose or the ear – as would the emanation of smells or fumes or noises."[79]

The test to be applied was simply:

> " ... whether what is being done interferes with the plaintiff in the comfortable and convenient enjoyment of his land, regard being had ... to the usages in this matter of civilised society, and regard being also had to the character ... of the neighbourhood."[80]

As regards the evidence, Lord Evershed MR stressed that it did appear:

> "... that the activities being conducted at No 12 ... are not only open, but they are notorious and such as to force themselves on the sense of sight at least of the residents in No 13. The perambulations of the prostitutes and their customers is something which is obvious, which is blatant, and which ... the ... plaintiff has shown *prima facie* to constitute not mere hurt to his sensibilities as a fastidious man, but ... to constitute a sensible interference with the comfortable and convenient enjoyment of his residence where live with him his wife, his son and his servants."[81]

In such *prima facie* circumstances the Court of Appeal held the lower court judge to have been fully justified in having issued an interlocutory injunction to preserve the situation pending trial of the action on full substantive evidence. Moreover, the need for such injunctive relief was referred to by Lord Evershed, in the following words, relevant to the issue

[78] At 653-654.
[79] At 654.
[80] *ibid.*
[81] *ibid.*

of the way in which, for the purposes of the law of nuisance, the character of a locality may change. His Lordship said:

> "It is obvious, having regard to the proximity of other streets with what I have called a less savoury reputation, that if this kind of use of houses is allowed to creep into Crookfield Street, the whole character of the street might very soon and very seriously change for the worse. That is a circumstance which it is proper to bear in mind in considering whether, pending the trial, an injunction should be granted to protect the plaintiffs in their use of their ... residence."[82]

In the short term these words very likely were intended to refer to the practical need not to allow "vice" to obtain a foothold; but looked at in the more medium term one can see that if no action of an effective kind be taken when such activities may first encroach upon a district, it may come to pass that such activity – at least in moderate degree – may become not a nuisance in that locality, but an aspect of the acceptable character of the locality.

An issue however remained, in *Thompson-Schwab*, as regards the breadth of the injunction which should issue. Was it too broad a prohibition to enjoin use of the premises "for the purposes of prostitution"? The Court of Appeal considered, indeed, that such an injunction was too broad. It would forbid activities which might not fall within the compass of the law of nuisance. In Lord Evershed MR's words:

> "... it could not be sustained that every use of a house for such purposes must constitute a nuisance."[83]

In other words something more than the mere use of premises for a purpose such as this was necessary, offering support to subsequent explanations that it was the blatant and notorious "coming and leaving" of the prostitutes to and from the premises which constituted the nuisance, rather than the nature of their activities once within the house in question. To this extent one must note that Lord Evershed MR's early statement that conduct need not impinge on the senses to constitute a nuisance does not need to seem to be illustrated by this particular decision. Certainly this was not a "smells", "noise" or "smoke" case. However, the reasoning behind the Court of Appeal's narrowing of the terms of the plaintiff's interlocutory injunction was that conduct – however immoral, or otherwise lowering in reputation and property value of a neighbourhood – will not involve a nuisance unless it manifests itself to the senses of those seeking to enjoy their properties within the neighbourhood.

The various examples given above have involved no more than illustration of the operation of the basic "locality principle" earlier described. We may, however, usefully use these examples also to consider two further important and related questions:

- Can a defence be raised, to a claim in nuisance, that the development or activity in question has the benefit of a grant of planning permission?
- Can a *single* new development or activity have the effect, on its own, of altering the nature of a locality so that it should not, in that altered locality, be considered a nuisance?

As to the first of these questions – whether a claim in nuisance may be met with a defence that the activity in question has been afforded planning permission – a fairly clear answer may be given. The grant of planning permission is not to be equated with the grant of statutory authority to commit a nuisance.[84] A grant of planning permission means no more than that the activity will not involve a breach of planning control. If the activity cannot be undertaken without the commission of a nuisance, the grant of planning permission will be of no avail in an action in nuisance brought by an affected person.

These principles are well illustrated by *Wheeler* v *JJ Saunders Ltd*.[85] Dr Wheeler and his wife lived adjacent to land used for the rearing of pigs. They sought to use outbuildings on their land for holiday accommodation. However, their plans – and also their own use and enjoyment of their property – were adversely affected by the construction and use, very close to the boundary between their property and that of the defendants, of two "Trowbridge" houses. These were units for high-intensity pig-rearing, comprising "accommodation" in each for some 400 pigs. The plaintiffs complained of the smell emanating from these units: the intensity of the smell resulting from both the number of pigs reared and the fact that the pigs defecated and urinated not onto straw but into a slurry reservoir. The defendants argued that since the units were built in accordance with grants of planning permission and the alleged nuisance flowed inevitably from the development so authorised, there could be no complaint of nuisance. The Court of Appeal rejected this contention. Staughton LJ explained:

> "I do not consider that planning permission necessarily has the same effect as statutory authority. Parliament is sovereign and can abolish or limit the civil rights of individuals ... The planning authority on the other hand has only the powers delegated to it by Parliament. It is not in my view self-evident that they include the power to abolish or limit civil rights in any or all circumstances."[86]

Peter Gibson LJ commented:

> "The defence of statutory authority is allowed on the basis of the true construction of the scope and effect of the statute. Parliament is presumed to have considered the competing interests in the particular circumstances ... and to have determined which is to prevail in the public interest ... But in the case of planning permission ... it is far

---

[84] For this defence, see below, p. 54.
[85] [1995] 2 All ER 697; [1995] Env LR 286.
[86] At 704 of the former report.

from obvious to me that Parliament must be presumed to have intended that ... it should have the same effect on private rights as direct statutory authority."[87]

And Sir John May concluded:

> "In my opinion ... the effect of the grant of planning permission cannot be treated ... as the equivalent of statutory authority ... [W]hile the inevitability of a nuisance could well be the ground for refusing planning permission, the grant of the latter could not in my view license such nuisance ... [E]ven if the nuisance complained of was an inevitable consequence of the ... planning permission ... I do not think that as a matter of law that permission can be said to have licensed that nuisance ..."[88]

The basic principles stated by the Court of Appeal in *Wheeler* confirm a clear distinction between the operation of the defence of statutory authority and the impact of a grant of planning permission. However, this is not to say that a grant of planning permission may not have some impact on the judicial determination of whether the activities so "permitted" are such as to amount to a nuisance. For one thing, the very fact that planning permission may have been granted in awareness of the impact which those activities would inevitably have, may influence a court in its general estimation as regards the matters of reasonable use/reasonable tolerance in the locality in question. In other words the same general factors which resulted in the planning authority seeing fit to grant planning permission may also be influential on the court in *its* judgment on the issue of reasonableness as between adjacent landowners/occupiers. However, there is nothing inevitable about any such equivalence of judgment.

A more controversial issue arises from the second of the two questions highlighted above: whether the grant and implementation of a planning permission may have the consequence of *changing* the nature of its locality for the purposes of assessing whether a nuisance has occurred: in other words changing it to a locality in which such conduct as was permitted by the planning permission – and is now engaged in by a developer – should not be characterised as a nuisance.

We described earlier the way in which the legal "character" of a locality may change, so that formerly inappropriate activity might become permissible. The process described was that of the emergence over a period of time of a number of such activities, with the continuing occurrence of those (nuisances) earlier in the field paving the way for the legitimacy of those commencing later (and themselves securing the legitimacy of the continuation of the earlier activities). The issue now to be considered is whether a *single* instance of the commission of an apparent nuisance (and let us assume, one permitted by a grant of planning permission) may, by

---

[87] At 711.
[88] At 713-714.

altering the nature of the locality in which it occurs, thereby produce the change which provides for its own legal justification. It will be evident that this is to go a step beyond the example formerly provided. In certain contexts, however, it seems an approach which has proven acceptable to the courts.

Discussion must begin with *Gillingham Borough Council* v *Medway (Chatham) Dock Co.*[89] The plaintiff local authority sought to protect the interests of residents[90] along two roads adjacent to the Old Chatham Royal Naval Dockyard (by this time a commercial port), by seeking a declaration that heavy vehicular traffic use of those roads at night amounted to a public nuisance; and also sought an injunction against continuance of such use. The action was brought not directly against those whose vehicles used those roads but, rather, against the owners and operators of the commercial port.

The history of the use of the dockyard/port is of some importance. The former Royal Naval Dockyard, dating from the sixteenth century, operated until its closure in 1982. The nature of its activities were such that it generated comparatively little heavy vehicular traffic to and from the dockyard, and particularly not at night. Matters became quite different as from early 1994 when the Medway Dock Company took over part of the site to develop and operate a commercial port: a "twenty-four hours a day" operation involving heavy vehicle movement at all hours. As Buckley J explained the position:

> "Although these roads must always have provided access to the dockyard ... they had not carried HGVs to any extent in the past. They are substantially residential roads."[91]

The evidence appeared strong that the intrusion on the peace and quiet of the residents of the two streets was sufficient for the lorry activity to have the quality of a legal nuisance in such an area. The principal issue of law was raised by way of defence. The operators of the commercial port were conducting their operations on the basis of, and in accordance with, a grant of planning permission dating from early 1983. When applied for, that application had been strongly objected to by local residents on grounds of the likely heavy vehicle noise. It was inevitable that a commercial port would wish to operate "around the clock" and would attract such traffic. Nevertheless, and notwithstanding the objectors' pleas, planning permission was granted and no conditions were attached limiting the scale of port activities or the times during which access was to be permitted. It was evidently the view of the local authority, in 1983, that its main priority was to gain the economic and employment benefits which the new port might provide. Those considerations – in the light of the then recent closure of the Dockyard – outweighed any adverse environmental effects.

---

[89] [1992] 3 All ER 923; [1992] 1 Env LR 98.
[90] Acting pursuant to s. 222 of the Local Government Act 1972.
[91] [1992] 3 All ER 923 at 928.

Five years later, however, the local authority's priorities became a little different, and it sought to utilise nuisance laws to curtail the activities it had "knowingly permitted" just a few years before.

On the matter of the relationship between nuisance liability and planning permission Buckley J took note of the general defence of statutory authority, and continued:

> "Doubtless one of the reasons for this approach is that Parliament is presumed to have considered the interests of those who will be affected ... and has decided that the benefits ... outweigh any necessary adverse side effects. I believe that principle should be utilised in respect of planning permission. Parliament has set up a statutory framework and delegated the task of balancing the scales between individuals, to the local planning authority ... If a planning authority grants planning permission for a particular construction or use ... it is almost certain that some local inhabitants will be prejudiced in the quiet enjoyment of their properties. Can they defeat the scheme by bringing an action in nuisance? If not, why not? It has been said no doubt correctly that planning permission is not a licence to commit a nuisance and that a planning authority has no jurisdiction to authorise a nuisance. However, a planning authority can, through its development plans and decisions, alter the character of a neighborhood. That may have the effect of rendering innocent activities which, prior to the change, would have been an actionable nuisance."[92]

Buckley J then explained:

> "It seems to me that I must judge the present claim in nuisance by reference to the present character of the neighbourhood pursuant to the planning permission for use of the dockyard as a commercial port."

And applying that test:

> "... these roads are now in the neighbourhood of and lead immediately to a commercial port which operates 24 hours a day. In those circumstances ... the undoubted disturbance to the residents is not actionable."[93]

Buckley J concluded this part of his judgment with the following broad statement:

> "In short, where planning consent is given for a development or change of use, the question of nuisance will thereafter fall to be

---

[92] At 934.
[93] *ibid.*

decided by reference to a neighbourhood with that development or use and not as it was previously."[94]

The decision in *Gillingham* has given rise to some difficulty of interpretation. Although accepting the basic principle that planning permission cannot authorise the commission of a nuisance, it may be thought that Buckley J went a long way towards securing that result by holding that reasonable user/reasonable tolerance must be judged by reference to expectations and circumstances in a locality where such activity as that granted planning permission exists. It would seem likely to be the case generally that it should be considered reasonable to engage in an activity which is (now) to be deemed characteristic of the district; and by the same token it will seem churlish of residents to seem to object to the occurrence of what is (now) characteristic to the locality. But given that the thing which has changed the nature of the locality is the very thing about which complaint is being made, this way of looking at the issue would seem over-generous to potential defendants and fail to acknowledge the true basis of the objections of plaintiffs.

For this reason judges in later cases have taken pains to place a limited interpretation on Buckley J's words. So, in the *Wheeler*[95] case emphasis was placed on the statement that planning permission cannot license a nuisance, with the point about such planning permission affecting the nature of the locality being held inapplicable to the particular issues raised in that case. Peter Gibson LJ noted that *Gillingham* involved:

"a major development altering the character of a neighbourhood with wide consequential effects, such as required a balancing of competing public and private interests before permission was granted. I can well see that in such a case the public interest must be allowed to prevail and that it would be inappropriate to grant an injunction …"[96]

However, his Lordship continued:

"I am not prepared to accept that the principle applied in the *Gillingham* case must be taken to apply to every planning decision. The court should be slow to acquiesce in the extinction of private rights without compensation as a result of administrative decisions which cannot be appealed and are difficult to challenge."[97]

And Staughton LJ, whilst agreeing with the actual decision in *Gillingham*, considered it to be clearly a quite different case from *Wheeler*:

---

[94] At 935.

[95] [1995] 2 All ER 697; [1995] Env LR 286.

[96] At 711 of the former report. Note that his Lordship was referring more to availability of remedy than to substantive issues. He contemplated the possibility of damages *in lieu* (on which, see below at p. 138).

[97] The reference to "cannot be appealed" refers to the absence of rights of appeal within the development control system for objectors in relation to a *grant* of planning permission. Appeals lie in favour of would-be developers who have been refused permission (or granted permission subject to conditions against which they wish to appeal).

"It would ... be a misuse of language to describe what has happened in the present case as a change in the character of a neighbourhood. It is a change of use of a very small piece of land ... It is not a strategic planning decision affected by considerations of public interest ..."[98]

In *Hunter* v *Canary Wharf Ltd*,[99] the House of Lords had little to say about the *Gillingham* decision since the argument that the grant of planning permission provided a defence to nuisance proceedings was not pursued. However, in giving the judgment of the Court of Appeal in *Hunter*,[100] Pill LJ expressed *per curiam* views on this point. After having referred to the Court of Appeal's decision in *Allen* v *Gulf Oil Refining Ltd*[101] where Cumming-Bruce LJ expressed the view that "...the planning authority has no jurisdiction to authorise a nuisance save (if at all) in so far as it has statutory power to permit the change of the character of the neighbourhood...",[102] Pill LJ continued:

"I respectfully agree with that statement. If, as might appear from a later passage in his judgment, Buckley J was deciding the case on the basis that where planning consent for a development is given and implemented, the question of nuisance will thereafter fall to be decided by reference to a neighbourhood with that development and not as it was previously, I have no difficulty with it. The changed character of the area may render innocent the nuisance. That is an application of what Cumming-Bruce LJ stated in *Allen's* case. If, however, as the defendants contend, Buckley J was purporting to broaden the defence of statutory authority so as to include the authority conferred by a planning permission under delegated powers, I have respectfully to disagree."[103]

Although the judges in *Wheeler* and in the Court of Appeal in *Hunter* have been at pains to distinguish *Gillingham*, whilst indicating that that earlier case was correctly decided on its own particular facts, the grounds for differentiation between the decisions are, perhaps, not substantial and may not withstand close analysis. Although there may certainly be a substantial factual difference between, at extremes, substantial developments granted planning permission as part of a strategic redevelopment of an area and permissions granted in respect of very much more minor and localised developments, it is not clear why a planning authority should be regarded as having power by its decision to overturn private rights in the one case but not the other.

What is behind the distinction between *Gillingham* and *Wheeler* seems to be a recognition by the courts that there are situations where there may be broad reasons of public interest supporting substantial and intrusive

---

[98] [1995] 2 All ER 697 at 706-707.
[99] [1997] 2 All ER 426. For the facts of this case, see above at p. 34.
[100] [1996] 1 All ER 482.
[101] [1979] 3 All ER 1008.
[102] At 1020.
[103] [1996] 1 All ER 482 at 492.

development which may "in the public interest" be regarded as outweighing the nuisance caused to neighbours.

Now, one can accept quite readily the proposition that where broad public interest considerations weigh strongly it may well be appropriate not to prohibit development even though that development may inevitably have an adverse impact on the locality and its residents. Certain kinds of "bad neighbour" development are essential in the public interest, even at some cost to its neighbours.

The real issue arises in relation to the proposition that where the public interest may warrant such development the private law rights of locals to the "market" and "amenity" values of their properties should be overturned. This is the crux of the matter, and the solution would seem to lie not, as in *Gillingham* and in *Wheeler*, in a discussion of "rights", but rather in the matter of "remedies". If, as no doubt is the case, from time to time it may be necessary in the broad public interest to afford planning permission to development which will inevitably result in a nuisance to local residents, we may very well want to prevent those residents having power to prevent such "permitted" development from being implemented, through obtaining private law injunctions. But this can be achieved by way of judicial denial of this discretionary remedy,[104] without need to go so far as to deny that a nuisance has been committed. The remedy of damages would remain. Moreover, such damages, as we shall see, may reflect not only loss or harm suffered up to the time of the court hearing, they may also be awarded so as to compensate, in lieu of an injunction, for future harm resulting from the judicial "authorisation" of the continuance of the nuisance. The result is that the cost of compensating those who are substantially adversely affected by the inevitable consequences of a development becomes a part of the cost of that development. In this way public interest objectives may be secured, albeit at what may be regarded as a "truer" economic cost.

Such a result is, of course, quite different from that provided by the conventional explanation of *Gillingham*, under which the public interest in developments not being prevented by private law injunctive relief is secured by a process of denial that the development has invaded private law rights.

The significance of duration and time

Unsurprisingly, the factors relevant to an assessment of the reasonableness of a defendant's conduct and of a plaintiff's objections, include both the *duration* of the alleged nuisance (temporary or of an indefinite or likely permanent nature; continual in nature or intermittent?) and also the *times* at which the alleged nuisance is experienced (for example, by day, by night, or both).

---

[104] As for example in *Miller* v *Jackson* [1977] 3 All ER 338 (above p. 42): but note the strength of the judicial presumption that the remedy by way of injunction shall be available (see below p. 137).

The significance of the intrusive conduct of the defendant being of a "temporary only" nature is well demonstrated by the approach the courts have taken to the adverse effects which building works may have beyond the boundaries of the site. Indeed, the approach has been elevated into what has been described as the "rule"[105] in *Harrison* v *Southwark and Vauxhall Water Co.*[106]

In that case Vaughan Williams J explained:

> "It frequently happens that the owners or occupiers of land cause, in the execution of lawful works in the ordinary use of land, a considerable amount of temporary annoyance to their neighbours; but they are not necessarily on that account held to be guilty of causing an unlawful nuisance. The business of life could not be carried on if it were so. For instance, a man who pulls down his house for the purpose of building a new one no doubt causes considerable inconvenience to his next door neighbour during the process of demolition; but he is not responsible as for a nuisance if he uses all reasonable skill and care to avoid annoyance to his neighbour by the works of demolition. Nor is he liable to an action, even though the noise and dust and the consequent annoyance be such as would constitute a nuisance if the same had been created by sheer wantonness, or in the execution of works for a purpose involving a permanent continuance of the noise and dust."[107]

This "principle" makes good sense. A reasonably tolerant neighbour will adopt a different attitude to the impact of a "nuisance" which he or she knows to be of a temporary nature, as compared with a nuisance which it is believed may be of indefinite, perhaps, permanent duration. Moreover, the limitations contained within the principle reflect the terms upon which such tolerance is commonly afforded. The tolerance relates to the noise, dust and other inconveniences necessarily consequential upon the adjacent operations, and does not extend to discomforts which might have been avoided by "use of all reasonable skill and care".

An example of a temporary nuisance which was held to have gone beyond the bounds of the *Harrison* v *Southwark* principle may be found in *De Keyser's Royal Hotel* v *Spicer Bros Ltd*:[108] a case also illustrating the relevance of the time of day (or more usually night) at which the plaintiff experiences the effects of the defendant's activities. In *De Keyser* a nuisance which was experienced from building works of an admittedly temporary nature transgressed the *Harrison* tolerance principle largely because of the continuance of the pile-driving operations through the night, thereby interrupting the plaintiff's sleep.

---

[105] See Buckley RA: *The Law of Nuisance*, 2nd edn (1997) at p. 10.
[106] [1891] 2 Ch 409.
[107] At 413-4.
[108] (1914) 30 TLR 257. See also *Matania* v *National Provincial Bank* [1936] 2 All ER 633.

In terms of the degree of quiet which an occupier of property may
reasonably expect there may clearly be a difference between daytime and
night-time. However, the fact that night-time noise may be a consequence
of a building schedule designed to reduce the overall period during which
inconvenience is experienced may be of relevance and may, in some
circumstances, render a defendant's conduct not a nuisance.

It is tempting in this context to make some sort of general comment, such
as that one may expect to be required to be quieter on one's property
during the night than during the day. However, although this may very
commonly be the case, it will not invariably be so. The Australian decision,
Daily Telegraph Co Ltd v *Stuart*,[109] provides a valuable reminder that the
various factors presently under review must be considered in relation to the
particular circumstances of each case. The plaintiffs owned a large office
building in Sydney. The building was occupied by persons engaged during
the standard working day on professional and clerical office work. The
defendants were conducting building operations on a nearby site. In the
course of this work they exposed the plaintiff's building to loud and
deafening mechanical drilling noise almost continuously throughout the
working day. In an application that an interlocutory injunction be extended,
Long Innes J commented:

> "In my view it is not reasonable for a builder to create a noise which
> makes it impossible for his neighbours to carry on their business,
> without making some effort either to conduct his operations only
> during hours when it will not have that effect, or during ordinary
> hours to carry out his operations in some less noisy method ... I,
> therefore, continue the injunction as asked; and also restrain the
> defendant ... from using the mechanical drills ... as they were used
> prior to the installation of this suit between the hours 9.30 am and
> 1 pm and between 2 pm and 5 pm on weekdays, and between 9.30 am
> and 12.30 pm on Saturdays. There is no evidence before me at
> present on which I could hold that the plaintiff carries on any
> business before 9 am or after 5 pm and I consequently express no
> opinion as to whether the use by the defendant of the ... drills before
> 9 am or after 5 pm on weekdays would constitute a nuisance."

Although the evidence did not, in the particular case, allow a conclusion to
be reached on this last point, one can see the possibility that within non-
residential, business, districts of cities the degree of noise acceptable at
night may well exceed that which is acceptable by day.

"Sensitivity" of the plaintiff

This factor is, perhaps, best introduced by reference to the words of
Luxmoore J in *Vanderpant* v *Mayfair Hotel Co Ltd*,[110] adopting earlier
language used by Knight-Bruce V-C in *Walter* v *Selfe*:[111]

---

[109] (1928) 28 SR (NSW) 291.
[110] [1930] 1 Ch 138.

" ... every person is entitled as against his neighbour to the comfortable and healthy enjoyment of the premises occupied by him, and in deciding whether, in any particular case, his right has been interfered with and a nuisance thereby caused, it is necessary to determine whether the act complained of is an inconvenience materially interfering with the ordinary physical comfort of human existence, *not merely according to elegant or dainty modes and habits of living, but according to plain and sober and simple notions among English people ..."*[112]

In other words a plaintiff will not succeed, whatever his or her own particular view of the matter, who is personally affected in a way which would not be regarded as overstepping the mark of acceptability by persons with a more averagely robust and tolerant approach to the exigencies of everyday living.

A stock illustration of this proposition may be found in *Robinson* v *Kilvert*.[113] The plaintiff rented the upper floor of premises from the defendant, and engaged there in the activity of storage of paper. The manufacturing activity of the defendant in the rooms below resulted in some warmth to the floor above. This consequence – commonly welcomed – was not of such degree as to cause any physical discomfort to the plaintiff, nor to cause damage to articles with no special sensitivity to moderate temperature. Some quantities of paper stored by the plaintiff were, however, unusually sensitive to heat and were damaged. The action in nuisance brought by the plaintiff was dismissed. Lopes LJ explained the principle:

"A man who carries on an exceptionally delicate trade cannot complain because it is injured by his neighbour doing something which would not injure anything but an exceptionally delicate trade."[114]

Likewise, to take an example from a different jurisdiction, in *Amphi-Theaters Inc* v *Portland Meadows*[115] the principle was applied by the Supreme Court of Oregon in a case brought by proprietors of an out-door cinema whose business was being damaged by the defendant's use of not otherwise objectionable floodlighting on adjacent land. The claim failed on account of the harm being suffered only because of the exceptionally sensitive nature of the plaintiff's business.

Some uncertainty exists as regards the scope of operation of the *Robinson* principle. We may wish to ask, for example, what may qualify as "abnormal sensitivity" for the purpose of that principle? What, for

---

[111] (1851) 64 ER 849.
[112] At 852 (emphasis added).
[113] (1889) 41 Ch D 88. For an example involving especial sensitivity to *noise*, see *Heath* v *Mayor of Brighton* (1908) 98 LT 718.
[114] (1889) 41 Ch D 88 at 97.
[115] (1948) 198 P (2d) 847.

example, of the case of a plaintiff who is adversely affected in the use of his or her property because of an allergic sensitivity to the effects of the activities of the defendant? Is such sensitivity to be regarded as normal or abnormal? In considering this issue it will, one expects, be relevant to ask how common, or how rare, is this particular allergic reaction? But even quite common allergic susceptibilities are not, in spite of current concerns, such as are likely to be experienced by more than a substantial minority of the population. Must one regulate one's conduct so as not to cause a nuisance in the enjoyment of property by a neighbour who suffers from such susceptibility? No very confident answer may be given.

The *Mackinnon* case

There is some authority to suggest that the plaintiff in *Robinson* v *Kilvert* would have been able to recover in relation to the damaged heat-sensitive paper had the facts been that the level of heat produced by the defendant's actions was sufficient to constitute a nuisance in relation to the ordinary use and enjoyment of the plaintiff's premises. Had the intensity of the heat been, in this way, more extreme – so as to have gone beyond what a reasonable owner or occupier might be expected to bear – the damages payable would have included compensation also in relation to the heat-sensitive paper. That item of harm would now not be regarded as a foundation upon which liability is based; but, rather, as an appropriate item in respect of which compensation should be paid arising out of a nuisance, adjudged to be such by reference to other effects and impacts.

An example of this approach may be found in the Canadian case, *Mackinnon Industries Ltd* v *Walker*.[116] Emissions of sulphur dioxide from a car plant operated by the defendant were regarded by the court as a nuisance to the plaintiff in terms of the consequences generally for vegetation on the plaintiff's land. In assessing the level of damages the court awarded compensation not only in relation to ordinary plants harmed, but also in relation to orchids which had a special sensitivity to atmospheric impurities. Notwithstanding the fact that harm to such orchids *alone* might well have not founded an action in nuisance, the court considered that in the light of the broader harm done a nuisance had been demonstrated and that compensation in relation to the orchids was recoverable as a part of the harm done by that nuisance.

This limitation on the principle in *Robinson* v *Kilvert* raises a number of questions, and may result in certain anomalies. Suppose that in *Mackinnon* the remedy sought had been an injunction. What, we might ask, should be the scope of that injunction? Should that injunction be such as to restrain the pollution of air to such degree as to provide protection not just for the general vegetation, but also for the orchids? Or would such an injunction only restrict pollution such as adversely to affect the *ordinarily sensitive* use and enjoyment of the property?

---

[116] [1951] 3 DLR 577.

The former possibility may, perhaps, be thought to extend the *Mackinnon* principle one step too far. It is one thing to say that one who has committed a nuisance must pay for all damage done by that nuisance. It is another to say that, for the future, such a person must conduct himself so that impacts on his neighbour are of a lesser degree than would have been required of him had no more substantial nuisance been earlier committed.

We may therefore prefer the latter possibility. The *Mackinnon* case suggests a generous approach to the measure of damages where a nuisance has been committed. It should not be regarded as extending the substantive ambit of nuisance liability, and so warranting the issuance of *injunctive* relief in relation to conduct which falls within the *Robinson* principle.

Malice

In some circumstances the presence of malice on the part of a defendant, as regards the consequences of his actions for the plaintiff, may render conduct a nuisance which might otherwise not be regarded as having that quality. Something done *in order to annoy* a neighbour may be a nuisance in circumstances in which precisely the same act done *in order to achieve a reasonable objective* in the defendant's ownership or occupation of his or her property might not. Where conduct of a defendant is actuated by a wish to spoil the use and enjoyment of a neighbour's property, rather than by a desire on the part of the defendant to make some reasonable and legitimate use of his or her property, a fundamental plank is removed from the "reasonable give and take" rationale. I may be expected to put up, to a reasonable degree, with the effects of your reasonable use and enjoyment of your property. There seems, however, to be no good reason why the law should require me to put up with the effects of behaviour which is unassociated with any reasonable use to which you may wish to put your land, and is simply behaviour engaged in order to adversely affect the use and enjoyment of my land.

These quite simple ideas may be readily illustrated. In *Christie v Davey*[117] the plaintiffs and the defendant lived side by side in semi-detached houses in Brixton. Mrs Christie was a teacher of music, and her family, generally, was musical. Throughout the day music emanated from the plaintiffs' house and could be heard by the defendant. The defendant, it seems, did not enjoy the sounds he heard and responded by making much noise himself by beating trays and by rapping on the dividing wall between the houses. The court granted the plaintiffs' claim for an injunction, to restrain the defendant from making such noise so as to vex and annoy the plaintiffs. North J explained:

> "In my opinion the noises which were made in the defendant's house were not of a legitimate kind ... They were made deliberately and maliciously for the purpose of annoying the plaintiffs."[118]

---

[117] [1893] 1 Ch 316.
[118] At 326.

The words which follow are also significant:

> "If what has taken place had occurred between two sets of persons both perfectly innocent, I should have taken an entirely different view of the case. But I am persuaded that what was done by the defendant was done only for the purpose of annoyance, and in my opinion it was not a legitimate use of the defendant's house to use it for the purpose of vexing and annoying his neighbours."[119]

A similar approach was adopted in *Hollywood Silver Fox Farm* v *Emmett*.[120] The plaintiffs were breeders of silver foxes on land adjoining that owned by the defendant. Following a dispute about a prominent advertising sign erected by the plaintiffs (the defendant considering the sign detrimental to his plans to develop a building estate) the defendant sent his son, on four evenings, to the point on his land closest to the vixens' pen, to fire there a gun. The noise from the gun had its intended consequence of causing fright to the vixens, and there was evidence that some for this reason did not mate. In these circumstances the plaintiffs sought and obtained damages and an injunction.

A neat contrast may be seen in the Canadian decision: *Rattray* v *Daniels*.[121] Here the defendant faced a predicament. Having just bought land he began to clear it by bulldozer. On being informed by his neighbour that the noise from these operations was adversely affecting mink in their breeding season – the mothers killing their young – he discontinued operations. It then appeared that the bulldozer necessary to clear the land was only available during the period of the year which coincided with the mink breeding. The following year the defendant cleared the land with the bulldozer notwithstanding complaint from the plaintiff, and in knowledge of the effects of these operations on the plaintiff's mink. The plaintiff's claim to damages, nevertheless, failed. Ford CJA noted that the situation was quite different from that in the *Hollywood Silver Fox Farm* case. In that case, he explained:

> "the defendant ... maliciously caused his son to discharge guns on his land as near as possible to the breeding pens ... for the purpose of injuring the plaintiff by interfering with the breeding of foxes. In the instant case the defendant proved clearly that there was no malice on his part but rather that he was unable to obtain the loan of a caterpillar at any other time of the year for use on the land. It so happened that the whelping season for the mink coincided with the time he was able to obtain the caterpillar to level his land in the hope that he might lease [the land] to a business concern that was interested in it ... The evidence indicated that there was no other reasonable or practical way that he could fit his land so as to lease it as contemplated. That he should desist from doing so because of the delicate nature of the

[119] At 326-327.
[120] [1936] 2 KB 468.
[121] (1959) 17 DLR (2d) 134.

business carried on by the plaintiff on her adjoining land would not … permit him reasonable use of his own land."[122]

Two points may be noted from this helpful statement. First, it is clear that mere awareness that one's actions will adversely affect a neighbour is not to be equated with malice. If one has a legitimate purpose as regards the use and enjoyment of one's own land the conduct will not fall within the "malice" principle. Rather, what will be in issue will be the ordinary operation of the "reasonable user" test: "In the light of such awareness of consequences was the defendant's user reasonable?" Much will, as the judgment suggests, depend on whether such consequences for the plaintiffs were or were not reasonably avoidable by reasonably practicable modification or moderation of the defendant's conduct.

Secondly, the judgment suggests that even those who engage in unusually sensitive land use activities – and who, as we have seen, are not permitted to use the law of nuisance to seek to impose exceptional constraints on their neighbour's conduct – may be protected from *malicious* interventions. To illustrate this point we may return to the *Hollywood Silver Fox Farm* case. The defendant had led evidence, not accepted as true by the judge, that the purpose of firing the guns was to scare away rabbits. Suppose, however, that this evidence had been believed; and suppose also that rabbits were a substantial pest on the defendant's land and that this was the only practicable means of reducing their menace. We now have an example of reasonable and non-malicious user on the part of the defendant; and, one presumes, user which ordinary, reasonably tolerant, neighbours would regard as reasonable agricultural land use. Following the principle in *Robinson* v *Kilvert*[123] it would seem, in such circumstances, that a neighbour, whose breeding animals were exceptionally sensitive to such noise, would be without redress in the law of nuisance.

Care may need to be taken to distinguish conduct which, because of its deliberate consequences for a plaintiff, may involve the commission of a nuisance, and conduct which is deliberate in those consequences because it involves reasonable measures to seek to abate a nuisance being committed *by the plaintiff*. The Australian case of *Fraser* v *Booth*[124] provides a nice example. Fraser had acted in various ways in the hope of frightening away his neighbour, Booth's, pigeons. He had deliberately made noises and even resorted to hosing them. Roper CJ Esq held, however, that his actions, although deliberate in their intent to adversely affect Booth in his use and enjoyment of his land, were not actionable in nuisance. The judge commented:

"This case … is quite different from *Hollywood Silver Fox Farm*. Here, the noises, … were made under the stress of annoyance from an existing nuisance in the hope of alleviating that annoyance, or having

---

[122] At 136-138.
[123] See above p. 61.
[124] (1949) 50 SR (NSW) 113.

it alleviated by the person responsible for it. They cannot be regarded as merely malicious and spiteful acts done simply to cause damage to the defendant ..."

In fact the evidence indicated that Fraser had also used firecrackers in his campaign against the pigeons. These were adjudged differently: this conduct went beyond reasonable acts to seek to abate Booth's nuisance, and involved, in themselves, the commission of a nuisance.[125]

A decision which requires carefully to be distinguished, within this line of "malice" cases, is *Bradford Corpn.* v *Pickles.*[126] The local authority drew water from land which it owned, and supplied that water to the people of Bradford. Prior to reaching the local authority's land the water percolated[127] through land belonging to the defendant. The defendant had begun to drain the water-bearing strata on his land, thereby reducing the volume of water reaching the plaintiffs. It was claimed by the local authority that the defendant's actions were not done in order to make any legitimate use of his own land or its water, but were done "maliciously" with a view to holding the local authority "to ransom", so that it would purchase from him his land or its water. Such motive, the local authority contended, rendered the defendant's actions unlawful, so that an injunction should issue. The House of Lords held to the contrary, even assuming the truth of the facts so pleaded. The speeches of their Lordships contain a number of very broad statements. So, for example, Lord Halsbury said:

"Motives and intentions in such a question as is now before your Lordships seem to me to be absolutely irrelevant."[128]

And Lord Watson stated that:

"... no use of property, which would be legal if due to a proper motive, can become illegal because it is prompted by a motive which is improper or even malicious."[129]

At first sight these statements might seem to fit uneasily alongside the approach taken by the courts in cases such as *Christie* and *Hollywood Silver Fox Farm*. However, here, as ever, context is critical: the statements set out above must be read not "at large", but in the light of the particular issue under consideration in the case itself.

To put the matter most simply: notwithstanding the use of the word "maliciously" in the plaintiffs' pleadings the case was really not one of malice at all: not, at least, in the sense used in the nuisance cases earlier described. Their Lordships were at pains to stress two important features of

---

[125] For another example of *unjustified* response to what may well have been a nuisance on the part of the plaintiff, see *Stokes* v *Brydges* [1958] QWN 5.
[126] [1895] AC 587.
[127] In undefined channels – i.e. through the soil and rock strata.
[128] [1895] AC 587 at 594.
[129] At 598.

the case. On the one hand the plaintiffs had not been deprived of any incident of land ownership to which they had any legal right: a landowner has no absolute right to an uninterrupted flow of underground water. Moreover, even if the utilisation of that flow could be regarded as an aspect of the plaintiffs' reasonable use and enjoyment of their land which was protected by the law of nuisance against interference by unreasonable user on the part of the defendant, there was really nothing about the defendant's conduct which could be so characterised. In the malice cases described earlier the sole motive of the defendant had been to act to the detriment of the plaintiff. In *Pickles* the matter was quite different. Certainly the plaintiffs were disadvantaged by the actions of the defendant. Certainly this was an intended consequence. But it was a consequence of the defendant having acted in a way which the law regarded as a perfectly proper use of a landowner's property: to obtain the commercial benefit of that asset (its groundwater). In the words of Lord MacNaghten:

" ...why should the defendant ... without fee or reward, keep his land as a store-room for a commodity which the corporation dispense, probably not gratuitously,[130] to the inhabitants of Bradford. He prefers his own interests to the public good. He may be churlish, selfish and grasping. His conduct may seem shocking to the moral philosopher. But where is the malice? [He] has no spite to the people of Bradford. He bears no ill-will to the corporation. They are welcome to the water, and to his land to, if they will pay the price for it."[131]

So regarded, the case was simply not one involving "malice" in the sense in which that concept has been used in the nuisance cases described earlier. The real issue in *Pickles* was whether such non-malicious and merely self-serving behaviour on the part of the defendant was, or was not, to be regulated by the ordinary nuisance rules about the reasonable user of land, and their Lordships held that in the context of the utilisation of percolating groundwater a different principle prevailed – a principle recognising absolute rights, rather than founded upon any principle of reasonable "give and take".[132]

Public benefit

It might have been expected that "public benefit" would rank as a *defence* to an action in nuisance rather than operating as simply one, amongst several, factors to be taken into account in the very assessment of whether some interference with the use and enjoyment of land amounts to such a nuisance.

---

[130] Lord Halsbury had referred to the local authority as a trading company in its function of selling water: desiring to make a profit.

[131] At 600-601.

[132] A different approach applies in respect of water which runs through defined channels – for example, the rules applicable to a landowner's actions affecting the quality and quantity of water flowing through rivers and streams.

This is not, however, the way in which the courts have approached this matter. Instead they have taken the view that although the value of a defendant's activities may be one factor relevant to the assessment of the level of reasonable tolerance to be expected of the plaintiff, beyond that level of reasonable tolerance his or her interests should not be sacrificed to the interests of the public as a whole. When the matter is regarded in terms of entitlement to damages we may, perhaps, say that beyond this point the damages payable to the plaintiff become a part of the price which the broader community must pay for the benefit which it may seek to gain from the defendant's activities.[133]

The matter was explained in strong terms in a case concerning the grant, or otherwise, of injunctive relief in relation to a nuisance: the words applying *a fortiori* as regards the logically anterior issue of whether a substantive nuisance has been demonstrated. Lindley LJ stated in *Shelfer* v *City of London Electric Lighting Co*:[134]

> "Neither has the circumstance that the wrongdoer is in some sense a public benefactor (for example, a gas or water company or a sewer company) ever been considered a sufficient reason for refusing to protect by injunction an individual whose rights are being persistently infringed. Expropriation, even for a money consideration, is only justifiable when Parliament has sanctioned it."[135]

As an example of a case in which a nuisance was restrained by injunction notwithstanding the "worthy cause" which gave rise to the nuisance, reference may be made to the Australian case, *McKenzie* v *Rowley*.[136] Here the dispute concerned the use made by the Salvation Army of land and buildings adjacent to the plaintiff's house. The plaintiff's complaints centred on the sounds from a brass band (playing and practising) and people singing, clapping hands and shouting ejaculations. An injunction was granted to restrain these activities to a level which would not involve a noise nuisance. In his judgment Murray CJ commented:

> "The right of people to assemble for [the exercise of religious worship] cannot be questioned and … the sounds which emanate from their devotions, as ordinarily conducted, cannot be held to be a nuisance. Still there must be a limit beyond which even worshipers may not be allowed to go. The happiness of human existence cannot be left to the mercy of whatever may be claimed to be done in the name of religion.
>
> It has been with great reluctance and deep regret that I have come to a decision unfavourable to the defendants. For I recognise the immense value of the work the Salvation Army has done, and is still doing, not only here, but in other parts of the world. The mistake that has been

---

[133] For issues relating to injunctions, see below at p. 137.
[134] [1895] 1 Ch 287.
[135] At 315-316. For the defence of statutory authority, see below p. 123.
[136] [1916] SALR 1.

made has been in forgetting that the plaintiff has a legal right to a certain degree of quietude in his own home."

More recently, the issue of public benefit or interest has arisen in a further case concerned with noise: *Dennis and Dennis v Ministry of Defence*.[137] Here, the first and second claimants owned and lived on the Walcot Hall Estate, situated near to Stamford, in Cambridgeshire. The Estate, which consisted of the Hall, a Grade 1 listed building, and a number of other buildings, cottages and other structures, several of which were Grade 2 listed, was also situated in close proximity to RAF Wittering, the "Home of the Harrier Jet." Since the late 1960s the aerodrome had become a purpose-built operating and training base for the aircraft: an aircraft famed for its ability to take off vertically and recognised as a noisy aircraft, perhaps even the noisiest, especially when executing a slow landing. The prevailing wind at the Walcot Estate was west to east. The Harriers took off into the wind and away from the Estate. However, when coming into land from the east, they flew directly over the Estate and very near to the Hall itself. The evidence of expert and lay witnesses was unanimous in supporting the view that the noise amounted to a very serious interference with the ordinary enjoyment of the Hall, whether judged from inside or outside the house. The effect of the noise was aggravated by its persistence and its unpredictability; there being a very rapid onset to the noise, with a corresponding "startle" effect. Following correspondence between the claimants and the Ministry of Defence (MoD), in which the latter expressed sympathy and apologies for the claimants' predicament but nevertheless stated that relocation of the aircraft to another base had been ruled out as being cost-prohibitive, the claimants instituted proceedings against the MoD in nuisance. The case thus raised what Buckley J termed an "important and problematic point of principle in the law of nuisance", namely "whether and in what circumstances a sufficient public interest can amount to a defence to a claim in nuisance".[138]

In the present context, it was submitted on behalf of the MoD that in none of the earlier cases in which the issue of public benefit had been considered had the matter been of such importance as it was in the present case. It was further submitted that the defence of the realm was a public interest of a different and greater order altogether from the commercial and other interests which had hitherto been considered by the courts. On behalf of the claimants, it was submitted that the private rights of the individual can never be overridden by the interests of the State, save perhaps in the case of a grave national emergency. Alternatively, it was submitted that if such rights could be overridden, the public rather than the individual ought to bear the costs of the damage which resulted from the interference.

On the facts of the case, Buckley J had little difficulty in concluding that the flying of Harriers over the Walcot Hall Estate amounted to a *prima facie* nuisance at common law. In His Lordship's judgment, such flying did

---

[137] [2003] EWHC 793 (QB).
[138] At para.30 of the judgment.

not amount to an ordinary use of land within the legal meaning of that phrase. Neither was Buckley J convinced by the argument that a consideration of the character of the neighbourhood tipped the balance against finding that the Harriers amounted to a nuisance. In his Lordship's judgment, the area in question remained essentially rural despite the establishment of the aerodrome in 1916, and in any case, "it would be odd if a potential tortfeasor could itself so alter the character of the neighbourhood over the years as to create a nuisance with impunity".[139] However, as his Lordship was at pains to stress, "it is not one factor that determines whether a legal nuisance has arisen". Although the character of the neighbourhood and the particular use of the land in question were relevant factors to consider, they were "only signposts to a conclusion, more or less important depending on all the circumstances".[140] Accordingly, it was necessary to have regard to another factor in the equation: the public interest.

In considering the question "What is the effect of a public interest in an activity continuing, where that activity would otherwise constitute a nuisance?", Buckley J observed that it would be "unsatisfactory to attempt a general answer" to such a question. Rather, the answer would "depend on all the circumstances, not least the strength of the public interest in question". Continuing on the same theme, his Lordship opined:

> "If public interest can be a relevant consideration, one solution would be that the particular public interest should be put in the scales at the stage when the court is seeking to balance the competing interests of the parties. As the cases indicate, very often the private interest will prevail. The alternative approach would be to exclude any public interest from consideration of whether a nuisance should be found and consider it as relevant only to remedy."[141]

Buckley J then proceeded to asses the merits of the two approaches which he had identified:

> "The problem with putting the public interest into the scales when deciding whether a nuisance exists, is simply that if the answer is no, not because the claimant is being over sensitive, but because his private rights must be subjugated to the public interest, it might well be unjust that he should suffer the damage for the benefit of all. If it is to be held that there is no nuisance, there can be no remedy at common law... If public interest is considered at the remedy stage and since the court has a discretion, the nuisance may continue but the public, in one way or another, pays for its own benefit."[142]

In the light of the considerations referred to above, and having regard to the facts of the case before him, Buckley J concluded that although the

---

[139] At para.34.
[140] At para.39.
[141] At para.44.
[142] At para.46.

flying of the Harriers amounted to a nuisance at common law, it was nevertheless a nuisance which was justified because of the public interest in RAF Wittering continuing to be used as an airbase for the training of pilots. The public interest did not, however, so override the private rights of the claimants that they were left without a remedy. Rather, it affected the type of remedy that would be granted. Thus rather than grant an injunction (or a declaration since the land in question was owned by the Crown), Buckley J held that the appropriate remedy would take the form of damages.[143]

THE RIGHT TO SUE IN PRIVATE NUISANCE

The leading authority on who may maintain an action in private nuisance is *Hunter* v *Canary Wharf Ltd*,[144] in which, it may be remembered,[145] the House of Lords considered appeals in two actions alleging nuisance arising out of the redevelopment of the London Dockland. In the first action several hundred plaintiffs claimed damages for alleged nuisance in the form of interference with television reception caused by the construction of Canary Wharf Tower. The second action involved a claim to damages to compensate for harm caused by allegedly excessive amounts of dust created by the London Development Corporation in its construction of the Limehouse Link Road. Certain preliminary points of law were sent for trial, one of which was whether it is necessary to have an interest in property affected by a nuisance in order to maintain a claim in private nuisance (and, if so, what interest in property might suffice to satisfy this requirement)? This issue was of significance to both actions. In each case the plaintiffs consisted of a considerable number of local people. All these individuals alleged that they had suffered or been inconvenienced in the ways described. However, not all were householders with an exclusive right to possession in respect of the places where they lived, whether as freeholders or tenants or even as licensees. In the words of Lord Goff:

> "They include people with whom householders share their homes, for example as wives or husbands or partners, or as children or other relatives."[146]

At first instance Judge Harvey QC had determined that such persons could not take the benefit of the rules of private nuisance: such protection was afforded only for the benefit of those with a right to exclusive possession of the property subject to the nuisance.

---

[143] The claimants were awarded an overall sum of £950,000 in damages to reflect the loss of capital value of the Estate, the loss of amenity and the loss of opportunity to exploit the property commercially caused by the existence of the noise nuisance. Since that sum was to be paid by the MoD, the decision in *Dennis* accords with a principle stated previously, i.e. that the broader community must pay for the benefit which it gains from the defendant's activities.

[144] [1997] 2 All ER 426; [1997] Env LR 488.

[145] For the facts of this case, see above at p. 34.

[146] At 434 of the former report.

The Court of Appeal,[147] however, adopted a more generous approach, Pill LJ explaining that:

> "A substantial link between the person enjoying the use and the land on which he or she is enjoying it is essential but ... *occupation of property, as a home, does confer upon the occupant a capacity to sue in private nuisance.*"[148]

In the House of Lords the majority (Lord Cooke dissenting) regarded this extension by the Court of Appeal of the ambit of private nuisance as inappropriate.

The traditional approach was described by Lord Goff as follows:

> " ... an action in private nuisance will usually be brought by a person in actual possession of the land affected, either as the freeholder or tenant of the land ..., or ... as a licensee with exclusive possession ...; though a reversioner may sue in respect of a nuisance of a sufficiently permanent character to damage his reversion."[149]

In one situation, however, a person in actual possession might sue in nuisance even though not being able to show any title to land. For this exceptional proposition their Lordships regarded *Foster* v *Warblington UDC*[150] as good authority. Here the local authority had discharged sewage into oyster beds on the foreshore. An oyster merchant who had for many years been in occupation of those beds, and who had throughout that period excluded all others from the beds, was held entitled to sue the local authority in nuisance notwithstanding that he possessed no demonstrable legal title to the land. In the words of Vaughan Williams LJ:

> " ... even if title could not be proved, in my judgment there has been such an occupation of these beds for such a length of time ... as would entitle the plaintiff ... to sustain this action ..."[151]

In other words *Foster* established that even wrongful possession might suffice to give standing for an action in nuisance, provided that possession was "exclusive".[152]

In the more recent case of *Pemberton* v *London Borough of Southwark*,[153] the Court of Appeal was required to consider a novel question: whether a

---

[147] [1996] 2 WLR 348.

[148] At 365 (emphasis added).

[149] [1997] 2 All ER 426 at 435.

[150] [1906] 1 KB 648.

[151] At 659-660.

[152] See also *Asher* v *Whitlock* [1865] LR 1 QB 1 and *Allan* v *Liverpool Overseers* [1874] LR 9 QB 180. Without going into intricacies of property law it may be helpful to draw attention to the statement of Lord Hoffmann in his speech in *Hunter*: "Exclusive possession distinguishes an occupier who may in due course acquire title under the Limitation Act 1980 from a mere trespasser. It distinguishes [also] a tenant holding a leasehold estate from a mere licensee" ([1997] 2 All ER 426 at 449).

[153] [2000] 2 EGLR 33.

"tolerated trespasser" can sue a local authority owner of premises in nuisance. The phrase "tolerated trespasser" first appeared in the speech of Lord Browne-Wilkinson in *Burrows* v *Brent London Borough Council*,[154] In effect, a "tolerated trespasser"[155] is a person who was formerly a secure tenant under Part IV of the Housing Act 1985, but whose tenancy has come to an end by reason of a court order for possession of the property.[156] Until that order is executed, however, the former tenant has a statutory right to remain in the property; he or she retains the exclusive occupation and possession of the property on payment of the rent. In *Pemberton*, the appellant became a tolerated trespasser when she failed to comply with the terms of a possession order granted by the Lambeth County Court. That order required her to pay a weekly installment on her rent arrears in addition to the current rent. The appellant nevertheless remained in the property and continued to pay to the council virtually all the rent to which it would have been entitled had she remained a secure tenant. Some five years later, she commenced proceedings against the council alleging that the flat that she occupied was infested with cockroaches, that the cockroaches had entered the flat from the common parts of the building and that the infestation had affected her enjoyment of the flat and had damaged her health and that of her two children as well as causing damage to her property in the flat. In its defence, the council argued that it had taken steps to eradicate the infestation and that the appellant had not always been cooperative in this process. More important, however, in the present context, was the argument that the appellant had no cause of action against the council because she was not their tenant and she did not have a sufficient interest in the property to support an action in nuisance. That argument was decisively and unanimously rejected by the Court of Appeal.

Roch LJ, who delivered the first opinion on the appeal, stated the legal position of the tolerated trespasser as follows:

> "As a tolerated trespasser the former tenant enjoys none of the rights of a tenant. The landlord cannot be required to repair the premises, nor does the former tenant have any rights under the Defective Premises Act 1972. The landlord has no right to evict the tolerated trespasser for any breach of the covenants which had been contained in the secure tenancy agreement. The tolerated trespasser could only be evicted for breach of the conditions on which he or she was being allowed to remain in the premises ... On the other hand, the tolerated trespasser is in occupation with the assent of the landlord and is under an obligation to make payments in respect of occupation. Those payments are normally the payments that would have to be paid by the tolerated trespasser had she remained a secure tenant together with additional sums off the arrears. The tolerated trespasser may be able to revive the secure tenancy be persuading the County Court

---

[154] [1996] 1 WLR 1448.

[155] In *Pemberton*, Clarke LJ referred to the concept as "a recent, somewhat bizarre, addition to the dramatis personae of the law" (at 37D).

[156] Such an order can be obtained under s.82(1) of the Housing Act 1985.

Judge to discharge or rescind the original order for possession or to make an order varying the date for the giving of possession, the original tenancy being revived under s.85(4) of the Act."[157]

Thus whilst a tolerated trespasser has an exclusive right to occupy the premises,[158] a landlord is under no obligation to effect any repairs that a property might need during the course of that possession. In these circumstances, therefore, the Court of Appeal held that a tolerated trespasser does have a sufficient interest in the relevant property in order to bring an action in nuisance. That ability to sue is not confined to bringing an action against a third party; it may also be exercised against a landlord. Thus in the words of Clarke LJ in the present appeal:

> "... if the council or another tenant causes such a noise in an adjoining flat that it would amount to a nuisance, the tolerated trespasser should be able to seek an injunction against the council or the tenant as the case may be to stop the noise."[159]

The requirement that occupancy involve exclusive possession provided the crucial distinction between the *Foster* case[160] and the decision, the following year, in *Malone* v *Laskey*.[161] In *Malone* the manager of a company lived in a house which was leased to that company. He occupied the house as a mere licensee. The plaintiff was not, however, the manager but the manager's wife. She lived with him in the house. She also was a mere licensee. Her claim arose out of injuries which she had suffered when a bracket supporting a water tank had fallen from the wall in the lavatory of the house; an event caused, it was alleged, by vibrations from an engine operating on the defendant's adjoining property. It was held in the Court of Appeal that she could not maintain a claim in nuisance.[162] The reasoning of the court was explained by Fletcher Moulton LJ. His Lordship drew attention to the fact that it was the husband's employers who were the tenants of the affected building, and noted:

> " ... if the premises had been injured or the enjoyment of them interfered with by the vibration it was open to them to take any one of three courses – they might come to the courts for an injunction to stop the vibration, or they might simply have tolerated it, or they might have authorised its continuance either gratuitously or for a valuable consideration. A person in the position of the plaintiff, who was in

---

[157] [2000] 2 EGLR 33 at 35D-E.

[158] In the words of Roch LJ in *Pemberton*: "possession or occupation by the tolerated trespasser may be precarious, but it is not wrongful and it is exclusive" (at 36M).

[159] At p 37J.

[160] See above at p. 72.

[161] [1907] 2 KB 141. Followed in, inter alia, *Cunard* v *Antifyre Ltd* [1933] 1 KB 551; *Oldham* v *Lawson* (No 1) [1976] VR 654.

[162] At the time of her action her claim in negligence could not succeed. This limitation was based upon a principle overturned in *A C Billings and Sons Ltd* v *Riden* [1958] AC 240. Nowadays, a plaintiff in Mrs Malone's position would succeed in negligence upon proof of breach of duty of care.

the premises as a mere licensee, had no right to dictate ... which course they should take."[163]

His Lordship then conjectured:

"They [i.e. the employer-tenants] seem to have voluntarily permitted the vibration to continue. Indeed, ... I have very little doubt that the proximity of the engine was by no means an unmixed evil to them, for it may well have affected the amount of rent paid by them for the premises."[164]

Regardless of whether or not this was the case, the question of what action, if any, to take in relation to a purely private nuisance was:

"a matter entirely for the tenant, and a person who is merely present in the house cannot complain of a nuisance which has in it no element of a public nuisance."[165]

This established principle, limiting actions in nuisance to those with proprietary interests or at least exclusive possession of the adversely affected land was, however, departed from in 1993 in *Khorasandjian* v *Bush*;[166] a decision which much influenced the Court of Appeal in *Hunter*, but which was overruled when that case came before the House of Lords.

In *Khorasandjian* the injunctive protection of the law was sought by a young woman (18 at the time of the hearing) in relation to threatening and abusive behaviour on the part of an older man with whom she had previously had a relationship. The issue before the Court of Appeal in *Khorasandjian* was whether the scope of the injunction to be issued could legitimately extend to a prohibition on the defendant making unwanted and harassing telephone calls to the plaintiff at her mother's home. By a majority it was held that the plaintiff could found a claim to an injunction upon the cause of action which she would possess in private nuisance; and this notwithstanding that she possessed no greater right to occupy or be present in her mother's house than had the injured wife to the property in *Malone*.

For a while the decision in *Khorasandjian* suggested the availability of remedies in private nuisance for the benefit of those who could show some "substantial link" – for example, regarding the premises as "home" – even though that connection was not one characterised by the possession of a proprietary interest (or mere exclusive possession, as in *Foster*). However, the majority of the House of Lords in *Hunter* regarded this as an inappropriate extension of the scope of operation of the tort of private nuisance. Lord Goff explained the *Khorasandjian* decision in the following words:

---

[163] [1907] 2 KB 141 at p. 153.
[164] At 153-154.
[165] At 154.
[166] [1993] QB 727.

> " ... what the Court of Appeal appears to have been doing was to
> exploit the law of private nuisance in order to create by the back door
> a tort of harassment ..."[167]

Lord Goff noted, in this connection, that it produced a tort of harassment
which was only partially effective: partially effective only because of it
being artificially limited to harassment which takes place against a plaintiff
in a place she regards as her "home". It would not operate in relation to
similar conduct by the defendant which she might experience at work,
while staying with a friend, or in her car via a mobile phone. Nevertheless,
in each of these instances the gravamen of the wrong was the same. It was,
their Lordships considered, a wrong approach to distort the fundamental
nature of the tort of private nuisance in order to provide a partial solution
only to a rather different problem.[168]

Lord Goff reiterated:

> "It follows that, on the authorities as they stand, an action in private
> nuisance will only lie at the suit of a person who has a right to the
> land affected. Ordinarily such a person can only sue if he has the right
> to exclusive possession. Exceptionally, ... as *Foster* shows, this
> category may include a person in actual possession who has no right
> to be there; and in any event a reversioner can sue in so far as a
> reversionary interest is affected. But a mere licensee on the land has
> no right to sue."[169]

In preferring the conventional approach in *Malone* to the broader
conception of nuisance in *Khorasandjian* their Lordships in *Hunter* were
determinedly returning the tort to its "protection of property" roots. Lord
Goff acknowledged this, referring to arguments put forward in favour of
the plaintiffs:

> " ... the extension of the tort in this way would transform it from a
> tort to land into a tort to the person, in which damages could be
> recovered in respect of something less than personal injury[170] and the
> criteria for liability were founded not upon negligence but upon
> striking a balance between the interests of neighbours in the use of
> their land. This is, in my opinion, not an acceptable way in which to
> develop the law."[171]

Such emphasis upon the "property-protection" nature of the tort lies behind
much of the speech of Lord Lloyd. His Lordship drew attention to the three
broad kinds of private nuisance:

---

[167] [1997] 2 All ER 426 at 438.

[168] It was noted also that the Protection from Harassment Act 1997 had, meanwhile, introduced a
statutory tort of harassment.

[169] At 438.

[170] i.e. for discomfort, inconvenience, annoyance.

[171] At 439.

> "They are (1) nuisance by encroachment on a neighbour's land; (2) nuisance by direct physical injury to a neighbour's land; and (3) nuisance by interference with a neighbour's quiet enjoyment of his land."[172]

In relation to the first two of these kinds of nuisance his Lordship noted that that there was no issue about limiting the right to sue to the owner, or occupier with exclusive possession. Since the basis of the claim was the damage to the land itself it was fully comprehensible that the right of action was so restricted. Lord Lloyd explained that the key to this lay in the measure of damages appropriate:

> " ... the measure of damages in cases (1) and (2) will be the diminution in the value of the land. This will usually (though not always) be equal to the cost of reinstatement. The loss resulting from diminution in the value of land is a loss suffered by the owner or occupier with the exclusive right to possession (as the case may be) or both, since it is they alone who have a proprietary interest, or stake, in the land. So it is they alone who can bring an action to recover the loss."[173]

The issue for Lord Lloyd was whether the same, or a different, principle should apply in cases of nuisance falling under the third heading: interference with a neighbour's quiet enjoyment of land. In this situation need the neighbour demonstrate loss in value of his or her own property in order to succeed? Or could neighbours who had experienced the nuisance, but not being property owners had suffered no property value loss, also take proceedings?

Lord Lloyd concluded that the same principle as regards measure of damages did and should apply to all three kinds of private nuisance. Moreover, the quantum of damages in a case falling within category (3) – interference with the quiet enjoyment of land – relates not to the number of persons whose enjoyment may have been affected, but to the effect that the nuisance may be regarded as having had on the value of the land. As Lord Lloyd explained:

> " ... the quantum of damages in private nuisance does not depend on the number of those enjoying the land in question."[174]

And again:

> "the reduction in ... value is the same whether the land is occupied by [a] family man or by [a] bachelor."[175]

---

[172] At 441.
[173] *ibid.*
[174] At 442.
[175] *ibid.*

Of course, if the activities causing the nuisance go beyond "mere" interference with quiet enjoyment of neighbouring property so as to cause persons to suffer personal injury or illness or damage to their goods, such persons may not be without redress. However, their cause of action will lie not in private nuisance but in negligence. Moreover, this requirement to sue for personal injury and other non-real property damage in negligence rather than nuisance applies also to those *with* property interests in the land affected. Lord Lloyd explained:

> "If the occupier of land suffers personal injury as a result of inhaling the smoke, he may have a cause of action in negligence. But he does not have an action in nuisance for his *personal* injury, nor for interference with his *personal* enjoyment."[176]

At this point a distinction drawn by Lord Lloyd should to be noted. His Lordship had earlier given, as an example of this third kind of nuisance, the emission of smoke from a factory. It might be that the effect of the smoke across a plaintiff's land would be such as to reduce the value of that land, so giving its owner a claim to compensation. We should note, however, Lord Lloyd's next comment:

> "The effect of smoke from a neighbouring factory is to reduce the value of the land. There may be no diminution in the market value. But there will certainly be loss of amenity value so long as the nuisance lasts."[177]

This concept of "amenity value", to be set alongside the idea of "market value", introduces some important and quite sophisticated ideas. In particular, it permits one who qualifies to sue in private nuisance to recover damages even in a case where no reduction in market value, consequent upon the nuisance, can be demonstrated. The damages for loss of "amenity value" will be assessed – in an admittedly somewhat "rough and ready" way – by reference to the harm to the enjoyment which might be made of the property: not, although clear overlap between these two things may exist, by reference to the spoiling of the plaintiff's personal enjoyment, comfort or whatever.

Lord Lloyd drew attention specifically to *Bone* v *Seale*,[178] a case in which, as has already been noted, odour nuisances affected two properties adjoining the defendant's pig farm.[179] Although no evidence existed to the effect that the odour nuisances had caused any reduction in the market value of either of these properties, the plaintiffs were each awarded £6000 by the trial judge to reflect the loss of amenity suffered by their properties over a 12-year period.

---

[176] *ibid.*
[177] *ibid.*
[178] [1975] 1 All ER 787.
[179] See above, p. 31.

That damages for harm to amenity value may be recovered is a matter of some significance. It suggests that the law acknowledges that land has a value to its owner over and above that sum for which it may be sold. However, *Bone* v *Seale* is also a case which provides evidence that in monetary terms courts may be wary of awarding substantial sums by way of such damages. The trial judge, as we have noted, awarded £6000 to reflect 12 years' of loss of amenity. The Court of Appeal considered that that sum was excessive and substituted for each of the plaintiffs the sum of just £1000.

These important distinctions and differentiations were very much at the heart also of the speech of Lord Hoffmann in *Hunter*. Referring to nuisance cases of Lord Lloyd's third type, involving not physical injury to land but interference with the quiet enjoyment of that land, Lord Hoffmann explained;

> "... there has been a tendency to regard cases in [this] category as actions in respect of the discomfort or even personal injury which the plaintiff has suffered or is likely to suffer. On this view, the plaintiff's interest in the land becomes no more than a qualifying condition or springboard which entitles him to sue for injury to himself.

> If this were the case, the need for the plaintiff to have an interest in land would indeed be hard to justify ... But the premise is quite mistaken. In cases of nuisances 'productive of sensible discomfort', the action is not for causing discomfort to the person but ... for causing injury to the land. True it is that the land has not suffered 'sensible' injury, but its utility has been diminished by the existence of the nuisance. It is for an unlawful threat to the utility of his land that the possessor or occupier is entitled to an injunction and it is for the diminution in such utility that he is entitled to compensation."[180]

Referring, as had Lord Lloyd, to *Bone v Seale*, Lord Hoffmann commented:

> "In that case it was said that 'efforts to prove diminution in value of the property as a result of this persistent smell over the years failed'. I take this to mean that it had not been shown that the property would sell for less. But diminution in capital value is not the only measure of loss. It seems to me that the value of the right to occupy a house which smells of pigs must be less than the value of the occupation of an equivalent house which does not. In the case of a transitory nuisance the capital value of the property will seldom be reduced. But the owner or occupier is entitled to compensation for the diminution in the amenity value of the property during the period for which the nuisance persisted. To some extent this involves placing a value upon

---

[180] [1997] 2 All ER 426 at 451.

intangibles. But estate agents do this all the time. The law of damages is sufficiently flexible to be able to do justice in such a case."[181]

It will be evident that in *Hunter* the House of Lords restored private nuisance to its traditional role as a tort protecting interests in land: as regards both its market value and its more intangible amenity value. In consequence the categories of person able to maintain the action are more confined than *Khorasandjian* had suggested; and additional consequences were noted, as we have seen, as regards the categories of harm for which an eligible plaintiff may recover compensation.

Lord Hoffmann, it may be remembered, was clear about one such implicit limitation:

> "So far as the claim for personal injury ... the only appropriate cause of action is negligence."[182]

What, though, of compensation for harm to goods? Can a plaintiff with an appropriate interest in land, who has suffered an actionable nuisance in relation to that land, claim also in nuisance in respect of harm which may have been suffered by his personal property (goods)? It might have been expected that if any claim which such a person might seek to make for *personal injury* must be brought within the tort of negligence rather than nuisance, the same would apply in relation to damages for *harm to goods*. In fact, however, it appears that such a claim may be brought as a part of a claim in nuisance. Lord Hoffmann reviewed what additional heads of damage might fall legitimately within a nuisance claim founded essentially on harm to the plaintiff's interest in land. His Lordship explained:

> "There may of course be cases in which, in addition to damages for injury to land, the owner or occupier is able to recover damages for consequential loss. He will, for example, be entitled to loss of profits which are the result of inability to use the land for the purposes of his business. Or if the land is flooded, he may be able to recover damages for chattels or livestock lost as a result."[183]

This statement requires some explanation if it is not to have potential to mislead. We are concerned here, as Lord Hoffmann states, only with matters which may be described as losses consequential upon some nuisance to land which the plaintiff has demonstrated. In other words, the harm to the land or the flooding creates the nuisance. The loss of profits or the harm to the cattle are not kinds of harm which can, in themselves, render the activities of the defendant a nuisance and constitute the basis for a nuisance claim. They may, however, as Lord Hoffmann indicates, be

---

[181] *ibid.*

[182] At 453. Note also that a plaintiff in a *negligence* action may not recover for "mere" distress, discomfort or inconvenience not resulting also in personal injury or psychiatric illness. See the decision of the House of Lords in *Hicks v Chief Constable of the South Yorkshire Police* [1992] 2 All ER 65.

[183] At 451-452.

relevant to the proper compensation of a plaintiff for the harm caused by a broader nuisance.

If we keep in mind this distinction between kinds of harm which may render a defendant's conduct actionable in nuisance, and kinds of harm which may qualify as compensable consequential harm, we may wonder also whether to this latter extent a plaintiff may seek compensation in relation to personal injury or illness associated with a nuisance. In other words, whilst it seems that such personal injury or illness on the part of a plaintiff is not relevant to the question whether a nuisance has been committed by the defendant (this relating solely to harm to land or to its use or enjoyment), in a case where such harm has occurred and a nuisance has been committed it may be that personal injury or illness may be compensable within the category of consequential loss.

Lord Cooke's dissent

A dissenting speech was delivered by Lord Cooke; and some attention may valuably be afforded to his views, if only as illustrating alternative possibilities foregone.

Lord Cooke began by acknowledging that the speeches of the majority produced what he referred to as a "major advance in the symmetry of the law of nuisance". Nevertheless, his Lordship was less sure than the majority that this enhanced symmetry strengthened also the "utility and justice of this branch of the common law", and he proceeded to describe the principles upon which he considered it would have been preferable for the law to have been developed.

At root, Lord Cooke explained, the decision which should be reached was not dictated by considerations of logic or symmetry. It might well be the case that a "logical" or "symmetrical" solution should be chosen, but that was a choice of policy for the judges. It was important not to lose sight of other, competing, factors which might suggest merit in a rather different set of principles. Lord Cooke explained:

> "... the choice is in the end a policy one between competing principles. ... [T]he lineaments of the law of nuisance were established before the age of television and radiation, motor transport and aviation, town and country planning, a 'crowded island', a heightened public consciousness of the need to protect the environment. All these are now among the factors falling to be taken into account in evolving the law."[184]

Whereas the majority had favoured fashioning their reasoning on the fundamental conception that, as regards right to sue, the same principles should apply in the case of nuisance in the form of interference with the enjoyment of land as with nuisance in the form of interference with land itself – both being species of interference with proprietary interests – for

---

[184] At 456.

Lord Cooke this was an open question. Having referred to Lord Westbury's distinctions as to conditions for liability as between the two categories of private nuisance,[185] his Lordship commented:

> "But just as a distinction has been drawn, as to conditions of liability, between material physical damage on the one hand and personal discomfort and the like on the other, so a distinction could perfectly logically be drawn between them as to right to sue."[186]

For Lord Cooke it seemed quite logical for the law of nuisance, concerned as it was with the protection of the amenity afforded by property, to recognise interests in that amenity going beyond those persons with proprietary interests and rights of exclusive possession singled out by his judicial colleagues. He explained this by reference to nuisances affecting a dwelling:

> "Where interference with an amenity of a home is in issue there is no *a priori* reason why [the law of private nuisance] should not include [in its protection], and it appears natural that it should include, anyone living there …"[187]

Malone v *Laskey*[188] could be viewed, according to Lord Cooke, as an understandable decision *of its time*. At its heart the claim was one for personal injuries suffered, rather than a claim founded upon loss of amenity caused by the noise and vibrations from the defendant's engine. Moreover, at the time of the decision the legal protection of wives (*vis à vis* husbands) was such that it was natural for the judges to have categorised the plaintiff as a person "merely present"[189] on the premises, and as having "no right of occupation".[190] Lord Cooke suggested that, 90 years on, it was no longer appropriate to view a wife's position in relation to the matrimonial home so lightly and quoted Clement JA in the Canadian case of *Motherwell* v *Motherwell*[191] where it had been stated that:

> "She has a status, a right to live there with her husband and children. I find it absurd that her occupancy of the matrimonial home is insufficient to found an action in nuisance."[192]

So much for wives:[193] What about children? Lord Cooke opined that:

---

[185] In *St Helen's Smelting Co* v *Tipping* (1865) 11 HL Cas 642. See above p. 27.

[186] At 457.

[187] *ibid.* It should be noted that Lord Cooke's sentence continued: " … who has been exercising a continuing right to enjoyment of that amenity." This would seem a reference not to any rights in the property itself: but rights to remain living there – as a spouse or as a child.

[188] [1907] 2 KB 141.

[189] per Fletcher Moulton LJ at 154.

[190] per Sir Gorell Barnes P at 151.

[191] (1976) 73 DLR (3d) 62.

[192] At 78.

[193] And, thought Lord Cooke, *de facto* partners (see [1997] 2 All ER 426 at 458).

"I am persuaded ... that they, too, should be entitled to relief for substantial and unlawful interference with the amenities of their home."[194]

This conclusion followed from a general trend in the law to view children as having rights and interests *of their own*; and not simply as being persons subject to potential protection by the exercise by parents or guardians of *their* rights on behalf of those children.

Lord Cooke found clear support for such development of the law in North American case-law. Having referred to the Canadian cases of *Motherwell* and *Devon Lumber Co Ltd* v *MacNeill*,[195] his Lordship noted the terms of the *Restatement, Second, of Torts*, summarising the general position taken by courts in the United States. Section 821E of this *Restatement* reads:

"d. Members of the family

... occupancy is a sufficient interest in itself to permit recovery for invasions of the interest in the use and enjoyment of the land. Thus members of the family of the possessor of a dwelling who occupy it along with him may properly be regarded as sharing occupancy ... When there is interference with their use and enjoyment of the dwelling they can therefore maintain an action for private nuisance. Although there are decisions to the contrary, the considerable majority of the cases dealing with the question have so held."[196]

The words of Sayre J in *Hosmer* v *Republic Iron and Steel Co*[197] were testimony to the substantial history of this broad North American approach:

"it is obvious that to maintain an action for an injury affecting the value of the freehold the plaintiff must have a legal estate. But if noxious vapors and the like cause sickness and death to one who has a lawful habitation in the neighborhood, no sufficient reason is to be found in the accepted definitions of nuisance, nor in that policy of the courts which would discourage vexatious litigation, nor in the inherent justice of the situation, as we see it, why the person injured, or his personal representative in case of death, should not have reparation in damages for any special injury he may have suffered, though he has no legal estate in the soil."[198]

Having taken comfort in North American jurisprudence, Lord Cooke returned to arguments of policy and expressed his preference for the broader approach to standing to sue described above; commenting that in

---

[194] *ibid.*
[195] (1987) 45 DLR (4th) 300: infant children of joint owner of house awarded damages for annoyance and discomfort from dust.
[196] Quoted by Lord Cooke at 460.
[197] (1913) 60 South 801.
[198] At 801-802.

comparison with the narrower approach favoured by the majority of their Lordships "it gives better effect to widespread conceptions concerning the home and the family".[199]

Indeed it was, for Lord Cooke, the notion of interests in the "home" which provided the key to the limits to the enlargement of the right to sue which he would have favoured. Beyond the clear cases of wives and children, there were more difficult issues as regards such persons as lodgers and *au pairs*. Lord Cooke regarded as an acceptable limiting criterion that which had been adopted by Pill LJ in the Court of Appeal in *Hunter*: occupation of property as a home. Considering the position of persons beyond wives and children, his Lordship explained:

> "Other resident members of the family, including such de facto partners and lodgers as may on the particular facts fairly be considered as having a home in the premises, could therefore be allowed standing to complain of truly serious interference with the domestic amenities lawfully enjoyed by them."

On the other hand:

> "... the policy of the law need not extend to giving a remedy in nuisance to non-resident employees in commercial premises".[200]

Having so explained why his Lordship would have preferred that the House had adopted a broader approach to the issue of right to sue in private nuisance, Lord Cooke proceeded also to express regret at the limitations expressed by the majority as regards recovery in private nuisance for harm in the form of personal injuries and damage to goods. It will be remembered that the reasoning of the majority discounted the possibility of personal injuries or damage to goods providing the foundation for an action in private nuisance: although, in cases where harm to land or its enjoyment sufficed to provide a cause of action in nuisance, compensation for damage to goods and personal injuries could (probably) be recovered as losses consequential upon that nuisance.

Lord Cooke, in contrast, would have preferred a broader approach. Those whom he would have given standing to sue should, he thought, be permitted to recover compensation for personal injuries suffered and goods damaged, as heads of damage in their own right: as founding the very cause of action in nuisance. To Lord Cooke a number of cases which the majority had regarded as somewhat inconsistent with principle and, therefore, anomalous, were to be regarded as demonstrating the scope of redress which the law should afford. Moreover, there was, his Lordship argued, some difficulty in seeing why a plaintiff who qualified to bring a civil action in *public* nuisance[201] (and who could by so doing recover for personal injuries) should be in a more advantageous position as compared

---

[199] [1997] 2 All ER 426 at 462.
[200] *ibid.*
[201] For which, see below, p. 159.

with a plaintiff in *private* nuisance. Equivalence should be achieved by adopting a more generous approach than had the majority of their Lordships as regards recovery for personal injuries in private nuisance. Furthermore, since the strict liability rule in *Rylands* v *Fletcher*[202] was, according to the *Cambridge Water Company* case,[203] to be regarded as a species of private nuisance, the same rule about recovery for personal injury should apply to each. In Lord Cooke's opinion, differing again from the approach implicit in the views of the majority, personal injury damages should be recoverable both under *Rylands* v *Fletcher* and in private nuisance.[204]

WHO MAY BE LIABLE IN NUISANCE?

Its creator

Unsurprisingly, a person by whose own positive act a nuisance arises will be a liable party in a nuisance action. Although such a person will very commonly be an owner or occupant of land neighbouring that of the plaintiff, it is important to note that the better view is that there exists no requirement either that the defendant possess any proprietary interest in land,[205] or even that the acts giving rise to the nuisance should have emanated from neighbouring land.

These points are illustrated by *Southport Corporation* v *Esso Petroleum Ltd*.[206] A small tanker, the *Inverpool*, became stranded in the Ribble estuary. In order to refloat the vessel, and *in extremis*, the master discharged some 400 tons of fuel oil. The oil drifted on the tide, was blown by the wind and eventually washed up on the foreshore belonging to the plaintiff local authority. The local authority claimed compensation in, *inter alia*, private nuisance. On the issue of such an action being brought in respect of actions emanating other than from neighbouring land, Devlin J commented at first instance:

> "It is clear ... that ... the nuisance must affect the property of the plaintiff, and ... in the vast majority of cases it is likely to emanate from the neighbouring property of the defendant. But no statement of principle has been cited to me to show the latter is a prerequisite to a cause of action, and I can see no reason why, if land or water belonging to the public or waste land is misused by the defendant ... he should not be liable for a nuisance in the same way as an adjoining occupier would be."[207]

---

[202] See below, p. 191.

[203] See below, p. 191.

[204] [1997] 2 All ER 426 at 463.

[205] Contrast, the position in respect of *plaintiffs* (above p. 71). Note also, that the creator of the nuisance who has gone out of occupation may be liable even though it may no longer be within the power of that person to abate the nuisance: see, for example, *Roswell* v *Prior* (1701) 12 Mod 635. For a harsh application, see *Fennell* v *Robson Excavations Pty Ltd* [1977] 2 NSWLR 486.

[206] [1953] 2 All ER 1204.

[207] At 1207-1208.

Liability of occupiers of land

In many instances the occupier of land from which a nuisance may have emanated will be the person who actually created that nuisance. In such circumstances this category adds nothing to the range of persons liable. However, there are circumstances where an occupier of land may be liable in respect of a nuisance created by others, or in respect of a nuisance resulting from the positive acts of no one, arising from events of nature or from the natural condition of the land. A number of different situations of liability *qua* occupier need, therefore, to be considered.

Liability of occupiers for independent contractors

In accordance with ordinary principles of vicarious liability an occupier will be liable for nuisances caused by employees acting within the scope of their employment. Such vicarious responsibility does not, however, extend to nuisances created by the activities of independent contractors. Nevertheless, the courts have taken pains to limit the capacity of an occupier to obtain the benefit of an activity which has given rise to a nuisance whilst at the same time avoiding liability by having employed contractors to undertake those activities.

For this purpose, a distinction is drawn between activities done by contractors which have a clear potential for causing a nuisance; and activities which should not, in principle, give rise to a nuisance unless the contractors are plainly at fault. In the former case the occupier will bear responsibility for the nuisance, notwithstanding engagement of the contractor. In the latter case the occupier will not be liable in nuisance, and such action must be taken against the actual creator of the nuisance – the independent contractor.

An illustration of occupier liability for activities conducted by contractors is provided by *Matania* v *National Provincial Bank Ltd*, the facts of which have already been noted.[208] The issue was whether the second defendants, who had engaged the contractors and who intended ultimately to occupy the altered premises, were liable for that nuisance. Shaw LJ explained the general position as regards contractors:

> "There is no doubt that Messrs. Adamson are independent contractors, and being independent contractors, save for exceptional circumstances, in the ordinary way those employing them would not be liable for their wrongful acts in negligence or in nuisance ..."[209]

His Lordship noted, however, that the position was different:

> "if the act done is one which in its very nature involves a special danger of nuisance being complained of ..."

---

[208] [1936] 2 All ER 633; see p. 32 above. Contrast, for example, *Angus* v *Dalton* (1881) 6 App Cas 740.

[209] [1936] 2 All ER 633 at 645.

Or, to put the matter in more graphic language, where:

"it be a case of a hazardous operation."[210]

The distinction so drawn may be regarded as between activities which are liable to cause a nuisance unless proper precautions are taken, and activities not likely to cause any nuisance unless conducted by the contractors carelessly.

Slesser LJ considered:

" ... it was hazardous as regards the possible nuisance to Mr Matania to bring the noise and dust immediately below his apartment. What is said is that with sufficient and proper precaution the result of that hazardous operation could have been avoided ..."[211]

In other words this case fell within the former of the two categories. In such circumstances the party engaging the contractor for the "hazardous" activity will be liable (along with the contractor) if the nuisance results from the contractor's failure to have taken the necessary precautions.

His Lordship concluded:

"I am of opinion that this was a hazardous operation ... and that, therefore, ... I think that the [second defendants] are responsible for the fact that neither they nor the contractors ... took those reasonable precautions which could have been taken to prevent this injury to the plaintiff."[212]

Liability of occupiers for acts of trespassers

The question of the liability of occupiers for nuisances caused by trespassers was considered by the House of Lords in *Sedleigh-Denfield* v *O'Callaghan*.[213] Without permission from the defendants – a monastic foundation – Middlesex County Council laid a water pipe in a ditch on their land. A grating, intended to prevent the pipe becoming blocked, was mis-positioned by the council workmen. Some three years later, during a heavy rainstorm the pipe became blocked owing to the misplaced grid and the water, unable to escape through the pipe, flooded onto the plaintiff's premises. The plaintiff's action raised the issue of the liability of an occupier for nuisance resulting from acts of a third-party trespasser. The evidence indicated that the defendants were aware of the council workers' activities at the time the pipe was placed in the ditch, and that the ditch had been cleaned out by the defendants periodically over the ensuing years.

---

[210] At 646.

[211] *ibid.*

[212] *ibid.* The reasonable precautions were: (i) refraining from carrying out the noisiest work when the plaintiff was teaching; and (ii) putting down dust sheets, see above p. 32. See also *Honeywill and Stein Ltd* v *Larkin Bros (London's Commercial Photographers) Ltd* [1933] All ER 77.

[213] [1940] AC 880; [1940] 3 All ER 349.

The House of Lords unanimously found the defendants liable for the nuisance. It was held that an occupier is liable for a nuisance created by another person (such as a trespasser) in circumstances where he or she may be regarded as having "continued" or "adopted" the nuisance. The issue for the court, therefore, was to elaborate upon the meaning of those governing concepts and to apply them to the evidence presented.

Viscount Maugham offered the view that:

> "an occupier of land 'continues' a nuisance if, with knowledge or presumed knowledge of its existence, he fails to take any reasonable means to bring it to an end, though with ample time to do so. He 'adopts' it if he makes any use of the erection [or other thing] which constitutes the nuisance."[214]

And Lord Atkin explained:

> "What is the meaning of 'continued'? In the context in which it is used, 'continued' must indicate mere passive continuance. If a man causes a nuisance by noise, vibration, smell or fumes, he is himself, in continuing to bring into existence the noise [etc.], causing a nuisance. Continuing in this sense, and causing are the same thing. It seems to me clear that, if a man permits an offensive thing on his premises to continue to offend – that is, if he knows that it is operating offensively, is able to prevent it, and omits to prevent it – he is permitting the nuisance to continue."[215]

And Lord Porter encapsulated the principle in the following succinct statements:

> "the occupier of land is liable for a nuisance existing on his property to the extent that he can reasonably abate it, even though he neither created it nor received any benefit from it. It is enough if he permitted it to continue after he knew, or ought to have known, of its existence. To this extent, but to no greater extent, he must be proved to have adopted the act of the creator of the nuisance."[216]

It will be evident that the liability of an occupier for nuisances created by an unauthorised third party is founded upon a finding of some culpability. As Lord Atkin explained: "[t]he occupier or owner is not an insurer". Rather, liability is founded on actual or presumed knowledge of the hazard or nuisance and a failure to have taken reasonable steps within his or her powers to have abated the nuisance or made safe the hazard. On the facts of the particular case their Lordships considered the defendant religious foundation to have failed in these responsibilities. Moreover, the evidence suggested that not only was it proper to conclude that the defendants had

---

[214] At 358 of the latter report.
[215] At 360.
[216] At 375.

"continued" the nuisance, it was fair also to regard them as having "adopted" the nuisance. Viscount Maugham noted:

"the respondents both continued and adopted the nuisance. After the lapse of nearly three years, they must be taken to have suffered the nuisance to continue, for they neglected to take the very simple step of placing a grid in the proper place, which would have removed the danger to their neighbour's land. They adopted the nuisance, for they continued during all that time to use the artificial contrivance of the conduit for the purpose of getting rid of water from their property without taking the proper means for rendering it safe."[217]

And Lord Atkin concluded:

"They knew the danger, they were able to prevent it, and they omitted to prevent it."[218]

Sedleigh-Denfield may valuably be contrasted with a decision the previous year from the High Court of Australia: *Torette House Pty Ltd* v *Berkman*.[219] The defendant had engaged a plumber, as an independent contractor, to perform certain services. In the course of his activities the plumber opened, and did not later turn off, a stop-cock on a pipe which discharged water beneath the floor of the defendants premises. This negligence on the part of the plumber led in due course to water damage to the neighbouring premises of the plaintiff. In an action against the defendant occupiers the High Court ruled that this was not a context in which an occupier bore liability for the negligence of an independent contractor.[220] Nor, in the circumstances, could the defendant be considered liable *qua* occupier. In the words of Dixon J:

"Some element of fault ... is necessary. Here there was no fault; the failure to discover the defect or to guard against its possible existence and consequence implied no neglect of the duty of an occupier ..., no want of prudence or of reasonable diligence and no omission to keep in repair."[221]

Liability of occupiers in respect of natural hazards

The fault-based approach in *Sedleigh-Denfield* has been held to be applicable also to the liability of occupiers for natural hazards arising upon and from their properties. Whereas liability is strict in relation to positive acts of creators of nuisances, non-feasance liability in nuisance is fault-based.

The leading authority on liability in connection with hazards arising by process of nature is *Leakey* v *National Trust for Places of Historic Interest*

---

[217] At 358-359.
[218] At 361.
[219] (1939) 62 CLR 637.
[220] See the principles described, above, at p. 86.
[221] (1939) 62 CLR 637 at p 659.

or Natural Beauty.[222] The case concerned the liability in nuisance of the National Trust in connection with its ownership of a piece of land called Burrow Mump.[223] The land comprised a steep-sloped conical hill and bordered the plaintiff's properties. At the border between the plaintiff's and the defendant's properties, the defendant's land took the form of an embankment. From time to time, as a result of natural forces, there had been slides of soil and rock onto the plaintiff's land. In 1976, following a substantial fall of material from the bank, the plaintiff commenced an action in nuisance. Argument in the Court of Appeal centred on the applicability of the rule established in *Goldman* v *Hargrave*[224] (an appeal to the Privy Council from Australia) as regards the law of England.

In *Goldman* v *Hargrave* a tall red gum tree on the defendant's land had been struck by lightning and caught fire. The defendant, an elderly man who lived alone in this lightly-timbered area of Western Australia, had cleared the land around the burning tree. The tree was then cut down and sawn into sections. The defendant decided then to allow the sections of tree to burn themselves out rather than positively to have doused with water the burning or smoldering sections of the tree. In so opting it was argued that he had failed to do something which he could have done without any substantial trouble or expense; and which, if done, would have eliminated or rendered unlikely the risk of the fire spreading. In fact, however, and again by process of natural forces, the weather became hotter and a strong wind arose, with the consequence that flames from the tree spread across the defendant's property and onto the land belonging to the plaintiff, destroying the latter's house and doing other substantial damage.

The Privy Council noted that this consequence of leaving the fire to burn itself out was foreseeable, and defined the legal issue in the following terms:

> "... the case is ... one where an occupier ... faced with a hazard accidentally arising on his land, fails to act with reasonable prudence so as to remove the hazard."[225]

Was there to be liability in such circumstances? The Privy Council determined that the principle in *Sedleigh-Denfield* applied so as to impose a general duty upon occupiers as regards hazards on their land; not just *man-made* hazards such as in *Sedleigh-Denfield* itself but also *natural* hazards.

The issue, then, was as to the content of that duty. The view of the Privy Council was as follows:

> "What is the standard of the effort required? What is the position as regards expenditure? It is not enough to say merely that these must be

---

[222] [1980] 1 All ER 17.

[223] See: http://www.bbc.co.uk/somerset/see/360/burrow/index2.shtml.

[224] [1966] 2 All ER 989; [1967] 1 AC 645.

[225] Per Lord Wilberforce at 991 of the former report.

'reasonable', since what is reasonable to one man may be very unreasonable, and indeed ruinous, to another: the law must take account of the fact that the occupier on whom the duty is cast has, *ex hypothesi*, had this hazard thrust upon him through no seeking or fault of his own. His interest, and his resources, whether physical or material, may be of a very modest character either in relation to the magnitude of the hazard, or as compared with those of his threatened neighbour. A rule which required of him in such unsought circumstances in his neighbour's interest a physical effort of which he is not capable, or an excessive expenditure of money, would be unenforceable or unjust. One may say in general terms that the existence of a duty must be based upon knowledge of the hazard, ability to foresee the consequences of not checking or removing it, and the ability to abate it.

… the standard ought to be to require of the occupier what is reasonable to expect of him in his individual circumstances. Thus, less may be expected of the infirm than the able-bodied."[226]

The opinion continued, emphasising the significance of relativities between the parties:

"… the owner of a small property where a hazard arises which threatens a neighbour with substantial interests should not have to do so much as one with larger interests of his own at stake and greater resources to protect them: if the small owner does what he can and promptly calls on his neighbour to provide additional resources, he may be held to have done his duty."[227]

Given that the action necessary to have put out the burning sections of the tree (by dousing with water) was well within the capacity and resources of the defendant, the plaintiff's claim succeeded.[228]

Returning to *Leakey*, the Court of Appeal concluded that the principle in *Goldman* should apply in English law and was fully applicable to the situation presented by the particular facts; the slip of soil or rock resulting from natural forces. The merits of the policy contained in *Goldman* was described by Megaw LJ as follows:

"If, as a result of the working of the forces of nature, there is, poised above my land, or above my house, a boulder or a rotten tree, which is liable to fall at any moment of the day or night, perhaps destroying my house, and perhaps killing or injuring me or members of my family, am I without remedy? … Must I, in such a case, if my protests

---

[226] At 996.

[227] *ibid.*

[228] The decision in *Goldman* was regarded as "controversial" at the time when the case was heard: see the remarks of Lord Phillips MR in *Marcic* v *Thames Water Utilities Ltd.* [2002] 2 All ER 55 at 69.

to my neighbours go unheeded, sit and wait and hope that the worst will not befall?

… I believe that few people would regard it as anything other than a grievous blot on the law if the law recognises the existence of no duty on the part of the owner or occupier. But take another example, at the other end of the scale, where it might be thought that there is, potentially, an equally serious injustice the other way. If a stream flows through A's land, A being a small farmer, and there is a known danger that in times of heavy rainfall, because of the configuration of A's land and the nature of the stream's course and flow, there may be an overflow, which will pass beyond A's land and damage the property of A's neighbours: perhaps much wealthier neighbours. It may require expensive works, far beyond A's means, to prevent or even diminish the risk of such flooding. Is A to be liable for all the loss that occurs when the flood comes, if he has not done the impossible and carried out the works at his own expense?

In my judgment, there is, in the scope of the duty as explained in *Goldman* … a removal, or at least a powerful amelioration, of the injustice which might otherwise be caused in such a case by the recognition of the duty of care. Because of that limitation on the scope of the duty, I would say that, as a matter of policy, the law ought to recognise such a duty of care."[229]

In terms of the subjective considerations relating to the setting of the standard of care required, Megaw LJ commented that:

"where the expenditure of money is required, the defendant's capacity to find the money is relevant. But this can only be in the way of a broad, and not a detailed, assessment."[230]

These final comments were offered by way of reassurance in relation to an argument, not accepted by Megaw LJ, that the subjective element in the standard of the duty might, if adopted, give rise to difficulties in the potential working of the law: increasing unpredictability in the outcome of cases. Megaw LJ regarded such concerns as "more theoretical than practical".

In the recent decision in *Marcic* v *Thames Water Utilities Ltd*,[231] Lord Phillips MR summarised the effect of the decisions in *Goldman* and *Leakey* thus:

"The two cases clearly establish that ownership of land carries with it a duty to do whatever is reasonable in all the circumstances to prevent

---

[229] [1980] 1 All ER 17 at 34-35.
[230] At 37.
[231] [2002] 2 All ER 55. Discussed below at p. 102.

hazards on the land, however they may arise, from causing damage to a neighbour."[232]

As Lord Phillips MR proceeded to observe in his judgment in *Marcic*, the approach adopted by the Court of Appeal in *Leakey* has since been applied in a number of different factual contexts, including – as described below – in relation to the collapse of a hotel and to damage caused to a neighbour's land by the encroachment of tree roots.

In *Holbeck Hall Hotel Ltd and another* v *Scarborough Borough Council*,[233] the first claimants were the freehold owners of a four-star hotel which had stood approximately 65 metres above sea level on the South Cliff, Scarborough. In 1980, they leased the property to the second claimants, English Rose Hotels (Yorkshire) Ltd, on a 21-year lease. The defendants, the Borough Council, were the owners of the land between the hotel grounds and the sea.[234] From 1893 onwards, there was evidence of slips and collapses along the stretch of coastline which included the stretch between the grounds of Holbeck Hall and the sea. These slips and collapses were the direct result of marine erosion. The Borough Council carried out remedial works on a number of occasions in order to halt the progress of the landslips. Nevertheless, in June 1993, a massive landslip took place in four stages. It led to the disappearance of the hotel's grounds and caused the ground under the whole of the seaward wing of the hotel to collapse. The remaining parts of the hotel were thereby rendered unsafe and had to be demolished. Fortunately, the progressive nature of the landslip meant that the hotel could be evacuated in good time so that no persons sustained any physical injury.

In respect of these events the claimants brought an action in the High Court in which it was alleged that the Borough Council were liable for the result of the collapse on the grounds that they were in breach of a duty at common law. On the basis of his finding that Scarborough were aware of the hazard caused by the potential failure of support to the claimant's land, Judge Hicks QC held that the council were under a measured duty of care to the claimants,[235] and that there had been a breach of that duty. Scarborough appealed against that decision.

Before the Court of Appeal, counsel for Scarborough made a number of submissions as to why the appellants should not be held liable for the

---

[232] At 70-71. But note that the principle was not applicable in *Marcic* itself, below p. 102.

[233] [2000] 2 All ER 705.

[234] The building which became the hotel had been built in 1880 and the relevant land had been conveyed to the Borough Council in two separate conveyances in 1887 and 1895, respectively.

[235] The use of the word "measured" in the present context serves to indicate that the scope of the duty of care is more restricted than if the defendant had done something to create a danger which resulted in a nuisance. The content of the "measured duty of care" is set out in the judgment of Lord Wilberforce in *Goldman* v *Hargrave*: see above at p. 90. In *Leakey*, Megaw LJ observed that: "The duty is a duty to do that which is reasonable in all the circumstances, and no more than what, if anything, is reasonable, to prevent or minimise the known risk of damage or injury to one's neighbour or to his property" ([1980] 1 All ER 17 at 35).

damage sustained by the claimants. Those submissions may be summarised thus:

- there is no duty to take positive steps to provide support for a neighbour's land. The principle in *Leakey* is not applicable to the right of support. Rather, it is confined to encroachment or escapes from the defendant's land onto the claimant's land;

- if the first submission was wrong, the judge's finding that Scarborough knew of the hazard to the claimant's land was wrong. Without carrying out extensive investigatory work, the appellants neither knew nor could have known of the catastrophic nature of the hazard. In the absence of such knowledge, no duty of care arose; and

- where in the authorities it is stated that a duty of care arises if a defendant knew or ought to have known, the concept "ought to have known" was confined to a situation where the defect giving rise to the hazard was patent and was capable of being observed by a reasonable landowner exercising reasonable care in the management of his estate.

In the context of the present discussion, it is the first of these submissions which is of the most interest. In order to determine whether or not the submission was correct, the court had in effect to consider the following question:

> "Does the principle enunciated in *Leakey's* case apply to cases of failure of support by the servient tenement to the land of the dominant tenement where there has been no withdrawal of support but mere omission?"[236]

In considering this question, Stuart-Smith LJ had regard to what he termed "the support cases".[237] These were a number of cases at first instance which established the rule "that while the dominant tenement had a right of support from the land of the servient tenement, the owner of the servient tenement was only liable if he did something to withdraw support".[238] The law on this point was, therefore, as stated by Lord Greene MR in *Bond* v *Nottingham Corporation*:[239]

> "The nature of the right of support is not open to dispute. The owner of the servient tenement is under no obligation to repair that part of his building which provides support for his neighbour. He can let it fall into decay. If it does so, and support is removed, the owner of the dominant tenement has no cause for complaint. On the other hand, the owner of the dominant tenement is not bound to sit by and watch the gradual deterioration of the support constituted by his neighbour's building. He is entitled to enter and take the necessary steps to ensure

---

[236] Per Stuart-Smith LJ [2000] 2 All ER 705 at 715.
[237] At 717.
[238] At 715.
[239] [1940] 2 All ER 12.

that the support continues by effecting repairs and so forth to the part of the building which gives the support. What the owner of the servient tenement is not entitled to do, however, is by an act of his own to remove the support without providing an equivalent. There is the qualification upon his ownership of his own building that he is bound to deal with it subject to the rights in it which are vested in his neighbour, and can only deal with it, subject only to those rights."[240]

In response to the submission that the principle established in *Sedleigh-Denfield*, *Goldman* and *Leakey* should be confined to cases where there has been an escape or an encroachment of a noxious thing from the defendant's land,[241] Stuart-Smith LJ remarked:

"... it is difficult to see what difference there is in principle between a danger caused by loss of support on the defendant's land and any other hazard or nuisance which affects the claimant's use and enjoyment of land. Encroachment is simply one form of nuisance; interference causing physical damage to the neighbour's land and building as a result of activities on the defendant's land is another form of nuisance. There seems no reason why, where the defendant does not create the nuisance, but the question is whether he had adopted or continued it, different principles should apply to one kind of nuisance rather than another. In each case liability only arises if there is negligence, the duty to abate the nuisance arises from the defendant's knowledge of the hazard that will affect his neighbour."[242]

It is clear from the foregoing, therefore, that the Court of Appeal in *Holbeck Hall* was of the opinion that no distinction could be drawn between a danger arising from a lack of support and a danger attributable to the escape or encroachment of a noxious thing. In other words, their Lordships rejected the submission that the *Leakey* principle did not apply to the right of support. Their Lordship's view on this point was not, however, fatal to the council's appeal for, in their opinion, the duty to prevent a hazard caused by a defect on the defendant's land only arose:

"... when the defect is known and the hazard or danger to the claimant's land is reasonably foreseeable, that is to say that it is a danger which a reasonable man with knowledge of the defect should have foreseen as likely to eventuate in the reasonably near future. It is the existence of the defect coupled with the danger that constitutes the nuisance; it is knowledge or presumed knowledge of the nuisance that involves liability for continuing it when it could reasonably be abated."[243]

---

[240] At 18.

[241] Counsel for the appellants in *Holbeck Hall* had pointed to the repeated use of the word "encroachment" by Megaw LJ during the course of his judgment in *Leakey*.

[242] [2000] 2 All ER 705 at 718.

[243] At 720.

The final part of this passage is important since it highlights the fault-based nature of liability for non-feasance nuisance. A defendant will thus be liable where the defect in question is *patent*. He will not be liable where that defect is *latent*, however, even if he would have discovered the defect on further investigation.[244] Applying this reasoning to the facts of the case before it, the Court of Appeal concluded that the full extent of the defect on the defendant's (and the claimant's) land was *latent* and hence liability did not arise. The council's duty to the claimants was confined to an obligation to take care to avoid damage which it ought to have foreseen without further geological investigation. Moreover, Stuart-Smith LJ was of the opinion that the scope of the duty:

> "... may also have been limited by other factors ... so that it is not necessarily incumbent on someone in Scarborough's position to carry out extensive and expensive remedial work to prevent the damage which they ought to have foreseen; the scope of the duty may be limited to warning claimants of such risk as they were aware of or ought to have foreseen and sharing such information as they had acquired relating to it."[245]

Tree roots

The encroachment of a neighbour's land by tree roots is, one would have thought, a natural hazard with which many people will be familiar. It is interesting to note, therefore, that despite the prevalence of encroachment by tree roots, there are only a handful of English cases on whether or not damages are recoverable for this phenomenon. The most important decision is that of the House of Lords in *Delaware Mansions Ltd and another* v *Westminster City Council*.[246]

The facts of *Delaware Mansions* were as follows. Westminster City Council was the owner of a London Plane Tree[247] which had probably been planted in the early 1900s. The tree stood in the footpath of the highway, Delaware Road, Maida Vale, approximately four metres from the boundary wall of Delaware Mansions. The Mansions consisted of 19 blocks which were divided into 167 flats. The tree had grown to such an extent that it was now almost as high as the five-storey brick Mansions. Its roots had caused the desiccation and shrinkage of the London clay soil on which the foundations of the flats were constructed. This had resulted in damage by cracking to 4 of the 19 blocks of flats. A report commissioned by managing agents for the first claimant and produced by a firm of structural engineers confirmed that this was the case and recommended that the tree be removed. Alternatively, if removal was not possible, the report

---

[244] See the remarks of Stuart-Smith LJ at 721.

[245] At 725.

[246] [2001] 4 All ER 737.

[247] The botanical name for this tree is *Platanus x acerifolia*. It is a cultivated hybrid species which closely resembles the American sycamore (*Platanus occidentalis*). It is often planted in city parks and alongside roads because of its ability to withstand urban conditions: see www.queensu.ca/pps/grounds/arboretum/London-planetree.com.

recommended underpinning. Following the transfer of the freehold in the Mansions to the second claimant, another firm of managing agents contracted an architect to look into the damage in a more detailed manner. He subsequently endorsed the view that the cracking had resulted from foundation damage, that remedial steps were required as a matter of urgency and that underpinning was necessary. The attention of the Council was drawn to the problem when it was sent a copy of the first report. Eventually it was agreed at a site meeting that root pruning would be carried out. However, the claimants also made it clear at this meeting that the underpinning works proposed in the original report would nevertheless have to proceed. Remedial works, including the insertion of piles, were therefore carried out at a cost of nearly £571,000.[248] In a subsequent action for damages, the claimants sought to recover the expense of the remedial works plus interest.[249]

At the trial, there was "a strong conflict of expert evidence".[250] However, it was accepted by the judge that the desiccation of the soil under the Mansions had been caused by tree roots. It was further accepted that the costs incurred by the claimants in carrying out the remedial works had been properly and reasonably incurred and that they would be recoverable from the Council provided that a legal cause of action could be incurred. The claim, however, was dismissed on the basis that most if not all of the structural damage to the Mansions had occurred before the transfer of the freehold to the claimants and that therefore only the previous landlord was able to sue in respect of that damage. On appeal, the Court of Appeal held that the second claimant could recover on the basis that the encroachment of tree roots amounted to a continuing nuisance. The Council appealed.

The unanimous opinion of the House of Lords was delivered by Lord Cooke of Thorndon. The reasoning of the Court of Appeal was, Lord Cooke felt, encapsulated in the following words taken from the judgment of Pill LJ:

> "Thus where there is a continuing nuisance, the owner is entitled to a declaration, to abate the nuisance, to damages for physical injury and to an injunction. He is in my judgment, and on the same principle, entitled to the reasonable cost of eliminating the nuisance if it is reasonable to eliminate it...
>
> A nuisance is present ...; acceptance of the need for remedial work establishes that. The actual and relevant damage is the cost of the necessary and reasonable remedial work. Underpinning has been held to be a reasonable way of eliminating the nuisance and the owner can

---

[248] This sum included the removal costs of leaseholders who had been required to vacate their flats whilst the remedial works were carried out. It should be noted that had the London Plane Tree been removed, underpinning would not have been necessary and the total cost of repair to the Mansions would have been the rather more modest figure of £14,000.

[249] The total claim was therefore for a sum of very nearly £835,500.

[250] Per Lord Cooke of Thorndon, [2001] 4 All ER 737 at 741.

recover the cost of doing it. There is no need to prove further physical damage resulting from the nuisance."[251]

Lord Cooke then proceeded to consider the English authorities on the encroachment of tree roots. His Lordship noted that there was dicta in cases such as *Lemmon* v *Webb*,[252] which suggested that the encroachment by roots could be equated with bough encroachment over a property and that in such circumstances the owner of the affected property had a right of abatement which would involve cutting the offending roots. Lord Cooke further noted, however, that this case was of "no help on damages" and accordingly it was to the "handful of reported cases decided in England on damages for root encroachment" that he turned.

A number of cases were briefly referred to by Lord Cooke during the course of his opinion. These included *Butler* v *Standard Telephones and Cables Ltd, McCarthy* v *Standard Telephones and Cables Ltd*,[253] *McCombe* v *Read*[254] and *Davey* v *Harrow Corporation*.[255]

In the course of delivering the judgment of the Court of Appeal in the last of these cases, Lord Goddard CJ had remarked:

> "The nuisance consists in allowing the trees to encroach from the land of their owner into that of his neighbour. The owner must keep his trees in, just as he must not allow filth to escape from his premises on to that of his neighbour..."[256]

Of the tree root encroachment cases referred to by Lord Cooke, it was, however, two more recent decisions which were of particular relevance to the issue to be considered in *Delaware Mansions*: *Masters* v *London Borough of Brent*[257] and *Solloway* v *Hampshire County Council*.[258] In *Masters*, the plaintiff had been met with the same argument advanced by Westminster City Council in the present case; that the damage caused by tree roots[259] had occurred prior to the plaintiff's acquisition of a proprietary interest in the land affected. However, that submission was rejected by Talbot J who held that:

> "Where there is a continuing nuisance inflicting damage on premises, those who are in possession of the interest may recover losses which they have borne whether the loss began before the acquisition of the interest or whether it began after the acquisition of the interest. The

---

[251] [2000] BLR 1 at 4-5.

[252] [1894] 3 Ch 1.

[253] [1940] 1 All ER 121.

[254] [1955] 2 All ER 458.

[255] [1957] 2 All ER 305.

[256] At 309.

[257] [1978] 2 All ER 664.

[258] (1981) 79 LGR 449.

[259] In *Masters*, the relevant damage was caused by the roots of a lime tree which stood in the pavement in front of the plaintiff's house. The roots had extracted moisture from the subsoil which had led to subsidence undermining the house's foundations.

test is: what is the loss which the owner of the land has to meet in respect of the continuing nuisance affecting his land?"[260]

In *Solloway* v *Hampshire County Council*, the plaintiff had at first instance recovered the cost of underpinning which was made necessary by the encroachment of the roots of a horse chestnut tree which was growing in the pavement owned by the defendant highway authority. On appeal, however, that decision was overturned by the Court of Appeal on the basis that since the decision in *Leakey's* case, it was necessary for a claimant to establish a reasonably foreseeable risk of damage by encroachment in order to recover damages. The three appellate judges who heard the appeal were each of the opinion that the cost to the appellant authority of taking steps to reduce or remove the risk of damage were in the circumstances disproportionate to that risk. In the words of Dunn LJ:

> "In my view there is no reason to suppose that many of the houses in Shirley Avenue could be eliminated from this risk. We were told that there is an avenue of trees all along that road and the evidence was that pockets of clay might exist elsewhere in Shirley Avenue. All the householders, it seems to me, would have to be approached, not only in Shirley Avenue but in any other street in Hampshire where there are trees adjacent to houses."[261]

With the exception of the decision in *Masters*, therefore, none of the authorities referred to by Lord Cooke dealt with the issue raised by the present appeal: whether a claimant was able to recover for remedial expenditure which had been incurred in respect of damage which had been caused prior to the claimant becoming the owner of the affected land. Accordingly, and noting that their Lordships must, in the absence of authority on the point, "to some extent break new ground in English law",[262] Lord Cooke ventured the following answer to the question posed by the case:

> "... I think that the answer to the issue falls to be found by applying the concepts of reasonableness between neighbours (real or figurative) and reasonable foreseeability which underlie much modern tort law and, more particularly, the law of nuisance. The great cases in nuisance decided in our time have these concepts at their heart."[263]

Applying these "governing concepts" to the present appeal, Lord Cooke opined:

---

[260] [1978] 2 All ER 664 at 669. Cited by Lord Cooke [2001] 4 All ER 737 at 744.

[261] (1981) 79 LGR 449 at 458. Cited by Lord Cooke [2001] 4 All ER 737 at 745.

[262] [2001] 4 All ER 737 at 746.

[263] At 747. The "great cases" to which Lord Cooke referred were: *Sedleigh-Denfield* v *O'Callaghan* [1940] AC 880; *Overseas Tankship (UK) Ltd* v *The Miller Steamship Co Pty, The Wagon Mound (No. 2)* [1967] 1 AC 617; and *Goldman* v *Hargrave* [1967] 1 AC 645.

"... I think there was a continuing nuisance ... until at least the completion of the underpinning and the piling in July 1992. It matters not that further cracking of the superstructure may not have occurred after March 1990. The encroachment of the roots was causing continuing damage to the land by dehydrating the soil and inhibiting rehydration. Damage consisting of impairment of the load-bearing qualities of residential land is, in my view, itself a nuisance ... Cracking in the building was consequential. Having regard to the proximity of the plane tree to Delaware Mansions, a real risk of damage to the land and the foundations was foreseeable on the part of Westminster ..."[264]

It is clear from this passage, therefore, that the council were liable to the claimants for the nuisance caused by the encroachment of tree roots. It should also be noted, however, that following this conclusion as to the council's liability, Lord Cooke was at pains to stress that the decision in *Solloway* v *Hampshire County Council* was "important as a salutary warning against imposing unreasonable and unacceptable burdens on local authorities or other tree owners".[265] In His Lordship's opinion:

"If reasonableness between neighbours is the key to the solution of the problems in this field, it cannot be right to visit the authority or owner responsible for a tree with a large bill for underpinning without giving them notice of the damage and the opportunity of avoiding further damage by removal of the tree. Should they elect to preserve the tree for environmental reasons, they may fairly be expected to bear the cost of underpinning or other reasonably necessary remedial works; and the party on whom the cost has fallen may recover it, even though there may be elements of hitherto unsatisfied pre-proprietorship damage or protection for the future. But, as a general proposition, I think that the defendant is entitled to notice and a reasonable opportunity of abatement before liability for remedial expenditure can arise."[266]

On the facts of the case, the House of Lords was satisfied that the council had been given "ample notice and time" before the claimant had undertaken the remedial works. In other words, since the claimant had acted reasonably in the circumstances it was able to recover the costs which it had incurred in carrying out the necessary remedial works once the council had declined to remove the tree.[267]

---

[264] At 749.

[265] *ibid.*

[266] *ibid.*

[267] For a recent example of a case where *Delaware Mansions* was applied, see *L E Jones (Insurance Brokers) Ltd* v *Portsmouth City Council* [2002] EWHC 857 (encroachment of tree roots causing damage to property giving rise to liability in nuisance and negligence). The decision of Judge Havery QC was subsequently affirmed by the Court of Appeal: see [2002] EWCA Civ 1723; [2003] 1 WLR 427.

Flooding

The principle established in *Goldman* v *Hargrave* and *Leakey* v *National Trust for Places of Historic Interest or Natural Beauty* has recently been further considered on several occasions in the context of flooding.

The first of these cases is the decision in *Bybrook Barn Garden Centre* v *Kent County Council*.[268] The first claimant was the owner of a garden centre in Ashford in Kent and the other claimants leased retail space within the garden centre. A natural watercourse, Bockhanger Dyke, flowed through the land owned by the first claimant. The defendant's predecessors had constructed a highway in about 1950 and, as part of that process, had also constructed a culvert under the highway through which the watercourse was intended to travel. The culvert had originally been fit for that purpose. However, subsequent major developments in the catchment area such as the construction of the M20 motorway and a business park had created a significant risk of flooding on the site. It was the claimants contention that the council as the highway authority were liable in nuisance for that risk of flooding. That claim was dismissed at first instance on the basis of the earlier Court of Appeal decision in *Radstock Co-operative and Industrial Society* v *Norton-Radstock UDC*.[269] The claimants accordingly appealed.

The question for the determination of the Court of Appeal was, in the words of Waller LJ, "an important one". Essentially it amounted to whether the defendants were responsible for the culvert which had not originally been the cause of a nuisance but which now was the cause of such a nuisance because it was no longer adequate to perform the function for which it was intended due to a change in the catchment area for which the defendants bore no responsibility.

In giving the judgment of the Court of Appeal in favour of the claimants, Waller LJ cited the following test from the judgment of Megaw LJ in *Leakey*:

> "The defendant's duty is to do that which it is reasonable for him to do. The criteria of reasonableness include, in respect of a duty of this nature, the factor of what the particular man – not the average man – can be expected to do, having regard, amongst other things, where a serious expenditure of money is required to eliminate or reduce the danger, to his means. Just as where physical effort is required to avert an immediate danger, the defendant's age and physical condition may be relevant in deciding what is reasonable, so also logic and good sense require that, where the expenditure of money is required, the defendant's capacity to find the money is relevant. But this can only be in the way of a broad, and not a detailed, assessment; and, in arriving at a judgment on reasonableness, a similar broad assessment may be relevant in some cases as to the neighbour's capacity to

---

[268] [2001] Env LR 30.
[269] [1968] Ch 605.

protect himself from damage, whether by way of some form of barrier on his own land or by way of providing funds for expenditure on agreed works on the land of the defendant."[270]

Applying this test to the facts of the case before him, Waller LJ concluded that there were several factors which pointed in favour of the defendants being liable in nuisance to the claimants. Chief amongst these were that the defendant's predecessors had chosen to construct the culvert to put the stream under the highway in the first place, and that the highway authority had the means at hand to prevent the flooding by enlarging the culvert. Although that operation may entail some financial cost to the defendants, this was not a case where it would be possible for them to contend that they did not have the money to undertake the work due to more pressing demands on their resources. Thus, the facts of the case were such that the highway authority was held to fall squarely within the scope of the *Leakey* duty.

Another flood nuisance claim arose in *Marcic* v *Thames Water Utilities Ltd.*[271] The claimant lived in a substantial family home situated near to the lowest point of a lane in a residential area in Stanmore, Middlesex. The property was subject to frequent flooding. It was first significantly affected by flooding on 9th June 1992. Thereafter, it was subject to the following flooding incidents: one in each of the years 1993, 1994, 1995 and 1996; two in 1997; four in 1999; and four or five in 2000. On each occasion, the flooding was accompanied by the back flow of foul water from the defendant's sewer system. By the time that the claimant commenced his action, the position had deteriorated to the extent that in 2001 it only took 15 minutes of heavy rainfall, or several hours of steady drizzle, for flooding to occur. When the claimant's front garden was flooded the water level reached the brickwork of the walls of the house above the level of the damp course; and often rose to a level about three-quarters of an inch below the level of the front door threshold. When the floodwaters subsided, deposits of sludge and debris were left in the back garden. The claimant had works carried out which took some of the floodwater from his front garden underneath the garage and to the bottom of his back garden. It was these works (which had cost £16,000) which were responsible for preventing the floodwater from entering his house. Nevertheless the house was affected by damp and may have been damaged structurally.

After making initial contact with his local authority, the claimant was eventually referred to the defendants, Thames Water Utilities Ltd, the relevant statutory sewerage undertaker for the purposes of the Water Industry Act 1991. It was apparent that Thames operated a points system as a way of determining priorities for spending money on the alleviation of flooding. Points were awarded for various factors such as whether the flooding was of foul or surface water, whether it was internal or external, the nature of the property affected and whether the customer had been

---

[270] [1980] 1 All ER 17 at 37.
[271] [2002] 2 All ER 55.

forced to vacate the property temporarily. The score was then compared with the cost of the necessary engineering project. Thames considered that the threshold for a viable engineering project was 100 points per million pounds. Given that the cost of the major of four projects identified by experts as necessary to alleviate the flooding in the present case was 30 points per million pounds, it followed that there appeared at that time to be no prospect of work being carried out in the foreseeable future to prevent flooding to the claimant's property.

The claim comprised two central strands: that the flooding of the claimant's property gave rise to liability at common law; and the novel argument that Thames' failure as a public authority to take steps to prevent the flooding constituted an infringement of the claimant's right to respect for his home and the peaceful enjoyment of his possessions as protected by Article 8 of, and Article 1 of the First Protocol to, the European Convention on Human Rights and Fundamental Freedoms (as incorporated into English law by the Human Rights Act 1998). At first instance, Judge Harvey QC rejected the common law claims but accepted that damages should be awarded under the HRA 1998. The Court of Appeal took the view that the common law claim should succeed, and accordingly did not consider the applicability of the "human rights" arguments. On 4th December 2003 the House of Lords unanimously upheld Thames Water's appeal, holding that the utility company was not liable at either common law or under the 1998 Act. The discussion below describes the decisions at first instance and in the Court of Appeal. The decision of the House of Lords is summarised in the Preface to this book.

The common law claims advanced by the claimant were in *Rylands* v *Fletcher*, nuisance, negligence and breach of statutory duty. In the opinion of Judge Havery QC, the claim amounted to a claim of non-feasance (i.e. a failure by Thames to perform its statutory duty to carry out the works necessary to prevent repetition of the flooding), and in his judgment a line of authority which could be traced back to the case of *Glossop* v *Heston and Isleworth Local Board*,[272] defeated the claimant's common claims.[273] The effect of these authorities was that:

> "... a statutory drainage undertaker is not liable to a person in its area who suffers damage by flooding where the claim is based on failure on the part of the undertaker to undertake works to fulfil its statutory duty of drainage of the area. That is so whether the cause of action is nuisance, the principle in *Rylands* v *Fletcher* or breach of statutory duty. It is clear that those authorities also cover the case of negligent non-feasance."[274]

---

[272] (1879) 12 Ch D 102.

[273] In addition to *Glossop*, the line of authority consisted of: *Robinson* v *Mayor and Corporation of the Borough of Workington* [1897] 1 QB 619; *Hesketh* v *Birmingham Corporation* [1924] 1 KB 260; *Pride of Derby and Derbyshire Angling Association Ltd* v *British Celanese Ltd* [1953] 1 All ER 179; and *Smeaton* v *Ilford Corporation* [1954] 1 All ER 923.

[274] [2001] 3 All ER 698 at 710.

On appeal, however, the Court of Appeal reached a quite different conclusion to Judge Havery QC on the question of Thames' common law liability for the flooding to the claimant's property. The judgment of the Court was delivered by Lord Phillips MR who chose to concentrate on the claim in nuisance.[275] It is sufficient here to have regard to that part of Lord Phillips MR's judgment which dealt with the issue whether the present case fell within the scope of the principle identified in *Goldman* v *Hargrave* and subsequently applied in *Leakey*.

Lord Phillips MR commenced with the observation that Thames were the owners of and were in control of the sewers from which the foul and surface water escaped prior to flooding Mr Marcic's property. Thames were, moreover, the owners of the system to which the relevant sewers were connected. Judge Havery QC had concluded that, in the words of Lord Phillips MR, "by passively using the sewers in order to carry out its statutory duty of draining its area" Thames had "passively permitted the nuisance to continue and thereby adopted the nuisance".[276] Whilst the Court of Appeal agreed with this part of the judge's analysis, it considered that "the matter can be put higher against Thames". In the words of Lord Phillips MR:

> "The sewers form part of a system which Thames are operating as a commercial venture in order to make profits for their shareholders. Thames are in no more favourable position than a landowner on whose property a hazard accumulates by the act of a trespasser or of nature. At all material times Thames have had, or should have had, knowledge of the hazard. If the principles identified in *Goldman* v *Hargrave* ... and *Leakey's* case are applied, these facts placed Thames under a duty to Mr Marcic to take such steps as, in all the circumstances, were reasonable to prevent the discharge of surface and foul water onto Mr Marcic's property."[277]

From this passage it is evident, therefore, that the Court of Appeal considered that Thames were *prima facie* liable in nuisance to the claimant.

However, in order for such liability actually to materialise, it was necessary to determine whether Thames' actions had been reasonable in the circumstances of the case. This in turn raised another question: On whom did the burden of proof lie? Did it lie with Mr Marcic to show that what Thames had done was not reasonable, or did Thames have to prove that they had done all that was reasonable?

---

[275] Prior to his remarks as regards liability in nuisance, Lord Phillips MR expressed support for the view expressed by Lord Denning MR in *Pride of Derby and Derbyshire Angling Association Ltd* v *British Celanese Ltd* [1953] 1 All ER 179, to the effect that the rule in *Rylands* v *Fletcher* was unlikely to apply "in all its strictness" to escapes of sewage on the basis that sewage works were constructed by local authorities for the general benefit of the community. This statement now must be considered in the light of the more recent statements on *Rylands* v *Fletcher* in *Transco plc* v *Stockport MBC* [2003] UKHL 61 (see below, p. 198).
[276] [2002] 2 All ER 55 at 78.
[277] *ibid.*

In determining this issue, the Court of Appeal had regard to a passage from the judgment of Lord Denning MR in *Southport Corporation* v *Esso Petroleum Co Ltd*[278] in which His Lordship had sought to identify the burden of proof as one of the principal differences between an action for public nuisance and an action for negligence. In Lord Denning's judgment, where the claim concerned public nuisance, "once the nuisance is proved and the defendant is shown to have caused it, the legal burden is shifted on to the defendant to justify or excuse himself."[279] If the defendant failed to discharge this burden of proof, he would accordingly be found liable. The Court of Appeal in *Marcic* agreed with this observation and with the following comment made by the editors of *Clerk & Lindsell on Torts*:

> "... in relation to private nuisance there seems no reason why the maxim *res ipsa loquitur* should not apply in appropriate cases to require the defendant to show that he was not at fault and was not negligent."[280]

Accordingly in the light of the authorities and academic opinion on the matter, the Court of Appeal concluded that:

> "Once a claimant has proved that a nuisance has emanated from land in the possession or control of the defendant, the onus shifts to the defendant to show that he has a defence in the claim, whether this be absence of 'negligence' in a statutory authority case or that he took all reasonable steps to prevent the nuisance, if it is a *Leakey* situation."[281]

Having regard to the facts of the present appeal, Lord Phillips MR noted that Thames had not sought to prove that it had taken all reasonable steps to prevent causing a nuisance to the claimant. Rather, it had sought to show that its system of priorities for determining when to take remedial action was a fair way of devoting limited resources to the widespread problem of flooding from its sewers. In the opinion of the Court of Appeal, had the defendants managed to establish this, they may also have been able to establish that they had done everything that was reasonable for the purposes of the *Leakey* test. However, Judge Havery QC had not been persuaded that Thames' system of priorities was a fair one and the Court of Appeal agreed with that conclusion. Indeed, their Lordship's went so far as to express the view that they could not reasonably accept that:

> "... a body with the actual and potential resources of Thames is in a position to rely on lack of resources to justify not merely no immediate steps, but taking no steps at all to abate a nuisance such as that suffered by Mr Marcic."[282]

---

[278] [1954] 2 All ER 561. For a fuller discussion of this case, see p. 166.
[279] *ibid* at 571.
[280] 17th edition (1995) at p. 904 (paras.18-28).
[281] [2002] 2 All ER 55 at 79.
[282] *ibid.*

Despite the Court of Appeal's reasoning on this matter, counsel for Thames submitted that the defendants could not be liable under the *Leakey* principle on two grounds: (i) that the *Leakey* duty of care could not extend so far as to require the defendants to acquire land in order to construct the necessary works so as to abate the nuisance; and (ii) that in order to abate the nuisance Thames would have to make use of their statutory powers, and that the *Leakey* duty could not be invoked to require this to happen.

In support of his first ground, counsel for Thames referred the Court of Appeal to *Job Edwards Ltd* v *Company of Proprietors of the Birmingham Navigations*,[283] where Scrutton LJ had remarked that: "surely a landowner cannot be required to execute permanent works on another person's land, if he could not ... stop the fire on his own land."[284] The Court of Appeal was, however, unimpressed by such an argument. In the words of Lord Phillips MR:

> "We do not read this statement as one of principle that a defendant can never be obliged to purchase land in order to abate a nuisance emanating from land that he already owns. It may be that the *Leakey* test will seldom involve such a duty, but where a massive corporation, such as Thames, is carrying on business as a sewerage undertaker, we consider that the common law duty to take reasonable steps not to permit a nuisance to continue will often involve the requirement to add to the substantial land areas that it already owns."[285]

The defendant's second ground, that regard could not be had to Thames' statutory powers when determining what it was required to do under the *Leakey* principle to abate the nuisance, was similarly rejected by the Court of Appeal. In the words of Lord Phillips MR:

> "The foundation of a claim in nuisance is the fact that the defendant has caused or permitted the nuisance to occur. It is the emanation of the nuisance from land within the control of the defendant that is the foundation of the claim to relief. The existence of the statutory power may become relevant when considering what the defendant could reasonably have done to prevent the nuisance. The duty to take reasonable steps to abate the nuisance is not, however, founded on the fact that the statutory power exists."[286]

Lord Phillips MR continued:

> "We are in no doubt that, when applying the *Leakey* test of duty to a sewerage undertaking such as Thames, the reasonableness of Thames' conduct must be judged having regard to all the steps that it

---

[283] [1924] 1 KB 341.
[284] At 360.
[285] [2002] 2 All ER 55 at 79.
[286] At 80.

is open to Thames to take to abate the nuisance, whether under statutory powers or otherwise."[287]

And concluded:

"It would be unrealistic, indeed an absurd, exercise to consider whether Thames had taken reasonable steps, having regard to their individual circumstances, to abate the nuisance, without including their statutory powers in those circumstances."[288]

For these reasons the Court of Appeal in *Marcic* held, inter alia, that the facts of the case were such as to bring it within the scope of the principle identified in *Goldman* v *Hargrave* and later applied in *Leakey*. Thames were therefore liable to the claimant for the nuisance that he had suffered and the *Glossop* line of authority on which Judge Havery QC had relied was held not to have survived the development of the law in those two cases. The issue of whether or not the defendant was in breach of section 6 of the Human Rights Act 1998 was therefore rendered "academic" for the Court of Appeal by this finding; but the decision of Judge Harvey on this point was nevertheless upheld. For the decision of the House of Lords, reversing the Court of Appeal, see the Preface to this book.

The *Leakey* duty was the subject of further judicial analysis in *Green* v *The Right Honourable Lord Somerleyton and others*,[289] a case which, like *Marcic*, was concerned with a claim in nuisance arising from flooding; in this instance the flooding of an area of marshland which the claimant owned and used as grazing for his cattle during the summer months. It had been argued at first instance before His Honour Judge Rich QC that applying *Leakey*, the defendants, the trustees of an area of marshland adjacent to the claimant's land, owed the claimant a duty to take reasonable steps to prevent his land from being flooded by water emanating from a lake on their land. It was further contended that the defendants were in breach of that duty in the context of a serious flooding incident which had occurred in December 1993, and also in respect of the intermittent flooding of the claimant's land which had occurred since that date. In finding against the claimant, however, the judge at first instance ruled that no *Leakey* duty arose on the facts of the present case. In his judgment, "the natural flow is not ... to be regarded as a hazard which would bring into play the duty of care held to arise in *Leakey's* case."

In the subsequent appeal, it was argued on behalf of the claimant that the *Leakey* duty arises in relation to naturally flowing water as it does in relation to water the flow of which has been artificially diverted. On behalf of the defendants, however, it was argued that the decisions in *Thomas & Evans Ltd* v *Mid-Rhonda Co-operative Society*[290] and the Australian case

---

[287] *ibid.*

[288] At 81.

[289] [2003] EWCA Civ 198; [2003] 11 EGCS 152.

[290] [1941] 1 KB 381.

of *Elston v Dore*[291] were authority for the contrary proposition (i.e. that no such duty arises in relation to naturally flowing water). It was further contended that *Thomas* remained good law despite the fact that in *Leakey*, Megaw LJ had erroneously treated it as a case in which a duty of care had arisen but had not been breached. In the alternative, counsel for the defendants argued that even if a *Leakey* duty did arise on the facts of the present appeal, the Trustees had nevertheless discharged that duty.

The judgment of the Court of Appeal was delivered by Jonathan Parker LJ.[292] In addressing the question of whether the defendants were liable in nuisance for the flooding to the claimant's land, his Lordship drew attention to the fact that the expression "naturally flowing water" was capable of bearing several meanings[293] and that the distinction between "natural" features of the landscape and those which could be said to be "artificial" in that they owed something to human agency was "not... an easy one to draw". Accordingly, his Lordship observed that:

> "So what at first glance may appear as a wholly 'natural' feature of the landscape may, on further examination, turn out to owe something to the intervention of man. To my mind, therefore, in the context of the English landscape a distinction between "natural" and "artificial" features is an inherently uncertain foundation on which to rest a decision as to the existence of liability in nuisance."[294]

A further introductory point made by Jonathan Parker LJ concerned the application of the *Leakey* duty in any particular case. In his Lordship's opinion, determining whether or not the duty applied to the facts of a case involved the same considerations that arose in the context of determining whether or not a tortious duty of care existed. Accordingly, it was necessary to consider whether a *Leakey* duty arose; if so, whether that duty had been breached; and what damage (if any) resulted from that breach.

Finally, Jonathan Parker LJ had regard to the decision in *Delaware Mansions* and noted that in reaching its conclusion on the issue of liability in nuisance, the House of Lords had emphasised that "reasonableness between neighbours is the key to the solution of the problems in this field...".[295] In his Lordship's opinion, the same guiding principle applied to the facts of the present case:

> "If reasonableness between neighbours is the key to the solution of problems concerning encroaching tree roots, I can see no reason in principle why it should not also be the key to the resolution of a dispute such as has arisen in the instant case. The more so because I

---

[291] (1982) 149 CLR 480.
[292] The other two members of the Court of Appeal were Schiemann LJ and Sir Christopher Staunton.
[293] e.g. water flowing in its natural direction, i.e. downhill, or water flowing in "natural" surroundings or at the very least, water flowing over a "natural" surface.
[294] [2003] EWCA Civ 198 at para.81.
[295] Per Lord Cooke [2001] 4 All ER 737 at 749.

cannot draw any sensible distinction between unreasonably allowing fire to escape onto a neighbour's land (the situation in *Goldman* v *Hargrave*, where the defendant was held liable for the resulting damage) and unreasonably allowing floodwater to do so."[296]

In the light of these preliminary observations it followed that the *Leakey* duty applies as much to floodwaters as it does to encroaching tree roots, unless such a conclusion was in conflict with existing authority. In short, therefore, whether or not the *Leakey* duty arose in the present case turned on the earlier authorities of *Thomas & Evans Ltd* v *Mid-Rhonda Co-operative Society*[297] and *Elston* v *Dore*.[298]

It will be remembered that a key argument in the defence case in the present proceedings was that *Thomas* was authority for the proposition that damage caused by the natural flow of water did not fall within the scope of the *Leakey* duty.

The facts of *Thomas* were that in 1892 an agreement had been entered into by the then owner of the land, which was later occupied by the appellants, and the local authority. The agreement provided for the construction by the local authority of a flood defence wall on the land to be paid for jointly by the authority and the land owner. The object of the wall was two-fold: it would protect the owner of the land's property; and it would also protect the nearby highway from flooding. As part of the agreement, the former owner of the land undertook not at any time thereafter to "pull down or remove such wall or any part thereof unless and until he shall have previously erected on the said land substantial buildings which would have the effect of preventing floods...". In 1939, the appellants wished to reconstruct certain buildings on the site. In order to do that, they proposed to demolish part of the wall and to substitute in its place the front wall of a new building which would also operate as river wall. Permission for such a development was granted by the freeholder's agents and work began. The original flood defence wall was demolished and a wall which was slightly shorter in length than the original wall was erected in its place. The gaps at either end of the new wall were left in order to facilitate other building operations on the site. It was always the appellants intention to fill those gaps once such operations had been completed. However, as the result of exceptional rains, the river Rhondda burst its banks and the floodwaters passed over the appellants' land, through the gaps in the new wall, across the highway and onto land owned by the respondents. The respondents accordingly brought an action in which they sought damages for the harm suffered to their land. At first instance, the county court judge took the view that by leaving the gaps in the wall in the course of their building operations the appellants had been negligent. In his opinion, the appellants ought to have taken precautionary action to prevent the floodwater passing onto the plaintiffs' land since the sudden rising of the river was an event

---

[296] [2003] EWCA Civ 198 at para.84.
[297] [1941] 1 KB 381.
[298] (1982) 149 CLR 480.

which ought to have been anticipated. Accordingly, the plaintiffs recovered the sum of £100 in damages.

In the subsequent appeal, it was contended on behalf of the appellants that they were under no common law duty to maintain the wall. The plaintiffs for their part contended that as occupiers of the adjoining property they were entitled to the protection of the wall, and that the flow of the floodwater through the gap amounted to an interference with their rights. The judgment of the Court of Appeal was delivered by Sir Wilfred Greene MR.[299] In allowing the appeal, the Master of the Rolls considered what rights, if any, were conferred on the respondents when the wall was erected pursuant to the agreement between the local authority and the appellants' predecessor in title. Sir Wilfred Greene opined:

> "They had no right to call upon Mr Idris Williams[300] or anybody else to erect a wall upon this land for the purpose of protecting their property. If Mr Idris Williams, for his own purposes, with or without the assistance and co-operation of the local Board, chooses to erect such a wall, on no principle of law known to me would a third person be entitled to insist on its continued existence. If this wall had been erected by the freeholder and taken down by the freeholder the next day, or a week, or a year afterwards, with the result that the floodwater took the course which it would have taken if the wall had never been there, I cannot see, on any principle known to me, that the respondents would have been entitled to complain."[301]

Later in his judgment, Sir Wilfred Greene MR further remarked:

> "As it seems to me, the simple ground for deciding this case is that the respondents had no right to have the wall erected, they had no right to insist on its continuance, they had no ground of complaint whatsoever against anybody who rightfully took it down, and the appellants in this case rightfully took it down under their licence from the freeholder."[302]

In the Australian case of *Elston* v *Dore*,[303] the appellants were the owners of land which they farmed for cane, whereas the respondent used his land for grazing purposes. The farms were situated in a low-lying area of North Queensland where the annual rainfall was very high. Accordingly from time to time, the whole area was inundated by floodwaters from the rivers Murray and/or Tulley. In order to alleviate the problems associated with flooding, the appellants obtained the respondent's permission to cut two drains on his land. The natural direction of the drainage was thereby changed, and if it had not been for the drains, floodwaters would not have

---

[299] The other two judges who heard the appeal were Clauson and Goddard LJJ.
[300] The owner of the land at the time that the agreement had been entered into with the local authority.
[301] [1941] 1 KB 381 at 389.
[302] At 393.
[303] (1982) 159 CLR 480.

flowed onto the respondent's land from the appellants' land. Eventually the respondent decided to block one of the drains and later it was completely filled in. As a result, the water that fell on the appellants' land drained away more slowly and some of it did not drain away at all so that the land remained flooded. The appellants suffered damage and accordingly asserted a cause of action against the respondent on three grounds, one of which was in nuisance. In holding that the respondent was not liable in nuisance, it was stated in the judgment of Gibbs CJ, Wilson and Brennan JJ that:

> "The respondent's action has not caused the appellants' lands to be damaged, invaded or interfered with. The damage which the appellants have suffered is due to the natural deficiency of their lands, and to the fact that other occupiers of land other than the respondent have impaired the natural drainage system ... and to the fact that the respondent would no longer provide an artificial means of drainage to carry from the appellants' lands water that would not naturally flow onto the respondent's land. The respondent had no duty to help the appellants in this way."[304]

In arriving at such a conclusion, the High Court of Australia had regard to the relevant authorities, including the decision in *Thomas* and what had been said about that case by Megaw LJ in *Leakey*.[305] In the opinion of the Australian court, Megaw LJ had erroneously interpreted the decision in *Thomas* as being that there had been nothing unreasonable in the action of the appellants in taking down the wall when in fact, Sir Wilfred Greene MR's judgment had proceeded on the basis that the appellants had no duty to act reasonably. In *Green* v *The Right Honourable Lord Somerleyton and others*, however, Jonathan Parker LJ considered that the High Court of Australia had itself been in error on this point. In his judgment, Megaw LJ had said nothing in *Leakey* to suggest that the test of reasonableness had been applied in *Thomas*.[306]

Having regard to the effect of *Thomas* on the facts of the case before him, Jonathan Parker LJ observed:

> "It is certainly the case that in *Thomas* this court held that there was no common law duty on the defendants to maintain the wall, and that it followed that the damage which the plaintiffs had suffered was not damage for which they were entitled to be compensated. But, in contrast to a statutory duty, the common law duty which underlies the tort of nuisance is not a duty which is writ in stone: it is a duty which reflects current attitudes and values, and as such is inherently susceptible to a process of development and refinement. In my judgment, the tort of nuisance is not to be made the prisoner of

---

[304] At 491.
[305] [1980] QB 485 at 522.
[306] [2003] EWCA Civ 198 at para.99.

precedent ... Life has moved on in the 63 years or so since *Thomas* was decided, and so has the law of nuisance."[307]

Thus in contrast to the judge at first instance, the Court of Appeal in *Green* concluded that *Thomas* was not authority for the proposition that the *Leakey* duty did not arise in relation to naturally flowing water. In the absence of any relevant easement, and given the parties' awareness of the propensity of the land to flood, the Trustees were therefore liable to the claimant in nuisance if and to the extent that the flooding of his land was attributable to their failure to do that which was reasonable in the circumstances.

As it turned out, however, although the Court of Appeal held in favour of the claimant as to the existence of a *Leakey* duty, on the facts it concluded that there had been no breach of that duty. In other words, there was nothing to suggest that the Trustees had acted unreasonably in relation to the 1993 flooding incident and the subsequent threat of further floods.

Landlords not in occupation

The courts have displayed some reluctance to regard a landlord not in occupation as responsible for nuisances caused by the activities of an occupying tenant. Such liability will arise, however, in situations where it may be said that the landlord *authorised* the nuisance.

An example may be found in *Tetley* v *Chitty*.[308] Here a local authority had leased to a co-defendant a site with a view to the latter running a Go-Kart Club. The Council were aware at the time of the grant of the lease that the noise which ensued was a likely consequence of the proposed use of the land.

It was held that the landlord local authority was an appropriate co-defendant. McNeill J concluded:

> "... the nuisance from noise generated by Go-Kart racing and practising was ... on the facts an ordinary and necessary consequence ... or a natural and necessary consequence [of that activity]. There was ... express or at least implied consent to do that which ... inevitably would amount to a nuisance."[309]

The requirements for liability would appear to be two-fold: express or implied consent to the tenant engaging in a particular activity (here go-karting), and an inevitability or a "very high degree of probability"[310] that the activity will result in a nuisance.

---

[307] *ibid.*
[308] [1986] 1 All ER 663. For a statutory nuisance case involving noise from a racing circuit, see *Sevenoaks DC* v *Brands Hatch Leisure Group Ltd* [2001] EHLR 114, discussed below at p. 468.
[309] At 671.
[310] See Pennycuick V-C in *Smith* v *Scott* [1973] Ch 314.

A similar approach and result may be found in an earlier decision: *Harris* v *James*.[311] A field was leased for the purpose of it being worked as a lime quarry, involving also the erection of lime kilns and the burning of lime. In his judgment for the plaintiffs against the landlords, Blackburn J explained:

> "... in the case before us the lime field was let for the very purposes of burning lime. No doubt, for any mischief arising from a careless or negligent use of the field, the landlord would not be liable, but for any mischief that arises from the natural and necessary result of what the landlord authorised or required or even authorised and did not require, I think that the landlord must be held liable."[312]

It is important to note, however, that mere foreseeability of the likelihood that tenants may commit a nuisance will not suffice to render a landlord liable. There is a difference between a landlord who lets land for a particular purpose which is in all probability going to cause a nuisance to neighbours, and a landlord who simply lets property to tenants whom there may be reason to suspect may behave in an un-neighbourly way.

The distinction is illustrated by *Smith* v *Scott*.[313] In this case the plaintiff suffered in the use and enjoyment of his home when the defendant local authority began to acquire neighbouring houses for letting to homeless persons. One such house was let to a family with a past record of anti-social behaviour towards neighbours: in other words the letting took place in circumstances in which the landlord local authority was aware of a likelihood that the tenants might cause a nuisance by their behaviour. Pennycuick V-C stated the position as regards liability in nuisance:

> "In general a landlord is not liable for nuisance committed by his tenant, but to this there is ... one recognised exception, namely, that the landlord is liable if he has authorised the tenant to commit the nuisance ... But this exception has ... been rigidly confined to circumstances in which the nuisance has either been expressly authorised or is certain to result from the purposes for which the property is let."[314]

Applying this test, Pennycuick V-C found the landlords not liable. They had not expressly authorised the activities which amounted to the actionable nuisance. What they *had* authorised was residence in the premises, subject to an express provision that the tenants should not cause a nuisance. Nor was it possible to find that nuisances were certain to result from residence on those premises. Unlike the situation in *Tetley*, where go-karting was inevitably going to cause a nuisance, residence in a house has no such objective probability. The fact that the particular tenants to whom the council had let property were likely to behave in a way which would amount to a nuisance did not suffice to render the landlord liable.

---

[311] [1874-80] All ER Rep 1142.
[312] At 1143.
[313] [1972] 3 All ER 645.
[314] At 648-649.

The decision in *Smith* v *Scott* is important in its demonstration of the quite narrow confines of the liability of defendants *qua* landlord.[315] The test stated may be regarded as rendering landlords liable only in circumstances where they may very nearly be regarded as having themselves created the nuisance in question, albeit via the instrument of a third party.[316] However, for the law to hold that one person has responsibility because a tort has been committed by another adult (third party) requires strong evidence that one is the instrument of the other, or strong policy justification (as in the case of the incidence of vicarious liability). Had the landlord in a case like *Smith* v *Scott* carefully selected the tenants *in the hope* that they would behave in a way which would involve a nuisance to the plaintiff the position might perhaps have been different (and this even if, formally, the terms of the tenancy might have forbidden the anticipated nuisance). But mere likelihood that an adult third party may behave tortiously will not suffice.

Judicial reticence as regards holding a landlord who is not in possession of land liable in nuisance for the actions of tenant occupants was confirmed also by the Court of Appeal in *Hussain* v *Lancaster City Council*.[317] The court upheld the striking out of the plaintiffs' action in nuisance (and negligence). The plaintiffs owned, and lived above, shop premises within the predominantly local authority-owned Rylands estate in Lancaster. Their statement of claim alleged that they had suffered from numerous incidents involving severe harassment, including racial harassment, from local authority tenants on the estate. Reference was made in the statement of claim to such matters as the shouting of threats and racist abuse, the kicking of footballs deliberately against (and shattering) the shop windows, the throwing of stones and bricks at the shop and its garage and an attempt to set fire to the shop premises by putting a lighted mattress against its door.

The plaintiffs sought to render the local authority liable on the basis of an alleged failure on the part of the authority to have taken appropriate and adequate steps to have caused those nuisances to the plaintiffs to have ceased. In particular, the plaintiffs alleged a failure by the local authority to

---

[315] The decision was approved and followed by the Court of Appeal in *Elizabeth* v *Rochester City Council* (unreported) 26th April 1993. Here, the plaintiff claimed that the defendants, in their capacity as landlords, were responsible for nuisance and annoyance allegedly caused to her by other tenants of the defendants. However, in dismissing an application for leave to appeal, Nourse LJ (delivering the judgment of the Court) stated that: "I am unable to see that it [the statement of claim] contains an allegation that the defendants ... ever expressly or impliedly authorised the other tenants to do any of the acts of which the plaintiff complains. Broadly stated, without such an allegation it would be quite impossible for the action to succeed."

[316] In *Southwark London Borough Council* v *Tanner* [1999] 3 WLR 939, Lord Millett made the following *obiter* remarks: "Once the activities complained of have been found to constitute an actionable nuisance, more than one party may be held legally responsible. The person or persons directly responsible for the activities in question are liable; but so too is anyone who authorised them. Landlords have been held liable for nuisance committed by their tenants on this basis. It is not enough for them to be aware of the nuisance and take no steps to prevent it. They must either participate directly in the commission of the nuisance, or they must be taken to have authorised it by letting the property..." (at 956).

[317] [1999] 4 All ER 125.

take steps to enforce terms in the residents' tenancy agreements forbidding such conduct,[318] or to have sought possession of properties let to the perpetrators.[319]

The Court of Appeal applied the principle in *Smith v Scott*,[320] that a non-occupier landlord could not be held responsible for nuisances committed by tenants except in so far as the court might regard the landlord as having authorised the commission of that nuisance: that is, where the nuisance is certain to result from the purposes for which the property was let. It was this simple, and restrictive, principle which was applicable.[321] The Court of Appeal rejected arguments presented by counsel for the plaintiffs to the effect that the broader liability principles in *Sedleigh-Denfield*[322] should be applied: that a local authority owner of land should bear responsibility where nuisances have been caused by tenants in occupation – responsibility being founded upon not having taken reasonable steps to have prevented those persons on one's land from having caused the nuisances.

The rejection of that principle produces, however, a quite stark contrast between two situations in which a nuisance action may be contemplated against a non-occupant owner of land in relation to the conduct on that land of other, occupying, persons. We seem to need to distinguish between:

- situations where the owner has granted a leasehold interest to those whose actions constitute the nuisance;

- situations where there may be persons more informally – perhaps unlawfully – present on the land and who may be causing the plaintiff a nuisance.

In the former situation the *Smith v Scott* principle will apply. In the latter, however, there may be scope for the *Sedleigh-Denfield* approach.

The broader potential for non-occupant landowner liability in the second of the two situations can be demonstrated by *Page Motors Ltd v Epsom and*

---

[318] "... do not do anything which may cause discomfort, annoyance, or nuisance ...; do not discriminate against or harass any residents ..."

[319] Under s. 84 and Sched. 2, Housing Act 1985.

[320] See above, p. 113.

[321] The principle in *Smith v Scott* was applied even more recently by the Court of Appeal in *Mowan v London Borough of Wandsworth* [2001] EHLR DG5. In this case, the plaintiff, a council tenant, complained that for a period of approximately ten years, another council tenant in the flat above carried on various acts which caused a nuisance. Such acts included: blocking the toilet of the neighbouring flat so as to cause the property to flood with sewage; leaving the taps on in the neighbouring flat so as to cause the property to flood with water; jumping up and down in the neighbouring flat so as to cause noise to permeate the flat below. The Court of Appeal was in no doubt that such acts amounted to a nuisance from which the plaintiff had suffered "serious harm". However, on the basis of the authorities, it was not a nuisance for which the council as landlord could be liable since it had not been authorised by them (neither were they liable in negligence since they did not owe the plaintiff a duty of care).

[322] See above, p. 87.

Ewell Borough Council.[323] Here the plaintiffs occupied business premises on an estate belonging to the defendant local authority. Their premises adjoined a piece of open land also belonging to the council. The proceedings related to nuisances which the plaintiffs alleged they had experienced, arising out of the conduct of gypsies who had been camping without permission for several years on that open land. The claim alleged nuisances in the form of smoke from the burning of rubbish and rubber, the obstruction of the plaintiffs' rights of way, failure to have controlled aggressive dogs and other conduct of an anti-social nature. The Court of Appeal approached the issue from the standpoint of the local authority being entitled, as against the gypsy trespassers, to immediate possession of the land. As such the principle in *Sedleigh-Denfield* applied: that an occupier – including as here a person with an immediate right to occupation – may be liable in nuisance for acts of a trespasser in circumstances where the defendant may be said to have adopted or continued the nuisance (for example, by not having taken reasonable steps to put an end to the conduct in question).

The facts of *Page Motors* presented a clear situation in which the court could hold there to have been such adoption or continuance. Quite apart from the council having taken no steps, over a five-year period, to regain possession of the land from the gypsy occupants, the council had taken certain positive steps to assist those trespassers – the provision of a water stand-pipe and skips for their disposal of refuse.

Page Motors was decided on the basis that the gypsies were *trespassers*, for whose actions, in the circumstances, the local authority bore liability in nuisance. The same principle seems applicable in cases where an owner of land permits another to go into occupation, but without there being a formal demise. This is demonstrated by the Court of Appeal decision in *Lippiatt* v *South Gloucestershire Council.*[324] In this case the plaintiffs were farmers who complained of nuisances caused by the activities of "travellers" who had settled for some three years on a strip of land, owned by the local authority, adjacent to the plaintiffs' farm. In due course the local authority secured the eviction of the travellers. The plaintiffs brought an action for damages in nuisance against the local authority. The evidence was that the local authority were well aware of the presence of the travellers from a quite early stage, and that its attitude was to "tolerate" the "unauthorised encampment". Indeed, the tolerance afforded was more than merely passive: the local authority provided some toilet facilities, skips and water bowsers. The Court of Appeal overturned the trial judge's decision to strike out the claim against the local authority. One of the reasons given, by Sir Christopher Staughton, was that the case fell on the *Page Motors* side of the divide, described above, between the principles applicable in cases where the owner retained occupation (or right of occupation) and cases where a leasehold interest had been granted by the property owner:

---

[323] (1981) 80 LGR 337.
[324] [1999] 4 All ER 149.

" ... there is in my judgment a difference between a case ... where the offenders were ... tenants of the defendant with an interest in the land, and the present case where they are either licensees of the council or else trespassers, and can be moved on. In the latter case, the council may be found to have adopted the nuisance by failing to exercise its power to turn out the travellers once their misbehaviour became apparent ..."[325]

One further point arising out of the decision in the *Hussain* case may conveniently be considered here. Quite apart from dismissal of the claim following application of *Smith* v *Scott*, the Court of Appeal considered the claim to be misconceived for another reason also. As Hirst LJ explained:

"So far as the scope of the tort [of nuisance] is concerned ... its essence is that the defendant's use of the defendant's land interferes with the plaintiff's use of the plaintiff's land ... In the present case the acts complained of unquestionably interfered persistently and intolerably with the plaintiffs' enjoyment of the plaintiff's land, but they did not involve the tenants' use of the tenants' land and therefore fell outside the scope of the tort."[326]

In other words, since the activities involving the harassment of the plaintiffs took place not from the tenants' homes, but from public spaces immediately outside the plaintiffs' shop and home, the law of private nuisance was, it was suggested, not applicable.

A number of questions arise in connection with this statement of principle. To begin with any such limitation of the tort of private nuisance to cases where the alleged nuisance arises out of the defendant's use of his or her property is to narrow the scope of the tort by comparison with earlier decisions and earlier understandings. Certainly a very common instance of nuisance is as depicted by Hirst LJ: but there is good authority for the view that the ambit of the tort is by no means so confined. For example, a nuisance may arise in circumstances such as those in *Southport Corporation* v *Esso Petroleum Co Ltd*:[327] fouling of a beach following the discharge of oil at sea; or which may arise out of a defendant's activities on a highway, and the effect of those activities on the use and enjoyment which the plaintiff may make on his adjacent land.[328]

If the words of Hirst LJ should not, therefore, be taken according to their literal meaning, what interpretation should be placed upon them? The answer would seem to be that the statements must be read in the light of the particular issue under consideration. When we are considering the liability which may attach (i) to a landlord for the acts of a tenant, or (ii) to

---

[325] At 160.

[326] [1999] 4 All ER 125 at 144.

[327] See below, p. 166.

[328] See, for example, *Thompson-Schwab* v *Costaki* [1956] 1 All ER 652 – above at p. 33: the nuisance comprised the *coming and going* of prostitutes and their clients rather than any activities within the neighbouring premises.

an owner for the acts of trespassers, it may indeed be relevant to ask whether the offending actions took place (a) on the defendant's land or (b) elsewhere. In *Hussain* the Court of Appeal regarded the fact that the alleged nuisance occurred away from the perpetrators' homes as an additional reason for holding that the claim disclosed no arguable cause of action against the local authority. Subsequently, in *Lippiatt* the Court of Appeal was called upon to consider the scope of a proposed general principle to the effect that before an owner of land may bear responsibility for a nuisance committed by persons who reside on his land (be it as tenants, trespassers or licensees) it must be shown that the nuisances in question arose out of the use made by those persons of that land. The Court reviewed the authorities and rejected any such general principle. Moreover, it was able to do so without shedding doubt on the correctness of the decision in *Hussain*, on that case's particular facts. Evans LJ distinguished and explained *Hussain* as follows:

> "The disturbance complained of in *Hussain's* case was a ... nuisance for which the individual perpetrators could be held liable, and they were identified as individuals who lived on council property; but their conduct was not in any sense linked to, nor did it emanate from, the homes where they lived."[329]

Evans LJ contrasted the situation of the nuisance caused by the travellers in *Lippiatt*. It was true that the alleged nuisances were not committed whilst the travellers were on the local authority land. The nuisances alleged involved their conduct whilst trespassing on the plaintiffs' adjacent farmland. Their conduct on the plaintiffs' land comprised such matters as: dumping rubbish; tethering goats, ponies and horses; steeling timber, gates and fences; and permitting dogs to chase the plaintiffs' sheep. Nevertheless, the case was, it was considered, very different from *Hussain*. Evans LJ explained:

> "Here, the allegation is that the travellers were allowed to congregate on the council's land and that they used it as a base for the unlawful activities of which the plaintiffs, as neighbours, complain. It is at least arguable that this can give rise to liability in nuisance, and so the claim should not be struck out."[330]

And in the words of Mummery LJ:

> "... nothing ... precludes a court from holding [that] an occupier of land may be liable for a nuisance which consists of a continuing state of affairs on his land where the nuisance manifests itself in the form of repeated acts on the plaintiff's land and those acts are, to the knowledge of the defendant, committed by persons based on his land and they interfere with the plaintiff's use and enjoyment of his land. ... It is reasonably arguable that the continuing presence of the

---

[329] [1999] 4 All ER 149 at 156-157.
[330] At 157.

travellers on the council's land constituted a nuisance to the plaintiff's use and enjoyment of their rights in their land, even though the travellers' activities involved using the council's land as a launching pad for repeated acts of trespass on the plaintiff's land.

It is not ... a case of the plaintiffs seeking to make the council vicariously liable for individual acts ... committed by third parties ... on [the plaintiffs'] land. It is rather a complaint of a continuing and potentially injurious state of affairs on the council's land ... The council let that state of affairs continue to exist on its land notwithstanding the complaints of the plaintiffs."[331]

---

[331] At 159.

Chapter 3

PRIVATE NUISANCE: DEFENCES

INTRODUCTION

This chapter focuses on two principal defences which may, in appropriate circumstances, defeat an otherwise good claim in nuisance: the defences of (i) statutory authority, and (ii) prescriptive right to commit the nuisance.

STATUTORY AUTHORITY

A defendant will not bear liability in nuisance if he or she is able to show that the interference suffered by the plaintiff is the inevitable result of the defendant having done something which is authorised by statute.

A modern example may be found in *Allen* v *Gulf Oil Refining Ltd.*[1] Some inhabitants of a small village near Milford Haven, in Dyfed, complained that they were experiencing nuisances in the form of smells, noise and vibrations, arising out of the defendant corporation's construction and operation of a nearby oil refinery. The refinery consisted of a vast complex of jetties on Milford Haven harbour (where the largest oil tankers could deliver crude oil), refining plant, pipes, pumping apparatus, storage tanks, a petrochemical plant and a private railway – extending in all to over 400 acres.

The issue raised as a preliminary point of law for decision by the House of Lords was whether the defendants could rely upon the terms of the Gulf Oil Refining Act 1965[2] as statutory authority for the construction and operation of the refinery, thereby freeing it from any liability in respect of any nuisances suffered by the plaintiffs arising inevitably out of the construction and operation of that refinery.

Setting out the basic principles, Lord Wilberforce noted:

> "It is now well settled that where Parliament by express direction or by necessary implication has authorised the construction and use of an undertaking or works, that carries with it an authority to do what is authorised with immunity from any action based on nuisance. The right of action is taken away ... To this there is made the qualification or condition, that the powers are exercised without 'negligence' – that word being used in a special sense so as to require the undertaker, as a condition of obtaining immunity ... to carry out the work and

---

[1] [1981] 1 All ER 353.
[2] A private Act which had been promoted by the defendants.

conduct in question with all reasonable regard and care for the interests of other persons."[3]

The 1965 Act did, indeed, provide clear statutory authority for the construction of a refinery at the location in question,[4] and it was held that by clear implication this authority extended also to the *operation* of the refinery so constructed. On that basis Lord Wilberforce[5] continued:

"The [plaintiff] alleges a nuisance ... The facts regarding these matters are for him to prove. It is then for the [defendants] to show, if they can, that it was impossible to construct and operate a refinery upon the site, conforming with Parliament's intention, without creating the nuisance alleged, or at least a nuisance ... To the extent that the environment has been changed from that of a peaceful unpolluted countryside to an industrial complex ... Parliament must be taken to have authorised it ... [T]he statutory authority ... confers immunity against proceedings for any nuisance which can be shown ... to be the inevitable result of erecting a refinery upon the site – not, I repeat, the existing refinery, but any refinery – however carefully, and with however great a regard for the interests of adjoining occupiers, it is sited, constructed and operated. To the extent and only to the extent that the actual nuisance exceeds that for which immunity is conferred, the plaintiff has a remedy."[6]

This test would appear reasonably straightforward. However, much will depend on how the matter of "inevitability" of harm is approached. One possibility is to hold that "inevitable" means consequences which are truly inescapable as a consequence of the authorised activity: inescapable however great the effort and resources which might be devoted to their avoidance. This interpretation would seem most to fit the language used by Lord Wilberforce in the passage quoted immediately above where the phrases "however carefully" and "however great a regard" are used. We should note, however, also the words which his Lordship used in the earlier extract to which we have referred. Here the language is that of immunity except where there has been a failure to "conduct operations with all reasonable regard for the interests" of affected persons.

The difference between these two broad formulations may, perhaps, be demonstrated by way of an example. Suppose it to be the case that it is not technically feasible, however much money is spent, to build and operate a refinery of the size envisaged by the statutory authority without causing a nuisance to persons who may reside close by. Clearly, any nuisance resulting from a state-of-the-art refinery, properly operated, will not be actionable. Suppose, next, that the refinery actually built is practically, but not quite, state-of-the-art, and is run practically, but not quite, with

---

[3] [1981] 1 All ER 353 at 356.

[4] Section 5.

[5] Lords Edmund-Davies, Diplock and Roskill agreed with Lord Wilberforce. Lord Keith delivered a dissenting opinion.

[6] [1981] 1 All ER 353 at 357-358.

maximum attention to the minimisation of external impacts. The reasons for having opted to fall short of the most benign method of operation have been, let us assume, economic: that the company has gone to very considerable expense and effort to keep nuisances to a relatively low level, but has not – in a competitive market – felt able to afford the much greater costs of technology which would have reduced impacts still further. In such a situation we may say that part of the nuisance was *not* inevitable in Lord Wilberforce's sense of "inevitable however hard" attempts are made at avoidance; but, equally, the nuisances may have been inevitable in the sense that they occurred notwithstanding the defendant having, let us concede, conducted the statutorily authorised activities "with all reasonable regard and care to the interests" of neighbours.

Of the two approaches so outlined, it is suggested that it is the "true inevitability" rather than "reasonably practicable inevitability" approach which is the one which Lord Wilberforce intended should apply. It is this language which his Lordship used in relation to the actual issue in the case, as distinct from in his broader preliminary formulation of principle. Further, the speech of Lord Edmund-Davies would seem to lend weight to this narrow approach to the statutory defence. His Lordship commented that the defendant was required to show that the nuisance in question was:

> "wholly unavoidable … quite regardless of the expense which might necessarily be involved in its avoidance."[7]

A contrary view had, however, been expressed by Viscount Dunedin half a century earlier in the House of Lords decision in *Manchester Corporation v Farnworth*.[8] In a case involving the construction, under statutory authority, of a generating station which emitted noxious fumes, Viscount Dunedin stated the basic principles set out above, and noted:

> "the criterion of inevitability is not what is theoretically possible but what is possible, according to the state of scientific knowledge at the time, having also in view a certain commonsense appreciation which cannot be rigidly defined, of practical feasibility in view of situation and expense."[9]

However, on the facts, it was held in *Farnworth* that the expense involved in operating without causing such a nuisance was *not* excessive; and their Lordships made clear that it was appropriate to regard Parliament as having intended, in the words of Viscount Sumner, to "require much care … to be taken".[10]

Whichever of the two broad approaches described above correctly represents the law it seems clear that the courts will not respond warmly to argument on the part of a defendant that the degree of expense which

---

[7] At 359.
[8] [1930] AC 171.
[9] At 183.
[10] At 201.

would need to be incurred to avoid the harm to the plaintiff is merely disproportionate to the harm which the nuisance is causing to the plaintiff. The Australian case, *York Bros (Trading) Pty Ltd* v *Commissioner for Main Roads*[11] provides an interesting illustration. The plaintiffs were owners of a shipyard on a river. Downstream the defendants were in the course of constructing a bridge, which when completed would, because of the relatively low level of its span, interfere with the plaintiffs' business by obstructing his rights to navigate the river. By way of defence the defendants pointed to authority under the Main Roads Act 1924 to build a bridge at the location in question. The defence did not, however, succeed. Having stated issues of principle as regards the defence of statutory authority, Powell J noted that this was not a case where a *particular design* of bridge was prescribed or authorised. Had that been the case:

> "it would seem hard to avoid the conclusion that the consequences naturally flowing from the construction ... of that work were intended, and thus made lawful by the statute."

Rather, the case was one in which authority was conferred in more general terms. Accordingly:

> "it was not the intention of the legislation that the rights of others should be invaded ... [S]uch invasion might be justified only if it can be demonstrated that ... if [the work] ... resulted in damage, there was, in the light of scientific knowledge then available no reasonable way in which the end described or permitted could have been achieved without doing the damage which ... resulted."

Powell J noted that, on the evidence, it was practically feasible to have chosen to have constructed a bridge of different design – a "lift span" bridge – which would not have interfered with navigation by the plaintiffs. The defendants countered, referring to Viscount Dunedin's dictum in *Farnworth*, that it was:

> "totally unreasonable to require the construction of a bridge, the cost of which would be 66 per cent greater merely so that one 'person' ... could continue its operations."

Powell J did not, however, accede to this argument, holding that the lift-span bridge alternative could not be regarded as "some fantastic method quite unsuited to the object in view". Rather, the alternative was to be regarded, notwithstanding the substantial additional cost to the public purse, as a feasible one and an injunction issued to restrain completion of the bridge in its initially proposed form.

It is clear that a nuisance will not be regarded as following inevitably from the pursuit of an activity authorised by Parliament in a situation where some discretion exists in terms of how or where those activities or operations are conducted. So, for example, in *Metropolitan Asylum District*

---

[11] [1983] 1 NSWLR 391.

v *Hill*,[12] the defendant sought to use the defence of statutory authority in relation to alleged nuisances arising from their use of a hospital for sufferers from small-pox and other infections and contagious diseases. The defence was held, however, not to apply, for reasons clearly summarised by Lord Watson:

> " ... if the legislators ... were to prescribe ... that a public body ... provide hospital accommodation for ... persons labouring under infectious disease, no injunction could issue ... provided that it was ... proved ... that the Act could not be complied with at all, without creating a nuisance. In that case the necessary result of that which they have directed to be done must presumably have been in the view of the legislature at the time the Act was passed.

> On the other hand ... the legislature [cannot] be held to have sanctioned ...a nuisance at common law, except ... where it has authorised a certain use of a specific building, which cannot be so used without occasioning nuisance, or in the case where the particular ... locality not being prescribed, it has imperatively directed that a building shall be provided within a certain area and so used, it being an obvious and established fact that nuisance would result."[13]

Moreover,

> " ... it is insufficient ... that what is contemplated by the statute cannot be done without nuisance, unless ... the legislature has directed it to be done. Where the terms of a statute are not imperative, but permissive, where it is left to the discretion of the persons empowered to determine whether the general powers committed to them .. be put into execution or not ... the fair inference is that the legislature intended that discretion to be exercised in strict conformity with private rights, and did not intend to confer licence to commit nuisance in any place which might be selected for the purpose."[14]

The asserted defence failed in *Hill* because the defendant had not demonstrated that such a nuisance as alleged was inevitable in *any* location at which they might have opted to place such patients. The case differed from *Farnworth* and *Allen* in that the location for the defendant's activities were not specified in the empowering Act. It was in that sense that it was appropriate to label the provisions of the Act "permissive" rather than "imperative".

It does not follow from *Hill* that the defence of statutory authority is limited to situations where a duty to act has been imposed on the defendant. After all, the Gulf Oil Refining Act did not oblige the defendant corporation in *Allen* to construct a refinery: it simply gave no option about where such a refinery was to be built, if it was to be built. It was,

---

[12] (1881) 6 App Cas 193.
[13] At 212-213.
[14] At 213.

accordingly, in *Allen*, not possible for the plaintiff to have sought to argue that the refinery could have been built in another location, away from the village, so that no nuisance would have been caused.

Of course, even where a defendant has a choice between locations at which he may elect to construct or conduct operations authorised by statute, it may be the case that the same degree of nuisance is inevitable whichever location may be selected. In such a case the defence will operate even though the legislation may be characterised as permissive as to location. Thus, in *London, Brighton and South Coast Rly Co* v *Truman*[15] occupiers of houses near to a railway station brought an action in nuisance in relation to noise nuisances following purchase by the railway company of land adjacent to the station for the purpose of accommodating cattle pending and after their being loaded and unloaded onto and from the company's trains. The defendant company sought to defend itself by reference to statutory powers conferred upon it to purchase land for this very purpose. The House of Lords found that the defence was applicable. Although the Act did not require the purchase and use of the particular piece of land in question it was inevitable that any land purchased would be adjacent to a railway station and therefore close to neighbours who would experience the noise necessarily associated with such use of land. Accordingly the plaintiff's claim could not succeed.

In each case where a defence of statutory authority is raised it is necessary to pay close attention to the wording and proper interpretation of the statutory provisions in question. In the cases so far considered, the statute was itself silent on the issue of the effect of its provisions on the private rights of those who may be adversely affected by its provisions. It is then, as we have seen, a matter of the courts asking whether by *necessary implication* the Act's provisions authorise both what the defendant has done, and the nuisances which may legitimately be regarded as inevitably attendant upon doing those things.

In some cases, however, the legislation may seem to address not only the matters authorised by its provisions but also the effect that the legislation shall have on private law rights of adversely affected persons. For example, in some statutes there exist explicit statements that nothing in the Act shall exonerate a defendant from liability in proceedings for nuisance. The courts have, however, been unwilling to give full effect to such apparent exclusion of the statutory authority defence.

The approach taken has been to have drawn a distinction between statutes which impose *duties* on a defendant to engage in particular activities, and statutory provisions which simply *empower* such actions. In cases where the defendant *must* exercise a certain function the basic principles described earlier will apply, notwithstanding the provisions of the Act about not exonerating the commission of nuisances. In other words, in cases of *duties*, and in spite of the Act's provisions about liability in

---

[15] (1885) 11 App Cas 45.

nuisance, there shall be no liability in relation to any nuisances which are the inevitable consequence of performance of that duty.

The position is different, however, in cases where the statute imposes no duty to perform the activities in question; where it merely gives a *power* to do so, which may or may not be exercised, at the discretion of the donee of that power. We have seen that where an Act is silent on the issue of liability in nuisance the position is that a statutory defence will lie in relation to any nuisance inevitably resulting from the exercise of that power: the position, it will be remembered, in *Allen* v *Gulf Oil Refining Ltd* itself. However, where a statute confers powers and includes a provision seeming to retain civil liability in relation to any nuisances caused, those who choose to exercise the statutory powers *will* be liable for any nuisances caused even though those nuisances may be an inevitable consequence of the exercise of the statutory powers. These principles may be illustrated by reference to *Dunne* v *North Western Gas Board*[16] and *Department of Transport* v *North West Water Authority*.[17]

In *Dunne* a number of plaintiffs had sustained various injuries as a consequence of 46 gas explosions. The explosions occurred due to the escape of gas from a gas main which had been caused by the bursting of an adjacent water main. The escaping gas had then travelled along a sewer, which itself had collapsed due to the burst water main, and had combined with air in the process. The resultant mixture was highly flammable and explosive. It was not clear how the gas had been ignited, although there were a number of possibilities, such as a stray match or cigarette. It was clear, however, that the explosions had occurred throughout the sewer system in a built up housing and industrial district measuring approximately 250 yards by 350 yards.

At first instance, neither defendant (the Gas Board and the Corporation as water undertaker) was found liable in negligence or for breach of statutory duty. However, although the Gas Board also escaped liability under the rule in *Rylands* v *Fletcher*,[18] it was found liable in nuisance. The Corporation was found liable under *Rylands* v *Fletcher* but not in nuisance.

In the Court of Appeal it was noted that both defendants carried out their relevant undertakings under statutory authority.[19] However, two important distinctions could be made between the statutory regimes. Whilst the acts of the Gas Board relevant to the proceedings were "enforced by obligation or duty",[20] the Corporation, as water and sewerage undertaker, acted under permissive powers only. Moreover, whilst the Gas Act 1948 contained a

---

[16] [1963] 3 All ER 916; [1964] 2 QB 806.

[17] [1983] 3 All ER 273.

[18] (1868) LR 3 HL 330. See below, Chapter 6.

[19] The Gas Act 1948 and the Liverpool Corporation Waterworks Act 1847, respectively.

[20] By virtue of s.1(1)(a) of the Gas Act 1948, the Gas Board was under mandatory powers to supply gas and "to develop and maintain an efficient, co-ordinated and economical system of gas supply for their area and to satisfy, so far as it is economical to do so, all reasonable demands for gas within their area."

provision retaining civil liability in respect of nuisances caused,[21] the Liverpool Corporation Waterworks Act 1847 had no "nuisance section".

The Court of Appeal held that neither defendant was liable in nuisance or under the rule in *Rylands* v *Fletcher*. In the case of the Gas Board, Sellers LJ (who gave the judgment of the Court) stated that:

> "Where there is a mandatory obligation with a saving or nuisance clause as here, or without one as in the *Chelsea Waterworks* case, there would be, in our opinion, no liability if what had been done was that which was expressly required by statute to be done or was reasonably incidental to that requirement and was done without negligence."[22]

With regard to the claim against the Corporation, however, the question of liability had to be assessed on the basis that they operated under permissive powers only. It was argued on behalf of the Corporation that in the absence of an express clause preserving liability for nuisance, there was no case where a water undertaker had been found to be liable without proof of negligence. In accepting the force of that argument and therefore exonerating the Corporation from liability, Sellers LJ cited a passage from the judgment of Lord Blackburn in *Geddis* v *Proprietors of the Bann Reservoir*.[23] In that case, Lord Blackburn had stated that:

> "For I take it… that it is now thoroughly well established that no action will lie for doing that which the legislature has authorised, if it be done without negligence, although it does occasion damage to anyone; but an action does lie for doing that which the legislature has authorised, if it be done negligently. And I think that if by a reasonable exercise of the powers, either given by statute to the promoters, or which they have at common law, the damage could be prevented it is, within this rule, 'negligence' not to make such reasonable exercise of their powers."[24]

In the second case, *Department of Transport* v *North West Water Authority*,[25] a water main for which the defendant water authority was responsible burst with the result that damage was caused to a stretch of trunk road for which the plaintiffs were responsible as both the street and highway authority. There was no negligence on the part of the defendants or their servants or agents in respect of the laying or maintenance of the burst main, and they had used all reasonable diligence to prevent the main becoming a nuisance. The issue between the parties was therefore whether

---

[21] Schedule 3 para.42 of the 1948 Act stated that: "Nothing in this Act shall exonerate an Area Board from any indictment, action, or other proceeding for any nuisance caused by them."

[22] [1963] 3 All ER 916 at 923. See more recently Lord Hoffmann's statement in *Transco plc* v *Stockport MBC* [2003] UKHL 61 that the effect of this principle is "to exclude the application of the rule in *Rylands* v *Fletcher* to works constructed or operated under statutory authority" (para. 31). This is correct provided we equate "authority" with "duty".

[23] (1878) 3 App Cas 430.

[24] At 455.

[25] [1983] 3 All ER 273.

or not the defendants were liable to pay damages to the plaintiffs in order to compensate them for the cost of repairing the damage to the highway caused by the escape of water from the main. This in turn depended upon the construction of section 18(2) of the Public Utilities Street Works Act 1950. The material part of that subsection provided that:

"If any nuisance is caused – (a) by the execution of code-regulated works,[26] or (b) by explosion, ignition or discharge of, or any other event occurring to, gas, electricity, water or any other thing required for the purposes of a supply or service afforded by any water undertakers which at the time of or immediately before the event in question was in apparatus of those undertakers the placing or maintenance of which was or is a code-regulated work... nothing in the enactment which confers the relevant power to which section one of this Act applies... shall exonerate the undertakers from any action or other proceeding at the suit... (i) of the street authority."

At first instance, there was some argument before Webster J as to whether the escape of water was a consequence of the defendants statutory *duty* to supply water under pressure or the exercise of their statutory *power* to lay water pipes in the highway. Webster J accepted the argument of counsel for the plaintiff on this point and held, therefore, that the escape was attributable to the performance of a statutory *duty*.

In his judgment Webster J summarised the common law rules governing the liability in nuisance of bodies exercising statutory authority in the form of four propositions.

"1.   In the absence of negligence, a body is not liable for a nuisance which is attributable to the exercise by it of a **duty** imposed on it by statute...

2.   It is not liable in those circumstances even if by statute it is expressly made liable, or not exempted from liability, for nuisance...

3.   In the absence of negligence, a body is not liable for a nuisance which is attributable to the exercise by it of a **power** conferred by statute if, by statute, it is **not** expressly either made liable, or not exempted from liability, for nuisance...[27]

4.   A body is liable for a nuisance by it attributable to the exercise of a power conferred by statute, even without negligence, if by statute it **is** expressly either made liable, or not exempted from liability, for nuisance..."[28]

Or perhaps more simply: items 1, 2 and 3 above state where liability for harm caused in the exercise of a statutory function is actionable only on proof of fault. Item 4, in contrast, describes the situation where strict

---

[26] These were defined in s.1(5) of the 1950 Act. For present purposes, it is sufficient to note that the laying of a water main amounted to code-regulated work under the Act.

[27] The decision in *Dunne* discussed above is authority for this proposition.

[28] [1983] 1 All ER 892 at 895 (emphasis added).

liability in nuisance or under *Rylands* v *Fletcher* will apply, i.e. where the function involves the exercise of a "power" in respect of which the statute has either expressly provided for strict liability or contains a provision providing that the statutory provisions shall not exonerate from legal liability.

On appeal the House of Lords affirmed the significance in this context of the distinction between statutory powers and statutory duties. Webster J had correctly held that the bursting of the water pipe was attributable to the water undertaker's performance of a *duty* to supply water under pressure, and not to the exercise of their *power* to lay the pipe. The wording of section 18(2) was not applicable to the case because it only applied in the context of "powers". There was no good reason to interpret it in such a way as to apply also to "duties". In a short judgment with which the other Law Lords who heard the appeal agreed, Lord Fraser drew attention to the fact that in rejecting a literal construction for section 18(2), Webster J had read additional words into the subsection in order to achieve consistency between both it and other provisions in the 1950 Act.[29] In Lord Fraser's opinion, this was an "unjustifiable" approach. It was certainly the case that, if possible, section 18(2) should be interpreted in a manner which was consistent with the scheme of the Act as a whole. However, as his Lordship further remarked:

> "But that is not to say that the subsection should be extended by adding a new provision which the draftsman has not included. That is especially true where, as here, the subsection as it stands can be given a sensible meaning. In my opinion the subsection is simply a non-exoneration clause of general application to undertakers acting in the exercise of a *power* (but not in the performance of a *duty*)..."[30]

Accordingly, the House of Lords held that where, as here, the nuisance was attributable to the performance of a statutory duty the undertaker was not liable for the nuisance in the absence of negligence even if the statute appeared expressly to make it liable or did not exempt it from liability for nuisance (i.e. situations 1 and 2 above).

Statutory authority: scope of injunctions and measure of damages

In some cases the question of statutory authority may be relevant even where a defendant is unable to show that the nuisance which he or she has caused is an inevitable consequence of the exercise of a statutory function. Although in such a case the defendant will have no *complete* defence to the plaintiff's claim, the issue of statutory authority may be relevant when it

---

[29] Most notably s. 19 of the Act which imposed absolute liability on undertakers in the event of damage being caused to a bridge or other property of a transport authority by reason of an explosion, etc. Webster J was perfectly well aware of the creative nature of his interpretation of s. 18(2). In his opinion, however, the words had not been added to make the subsection accord with his view of what was right or reasonable. Rather, they had been added "so as to give the subsection the construction which, in my view, in its context, is properly to be given" ([1983] 1 All ER 892 at 900).

[30] [1983] 3 All ER 273 at 276-7 (emphasis added).

comes to the matter of remedies. If an injunction is sought it should be limited in its scope to that or those aspects of the nuisance which may be regarded as in excess of what may properly be regarded as authorised by the statute. Equally, in terms of the measure of damages to be awarded, these should compensate only in relation to the degree of nuisance which is unauthorised, taking note that there may be statutory authorisation of some lesser degree of nuisance.

It is for these reasons that Lord Wilberforce, in *Allen* v *Gulf Oil Refining Ltd* used the following carefully worded phrase:

> "To the extent *and only to the extent* that the actual nuisance caused by the actual refinery and its operation exceeds that for which immunity is conferred, the plaintiff has a remedy."[31]

The matter may be illustrated also by *Tate and Lyle Industries Ltd* v *Greater London Council*.[32] The plaintiffs owned and operated a sugar refinery on the north bank of the River Thames. In 1922 and then again in 1964, they were granted a licence to construct a jetty by the Port of London Authority (PLA). The two jetties were used by the plaintiffs for loading and unloading raw and refined sugar. Between 1964 and 1966, the predecessor of the Greater London Council (GLC) and later the GLC itself, constructed two ferry terminals in the river in the exercise of powers conferred on it by statute[33] and with the approval of the PLA. The effect of constructing the terminals was to cause siltation of the river bed. As a result, the plaintiffs were unable to operate the jetties without carrying out additional dredging. This they did at their own expense, between 1967 and 1974, with the consent of the PLA. The plaintiffs subsequently brought an action for damages against the GLC and the PLA for the additional dredging costs which they had incurred.

They succeeded at first instance, but the GLC and the PLA successfully appealed to the Court of Appeal. Before the House of Lords, the plaintiff's claim was based on breach of riparian rights; breach of contractual rights; negligence; nuisance; and public nuisance. Although the plaintiffs did not succeed under any of the first four heads, the majority of the House of Lords[34] held that they were able to maintain an action in public nuisance. This was because the Thames was a navigable river over which the public enjoyed a right of navigation, such right having been interfered with in the case of the plaintiffs due to the construction of the ferry terminals having caused them special damage by rendering their jetties inoperable without additional dredging.

In its defence, the GLC had argued that it was excused from liability for any public nuisance which it may have caused by the terms of the London County Council (Improvements) Act 1962, which authorised the

---

[31] [1981] 1 All ER 353 at 358 (emphasis added).
[32] [1983] 1 All ER 1159; [1983] AC 509.
[33] See s. 17 of the London County Council (Improvements) Act 1962.
[34] Lord Diplock dissented.

operations in respect of which the compliant was made. However, in delivering the judgment of the majority, Lord Templeman noted that the defence of statutory authority was subject to the qualification identified by Lord Wilberforce in *Allen* v *Gulf Oil Refining Ltd* (i.e. that the relevant statutory powers were exercised without "negligence" – as that word was defined in *Allen* itself). The effect of that qualification in the present case could be stated thus:

> "...Parliament authorised the terminals and thereby granted immunity from the consequences of the terminals provided that the GLC paid 'all reasonable regard and care for the interests' of public navigation and for the interests of Tate & Lyle liable to suffer particular damage from any interference with the right of public navigation."[35]

Applying this reasoning to the facts of the case before them, the majority of their Lordships considered that the statutory provision[36] only conferred immunity in respect of siltation that was an inevitable consequence of the execution of works. It did not, therefore, confer immunity in respect of additional siltation which was caused by the particular design of the terminals chosen by the GLC. Moreover, the requirement imposed upon the GLC by section 50(3)(a) of the London County Council (Improvements) Act 1962 to submit plans and particulars of river works to the PLA prior to construction did not transfer to that body the duty to ensure that the design of the terminals did not cause unnecessary siltation. The PLA was entitled to assume that the GLC had chosen a competent designer who would ensure that the design did not have any unnecessary adverse affect. Neither did the majority of their Lordships consider that section 50(3)(a) relieved the GLC of its duty to design the terminals "with all reasonable care for the interests of other persons".

Given the finding that the GLC were liable, it became necessary for the House of Lords to assess the level of damages to be awarded. The cost of additional dredging required to remedy the siltation was £540,000. The trial judge found that had an alternative design been employed, it would have resulted in only one quarter of the accretion which was caused by the design which was in fact used. In other words, one-quarter of the cost of additional dredging was the inevitable consequence of the exercise by the GLC of its statutory powers to construct the terminals. The GLC could not therefore be liable for this sum. However, since the remaining three-quarters of the additional dredging expenditure was not covered by statutory authority, this was the sum (£405,000) which the plaintiffs were entitled to recover from the GLC.

PRESCRIPTIVE RIGHT TO COMMIT NUISANCE

There is clear authority to the effect that it is possible in law to acquire by prescription the right, in the form of an easement, to commit a private

---

[35] [1983] 1 All ER 1159 at 1171.
[36] Section 17 of the 1962 Act.

nuisance. The rules applicable will be summarised below. However it may be helpful to point out that severe difficulties may present themselves for any defendant who may seek to assert any such prescriptive right. The defence is one which operates within quite narrow confines.

For a plea of "prescriptive right" to succeed it is necessary for the defendant to be able to show that throughout the period of time necessary to secure the right by prescription (20 years) the activity about which proceedings have been commenced was carried on in a way which amounted to an actionable nuisance. The final words "as an actionable nuisance" are important. Merely to have undertaken an activity for 20 years will not suffice if, in all the circumstances, that activity did not amount to an actionable nuisance throughout that long period.

The point is well illustrated by *Sturges* v *Bridgman*, the facts of which have been discussed previously.[37] It will be remembered that prior to the construction of the consulting room, the use by the defendant of the mortars in his confectionery business had caused no substantial annoyance or inconvenience to the plaintiff or any previous occupier. The Court of Appeal held that no prescriptive right to operate the mortars had been acquired, notwithstanding that they had been operated in the same way for more than 20 years. The key to the reasoning of the court was that a right by prescription is based upon the notion that the owner of the land against which the right has been acquired has failed, for 20 years, to have taken physical or legal steps to have put a stop to the actions of the other party. It follows that if through part or all of the 20-year period the activities did not amount to an actionable nuisance, there was nothing that could have been done at that time to stop the defendant in his, at that time quite lawful, activities. Accordingly, that period of time cannot be counted for the purposes of the prescription period. The matter was well explained by Thesiger LJ:

> "here then arises the objection [that] ... that which was done ... was in its nature such that it could not be physically interrupted; it could not at the same time be put a stop to by action. Can user which is neither preventable nor actionable found an easement? We think not."[38]

And, speaking more generally, his Lordship explained:

> " ... the laws governing the acquisition of easements by user stands thus: consent or acquiescence of the owner of the servient tenement lies at the root of prescription ... [H]ence the acts or user ... must be, in the language of the civil law, *nec vi nec clam nec precario*;[39] for a man cannot, as a general rule, be said to consent to or acquiesce in the acquisition by his neighbour of an easement through an enjoyment of which he has no knowledge, actual or constructive, or

---

[37] (1879) 11 Ch D 852; see above, p. 46.

[38] (1879) 11 Ch D 852 at 863.

[39] Not forcibly, secretly or by permission.

which he contests and endeavours to interrupt, or which he temporarily licences."[40]

And returning to the particular issue:

"... until the noise ... became an actionable nuisance, which it did not at any time before the consulting room was built, the basis of the presumption of consent, ... the power of prevention physically or by action, was never present."[41]

The Court of Appeal accordingly confirmed the injunction granted below.

This principle, when allied to the notion that it is no defence that a plaintiff came to a nuisance[42] may seem at first sight to work rather hard upon defendants. An example provided by Thesiger LJ serves, however, as a valuable reminder of the competing considerations in issue, and the rationale behind the approach adopted by the Court of Appeal:

"It is said that if this principle is applied ... to its logical extremes, it could result in the most serious practical inconveniences ... The case is put of a blacksmith's forge built away from all habitations, but to which, in course of time habitations approach ... The smith, in the case supposed, might protect himself by taking a sufficient curtilage to ensure what he does from being at any time an annoyance to his neighbour."[43]

The requirement that the owner of the servient tenement should have "sat" upon his rights for a 20-year period is well demonstrated by *Liverpool Corporation* v *H Coghill and Son*.[44] For a period exceeding 20 years the defendants had discharged liquid waste from their chemical plant into the plaintiff's sewers. For much of the 20 years this conduct was unknown to the plaintiffs, their suspicions only being raised when crops on their sewage "farm" became damaged. It was held by Eve J that the prescription period only ran from the point at which the nuisance became known to the plaintiff.

It may be noted that in one way this decision is stricter than that in *Sturges*. In *Sturges* no nuisance was being committed until the plaintiff's consulting room was built and his enjoyment of his land began to be interfered with. In *Coghill* the activities causing actual harm to the defendant's property (as distinct from "mere" harm to its enjoyment) had been an actionable nuisance for over 20 years. Nevertheless, the plaintiff was not debarred by prescription because of his absence of knowledge of that harm.

---

[40] At 863.
[41] At 864-865.
[42] See above, p. 43.
[43] (1879) 11 Ch D 852 at 865.
[44] [1918] 1 Ch 307.

In addition to these requirements in relation to the "20-year" rule there are certain other aspects of the requirements of the prescription defence which may present difficulties for a defendant. Three, in particular, deserve mention.

First, it is clear that one cannot acquire by prescription a right to commit an offence. This principle goes beyond merely the proposition that there can be no claim of prescriptive right by way of defence to actual criminal proceedings. It extends also to prevent conduct, in which a plaintiff may well have acquiesced for a 20-year period, from becoming defensible in a private nuisance claim brought by that plaintiff. So, for example, it is clear that if the nuisance in question amounts to a *public* nuisance,[45] in addition to being a private nuisance in relation to the plaintiff's land, the defence of prescription will be inapplicable in relation (i) to any criminal proceedings brought in relation to the public nuisance, (ii) to any action for damages brought by any who may have suffered special damage arising out of the public nuisance,[46] and (iii) to any actions brought by persons who may have claims in private nuisance. The significance of this general principle may, of course, have increased in recent times, as the ambit of the criminal law in relation to activities which harm, or threaten to harm, the environment has widened.[47]

Second, even an actionable nuisance engaged in *nec vi nec clam nec precario* will not found a defence of prescriptive right unless that "right" is capable of being defined with sufficient certainty and precision as to be capable of forming the subject matter of a legal grant.[48] In the recent case of *Dennis and Dennis* v *Ministry of Defence*,[49] it was contended, inter alia, that the MoD had acquired by prescription the right to fly Harrier jets over the claimants' property. However, that argument failed on two grounds,[50] one of which was concerned with whether or not the "right" to fly over the property could have been capable of forming the subject matter of a grant. In the judgment of Buckley J, it was not possible to see how a conveyancer could have drafted a grant which satisfied the requirements of certainty and precision, particularly since no one had measured decibels over the 20-year period or determined the precise flights paths that had been flown by the jets.[51]

---

[45] For public nuisances, see below, p. 267.

[46] For this action, see below, p. 159.

[47] See, generally, Chapter 7, below.

[48] *Hulley* v *Silversprings Bleaching and Dyeing Co* [1922] 2 Ch 268; *Woodman* v *Pwllbach Colliery Co Ltd* [1914] 11 LT 169 (CA); [1915] AC 634 (HL).

[49] [2003] EWHC 793 (QB). For the facts of this case, see above at p. 69.

[50] The other ground was that the claimant's written complaints to the MoD about the flying of jets over his property defeated any suggestion that he had either consented (tacitly or otherwise) or acquiesced in the commission of the nuisance. In other words, the user was not "as of right" as is required by the defence.

[51] In the words of Buckley J: "Sometimes the Harriers seemed to 'fly between the chimneys' as one witness mentioned. At other times they were generally overhead and at yet other times simply very close" (at para.53 of the judgment).

The third limitation on the defence is provided by what we may regard as a judicial application of the principle of "best practicable means". It appears from *Shoreham-by-Sea UDC* v *Dolphin Canadian Proteins*[52] that a defendant who may have satisfied the requirements of prescription may nevertheless be required to exercise that right in such a way as to cause to the plaintiff the least practicable nuisance associated with continuance of those activities. In the words of Donaldson J, the prescriptive right:

> " ... can go no further than to entitle the person concerned to carry on the business to which the prescriptive right attaches in the best practicable way, that is to say, the way that causes the least practicable nuisance applying reasonable standards ..."[53]

Moreover, as new techniques or technology may render practicable the operation of business with less in the way of consequential nuisance, the limitations on the ambit of the defendant's prescriptive right will increase. Donaldson J explained that the standards applicable would be the standards practicable at the time of present assertion of the nuisance, albeit that those standards may differ from what may have been practicable through the prescription period.

---

[52] (1973) 71 LGR 261.
[53] At 267.

Chapter 4

PRIVATE NUISANCE: REMEDIES

There are three principal remedies which may come into play in a case where a private nuisance been committed by a defendant. These comprise:

- Injunctive relief
- Damages
- Abatement action

INJUNCTIVE RELIEF

A typical instance of nuisance will be a complaint on the part of the plaintiff in respect of ongoing activity on the part of the defendant. In such circumstances it will be of no surprise that, quite apart from any right to damages to provide compensation for certain kinds of harm resulting from the nuisance, a plaintiff may seek relief in the form of an injunction. Pending trial of the action the plaintiff may seek an *interim* or *interlocutory* injunction. On successfully demonstrating nuisance at trial the plaintiff will hope to succeed also in his or her claim to a remedy by way of a permanent injunction against the continuance of the nuisance. In most cases such injunctive relief will relate to conduct upon which the defendant has been engaged, requiring that the defendant should discontinue or moderate such behaviour so as not to continue to cause a nuisance. If such behaviour has discontinued during the course of the legal proceedings but there is reason to believe it may be recommenced, a court may award an injunction prohibiting such recurrence. Furthermore, even where no nuisance has yet occurred a plaintiff may be successful in obtaining an injunctive relief where he or she is able to demonstrate a clear threat that the defendant may engage in activities which will involve a nuisance: a *quia timet* injunction.

A discretionary remedy

Whereas a plaintiff who has suffered a recoverable form of loss may claim the common law remedy of damages *as of right*, the remedy of injunction, deriving from the former equitable jurisdiction of the Court of Chancery, is in principle available not as of right but at the *discretion* of the court. The scope of this remedy will, therefore, depend very much on the approach taken by the judges as regards their exercise of this discretion.

The starting-point is to note the general approach of the courts towards equitable relief: that it is available in order to do justice in situations where the common law remedy of damages alone would provide a substantially inadequate remedy. The fundamental issue, generally, in relation to the availability of equitable relief will be whether in the view of the judges an award of a sum of money will provide adequate compensation for a wrong being suffered at the hands of the defendant. In some contexts of civil wrongdoing the judges have been rather unwilling to make such a general assumption. So, for example, it is well known that the equitable remedy of specific performance is rarely considered appropriate in relation to a seller's failure to have delivered in a contract for the sale of goods. The purchaser is considered to be granted an adequate remedy if, rather than being judicially awarded the specific item which should have been delivered, he is awarded whatever sum of money may allow him to buy an equivalent item elsewhere.

It will be necessary, shortly, for us to consider the approach of the judges to this issue in the particular context of the law of private nuisance. Is an award of money to compensate for a nuisance experienced likely to constitute an adequate form of relief, or will the courts take the view that, generally, justice will only be done by making an award which will allow the plaintiff to be quit of the nuisance in question?

Before an answer may be afforded to this important question it is important to note an important feature of the law as regards the power of the courts to award *damages*. At common law damages could be awarded only in relation to harm which had been suffered up to the date of the award. In other words, if injunctive relief were refused and the nuisance continued, it would be necessary for the plaintiff to commence proceedings periodically in order to recover compensation, period by period, in respect of that nuisance. This particular inadequacy in the law resulted, in the mid-nineteenth century, in legislative intervention: the Chancery Amendment Act 1858 (Lord Cairns' Act). This legislation conferred power on the courts to award damages *in lieu* of the grant of an injunction. This overcame the principal shortcoming of common law damages, and opened up the possibility that courts might take a broad view that such damages (for past harm and also for harm *in futuro*) would render the award of injunctive relief not necessary in the ordinary case in order to achieve justice. Without wishing to spoil the story which follows, it may however be helpful to anticipate its general conclusion and to indicate here that, notwithstanding this option apparently being very much open to the judges, the courts have generally remained quite firmly of the view that a plaintiff should generally be entitled to injunctive relief – and that an award of damages, even on the basis just described, will in general not provide adequate protection in respect of that person's legal rights.

In the discussion which follows we shall begin by considering the scope of operation of Lord Cairns' Act, and then move on to describe the approach which the courts have adopted to the more general issue as regards the "right" to injunctive relief.

Chancery Amendment Act 1858: Lord Cairns' Act

This Act provided the courts with a power to award damages in lieu of the award of an injunction. The key provision was contained in section 2:

"In all cases in which the Court of Chancery has jurisdiction to entertain an application for an injunction against a breach of any covenant, contract, or agreement, or against the commission or continuance of any wrongful act ... it shall be lawful for the same court, if it shall think fit, to award damages to the party injured, either in addition to or in substitution for such an injunction or specific performance; and such damages may be assessed in such manner as the court shall direct."

The 1858 Act is no longer in force. However, the jurisdiction to award damages in lieu of an injunction continues, being now exercised within the terms of section 50 of the Supreme Court Act 1981.

The implications of this jurisdiction for plaintiffs will be evident, comprising as it does a power to award *damages* in respect of future harm in place of an award which would require that the defendant modify or moderate conduct so that that future harm does not occur. Although some plaintiffs may consider that such a "once and for all" monetary award will provide an acceptable remedy in the circumstances, even notwithstanding the continuance of the nuisance, in many – perhaps most – situations we might expect a plaintiff to continue to argue for injunctive relief. In short, the jurisdiction provided by the legislation seems more likely to favour defendants as compared with plaintiffs. The power which the courts have been given may be described as a power to "set a price" at which it will permit the defendant to continue to invade the private law rights of the plaintiff as regards the quality of his or her land, or as to his reasonable use and enjoyment of that land. To put the matter slightly differently, in any case where a plaintiff would prefer an award of injunctive relief, for a court to award damages *in lieu* is, in effect, to confiscate – albeit with compensation – the plaintiff's private law rights. When so considered it may come as little surprise that the courts have displayed some reticence as regards their utilisation of the powers which the legislation has conferred upon them.

The classic statement of general principle as regards the exercise of the powers under Lord Cairns' Act is to be found in a decision of the Court of Appeal in 1895: *Shelfer* v *City of London Electric Lighting Company.*[1] The plaintiff's claim was of nuisance in the form of noise and vibrations experienced in his house as a consequence of the operations of the defendants. At first instance the plaintiff was refused an injunction, damages being awarded *in lieu*. On appeal, the Court of Appeal regarded this fairly standard case of nuisance as not one in which it was appropriate to exercise the power under the 1858 Act, and awarded the plaintiff an injunction. In terms of principle Lord Lindley explained;

"Ever since Lord Cairns' Act was passed the Court of Chancery has repudiated the notion that the legislature intended to turn that court into a tribunal for legitimising wrongful acts; or in other words, the

---

[1] [1895] 1 Ch 287.

court has always protested against the notion that it ought to allow a wrong to continue because a wrongdoer is able and willing to pay for the injury he may inflict."[2]

Moreover, public benefit from the activities in question had not, according to Lord Lindley, provided justification for sacrificing the private law rights of the plaintiff:

"Neither has the circumstance that the wrongdoer is in some sense a public benefactor (e.g. a gas company or water company or a sewer authority) ever been considered a sufficient reason for refusing to protect by injunction an individual whose rights are being persistently infringed. Expropriation, even for a money consideration, is only justifiable when Parliament has sanctioned it."

His Lordship then warned:

"Without denying the jurisdiction to award damages instead of an injunction … such jurisdiction ought not to be exercised in such cases except under very exceptional circumstances."

And continued, as regards such "exceptional circumstances":

"I will not attempt to specify them, or to lay down rules for the exercise of judicial discretion. It is sufficient to refer, by way of example, to trivial and occasional nuisances; cases in which a plaintiff has shown that he only wants money; vexatious and oppressive cases; and cases where the plaintiff has so conducted himself as to render it unjust to give him more than pecuniary relief …"[3]

In relation to the examples given one might make the following immediate comment. Apart from the first – cases where the nuisance is trivial and occasional – the circumstances in which the jurisdiction to award damages might appropriately be exercised seem to be very much the sort of reasons why a court (of equity) might, quite apart from any issue of awarding damages *in lieu*, exercise its discretion to refuse injunctive relief to an applicant. In other words it seems that except in the trivial/occasional nuisance context Lord Lindley was not, in fact, providing examples of cases where the "new" jurisdiction to award damages was genuinely *in compensation for* the denial of an otherwise likely award of an injunction. If this is correct the result is that the new jurisdiction seems not much to diminish the breadth of the remedies available in cases where a serious nuisance would formerly have given a good claim to an injunction. The main change, rather curiously, being to enhance the rights to damages of those who might have formerly, in the exercise of judicial discretion, been denied injunctive relief.

---

[2] At 315-316.
[3] At 316-317.

Further guidance from *Shelfer* is to be found in the judgment of A L Smith LJ. Perhaps somewhat exaggerating its practical utility, his Lordship enunciated what he described as a "good working rule" as regards this jurisdiction to award damages *in lieu* of an injunction. According to his Lordship damages *in lieu* might be given:

(i)   if the injury to the plaintiff's legal right is small; and
(ii) is capable of being estimated in money; and
(iii) can be adequately compensated by a small money payment; and
(iv) it would be oppressive to the defendant to grant an injunction.

It will be noted that A L Smith LJ adopted an approach of a similarly restrictive nature to that of Lord Lindley. Both of their Lordships, for example, seem to have reserved the use of the jurisdiction generally to cases where a *small sum* by way of damages might adequately compensate for a continuing nuisance of a *quite minor* nature. And note also the indication in A L Smith LJ's formulation that *all* of the four requirements should be satisfied before the jurisdiction should appropriately be exercised. So, for example, we should assume that the fourth item was intended as a separate and distinct requirement to be satisfied, and that the "good working rule" will not be satisfied just because the first three of the matters listed may be found to be a feature of the case.[4]

It will be evident that in the exercise and application of the *Shelfer* principles much may depend on the interpretation afforded by the courts to the requirement of it being "oppressive" to the defendant for the court to prohibit the defendant from continuing his behaviour, giving rise to the minor nuisance in question. If the standard case, as we must assume, would *not* involve such unfairness to a defendant, what special circumstances, we must ask, might suffice to satisfy this fourth requirement?[5]

The principles stated and applied in *Shelfer* have been influential in a number of subsequent cases. In *Wood* v *Conway Corporation*[6] the plaintiff's claim related to quantities of fumes and smoke which it was shown were being emitted from gasworks operated by the defendant, and which were rendering a part of the plaintiff's land uninhabitable. The defendant sought to continue operations, arguing that damages should be awarded but that an injunction should not be granted. The Court of Appeal acknowledged the likely serious financial consequences for the defendant

---

[4] See, for example, in the context of trespass to land, *Kelsen* v *Imperial Tobacco Co (of GB and Ireland)* [1957] 2 QB 334: injury small and damages would be nominal, but not oppressive to defendant to grant injunction ordering the removal of trespassing advertising sign.

[5] Note the words of A L Smith LJ: "It is impossible to lay down any rule as to what, under the different circumstances of each case, constitutes either a small injury, or one that can be estimated in money, or what is a small money payment, or an adequate compensation, or what would be oppressive to the defendant. This must be left to the good sense of the tribunal which deals with each case ... For instance, an injury to the plaintiff's legal right to light to a window in a cottage represented by £15 might well be held to be not small but considerable, whereas similar injury to a warehouse or other large building represented by ten times that amount might be held to be inconsiderable ..." ([1895] 1 Ch 287 at 323).

[6] [1914] 2 Ch 47.

in not being able to operate its gasworks lawfully in the future, and noted that these consequences were likely to be financially greater than the sum of money which would adequately compensate the plaintiff. Nevertheless, the court concluded that it would not be fair to the plaintiff to refuse an injunction and award damages *in lieu*. The case was not one where future harm could readily be estimated in terms of magnitude, and nor was the kind of harm such as could with confidence be compensated in monetary terms. Notwithstanding some temptation, the Court of Appeal considered the case not to be one to which the 1858 Act's powers were applicable, and awarded the injunction sought by the plaintiff.

Likewise, in *Elliott* v *London Borough of Islington*,[7] the Court of Appeal refused to accept that the claim fell within the *Shelfer* preconditions to the award of damages *in lieu* of an injunction. The claim was one in which roots from the defendant's tree had caused movement in the plaintiff's garden wall. It was held that the plaintiff was not claiming in respect of a nuisance which could properly be described as only minor, even though the movement in the wall was quite small. The plaintiff was entitled to expect injunctive support from the court, and it was not appropriate for the court to require that the plaintiff settle for a sum by way of compensation for the continuing invasion of his private rights.

An example, by way of contrast, of a case in which this jurisdiction was exercised in favour of granting damages *in lieu* of an injunction is provided by *Jaggard* v *Sawyer*.[8] The case was not one of nuisance but of breach of a covenant, between neighbouring owners of residential property, forbidding the use of land not built upon on the residential estate for any purpose other than that of a garden. The defendant had begun to build a house on a piece of such land and, when the building was quite advanced, the plaintiff sued for breach of covenant. Was the plaintiff entitled to an injunction requiring the building to be taken down? Or would damages, and damages *in lieu*, be awarded, thereby permitting the building to be completed subject to payment of compensation to the plaintiff in respect of the past and the ongoing breach of the property covenant?

The Court of Appeal upheld the trial judge's refusal of an injunction, leaving the plaintiff instead to the satisfaction afforded by damages. In his leading judgment Sir Thomas Bingham MR (as he then was) considered each of the four *Shelfer* conditions in turn, and concluded in relation to each:

- that the trial judge had been correct to regard the injury to the plaintiff's right as small. No impairment of visual amenity had been caused to the plaintiff; nor was there any demonstrable diminution in the value of his property;

---

[7] [1991] 10 EG 145.
[8] [1995] 2 All ER 189. See also, the very similar, *Bracewell* v *Appleby* [1975] Ch 408.

- that the trial judge was correct in taking the view that the injury to the plaintiff's right could be estimated in financial terms. That sum would be based upon the amount which a reasonable neighbour would charge for granting release from such a term in a covenant;[9]

- that the trial judge correctly considered that the injury to the plaintiff's legal rights could adequately be compensated by a small money payment. It will be remembered that the evidence did not suggest that the plaintiff was *substantially* affected by the development. Her action was to seek to secure that her neighbours obeyed the rules, rather than to seek a remedy in respect of a substantial problem affecting her property;

- that the trial judge had concluded correctly that in all the circumstances it would be oppressive to the defendant to grant injunctive relief.

It was the final of these four issues upon which most argument centred before the Court of Appeal. Sir Thomas Bingham MR made clear that the test of "oppressive to the defendant" was quite different from any test based upon finding where the "balance of convenience" between the parties might lie. In considering the facts of the particular case it was relevant that the plaintiff had failed at a somewhat earlier stage, before the construction of the now nearly-completed building, to have taken proceedings to have secured interlocutory relief. It was also relevant to consider whether the defendant had built in "blatant and calculated" disregard for the plaintiff's rights: a possibility found by the trial judge not to have been the case.[10] On the basis of such findings, the Court of Appeal upheld the trial judge's conclusion that the award of injunctive relief would indeed, in the particular circumstances, be oppressive to the defendant. Accordingly this was found to be a case where the court *should* exercise the jurisdiction, which Sir Thomas Bingham MR described as one which was only "rarely and reluctantly" exercised, to allow the wrongdoing to the plaintiff to continue and to award damages *in lieu* of the award of injunctive relief.

Injunctions "as a matter of course": the general equitable discretion

Although it is correct to say that injunctions, being equitable remedies, are not available as of right, it is of equal importance to note that in the context of actionable nuisances this remedy is commonly said to be available "as a matter of course". In other words in the absence of factors which will

---

[9] Following the approach to quantification in *Wrotham Park Estate Co* v *Parkside Homes Ltd* [1974] 1 WLR 798, Sir Thomas Bingham took the view that in such an assessment the neighbour should not be assumed to be "eager" to sell; but neither would a reasonable neighbour, not adversely affected by the proposed work, extract a "ransom" price. Contrast the power to seek to extract such a "ransom" in cases where a court is unwilling to award damages *in lieu* of an injunction. See, for example, *Anchor Brewhouse Developments Ltd* v *Berkley House (Docklands Developments) Ltd* [1987] EGLR 173 per Scott J.

[10] It seems that the defendant continued building in the belief, engendered by the plaintiff's solicitors, that the plaintiff would be satisfied by a monetary payment in compensation.

generally disentitle an applicant from being granted a discretionary equitable remedy, a plaintiff in a private nuisance case may expect that the court will exercise its discretion in his or her favour. In particular, it should be noted that the judges have generally been unwilling to refuse an injunction on grounds that such a remedy may be disproportionately burdensome upon the defendant, or on the ground that considerations of general public interest might seem to weigh in favour of permitting continuation of the nuisance-causing activities of the defendant.

A good example of a court not regarding the burden of complying with an injunction as relevant to its discretion is provided by *Pride of Derby* v *Derbyshire Angling Association* v *British Celanese Ltd.*[11] In this case, the Court of Appeal held that an actionable nuisance had been created where stretches of two rivers had been polluted by effluent discharged from the defendants works. With regard to the granting of a remedy, counsel for Derby Corporation (the second defendant) argued that an injunction should not issue. He argued that to require the Corporation to dam back the sewage would cause a nuisance to the inhabitants of Derby, and he pointed out that the Corporation was prohibited from extending its sewage disposal works by statutory provisions[12] which required the consent of the Minister of Works for such an extension. At first instance, Harman J had granted an injunction against all three defendants.[13] The Court of Appeal was unimpressed by the argument that an injunction was an inappropriate remedy. Sir Raymond Evershed MR stated the general rule with regard to the granting of injunctive relief as follows:

> "It is, I think, well settled that, if A proves that his proprietary rights are being wrongfully interfered with by B, and that B intends to continue his wrong, then A is prima facie entitled to an injunction, and he will be deprived of that remedy only if special circumstances exist, including the circumstances that damages are an adequate remedy for the wrong that he has suffered."[14]

Applying this rule to the facts of the case before him, Sir Raymond Evershed MR continued:

> "In the present case, it is quite plain that damages would be a wholly inadequate remedy for the plaintiff association. The general rule which I have stated applies, in my opinion, to local authorities as well as to other citizens. Equally, of course, the court will not impose on a local authority, or on anyone else, an obligation to do something which is impossible, or which cannot be enforced, or which is unlawful. Therefore, the practice is adopted in the case of local authorities of granting injunctions, and then suspending their operation for a time, long or short … [T]he Defence General Regulations, 1939, reg. 56A, is, beyond doubt, a matter proper to be

[11] [1953] 1 All ER 179; [1953] Ch 149.
[12] The Defence (General) Regulations 1939, reg.56A.
[13] [1952] 1 All ER 1326.
[14] [1953] 1 All ER 179 at 197.

considered, but the mere fact that, without obtaining a licence, the authority would be unable in any case to do the work is not, in my judgment, a sufficient reason why the ordinary procedure should not be followed."[15]

The two other judges who heard the appeal, Denning and Romer LJJ, also expressed views on the question of injunctive relief. After having rehearsed counsel for the Corporation's arguments as to why an injunction should not be granted, Denning LJ (as he then was) remarked that:

"These are strong reasons for suspending the injunction, but are no reasons for not granting it. The power of the courts to issue an injunction for nuisance has proved itself to be the best method so far devised of securing the cleanliness of our rivers ..."[16]

In a comparatively brief third judgment in the appeal, Romer LJ paid particular attention to the question whether an injunction should be granted against the Corporation. His Lordship explained the legal position as follows:

"Anyone who creates an actionable nuisance is a wrongdoer, and the court will prima facie restrain him from persisting in his activities. If special circumstances be shown, the court may leave the injured party to his remedy in damages, but, in my judgment, the mere fact, in itself, that the wrongdoer is a local authority (however important) has never been, and ought not now to be, regarded as a circumstance of this character. Local authorities have great and important duties to discharge, and the court, in deciding what order it should make, would, undoubtedly, take those duties into consideration, and would no more make an order that was virtually impossible for an authority to perform than it would order a private individual to perform an act which it was not in his power to do ... [W]hy ... no injunction should be granted at all – with the result that the plaintiffs would be compelled to bring one action after another for damages in the future – I am wholly at a loss to see."[17]

Accordingly, the Court of Appeal followed the course adopted by Harman J and granted an injunction, suspending its operation for a reasonable time.

The position may be different in a case where what is sought by the plaintiff is not the grant of a prohibitory injunction but the award of a mandatory injunction.[18] The courts are generally rather more cautious as regards the award of mandatory injunctions, as compared with their

---

[15] At 197-8.

[16] At 204.

[17] At 205-6.

[18] A prohibitory injunction is an order from the court that a defendant should not engage in certain activities which have been shown to have caused, to be causing, or to be likely to cause a nuisance; or to cease to conduct those activities in a way which causes such a nuisance. By contrast, a mandatory injunction is an order that a defendant should undertake certain actions of a positive nature, necessary in order that a nuisance should come to an end.

approach to prohibitory injunctions. Indeed, the statement that injunctions are awarded as a matter of course in nuisance cases should, probably be regarded as accurate only in relation to prohibitory injunctions. A plaintiff seeking a mandatory injunction must, it seems, go further and demonstrate to the satisfaction of the court that without the award of such a remedy he or she will not be afforded a remedy against serious interference with his or her rights.[19]

Given such reticence as regards mandatory injunctions it may be unsurprising that the House of Lords in *Redland Bricks* v *Morris*[20] indicated that the relative "cost" implications for the plaintiff and the defendant of the making, or not making, of such an order was relevant to its exercise of discretion. The plaintiff owned land adjoining that belonging to the defendant brick company. Excavation of earth and clay from the defendant's land resulted in a loss of support for the plaintiff's land, with resultant slippage. Although the value of the plaintiff's land, subject to the nuisance, was less than £2,000 the trial judge ordered, by way of mandatory injunction, that the defendants should refill the excavated land in order thereby to restore support for the plaintiff's property. The estimated cost of such work was some £35,000. In the House of Lords, opinions were expressed that in relation to mandatory injunctions much depended, in a case such as this involving apparently disproportionate cost and benefit, on the court's overall judgment of the conduct of the defendant. The high relative cost of works necessary to put an end to a nuisance would not militate against the award of an injunction where the nuisance had been committed in wanton disregard of the rights of the plaintiff. However, such was not the position in the instant case, where the harm to the plaintiff had been an unintended consequence of reasonable activities on the part of the defendant. In such a case the relative costs and benefits as between the parties *was* a consideration very relevant to the exercise of discretion as regards the award of an injunction in mandatory form.

The public interest?

We noted earlier, when considering the defence of statutory authority,[21] that the courts acknowledge that Parliament may expressly or implicitly have enacted legislation which may have the consequence that the interests of individuals are subjugated to what Parliament may have regarded as the general public interest. The issue here to be considered is whether, quite apart form any such statutory guidance, the *judges* will make relative assessments of private and public interests in their exercise of discretion to award or withhold the remedy by way of injunction.

The general approach of the judges has been that such a roving commission is *not* appropriate to the civil courts: that those who commit

---

[19] See, for example, the statement by Turner LJ in *Durrell* v *Pritchard* (1865) 1 Ch App 244 at 250.
[20] [1970] AC 652.
[21] See, above, p. 121.

actionable nuisances should ordinarily expect, in the absence of Parliamentary sanction for those activities, a court to order against it not only for damages, but also the award of injunctive relief.

An example of this approach may be found in *A-G v Birmingham Borough Council.*[22] The local authority was found to be committing a nuisance by its discharge of sewage from Birmingham into a river belonging to the person for whose benefit the Attorney-General had brought the proceedings. Commenting on arguments that if sewage could not be so discharged the health implications for the residents of the town might be calamitous, Page-Wood V-C explained that it was "a matter of absolute indifference" whether the award of an injunction had implications just for the defendant, or also for a population of some 25,000 people. It was not for the court to take such broader public interest considerations into account. If the consequences, genuinely, of a defendant being prohibited from committing a nuisance were of such gravity, then it might be appropriate for Parliamentary (i.e. statutory) sanction for such conduct to be sought.

A similar approach was adopted in a case in the Irish Republic: *Bellew v Cement Ltd.*[23] Here the plaintiff sought and was granted (at first instance) an interlocutory injunction restraining the defendants from continuing to carry on blasting operations at their quarry. The blasting had taken place at a distance of between 100 and 150 yards from the plaintiff's house on land which the plaintiff had sold to the defendants. Moreover, there was evidence that in response to the plaintiff's complaints, the defendants had substantially reduced the maximum amount of explosives used in any one blast from 1,115 lbs to 150 lbs. Nevertheless, on appeal, the majority of the Irish Supreme Court considered that the plaintiff had established a *prima facie* case for the existence of a nuisance which ought to be restrained by an interlocutory injunction pending the trial of the action. With regard to the effect of the remedy upon the public convenience, Maguire CJ stated that:

> "I am afraid that I cannot attach very much importance to the effect of this injunction upon the public convenience. It is suggested that, to restrain the company in the way in which the injunction would restrain them, would have a serious effect on building operations throughout the entire country. I am not altogether clear how far it was intended to press the argument, but I am of the opinion that the court is not entitled to take the public convenience into consideration when dealing with the rights of private parties. This matter is a dispute between private parties, and I think that the court should be concerned, only, to see that the rights of the parties are safeguarded."[24]

---

[22] (1858) 22 JP 561. See also *Manchester Corporation v Farnworth* [1930] AC 171.
[23] [1948] IR 61.
[24] At 64.

Both O'Byrne and Black JJ dissented from the majority on the facts alone. Neither judge was satisfied that the plaintiff had established a prima facie case for the existence of a nuisance. On the question of injunctive relief, O'Byrne J remarked that:

> "If Mr Bellew had made out a clear case for an interlocutory injunction, I do not think that the court would be entitled to have regard to questions of public convenience; but where, as in this case, public convenience is involved, the court should be careful to see that a clear case has been established before an injunction is granted."[25]

Black J went further in his judgment, however, when he contended that whilst considerations of public convenience could not justify a refusal to grant a remedy where a nuisance existed, they could nevertheless influence a court's choice of remedy. In his opinion:

> "... it must be plain that the inconvenience of the company entailed by an injunction would transcend, perhaps a hundred-fold, the inconvenience that would result to the plaintiff from its refusal pending the trial. Nor, is it the defendants alone that would suffer. To stop their work, must have grave consequences for the public at a time when, as stated, more than four-fifths of the entire cement used in this country is produced by the defendants, and at a time when houses are badly wanted, and when the building trade is expected to be about to awake from its long torpor. No doubt, as has often been laid down, public inconvenience cannot justify refusal of a remedy for a nuisance. It is another matter to say that it cannot, or ought not to, affect the way in which a nuisance should be dealt with."[26]

This general principle was also asserted, more recently, by the Court of Appeal in *Kennaway* v *Thompson*.[27] A motor boat racing club was found to be causing a nuisance by its racing and other activities on Mallam Water. The nuisance was experienced by the plaintiff, a lady residing in a house beside the lake. The trial judge had awarded damages but had refused an injunction on the grounds of the effect that such an injunction would have on the club, and on a section of the public: that is, those persons who gained enjoyment by racing motor boats or by watching such races. On appeal the plaintiff argued that she was subject to a substantial noise nuisance. It was no justification – warranting an award limited to damages only – that that nuisance might provide some benefit to a section of the public. The Court of Appeal granted the injunction denied below, giving short shrift to notions that the public interest should be allowed to prevail over the private interest.[28]

---

[25] At 66.

[26] At 70.

[27] [1980] 3 All ER 329.

[28] Note, however, that given that some boat activity could continue without constituting a nuisance, the task for the court was to devise an injunction worded in a way which permitted such

Kennaway is significant also for the doubt cast by the Court of Appeal on certain statements made by a differently constituted Court of Appeal just three years earlier: in *Miller* v *Jackson*[29] – the case, it may be recalled, of the plaintiffs who became subject to a nuisance when they moved to a house recently built beside an overly-small cricket ground. In *Miller* a majority of the Court of Appeal (Geoffrey Lane and Cumming-Bruce LJJ) took the view that the playing of cricket on the ground now constituted an actionable nuisance; but, also by a majority (Cumming-Bruce LJ and Lord Denning MR), it was decided that no injunction should issue.

In explaining why he would refuse an injunction even had he considered there to have been committed an actionable nuisance, Lord Denning MR, expressed himself in broad terms:

> "This case ... should be approached on principles applicable to modern conditions. There is a contest here between the interest of the public at large; and the interest of a private individual. The *public* interest lies in protecting the environment by preserving our playing fields in the face of mounting development, and ... enabling our youth to enjoy all the benefits of outdoor games ... The *private* interest lies in securing the privacy of the [plaintiff's] home and garden without intrusion or interference ..."[30]

In the context of that contest either the plaintiff or the defendant (cricket club) would have to move:

> "Either the cricket club has to move: but goodness knows where ... Or Mrs Miller has to move elsewhere."[31]

And his Lordship continued:

> "as between their conflicting interests, I am of opinion that the public interest should prevail over the private interest. The cricket club should not be driven out. In my opinion the right exercise of discretion is to refuse an injunction ..."[32]

Cumming-Bruce LJ spoke in similar vein, considering that it was legitimate to take factors of public interest into account in exercising discretion as to the award of injunctive relief. Moreover, although his Lordship accepted that it provided no *defence* that the plaintiff had come to the nuisance, this was of relevance as regards the issue of remedies.

These statements, which share some similarities with the dictum of Black J in *Bellew*, seem out of line with the general run of authority. Lord Denning MR, indeed, seemed to acknowledge that a new and broader approach than

---

activity to continue up to a level at which the court considered it to become an actionable nuisance.

[29] [1977] 3 All ER 338.
[30] At 345.
[31] *ibid.*
[32] *ibid.*

was to be found in the earlier cases was necessary to meet his view of the needs of more modern times. Cumming-Bruce LJ purported to follow earlier authority, but his Lordship's reliance on a dictum of Lord Romilly MR in *Raphael* v *Thames Valley Rly Co*[33] has been demonstrated to have been misconceived, in the light of the statements of Lord Chelmsford LC when *Raphael* was reversed on appeal: the public inconvenience which might follow from the award of an equitable remedy being held not to be a matter relevant to its grant or refusal.[34]

The recent decision of Buckley J in *Dennis and Dennis* v *Ministry of Defence*[35] does, however, provide further support for the view that the public interest may be taken into account when a court is exercising its discretion as to the nature of the remedy to grant following a finding that a nuisance exists.[36] It was beyond doubt in *Dennis* that the flying of Harrier jets amounted to an actionable nuisance; all the evidence heard during the trial pointed to such a conclusion. However, since the public interest in the defence of the realm demanded that RAF Wittering continue to be used as an airbase for the training of pilots, it was held that it was a nuisance which would not be restrained by way of an injunction. Rather, the claimants would be compensated by an award of damages. In reaching such a conclusion, Buckley J balanced the nature of the public interest, the defence of the realm and the enormous cost of relocating RAF Wittering to another location against the property rights of the claimants, including the fact that the Estate had been occupied by the first claimant since childhood and that it was hoped that his children would enjoy and continue to maintain the Estate in due course. It was further noted that the diminution of the market value of the Estate could be compensated financially and that there had been considerable delay in instituting the proceedings. In the conclusion to this aspect of his judgment, Buckley J observed:

> "I do not believe that the conclusion at which I have arrived is prohibited by authority. The facts of this case are extreme and not analogous to others to which I have been referred. I am conscious that there is no authority directly in point which supports my solution."[37]

---

[33] (1866) LR 2 Eq 37 at 46.

[34] See Buckley RA: *The Law of Nuisance*, 2nd edn (1996) at p. 143 note 14. It is, perhaps, worth noting that *Miller* was a rather "harder" case than *Kennaway*. In *Kennaway* it was possible for an injunction to issue which would *regulate* the activities of the motor boat enthusiasts so that no further nuisance was caused to the plaintiff, but without prohibiting all substantial activity on their part. In other words the conflict between the private rights of the plaintiff and the more general public interest proved, it seems, more apparent than real. By contrast, in *Miller* the Court of Appeal proceeded upon the assumption that any injunction which preserved the private law rights of the plaintiff would prevent the game of cricket being played in a properly competitive fashion on the small ground.

[35] [2003] EWHC 793 (QB). For the facts of the case, see above at p. 69.

[36] In delivering his judgment in *Dennis*, Buckley J noted that in the earlier cases of *Miller* v *Jackson* and *Kennaway* v *Thompson*, the point at issue, whether and in what circumstances a sufficient public interest could amount to a defence to a claim in nuisance, had arisen "in a less dramatic form" than in the case before him: see para.30 of the judgment.

[37] [2003] EWHC 793 (QB) at para.49.

DAMAGES

We need to divide discussion of damages as a remedy in nuisance into two main parts: the appropriate *measure* of damages, and the rules which may apply as regards *remoteness of recoverable losses*.

Measure of damages

The starting-point of discussion of the measure of damages in private nuisance must be to remind ourselves of certain general propositions as regards the purposes and aims of awards of damages generally in the law of tort. We shall see that the nuisance cases on measure of damages involve the application of these general principles in the particular context of this tort.

The objective of an award of damages in the law of tort may be said to be to award that amount of money which may be regarded as putting the plaintiff into the position he would have been in had he not sustained the wrong in question:[38] in other words, to give the injured party, so far as money can, reparation for the wrongful act.[39]

It will be evident that the aim is compensation: in the ordinary case it is not the aim of an award of damages to go further, and seek to exact retribution on the defendant for his or her wrongful act.[40] It is true that there are exceptional situations[41] where an award of damages going beyond what is necessary to compensate the plaintiff – an award of exemplary damages – is permitted. But this is not the normal situation and may, for the moment, be ignored.[42]

What must concern us here is the way in which these basic compensatory aims are sought to be achieved by the courts in relation to the tort of private nuisance. We shall be concerned, essentially, with two questions:

(i) In cases of tangible/physical harm may a plaintiff elect between (a) seeking damages to compensate for loss of market value, and (b) seeking damages to reflect the cost of reinstatement, repair or cleanup action?

(ii) In cases of intangible harm (amenity loss) what level of award of damages may be appropriate?

---

[38] See, for example, Lord Blackburn in *Livingstone* v *Rawyards Coal Co* (1880) 5 App Cas 25 at 39.

[39] See, for example, Viscount Dunedin in *Admiralty Commissioners* v *SS Susquehanna* [1926] AC 655 at 661.

[40] See per Denning LJ in *Philips* v *Ward* [1956] 1 WLR 471 at 473: "the injured person is to be fairly compensated …, neither more nor less".

[41] As described in *Rookes* v *Barnard* [1964] AC 1129; [1964] 1 All ER 367.

[42] But see below, p. 168.

Tangible damage: loss in value or cost of repair as the measure of damages?

It will be evident that the object of seeking to compensate a plaintiff for tangible damage to his or her land may be achieved in either of these two ways. As Donaldson LJ explained in *Dodd Properties (Kent) Ltd* v *Canterbury City Council*:[43]

> "The general object ... is, so far as is possible ..., to place the plaintiff in the position which he would have occupied if he had not suffered the wrong complained of ... In the case of a tort causing damage to real property, this object is achieved by the application of one or other of two quite different measures of damages ... The first is to take the capital value of the property in an undamaged state and to compare it with its value in its damaged state. The second is to take the cost of repair or reinstatement. Which is appropriate will depend on a number of factors."[44]

Given that the sums of money necessary to achieve each of these objectives may be substantially different it is important to consider what factors are relevant to, and what principles govern, a court's decision as regards which measure to award. In principle a range of approaches is possible. We might limit the plaintiff to the smaller of the two sums; or we might allow the plaintiff a free choice between the two options; or some principles might develop limiting the breadth of such freedom of choice. As will be seen, it is the third of these possible approaches which may be said best to characterise the approach the courts have adopted.

We may begin with a statement from the Court of Appeal of New South Wales. In *Evans* v *Balog*[45] Samuels JA noted:

> "In a case such as the present, involving tortious damage to a building, it cannot be said that the normal measure of damages is the amount of diminution of the value of the land ... [A]n equally admissible measure is the cost of reinstatement and restoration ..."

Reference to certain cases followed, and then Samuels JA explained that nothing in those decisions went:

> "against allowing the cost of reinstatement where the circumstances are such that it is only by that means that fair compensation may be made."

And then approval was given to statements in *McGregor on Damages*. The real issue according to *McGregor* is:

> "the reasonableness of the plaintiff's desire to reinstate the property."

---

[43] [1980] 1 All ER 928.
[44] At 937.
[45] [1976] 1 NSWLR 36.

Such reasonableness would be assessed in part by the *advantages to him* of reinstatement in comparison with the *extra cost to the defendant* in having to pay damages for reinstatement rather than damages calculated by reference to the diminution in the value of the land.[46]

Amenity value damages

The courts will award damages over and above, and independently, of any loss in capital value (or cost of repair/reinstatement) in order to compensate for loss of amenity value resulting from the defendant's nuisance. An example of a situation where this may be the appropriate measure of damages would be where a nuisance has occurred in the form of interference with the use and enjoyment of land. When the nuisance terminates, voluntarily or in response to an injunction, any adverse effect on the capital value of the affected land should also cease; the cessation of the nuisance restoring the land to its full market value. In such circumstances the plaintiff's claim to compensation would focus on the intangible lost amenity value of the land during the period of the nuisance.[47]

It will be evident that the "amenity loss" recoverable in such cases as these will not be capable of precise measurement. The task for the court in this situation is very much akin to that experienced when sums are awarded for non-material losses in personal injury cases. Indeed, this similarity was noted and commented upon in *Bone* v *Seale*.[48] The plaintiffs succeeded in demonstrating that for a period of some twelve and a half years they had experienced odour nuisances from the defendant's pig farm. It was not, however, possible to demonstrate that the value of their property had been affected. The damages to be awarded would, therefore, simply reflect a sum regarded by the court as properly compensating the plaintiffs for the lowered amenity enjoyment of the ownership of their property.[49] At first instance, the plaintiffs were awarded each the sum of £6000:[50] calculated

---

[46] Another way of presenting essentially the same question is to ask: if the plaintiff had done the damage himself and was in possession of reasonably ample funds, would the plaintiff have spent from his own funds the sums he seeks in reinstatement damages from the defendant? It is common experience that we all spend sums maintaining and repairing the quality of our property, without there being any *necessary* connection between such expenditure and the protection of the property's market value.

[47] Contrast the claims of (i) a former owner who sold at a depleted price because of the existence of the nuisance, and (ii) an owner who can demonstrate lost rental income in connection with the land as a consequence of the nuisance. Each of these plaintiffs may recover more substantial sums than just that recoverable in a "loss of amenity" claim.

[48] [1975] 1 All ER 787. See above, at p. 31.

[49] In the light of the confirmation in *Hunter* (above, p. 71) that the tort of private nuisance protects rights in property rather than the comfort and convenience of individuals generally, it has been thought appropriate to couch the harm for which compensation is awarded not in terms of the lowered enjoyment of the use of the property, but as lowered enjoyment of the "ownership" of "their" property.

[50] Note that in respect of *this* kind of damage the amount which a defendant may have to pay may depend on the number of owners whose enjoyment has been affected. This statement assumes that the courts will not develop a principle that where there is more than one owner each suffers less amenity value loss than if each was a sole owner (on the principle that each is less harmed because

on the basis that each had suffered at a rate of £500 per year throughout the period of the nuisance. On appeal this sum was reduced very substantially – to just £1000 per plaintiff. In explaining why the trial judge's award was too high the Court of Appeal noted the relatively low sums awarded for loss of amenity in personal injury cases. Stephenson LJ noted:

> "There is, as it seems to me, some parallel between the loss of amenity which is caused by personal injury and the loss of amenity which is caused by a nuisance of this kind. If a parallel is drawn between those two losses, it is at once confirmed that this figure [£6000] is much too high. It is the kind of figure that would only be given for a serious and permanent loss of amenity as a result of a very serious injury, perhaps in the case of a young person."[51]

In other words, given that damages in personal injury claims do not compensate very generously for *mere* interference with the enjoyment of one's body (to hear, to talk, to walk, etc.), nor even pain and suffering associated with such injuries, so damages in the law of private nuisance should not be disproportionately generous as regards compensation[52] for mere interference with the enjoyment of ownership. In both cases, of course, overall levels of damages may be greater than just these small "amenity loss" items. In the case of personal injuries actions the damages may likely be swelled by "loss of earnings" claims and other material losses consequential upon the injury. In nuisance claims the overall level of damages may be swelled by demonstrable diminution in the capital value of the land, together with other material losses consequential upon the nuisance experienced.[53]

Remoteness of damage

A defendant whose conduct has given rise to a private nuisance experienced by the plaintiff is, in principle, required to pay such a sum by way of damages as will put the plaintiff in the position the plaintiff would have been had the tort not been committed. This principle of full compensation for all loss flowing from the nuisance is, however, subject to an important limiting provision: items of loss which are in law regarded as *too remote* consequences of the actions of the defendant will not be recoverable in the action for damages.

The question therefore arises: what principles govern the categorisation of kinds of harm flowing from the defendant's conduct as being "too remote"

---

each has a lesser ownership). It is suggested that to go so far would be to take the logic of private nuisance being a "property" tort rather too far.

[51] [1975] 1 All ER 787 at 793.

[52] This is not, of course, to suggest that the law does not regard such harm as a serious invasion of an owner's rights. It is merely to have chosen not to have been willing to estimate compensation in substantial sums. The seriousness with which the law views the matter is demonstrated by the availability "as a matter of course" of injunctive relief in order to protect this property interest (see above p. 143).

[53] For examples, see above p. 160.

or "not too remote"? Are the applicable principles, for example, to be the same as the ones which govern this matter in the tort of negligence?

Since the decision of the Privy Council in *Overseas Tankship (UK) Ltd* v *Miller Steamship Co Pty Ltd*[54] it has been clear that where damages are sought in relation to a *public* nuisance caused by a defendant,[55] the same rules do apply as in the law of negligence.[56] More recently, in 1993, in *Cambridge Water Company Ltd* v *Eastern Counties Leather plc*,[57] the House of Lords extended the ambit of those remoteness principles to both liability in private nuisance and also to strict liability under the rule in *Rylands* v *Fletcher*. These cases are more fully considered below.[58]

ABATEMENT OF NUISANCES: SELF-HELP

In addition to the judicial remedies of damages and injunctive relief, an extra-judicial remedy of abatement or "self-help" has been recognised by the courts. This remedy, involving the victim taking steps personally to put an end to the nuisance, is of some practical significance; albeit that the judges, as will be seen, have been at pains to keep the bounds of this privilege within quite close confines. Indeed, it has even been stated in the highest court that abatement by the party affected is:

"a remedy the law does not favour and is not usually advisable."[59]

The remedy is most suited to situations where the fact of the nuisance is clear and indisputable and where the nuisance can be abated without the victim needing to enter onto other land. So, for example, it may be an efficient and judicially acceptable method of putting an end to a nuisance in cases where all that is required is the cutting back of the branches from an overhanging tree,[60] or the chopping back of an encroaching root. Thus Bracton stated the rationale for abatement in the following terms:

---

[54] [1967] 1 AC 617: "*Wagon Mound II*".

[55] For claims to damages in public nuisance, see Chapter 5.

[56] The principle laid down in the earlier *Wagon Mound* decision: the test of *foreseeability* of the kind of harm.

[57] [1994] 2 AC 264.

[58] See below, Chapter 6.

[59] Per Lord Atkinson in *Lagon Navigation Co* v *Lambeg Bleaching Dyeing and Finishing Co* [1927] AC 226 at 244. Similarly in *Sedleigh-Denfield* v *O'Callaghan* [1940] 3 All ER 349, Lord Wright observed that: "No doubt there may be a common law right to abate extrajudicially, but that is a right which involves taking the law into a man's own hands, and which is much to be discouraged, particularly if it involves entering onto the other party's land" (at 369). This judicial dislike of the remedy of abatement has also emerged in other contexts. Thus in *R* v *Chief Constable of the Devon and Cornwall Constabulary, ex p Central Electricity Generating Board* [1981] 3 All ER 826, where the applicant Board sought an order of mandamus to compel the Chief Constable to have his officers remove protesters from a piece of land which was being surveyed in order to assess its suitability as the site of a power station, Lawton LJ considered that there were "many reasons why self-help should be discouraged" in the present context. Chief amongst these was that "as soon as one person starts to, or makes to, lay hands on another there is likely to be a breach of the peace" (at 834).

[60] *Lemmon* v *Webb* [1895] AC 1.

"And the reason why the law allows this private and summary method of doing one's self justice, is because injuries of this kind, which obstruct or annoy such things as are of daily convenience and use, require an immediate remedy; and cannot wait for the slow progress of the ordinary forms of justice."[61]

In situations where some degree of judgment is necessary before a view may be reached as to whether a nuisance is being committed the remedy by way of self-help will be less appropriate. As Eyre CJ noted in *Kirby* v *Sudgrove*:[62]

"Abatement ought only to be allowed in clear cases of nuisance where the injury is apparent on the first view of the matter."[63]

It was, accordingly, held in *Kirby* not to be justified in a case where the alleged wrongdoing was the planting of trees on common land. This might, or might not, have amounted to an actionable interference with the defendant's rights of common over that land: but the matter was one of degree and the matter therefore was one in which judicial resolution was necessary, and the defendant's actions in cutting down the trees was unlawful.[64]

In addition to clear and simple cases where a nuisance may be abated without the victim entering onto other property, the courts have acknowledged that abatement action may be legitimate where it is reasonable to take immediate action in an emergency situation, rather than to allow substantial damage to occur and then seek compensation in a court of law. In such circumstances the victim may enter, without notice if giving notice is impracticable, onto other land to abate the nuisance. As Best J explained in *Earl of Lonsdale* v *Nelson*:[65]

"The security of lives and property may sometimes require so speedy a remedy as not to allow time to call on the person on whose property the mischief has arisen, to remedy it."[66]

---

[61] See 3 Bl Com (17th edn 1830) at p. 5, referred to by Lloyd LJ in *Burton* v *Winters* [1993] 3 All ER 847 at 850.

[62] (1797) 3 Anst 892.

[63] See also *Burton* v *Winters* [1993] 3 All ER 847, where Lloyd LJ observed that: "Self-redress is a summary remedy, which is justified only in clear and simple cases, or in an emergency" (at 851).

[64] In *Burton* v *Winters* [1993] 3 All ER 847, where the question at issue for the Court of Appeal was whether the plaintiff was entitled to exercise her common law right of abatement in respect of a nuisance created on her land by the construction of her neighbour's garage, Lloyd LJ felt that this was not an appropriate case for self-redress. The reasoning underpinning this conclusion was that there was no emergency and "there were difficult questions of law and fact to be considered" ([1993] 3 All ER 847 at 851).

[65] [1823] 2 B & C 302.

[66] At 311. This statement was later affirmed by Beldam LJ in *Co-operative Wholesale Society Ltd* v *British Railways Board*, *The Times*, 20 December 1995. In this case His Lordship was of the opinion that: "the right of abatement should be confined to cases where the security of lives or property require immediate or speedy action or where it can be exercised simply without recourse to the expense and inconvenience of legal proceedings in circumstances unlikely to give rise to

Outside situations of emergency there is generally a requirement that prior to a victim entering onto another's land to abate a nuisance, the victim should have given notice of this intent to the neighbour. Given evident judicial concern about the potential for abatement action to be met with hostile response on the part of the neighbouring landowner this rule would appear to involve good sense. A neighbour who has been given notice, and hence an opportunity himself or herself to put matters right, may be less incensed at the sight on his or her land of the victim putting a stop to the nuisance, than if such actions of abatement were to be done summarily and without warning.

The exact scope of this rule about notice needs, however, to be noted. It clearly applies to cases where the present occupier of the land upon which the nuisance exists was not the person who created that nuisance, and not having adopted or continued the nuisance bears no potential personal liability in respect of that nuisance. It is less clear, however, whether the requirement of notice before entering to abate a clear nuisance applies in relation to neighbouring occupiers who have themselves created the nuisance, or who may be regarded through adoption or continuance as having responsibility for a nuisance created by another (perhaps a trespasser or a predecessor in title).

The weight of authority would seem to suggest that in relation to persons who bear such legal responsibility for the nuisance the obligation to afford prior notice does *not* apply. An example of this approach may be found in *Jones* v *Williams*,[67] in which Parke B noted:

> "It is clear, that if the plaintiff himself was the original wrongdoer, by placing filth upon the *locus in quo*, it might be removed by the party injured, without any notice …; and so, possibly, if by his default in not performing some obligation incumbent upon him, for that is his wrong also."

However, Parke B continued with words suggesting that one who has *continued* a nuisance created by a predecessor in title is a person to whom notice must be given. His Lordship said:

> " … a notice … is necessary … in the case of a nuisance continued by an alienee …"

One may wonder a little at these distinctions. It may be readily explicable that the notice/request requirement may be waived in situations of emergency. It also seems to make sense that an "innocent" occupier should, where reasonably practicable, be served some form of request/notice prior to abatement action occurring. What is less clear is why this rule of commonsense and courtesy, designed to avoid unnecessary inflammation of passions between neighbours – in a context where

---

argument or dispute. Where a simple and speedy application to a court can be made, I would not regard a remedy of self-help as appropriate or desirable."
[67] (1843) 11 M&W 176.

passions may likely very readily be stirred – should not apply also where the occupier created the nuisance. Moreover, even if we can see some good reason for not applying the rule to such a person, it is not very obvious why a distinction should exist between the creator of a nuisance (no need to give notice) and the person who is to be regarded as having "continued" a nuisance created by another.

It might be thought that there would be good sense in extending the prior notice/request requirement, simple as it is, to all cases of non-emergency abatement action. Indeed, although the weight of judicial comment would seem to support the distinctions initially stated above, there do exist some indications of support for the more straightforward and simple alternative proposed. So, for example, in *Lemmon* v *Webb*,[68] Lord Herschell considered the authorities and observed that:

> "They are cases where a nuisance has existed on neighbouring soil, where the person complaining of the nuisance could only get rid of it by going onto the soil of his neighbour; and there no doubt it has been held that he cannot justify going onto the soil of his neighbour to remove the nuisance except in a case of emergency, unless he has first given his neighbour notice to remove it. That is because his act involves an interference with his neighbour's soil – involves a trespass."[69]

And Lord Davy said:

> "It is true that where a person desires to abate a nuisance, which can only be abated by going on the land of the person from whom the nuisance proceeds, he must usually give notice of his intention to do so. That seems to me to be reasonable, because his act of going upon his neighbour's land in prima facie a trespass, and I can understand that he should be bound to give notice of his intention to do that which would be prima facie a trespass before doing it."[70]

---

[68] [1895] AC 1.
[69] At 5.
[70] At 8.

Chapter 5

THE ACTION FOR DAMAGES ARISING OUT OF PUBLIC NUISANCE

INTRODUCTION

The law of public nuisance is essentially a branch of the criminal law and not the law of tort. For this reason we shall consider the *substance* of such criminal liability, not here, but in Part II, below.[1] The aim of this chapter is to describe the circumstances in which an individual may bring civil proceedings for damages and/or an injunction in a case where a defendant has committed a public nuisance. A separate treatment is justified on the basis that "the major importance of public nuisance today is in the civil remedy which it affords".[2]

The circumstance which triggers such private law rights is the individual being able, on the facts,[3] to demonstrate that he or she has suffered "special damage"[4] over and above, or different to, that suffered by other members of the public. In other words, merely to have experienced that which others have suffered, and which has resulted in the defendant's actions being characterised as a public nuisance, will not suffice to allow any individual to recover compensation.[5]

---

[1] See below, Chapter 8.

[2] Smith and Hogan, *Criminal Law* (10th edn, (2002) Butterworths) at p. 772.

[3] In *Wildtree Hotels Ltd and others* v *London Borough of Harrow* [2000] 3 All ER 288, Lord Hoffmann remarked that: "This rule offers considerable scope for dispute on the facts and some of the decisions on injurious affection reflect different judicial views on what amounts to particular damage" (at 293). In *Blundy, Clark and Company Ltd* v *London and North Eastern Railway Company* [1931] 2 KB 334, Greer LJ noted that: "What amounts to such special or peculiar damage is a question of some difficulty..." (at 360).

[4] In some of the authorities, the phrase "particular damage" is preferred. Thus in *Harper* v *G N Haden & Sons Ltd* [1933] Ch 298, Lawrence LJ observed that: "A private individual can maintain an action in respect of a wrongful obstruction of the highway; but, in order to do so, he must establish that he has suffered some *particular*, direct and substantial loss or damage beyond what is suffered by him in common with all other members of the public affected by the nuisance" (at 308 (emphasis added)).

[5] If a victim of a public nuisance satisfies the requirements for a claim in *private* nuisance (for example, being a property owner whose property, or whose enjoyment of that property, has been adversely affected) the fact that he or she may not have suffered above or beyond others in the locality (and so not have suffered such "special" damage) will act as no bar to the *private* nuisance claim. The value of the action arising out of public nuisance is that it may provide a remedy for persons who, for some reason described above in Chapter 2, may not be able to claim in private nuisance (or for whom the action arising out of the public nuisance may allow a more broadly founded claim than is permissible in private nuisance – for example, allowing recovery in relation to personal injury or illness suffered).

THE REQUIREMENT OF "SPECIAL DAMAGE"

In *Benjamin* v *Storr*,[6] Brett J made the following well-known statement of general principle:

> "By the common law of England, a person guilty of public nuisance might be indicted; but if injury resulted to a private individual, *other and greater than that which was common to all the Queen's subjects*, the person injured has his remedy by action ..."[7]

This requirement of special or particular damage may be traced back to early times. In a Year Book case of 1536 Fitzherbert J is reported to have referred, in the crude Law French of the time, to the need for:

> *"plus grand hurt ou incommodity y ce que chacun homme ad."*[8]

To put the matter in reverse, we may adopt the language of Scholl J in the Australian case of *Walsh* v *Ervin*[9] and say that:

> "no one should have an action for that which everyone suffered."

Returning to the Year Book case of 1536, Fitzherbert J uttered a dictum which has since been much quoted:

> "I agree well that each nuisance in the King's highway is punishable in the Leet and not by action, unless it be where one man has suffered greater hurt or inconvenience than the generality have; but he who has suffered such greater displeasure or hurt can have an action to recover the damage which he has by reason of this special hurt. So if one makes a ditch across the highway, and I come riding along the way in the night and I and my horse are thrown into the ditch so that I have great damage and displeasure thereby, I shall have an action here against him who made this ditch across the highway, because I have suffered more damage than any other person."[10]

In his seminal article on the law of nuisance, F H Newark argued that this case had "set the law of nuisance on the wrong track".[11] The basis for such a forthright view lies not so much in the words of Fitzherbert J as in the words of Baldwin CJ. In giving judgment, the latter's explanation as to why the claimant should not succeed was that "if one person shall have an action for this, by the same reason every person shall have an action, and so he will be punished a hundred times on the same case." In Newark's opinion, Baldwin CJ's error lay in his having given the wrong reason for rejecting the action. Instead of restating the established rule that the existence of a criminal punishment was a bar to a private action, Baldwin

---

[6] (1874) LR 9 CP 400.
[7] At 407 (emphasis added).
[8] YB 27 H VII fo 27: referred to by Scholl J in *Walsh* v *Ervin* [1952] VLR 361.
[9] [1952] VLR 361.
[10] YB 27 H VII fo 27 pl.10.
[11] "The Boundaries of Nuisance" (1949) 65 LQR 480.

CJ had attempted to rationalise the rule and in so doing, had placed too great an emphasis upon the need to avoid over-punishing the defendant.[12] Indeed, as J R Spencer has argued, it is:

"... a singularly weak reason to modern legal minds, because nowadays we think that civil proceedings are about compensation rather than about punishment, and it is hard to see why someone who has suffered by another person's criminal act should have to bear the loss because the defendant's misbehaviour has been bad enough to affect ninety-nine other people too."[13]

The substantial issues raised for a court to determine will be of two kinds. One is whether it is necessary that the particular damage suffered by the plaintiff should not only be *greater* than that suffered by others generally, but also be *different in kind*. The other issue will be what, on the facts of each case, will be regarded as amounting to particular damage which is other and greater than that suffered by persons generally. The courts have regarded the latter issue as essentially one of fact for determination by the court of first instance, whereas the former has been the subject of some judicial discussion.

The majority of cases reviewing the issue of special damage have been civil actions arising out of public nuisances in the form of the obstruction of public rights of way or public rights of navigation.[14] From early times clear statements were made by the judges, in this context, that one who had suffered mere inconvenience would not qualify as a plaintiff in a civil action.

However, in so far as such statements appear in cases in which the degree of inconvenience suffered by the plaintiff was really no more than that suffered by others,[15] the statements need not be regarded as ruling out recovery on the part of one who can show a special degree of inconvenience suffered, over and above that suffered generally.

This raises immediately the fundamental question: may such *greater* hurt, but of the same *kind* as suffered by others, qualify as special damage? In numerous cases the judges were able to avoid having to decide this particular question. The cases which came before them were commonly claims based upon demonstrable financial harm having resulted directly to the plaintiff from the commission by the defendant of the public nuisance. Typical instances would be cases where, following obstruction of a right of way, it had become necessary in the plaintiff's conduct of his business to incur greater costs by having to proceed by a longer route. Such plaintiffs,

---

[12] Newark remarks that: "If a hundred private wrongs have been done a hundred private actions may well be brought", *ibid* 483.

[13] "Public Nuisance – A Critical Examination" [1989] 48 CLJ 55 at 73.

[14] See, for example, *Iveson* v *Moore* (1699) 1 Ld. Raym. 486, *Rose* v *Miles* (1815) 4 M & S 101, and *Greasly* v *Codling* (1824) 2 Bing 263.

[15] See, for example, *Winterbottom* v *Lord Derby* (1867) LR 2 Ex 316: obstruction of a public highway causing plaintiff to take a less convenient detour did not result in him suffering damage any different to that suffered by other members of the public.

able to show pecuniary expense flowing from the public nuisance, generally were successful.[16] The basis of their claims was explained by Gibson J, following a careful review of the authorities, in the Irish case, *Smith* v *Wilson*:[17]

> "Mere inconvenience, as in *Winterbottom* … may not be enough; but where premises are prejudicially affected by a [right of way] being permanently stopped, and replaced by a circuitous and longer way … direct damage may be inferred."[18]

The final words of this quotation are significant. Not only would the judges regard such additional expense as constituting special damage: they became willing, in appropriate cases, to make *inferences* that, given the nature of a plaintiff's activities and his or her use of the obstructed route, such financial expense had resulted from the nuisance.

Proof, or inference, of *financial* loss following directly from a public nuisance also eased the lot of plaintiffs seeking to show special damage in cases where obstruction to the highway had hindered access by customers or suppliers to the plaintiff's business premises.[19] *Benjamin* v *Storr*[20] provides a well-known example. In the course of the defendants' business as auctioneers vans were continually loaded and unloaded on the street outside a coffee-house run by the plaintiff. The vehicles blocked light to the premises and obstructed access by customers. The horses, used to pull the vans, emitted odours which rendered the use of the coffee-house unattractive to customers. It was held that the public nuisance by way of obstructing the highway had had direct consequences in the form of special damage to the plaintiff's business, and the action therefore succeeded.[21]

---

[16] In *Blundy, Clark and Company Ltd* v *London and North Eastern Railway Company* [1931] 2 KB 334, for example, Greer LJ opined: "In my judgment it is the law that where a plaintiff has property near a highway which he uses for the purposes of his business, and the highway, whether a canal or a roadway, is unlawfully obstructed, and he is thereby put to greater expense in the conduct of his business, or suffers loss by the diminution of his business, he is entitled to recover damages as a person who has suffered special or peculiar damage beyond that which has been suffered by other members of the public wanting to use the highway or waterway" (at 365).

[17] [1903] 2 IR 45.

[18] At 76.

[19] Of course, if persons generally had suffered such losses there would be nothing *special* in the plaintiff's claim. See, for example, *Martin* v *London County Council* (1899) 80 LT 866 per Smith LJ at 867.

[20] (1874) LR 9 CP 400.

[21] A plaintiff's business may also be adversely affected where a public nuisance results in the obstruction of its employees rather than its customers or suppliers: see *Gravesend Borough Council* v *British Railways Board* [1978] 3 All ER 853, where Slade J held that the Port of London Authority had *locus standi* to sue the Board in respect of its decision to offer a reduced ferry service between Gravesend and Tilbury. This would have meant that some of the Authority's employees would have to leave work early in order to catch the last ferry. Since a public ferry was a public highway, albeit of a special kind, it would be a public nuisance to hinder or obstruct the passage of the public along that highway. Moreover, Slade J considered that the cost of training staff in order to fill the gaps left by those who had departed early (£14,000) amounted to special damage other than and beyond the general inconvenience and injury likely to be suffered by the public. On the facts, however, the claim failed.

In this case evidence was presented to suggest the degree of harm done to the plaintiff's business. However, just as in the "detour" cases considered above, here also the judges have displayed a willingness to *infer* that a public nuisance must have caused financial harm to a plaintiff's trade or business. *Lyons, Sons and Co v Gulliver*,[22] for example, involved a public nuisance caused by the popularity of performances of *Charley's Aunt* at the Palladium Theatre. Queues rendered access to neighbouring businesses more difficult, and Cozens-Hardy MR explained that it was not necessary, in such a case, for evidence of financial loss to be presented to the court:

> "I cannot bring myself to doubt that this is a serious nuisance and annoyance, by which the plaintiffs are specially affected, and that it is not a case in which it is at all necessary for them to say 'We can prove that we have lost … by reason of this.'"[23]

In cases such as these, where pecuniary damage may be proven or inferred to have followed directly from the defendant's nuisance, the courts may regard the harm suffered as being, in the words of Brett J referred to above, both "other and greater" than that suffered by persons generally. What, though, of cases where no such proof or inference of *pecuniary* loss is possible. For example, where a plaintiff may be able to point to inconvenience substantially greater in degree than persons generally but, not being involved in any business or trade, may find it difficult to show pecuniary damage. Should such a plaintiff receive general damages in respect of his or her exceptional discomfort and inconvenience, or be barred on the ground that his or her suffering has been only the same in *kind* as others generally?

No confident answer may be given to this question. However, the matter was subject to some careful consideration by Scholl J in the Supreme Court of Victoria in *Walsh v Ervin*,[24] who concluded that "proved general damage, for example, inconvenience and delay" would suffice:

> "provided it was substantial, that it is direct and not consequential, and that it is appreciably greater in degree than any suffered by the general public."[25]

Such a plaintiff would, according to Scholl J, satisfy the essential requirements stated several centuries earlier in the test proposed by Fitzherbert J, involving demonstration of:

> "greater hurt, or inconvenience, than every man had."[26]

---

[22] [1914] 1 Ch 631.

[23] At p 641. In cases like *Benjamin* and *Lyons* there seems no reason why the conduct of the defendant could not have been categorised as a private nuisance to the use and enjoyment of the plaintiffs' properties. As such the willingness of the judges to grant damages arising out of the public nuisance is unremarkable. On the facts, however, the claim failed.

[24] [1952] VLR 361.

[25] At 371.

The *Halsey* case

It will be evident that a claim for damages and/or injunctive relief may involve allegations both of private nuisance and of special damage arising out of a public nuisance.

No better illustration of such an instance can be given than *Halsey* v *Esso Petroleum Co Ltd.*[27] The plaintiff claimed an injunction and damages arising out of the operation of the neighbouring defendant's oil distribution depot. The trial judge, Veale J, characterised the litigation in the following terms:

> "This is a case, if ever there was one, of the little man asking for the protection of the law against the activities of a large and powerful neighbour."[28]

The plaintiff's claim was in respect of:

- smells from the defendant's operations;

- deposits consisting of noxious acid smuts (some the size of a sixpence), falling on and damaging such items as clothes put out to dry, the defendant's motor car parked outside his house, the paintwork of his house, and fabrics within his house;

- noise from boilers, pumps and vehicles.

Veale J noted that in assessing whether the smells and noises constituted a legal nuisance the nature of the locality was a relevant consideration;[29] and indicated that the plaintiff's terraced house was in a residential area, albeit situated close to a strip of industrial development along the River Thames – development which included a variety of types of industrial activity, including other oil storage depots. Having so described and characterised the locality, Veale J explained:

> "So far as the present case is concerned, liability for nuisance by harmful deposits could be established by proving damage by the deposits to the property in question, provided, of course, that the injury was not merely trivial. Negligence is not an ingredient of the cause of action, and the character of the nieghbourhood is not a matter to be taken into consideration. On the other hand nuisance by smell or noise is something to which no absolute standard can be applied. It is always a question of degree whether the interference with comfort and convenience is sufficiently serious to constitute a

---

[26] *ibid.* Scholl J was much influenced also by the words of Luxmoore J in *Vanderpant* v *Mayfair Hotel Co Ltd* [1930] 1 Ch 138: "[H]e will have satisfied the necessary conditions to enable him to maintain this action, because he would have established the fact that he had sustained an injury affecting him particularly, *in a manner beyond that in which other members of the public are in fact affected* ..." (emphasis added).

[27] [1961] 2 All ER 145.

[28] At 149.

[29] See further on this factor, above, p. 42.

nuisance. The character of the neighbourhood is very relevant and all the relevant circumstances have to be taken into account."[30]

And later:

> "The standard in respect of discomfort and inconvenience from noise and smell that I have to apply is that of the ordinary reasonable and responsible person who lives in this particular area ... This is not necessarily the same as the standard which the plaintiff chose to set ... for himself. It is the standard of the ordinary man, and the ordinary man, who may like peace and quiet, will not complain for instance of the noise of traffic if he chooses to live on a main street in an urban area, nor of the reasonable noises of industry, if he chooses to live alongside a factory."[31]

Veale J reviewed the evidence as regards each item of alleged nuisance. In relation to the nuisances involving harm to the plaintiff's use and enjoyment of his property he concluded:

- that no complaint could be made of occasional oily background smells.[32] However, the periodically occurring more pungent and nauseating smells which had arisen in recent years were a different matter – going far beyond triviality and involving a nuisance to local residents.

- that the noise experienced at night from the plant (boilers and pumps) amounted to an actionable nuisance: in particular, the noise from the defendant's boiler-house, situated near to the plaintiff's house which, when at its worst, caused the plaintiff's windows and doors to vibrate "terrifically".

- that the vehicle noise involved an actionable nuisance.

On the last of these matters, Veale J commented:

> "At intervals through the night tankers leave and come to the ... depot. It has been urged on me that the public highway is for the use of all, and that is true. But it must be borne in mind that these tankers are not ordinary motor cars; they are not ordinary lorries which make more noise than a motor car; they are enormous vehicles ... which, apart from the loud noise of their engines, may rattle as they go .... They all enter the depot almost opposite the plaintiff's house .... This ... now happens every night."[33]

On the basis of these various findings Veale J found there to be a liability to damages in *private* nuisance in respect of the smells and noise. The

---

[30] At 151. See further on the differing approach to material and non-material harm, above p. 28.
[31] At 151-152.
[32] It is not clear whether this was because of the application of the "locality" principle, or because the defendant had demonstrated a prescriptive right to emit such a level of odour.
[33] At 156.

claims in respect of the damage caused by the smuts to the plaintiff's car and clothes, however, raised issues outside the scope of protection afforded by private nuisance. Nevertheless, Veale J held that such damage involved special damage suffered by the plaintiff arising out of the public nuisance caused to the local community by the operation of the depot.[34]

The plaintiff was awarded £5 in respect of his modest claim for damaged linen; £30 to permit him to have a new coat of paint applied to his car – Veale J commenting: "I do not think a perfect result would be necessary"; and £200 by way of general damages.

It will be remembered that the plaintiff had also sought injunctive relief. Veale J noted that the court should be wary of exercising discretion to refuse an injunction[35] and held:

- "There will be an injunction restraining the defendants ... from so operating their plant ... and from so driving their vehicles as, by reason of noise, to cause a nuisance to this plaintiff between the hours of 10.00 pm and 6.00 am";

- that an injunction should issue prohibiting, day and night, nuisance by smell comprising the pungent and nauseating smells as periodically experienced (but not extending to prohibition of the general background oily smells);

- that provided the defendants gave an undertaking to construct a new chimney such as would avoid the issuance of smuts, no injunction (or damages *in lieu*) would be awarded in relation to that matter.

Halsey is a good illustration of how a plaintiff may be able to recover for physical damage to his property caused by the existence of a public nuisance. Similarly in *Southport Corporation* v *Esso Petroleum Co Ltd*,[36] Devlin J held that the owners of an area of foreshore had a good cause of action in nuisance where the larger part of 400 tons of oil had been deposited on their land and they had suffered damage. However, to emphasise a point which was made previously,[37] one advantage which an action arising out of a public nuisance has over a private nuisance claim is that it may provide a plaintiff with a remedy where a remedy does not exist in private nuisance. Thus a plaintiff who has sustained physical injuries to

---

[34] Veale J also regarded the principle of *Rylands* v *Fletcher* as applicable to the escape of acid smuts and the damage to the motor vehicle paintwork. Note, further, that Veale J was willing to regard the noise from vehicular use of the highway as involving unreasonable user of the highway and, thus, a public nuisance: the plaintiff had suffered more from this noise than others, and so special damage was proven. Veale J did not advert to the issue whether it was necessary for such special damage to be different in kind as well as greater than that experienced by others. As the *plaintiff* could maintain this claim also in private nuisance the matter was not one of real significance. What, though, of a claim which might have been made by members of his family as regards their own "special" damage?

[35] See further on injunctions "as a matter of course", above, p. 143.

[36] [1953] 2 All ER 1204.

[37] See above, p. 159, fn. 5.

his *person* as a consequence of a public nuisance may be able to recover. A well known case which illustrates this point is *Castle* v *St Augustine's Links.*[38] Here the plaintiff, a minicab driver, was driving along a road when a ball struck from an adjacent golf course hit his cab's windscreen. The impact of the ball caused the windscreen to shatter and a fragment of glass became embedded in his eye. The injury was such that the eye had to be removed several days later. It was held by the Court of Appeal that the siting of a golf tee and hole parallel to the highway amounted to a public nuisance and that both defendants (the club and the player who had struck the ball) were liable to the plaintiff in damages for the harm that he had sustained as a result.

Similarly in *Slater* v *Worthington's Cash Stores Ltd,*[39] the plaintiff was standing outside the defendant's shop in Leicester whilst her mother made a purchase inside, when a large mass of snow fell from the roof of the shop and crushed her under its weight. The plaintiff suffered a number of injuries including the fracture of a vertebrae in her back. In an action for damages alleging nuisance or alternatively negligence Oliver J held that the accumulation of snow on a sloping roof overhanging a public street amounted to a public nuisance. This was particularly so given that four days had passed since the snow storms had ceased and yet the defendants had done nothing to abate the nuisance or make people aware of the potential danger. Accordingly, since the plaintiff had suffered special damage in the form of personal injuries, she was entitled to recover.

Although "special" damage is not susceptible to precise definition it would seem possible to identify a number of heads under which special damage may be found. Thus a plaintiff may recover damages in respect of a public nuisance where the "special" damage which he or she has suffered has taken the form of personal injury, injury to property, or pecuniary loss arising from loss of business. To these three heads can be added a fourth: that the plaintiff has suffered a depreciation in the value of his land as the direct consequence of a public nuisance.

A leading case on this category of special damage is *Caledonian Railway Co* v *Walker's Trustees.*[40] The Trustees were in possession of a spinning mill 90 yards from an important thoroughfare in Glasgow which could be accessed from two sides of the mill. Under the Scottish Railways Clauses Act 1845, the railway company completely cut off one access, substituting a deviated route over a bridge with steep gradients. The other access was diverted and made less convenient. The Trustees claimed compensation for the diminished value of their premises caused by the detour and gradients. The House of Lords affirmed the decision of the Second Division of the Court of Session and held that the Trustees were entitled to compensation under the statute. In giving judgment, Lord Watson observed that:

---

[38] (1922) 38 TLR 615.
[39] [1941] 1 All ER 245.
[40] (1882) 7 App Cas 259.

"When an access to private property by a public highway is interfered with, the owner can have no action of damages for any personal inconvenience which he may suffer, in common with the rest of the lieges. But should the value of the property, irrespective of any particular uses which may be made of it, be so dependent upon the existence of that access as to be substantially diminished by its obstruction, then I conceive that the owner has, in respect of any works causing such obstruction, a right of action."[41]

WHAT TYPE OF DAMAGES ARE RECOVERABLE?

In an earlier chapter the essentially compensatory nature of awards of damages in the law of tort was noted.[42] The aim of such an award is, generally, to compensate the plaintiff for the harm suffered as a consequence of the commission of a tort, rather than to seek to punish or deter the tortfeasor for his or her wrongdoing. Such *ordinary* damages are what a plaintiff will recover if he or she is successful in an action arising out of a public nuisance. However, English Law does recognise that there may be exceptional circumstances in which it is appropriate for a court to award damages other than *ordinary* damages, e.g. to award *exemplary* or *punitive* damages.

Exemplary damages

Can *exemplary* damages be recovered by a plaintiff in an action in respect of a public nuisance? The starting point must be the House of Lords decision in *Rookes* v *Barnard*.[43]

In this case the appellant, a draughtsman at London Airport, was, like all the other draughtsmen at the airport, a member of a particular trade union: the AESD.[44] He resigned his membership of that trade union following a disagreement. A resolution was passed at a union branch meeting of the union to the effect that their employer (BOAC) should be informed that all the other draughtsmen would withdraw their labour if the appellant was not removed from the design office by a stipulated time and date. Each of the three respondents spoke in favour of the resolution. In response to the resolution presented to them BOAC initially suspended the plaintiff and then ultimately terminated his contract of employment. The appellant brought an action against the respondents claiming damages against them for using unlawful means to induce his employer to terminate his employment and for conspiring to do so. He succeeded at first instance and was awarded £7,500 damages by the jury. That decision was subsequently reversed by the Court of Appeal.[45] On appeal to the House of Lords their Lordships reviewed the summing up of the trial judge, in the course of

---

[41] At 303.
[42] See above, p. 151.
[43] [1964] 1 All ER 267; [1964] AC 1129.
[44] The Association of Engineering and Shipbuilding Draughtsmen.
[45] See [1961] 2 All ER 825.

which the trial judge had directed that the jury might award exemplary damages.

After making some general observations as to the nature of exemplary damages and how these might be distinguished from ordinary damages Lord Devlin, with whom the other Law Lords concurred, proceeded to examine the authorities in order to determine the circumstances in which exemplary damages might be awarded within the law of tort. Cases such as *Wilkes* v *Wood*,[46] *Huckle* v *Money*,[47] *Bell* v *Midland Railway Co*,[48] *Owen and Smith (Trading as Nuagin Car Service)* v *Reo Motors (Britain) Ltd*[49] and *Williams* v *Settle*[50] led His Lordship to two initial conclusions:

> "First, that your Lordships could not without a complete disregard of precedent, and indeed of statute, now arrive at a determination that refused altogether to recognise the exemplary principle. Secondly, that there are certain categories of cases in which an award of exemplary damages can serve a useful purpose in vindicating the strength of the law, and thus affording a practical justification for admitting into the civil law a principle which ought logically to belong to the criminal."[51]

His Lordship identified three such categories.

Into the first of these could be placed:

> "…oppressive, arbitrary or unconstitutional action by the servants of the government."[52]

This category of exemplary damages could therefore be justified by the need to ensure that government power is exercised properly by its servants in accordance with their duty of service.

Into the second category fell those cases in which:

> "…the defendant's conduct has been calculated by him to make a profit for himself which may well exceed the compensation payable to the plaintiff."[53]

Exemplary damages may be awarded in this category of case "whenever it is necessary" in the words of Lord Devlin, "to teach a wrongdoer that tort does not pay".[54]

---

[46] (1763) Lofft. 1.
[47] (1763) 2 Wils. 205.
[48] (1861) 10 C.B.N.S. 287.
[49] [1934] All ER Rep 734.
[50] [1960] 2 All ER 806.
[51] [1964] 1 All ER 367 at 410.
[52] At 410.
[53] At 410.
[54] At 411.

In addition to identifying these two categories as part of the common law, Lord Devlin also allowed for a third category where exemplary damages had been expressly authorised by statute.[55]

As well as identifying these categories where the award of exemplary damages was permissible Lord Devlin identified three considerations which he felt ought always to be borne in mind when considering such an award. His Lordship stated these considerations as follows:

> "First, the plaintiff cannot recover exemplary damages unless he is the victim of the punishable behaviour. The anomaly inherent in exemplary damages would become an absurdity if a plaintiff totally unaffected by some oppressive conduct which the jury wished to punish obtained a windfall in consequence. Secondly, the power to award exemplary damages constitutes a weapon that, while it can be used in defence of liberty... can also be used against liberty. Some of the awards that juries have made in the past seem to me to amount to a greater punishment than would be likely to be incurred if the conduct were criminal. I should not allow the respect which is traditionally paid to an assessment of damages by a jury to prevent me from seeing that the weapon is used with restraint... [T]hirdly, the means of the parties, irrelevant in the assessment of compensation, are material in the assessment of exemplary damages."[56]

Lord Devlin's assessment of the limited scope for exemplary damages in English Law was confirmed just a few years later by the House of Lords' decision in *Cassell & Co Ltd* v *Broome*.[57] In particular, in that later case their Lordships concluded that although Lord Devlin had enumerated the categories and stated the considerations which would apply, he was not seeking to substitute a broad rational principle in place of the law which had applied up until that earlier case. In the words of Lord Diplock:

> "...*Rookes* v *Barnard* was not intended to extend the power to award exemplary or aggravated damages to particular torts for which they had not previously been awarded, such as negligence and deceit. Its express purpose was to restrict, not to expand, the anomaly of exemplary damages."[58]

It is in this respect that the issue arises: are exemplary damages available in an action for damages arising out of public nuisance? This matter was in issue in *AB and others* v *South West Water Services Ltd*.[59] This case arose out of the accidental contamination of a drinking water supply at

---

[55] The example which Lord Devlin used to illustrate the point was the Reserve and Auxillary Forces (Protection of Civil Interests) Act 1951. Section 13(2) of that Act provided: "In any action for damages for conversion or other proceedings which lie by virtue of any such omission, failure or contravention, the court may take account of the conduct of the defendant with a view, if the court thinks fit, to award exemplary damages in respect of the wrong sustained by the plaintiff".

[56] [1964] 1 All ER 367 at 411.

[57] [1972] 1 All ER 801; [1972] AC 1027.

[58] At 874 of the former report.

[59] [1993] 1 All ER 609.

Camelford in Cornwall by the introduction into that supply of approximately 20 tonnes of aluminium sulphate. The plaintiffs, who numbered 180, claimed to have suffered a variety of ill effects as a consequence of drinking the contaminated water. Individual writs and the master statement of claim alleged a number of different causes of action, including public nuisance, breach of statutory duty to take all reasonable care to provide a wholesome water supply,[60] negligence and the rule in *Rylands* v *Fletcher*. The defendants admitted that they were liable for breach of statutory duty and that they should therefore pay compensatory damages. However, they contested the plaintiff's claim that they were also entitled to exemplary and/or aggravated damages. This latter claim was based on a number of facts alleged to have occurred. These included:

- that the servants or agents of South West Water had acted in an arrogant and high-handed manner in ignoring complaints made by customers;

- that they wilfully and deliberately misled the plaintiffs as to the true state of affairs by sending a circular letter in which it was stated that the water was safe to drink;

- that the defendants withheld any accurate or consistent information as to what had happened and in respect of the state of the water; and

- that the defendants failed to give any proper information to the public health authorities, hospitals, doctors, pharmacists and their own customers as to any precautions that should be taken to minimise the ill effects of drinking the water.

At first instance, Wright J refused to strike out the claim for exemplary and aggravated damages on the basis that there was an arguable case that they might be recoverable in the public nuisance proceedings.[61] Before the Court of Appeal, counsel for the defendants made three main submissions on this issue: (i) that public nuisance was not a cause of action that could found a claim for exemplary damages; (ii) that if that submission was wrong, the allegations in the case did not bring the case into either of the two categories identified by Lord Devlin in *Rookes* v *Barnard*; (iii) that in any event, this was not an appropriate case for exemplary damages: it was really a claim for damages for personal injury.

The leading Court of Appeal judgment was delivered by Stuart-Smith LJ. His Lordship referred to several cases in which broad obiter statements had been made as to the availability of exemplary damages.[62] However, in none of these cases had the point expressly been argued that exemplary damages were not available in respect of public nuisance because there had been no

---

[60] Contrary to s. 31 and Schedule 3 to the Water Act 1945.

[61] See [1992] 4 All ER 574.

[62] Stuart-Smith LJ referred, amongst other cases, to *Bradford Metropolitan City Council* v *Arora* [1991] 3 All ER 545; a case concerning allegations of sex and race discrimination; and *Guppys (Bridport) Ltd* v *Brookling, Guppys (Bridport) Ltd* v *James* (1983) 14 HLR 1, a trespass case.

such award prior to the decision in *Rookes* v *Barnard*. Accordingly, Stuart-Smith LJ stated that:

> "...in my judgment there is no binding authority of this court which compels us to disregard the dicta of the House of Lords in *Cassell & Co Ltd* v *Broome*...[A]nd accordingly I would hold that before an award of exemplary damages can be made by any court or tribunal the tort must be one in respect of which such an award was made prior to 1964."[63]

In other words it was quite possible for the facts of a case to fall within the scope of one of Lord Devlin's categories but not satisfy the "cause of action test".[64]

What causes of action had, prior to Lord Devlin's speech, been regarded as those in respect of which exemplary damages might be awarded?

These were summarised by the Law Commission in a Report in 1997 as comprising the following: malicious prosecution; false imprisonment; assault and battery; defamation; trespass to land or goods; private nuisance; and, tortious interference with business. However, the Law Commission regarded the limitation of exemplary damages to cases where historically such damages had, perhaps more by chance than design, been awarded as irrational.[65]

An opportunity arose quite recently in *Kuddus* v *Chief Constable of Leicestershire Constabulary*[66] for the courts to reconsider these fundamental questions. In this case the appellant had complained to the police that a number of his personal possessions had been stolen from his flat. He was informed by an officer that the matter would be investigated. However, some two months later the officer forged the appellant's signature on a written statement withdrawing the complaint of theft. The result was that the police investigation was discontinued. A claim for exemplary damages in proceedings for misfeasance in public office brought by the appellant was struck out in the Leicester County Court. A subsequent appeal was dismissed by the Court of Appeal (Auld LJ dissenting). However, the appellant's appeal to the House of Lords succeeded: all five Law Lords who heard the case delivering a speech.

Lord Slynn delivered the first speech. After having drawn attention to Lord Devlin's remarks concerning the categories of case in which an award of exemplary damages may be appropriate,[67] Lord Slynn observed that:

---

[63] [1993] 1 All ER 609 at 620.

[64] See the Law Commission's Report No.247, *Aggravated, Exemplary and Restitutionary Damages* (December 1997) (para.4.24).

[65] See the Summary section of the above named report.

[66] [2001] 3 All ER 193.

[67] See above at pp. 169-170.

"It seems to me that there is nothing in Lord Devlin's analysis which requires that in addition to a claim falling within one of the two categories it should also constitute a cause of action which had before 1964 been accepted as grounding a claim for exemplary damages."[68]

Thus in short, for Lord Slynn, the "cause of action" test which the Court of Appeal had applied in *AB and others* v *South West Water Services Ltd* could not be based on the decision in *Rookes* v *Barnard* alone, but only on the combined effect of that case and the later House of Lords decision in *Cassell & Co Ltd* v *Broome*. Accordingly, it was necessary to look carefully at that case.[69]

In *Cassell & Co*, Lord Hailsham (with whom Lord Kilbrandon agreed) had noted in the context of Lord Devlin's first category that as well as covering servants of the government such as the police and other local officials exercising a power of arrest without warrant, it:

"*may be that in the future it will be held to include* other abuses of power without warrant by persons purporting to exercise legal authority ... I am not prepared to say without further consideration that a private individual misusing legal powers of private prosecution or arrest ... *might not at some future date* be assimilated into the first category."[70]

In Lord Slynn's opinion, this passage (with the added emphasis) provided support for the view that "Lord Hailsham was prepared in some respects to be more flexible than a rigid adherence to the 'pre-1964 cause of action' test suggests."[71] After having quoted quite lengthy passages from the speeches of Lords Reid, Wilberforce and Diplock in the same appeal, Lord Slynn stated that:

"... Lord Hailsham and Lord Kilbrandon appeared to attach importance to the existence of the pre-1964 cause of action test. It is arguable that Lord Reid and Lord Wilberforce took the same view. I am not, however, satisfied that it was their intention. Lord Reid lays much emphasis on 'principles' and 'categories' and 'class of case' rather than on specific or precise causes of action. It seems to me, despite his general agreement with Lord Hailsham, that Lord Wilberforce contemplated a wide interpretation of both 'government' and the excessive use of executive power. Accordingly, although I well understand the approach of the Court of Appeal in *AB* v *South West Water Services Ltd*, I do not consider that the House is bound by a clear or unequivocal decision in *Cassell & Co Ltd* v *Broome* to hold

---

[68] [2001] 3 All ER 193 at 196.

[69] In adopting this approach, Lord Slynn was in agreement with Lord Bingham MR (as he then was) who had observed in *AB and others* v *South West Water Services Ltd* that while the cause of action test "may involve a misreading of their Lordships' speeches in *Cassell & Co Ltd* v *Broome*" it was nevertheless "the basis upon which the Court of Appeal should, until corrected, proceed" ([1993] 1 All ER 609 at 626).

[70] [1972] 1 All ER 801 at 829-830 (emphasis added by Lord Slynn).

[71] [2001] 3 All ER 193 at 198.

that the power to award exemplary damages is limited to cases where it can be shown that the cause of action had been recognized before 1964 as justifying an award of exemplary damages."[72]

Thus in Lord Slynn's opinion, the approach which the Court of Appeal had adopted in *AB and other* v *South West Waters Services Ltd* was based on a misreading of their Lordships speeches in *Cassell & Co*, albeit the misreading was excusable given that it was "not easy to be sure whether the House ... ruled that the 'pre-1964' test had to be satisfied".[73] In further explaining the basis for his rejection of the cause of action test, Lord Slynn remarked that:

> "I do not think that courts should be required to undertake a trawl of the authorities in order to decipher whether awards of damages for misfeasance [in public office] pre-1964 might have included an award for exemplary damages. Such a task would be all the more difficult given the fact ... that the distinction between exemplary and aggravated damages was not until *Rookes* v *Barnard* clearly articulated. To adopt such a rigid rule seems to me to limit the future development of the law even within the restrictive categories adopted by Lord Devlin in a way which is contrary to the normal practice of the court ..."[74]

Lord Mackay delivered the second speech in *Kuddus* and asked whether it should be permissible for the defendant to accept that his officer's conduct fell within the scope of Lord Devlin's first category and yet still argue that the appeal ought to be dismissed on the basis that misfeasance in public office was not a cause of action recognized prior to *Rookes* v *Barnard* as founding a claim to exemplary damages. For Lord Mackay:

> "The genius of the common law is its capacity to develop and it appears strange that the law on this particular topic should be frozen by reference to decisions that had been taken prior to and including *Rookes* v *Barnard*."[75]

However, in Lord Mackay's opinion, this would not represent an illogical position if it was accepted that the inherent anomaly in exemplary damages meant that they should not be extended beyond their existing limits. In other words, Lord Mackay contended that:

> "... if one has accepted that damage has been done to the rationality of the law by the introduction of an anomaly which cannot be removed but which should not be enlarged, the consequence that the extent to which the anomaly persists is determined by the extent to which it has prevailed prior to the decision to limit it is a perfectly natural and reasonable result. In my opinion therefore criticism of *AB*

---

[72] *ibid*. at 200.
[73] *ibid*. at 197.
[74] *ibid*. at 200.
[75] *ibid*. at 202.

v *South West Water Services Ltd* on the basis that it is illogical is not well founded."[76]

It was therefore necessary to determine whether the decision in *AB and others* v *South West Water Services Ltd* was capable of being justified by the reasons on which it was based, which in turn required an examination of the principles on which *Rookes* v *Barnard* and *Cassell & Co Ltd* v *Broome* had been decided. As far as the latter case was concerned, Lord Mackay echoed the earlier remarks of Lord Slynn when he observed that he had not found the dicta very easy to construe.[77] However, Lord Mackay considered that:

> "... there is no basis in *Rookes* v *Barnard* for the view that the power to award exemplary damages exists only in torts which had been decided to have that character prior to 1964. A fair reading of the dicta in *Cassell & Co Ltd* v *Broome* do not effectively insert such a basis into the law and accordingly I am of the opinion that *AB* v *South West Water Services Ltd* was wrongly decided."[78]

The third speech was delivered by Lord Nicholls. With regard to the decision in *Rookes* v *Barnard*, Lord Nicholls drew attention to the two different interpretations which can be applied to Lord Devlin's categorisation. Put simply, the first of these interpretations requires that it is the factual circumstances of the case which determines the availability of exemplary damages rather than the cause of action. Thus provided that a defendant's conduct falls within the scope of either of Lord Devlin's categories[79] a claimant will be able to recover exemplary damages irrespective of the nature of the claim or the tort involved. This interpretation, which found favour with Widgery LJ in *Mafo* v *Adams*,[80] would allow the law to develop in that the availability of exemplary damages would not be confined to torts in respect of which recovery had occurred prior to 1964.

The second interpretation of Lord Devlin's categorisation is rather more limited. It holds that in *Rookes* v *Barnard*, Lord Devlin was not seeking to rationalise the law of exemplary damages. Rather, he was imposing a further limitation on recovery in that it was confined to those torts which had previously attracted the award of exemplary damages.

In Lord Nicholls' analysis, the first of these two interpretations had been rejected by the House of Lords in *Cassell & Co Ltd* v *Broome*. In support of this view, Lord Nicholls cited what he described as the "unambiguous

---

[76] *ibid.* at 203.

[77] *ibid.* at 205. Lord Hutton also stated that he found it "difficult to obtain clear guidance from the dicta in *Cassell & Co Ltd* v *Broome*" (at 216).

[78] *ibid.* at 205-206.

[79] As we shall see, Lord Nicholls felt that the categorisations could themselves be subject to criticism.

[80] [1969] 3 All ER 1404 at 1410-1411. These observations were expressly disagreed with by Lord Hailsham in *Cassell & Co Ltd* v *Broome* [1972] 1 All ER 801 at 828 – noted by Lord Nicholls, [2001] 3 All ER 193 at 208.

and forthright" view of Lord Diplock in *Cassell* where his Lordship had observed that:

> "*Rookes* v *Barnard* was not intended to extend the power to award exemplary or aggravated damages to particular torts for which they had not previously been awarded, such as negligence and deceit. Its express purpose was to restrict, not to expand, the anomaly of exemplary damages."[81]

It followed therefore, in Lord Nicholls' opinion that the majority of the House of Lords[82] in *Cassell* had adopted the first interpretation of Lord Devlin's categorisation, and that this interpretation had been "faithfully applied" by the Court of Appeal in *AB and others* v *South West Water Services Ltd* when it had determined that exemplary damages were not available in claims for public nuisance and negligence. Such reasoning therefore begged the question: what approach should the House of Lords now adopt in determining the appeal in *Kuddus*?

In Lord Nicholls' opinion, a way forward for their Lordships would be to decide that the law relating to exemplary damages should proceed on the basis of the first interpretation of Lord Devlin's categorisation.

> "It would mean that in the future, if the necessary factual circumstances are present, exemplary damages will be available across the board in every tort, including those torts where the absence of exemplary damages has long been established. This would revolutionise the law's approach to exemplary damages. It would mean that, far from being an undesirable anomaly whose use is to be restricted, exemplary damages are now regarded as a convenient tool which the law should seize and be able to use more widely."[83]

But was this the direction in which the law should develop? Lord Nicholls considered that three issues arose: whether the present state of the law on exemplary damages was satisfactory; whether, nonetheless, the matter was best left to Parliament; and finally, if the answers to the first two questions were in the negative, what should now be the law relating to exemplary damages?

In Lord Nicholls' opinion, the first and second questions could both be answered swiftly in the negative. Although the Law Commission had made the case for Parliamentary intervention,[84] government had taken the view that it would not legislate whilst there did not appear to be a clear consensus on the way forward.[85] Accordingly, it was necessary to have

---

[81] [1972] 1 All ER 801 at 874 – noted by Lord Nicholls, *ibid*.
[82] The views of Lords Hailsham, Wilberforce and Diplock.
[83] [2001] 3 All ER 193 at 209.
[84] See its report *Aggravated, Exemplary and Restitutionary Damages* (Law Com No 247) (1997), at para.5.3.
[85] See *Hansard* (HC Debates), 9 November 1999, col.502.

regard to the third issue, namely what stance should the law adopt on exemplary damages?

Lord Nicholls alluded to what he termed the "vitality" of the principle of exemplary damages.

> "The availability of exemplary damages has played a significant role in buttressing civil liberties, in claims for false imprisonment and wrongful arrest. From time to time cases do arise where awards of compensatory damages are perceived as inadequate to achieve a just result between the parties ... On occasion conscious wrongdoing by a defendant is so outrageous, his disregard of the claimant's rights so contumelious, that something more is needed to show that the law will not tolerate such behaviour. Without an award of exemplary damages, justice will not have been done. Exemplary damages, as a remedy of last resort, fill what otherwise would be a regrettable lacuna."[86]

Given the strength of the case for the retention of exemplary damages as a "remedial tool",[87] Lord Nicholls then moved on to consider *the* fundamental practical question, namely when "this tool should be available for use". His conclusions on this matter, which were not comprehensive given the limited nature of the submissions made by the parties on this point, and which were in any case *obiter*, are nevertheless worth noting.

For Lord Nicholls, the "underlying rationale" of exemplary damages:

> "...lies in the sense of outrage which a defendant's conduct sometimes evokes, a sense which is not always assuaged fully by a compensatory award of damages, even when the damages are increased to reflect emotional distress."[88]

Lord Nicholls took advantage, in this context, of the opportunity provided to comment upon Lord Devlin's categories. In relation to the first category, oppressive, arbitrary or unconstitutional action by the servants of the government, Lord Nicholls doubted whether it remained appropriate to exclude bullying by private companies from the reach of exemplary damages. In his opinion, the "enormous power" of some national and international companies cast doubt on the soundness of the distinction which Lord Devlin had made some 40 years previously.[89] Moreover, Lord Nicholls considered that:

---

[86] [2001] 3 All ER 193 at 210.

[87] Lord Nicholls also drew attention to how exemplary damages have been "perceived to be useful and valuable" in other common law jurisdictions such as Canada, Australia and New Zealand.

[88] [2001] 3 All ER 193 at 210.

[89] The reasoning here corresponds with that which has been applied by some judges when determining whether or not a non-public body should be susceptible to judicial review: see, for example, the remarks of Lloyd LJ in the leading case of *R v Panel on Takeovers and Mergers, ex parte Datafin* [1987] QB 815, where he remarked that the Panel had "enormous power" and a "giant's strength" prior to observing that: "The fact that it is self-regulating, which means

"...the validity of the dividing line drawn by Lord Devlin when formulating the first category is somewhat undermined by his second category, where the defendants are not confined to, and normally would not be, government officials or the like."[90]

Turning to the second category, wrongful conduct expected to yield a benefit in excess of any compensatory award likely to be made, Lord Nicholls noted that "the law of unjust enrichment has developed apace in recent years". In his opinion, if the law did need to be developed further, it should be on the same basis as for the first of Lord Devlin's categories, i.e. in the case of "outrageous conduct on the part of the defendant". Thus for Lord Nicholls, there was:

"... no obvious reason why, if exemplary damages are to be made available, the profit motive should suffice but a malicious motive should not."[91]

Lord Hutton delivered the fourth speech in *Kuddus*. He expressed:

"...no concluded opinion on the question whether exemplary damages should continue to be awarded in England, but I think that a number of cases decided by the courts in Northern Ireland during the past 30 years of terrorist violence give support to the opinion of Lord Devlin in *Rookes* v *Barnard* that in certain cases the awarding of exemplary damages serves a valuable purpose in restraining the arbitrary and outrageous use of executive power and in vindicating the strength of the law."[92]

The cases referred to in this statement were *Lavery* v *Ministry of Defence*[93] and *Pettigrew* v *Northern Ireland Office*.[94] In the former case, exemplary damages were awarded on appeal where a solider who was part of an army patrol had, without any provocation whatsoever, kneed a 16-year-old boy in the groin, struck him on the head with the butt of his rifle and then handcuffed him. In the latter case, the plaintiff had been a prisoner in the Maze prison who had helped other prisoners to escape. During the escape, one prison officer died and another was seriously wounded. Once order had been restored, a number of prisoners were transferred from one prison block to another. During the process of transfer, the plaintiff was punched and kicked by prison officers and dog-handlers did not properly restrain their dogs from nipping and biting him. An award of exemplary damages in this case was made to "mark the disapproval of the court, to teach that such conduct does not pay, and to act as a deterrent against this type of

---

presumably, that it is not subject to regulation by others ... makes it not less but more appropriate that it should be subject to judicial review by the courts" (at p 845). Nicholls J (as he then was) was the third member of the Court of Appeal (after Sir John Donaldson MR and Lloyd LJ) that heard the appeal in *Datafin*.

[90] [2001] 3 All ER 193 at 210.

[91] *ibid*. at 211.

[92] *ibid*. at 212.

[93] [1984] NI 99.

[94] [1990] NI 179.

conduct against prisoners being repeated in the future."[95] In Lord Hutton's opinion:

"... the power to award exemplary damages in such cases serves to uphold and vindicate the rule of law because it makes clear that the courts will not tolerate such conduct. It serves to deter such actions in future as such awards will bring home to officers in command of individual units that discipline must be maintained at all times."[96]

Moreover, for Lord Hutton, an award of exemplary damages was a useful tool "where one of a group of soldiers or police officers commits some outrageous act in the course of a confused and violent confrontation" since such an award was not dependent upon identifying the wrongdoer. In these circumstances:

"... an award of exemplary damages to mark the court's condemnation of the conduct can be made against the Minister of Defence or the Chief Constable under the principle of vicarious liability even if the individual at fault cannot be identified."[97]

The final speech in *Kuddus* was that of Lord Scott. Although Lord Scott agreed that the appeal should be allowed, this was with some reluctance. Indeed, rather than extend the exemplary principle, Lord Scott would have been "receptive to a submission that exemplary damages awards should no longer be available in civil proceedings".[98]

Lord Scott commenced his speech by drawing attention to the anomalous character of exemplary damages in the light of what he termed "the fundamental principle of damages", i.e. that they are compensatory rather than punitive. In support of this view, Lord Scott cited several passages from speeches delivered in *Cassell & Co Ltd* v *Broome*, including the following remarks from Lord Diplock which were made in respect of Lord Devlin's first category:

"... in view of the developments, particularly in the last 20 years, in adapting the old remedies by prerogative writ and declaratory action to check unlawful abuse of power by the executive, the award of exemplary damages in civil actions for tort against individual government servants seems a blunt instrument to use for this purpose today."[99]

In Lord Scott's opinion:

"One of the great developments of the common law since the time of *Rookes* v *Barnard* has been in the area of public law and judicial

---

[95] *ibid.* at 181-182. Lord Hutton gave judgment in this case.
[96] [2001] 3 All ER 193 at 214.
[97] *ibid.* at 215. Note that Lord Hutton doubted whether the behaviour in *Kuddus* itself was of sufficient gravity to bring it within Lord Devlin's first category.
[98] *ibid.* at 222.
[99] [1972] 1 All ER 801 at 873.

review to which Lord Diplock referred. Oppressive, arbitrary and unconstitutional acts by members of the executive can be remedied through civil proceedings brought in the High Court. The remedies the court can provide include awards of damages, declarations of right and, in most cases, injunctions. The developments since Lord Diplock's remarks in *Cassell & Co Ltd* v *Broome* have transformed the ability of the ordinary citizen to obtain redress. The continuing need in the year 2001 for exemplary damages as a civil remedy in order to control, deter and punish acts falling within Lord Devlin's first category is not in the least obvious."[100]

It may be remembered that in making the case for the retention of exemplary damages, Lord Hutton had referred to two cases decided by the courts in Northern Ireland. By contrast, Lord Scott was not convinced that these judgments evidenced the need for an award of exemplary damages. In his words:

"... I do not follow why an appropriate award of aggravated damages[101] would not have served to vindicate the law just as effectively as the fairly moderate awards of exemplary damages that were made. The condemnation by the trial judge of the conduct in question would have been expressed no differently. As to deterrence, in a case where the defendant is not the wrongdoer, and the damages are in any event going to be met out of public funds, how can it be supposed that the award of exemplary damages adds anything at all to the deterrent effect of the trial judge's findings of fact in favour of the injured person and his condemnation of the conduct in question? The proposition that exemplary damage awards against such defendants as the Ministry of Defence or the Northern Ireland Office, or, for that matter, the defendant, can have a deterrent effect is, in my respectful opinion, fanciful. It is possible that exemplary damages awards against the actual wrongdoers which they would have to meet out of their own pockets would have a deterrent effect upon them and their colleagues. But that is not what happened in either of the two cases."[102]

Furthermore, the question whether exemplary damages could be recovered where a defendant's alleged liability is merely vicarious was, in Lord Scott's opinion, a point of "considerable importance" not raised in argument in the present appeal. In his Lordship's opinion, however:

"The objection to exemplary damages awards in vicarious liability cases seems to me to be fundamental. The only acceptable justification of exemplary damages awards in cases falling within

---

[100] [2001] 3 All ER 193 at 221.
[101] For this distinction see further below, p. 184.
[102] *ibid.* at 222.

Lord Devlin's first category ... is that the conduct complained of has been so outrageous as to warrant a punitive response."[103]

However, Lord Scott continued:

"The other side of the coin is, in my opinion, equally valid: the defendant should not be liable to pay exemplary damages unless he has committed punishable behaviour. This principle leaves no room for an award of exemplary damages against an individual whose alleged liability is vicarious only and who has not done anything that constitutes punishable behaviour."[104]

Finally, Lord Scott observed that:

"It appears to me that, silently and without any proper or principled justification for it, a system of vicarious punishment of public employers for the misfeasances of their employees has crept into our civil law... In my opinion vicarious punishment, via an award of exemplary damages, is contrary to principle and should be rejected."[105]

How to sum up the decision in *Kuddus*? It is clear from their Lordships that the law took a wrong turn when the decisions in *Rookes* v *Barnard* and *Cassell & Co Ltd* v *Broome* were construed to mean that in order for a claimant to recover exemplary damages he had to satisfy the "cause of action" test in addition to showing that his claim fell within one or other of Lord Devlin's two categories. The Court of Appeal decision in *AB and others* v *South West Water Services Ltd* has therefore been overruled and the issue now arises how far the decision in *Kuddus* has opened the door for a claimant to recover exemplary damages where he is the victim of a public nuisance.

Although the decision in *AB and others* v *South West Water Services Ltd* is no longer good law, it provides a useful starting point for considering this question. The Court of Appeal noted the earlier case of *Bell* v *Midland Railway Co.*[106] In discussing that case Stuart-Smith LJ said that he was:

"...quite satisfied that, if exemplary damages are to be awarded for nuisance, such awards should be confined to those cases of private nuisance where there is deliberate and wilful interference with the plaintiff's rights of enjoyment of land where the defendant has calculated that the profit or benefit for him will exceed the damages he may have to pay...[W]here there has been a public nuisance, a plaintiff who can show particular damage can sue in tort. But it is an

---

[103] *ibid.* at 226.
[104] *ibid.*
[105] *ibid.* at 228.
[106] (1861) 10 C.B.N.S. 287, 142 ER 462.

entirely different class of case; there is no conduct deliberately and wilfully aimed at the plaintiffs as individuals."[107]

Thus in the opinion of Stuart-Smith LJ there was logic to the idea that exemplary damages might be recoverable in a claim for private nuisance, but not in respect of a public nuisance.

Sir Thomas Bingham MR was also at pains to emphasise the difference between private and public nuisance, expressing the view that the anomalous position of exemplary damages would seem even more so where the defendant's conduct had already attracted the sanctions of the criminal law.[108] Moreover, at a practical level, Sir Thomas Bingham MR considered that there were objections to an award of exemplary damages for public nuisance. These difficulties related to calculation of the award, given the potential size of the class of plaintiffs. In his Lordship's words:

> "...in the case of a public nuisance affecting hundreds or even thousands of plaintiffs, how can the court assess the sum of exemplary damages to be awarded to any one of them to punish or deter the defendant without knowing at the outset the number of successful plaintiffs and the approximate size of the total bill for exemplary damages which the defendant must meet?"[109]

Quite apart from such general concerns as regards the applicability of exemplary damages to public nuisance cases both Stuart-Smith LJ and Sir Thomas Bingham MR considered whether the actual facts of the case before them fell within the scope of either of the categories referred to by Lord Devlin. They both concluded that they did not.

With regard to the first category – oppressive, arbitrary or unconstitutional action by the servants of the government – Stuart-Smith LJ observed in respect of South West Water:

> "At the time of these events the defendants were a nationalised body set up under statute for a commercial purpose, namely the supply of water. They have since been privatised, but carry on essentially the same functions. Although it is conceivable that governmental functions could be delegated or entrusted to a nationalised industry with appropriate powers to carry out such functions, perhaps for example with powers of entry and search, I do not think it can possibly be argued that the defendants' servants or agents were performing such a function in this case. A serious mishap had occurred in the course of the defendants' commercial operations, their reaction to it was open to serious criticism if the allegations in the statement of claim are true ... [B]ut their conduct was not an exercise of executive power derived from government, central or local, and no

---

[107] [1993] 1 All ER 609 at 621.
[108] South West Water had been prosecuted for a public nuisance.
[109] [1993] 1 All ER 609 at 627. Remarks of a similar nature were also made by Stuart-Smith LJ at 624.

amount of rhetoric describing it as arbitrary, oppressive, unconstitutional, arrogant or high-handed makes it so."[110]

Dealing with the same issue, Sir Thomas Bingham MR rejected any analogy that might be drawn between the first category and the identification of either a "public body" for the purposes of an application for judicial review, or an "emanation of the state" in the context of requiring a Member State to comply with its European Community Law obligations. In his Lordship's opinion:

> "We are here concerned with a judge-made principle of domestic private law, devised to address a particular problem, and other rules arising in different contexts seem to me to have little bearing".[111]

With regard to the conduct complained of, Sir Thomas Bingham MR observed that it was:

> "…quite unlike the abuses of power which Lord Devlin had in mind and I cannot regard the defendants … as wielding executive or governmental power. They were a publicly owned utility acting as a monopoly supplier of a necessary commodity, enjoying certain statutory powers and subject to certain obligations, but they were not acting as an instrument or agent of government."[112]

Turning to the second category identified by Lord Devlin – conduct calculated by a defendant to make himself a profit which will exceed the compensation payable to the plaintiff – Stuart-Smith LJ stated that:

> "The essence of the second category is that the tort is knowingly committed for the purpose of gaining some pecuniary or other advantage. The award is to show that tort does not pay. It cannot possibly be said that the defendants continued the nuisance for this purpose. In my judgment what the allegation amounts to is an attempt by the defendants to cover up the fact that they had committed a tort. That may be reprehensible but not uncommon conduct. The object of such conduct may well be to limit the amount of damages payable to the … victim, but that is an entirely different concept from that involved in the second category."[113]

---

[110] At 622.

[111] At 628.

[112] At 628.

[113] At 623. In the post *Kuddus* case of *Galun* v *Wright-Bevans* [2002] EWHC Ch 1099, the plaintiff recovered, inter alia, the sum of £35,000 in *exemplary* damages where the development of a garage block by the first defendant had effectively prevented the claimant's use of a right of way from the road. Such a right of way had only been abandoned on the basis of an assurance given by the first defendant that an alternative means of access would be made available. In the opinion of Kirkham J, it was "quite plain that what the first Defendant was aiming to do was to make a profit on the deal, and in achieving this it seems to me that he simply rode roughshod over the Claimant's rights and in complete disregard of the promise which he had made to the Claimant to provide rights over the new access road". The first defendant's conduct therefore fell within the second category identified by Lord Devlin in *Rookes* v *Barnard*.

These views were of course *obiter*. Nevertheless, they constitute quite a powerful argument that judges should be circumspect on their application of the principles surrounding the award of exemplary damages to public nuisance claims. Although the recovery of exemplary damages for a public nuisance may have moved a step closer with the dismantling of the cause of action test, there are still significant obstacles for a claimant to overcome.

Aggravated damages

It may be remembered that the plaintiffs in *AB and others* v *South West Water Services Ltd* sought *aggravated* damages in addition to, or as an alternative to, exemplary damages. Since the decision of the House of Lords in *Rookes* v *Barnard* 'aggravated damages' have been recognised as a further distinct category of damages. In that case, Lord Devlin remarked that:

> "... it is very well established that in cases where the damages are at large the jury (or the judge if the award is left to him) can take into account the motives and conduct of the defendant where they *aggravate* the injury done to the plaintiff. There may be malevolence or spite or the manner of committing the wrong may be such as to injure the plaintiff's proper feelings of dignity and pride. These are matters which the jury can take into account in assessing the appropriate compensation."[114]

Although the compensatory nature of aggravated damages is clear from the final sentiment expressed in this passage, reference to the motive of the defendant does serve to confuse matters in that it also suggests that there is a punitive element to this head of damages. The Law Commission has drawn attention to what it describes as the "continuing confusion in the case law" regarding the purpose and function of aggravated damages. Despite Lord Devlin's attempts to clarify matters in *Rookes* v *Barnard*, its Report notes that "the residual perception is arguably that they retain a quasi-punitive quality".[115]

Accordingly, in order to clarify the law, the Law Commission has proposed that legislation be enacted to provide that aggravated damages only be awarded to compensate a person for his or her mental distress and, that the label "damages for mental distress" be used rather than aggravated damages. Moreover, the Law Commission has stressed that the compensatory nature of this head of damages should be preserved. To date, no such legislation has appeared on the statute book.

Returning to *AB and others* v *South West Water Services Ltd*, the plaintiff's claim for aggravated damages for the "high-handed" way in which the defendants dealt with the incident failed. Both Stuart-Smith LJ

---

[114] [1964] 1 All ER 367 at 407 (emphasis added).
[115] *Aggravated, Exemplary and Restitutionary Damages*, para. 2.3.

and Sir Thomas Bingham MR were of the opinion that any prolonged pain and suffering which the plaintiffs had endured as a consequence of the nuisance could be compensated by way of ordinary damages, even where this had been exacerbated by the defendants' conduct.

A CONTINUING NEED FOR PUBLIC NUISANCE?

At one time, it was a defence for someone sued for private nuisance to be able to show that the nuisance in question was in fact public in nature.[116] As we have seen, however, the overlap between public and private nuisance is now such that both are often pleaded by the same claimant in proceedings before a court. Since this is the case, we must inevitably ask ourselves whether there is still a place for public nuisance in the corpus of the law. In other words, is it sufficiently distinct from private nuisance to merit a separate existence?

The short answer to this question would appear to be "yes". Although there is a significant overlap between public and private nuisance, some important distinctions do still remain. For example, there is the issue of duration. This was highlighted by Denning LJ during the course of his judgment in the *PYA Quarries* case. In that case, his Lordship observed that:

> "... a private nuisance always involves some degree of repetition or continuance... But an isolated act may amount to a public nuisance if it is done under such circumstances that the public's right to condemn it should be vindicated."[117]

A further distinction relates to the issue of private nuisance as a tort which exists to protect proprietary interests. Until quite recently, the law of private nuisance was developing in such a way that the requirement of a proprietary interest in land in order to be able to sue no longer appeared to be significant. This much was evident from the decision of the Court of Appeal in *Khorasandjian* v *Bush*.[118] However, as has been noted,[119] that decision was overruled by the House of Lords in *Hunter* v *Canary Wharf Ltd*,[120] where it was firmly reasserted by the majority of their Lordships that a person who had no rights to the land affected by a nuisance cannot bring an action in private nuisance. The consequence of this decision for public nuisance ought not to be overlooked. Whilst it may be overstating the case to say that *Hunter* has breathed new life into the law of public nuisance,

---

[116] See J R Spencer, [1989] 48 CLJ 55 at 59. Such a defence succeeded in ousting the jurisdiction of the courts of common law in that public nuisance was (and is) a crime and hence was a matter for the exclusive jurisdiction of the criminal courts. However, as the author notes, that exclusivity ceased in the sixteenth century when the common law courts recognized the right of the individual to sue in respect of a public nuisance where he or she could show that they had suffered some form of "special" damage.

[117] [1957] 2 QB 169 at 192.

[118] [1993] 3 All ER 669.

[119] See pp. 75-76 above.

[120] [1997] 2 All ER 426.

their Lordships decision has served to reinforce the important distinction between it and private nuisance, i.e. the need for a proprietary interest. Had their Lordships in *Hunter* endorsed the decision in *Khorasandjian*, the natural consequence of such a ruling may have been the disappearance of public nuisance as a separate form of nuisance, at least in terms of nuisances arising from noise, smells, smoke, fumes, etc.

Thus it might be argued that prior to the decision in *Hunter*, public nuisance was under threat from the development of the law of private nuisance. It might also be argued that it has faced an equally significant threat from a different direction; statute. Much of the ground which public nuisance formerly occupied has now been taken over by statute, principally in the form of the statutory nuisance provisions.[121] In the environmental context, therefore, it would seem that public nuisance has largely been left to fill the gaps which may exist in that statutory regime.

---

[121] See Part III of the Environmental Protection Act 1990, discussed in Chapters 11 and 12.

Chapter 6

STANDARD OF LIABILITY, REMOTENESS OF DAMAGE AND PROOF OF CAUSALITY: COMMON LAW PRINCIPLES IN ACTION

INTRODUCTION

The previous four chapters have examined in some detail the scope of civil liability in the contexts of private nuisance and public nuisance. These torts have been treated extensively because they may legitimately be regarded as the principal "environmental" torts.

In this chapter we consider the application of the tort of negligence and the strict liability *"Rule in Rylands* v *Fletcher"* to claims in this context. However, in relation to these torts a rather different approach is adopted. Rather than seek to produce here a version "in miniature" of what may be found in any of the standard works on the English law of tort, this chapter focuses quite closely on a number of cases decided by the English courts in recent years. These cases shed a good deal of light on the inter-relationship between the principles of nuisance, negligence and *Rylands* v *Fletcher*, and as such may be regarded as providing a useful insight into these common law principles "in action".

The principal issues explored in these cases will be:

(i) the respective ambits of strict liability and fault-based liability in the context of operations which may have some propensity to do harm by way of pollution;

(ii) the application in such cases of rules relating to "remoteness of damage"; and

(iii) the basic principles which apply to the requirement that a causal connection should exist between the conduct of the defendant and the harm suffered by the claimant.

STANDARD OF LIABILITY AND REMOTENESS OF DAMAGE: *CAMBRIDGE WATER COMPANY* v *EASTERN COUNTIES LEATHER*[1]

The material facts

The material facts of this case were essentially quite simple. A company producing leather products (ECL) had over a quite substantial period of time used solvent de-greasing chemicals as part of its leather preparation process at Sawston Mill, an "industrial village", a few miles outside

---

[1] [1994] 1 All ER 53; [1994] 2 AC 264.

Cambridge.[2] Quantities of the chemicals were from time to time spilled, with the result that over a period of time, they made their way down through the surface of the ground or floor, through the soil beneath, and down into the rock strata below. Here the chemical became absorbed into the saturated rock, so contaminating the groundwater. The chemical then moved very slowly laterally through the saturated rock, driven under hydrogeological pressure. In due course it reached an extraction bore-hole, a mile or more away, used for domestic water supply purposes by Cambridge Water Company (CWC). The water from the bore-hole, being so contaminated, failed to meet drinking water standards which had, subsequent to the spillages, been set by the European Community.[3] The cost to CWC of securing and bringing into operation an alternative "clean" domestic water supply – a new bore-hole further up the aquifer – was in excess of £1 million. The water supply company claimed compensation from the polluting leather company in respect of this expense.

The case proceeded from first instance, through the Court of Appeal, to final decision in the House of Lords. In each court emphasis focused on somewhat different arguments. For this reason we consider below not just the issues which arose for decision in the highest court, but also some of the matters reviewed in the lower courts.[4]

Establishing the facts

The summary of material facts presented above disguises the technical complexity of the survey work which was necessary in order to prove those facts. At the time when CWC first became aware of the contamination of their bore-hole the company was unaware of the source of that contaminant: remember that the chemical had moved laterally through the underground strata for about a mile from the point of spillage. The claimant company commissioned the British Geological Survey (BGS) to survey the area surrounding the bore-hole in order to assess the direction of flow of groundwater,[5] an exercise which required not only the drilling of numerous test bore-holes but also the modelling of the effects of the water company's water extraction activities on the "natural" flow of the underground water. On the basis of such survey data, gained from a survey period extending over more than a year, the BGS was able to chart a line at ground level – somewhere along which might be discoverable the point at which the chemicals had been spilled to ground. On tracking that line the

---

[2] Chief amongst these was the solvent perchloroethene (PCE).

[3] These were set out in the Drinking Water Directive, 80/778/EEC.

[4] For the first instance judgment of Kennedy J, see [1993] Env LR 116; for the Court of Appeal, see [1993] Env LR 287.

[5] The direction and rate of groundwater flows cannot be reliably assessed by reference to the lie of the surface of the land. Much depends on the underground strata and hydrogeological pressures, resulting sometimes in groundwater flowing in an opposite direction to that which would be anticipated by reference only to surface topography.

defendant tannery site (a likely user of the offending chemical) was identified.[6]

Some general considerations

Before considering the law applicable to these facts a number of significant general features of the claim may usefully be noted.

First, the claim (to over £1 million) was fairly substantial. The defendant company was by no means a "small business", but was not what one would regard as a large corporation. The company employed a little over a hundred employees at its production site in a rural area not far from the city of Cambridge. The truth is not a matter of public record, but at the time of the litigation it was widely thought that the defendant's liability insurance was not such as to cover the claim, or to cover the claim in full. As the case moved through the courts, and inexorably towards the House of Lords, the litigation attracted a fair amount of attention in the financial and business press.[7] The general assumption in this coverage was that if the company were to be held liable to pay the damages sought the consequence, in the absence of insurance protection, would be that the company would be forced into closure, resulting in social and economic harm within the local rural community.[8]

A second aspect of the case which deserves initial comment may be identified by asking: What did the sum of more than £1 million claimed in the action represent? Notwithstanding that *Cambridge Water* is commonly described as an environmental damage case, it should be noted that this very substantial sum did not represent what might be described as cleanup

---

[6] It is believed to be the case that initial modelling of groundwater flows, not taking into account the effects of bore-hole water abstraction in drawing groundwater towards the bore-hole, had produced a ground level flow line which disclosed no potential culprit. The survey undertaken by BGS has subsequently become the leading authoritative scientific work on the behaviour and characteristics of chlorinated organic industrial solvents in groundwater.

[7] It is interesting to note how the general tenor of press coverage altered as the case proceeded through the various courts. At first it was written about as a case where an alleged polluter was to be "brought to book" and made to pay for harm caused. In due course, concern began to focus rather more on the evils which might follow (in this case, and more generally) by a ruling in favour of liability. The water company, which began as the "unfortunate victim seeking redress" became cast, eventually, as almost the uncaring "villain of the piece"!

[8] Whether or not this assumption was ever well-founded may be a matter of some doubt. Assuming that, in the absence of insurance coverage, a company cannot pay a debt out of current liquid assets it may seek to borrow such sums. Whether it may be successful in finding a lender will depend very much on the value of its assets (especially land) in order that it may provide security for the loan, and also the ongoing profitability of the business in order that it may be able to cover loan repayments. In this situation the company will continue to operate and employ staff, albeit subject to loan repayment obligations. In a more extreme case where no loan can be secured to pay the judgment debt the company may be forced into administration (or similar). In such a case the ongoing business will be sold to a new company and the proceeds of that sale will be used, so far as the purchase price permits, to pay debts owed by the insolvent company. The new operator of the business will take over the concern quit of the judgment debt. If the business is essentially profitable there is no reason why the net result should involve the workforce losing their jobs. New company and new management certainly, but not an end to the businesses operations. The spectre described in some parts of the press of social deprivation following closure of a village's economic life-line, would seem to have been somewhat fanciful.

costs. It did not reflect money spent de-contaminating the water supply
from the contaminated bore-hole, and still less did it represent sums spent
seeking to de-contaminate the groundwater aquifer more generally. The
water supply company had, it seems both for technical and for economic
reasons, chosen instead to disconnect the polluted water-supply bore-hole
from its mains supply pipelines, and to spend the sum claimed (£1 million
plus) in finding and connecting to its distribution network a different water
supply source. The case is not, therefore, one involving a claim in respect
of the cost of environmental cleanup. Rather the claim related to economic
loss consequential on damage having been done to an asset belonging to
the water company. To adopt the language of the sale of goods, the
measure of damages sought reflected the cost of *replacement* rather than
the cost of *repair* of the item harmed.[9]

This prompts further questions. Environmental lawyers may,
understandably, prefer civil liability rules which seem to favour the repair
of environmental assets, rather than simply allow recoupment of the cost of
moving towards the exploitation of another, as yet untainted,
environmental resource. If we find that the law holds a defendant liable to
pay compensation on the basic facts described above, we would want
therefore also to ask whether there would also have been liability to full
damages had the water company chosen what we may assume to have been
a more expensive option of having installed and operated expensive water
purification equipment, and thereby allowing it to continue to supply for
public consumption water obtained from the tainted bore-hole. Would the
defendant be required to pay compensation to cover the full cost of this
more expensive option, or could the defendant argue (as is commonly
allowed within our general law on damages) that the plaintiff should have
taken reasonable steps to mitigate the damage (loss) flowing from the
defendant's wrongful acts, and that this would here have required
"replacement" rather than "repair" of the damaged asset? As and when
they may be called upon so to adjudicate, the judges will be faced here
with a stark choice between issues of economic efficiency within a system
of civil compensation and issues of more general environmental public
policy.

A third preliminary comment on the case is this. *Cambridge Water*
illustrates a feature of environmental damage cases which may set them
apart from certain other contexts of civil liability for which special pro-
claimant liability principles may be regarded as appropriate. It will be
evident from the facts described above that this is a context in which quite
small enterprises (even individuals acting alone) have the capacity to do
very significant (and costly to compensate/repair) environmental damage.
Without seeking to exaggerate the point there may be a significant
difference between litigation in this context and litigation in other
"disaster" contexts. Aeroplane manufacturers, oil tanker owners and
operators and pharmaceutical companies have, in the modern world, to be

---

[9] For action by the Environment Agency to seek that ECL should take steps to clean up the
polluted aquifer, see the facts of *Eastern Counties Leather Plc* v *Easter Counties Leather Group
Ltd* [2002] Env LR 34 (Ch D); [2003] Env LR 13 (CA).

substantial entities in order to do business at all. In the context of environmental damage there exists no such essential, inherent, correlation between corporate size and capacity to do harm. Some care should perhaps therefore attach to the design of proposals for wide-ranging civil liability rules in the environmental damage context.

And one further preliminary point. Let us assume that the claim in a case such as this will succeed, and that the damages are paid in full. Who exactly will benefit from such an award? The answer can only be a matter of conjecture. However, we can be confident that the environment will not benefit directly.[10] It has already been noted that the sum claimed did not reflect cleanup costs. Nor would there be any obligation on a plaintiff to use any sums recovered for cleanup purposes.

If benefit to the environment from the award of damages is unlikely, who might be likely to benefit? Maybe the customers of the water company? After all, we can fairly presume that the costs which form the subject-matter of the claim have, during the period it has taken to bring the claim, been borne by those who have paid charges for their water supply. It may now be time for those customers to benefit? Or maybe the plaintiff company would have other ideas? Maybe there would be felt to be better uses to which to put this money as compared with reductions in subsequent water bills? Maybe it would be put towards capital investment projects (for eventual customer benefit); maybe it would go to fund better pay for employees of the company; maybe it would be used to enhance the remuneration of the directors who so doggedly fought the case; maybe the financial benefit should simply contribute to annual profits and be declared in shareholder dividends? The point to remember is that under English law a plaintiff is free to use his damages as he or she pleases. This fact may be relevant to the role to be played by "civil liability" within the broader context of liability for environmental damage.

The decision at first instance: Kennedy J

Kennedy J noted that the plaintiff had argued its claim chiefly on the *Rule in Rylands* v *Fletcher*, but also in nuisance and in negligence. The application of each of these causes of action was considered in turn.

The ambit of the strict liability principle in *Rylands* v *Fletcher* is commonly described in the words used by Blackburn J in the Exchequer Chamber in the case of that name. In considering the liability of a landowner who had stored large quantities of water in a reservoir on his land, where water had escaped through underground channels onto his neighbour's land and thereby done harm, Blackburn J formulated a principle which made liability independent of the plaintiff having to show fault on the part of the defendant neighbour.

---

[10] There is perhaps some possibility that there may be environmental benefit of an *indirect* nature: such benefit which would follow should the clear imposition of civil liability in a case such as this lead to greater care being taken by companies that their activities should not cause environmental damage.

"We think the true rule of law is, that the person who for his own purposes brings onto his lands and collects and keeps there anything likely to do mischief if it escapes, must do so at his peril, and, if he does not do so, is prima facie answerable for all the damage which is the natural consequence of the escape. He can excuse himself by shewing that the escape was owing to the plaintiff's default: or perhaps that the escape was the consequence of *vis major*, or the Act of God; but as nothing of that sort exists here it is unnecessary to inquire what excuse would be sufficient. The general rule, as stated above, seems on principle just. The person whose ... mine is flooded by the water from his neighbour's reservoir, or whose cellar is invaded by the filth from his neighbour's privy ... is damnified without any fault of his own; and it seems both reasonable and just that the neighbour, who has brought something on his own property which was not naturally there, harmless to others so long as it is confined to his own property, should be obliged to make good the damage which ensues if he does not succeed in confining it to his own property. But for his act in bringing it there no mischief could have accrued, and it seems but just that he should at his peril keep it there so that no mischief may accrue, or answer for the natural and anticipated consequences."[11]

Blackburn J's classic formulation of this principle was expressly approved by Lord Cairns on appeal in the House of Lords.[12] Lord Cairns commented on the notions of "natural" and "non-natural" use of land in the following terms:

"... [I]f the defendants, not stopping at the natural use of their close, had desired to use it for any purpose which I may term a non-natural use, for the purpose of introducing into the close that which in its natural condition was not in or upon it, for the purpose of introducing water ... in quantities ... and if in consequence of their doing so, the water came to escape and to pass off into the close of the plaintiff, then it appears to me that that which the defendants were doing they were doing at their own peril ..."[13]

Lord Cranworth similarly explained:

"If a person brings, or accumulates, on his land anything which, if it should escape, may cause damage to his neighbour, he does so at his peril. If it does escape, and cause damage, he is responsible, however careful he may have been, and whatever precautions he may have taken to prevent the damage."[14]

---

[11] [1866] 1 Exch. 265 at 280.

[12] [1868] 3 App.Cas 330; [1861-73] All ER Rep 1.

[13] At 13 of the latter report.

[14] At 14. It will be noted that there were only two opinions delivered in the House of Lords in respect of the appeal. For an interesting discussion as to whether or not the House was therefore

Applying these statements, Kennedy J held first that the solvent chemicals which had been stored at the defendant's works fell within the category of substances "likely to do damage if they escaped". On that basis the next question was how such storage, in the quantities as had occurred, should be viewed in terms of the requirement that the storage or accumulation be a "non-natural" rather than a "natural" use of the defendant's land.

On this matter Kennedy J took the view that the law had moved on somewhat since the decision in *Rylands*, mitigating the rigour of that rule. Kennedy quoted from Lord Moulton in *Rickards v Lothian*.[15]

> "It is not every use to which land is put that brings into play that principle. It must be some special use bringing with it increased danger to others, and must not merely be the ordinary use of land or such use as is proper for the general benefit of the community."[16]

The final words of this quotation suggest that whether or not a use of land should be regarded as "natural" or "non-natural" for this purpose may depend, at least in part, on an assessment of whether the use serves to benefit only the defendant or whether the use is one from which "general benefit" may attach.[17] Indeed, Kennedy J adopted this principle:

> "... [I]n considering whether the storage of organochlorines as an adjunct to a manufacturing process is a non-natural use of land, I must consider whether that storage created special risks for adjacent occupiers and whether the activity was for the general benefit of the community."[18]

Applying this test he concluded that the storage of the chemicals by ECL did not amount to a non-natural user of land for the purpose of the application of the *Rule in Rylands v Fletcher*.

As we shall see below, when the case came on appeal to the House of Lords a quite different view was expressed by Lord Goff in his leading speech, eschewing the importation of notions of "community benefit" into the issue of natural/non-natural use. For Kennedy J, however, this notion allowed the "innumerable small works that one sees up and down the country with drums stored in their yards" to fall outside the principle in *Rylands*. Although such storage might present some hazards such hazards

---

quorate (the Standing Orders at the time required that at least three Law Lords hear an appeal), see Heuston, 'Who was the Third Lord in *Rylands v Fletcher*?' (1970) 86 LQR 160.

[15] [1912] AC 263.

[16] At 279.

[17] Note also similar statements in *Read v J.Lyons & Co* [1947] 156: Lord Simon at 169 and Lord Macmillan at 174. Note also that in *British Celanese Ltd v A H Hunt (Capacitors) Ltd* [1969] 1 WLR 959, Lawton J held that: "the manufacture of electrical and electronic components in 1964, which is the material date, cannot be adjudged to be a special use nor can the bringing and storing on the premises of metal foil be a special use in itself... The metal foil was there for use in the manufacture of goods of a common type which at all material times were needed for the general benefit of the community" (at 963).

[18] [1993] Env LR 116 at 139.

were "part of the life of every citizen" and therefore not such as to attract the special strict liability principle.[19]

Having for this reason found against the plaintiff's claim under *Rylands* v *Fletcher* Kennedy J moved on to consider the claims in nuisance and in negligence. The evidence before him suggested that the defendant's handling of the solvent chemical during the years in question (from about 1950 to 1976) could properly be characterised as having not displayed reasonable care. The chemical was supplied in large drums and spillages occurred with some regularity as the contents of these drums were emptied for use.[20] Accordingly, the criterion of "carelessness" within the law of negligence was satisfied.

The key issue, however, in the context of both the nuisance and negligence claims, was whether the harm which had been suffered by the plaintiff fell within the rules of "remoteness of damage" which governed the scope of liability.

Kennedy J took the view that the same principle of remoteness of damage applied to the claim in nuisance as to the claim in negligence. Applying the broad principles which had been laid down by the Privy Council in the *Wagon Mound*,[21] Kennedy J considered two principal questions:

- what *kind of harm* was at the time of the spillages a foreseeable consequence of the carelessness in the handling of the solvent?
- whether the kind of harm which had actually occurred was to be regarded as the *same kind of harm* as was foreseeable?

The evidence in the case was clear that all spillages of the chemical had ceased in 1976, when a pumped supply was substituted for supply in drums. The key question was therefore the state of awareness of a reasonable operator in the decades immediately before 1976 as to the kinds of harm that might follow from such spillages. Kennedy J assessed the evidence as follows. It was certainly the case that there was awareness that in a confined space a person might be overcome by fumes arising from a spillage. However, such illness was a quite different kind of harm from that which the plaintiff had suffered. That the former kind of harm was foreseeable did not suffice to render the plaintiff's harm not too remote. It was true that both could be characterised as being harm resulting from "pollution", but Kennedy J considered that the concept of "pollution" as describing both the foreseen and the actual kinds of harm was too broad a categorisation. It was not the case that just because one kind of "pollution harm" was a foreseeable consequence of the spillage of the solvent the defendants should be liable for all kinds of pollution which may have ensued, whether or not what had ensued was itself foreseeable.

Kennedy J explained the evidence on this matter as follows:

---

[19] *ibid.*
[20] From 1976 a piped supply replaced loading by drums, and spillages ceased to occur.
[21] [1961] AC 388.

"The reasonable supervisor alive to the pattern of [the] … spillages would not, in my view, foresee any environmental hazard from those lesser spillages: he would, I believe, have supposed that the majority would have evaporated harmlessly either directly or by drying out of the ground, and as to that proportion that would remain, I entirely doubt whether, even if he has reflected upon the way in which an aquifer is re-stocked, he would have concluded that detectable quantities of solvent would be found down-catchment."[22]

It followed that the claims in both nuisance and negligence[23] failed on the grounds that the kind of harm which the plaintiff had suffered was not a kind of harm which was reasonably foreseeable as a consequence of the spillages at the time the spillages had occurred, and that the kinds of harm which were foreseeable as consequences were, for the purpose of remoteness of damage, legally different in kind from the harm which had actually eventuated.

Accordingly the plaintiff's claim failed at first instance.

The Court of Appeal

The Court of Appeal allowed the appeal by CWC, holding that the matter was governed entirely by an earlier authority of the Court of Appeal – *Ballard* v *Tomlinson*[24] – which could not be distinguished and was binding both on the court of first instance and on itself. *Ballard* was said by the Court of Appeal to decide that:

"…[W]here the nuisance is an interference with a natural right incident to ownership, then the liability is a strict one. The actor acts at his peril in that if his actions result by the operation of ordinary natural processes in an interference with the right then he is liable for any damage suffered by the owner. In the present case, the [solvent] was found to have been spilt by the actions of the respondent's servants and the damage which was suffered by the appellant resulted from the operation of ordinary natural forces. Accordingly, in our

---

[22] [1993] Env LR 116 at 142.

[23] It was noted above that Kennedy J had found that the spillages were a consequence of carelessness on the part of the defendants. This finding has attracted little attention, but is, perhaps, a surprising finding in the light of the evidence (see further below) that a reasonable operator during the years in question would not have been aware of the groundwater pollution potential of these chemicals. Certainly the spillages could easily have been avoided by taking a little more care. But, in the absence of foreseeable harm, why would the hypothetical reasonable person have taken more care than had ECL? The evidence seemed to be rather the reverse: that in the years in question reasonable operators dealt with these chemicals in such a way that spillages were by no means uncommon. The authors understand that it was regarded as good standard practice at this time to dispose of surplus supplies of these chemicals by pouring on the ground, in order that no one might be harmed by mistaken ingestion, or by inhalation of fumes in a confined space.

[24] (1885) 29 Ch D 115.

judgment, *Ballard* v *Tomlinson* is determinative in favour of the appellant."[25]

Ballard, according to the Court of Appeal, was a decision which imposed liability without need to address the sophistications as regards the scope of liability which had been considered by Kennedy J.

The House of Lords

The House of Lords restored judgment in favour of the defendants, but for reasons which differed in some important respects from those given by Kennedy J. Rather remarkably, given that the judgment denied liability on the facts, the House of Lords decision has breathed some substantial life back into the strict liability rule in *Rylands* v *Fletcher*.

Lord Goff spoke for a unanimous House. Giving short shrift to the decision of the Court of Appeal Lord Goff explained that that court had misinterpreted a number of statements in *Ballard,* and had regarded the case as establishing a broader strict liability principle than was necessary on its own particular facts or could legitimately be regarded as following from the tenor of the judgments in the case. *Ballard* was no more than an application, on its facts correctly in its plaintiff's favour, of the ordinary principles of nuisance and *Rylands* v *Fletcher*.[26]

Turning to the particular issues of liability under *Rylands* v *Fletcher* and in nuisance which fell to be considered, Lord Goff discussed whether the rules of remoteness of damage which had developed within the law of negligence (i.e. the *Wagon Mound* principle) were applicable also to claims in these other two torts. He concluded that the same principles should indeed apply:

> "...[I]t appears to me to be appropriate ... to take the view that foreseeability of damage of the relevant type should be regarded as a prerequisite of liability in damages under the rule [in *Rylands* v *Fletcher*]. Such a conclusion can ... be derived from Blackburn J's original statement of the law; and I can see no good reason why this prerequisite should not be recognised under the rule, as it has been in the case of private nuisance."[27]

Applying the trial judge's view of the evidence to this conclusion of law Lord Goff noted that:

> " ... [S]ince those responsible at ECL could not at the relevant time reasonably have foreseen that the damage in question might occur, the claim ... must fail."[28]

---

[25] [1993] Env LR 287 at 295.
[26] [1994] 1 All ER 53 at 67-69.
[27] At 76.
[28] At 78.

Notwithstanding this conclusion Lord Goff proceeded to consider whether the principle in *Rylands* v *Fletcher* would, even on a contrary view, have been applicable. As noted earlier, Kennedy J had come to the conclusion that the storage of the solvent chemicals had not, on the facts, involved a non-natural use of the land in question, and so had held that liability under *Rylands* v *Fletcher* was not engaged.

Lord Goff expressed, obiter but nevertheless influentially, a quite different opinion. Whilst acknowledging that "over the years the concept of natural use ... has been extended to embrace a wide variety of uses, including not only domestic uses but also recreational uses and even some industrial uses"[29] Lord Goff indicated that in his view Kennedy J had erred in regarding the community benefit associated with a use of land as relevant to the question whether the user was "natural" or "non-natural" for this purpose. Whereas it might be that the provision of services to a local community may be regarded quite properly as a natural use of land, the idea that the scope of the strict liability principle should widen or narrow depending on whether the activities could be regarded as serving "the wider interests of the local community or the general benefit of the community at large" should be resisted. Such an approach had been taken by Kennedy J when he had regarded the creation of employment in the village of Sawston as conferring a benefit on the local community and, as such, as warranting his conclusion that the storage of the solvent should, for the purposes of the liability rule, be categorised as a natural use of land. In Lord Goff's opinion the issues of whether a use of land was "natural" or "non-natural", and whether it conferred social or community benefit, were essentially unrelated. Without feeling the need to define the former concepts further he concluded starkly:

> "I am bound to say that the storage of substantial quantities of chemicals on industrial premises should be regarded as an almost classic case of non-natural use; and I find it very difficult to think that it should be thought objectionable to impose strict liability for damage caused in the event of their escape."[30]

Lord Goff commented that his reassertion of the breadth of the ambit of liability under *Rylands* v *Fletcher* (i.e. the breadth of the concept of non-natural user) should not prove unpalatable even to those who had formerly sought to limit the principle by reference to such "community benefit" ideas. This was because *Cambridge Water* had itself substituted a different, but in his view more appropriate, limiting factor to the scope of liability under the rule. As Lord Goff explained:

> "It may be that, now that it is recognised that foreseeability of harm of the relevant type is a prerequisite of damages under the rule, the

---

[29] *ibid.*
[30] At 79.

courts may feel less pressure to extend the concept of natural use to circumstances such as those in the present case."[31]

Conclusions

The obiter[32] statements of the House of Lords modified former understandings about the notions of natural and non-natural use of land within the rule in *Rylands* v *Fletcher*, extending substantially the range of uses of land to which this rule applies. At the same time the House affirmed the idea that even where liability is strict (in the sense that the harm done could not have been averted even by having taken reasonable care) there will be liability to compensate only for those aspects of damage done which may be regarded as of the kinds which might reasonably have been foreseen at the time the actions or events in question took place.

Has the net effect of the decision been to enlarge or narrow the scope of civil liability? The contemporary "headlines" certainly suggested the latter. "No liability for historic pollution" was a common summation. In fact the better view may be that the case marks a quite substantial extension of civil liability. Assuming that Lord Goff's statements, quoted above, about storage of everyday industrial chemicals involving the non-natural user of land correctly represent the law, the ambit of strict liability for harm caused by escapes may be regarded as having been substantially broadened. The limitation to liability conferred by the rules of remoteness of damage may well prove more apparent than real. If the courts adopt, in nuisance and *Rylands* v *Fletcher* cases, the same approach to the question whether foreseeable harm was of the same kind as that which actually occurred as they have adopted in negligence cases post-*Wagon Mound*, we may expect to see two things. First, that under these remoteness rules there is no requirement that the defendant should have been able to have foreseen precisely the harm which has resulted; and second, that it does not matter for liability that the mechanism by which broadly foreseeable harm resulted could not precisely have been foreseen. Successful arguments from defendants that they are protected from liability by such remoteness rules may prove few and far between.

The decision in *Cambridge Water* figured large in the very recent House of Lords case: *Transco plc* v *Stockport MBC* (19th November 2003). Their Lordships declined an invitation to overturn the principle in *Rylands* v *Fletcher*, preferring instead to "restate" the rule so as to render its scope of operation more clear. In so doing their Lordships emphasised:

(i)　the need for an "escape";
(ii)　the action does not lie for death or personal injury;

---

[31] *ibid.*

[32] Remember that the decision's extension to our understanding of the scope of strict liability occurred in a case in which the trial judge had expressly held that the defendants had been careless in their handling of the solvents.

(iii) the defendant must have done something giving rise to an exceptionally high risk of danger or mischief in the event of an escape;

(iv) the use of the land must have been exceptional or extraordinary (but not necessarily an unreasonable use of the land);

(v) "public interest" is not relevant to the scope of liability.

Their Lordships confirmed that *Cambridge Water* involved correct understanding of the rule: the storage of solvents created the sort of risk referred to in (iii) above, and the defendants' actions had involved an exceptional and extraordinary (albeit reasonable) use of land. In the words of Lord Bingham, *Cambridge Water* was the kind of case where, had there been foreseeability of the kind of damage which had ensued, it would have been "just" to have imposed liability even in the absence of fault.

REMOTENESS OF DAMAGE: *SAVAGE* v *FAIRCLOUGH*

On this matter only time will tell. For the moment the decision in *Savage* v *Fairclough*[33] is instructive. Like *Cambridge Water* this case involved the pollution of a water supply, albeit on a much reduced scale. The plaintiffs owned a Grade II listed cottage near Lenham in Kent. The cottage had a private water supply fed by a spring. Water from the spring was collected in a tank and then electrically pumped to a holding tank in the roof of the cottage. The defendants owned a pig farm approximately one mile from the cottage. They had also acquired a neighbouring property and various other parcels of land over a number of years. The plaintiffs claimed that the defendant's intensive pig farming unit coupled with the use of inorganic nitrogen fertilisers on their adjacent farmland had caused the plaintiffs' water supply to become polluted with nitrate. They accordingly instituted proceedings against the defendants for damages for negligence and nuisance, although the negligence claim was not pursued at trial. The defendants were successful before Mellor J and the plaintiffs appealed.

The judgment of the Court of Appeal was delivered by Mummery LJ. Before we consider the reasoning underpinning the Court's decision to dismiss the appeal, it is worth noting that the judgment of the Court commenced with the following observation about the litigation:

> "Both sides are legally aided on this appeal. The total costs to date are estimated to be £150,000. The drinking water supply is still polluted. The experts agree that the only long term solution is to lay on mains water. The estimated cost of that is £30,000. The professional expertise, the human effort and anxiety and most of the public money invested in this lawsuit could have been better spent. Efforts have been made at various times to settle, but without success."[34]

---

[33] [2000] Env LR 183.
[34] At 184.

Moving to the Court of Appeal's substantive decision, the Court agreed with Mellor J that the case turned on the question of foreseeability. The critical question had been put by the trial judge in the following terms:

> "Would or should such a farmer [the hypothetical good farmer] have in the circumstances in which the defendants found themselves appreciated that to follow good farming practice would give rise to a real risk of contamination of the plaintiffs' water supply? More precisely, on the facts as I have found them, would such a farmer have appreciated that the application of pig manure supplemented by chemical fertiliser, both falling within the limits regarded as good practice, would give rise to such a risk? That notional farmer would not be endowed with hindsight nor, of course, with foresight of the changes in practice that were still to some, changes reflected by the 1991 Code [of Good Agricultural Practice]."[35]

Both Mellor J and the Court of Appeal concluded that the evidence defeated the plaintiff's claim. This evidence did not suggest that the use of the pig unit was the cause of any significant pollution of the spring. Further, the evidence was that both the inorganic fertiliser and the pig manure were spread on the defendants' fields in accordance with what was regarded as good farming practice at the relevant time. Moreover, it seemed also to be the case that throughout the period 1983-88 the defendants had relied upon the advice of an expert agronomist whose view it was that there had been no excessive application of nitrogen to the crops during the relevant period. Two other pieces of evidence were also noted by the Court of Appeal. First, that the last spreadings of pig manure and inorganic fertiliser in any significant quantity had been in 1987 and 1991 respectively. Secondly, that the position of the spring which was the source of the plaintiffs water supply had not been known until excavation work had been carried out in 1988. Collectively these factors provided the basis for concluding that the defendants could not have foreseen at the relevant time that their use of pig manure and inorganic fertiliser, in accordance with the accepted standards of good agricultural practice, would cause harm to the plaintiffs water supply. Accordingly, they were not liable in nuisance to the plaintiffs.

ISSUES OF CAUSALITY: *GRAHAM AND GRAHAM v RE-CHEM INTERNATIONAL*[36]

Both *Savage* and *Cambridge Water* provide salutary reminders that the mere fact that a causal link may exist between a defendant's activities and the claimant's loss should not give rise to any assumption that civil liability will follow. In contrast, the next case, *Graham and Graham* v *Re-Chem International* provides a rather different and more basic warning: that a

---

[35] At 191. The Code of Good Agricultural Practice is a statutory code made pursuant to s. 97 of the Water Resources Act 1991.

[36] [1996] Env LR 158. See also (1995) ENDS Report 245 at 17-19; and [1995] 7 Environmental Law and Management 175.

claimant who believes quite genuinely that he or she has suffered harm at the hands of a defendant may discover, following exhaustive examination of evidence in court, that this has not – on a balance of probabilities – in fact been the case.[37]

The facts

The claim in *Graham* was brought by a farmer and his wife. Their cattle had lost weight and become ill, with disastrous financial consequences for their farming business. In the vicinity of the farm was a hazardous waste incinerator operated by the defendant company. The farmer plaintiff took the view that the sickness suffered by his cattle was a consequence of their ingestion of toxic emissions from the nearby incinerator. The defendants opted to defend the claim made against them and a trial of quite monumental dimensions ensued. The presentation and examination of the evidence, including that of a very substantial number of expert witnesses, lasted well in excess of a hundred days.[38]

The conclusion reached eventually by the trial judge, Forbes J, on all the evidence presented, was that no link had been demonstrated between the emissions from the incinerator and the illness suffered by the cattle. It should be stressed that in accordance with the rules about proof in civil cases the judge did not require proof that the incinerator was the sole cause of the illness. It would have been sufficient if there had been probative evidence that the incinerator was one amongst several contributors to the illness of the cattle. Nor was the judge seeking proof of such contribution beyond the "balance of probabilities" – the "more likely than not" test. On all the evidence presented the trial judge simply took the view that these minimum evidential requirements of proof had not been satisfied by the plaintiffs and so the claim was ruled unsuccessful.

It might be asked: Was the problem faced by the plaintiffs fundamentally that their claim involved a "David versus Goliath" struggle in which they were unfairly disadvantaged: an unequal match between a small farmer and a large corporation? If this were the case it might also be linked to the harbouring of some suspicion that in truth the farmer's cattle *had* been harmed by the incinerator's emissions; and that it was simply a matter of the individual plaintiffs having not been able at the trial to produce adequate evidence of that causal link.

Any such conclusions would seem, however, unjustified. For one thing the plaintiffs were very substantially supported in this case by the legal aid system. Although the legal costs incurred by the defendant company were substantially greater than those of the plaintiffs, there is no reason to think that the plaintiffs were for financial reasons unable to present all the evidence which might have seemed to have supported their claim.

---

[37] Note also *Reay v British Nuclear Fuels Ltd* [1994] Env LR 320.

[38] It may also be noted also that the interval of time between the harm occurring and the court judgment was, as in the *Cambridge Water* case, some 10 years.

Nor is this a case where one might be justified in suspecting that a causal link did in fact exist, it merely being the case that as yet scientists have not been able adequately to explain or demonstrate that link. There may well be cases where such suspicion is not illegitimate. But *Graham* is not such a case.

This can be demonstrated in the following way. The very substantial costs incurred by the defendants reflected the fact that their own evidence went beyond seeking to rebut the plaintiffs' evidence as regards the toxic nature of emissions from their incinerator, their ingestion (directly or indirectly) by their cattle, and the adverse effects that thereby resulted.[39] The defendants sought to go further than this and seek to demonstrate that the true cause of the plaintiffs' cattle becoming ill was rather different, and was something in respect of which they had not the slightest involvement.

The defendants sought to prove that the plaintiffs' cattle had suffered from a condition known as "fat cow syndrome". Moreover, they argued that the cause of that syndrome had been the plaintiffs' own actions in the way they had fed and grazed the cattle. The defendants examined in detail the husbandry records of the farm over a period of time during which it was important to the farmer[40] to have well-fattened cattle. The high protein diet and lush grazing being offered at this time to the cattle was, the defendants contended, unwittingly having the effect, quite literally, of killing them by kindness. The trial judge, having, as described earlier, held that there was no proven link between the incinerator and the illness suffered by the cattle, then proceeded to accept the evidence and arguments of the defendant company as regards "fat cow syndrome". Whilst Forbes J recognised that there was no single explanation for all the symptoms of ill-health experienced by the dairy herd during the relevant period, "fat cow syndrome" was regarded as the "principal cause" of the illness. This coupled with a number of subsidiary and contributory causes such as a lack of veterinary treatment and various mineral and vitamin deficiencies in the herd had only served to add to and exacerbate the problems experienced by the plaintiffs. The plaintiffs' ardent, even obsessive, belief that Re-Chem International was responsible for their problems meant, it seems, that they had closed their eyes to all other possible explanations for their herd's ill-health. Ultimately, the plaintiffs lost the case not because they could not prove harm which had been caused to them by the defendants, but because in truth they had been the masters of their own misfortune.

---

[39] Many of these claims were in fact challenged by the defendants, apparently to the satisfaction of the judge. Particular problems for the plaintiffs arose from the facts that the prevailing wind blew in a direction which did not help their arguments, other farmers nearby had not suffered similarly, and the evidence of similar illness following similar exposures in other parts of the world was regarded by the judge as quite unconvincing.

[40] In terms of the advent of the EU dairy quota scheme.

CAUSALITY: FURTHER COMPLEXITIES – THE *CROWN RIVER CRUISES* CASE

A failure to establish causation is a fatal blow to a claim, whether in nuisance, negligence or some other cause of action. However, as the judgment of Forbes J in *Graham* v *Re-Chem International* clearly illustrates, it has been clear for a good while that it is not necessary for a plaintiff to show that the defendant's conduct was the sole cause of the harm which the plaintiff has suffered. It is enough that the conduct in question materially contributed to the harm.

Where, however, several defendants are party to the proceedings, the issue of causation may become quite involved. There may be a number of potential outcomes to the litigation and a trial judge will have to ensure that the decision which he or she reaches is supported by the facts as found. It may be that the judge will find that none of the defendants materially contributed to the plaintiff's harm, in which case liability will not have been established. Alternatively, the judge may conclude that the conduct of one defendant in particular was of such an overwhelming nature as to have effectively broken the chain of causation which existed between the harm suffered by the plaintiff and the conduct of one or more of the other defendants to the proceedings. If this is the case, the defendant's intervening act will render him or her liable as the sole cause of the harm suffered.

What, however, will be the position if a second defendant's conduct did not in this way break the chain of causation but instead constituted a further cause of the harm suffered? The decision in *Crown River Cruises* v *Kimbolton Fireworks Ltd and London Fire & Civil Defence Authority*[41] illustrates how a court may deal with such a case.

The litigation in this case arose out of a fireworks display held on the River Thames to commemorate the fiftieth anniversary of the Battle of Britain. The display itself (organised and executed by the first defendants) was mounted upon a pontoon on the bow of the tug *Revenge*. The *Revenge* was stationed approximately mid-river between Blackfriars Bridge and Waterloo Bridge. Shortly before the display started the river between the two bridges was closed and the movement of vessels during the display was prevented. The plaintiffs owned two dumb barges, *Sago* and *Surround*, which were moored between the two bridges some 100-200 metres from the *Revenge*. The barges were used as moorings from which the plaintiffs operated passenger vessels up and down the Thames. One of these passenger vessels, *Suerita*, had a wedding party on board during the display. When the display was at an end, *Suerita* departed for a cruise down the river. Not long after 9.00pm the second defendants, the London Fire & Civil Defence Authority, received a call that smoke had been seen coming from *Surround*. It appeared that the fire had been caused by hot falling debris from the fireworks display. The crew of a fireboat attended, and later departed the scene in the belief that the fire had been

---

[41] [1996] 2 Ll. Rep 533.

extinguished. At about 1.00am *Suerita* returned from her cruise and adopted her usual mooring berth alongside *Surround*. In the early hours of that same morning a muffled explosion was heard and fire was seen on board *Suerita*. The second defendants re-attended and discovered a serious fire aboard both *Suerita* and *Surround*. The fires were extinguished, but not before they had caused substantial damage to both vessels. The plaintiffs sued the first defendants for the damage caused to their vessels in negligence, nuisance and the Rule in *Rylands* v *Fletcher*. The plaintiffs claimed against the second defendants for damage to their vessels caused by the second defendants failure to properly extinguish the initial fire on board *Surround*.

With regard to the liability of the first defendants, Potter J initially considered whether or not they had been negligent. He concluded that they had. After asserting the general principle that a wrongdoer "is only liable for damage which is reasonably foreseeable", Potter J concluded that the damage to the vessels had indeed been foreseeable. In his Lordship's opinion, the first defendants had taken "the understandable, but nonetheless foreseeable and unjustifiable, risk of some damage occurring in the course of the display".[42] The essential question therefore became whether the second defendants' negligent conduct in failing properly to extinguish the initial fire amounted to a break in the chain of causation. In other words, did their conduct amount to a *novus actus interveniens*?

It is a well-established principle that whether or not the chain of causation has been broken is a question to be determined in a common sense manner rather than by the application of a precise test. Thus in *Stapeley* v *Gypsum Mines Ltd*,[43] Lord Reid stated that:

> "The question must be determined by applying common sense to the facts of each particular case. One may find that, as a matter of history, several people have been at fault and if any one of them had acted properly the accident would not have happened, but that does not mean that the accident must be regarded as having been caused by the faults of all of them. One must discriminate between those faults which must be discarded as being too remote and those which must not. Sometimes it is proper to discard all but one and to regard that one as the sole cause, but in other cases it is proper to regard two or more as having jointly caused the accident. I doubt whether any test can be applied generally."[44]

Applying a common sense approach to the facts of the present case, Potter J concluded that the conduct of the second defendants did *not* break the chain of causation. In so concluding, it appears that his Lordship was much influenced by the belief that the second defendants' conduct did not amount to a positive act but, rather, that it constituted a failure to prevent

---

[42] At 541.
[43] [1953] 2 All ER 478; [1953] AC 663.
[44] At 486 of the former report.

the spread of the fire.[45] Thus their negligent omission was not a new cause of the damage to the plaintiffs' vessels; it was simply a further link in the chain of causation between that damage and the first defendants' negligence.

CAUSALITY – THE MESOTHELIOMA PROBLEM: *FAIRCHILD* v *GLENHAVEN FUNERAL SERVICES LTD*[46]

Introduction: the nature of mesothelioma

In *Fairchild* the House of Lords heard four conjoined appeals, each raising substantially the same issue. Each of the claimants had contracted the lung disease "mesothelioma" after having worked for several employers in various industries in which at various times they had been exposed to asbestos.

The nature of mesothelioma, as distinct from asbestosis and other asbestosis-related diseases, is that it may be triggered by a single asbestos fibre. Certainly it appears to be the case that the greater the exposure to asbestos fibres the greater the risk that a fibre may trigger mesothelioma. However, it is equally the case that a person may be exposed to fibres regularly over a substantial period without contracting the disease. And most problematically of all in terms of the application of rules of causality, where a person had been exposed to asbestos by each of several successive employers it was not possible to identify the point at which the disease was triggered. One reason for this is that the symptoms of the disease commonly do not appear for one or more decades after the time of exposure to the fibre which triggered that condition.

The fundamental legal problem

The essential problem confronting the claimants in their quest for compensation was explained by Lord Bingham in the House of Lords by way of the following question:

> "If (1) C was employed at different times and for differing periods by both A and B, and (2) A and B were both subject to a duty to take reasonable care or to take all practicable measures to prevent C inhaling asbestos dust because of the known risk that asbestos dust (if inhaled) might cause a mesothelioma, and (3) both A and B were in breach of that duty in relation to C during the periods of C's employment by each of them with the result that during both periods C inhaled excessive quantities of asbestos dust, and (4) C is found to be suffering from a mesothelioma, and (5) any cause of C's mesothelioma other than the inhalation of asbestos dust at work can be effectively discounted, but (6) C cannot (because of the current limits of human science) prove, on the balance of probabilities, that

---

[45] Potter J observed that: "This is not a case where the actions of the fire brigade positively promoted the fire; they simply failed to put it out" ([1996] 2 Ll. Rep 533 at 543).
[46] [2002] 3 All ER 305; [2003] 1 AC 32.

his mesothelioma was the result of his inhaling asbestos dust during his employment by A or during his employment by B, ... is C entitled to recover damages against either A or B or against both A and B?"[47]

The Court of Appeal had found against the claimants, doing so by reference to what is usually called the "but for" test.[48] Under this test if a claimant cannot show on a balance of probabilities that "but for" the acts of the defendant he would not have suffered the harm in question then that defendant cannot be considered to be a legal cause of the claimant's harm. In a situation where it may be certain that harm was caused by either A or B, but where it is quite uncertain whether the person who caused the harm was A or B, the traditional conclusion drawn has been that neither A nor B will bear liability. In relation to each of A and B the conclusion to be drawn would be that it cannot be said to be more likely than not that the harm would not have occurred but for that person's actions. Accordingly, the Court of Appeal held, to use the example given above, that claimant C had not proved against A that his mesothelioma would on a balance of probabilities not have occurred but for the breach of duty by A; nor had C shown against B that his mesothelioma would not have occurred but for the breach of duty by B. Accordingly C failed against both A and B.

The issue for the House of Lords, on appeal, was whether, in the special circumstances confronting such claimants, policy required a modified approach to proof of causation. On this matter the Law Lords were unanimous in favour of a departure from established principle in order that the claimants should not be left without remedy.[49]

Each of Their Lordships delivered a separate speech and each conducted a quite full review of English and overseas judicial decisions. In reading the speeches it is evident that *Fairchild* may properly be considered to be the latest in a line of cases in which, when confronted by the apparently harsh operation of established principles of causality, the courts have (although not always with conspicuous clarity) modified or provided an exception to that principle.

This may be demonstrated by the discussion which follows of two earlier House of Lords decisions: *Bonnington Castings Ltd* v *Wardlow*[50] and *McGhee* v *National Coal Board*.[51] When these two cases have been considered we shall return to the particular solution devised by the House of Lords for *Fairchild* itself.

---

[47] At 309 of the former report (para.2 of the judgment).

[48] See [2002] 1 WLR 1052.

[49] Feeny, Laleng and Cooper have argued that the House of Lords decision "was never realistically in doubt" since the facts of the case coupled with the attendant public and media interest made it "extremely unlikely that the judgment of the Court of Appeal would be upheld": see "Mesothelioma, Asbestos and Causation" [2003] JPIL 1.

[50] [1956] 1 All ER 615; [1956] AC 613.

[51] [1972] 3 All ER 1008; [1973] 1 WLR 1.

The *Bonnington Castings* case

In this case the claimant contracted pneumoconiosis as a consequence of having over a period of time inhaled silica dust. The inhaled dust emanated from two sources at his place of employment. One source was a "pneumatic hammer". The dust coming from this hammer was not, however, a consequence of any breach of duty owed to the claimant employee. The other source was a "swing grinder", and the dust arose here as a consequence of a breach of the employer's duty of care. The issue was whether it could be said that the breach of duty in relation to the swing grinders had caused the claimant's illness?

The leading speech in the House of Lords in *Bonnington* was that of Lord Reid. As will appear, by a slight reformulation of the traditional statement of what is required for proof of causality, and by drawing attention to the mechanism by which dust may cause pneumoconiosis, Lord Reid was able to conclude that the employer was liable.

In terms of the *principle* to be applied Lord Reid made plain that:

> "The employee must, in all cases, prove his case by the ordinary standard of proof in civil actions; he must make it appear at least that, on a balance of probabilities, the breach of duty caused, *or materially contributed to*, his injury."[52]

Note here the reference to "material contribution to injury" as, it would appear, a sufficient alternative to the defendant being shown to have *caused* the injury. This is a matter to which we shall return.

As regards the mechanics by which pneumoconiosis may be contracted, Lord Reid explained that, unlike mesothelioma (where a cancerous cell may be triggered by a single fibre) the illness in *Bonnington* was of a kind which is caused by the gradual accumulation in the lungs of minute particles of silica dust inhaled over a period of years. In this respect pneumoconiosis is more akin to asbestosis than to mesothelioma.

Applying the above statement of principle to the nature of the illness as described above, Lord Reid came to the conclusion that any source from which dust had got into the claimant's lungs could, so long as not *de minimis*, properly be regarded in law as having made a "material contribution to the injury", and as such could be regarded as rendering any party in breach of duty as regards that source liable in damages.[53] Moreover, such liability would be to compensate the defendant for the whole of the illness.[54] On the facts of *Bonnington* it may very well have been the case that more inhaled dust came from the "innocent" source (i.e. the pneumatic hammer) than from the source which arose out of breach of

---

[52] [1956] 1 All ER 615 at 618 (emphasis added).

[53] At 618-619.

[54] Subject, where there may be other persons also whose breaches of duty may also be so regarded as having caused or contributed to the harm, to rights of contribution amongst those joint tortfeasors.

duty (i.e. the swing grinder). Nevertheless, as the amount inhaled from the swing grinder source was sufficient to be regarded as having made a "substantial" or "material" contribution to the claimants injury, and was not a *de minimis* contributor, the employer was liable to compensate the claimant for the whole injury suffered.

The *McGhee* case

In this case the claimant had been employed by the National Coal Board for some 15 years. For most of that time he worked in pipe kilns, but for a relatively short period he worked in a brick kiln. In each kind of kiln the work brought the claimant's skin into contact with much dust and grit, and the claimant contracted a dermatitic condition. The trial judge held that it was exposure to dust in the brick kiln which had caused the claimant's dermatitis.

The next question was what breach of duty might be found in relation to the exposure to the brick kiln dust. The trial judge was willing to accept that the absence of adequate showers at the workplace was a breach of the employer's duty of care, but was not willing on the evidence presented to find that "but for" that breach of duty in relation to the showers the claimant would not have suffered the dermatitis. This conclusion followed from expert testimony to the effect that it could not be said that the provision of showers (i.e. compliance with the duty) would have prevented the disease. It could only be said that such showers would have reduced the risk of the disease occurring. On that basis the trial judge, and later the Scottish First Division, concluded that the employer was not liable.

The issue for the House of Lords was whether there should or should not be liability in a case where the absence of showers could be said to have increased the risk of something occurring, but where it could not be said that had the showers been provided the injury would "more likely than not" not have occurred. Their Lordships decided that there should be liability in such a case, Lord Reid explaining that in his opinion:

> "From a broad and practical viewpoint I can see no substantial difference between saying that what the [defendants] did materially increased the risk of injury to the appellant and saying that what the [defendants] did made a material contribution to his injury."[55]

As such Lord Reid characterised the distinction utilised by the court below, between materially increasing the risk that a disease will occur and making a material contribution to its occurrence, as founded too much on "logic" or "philosophy" and as too little a reflection of the "practical way in which the ordinary man's mind works in the every-day affairs of life".[56]

---

[55] [1972] 3 All ER 1008 at 1011.
[56] *ibid.*

A keen awareness that the rules of causation should reflect practical possibilities in terms of evidence and proof appears also in the following statements from Lords Wilberforce and Simon.

The former acknowledged that merely to show that a breach of duty had led to an increased risk of harm was not sufficient for liability. Nevertheless:

> "... the question remains whether a [claimant] must necessarily fail if, after having shown a breach of duty ... he cannot positively prove that this increase of risk caused or materially contributed to the disease while his employers cannot prove positively to the contrary."[57]

In such circumstances it might certainly be logical to say that the claimant should fail. However, Lord Wilberforce considered that there were good reasons not to adopt such an approach:

> "First, it is a sound principle that where a person has, by breach of duty of care, created a risk, and injury occurs within the area of that risk, the loss should be borne by him unless he shows that it had some other cause. Secondly, from the evidential point of view, one may ask, why should a man who is able to show that his employer should have taken certain precautions, because without them there is a risk, or an added risk, of injury or disease, and who in fact sustains exactly that injury or disease, have to assume the burden of proving more: namely that it was the addition to the risk, caused by the breach of duty, which caused or materially contributed to the injury? In many cases ... this is impossible to prove, just because honest medical opinion cannot segregate the causes of an illness between compound causes. And if one asks which of the parties, the workman or the employers should suffer from this inherent evidential difficulty, the answer as a matter of policy or justice should be that it is the creator of the risk ..."[58]

And Lord Simon stated that:

> " ... where an injury is caused by two (or more) factors operating cumulatively, one (or more) of which factors is a breach of duty and one (or more) is not so, in such a way that it is impossible to ascertain the proportion in which the factors were effective in producing the injury or which factor was decisive, the law does not require a ... plaintiff to prove the impossible, but holds that he is entitled to damages for the injury if he proves on a balance of probabilities that the breach or breaches of duty contributed substantially to causing the injury."[59]

---

[57] At 1012.
[58] *ibid.*
[59] At 1014.

Applying this principle to the facts of the case Lord Simon concluded:

> "In this type of case a stark distinction between breach of duty and causation is unreal. If the provision of shower baths was ... a precaution which any reasonable employer in the [defendant's] position would take, it means that such an employer should have foreseen that failure to take the precaution would more probably than not, substantially contribute towards injury; this is sufficient prima facie evidence."[60]

To conclude we may quote the words of Lord Bingham in *Fairchild*. In his view *McGhee* was a case in which the House recognised that the claimant:

> " ... faced an insuperable problem of proof if the orthodox test of causation was applied, but [regarded the case as one in which justice demanded a remedy for the [claimant]";

and where therefore:

> "... a majority of the House adapted the orthodox test to meet the particular case."[61]

The *Fairchild* decision

In *Fairchild* each member of the House of Lords reviewed the above decisions, and also a substantial number of others from England and elsewhere,[62] and concluded that the evidence of the case-law was that in an appropriate case it was possible to devise rules of causation which would prevent the orthodox approach to causation defeating a claimant's case.

The issue was whether *Fairchild* was an appropriate case, and this was answered in turn by each Law Lord in the affirmative.

Lord Bingham acknowledged that such a conclusion might well result in some cases in injustice to a defendant. In his words:

---

[60] *ibid.*

[61] [2002] 3 All ER 305 at 324 (para.21 of the judgment).

[62] Lord Bingham, for example, considered "the wider jurisprudence" to emerge from Germany, France, California, Canada, Norway and Australia: see 326-334. His Lordship also had regard to academic writings and European Civil Code provisions relating to causation. Nevertheless, Lord Bingham did observe that "Development of the law in this country cannot of course depend on a head-count of decisions and codes adopted in other countries around the world, often against a background of different rules and traditions" (at 334 (para. 32)). In a comment on *Fairchild*, Morgan draws attention to the fact that "the citation of modern European authorities came at the behest of the House of Lords, and not the initiative of counsel": see "Lost Causes in the House of Lords: *Fairchild* v *Glenhaven Funeral Services*" (2003) 66 MLR 277 at 282, where the author relies on the following words of Lord Rodger: "The Commonwealth cases were supplemented, at your Lordships' suggestion, by a certain amount of material describing the position in European legal systems" (at 382 (para. 165)).

"It can properly be said to be unjust to impose liability on a party who has not been shown, even on a balance of probabilities, to have caused the damage complained of."[63]

Nevertheless:

"… there is a strong policy argument in favour of compensating those who have suffered grave harm, at the expense of their employers who owed them a duty to protect them against that very harm and failed to do so, when the harm can only have been caused by breach of duty and when science does not permit the victim accurately to attribute, as between several employers, the precise responsibility for the harm he has suffered. I am of opinion that such injustice as may be involved in imposing liability on a duty-breaking employer in these circumstances is heavily outweighed by the injustice of denying redress to a victim."[64]

A crucial argument in favour of this conclusion was regarded by Lord Bingham as being that:

"Were the law otherwise, an employer exposing his employees to asbestos dust could obtain complete immunity against mesothelioma (but not asbestosis) claims by employing only those who had previously been exposed [i.e. before the present employment] to excessive quantities of asbestos dust. Such a result would reflect no credit on the law."[65]

Accordingly, for Lord Bingham the *Fairchild* case could properly be regarded, like the cases discussed above, as a case where:

"… the conduct of A and B in exposing C to a risk to which he should not have been exposed [made] a material contribution to the contracting by C of the condition against which it was the duty of A and B to protect him."[66]

Lord Nicholls agreed with this conclusion, regarding any other outcome as:

" … deeply offensive to instinctive notions of what justice requires and fairness demands."[67]

For this reason Lord Nicholls was willing to accept that:

"So long as it was not insignificant, each employer's wrongful exposure of its employees to asbestos dust, and hence to the risk of contracting mesothelioma, should be regarded by the law as a sufficient degree of causal connection. This is sufficient to justify

---

[63] At 334-335 (para. 33).
[64] At 335 (para. 33).
[65] *ibid.*
[66] *ibid.* (para. 34).
[67] At 336 (para. 36).

requiring the employer to assume responsibility for causing or materially contributing to the onset of the mesothelioma when, in the present state of medical knowledge, no more exact causal connection is ever capable of being established. Given the present state of medical science, this outcome may cast responsibility on a defendant whose exposure of a claimant to risk …had no causative effect. But the unattractiveness of casting the net of responsibility as widely as this is far outweighed by the unattractiveness of the alternative outcome."[68]

Lord Hoffmann spoke in similar vein:

"My Lords, as between the employer in breach of duty and the employee who has lost his life in consequence of a period of exposure to risk to which that employer has contributed, I think it would be both inconsistent with the policy of the law imposing the duty and morally wrong for your Lordships to impose causal requirements which exclude liability."[69]

Given that their Lordships were of the view that the claims in *Fairchild* should succeed the question is raised: upon what principle should such departure from orthodoxy be based?

Their Lordships took pains to stress that the exception should be of quite limited application – no "coach and horses" being driven through conventional principles. But in terms of how to explain the narrow exception it was Lord Rodger of Earlsferry whose speech examined this matter most closely.

Lord Rodger explained the exception to orthodoxy in terms of six principles, as follows:

"First, the principle is designed to resolve the difficulty that arises where it is inherently impossible for a claimant to prove exactly how his injury was caused. It applies, therefore, where the claimant has proved all he possibly can, but the causal link could only ever be established by scientific investigation and the current state of the relevant science leaves it uncertain exactly how the injury was caused and, so, who caused it. *McGhee*'s case and the present cases are examples. Secondly, part of the underlying rationale of the principle is that the defendant's wrongdoing has materially increased the risk that the claimant will suffer injury. It is therefore essential not just that the defendant's conduct created a material risk of injury to a class of persons but that it actually created a material risk of injury to the claimant himself. Thirdly, it follows that the defendant's conduct must have been capable of causing the claimant's injury. Fourthly, the claimant must prove that his injury was caused by the eventuation of the kind of risk created by the defendant's wrongdoing … By

---

[68] At 337 (para. 42).
[69] At 341 (para. 63).

contrast, the principle does not apply where the claimant has merely proved that his injury could have been caused by a number of different events, only one of which is the eventuation of the risk created by the defendant's wrongful act or omission ... Fifthly, this will usually mean that a claimant must prove that his injury was caused, if not by exactly the same agency as was involved in the defendant's wrongdoing, at least by an agency that operated in substantially the same way. A possible example would be where a workman suffered injury from exposure to dusts coming from two sources, the dusts being particles of different substances each of which, however, could have caused the injury in the same way ... Sixthly, the principle applies where the other possible source of the claimant's injury is a similar wrongful act or omission of another person, but it can also apply where, as in *McGhee*'s case, the other possible source of the injury is a similar, but lawful, act or omission of the same defendant. I reserve my opinion as to whether the principle applies where the other possible source of injury is a similar but lawful act or omission of someone else or a natural occurrence."[70]

The decision in *Fairchild* thus seems to represent a victory for justice, at least from the viewpoint of the claimant. The earlier Court of Appeal decision had provoked adverse comment in some quarters, principally because it was regarded as a victory for principle and injustice.[71] Accordingly, their Lordships' relaxation of the rules of causation where several tortfeasors are jointly responsible for harm suffered will be regarded by some as a welcome development in situations where the limits of scientific knowledge make it impossible to establish (for the time being) which of the tortfeasors actually caused the harm in question. In some respects, therefore, English common law on causation now shares distinct similarities with the following provision of the Greek Civil Code:

"If damage has occurred as a result of the joint action of several persons, or if several persons are concurrently responsible for the same damage, they are all jointly and severally implicated. The same applies if several persons have acted simultaneously or in succession and it is not possible to determine which person's act caused the damage."[72]

Nevertheless, while the outcome in *Fairchild* is undeniably satisfactory from the viewpoint of a claimant who has suffered harm as a consequence of a breach of duty but who cannot prove which of several potential tortfeasors actually caused the harm, enabling the claimant to recover damages in these circumstances may seem less just as far as defendants and their insurers are concerned. Thus it has been argued that:

---

[70] At 383-384 (para. 170).

[71] See, for example, Miller "Why the House of Lords must overturn the *Fairchild* decision" (2002) 152 New Law Journal, 319-320.

[72] Article 296, cited by Lord Bingham in *Fairchild* at 328 (para. 26).

"The reality is that these are historic liabilities and that the effect of the judgment will be to require solvent defendants and insurers where many defendants have disappeared and important insurers have become insolvent, to contribute to the compensation of claimants to a far greater extent than these defendants and insurers could reasonably have anticipated their liability to be at the time the relevant risk occurred and was insured."[73]

This may well constitute a significant line of policy argument as further cases come before the courts, and the judges are invited little by little to develop further the *Fairchild* inroad into the "but for" principle.

---

[73] See Feeny, Laleng and Cooper [2003] JPIL 1.

Part II
CRIMINAL LIABILITY

CRIMINAL LIABILITY IN THE ENVIRONMENTAL CONTEXT

INTRODUCTION

Within the large corpus of environmental laws in the United Kingdom there exist a substantial number of different criminal offences. In addition to the *common law* offence of public nuisance,[1] which retains some modern significance, each of the numerous statutes which comprise the main body of our environmental legislation contains provisions creating criminal offences associated with the matter or matters with which the particular legislative provisions deal.

Criminal offences contrasted with administrative penalties

In the United Kingdom, in the environmental law context, we know nothing of the continental concept of the "administrative offence" or "administrative penalty". If our Parliament has thought fit to have imposed a penal sanction in respect of some form of conduct this has been done by utilising the process of the ordinary criminal law. It has not become a feature of penal liability in this context, or generally in others,[2] for statutes to have afforded powers upon *administrative* bodies to impose penalties.[3] Comparisons between the United Kingdom and other jurisdictions will, for this reason, quite likely show quite significant differences in the extent to which the ordinary criminal courts become involved in environmental cases. As ever, conclusions from comparative study must therefore be drawn with care.

THE BROAD VARIETY OF OFFENCES

In addition to being very numerous, environmental offences take a wide variety of forms. Some are designed to seek to assist in a quite direct way in the protection of the environment. For example, by proscribing conduct

---

[1] See Chapter 8.

[2] Compare, however, in a quite different context, the provision of powers of such nature to certain of the regulatory bodies established to monitor and supervise the performance of the industries and services privatised over the last two decades: for example, the power to impose financial penalties where performance standards set in franchise agreements have not been met.

[3] As distinct from administrative powers to impose *directions*, and administrative powers to *recoup costs incurred* in certain activities. These important administrative powers form the content of Part III of this book. For an argument in favour of the Environment Agency being accorded the power to levy administrative penalties on environmental offenders, see Ogus and Abbot, 'Sanctions for Pollution: Do we have the Right Regime?' (2002) 14 JEL 283, discussed more fully at fn. 23 below. See also the recently published DEFRA sponsored report, *Environmental civil penalties: A more proportionate response to regulatory breach*, in which the authors (Michael Woods and Professor Richard Macrory) make the case for a new system of civil penalties for environmental offences.

which pollutes, or endangers, a particular environmental medium. Thus, as we shall see, there is an offence, quite frequently prosecuted, of "causing or knowingly permitting" polluting or like matter to enter "controlled waters";[4] and there is a similarly broad offence which seeks to protect land from being contaminated by the deposit of waste.[5] It will not be possible, in the discussion which follows, to examine the details of all such "front-line" offences. However, the treatment which will be afforded certain of the offences will demonstrate the quite substantial breadth of criminal liability, and the potential at least for quite significant penalties to be imposed in the more serious cases.

Beyond these "primary" environmental offences there exist a variety of other offences, designed to support and reinforce the operation of the numerous statutory schemes of regulation and control. Each of the several regimes of environmental permitting which operates in Britain is supported by a range of associated criminal offences. So, within the legislative provisions which establish and define schemes of regulation – such as, for example, over the development of land, the operation of processes falling within the ambit of integrated pollution (prevention and) control or local authority air pollution control, activities in the context of waste management, or which involve discharges to water, or of trade effluent to sewers – there will be found ancillary provisions as to criminal liability. The details, and thus the precise scope or potential for criminal liability, will be found within each piece of regulatory legislation. To a degree the provisions will be found to take a common form; but the pattern is by no means identical from one context to another, and so general statements as regards these provisions must be treated with some care. For example, we may say that provision is *generally* made that it shall be an offence to conduct operations or engage in activities which require a permit without such a permit having been obtained (or in breach of the terms of the permit obtained). However, although this statement is generally true, it is not accurate as regards one very important scheme of environmental regulation. It misrepresents the position in relation to planning controls over the development of land. It is not, in the main, a criminal offence simply to act in breach of planning controls: merely to have developed land without planning permission (where this is required) does not of itself involve the commission of a criminal offence. In this particular context criminal liability is one stage further removed than is the case with other permitting schemes. It arises only if the planning authority chooses, in the exercise of discretion, to serve an enforcement notice on the person in breach of planning control, and that person continues to act in contravention of that enforcement notice.[6]

The legislation which establishes a scheme of regulatory control will also, typically, be found to contain a variety of further offences relating, for

---

[4] Water Resources Act 1991 s. 85. See further, below, Chapter 9.

[5] Environmental Protection Act 1990 s. 33. See further, below pp. 372-385.

[6] Note, in similar vein, the incidence of criminal liability as regards statutory nuisances. See Chapter 11.

example, to the giving of false information to the agency charged with operating those controls, to the obstruction of officers of that agency in the exercise of their powers and duties, to requirements as to the maintenance of proper records, and so on. In the discussion which follows no attempt will be made to treat these numerous secondary offences either comprehensively or in any detail.

PROSECUTORIAL DISCRETION

Against this background, of a considerable number of more and less serious criminal offences, it is important to note the recognition under English law of substantial prosecutorial *discretion.* In some jurisdictions a duty may exist requiring public authorities that are in possession of evidence to support a criminal charge to commence criminal proceedings; and this duty may well be subject to judicial enforcement at the instance of an interested third party.

In Britain the position is quite different. In relation to criminal offences generally, and environmental offences involve no exception to this general principle, the existence of probative evidence against a suspect imposes no duty on any prosecutor to commence criminal proceedings. The decision to prosecute, or not to prosecute, is regarded for prosecuting authorities as a matter not of legal duty but of discretion, to be exercised case by case as the general public interest may seem to require. Amongst cases where the evidence may be equally strong there may be some in which the public body with responsibility for enforcement considers the public interest to warrant a prosecution being initiated, and there may be others where some lesser action – a warning or a caution – may be felt to be a quite adequate response. Provided a decision has been reached – to prosecute or not – on the basis of an assessment of relevant facets of the public interest, the decision of the prosecuting authority will not be challengeable.[7]

It is unsurprising that, just as with prosecution decisions in other contexts of the criminal law, much interest centres on the approach to the "public interest" which is taken by prosecutors who have responsibilities in relation to environmental offences. How should one characterise their general approach? Is it to prosecute offences as a matter of regular course, subject to non-prosecution in exceptional situations only? Or is the situation more one where prosecution is reserved for the more serious instances only, or in relation only to the more intransigent suspects, with cautions, warnings and constructive support towards future compliance with legal obligations being more the order of the day in the typical case?

These matters will be considered later. For the moment we may simply note that no simple picture will emerge and, moreover, any picture presented may change over time – one approach giving way or moving

---

[7] Judicial review of a prosecutor's general policy or of an individual decision will be a possibility, however, where that policy or decision can be said to contravene any of the *Wednesbury* principles – see *R* v *Metropolitan Police Commissioner, ex parte Blackburn* [1968] 1 All ER 763 and *R* v *General Council of the Bar, ex parte Percival* [1990] 3 All ER 137.

towards another. Even following the amalgamation and rationalisation produced by the Environment Act 1995[8] a variety of different agencies continue to enforce different pieces of environmental legislation; and that legislation is itself varied and operates in a wide variety of contexts. It would be surprising if any simple overall picture were to emerge. Considerations and approaches appropriate in the contexts, for example, of nuclear safety and the littering of streets may be very different, and such as legitimately to demand quite different responses.

What should be noted, however, is that over the last decade or so this matter of prosecutorial discretion has become more widely acknowledged and discussed than was earlier the case.[9] Further, in an attempt to enhance "transparency" in their decision-making, prosecuting authorities have sought to explain the basic principles upon which their public interest assessments are made. We shall consider shortly the documents quite recently developed and published by the Environment Agency on this matter.[10]

The discretion of public authorities *not* to prosecute might seem, at first sight, akin to a power to license criminal activity. This, however, would substantially misrepresent the position, principally for two reasons. To begin with there exists, unless taken away by statute, a general power in any individual to initiate *privately* a prosecution which the responsible state agency may, for whatever reason, have chosen not to have brought: the power of prosecution is not a state monopoly. Understandably this power of private prosecution is not one which is frequently, or lightly, exercised. Nevertheless, as will be seen, it may be regarded as a potentiality which lurks always in the background, enhancing the utility of the criminal law as a mechanism for the securement of environmental control. Businesses may never quite be sure that a decision by a state agency not to prosecute will be an end to the matter. Moreover, the decision of the state agency as regards prosecution may itself be influenced by its own appreciation that, should *it* decide not to prosecute, a private prosecution might, perhaps to its embarrassment, be initiated.[11]

A second point to note is that the courts have taken a consistent view that prosecutors should not feel disentitled by previous absence of prosecution from changing their prosecution policy even where by doing so they may defeat expectations of non-prosecution which may have been engendered.

---

[8] Establishing, in April 1996, for England and Wales, the Environment Agency: taking over, principally, the functions of the former National Rivers Authority, Her Majesty's Inspectorate of Pollution and the local authority Waste Regulatory Authorities.

[9] See, for example, Hilson "Discretion to Prosecute and Judicial Review" [1993] Crim LR 739-747.

[10] See below, p. 222.

[11] Following the running aground of the *Sea Empress* off the port of Milford Haven in February 1996, more than a year passed before the Environment Agency announced that the Port Authority was to be prosecuted. In the meantime, Friends of the Earth had publicly stated that if the Agency did not prosecute, then it would do so itself. For an example of a successful private prosecution in relation to s. 85(3) of the Water Resources Act 1991, see *R v Anglian Water Services* [2003] EWCA Crim 2243, discussed further below.

Defendants who have sought to argue that earlier inaction has in some way afforded them a licence or liberty to act in breach of the criminal law have been afforded short shrift. However, a limit to this should be noted. A prosecutor may be estopped from bringing a prosecution where a defendant has been afforded an assurance, undertaking or representation that no further action will be taken on the basis that the prosecution amounts to an abuse of process.[12] An argument along these lines failed on the evidence in *Environment Agency* v *Stanford*.[13] The respondent, S, carried out waste management activities at a site in Lingfield, Surrey, without a licence contrary to section 33 of the Environmental Protection Act 1990. He applied to register the activities as being exempt from the need for a licence in accordance with regulation 17 of the Waste Management Licensing Regulations 1994.[14] An Environment Agency officer visited the site and subsequently wrote to S. In his letter the officer noted that the current position constituted an offence. He also drew attention to the steps necessary to bring the site within the terms of the Regulations. Four further site visits occurred. Following the third of these, the Agency officer sent S a letter in which he indicated that the works necessary to comply with the exemption should be completed by a set deadline. That deadline had not passed at the time of any of the five site visits. However, the work was not completed on time and the Agency took the decision to prosecute S for five alleged breaches of section 33 of the 1990 Act. At the trial, the Justices ruled that the prosecution should be stayed as an abuse of process on the ground that S had been led to believe that he would not be prosecuted if he carried out the necessary works within the stipulated deadline. The Environment Agency's appeal against that decision was upheld by Lord Bingham CJ and the matter was accordingly remitted back to the Justices with a direction to continue the hearing. In the words of Lord Bingham CJ, there was:

> "... in the findings which I have read at length nothing whatever to support the justices' findings that Mr Stanford was led to believe that he would not be prosecuted for past offences if he completed by July 1; that the Agency had gone back on any implied understanding; that Mr Stanford had reasonably gained the impression that he would not be prosecuted if the work was done by July 1; or that he had been led to entertain a belief to that effect. It is true that the Agency had arguably not made plain that it would consider prosecution, but there was no reason why it should be so. It had on at least two occasions reminded Mr Stanford in writing that he was committing offences. Even if Mr Stanford's case is put at its very highest and a condition was imposed that he would not be prosecuted if he completed by the first week of July, that condition was not met."[15]

---

[12] See *R* v *Croydon Justices, ex p Dean* [1993] QB 769.

[13] [1999] Env LR 286.

[14] SI 1994/1056.

[15] It is worth noting that towards the end of his judgment, Lord Bingham stressed that the jurisdiction to stay proceedings was one which should be exercised "with the very greatest caution". For further examples of the same judicial reluctance to exercise the jurisdiction in an

PROSECUTION OF INDIVIDUALS AND CORPORATIONS

Where it is decided that substantial probative evidence of an offence exists, and that the public interest requires that a prosecution be brought, the prosecutor will need to make certain important decisions as regards the identity of the defendant to face charges. Most environmental offences are committed in the course of industrial or business activity. Certainly it is likely to be possible to point to individuals, often quite lowly employees, whose personal actions have involved the commission of the environmental offence in question. Such individuals, if prosecuted, would bear criminal liability; no defence of "only doing my job" being countenanced.

However, the value (and equity) of prosecuting such individuals may be doubted. Attention should focus, instead or in addition, on the criminal liability which may attach in such circumstances to, on the one hand, the *company* for which the employees may work and, on the other hand, to more *senior individuals involved in the running of that company.* In other words we shall need to consider the principles which govern the criminal liability of corporations and the criminal liability which may attach personally to directors and similar officers of companies where offences have been committed by those companies.

The material which follows in Part II of this book will, in the light of this preliminary discussion, appear in the following sequence:

- Prosecution policies
- Corporate criminal liability and the personal criminal liabilities of directors, etc.
- The offence of public nuisance
- Principal offences in the contexts of water and waste.

PROSECUTION POLICIES

The Environment Agency, quite soon after it was established, made public its enforcement and prosecution policy.[16] The existence of such a policy reflects the fact that the Agency has to be selective as to the circumstances

---

environmental context, see *R v Aylesbury Justices, ex parte Kitching* [1997] Env LR D16 and *R v Leeds Stipendiary Magistrate ex parte Yorkshire Water Services (No.2)*, CO/4834/99, 15 December 1999. In the former case, the applicant, the owner of a woodland, argued that letters and oral statements made by an employee of the Forestry Association (a subordinate agency to the Forestry Commission) constituted an assurance that he would not be prosecuted for an offence contrary to s. 17(1) of the Forestry Act 1967 in respect of the unlicensed felling of trees. On the facts of the case, however, the High Court (Pill LJ and Astill J) concluded that there was nothing in the correspondence which could be sensibly regarded as an assurance that the applicant would not be prosecuted (or that the employee had the authority to give such an assurance on behalf of the Commission). Accordingly, the application was dismissed. In the latter case, Rose LJ and Smith J rejected a renewed application for leave to apply for judicial review in respect of a decision by the stipendiary magistrate to refuse to stay proceedings in relation to the supply of water, allegedly unfit for human consumption, contrary to s. 70 of the Water Industry Act 1991, on the grounds of an abuse of process.

[16] November 1, 1998.

in which it will take enforcement action or initiate a prosecution; budgetary constraints are an obvious limiting factor upon such action. The document sets out the general principles which the Agency intends to follow in relation to enforcement and prosecution.

With regard to enforcement, it is stated that the Agency "believes in firm but fair regulation". Four principles underlie this policy: proportionality; consistency; transparency; and, targeting.[17] In relation to "proportionality" the policy states that: "The enforcement action taken by the Agency will be proportionate to the risks posed to the environment and to the seriousness of any breach of the law." There is nothing very surprising about this principle. Proportionality ought to be the watchword of any agency with regulatory functions to perform. Similarly the second principle underlying the Agency's enforcement policy, "consistency", springs no shocks. Given that decisions relating to enforcement action involve an exercise of discretion on the part of the Agency's officers, it is important that significant and not apparently explicable variations should not emerge as between regions or, within any region, within any period of time. Public confidence in the Agency's ability to regulate is therefore dependent upon a consistent approach and upon the third principle, "transparency". As far as the Agency is concerned, transparency "means helping those regulated and others, to understand what is expected of them and what they should expect from the Agency". Moreover, it "means making clear why an officer intends to, or has taken enforcement action". The fourth principle, the "targeting" of enforcement action against those whose activities give rise to or risk serious environmental damage, is yet further evidence, if such were needed, of both the impossibility and the undesirability of taking enforcement action against all those who transgress environmental laws. Given the range and scale of conduct covered by environmental offences, it would be wrong for enforcement action to be taken in all cases. Targeting is therefore an appropriate approach, provided that it is carried out in a manner which is neither disproportionate nor inconsistent.

Turning to the matter of prosecution, the Agency's policy states that:

> "The use of the criminal process to institute a prosecution is an important part of enforcement. It aims to punish wrongdoing, to avoid a recurrence and to act as a deterrent to others. It follows that it may be appropriate to use prosecution in conjunction with other available enforcement tools, for example, a prohibition notice requiring the operation to stop until certain requirements are met. Where the circumstances warrant it, prosecution without prior warning or recourse to alternative sanctions will be pursued."

The above statement reflects conventional wisdom on the purpose of bringing a prosecution. It stresses, amongst other things, the punitive and deterrent aspects of a prosecution. However, the statement also emphasises

---

[17] The same four principles underlie the Health and Safety Executive's prosecution policy: see Hawkins, *Law as Last Resort* (2002) Oxford University Press, p. 186.

an important feature of environmental offences, namely that unlike many criminal offences, enforcement action in respect of these offences may consist of something other than, or additional to, a prosecution.

In deciding whether or not to bring a prosecution, the Agency's policy states that regard will be had to the *Code for Crown Prosecutors*.[18] The *Code* identifies two stages in the decision to prosecute: (i) the evidential test; and (ii) the public interest test. Not surprisingly, both the *Code* and the Environment Agency's policy are unequivocal on the question whether a prosecution should be initiated which does not satisfy the evidential test. In the words of the latter:

> "A prosecution will not be commenced or continued by the Agency unless it is satisfied that there is sufficient, admissible and reliable evidence that the offence has been committed and that there is a realistic prospect of conviction. If the case does not pass this evidential test, it will not go ahead, no matter how important or serious it may be."

Assuming that the evidential test – that success in the prosecution is "more likely than not" – is satisfied, it will then be necessary to consider whether a prosecution is justified in the public interest. The following public interest factors will be taken into account when deciding whether or not to prosecute:

- the environmental effect of the offence;
- the foreseeability of the offence or the circumstances leading to it;
- the intent of the offender, individually and/or corporately;
- the history of offending;
- the attitude of the offender;
- the deterrent effect of a prosecution on the offender and others;
- the personal circumstances of the offender.

This list is not exhaustive. Precisely which factors apply will depend upon the particular circumstances of the case. However, in certain specified circumstances, where the sufficiency of evidence test is satisfied, there is a presumption that the Agency will normally bring a prosecution. These circumstances are as follows:

- incidents or breaches which have significant consequences for the environment or which have the potential for such consequences;
- carrying out operations without a relevant licence;
- excessive or persistent breaches of regulatory requirements;
- failure to comply or to comply adequately with formal remedial requirements;
- reckless disregard for management or quality standards;
- failure to supply information without reasonable excuse or knowingly or recklessly supplying false or misleading information;
- obstruction of Agency staff;

---

[18] Issued under section 10 of the Prosecution of Offences Act 1985.

- impersonating Agency staff.

In order to seek to ensure that its enforcement and prosecution policy is operated in an efficient and effective manner, the Agency has also published some functional guidelines. These guidelines take account of the Common Incident Classification Scheme (CICS), a national system for recording incidents, assessing the level of response and, categorizing incidents. For the purposes of the CICS, an incident is a specific event which comes to the attention of the Agency, is of concern to the Agency, and which may have an environmental and/or operational impact. The scheme provides a categorisation for those incidents which result in an actual or potential impact on the environment. Accordingly, in the context of environmental protection,[19] Category 1 incidents involve a "major" environmental impact, Category 2 incidents a "significant" impact and Category 3 incidents, a "minor" impact. The fourth category is reserved for those incidents where there is no environmental impact.

The guidance in respect of the Agency's environmental protection and water resources functions is the same when determining the appropriate enforcement action to take in the light of the environmental impact of the incident. Accordingly, the guidance states that:

> "If the impact or potential impact is Category 1, prosecution will normally result. If it is Category 2, prosecution or formal caution[20] will be the normal course of action, the choice being determined by reference to other factors... If it is Category 3, a warning[21] will usually be sufficient, unless other factors determine a more severe course of action, e.g. a repeated offence."[22]

Despite the existence of a prosecution policy, it should be noted that there would appear to be significant discrepancies between the policy and what the Agency actually does in practice. Thus, for example, in 1999, of the 953 Category 1 and 2 incidents involving water pollution, only 230 resulted in a prosecution.[23] Figures such as these therefore cast some

---

[19] The guidance takes account of the various enforcement functions which the Agency undertakes and is, therefore, function-specific. Accordingly, in addition to a section on environmental protection, there are further sections which relate to: water resources; fisheries; flood defence; and navigation.

[20] The guidance uses the term "formal caution" to distinguish it from a caution given by an Agency officer prior to asking questions concerning an offence. In effect, a formal caution amounts to a written acceptance by the offender that he has committed the offence in question. It should therefore only be used in cases where it is considered that a successful prosecution could be brought.

[21] According to the guidance, this may take one of two forms, either: (i) a written warning in a letter format; or (ii) a warning given on site by an investigating officer and recorded either on the site inspection report or a special form designated for the purpose.

[22] See s. 2, para. 3.1 and s. 3, para. 3.1, respectively.

[23] See *Water Pollution Incidents in England and Wales 1999*, p. 19, and table 18, p. 37, respectively. Despite the low level of prosecutions for environmental offences, it does compare favourably with the Agency's use of its administrative powers: the power to revoke or suspend environmental licences or consents. It has been reported, for example, that between its establishment in 1996 and February 2001, the Agency revoked a mere six waste management

perspective upon the Agency's very high success rate when bringing prosecutions for environmental offences. Although a conviction may be the outcome in approximately 95% of such cases, it suggests that the Agency applies the evidential test referred to above with a considerable degree of rigour.

In a regulatory body the size of the Environment Agency, it is almost inevitable that there will be variation in decision-making when Agency officers are deciding whether or not to prosecute an offender. What Hawkins has termed the "fragmentation of discretion"[24] creates the very real possibility that decisions relating to prosecutions will ultimately prove to have been inconsistent when analysed on a regional or national basis. As Hawkins explains:

> "It is difficult to escape the conclusion that so far as prosecution is concerned, the symbolic and organizational imperatives to which inspectors are routinely subjected serve to attenuate or even to smother the force of formal enforcement policy in shaping the inspector's decision field."[25]

CORPORATE CRIMINAL LIABILITY

In this section the primary focus will be upon the various techniques which the law has adopted in order to make corporations criminally liable for the actions of their employees, rather than upon the broader question whether criminal liability *ought* to be affixed to corporations. Of these techniques, the most notable are vicarious liability and what has become known as the principle of "identification".[26]

---

licences (HC Written Answers, 26 February 2001, col. 314). Ogus and Abbot suggest that the statistics reveal that "revocation notices are served in only the most serious of cases and the power of suspension is exercised with extreme caution". However, as they also note, since the penalties for a prosecution are "generally, and paradoxically, less severe", it is not surprising that "the Agency exercises its powers of prosecution more readily than those of suspension and revocation". The authors proceed to evaluate the different aspects of enforcement policy which they have described by having regard to various model enforcement pyramids and bearing in mind throughout, that "the goal of the system should be optional compliance" i.e. "the point at which the marginal social benefits accruing from compliance are equivalent to the marginal social costs incurred in securing that level of compliance". Their solution to the "problem" of the Agency's cautious approach to the prosecution of environmental crimes would be to give the Agency "powers to levy administrative financial charges from offenders without the procedures and onus of proof with which the criminal process protects defendants, but which also inhibits prosecution". Accordingly, they recommend that the German system of "administrative offences" (*Ordnungswidrigkeiten*) "provides an excellent model for this purpose": see "Sanctions for Pollution: Do we have the Right Regime?" (2002) 14 JEL 283-298.

[24] *Law as Last Resort* (2002), p. 204.

[25] *ibid.* Hawkins was referring to Health and Safety inspectors. However, there is no reason to think that his observations in relation to this group of persons are not equally applicable to those officers of the Environment Agency who carry out the day-to-day regulatory functions of that body.

[26] A further technique referred to in the literature on corporate criminal liability is the "aggregation doctrine" or, to give it its American name, the "collective knowledge doctrine". Under this doctrine, whether or not a corporation will be criminally liable should be determined

The principle of identification[27]

The origins of the "identification" principle can be traced to a dictum of Viscount Haldane LC in the civil case of *Lennard's Carrying Co Ltd* v *Asiatic Petroleum Co Ltd*[28] where his Lordship observed that:

> "... a corporation is an abstraction. It has no mind of its own any more than it has a body of its own; its active and directing will must consequently be sought in the person of somebody who for some purposes may be called an agent, but who really is the directing mind and will of the corporation."[29]

Subsequently Denning LJ (as he then was) addressed the issue of the "directing mind and will" of a company in another civil case, *H L Bolton (Engineering) Co Ltd* v *T J Graham & Sons Ltd.*[30] In order to emphasise the point he was making, Denning LJ made use of a vivid metaphor which compared the company with the human body:

> "A company in many ways may be likened to a human body. It has a brain and a nerve centre which controls what it does. It also has hands which hold the tools and act in accordance with directions from the centre. Some of the people in the company are mere servants and agents who are nothing more than hands to do the work and cannot be said to represent the mind or will. Others are directors and managers who represent the directing mind and will of the company, and control what it does. The state of mind of those managers is the state of mind of the company and is treated by the law as such."[31]

The introduction of the "identification" principle into the *criminal* law took place in 1944 as a result of three cases decided in that year: *DPP* v *Kent*

---

by aggregating all the acts and mental states of the relevant persons within the company in order to see whether collectively those acts and mental states would amount to the criminal offence had they been done and held by a single person. The doctrine has been rejected by the English courts and has also been the subject of criticism in some academic quarters: see, for example, *R* v *HM Coroner for East Kent, ex parte Spooner* (1989) 88 Cr App R 10 and Clarkson "Corporate Culpability" [1998] 2 Web JCLI, part 4(ii).

[27] In *R* v *HM Coroner for East Kent, ex parte Spooner* (1989) 88 Cr App R 10, Bingham LJ (as he then was) explained the distinction between vicarious liability and the liability of corporations under the "identification" principle in the following terms: "It is important to bear in mind an important distinction. A company may be vicariously liable for the negligent acts and omissions of its servants and agents, but for a company to be criminally liable for manslaughter ... it is required that the mens rea and actus reus of manslaughter should be established not against those who acted for or in the name of the company but against those who were to be identified as the embodiment of the company itself" (at 16). This passage was cited in *Legislating the Criminal Code: Involuntary Manslaughter* (Law Com No.237) (1996), at para. 6.34.

[28] [1915] AC 705.

[29] At p. 713.

[30] [1957] 1 QB 159.

[31] At p. 172.

and Sussex Contractors Ltd;[32] *R* v *ICR Haulage Ltd*;[33] and *Moore* v *Bresler*.[34]

In *DPP* v *Kent and Sussex Contractors Ltd* the respondent company had informations preferred against it in which it was alleged that for the purposes of the Motor Fuel (No.3) Rationing Order 1941, it had, with intent to deceive, made use of a document, signed by the transport manager of the company, which was false in a material particular. It was also alleged that in furnishing information in the document for the purposes of the order, it had made a statement which it knew to be false in a material particular. The offences in question were stated to be contrary to Regulations 82(1)(c) and 82(2) of the Defence (General) Regulations 1939. Before the justices, however, the informations were dismissed on the basis that a body corporate could not in law be guilty of the offence charged because an act of will or state of mind which could not be imputed to a corporation was implicit in the commission of the offences. In allowing the appeal, Viscount Caldecote LCJ sought to explain how a criminal intent could be imputed to a company in the following terms:

> "I think that a great deal of [counsel for the company's] argument on the question whether there can be imputed to a company the knowledge or intent of the officers of the company falls to the ground, because although the directors or general manager of a company are its agents, they are something more. A company is incapable of acting or speaking or even of thinking except in so far as its officers have acted, spoken, or thought... In the present case the first charge against the company was of doing something with intent to deceive, and the second was that of making a statement which the company knew to be false in a material particular. Once the ingredients of the offences are stated in that way it is unnecessary, in my view, to inquire whether it is proved that the company's officers acted on its behalf. *The officers are the company for this purpose* ..."[35]

In the second case, *R* v *ICR Haulage Ltd*,[36] the appellant company had been charged with the common law offence of conspiracy to defraud. Its submission that an indictment alleging such an offence could not lie against a limited company had been rejected at first instance and the company was convicted and fined. In dismissing its appeal Stable J had regard to a number of authorities, including *DPP* v *Kent and Sussex*

---

[32] [1944] 1 KB 146.

[33] [1944] KB 551.

[34] [1944] 2 All ER 515. These three cases are cited in, for example, *Legislating the Criminal Code: Involuntary Manslaughter* (Law Com No.237) (1996) at paras 6.30-6.31.

[35] [1944] 1 KB 146 at 155 (emphasis added). Hallett J, who also heard the appeal, explained as follows the rationale for accepting the existence of corporate criminal liability in the present case: "... if every person desiring to obtain petrol coupons has a duty imposed by statutory authority to furnish honest information, it seems strange and undesirable that a body corporate desiring to obtain petrol coupons and furnishing dishonest information for that purpose should be able to escape the liability which would be incurred in like case by a private person" (at 158).

[36] [1944] 1 KB 551.

Contractors Ltd which, he noted, might be argued to be distinguishable on the facts from the present case in that it was concerned with offences "charged under a Regulation having the effect of a statute", whereas the offence in question in *IRC Haulage* was enshrined in the common law. Stable J was, however, of the view that such a distinction had no material bearing on the issue to be determined by the court. In his judgment, therefore:

> "both on principle and in accordance with the balance of authority, the present indictment was properly laid against the company, and the learned commissioner rightly refused to quash."[37]

In the third of the three 1944 cases, *Moore* v *Bresler Ltd*,[38] Viscount Caldecote LCJ (once again) expressed the judgment of the court as follows:

> "The sales undoubtedly were fraudulent, but they were sales made with the authority of the respondent company by these two men as agents for the respondent company ... These two men were important officials of the company, and when they made statements and rendered returns ... they were clearly making those statements and giving those returns as officers of the company ... Their acts, therefore, ... *were the acts of the company*."[39]

It is clear from these cases that the "identification" principle affixes criminal liability to a company in respect of the acts or states of mind of those who can be said to exercise control over the company. In other words, the actions of the controlling officers of a company are regarded in law as having been the actions of the company itself.[40]

This principle reached its high point in the decision of the House of Lords in *Tesco Supermarkets Ltd* v *Nattrass*,[41] a case involving the prosecution of Tesco for the commission of an offence under the Trade Descriptions Act 1968. It was alleged that Tesco had acted contrary to section 11(2) of that Act in that it had indicated by way of an advertisement in one of its stores that it was offering goods for sale (a particular brand of washing powder) at a price lower than that at which it was in fact offering it for sale. In its defence, Tesco relied on the terms of section 24(1) of the 1968 Act. This

---

[37] At 559. Stable J was at pains to stress, however, that the decision was confined to the validity of the indictment on its face. It did not amount to a decision "that in every case where an agent of the limited company acting in its business commits a crime the company is automatically to be held criminally responsible" (*ibid.*).

[38] [1944] 2 All ER 515.

[39] At 516-517 (emphasis added).

[40] One commentator has expressed the position thus: "It is not status *per se* which matters; what is critical is that the persons in question have the authority to determine and direct company policy. The liability is not technically vicarious. Rather, the designated officials are thought to be so identified with the company that they embody its mind and will; they *are* the company": see Gobert, "Corporate Criminality: New Crimes for the Times" [1994] Crim LR 722 at 723.

[41] [1971] 2 All ER 127.

made provision for a due diligence defence.[42] In other words, if a defendant could show, for example, that the commission of the offence was due to the act or default of another person and that it had taken all reasonable precautions and exercised all due diligence to avoid the commission of such an offence by itself or by a person under his control, it was thereby absolved from liability. A question for the House of Lords, therefore, was whether the manager of the store was "another person" for the purposes of section 24(1). Their Lordships concluded that he was.

In reaching this conclusion, their Lordships considered the role of the store manager in the context of the operation of the company. That role, which involved day-to-day responsibility for the running of a particular store, did not involve the exercise of management functions delegated to him by the company. The company remained in control. In the case of a limited company such as Tesco, a failure to exercise due diligence would only occur where that failure was that of a director or senior manager in actual control of the company's operations who could be identified with the controlling mind and will of the company. In other words, a store manager in a company of this size (Tesco owned several hundred supermarkets at the time) was too far down what Lord Morris termed the "ladder of responsibility" for his actions to be said to be those of the company.[43] Lord Pearson explained the position thus:

> "In the present case the company has some hundreds of retail shops, and it would be far from reasonable to say that every one of its shop managers is the same person as the company ... Supervision of the

---

[42] In an interesting discussion on corporate criminality, Gobert has argued that rather than requiring the Crown to prove *mens rea*, a preferable approach would be to require a corporate defendant to establish due diligence. Although he acknowledges that such a defence has on occasion been incorporated into statute (e.g. s. 24(1) of the 1968 Act), he makes the case for an "across-the-board defence which would protect a corporate defendant from liability where the company has made a conscientious and reasonable effort to prevent the substantive crime which has occurred". In his opinion, "the burden should not be subject to discharge by mere proof of an unawareness of the dangers on the part of management without also showing that it was not reasonable to expect the company to have been aware of risks". Neither "should it be enough for the company to establish that its operation conformed to that which was prevalent in the industry" since "although compliance with an industry wide standard may be evidence of due diligence, the possibility must nevertheless be entertained that the entire industry has acted in a culpable manner". Thus for Gobert, in order for a company to succeed under the due diligence defence, it would be necessary for it to establish (because it will be in the best position to know what it has done to protect against the commission of a crime) on the balance of probabilities that "it took reasonable and appropriate steps under the circumstances to prevent harm from occurring": see "Corporate Criminality: New Crimes for the Times" [1994] Crim LR 722 at 729-730.

[43] Commenting on the decision in *Nattrass*, Professor Glanville Williams remarked that: "There is no absolute right and wrong about this, but the practical effect of *Tesco* appears to be to confine the identification doctrine to the behaviour of a few men meeting, say, in London, when the activities of the corporation are country-wide or even world-wide. It would seem on the whole to have been more sensible to have extended identification to cover the person or persons in control of local branches" (*Textbook on Criminal Law* (2nd edn 1983), p. 973, cited in *Legislating the Criminal Code: Involuntary Manslaughter* (Law Com. No.237) (1996) at p. 78, fn 62. Gobert has also criticised their Lordships' focus in *Nattrass* as having been "too narrow". In his opinion, "The law must be concerned not only with whether senior management has exercised due diligence, but whether there was due diligence throughout the company's organisational structure": see "Corporate Crime: New Crimes for the Times" [1994] Crim LR 722 at 732.

details of operations is not normally a function of higher management; it is normally carried out by employees at the level of foreman, chargehands, overlookers, floor managers and 'shop' managers (in the factory sense of 'shop')."[44]

In order for Tesco to rely successfully upon the section 24(1) defence, however, both limbs of that provision had to be satisfied. It was not enough to show that the act or default was that of "another person". It also had to be established that it had taken all reasonable precautions and exercised all due diligence to avoid the commission of an offence. The House of Lords accepted that, on the facts, Tesco had devised a proper system for the management of the store and had done all that they could to ensure that the system was implemented.

In *Nattrass*, Lord Reid sought to draw a distinction between the principle of identification and the doctrine of vicarious liability, as follows:

"A living person has a mind which can have knowledge or intention or be negligent and he has hands to carry out his intentions. A corporation has none of these; it must act through living persons, though not always one or the same person. Then the person who acts is not speaking or acting for the company. He is acting as the company and his mind which directs his acts is the mind of the company. There is no question of the company being vicariously liable. He is not acting as a servant, representative, agent or delegate. He is an embodiment of the company or, one could say, he hears and speaks through the persona of the company, within his appropriate sphere, and his mind is the mind of the company. If it is a guilty mind then that guilt is the guilt of the company. It must be a question of law whether, once the facts have been ascertained, a person in doing particular things is to be regarded as the company or merely as the company's servant or agent. In that case any liability of the company can only be a statutory or vicarious liability."[45]

Although the distinction which is described in this passage has clearly been both recognised and applied by the courts, it might be argued that there is more than a tinge of artificiality about it. If one were to consider the principle of identification from the perspective of vicarious liability, might it not be possible to argue that what the principle really amounts to is a special and limited form of vicarious liability for the acts or omissions of those in senior management positions within the company? By virtue of their position within a company and the control which they are able to exert over company policy and direction, the company is accordingly vicariously liable for all that the senior managers do within the course of their employment. Viewed in this way, the distinction between the identification principle and vicarious liability becomes more apparent than real.

---

[44] [1971] 2 All ER 127 at 148-150.
[45] At 131-132.

The "ameliorated" identification doctrine: *Meridian Global*

It has been suggested that as a result of the decision of the Privy Council in *Meridian Global Funds Management Asia Ltd* v *Securities Commission*[46] the "days of the identification doctrine, in its classic form, are numbered".[47] In this case, the Privy Council upheld the lower court judgments of Heron J, and of the New Zealand Court of Appeal,[48] to the effect that an employee of an investment management company amounted to the directing mind and will of the company and that, therefore, his knowledge was attributable to the company, with the result that the company was in breach of a duty under section 20(3) of the Securities Amendment Act 1988 (NZ) to give notice that it had become a substantial security holder in a public issuer.

Stated in these relatively bald terms, the decision does not appear to be of any great significance. Indeed, it might even be thought to have been merely a further example of the application of the classic identification principle. However, the significance of the decision becomes apparent when it is appreciated that the employee in question was an investment manager of the company. As one commentator has pointed out, "under the classic identification doctrine such an investment manager would not be sufficiently senior to represent the "mind" of the company".[49] Nevertheless, Lord Hoffmann (delivering the Privy Council opinion) refused to be constrained by the classical formulation of the principle. Instead, his Lordship observed that in cases such as the present:

> "... the court must fashion a special rule of attribution for the particular substantive rule. This is always a matter of interpretation: given that it was intended to apply to a company, how was it intended to apply? Whose act (or knowledge, or state of mind) was *for this purpose* intended to count as the act etc. of the company? One finds the answer to this question by applying the usual canons of interpretation taking into account the language of the rule (if it is a statute) and its content and policy?."[50]

Thus under what has been termed the "ameliorated identification doctrine",[51] a company may be held to be criminally liable even though the employee in question does not hold a position within the company which would previously have been regarded as sufficient for him or her to have been said to have been the directing mind and will of the company. In other words, *Meridian* suggests an approach to the principle of identification which moves away from an emphasis on status and focuses instead on context and responsibility. Thus a comparatively junior member of a company's management team may still be regarded as the controlling mind and will of the company for the purposes of establishing criminal liability

---

[46] [1995] 2 AC 500.
[47] Clarkson, "Corporate Culpability" [1998] 2 Web JCLI.
[48] [1994] 2 NZLR 291.
[49] Clarkson, "Corporate Culpability" [1998] 2 Web JCLI.
[50] [1995] 2 AC 500 at 507.
[51] Clarkson, "Corporate Culpability" [1998] Web JCLI.

where that person has responsibility for the relevant area of company activity to which that criminal liability applies. Applying this reasoning to the environmental context it would mean, therefore, that where a company has been charged with the commission of an environmental offence, the acts or knowledge of the person in that company with responsibility for environmental issues (including compliance with legal requirements) could be imputed to be the acts or knowledge of the company for the purposes of determining liability.

There is, however, a potentially significant limitation to the ambit of this version of the identification principle since "it still requires an individual to be identified within the corporate structure whose acts and knowledge can be attributed to the company".[52] As has been pointed out:

> "If the company's structures are impenetrable or if its policies are so "sloppy" that no person has been made responsible for the relevant area of activity, a company can still shield itself from corporate criminal liability."[53]

Vicarious liability

The principle of vicarious liability is well established in the law of tort. It means, in essence, that an employer is responsible for the acts or omissions of his or her employees which are committed within the course of their employment.

The important question in the context of the present chapter is whether or not an employer may be vicariously liable not only for the torts so committed by his employees, but also liable under the *criminal law* for the *criminal acts* or omissions of his employees (committed within the course of their employment).

In its report *Legislating the Criminal Code: Involuntary Manslaughter*,[54] the Law Commission drew attention to the "long-established principle of the common law" that vicarious liability does not form part of the criminal law. Thus in *Huggins*,[55] Raymond CJ had opined:

> "It is a point not to be disputed but that in criminal cases the principal is not answerable for the act of his deputy, as he is in civil cases; they must each answer for their own acts, and stand or fall by their own behaviour."

However, as the Law Commission report then proceeded to note, this general principle is subject to three exceptions. Thus vicarious criminal

---

[52] *ibid.*
[53] *ibid.*
[54] Law Com No. 237 (1996).
[55] (1730) 2 Ld Raym 1574, 92 ER 518.

liability may arise in the context of public nuisance,[56] criminal libel,[57] and certain statutory offences.[58]

In the case of statutory offences, the question whether or not a statutory provision imposes vicarious liability is a matter of construction which, it has been held depends on:

> "the object of the statute, the words used, the nature of the duty laid down, the person upon whom it is imposed, the person by whom it would in ordinary circumstances be performed, and the person upon whom the penalty is imposed."[59]

In a case where the proper construction of a statutory offence is that it does impose vicarious liability, the fact that an employee may have acted contrary to the express instructions of a corporate employer will not necessarily exclude the company from being found vicariously liable for its employee's acts.[60] Thus in *Director General of Fair Trading* v *Pioneer Concrete (UK) Ltd,*[61] where the Director General had obtained injunctions from the Restrictive Practices Court restraining the respondent companies from giving effect to agreements made with other companies relating to the supply of ready-mixed concrete in contravention of section 35(1) of the Restrictive Trade Practices Act 1976, the respondent companies had given express instructions to their employees to refrain from making or putting into effect any such agreements. Nevertheless, unbeknown to the respondent's management, certain of their employees had entered into such agreements in breach of the injunctions. In the subsequent proceedings for contempt which were brought by the Director General before the Restrictive Practices Court, it was accepted by the respondents that they were in contempt and they were duly fined. On appeal the Court of Appeal ruled in favour of the respondents. In the words of Russell LJ:

> "In our judgment an employer does not become party to an agreement or an arrangement if he prohibits his employee from entering into it, provided that the prohibition is in clear and unequivocal terms and is in no sense a sham. If the employee then chooses to enter into an

---

[56] See Chapter 8 for a fuller discussion of vicarious liability in the context of public nuisance.

[57] See, for example, *Pharmaceutical Society* v *London and Provincial Supply Association* (1880) 5 All Cas 857.

[58] See paras 6.8 and 6.9 of the Law Commission Report. Addressing the issue of vicarious liability for statutory offences in *Chisholm* v *Doulton* (1889) 22 QBD 736, Cave J remarked that: "A master is not criminally responsible for a death caused by his servant's negligence, and still less for an offence depending on the servant's malice; nor can a master be held liable for the guilt of his servant in receiving goods knowing them to have been stolen. And this principle of the common law applies also to statutory offences, with this difference, that it is in the power of the Legislature, if it so pleases, to enact ... that a man may be convicted and punished for an offence although there was no blameworthy condition of mind about him" (at 741).

[59] Per Atkin J in *Mousell Bros Ltd* v *London and North-Western Railway Co* [1917] 2 KB 836 at 845, cited in *Legislating the Criminal Code: Involuntary Manslaughter*, Law Com. No.237 (1996) at para. 6.10.

[60] See *Coppen* v *Moore (No.2)* [1898] 2 QB 306 and *Canadian Pacific Railway Co* v *Lockhart* [1942] AC 591.

[61] [1995] 1 AC 456; [1995] 1 All ER 135.

agreement or arrangement contrary to the instructions, then the employer does not become a party to the agreement or arrangement in the absence of the employee being cloaked with ostensible authority … It is the *prohibition*, and the prohibition alone which takes the employer outside the agreement or arrangement."[62]

On appeal to the House of Lords, however, it was unanimously held that the respondents were in contempt in that they were vicariously liable for the acts of their employees committed within the scope of their employment. Having regard to the passage from the Court of Appeal's judgment cited above, Lord Templeman remarked:

"My Lords, I cannot accept this pronouncement. It would allow a company to enjoy the benefit of restrictions outlawed by Parliament and the benefit of arrangements prohibited by the courts provided that the restrictions were accepted and implemented and the arrangements were negotiated by one or more employees who had been forbidden to do so by some superior employee identified in argument as a member of the 'higher management' of the company or by one or more directors of the company identified in argument as 'the guiding will' of the company."[63]

Lord Nolan, who delivered the other reasoned opinion in the appeal, examined the decision in *Coppen* v *Moore (No.2)*,[64] and concluded that:

"The principal significance of this case, and of the cases to which it refers,[65] as it seems to me, lies in the acceptance of the proposition that even in the case of a statute imposing criminal liability, and even without any express words to that effect, Parliament may be taken to have imposed a liability on an employer for the acts of his employees, provided that those acts were carried out in the course of the employment. *Further, the liability may be imposed even though the acts in question were prohibited by the employer.*"[66]

Vicarious liability in an environmental context can be seen in the case of *National Rivers Authority* v *Alfred McAlpine Homes East Ltd.*[67] Here the respondent company was engaged in building houses on a new residential development at the material time. A stream, which was "controlled water" within the meaning of section 104 of the Water Resources Act 1991, ran through the development. A water quality engineer employed by the NRA

---

[62] [1994] ICR 57 at 66-67.

[63] [1995] 1 All ER 135 at 141-142.

[64] [1898] 2 QB 306.

[65] These were, respectively, *R* v *Stephens* (1866) LR 1 QB 702, *Mullins* v *Collins* (1874) LR 9 QB 292 and *Bond* v *Evans* (1888) 21 QBD 249.

[66] [1995] 1 All ER 135 at 149 (emphasis added). Clarkson has identified this aspect of vicarious liability as being "over-inclusive". In his opinion, it dictates that "a company can be penalized for the fault of an employee for whom the company ought not to be held responsible in that the company may have done everything within its power to prevent the wrongdoing": see "Corporate Culpability" [1998] 2 Web JCLI.

[67] [1994] 4 All ER 286.

carried out an inspection of the stream and found that downstream of the development, the water was cloudy and contained a number of dead and distressed fish. He interviewed the company's site agent and its site manager and both admitted that the pollution had been caused by washing wet cement into the stream during the construction of a water feature on the development. The NRA accordingly prosecuted the company for an offence contrary to section 85 of the Water Resources Act 1991.

Before the justices, the company submitted that on the facts, there was no case to answer. Its submission was accepted, hence the appeal brought by the NRA. The question posed for the consideration of the Divisional Court was:

> "Whether [the justices] were correct to conclude that an offence under s.85 of the Water Resources Act 1991 could only be committed by a company if the offence was committed by a person exercising the 'controlling mind and will' of the company, such as a director, manager, secretary or some similar officer of the company, and therefore correct to find that there was no case to answer and to dismiss the information."[68]

The first speech in the successful appeal was delivered by Simon Brown LJ. After having stated the facts of the case, his Lordship proceeded to cite quite extensively from the speeches delivered in *Alphacell Ltd* v *Woodward*,[69] the leading authority on the nature of the "causing" water pollution offence.[70] Although in *Alphacell* none of their Lordships expressly referred to the principle of vicarious liability, for Simon Brown LJ (and for Morland J) their Lordship's dicta supported the view that the case is "an illustration of vicarious liability rather than a case where the House of Lords concluded that those representing the directing mind and will of the company had themselves personally caused the polluting matter to escape".[71]

In truth, the reference to *Alphacell* serves to demonstrate that rather different issues arise in terms of corporate liability depending on whether the offence in question is one involving *mens rea*, or is one of strict liability. In the former context it is evident that a court must be satisfied not only that the company did the act or omission which constitutes the offence (the *actus reus)* but also that *mens rea* requirements are satisfied by an appropriate person within the company. This is the issue we have considered above in the discussion of the "identification" doctrine and the "ameliorated identification" doctrine.

---

[68] In other words, therefore, the issue for the Divisional Court to consider was whether liability for a s. 85 offence was founded, in the corporate context, on the principle of identification alone, or whether an employer could also be vicariously liable for the commission of an offence by one of its employees.

[69] [1972] 2 All ER 475.

[70] This case will be considered more fully below, Chapter 9.

[71] Per Simon Brown LJ [1994] 4 All ER 286 at 293.

In cases, however, where criminal liability is strict the issue of identifying an appropriate individual as having the necessary *mens rea* does not arise. The only question is whether the acts of a company's employees, done in the course of their employment, can be regarded as acts of the company. It is unsurprising that the courts should have been reluctant to countenance corporate arguments suggesting that this has not been the case.

There are strong policy reasons why such liability, whether or not it be truly "vicarious", ought to apply to strict liability environmental offences, such as "causing" water pollution. In a vast majority of cases, the act or omission which has led to the pollution of a watercourse is likely to be that of an employee occupying a relatively lowly position in the chain of command within a company. If a company were able, in such circumstances, to avoid the imposition of strict criminal liability by arguing that the acts in question were those of its employees and not its own acts, the potential for the legislation effectively to protect the environment would be seriously compromised.[72]

It may be that the harshness inherent in strict liability environmental offences is further compounded by the possibility of such broad corporate liability in respect of these offences. This might be thought to weigh in favour of a limited approach to the question "whose acts or omissions should be regarded as those of the company?" In fact the better view is probably that as the same policy arguments support both strict and such broad corporate liability it would be rather odd to deny application of the latter because of the existence of the former.

PERSONAL CRIMINAL LIABILITY: DIRECTORS AND OTHERS

There may be occasions when the acts or omissions which involve commission of one of the environmental offences with which we are concerned have actually been performed (or neglected) personally by a director or similar officer of company. In relation to the primary pollution offences this may, perhaps, be relatively unusual; the individual culprit more usually being some rather more lowly employee. But even such primary pollution offences may perhaps not infrequently be committed by directors and similar officers of quite small companies, individuals with a relatively "hands on" involvement in the operations of "their" businesses. Even in rather larger companies the potential for a director or similar officer to commit personally what we have referred to as secondary-style offences (for example, the giving of false information, etc.) is by no means a remote possibility.

---

[72] Clarkson has remarked that: "The arguments in favour of vicarious liability are largely pragmatic. It by-passes all the problems associated with the other doctrines such as finding a person sufficiently important in the corporation who has committed the crime. As long as someone (anyone) acting in the course of their employment has committed a crime the company can be held liable. It prevents companies shielding themselves from criminal liability by delegating potentially illegal operations to employees": see "Corporate Culpability" [1998] 2 Web JCLI. Pretty much the same justfications apply to the imposition of strict liability in criminal law.

When, however, reference is made to the *personal* criminal liability of directors and similar officers of companies, that reference is generally not to this ordinary responsibility for their *own* offences. Rather, reference is being made to provisions in legislation which may render those responsible for the running of companies personally criminally liable for offences committed *by* those companies *through the actions of others* within those companies. This is, we might say, a form of derivative criminal liability. It is founded not upon the director defendant having himself or herself done those things proscribed by the criminal offence; it is a responsibility imposed upon such a person, in prescribed circumstances, deriving from the fact that their company has been ascribed criminal responsibility.

Such derivative criminal responsibility on the part of those who run companies does not exist as a general principle of corporate criminal law. It operates only in cases where statute specifically so provides, and then in accordance with the limits or scope specified in that statute. The matter is, however, rendered less complex than might otherwise have been the case, by the fact that such "personal liability" provision is quite commonplace in environmental (and similar – e.g. health and safety) legislation, and the provisions which are there to be found take a standard form.

A typical example may be found in section 157 of the Environmental Protection Act 1990. This provides:

> "157(1). Where an offence under any provision of this Act committed by a body corporate is proved to have been committed with the consent or connivance of, or to have been attributable to any neglect on the part of, any director, manager, secretary or other similar officer of the body corporate or a person who was purporting to act in any such capacity, he as well as the body corporate shall be guilty of that offence and shall be liable to be proceeded against and punished accordingly.

> (2) Where the affairs of a body corporate are managed by its members, subsection (1) above shall apply to the acts or defaults of a member in connection with his functions of management as if he were a director of the body corporate."

In order to appreciate the scope of liability under this typical provision we shall need to consider:

- Who may be liable: in particular, the meaning of "similar officers"?
- The scope of such liability: the meanings of "consent", "connivance" and "neglect"?

Who may be liable?

The issue here is the scope of the phrase: "director, manager, secretary or similar officer of a body corporate or a person who is purporting to act in such capacity".

Some guidance is afforded by the decision of the Court of Appeal in *R* v *Boal*.[73] The defendant was assistant general manager of Foyles booksellers, in Charing Cross Road. Officers from the London Fire and Civil Defence Authority inspected the shop on a day when the defendant was in charge, the general manager being on leave. Serious breaches of the premises' fire certificate were discovered and prosecutions were brought in the Crown Court, under the Fire Precautions Act 1971, against the company and also personally against the defendant in his capacity as a "manager". The 1971 Act contained a derivative personal criminal liability section in standard form: section 23. The defendant, who evidently (and no doubt with some pride) regarded himself as a "manager" of Foyles, pleaded guilty and was convicted. On appeal against sentence the appeal court voiced doubts about whether it was correct to have regarded the defendant as a "manager of the body corporate", and so granted leave to appeal against conviction also.

Following a review of decisions where, under other legislation and in a variety of differing contexts the courts had considered the meaning of the word "manager", the Court of Appeal concluded that the term might bear a broad or narrow meaning according to that context. In the context of the imposition of a criminal liability it would be appropriate to follow the approach in those cases which had taken a narrow view as to those whose functions brought them within this category. Approval was, accordingly, afforded to the words of Blackburn J in *Gibson* v *Barton*:[74]

> "A manager would be, in ordinary talk, a person who has the management of the whole affairs of the company; not an agent who is to do a particular thing, or a servant who is to obey orders, but a person who is entrusted with power to transact the whole affairs of the company."

Approved also was Lord Denning MR's reference in *Registrar of Restrictive Trading Agreements* v *W H Smith and Sons Ltd*,[75] to a manager being:

> " … a person who is managing in a governing role the affairs of the company itself."

The issue for the Court of Appeal was, therefore, whether the position of the defendant in the company, Foyles, matched these descriptions. Given the rather strange way in which the appeal had arisen the Court was under some difficulty as regards evidence of fact. It was noted that in some respects the defendant was a person of considerable seniority. There were only two directors of the company, and the only employee more senior than the defendant was the general manager who was on leave at the time of the inspection. Nevertheless, the court noted that the defendant's position as assistant general manager was more one confined to particular tasks –

---

[73] [1992] 3 All ER 177.
[74] (1875) LR 10 QB 329.
[75] [1969] 3 All ER 1065.

books purchasing, counting takings – than one relating more broadly to the management of the company. The Court of Appeal was therefore unwilling to regard the defendant as falling within the ambit of the statutory description of persons subject to derivative personal criminal liability.

Simon Brown J explained that:

> "Whilst declining to accept the full width of [counsel for the defendant's] submissions – which include the proposition that not even … the general manager could properly be said to fall within section 23 – we are certainly disposed to agree that [the defendant] could well have been regarded as responsible only for the day to day running of the bookshop rather than enjoying any sort of governing role in respect of the affairs of the company itself."

It would appear from *Boal* that a distinction must be drawn between being involved in the management of a company and (merely) being responsible for the management of an activity in which the company engages.

A broadly similar distinction may be found in *Woodhouse* v *Walsall Metropolitan Borough Council*.[76] The defendant was employed by Caird Environmental Ltd as the "General Manager" of the largest of its waste sites. His contract made him responsible for:

- the commercial operation of the site;
- co-ordinating activities of a management team;
- improving and maintaining operational performance;
- site development.

He was responsible to Caird's "Director of Special Waste Disposal", who prepared a monthly report to the company's board from information supplied by the defendant.

The magistrates convicted the defendant, finding him to fall within the derivative criminal liability requirement of being a "manager" of Caird. Their decision was much influenced by the statement made by Simon Brown J in *Boal* that:

> " … the intended scope of section … is … to fix with criminal liability only those who are in a position of real authority."

For the magistrates the defendant could be regarded as such a person, given his management power in relation to his particular site, and also certain "peripheral responsibilities" as regards two other sites.

On appeal the Divisional Court regarded the magistrates as having misinterpreted the words of Simon Brown J. In regarding "real authority" as relating to power in relation to an aspect of the company's business

---

[76] [1994] Env LR 30; [1994] 1 BCLC 435.

(running the waste site) the magistrates had failed to note that Simon Brown J had described "managers" also as:

> "The decision makers within the company who have both the power and the responsibility to decide corporate policy and strategy."

In short, the concept related to those who determined what the company should do, and had power to direct its employees on those matters. It did not apply to those who, ultimately, were at the direction *of the company* as regards performance of their functions, even where those persons were, in other respects, persons with "real authority" within the organisation.

McGowan LJ summarised the position as follows:

> "Merely to speak of 'in real authority' amounts ... to nothing ... Had [the magistrates finished Simon Brown J's sentence] ... they could not possibly have arrived at the conclusion they did, because there was nothing in the evidence which could properly have led them to conclude that the [defendant] was a decision-maker within the company having both the power and responsibility to decide corporate policy and strategy."

Consent, connivance, or neglect

This formula is found in a number of statutes which impose criminal liability on corporate bodies. In *R* v *Wilson*,[77] Evans LJ expressed the view, in the context of the Insurance Companies Act 1982,[78] that it creates an "essentially parasitic" offence in that it is ancillary to the offence committed by a body corporate. On the basis of the words used, it is an offence which may be committed in a number of alternative ways. Where the prosecution is unable to specify which of the alternatives applies to a defendant, it is often charged as one offence and the various ways in which it may be committed are stated in the alternative. An indictment alleging the various alternatives will not therefore be duplicitous.[79]

---

[77] [1997] 1 All ER 119.

[78] Section 91(1) of that Act imposes criminal liability on directors in exactly the same terms as s. 157(1) of the Environmental Protection Act 1990.

[79] See *R* v *Leighton and Town and Country Refuse Collections Ltd* [1997] Env LR 411. In giving the judgment of the Court of Appeal in that case, Auld LJ observed that this "well established practice does not seem to have its origin in Rule 7 of the Indictment Rules, though it is consistent with it". Rule 7 provides that: "Where an offence created by or under an enactment states the offence to be the doing or the omission to do any one of any different acts in the alternative, or the doing or the omission to do any act in any one of any different capacities, or with any one of any different intentions, or states any part of the offence in the alternative, the acts, omissions, capacities or intentions, or other matters stated in the alternative in the enactment or subordinate instrument may be stated in the alternative in an indictment charging the offence" (SI 1971/1253). Continuing on the same theme, Auld LJ further observed that "since the middle of the 19th century at least" it had been common practice to put in one charge the aiding and abetting of an offence and that the "same principle and practice are clearly applicable to statutory formulations" of the sort which the court in *Leighton* were concerned" (at 419).

Some guidance as regards the meaning of "consent, connivance or neglect" was afforded by the Divisional Court in *Huckerby* v *Elliott*:[80] albeit in a rather different context to that of environmental liability. Windmill Clubs Ltd had pleaded guilty and been convicted by magistrates in Leeds of having operated premises in which *chemin de fer* was played, without being the holder of an appropriate gaming licence under the Finance Act 1966. A charge was also brought against one Frank Lunn, the secretary and director of the company, under section 305(3) of the Customs and Excise Act 1952, in similar terms to the personal criminal liability provisions set out above. Lunn, also, pleaded guilty. The charge against Mavis Huckerby, the appellant, was also brought under section 305, charging that she was a director of the company and that the offence of the company was attributable to her neglect as a director of the company.

The evidence before the Divisional Court made evident that, in the words of Lord Parker CJ:

> "although [the appellant] was a director, she knew very little about the conduct of the New Embassy Club."

The conduct of that club, when the unlicensed gaming had occurred:

> "was quite clearly left to Mr Lunn who was ... not only the secretary but her co-director, and to Mr Beveridge, who was the manager. She did not, for instance, know how long *chemin de fer* had been played ..."

On this evidence the stipendiary magistrate had found the appellant guilty. Having noted that it was Mr Lunn who was in much closer touch with operations at the New Embassy Club than the appellant, he continued:

> "it does seem to me that even if a secretary of the company had taken it upon himself to break the law, it must surely be for the director of the company to exercise some degree of control over what is going on or there is no point in being a director. To escape liability by saying 'I have delegated all my duties to a servant' seems to me to make a nonsense of the position of a director. I feel this: that a servant of a company ... is more likely to be encouraged in breaking the law if he knows that his superiors as directors are slack or lax in their supervision of the company. Similarly a secretary or director may be inclined to consent to the commission of an offence if he knows that his fellow directors are not supervising the running of the company properly. If that state of affairs exists then the neglect of the directors to carry out their duties is clearly leading to the commission of the offence, albeit indirectly, and clearly the commission of the offence is attributable to neglect on the part of the directors."

On the appeal, Lord Parker CJ regarded these words as expressing the duties of directors in a way which was much too wide. Far from it being

---

[80] [1970] 1 All ER 189.

the case that a director might face criminal liability on grounds of having allowed a generally lax attitude to persist in the company – and without, it seems, need for particular neglect in relation to the particular offence in question – the true situation was that:

> "it is perfectly proper for a director to leave matters to another director or to an official of the company, and ... he is under no obligation to test the accuracy of anything that he is told by such a person, or even to make certain that he is complying with the law."

On the basis that Mr Lunn was known to be taking charge of the operation of the Embassy Club and that the appellant had no reason to distrust him or doubt his competence, this was not a case where the prosecution had demonstrated that the offence was the consequence of any neglect on the appellant's part.

Ashworth J expressed agreement with Lord Parker CJ, but added some words commenting on the stipendiary magistrate's interpretation of the general words "consent, connivance and neglect". As regards "consent", Ashworth J agreed with the statement that:

> "a director consents to the commission of an offence by his Company [when] he is well aware of what is going on and agrees to it."[81]

For this reason there was no doubt that Mr Lunn had rightly pleaded guilty and been convicted: "he knew what was going on and agreed with it ..."

On the meaning of "connivance" the magistrate had said:

> "Where he connives at the offence committed by the company he is equally well aware of what is going on but his agreement is tacit, not actively encouraging what happens but letting it continue and saying nothing about it."

Ashworth J commented that it was "enough ... to say that I do not disagree with that". It was, rather, with the magistrates view of "attributable to neglect" that more difficulty was experienced. The magistrate had said, as regards this limb:

> "it would seem to me that the offence which is being committed may well be without his knowledge but it is committed in circumstances where he ought to know what is going on and he fails to carry out his duty as a director to see the law is observed."

Ashworth J was unwilling to accept the existence of any such broad duty on directors to "see that the law is observed".

---

[81] In *Attorney General's Reference (No.1 of 1995)* [1996] 4 All ER 21, Lord Taylor CJ referred to the "rather general nature" of Ashworth J's dictum and observed that it "does not throw much light on the issue which has been raised in the present case" (at 26).

"For my part I do not accept that as a right contention at all. It seems to me that in effect to express the duty in that way is to make it absolute."

The word "neglect" was not to be interpreted as involving failure to have achieved this absolute objective. There was nothing in the evidence to suggest neglect on the part of the appellant in not having taken positive steps to check and ensure that no offences were being committed. Ashworth J concluded:

" ... it would be wrong to say that she was neglecting her duty if she failed to make specific inquiry whether a licence had been obtained ..."

Huckerby v *Elliott* would seem to sound important warnings against over-eager attribution of neglect, and hence personal criminal liability, where a company of which the defendant is a director has committed an offence under environmental legislation. It provides a reminder that such personal liability will accrue only upon a finding that a director has failed in the duties the law casts upon persons in that capacity, and that the law does permit a director of an apparently well run company, which appears to be attending to its legal obligations in the environmental and other fields, to take something of a back seat in terms of personal monitoring or supervision of activities.[82] In *Huckerby* reference was made with approval to the statements about the duties of directors to be found in the judgment of Romer J in *Re City Equitable Fire Insurance Co Ltd:*[83] that it is perfectly proper for a director to leave matters to another director or to an official of the company, and that he is under no obligation to test the accuracy of anything he is told by such a person, or even to make certain that that person is complying with the law. It should be noted, however, that Romer J expressed this matter subject to, in his words: "the absence of grounds of suspicion".

SENTENCING FOR ENVIRONMENTAL OFFENCES

Where a defendant has been found guilty of having committed an environmental offence, it will fall to a judge or magistrate to determine the sentence to be imposed. Imprisonment is of course a possibility in some cases, but custodial sentences are rare in respect of environmental offences.

---

[82] In cases of this kind, where delegation is pleaded or relied upon, the facts of the particular case will have to be closely examined. Thus in *Hirschler* v *Birch* [1987] RTR 13, where the defendant (the managing director of a company) had been minded to import several thousand sets of high-level vehicle brake lights and had made enquiries of a co-director as to their legal status in the UK, justices convicted him of an offence contrary to s. 20 of the Trade Descriptions Act 1968 on the basis that his neglect was apparent from the precipitate confirmation of the sale and his failure to assure himself that an authoritative source had been consulted as to the legality of the lights. His appeal against conviction was dismissed. In the opinion of Woolf LJ and Macpherson J, the facts of the case could be distinguished from those of *Huckerby* v *Elliott*. The justices had found that the defendant had not done what he should have done and although the case was "undoubtedly near the line", the appeal court was not prepared to attack the justices' findings.
[83] [1925] Ch 497.

A far more likely outcome will be the imposition of a fine. Where a defendant has been convicted of a summary offence, magistrates are entitled to form their own view as to the amount of a fine, subject to the statutory maximum levels. In the case of a trial on indictment, a Crown Court judge has the power to impose an unlimited fine on a defendant.

In each case, the levying of a fine calls for the exercise of discretion on the part of the judge or magistrate. Various considerations need to be taken into account in arriving at a figure which properly reflects the gravity of the crime. One such consideration is of course the need to deter other potential defendants from committing the same or a similar environmental offence. Another involves the consideration of factors which might aggravate the offence, such as a defendant's previous convictions for environmental offences or their unco-operative attitude towards the enforcing agencies. Still further, a judge or magistrate will need to have regard to any mitigating factors which might exist, such as a previously good environmental record or the entry of a guilty plea. Collectively these considerations ensure that the task of determining an appropriate sentence is by no means a straightforward one.[84] It is perhaps not surprising, therefore, that sentencing for environmental offences has been the subject of quite forceful criticism from some quarters.

The Environment Agency has been in the vanguard of those who are concerned at the low levels of fines imposed on those who pollute the environment. In the context of fines imposed for water pollution offences, its Chief Executive has gone on record as saying that:

> "These fines of a few thousand pounds are no deterrent to multi-million pound companies – we want fines that reflect the seriousness of the crime".[85]

The available statistics suggest that these concerns are not without foundation. Thus although a magistrate has the power to impose a fine of up to £20,000 for the offences of causing or knowingly permitting water pollution,[86] this statutory maximum has, it appears, only been imposed on one occasion to date, in 1998.[87]

The growing public awareness of the harm done to the environment by pollution, coupled with concerns such as those referred to above about the generally low level of fines for environmental offences, thus provided the

---

[84] For a detailed and illuminating discussion of the kinds of arguments advanced by defendants in prosecutions for environmental offences, see de Prez, "Excuses, excuses: The ritual trivialisation of environmental prosecutions" (2000) 12 JEL 65. The research which underpins the discussion took the form of 25 environmental prosecutions which were observed by the author.

[85] See *Water Pollution Incidents in England and Wales 1998* (The Environment Agency, 1999) para.8.4, p. 36.

[86] See s. 85 of the Water Resources Act 1991.

[87] See *Water Pollution Incidents in England and Wales 1998*, para.8.4, p. 36. The case in question was *Environment Agency* v *Shell UK Ltd*, 19th October 1998, and the fine was imposed in respect of the escape of 140 tons of refined oil into the Manchester Ship Canal, *ibid.* para. 7.7.3, p. 34.

catalyst for a direction issued by the Home Secretary to the Sentencing Advisory Panel in July 1999. This required the Panel to consider various environmental offences[88] and to issue an Advice to the Court of Appeal in due course.

The Sentencing Advisory Panel is an independent advisory non-departmental public body sponsored by the Home Department.[89] Its remit is to provide the Court of Appeal (Criminal Division) with views on sentencing matters so as to assist the Court in framing sentencing guidelines or making amendments to those already in existence. Following a period of consultation with various organisations with whom the Panel is required to consult, together with various other individuals and organisations working in the environmental field, the Panel published its Advice to the Court of Appeal.[90]

Given that the statistical information available to the Panel indicated a very high incidence of fines being imposed for environmental offences,[91] it is not surprising that the Panel took the view that "fines should be the starting point for sentencing of both *persons* and *companies* for environmental offences."[92] In the opinion of the Panel, environmental offences lend themselves to the imposition of fines for two main reasons:

(i) they are non-violent offences which involve no immediate physical threat to the person; and

(ii) they are offences which are "generally committed in situations where the defendant has failed to devote proper resources to preventing a breach of the law."[93]

Despite their high incidence, fines are of course but one form of sentence which might be imposed by a magistrate or judge in respect of many environmental offences. Accordingly part of the Panel's Advice is given over to a consideration of sentencing alternatives to fines.

---

[88] The five offences covered by the direction were: carrying on a prescribed process without, or in breach of, an authorisation (s. 23 of the Environmental Protection Act 1990); depositing, recovering or disposing of controlled waste without a site licence or in breach of its conditions (s. 33 of the Environmental Protection Act 1990); polluting controlled waters (section 85 of the Water Resources Act 1991); abstracting water illegally (s. 24 of the Water Resources Act 1991); and failing to meet packaging, recycling and recovery obligations, or to register or to provide information (s. 93 of the Environment Act 1995 and the Producer Responsibility Obligations (Packaging Waste) Regulations 1997, SI No. 648).

[89] It was established under s. 81 of the Crime and Disorder Act 1998.

[90] This took place on 1st March 2000. See further, Parpworth, "Environmental Offences: views from the Sentencing Advisory Panel for England and Wales" [2000] Env. Liability 91.

[91] The Home Office statistics for 1997 and 1998 provided the sentencing profile for three of the five environmental offences falling within the scope of the Home Secretary's direction (ss. 23 and 33 of the Environmental Protection Act 1990 and s. 85 of the Water Resources Act 1991). These revealed that where an individual had been convicted, 71% were fined, 23% were discharged, 2% received a community sentence and 4% received a custodial sentence. Where a company had been convicted for an environmental offence, 96% were fined and 4% were discharged.

[92] Advice, para.14.

[93] *ibid.*

One such alternative is the imposition of a custodial sentence. As was noted above, a term of imprisonment is rarely imposed upon a person who has committed an environmental offence. For a custodial sentence to be the appropriate form of punishment, the Panel has taken the view that:

> "a case would need to combine serious damage, or the risk of serious damage, with a very high degree of culpability on the part of the offender."[94]

Moreover, the Advice indicates that imprisonment ought only to be considered where (i) the offence amounts to a deliberate or reckless breach of the law or the defendant acted from a financial motive (profit or cost-saving) and (ii) human health has been damaged or put at risk; or, the pollutant was noxious, widespread or pervasive, or liable to spread widely or have long-lasting effects.[95]

It is clear from the foregoing that the custody threshold for environmental offences is a high one. This point is illustrated by the decision in *R* v *O'Brien* and *R* v *Enkel*,[96] where the defendants, who had illegally dumped 2000 rubber tyres, had been convicted of various environmental offences[97] in respect of their behaviour and sentenced to a term of eight months imprisonment.[98] On appeal, the Court of Appeal held that the custody threshold had not been passed in the present case due to the fact that the tyres were not dangerous, that there had been no long term effect on the environment, that there had been no repeated breaches of the law and that the defendants had pleaded guilty (albeit at the last minute). In the opinion of Goldring J, "the justice of the case would have been met by a fine or a community service order" rather than by a term of imprisonment.

It is worth remembering that in reaching such a conclusion, the Court of Appeal was dealing with the particular facts of the case before it rather than seeking to express a more general view about sentencing in respect of environmental offences. However, with reference to the views of the Sentencing Advisory Panel[99] referred to above, it would seem that this is just the type of case which would not justify a term of imprisonment in the opinion of that body. The mitigating factors identified by Goldring J, in particular the absence of a long-lasting effect on the environment, caused the offence to fall below the custody threshold, even though the Court of Appeal did accept that "the appellants became involved in the offences because they saw a chance of making a quick profit". In short, applying the

---

[94] Advice, para. 29.

[95] *ibid.*

[96] [2000] Env LR 653.

[97] Section 33 of the Environmental Protection Act 1990.

[98] The maximum sentence for a conviction on indictment for this offence is two years: s. 33(8)(b).

[99] The Court of Appeal in *R* v *O'Brien* was sent documents expressing the Panel's interest in this type of offence. However, Goldring J spoke for the Court when he observed that: "We are a little surprised that counsel for the Environment Agency … knows nothing about that matter and has had no submissions to make" ([2000] Env LR 653 at 655).

criteria suggested by the Panel, the appellants motive was cancelled out by the mitigating factors.

Prison is of course not the only alternative to a fine where an environmental offence has been committed. In addition to community sentences, the Advice draws attention to two further alternatives which may have some utility in the environmental field: compensation orders and deprivation orders. The power to grant these orders is conferred upon the courts by the terms of the Powers of Criminal Courts (Sentencing) Act 2000.[100]

Compensation orders are particularly useful where there is an identifiable victim of a crime. In the environmental context, this could be a person or company (or their insurers) who has incurred expense in the form of clean-up costs. The Panel has taken the view that where an environmental offence has been committed, a court "should always consider making a compensation order" and that "it should give reasons if it decides not to do so".[101] However, despite their apparent attraction, compensation orders do have an important drawback. At the time of writing, the statutory maximum level for the award of compensation by a magistrates court is £5,000. An unfavourable comparison can therefore be made between this figure and the statutory maximum level of fine for a summary offence, i.e. £20,000. Such matters are strictly beyond the remit of the Sentencing Advisory Panel and for that matter the courts. However, in its Advice, the Panel has undertaken to bring this inconsistency to the attention of Ministers.[102] Moreover, it is worth noting that the House of Commons Environment, Transport and Regional Affairs Select Committee has added its support for an increase in the monetary limit on compensation orders imposed by magistrates.[103]

Deprivation orders involve the confiscation of equipment which has been used in the commission of an offence. They may be issued in addition to or as an alternative to the imposition of a fine. In an environmental context, there is an obvious attraction in deprivation orders, particularly where a defendant has previous convictions for the same offence and a court takes the view that confiscation is the only effective means of ensuring that he or she will not re-offend.

Although the Sentencing Advisory Panel's Advice to the Court of Appeal has been broadly welcomed since its publication,[104] it is, as its name implies, merely advice to that Court. The Court of Appeal is under no obligation to follow it, although clearly it must have regard to any Advice

---

[100] Sections 130 and 143, respectively. Previously the powers to grant such orders were to be found in ss. 35 and 43, respectively, of the Powers of Criminal Courts Act 1973.

[101] Advice, para. 30.

[102] Advice, para. 31.

[103] See its Sixth Report for the 1999-2000 session, *The Environment Agency*, para. 98.

[104] See, for example, the views of the House of Commons Environment, Transport and Regional Affairs Select Committee expressed in its Sixth Report for the 1999-2000 session, *The Environment Agency*, at para. 98.

which it receives from the Panel. In the time that has passed since its establishment, the Panel has published several Advices on sentencing matters across a range of offences. These have met with a varied response from the Court of Appeal. In the case of the Advice on sentencing for the importation and possession of opium,[105] the Court adopted the recommendations of the Panel when it determined the appeal in *R v Mashaollahi*.[106] This is perhaps not so very surprising given that the Court of Appeal had itself referred the matter to the Panel under the terms of section 81(2) of the Crime and Disorder Act 1998. However, the Panel's Advice on sentencing for environmental offences received a rather more lukewarm response in *R v Milford Haven Port Authority*.[107]

The appeal in this case arose from the decision of Steel J in the Cardiff Crown Court in *Environment Agency v Milford Haven Port Authority and Andrews*.[108] The trial was concerned with the much publicised running aground of the *Sea Empress* as it attempted to enter the Port of Milford Haven whilst being piloted by a person supplied by the Port Authority under a compulsory scheme. The incident led to the escape of more than 70,000 tons of crude oil from the ship into the sea. A large-scale cleanup operation followed and this coupled with the type of oil, the time of year and the prevailing weather conditions, served to lessen the environmental impact of the spillage to a level below that of original forecasts. However, despite these measures and the element of good fortune involved, the spillage still had a significant impact upon the sea bird population and caused fishing and crab and lobster harvesting to be banned in the area for a period of three and six months respectively. The total cleanup cost was estimated at £60 million, although as Steel J pointed out in giving his judgment, this figure "does not reflect the financial impact on tourism or commercial fisheries measured in total in further tens of millions of pounds".[109]

The Port Authority was prosecuted by the Environment Agency on two counts: (i) that it had caused the pollution of controlled waters contrary to section 85(1) of the Water Resources Act 1991; and (ii) that it had committed a public nuisance. It pleaded guilty to the first count on the basis of the strict liability nature of the offence,[110] and the second charge was ordered by Steel J to lay on the file. The issue on which the Port Authority appealed was not, therefore, whether it was criminally liable for the oil spillage. Instead, its appeal centred upon the extent of its liability.

In the Crown Court, Steel J had assessed the extent of that liability at £4 million, following a consideration of various arguments which had been

---

[105] Published in May 2000.
[106] [2001] Cr App R 6.
[107] [2000] Env LR 632.
[108] [1999] Lloyd's Rep 673.
[109] At 679.
[110] See Chapter 9.

put to him in mitigation.[111] The level of fine was welcomed by, amongst others, the Environment Agency. Its Chief Executive was reported as saying that it represented "an important landmark in environmental protection" which would "cause the businessmen who cynically calculate that a bit of environmental damage and the usual low fine are a cheaper and more acceptable alternative to operating their factories and equipment properly, to think again".[112] Certainly it is worth noting that the fine comfortably eclipsed the previous highest fine for an environmental offence (£1 million) which had been imposed upon Shell UK Ltd for causing 156 tons of crude oil to pollute the River Mersey. For this reason, therefore, the decision might have represented the beginning of a new chapter in the relationship between the courts and the environment so that Lord Woolf's rhetorical question "are the judiciary environmentally myopic" could have been answered in the negative.[113] However, on appeal the Court of Appeal took a rather different view as to the extent of the Port Authority's liability.

The judgment of the Court of Appeal was delivered by the then Lord Chief Justice, Lord Bingham. Following a summary of Steel J's reasoning for setting the level of fine at £4 million, Lord Bingham embarked upon a review of a number of cases which, it had been argued, were of assistance in the present context. The majority of these cases related to prosecutions brought under health and safety legislation and therefore in his Lordship's opinion, they did not provide "anything approaching an exact analogy". One health and safety case was, however, regarded as of substantial assistance to the determination of the appeal: *R* v *F Howe & Son (Engineers) Ltd.*[114]

Howe involved a prosecution under the Health & Safety at Work etc. Act 1974 and associated legislation in respect of a fatal accident which occurred at the appellants' precision engineering factory. At the trial before Fanner J in the Bristol Crown Court, the appellants pleaded guilty on four counts and were fined a total of £48,000 and ordered to pay £7,500 costs. They appealed on the basis that the total fine was excessive. In delivering the judgment of the Court of Appeal, Scott Baker J made some general remarks in relation to sentencing for health and safety offences. He observed that:

> "Disquiet has been expressed in several quarters[115] that the level of fine for health and safety offences is too low. We think there is force

---

[111] These involved five arguments: a guilty plea; the payment of the prosecution's costs; the status of the defendants; the financial impact of the casualty; and the means of the defendant.

[112] (1999) 288 ENDS Report, p. 50.

[113] This was the title which Sir Harry Woolf (as he then was) chose for the fifth annual Garner Environmental Law Lecture delivered on 23rd October 1991: see (1991) 4 JEL 1. For a discussion of one of the key issues considered during the course of that lecture, whether or not there is a need for a specialist environmental court or tribunal, see further below at pp. 257-265.

[114] [1999] 2 All ER 249.

[115] This disquiet had been voiced by, amongst others, two former Lord Chancellors: see the remarks of Lord Hailsham in his Presidential Address to the Magistrates' Association, *The Magistrate*, 39(12) 194, cited in Holgate, "Proper Penalties for Breach of Health, Safety and

in this and that the figures with which we have been supplied support the concern. There has been increasing recognition in recent years of the seriousness of health and safety offences. The circumstances of individual cases will, of course, vary almost infinitely and very few cases have reached this court. Accordingly it is difficult for judges and magistrates, who only rarely deal with these cases, to have an instinctive feel for the appropriate level of penalty."[116]

As has previously been noted,[117] remarks of a very similar nature have been made in relation to environmental offences. The judgment in *Howe* then proceeded to identify various factors which ought to be taken into account when determining the level of fine in a health and safety case. In so doing, however, the Court of Appeal sought to "emphasise that it is impossible to lay down any tariff or to say that the fine should bear any specific relationship to the turnover or net profit of the defendant".[118] In other words, therefore, "each case must be dealt with according to its own particular circumstances".[119]

Nevertheless, the relevant factors which were identified were as follows:

- in assessing the gravity of the breach of the law, regard should be had to how far short of the appropriate standard the defendant fell in failing to meet the reasonably practicable test;
- generally where death is a consequence of the criminal act,[120] it should be regarded as an aggravating feature of the offence. The penalty should reflect public disquiet at the unnecessary loss of life;
- deliberately breaching health and safety legislation with a view to financial profit seriously aggravates the offence;
- the size of a company and its financial strength or weakness cannot affect the degree of care that is required where safety is concerned;
- the degree of risk and extent of the danger created by the offence;
- whether the offence was an isolated incident or continued over a period of time; and
- the resources of the defendant and the effect of the fine on its business.

In addition to the above, the Court of Appeal identified certain other aggravating factors. Foremost amongst these were a failure to heed warnings, and where a defendant had deliberately profited financially from a failure to take the necessary health and safety measures or has run a risk to save money. Particular *mitigating* factors which the Court identified included a prompt admission of responsibility and a timely plea of guilty;

Environmental Protection Legislation", *Environmental & Waste Management* 2(3) 1999, 159 at n. 7; and those of Lord Irvine of Lairg to the York and District Magistrates' Association in April 1998, also cited in Holgate, at p. 159.

[116] At 254.

[117] See above at p. 245.

[118] [1999] 2 All ER 249 at 254. The Sentencing Advisory Panel arrived at essentially the same conclusion in its Advice to the Court of Appeal: see para. 23.

[119] At 254.

[120] A clear distinction exists here between the most serious health and safety cases, which often involve human fatalities, and environmental cases which do not.

steps to remedy deficiencies after they had been drawn to the defendant's attention; and a good safety record.

Applying these factors to the facts of the case before it, the Court of Appeal in *Howe* took the view that the total fine imposed was indeed excessive. Although it accepted that the case was a bad example since there had been a "flagrant disregard for the safety of the company's employees",[121] it nevertheless felt that the offences were not so bad that the defendant ought not to be in business. In the opinion of the Court of Appeal, the trial judge had given inadequate weight to the financial position of the defendant. The small size of the company[122] coupled with its modest turnover and annual profit meant that a fine of £48,000 represented a substantial financial burden. Accordingly, the Court of Appeal substituted a total fine of £15,000 which, when added to the costs of £7,500, meant that the total financial burden placed on the company had been reduced from £55,500 to £22,500.[123]

In a comment on the *Howe* decision, it has been argued that "many of the principles" laid down in the case "appear equally applicable to the environmental field".[124] Accordingly, it is no great surprise to learn that they had a notable influence on the submissions made by counsel for the Port Authority in *Milford Haven*. Thus it was argued that, in setting the level of fine at £4 million, Steel J had given inadequate recognition to the relative lack of culpability of the appellants,[125] been wrong to deny the appellants full credit for their guilty plea, failed to appreciate that the status of the appellant as a public trust was relevant to the issue of assessing the appropriate level of fine, and had misunderstood the financial position of the company.

In support of the first of these submissions, counsel for the Port Authority pointed to the fact that in the commission of the offence there had been an absence of aggravating factors such as corner-cutting on operational or safety measures in order to maximise profit or to seek a competitive advantage, a record of previous offending, a history of non-compliance,

---

[121] [1999] 2 All ER 249 at 255.

[122] At the time of the fatal accident it employed 12 people. This had reduced to 10 by the time of the appeal.

[123] The decision in *Howe* was welcomed by both the Chairman of the Health and Safety Commission and the Director General of the Health and Safety Executive: see Health and Safety Executive Press Release C49:98, 16th November 1998. It was also later applied in *R v Rollco Screw and Rivet Co Ltd* [1999] Cr App R(S) 436 where Lord Bingham remarked that Scott Baker J's observations amounted "in our judgment to a very clear and correct statement of the principles which should guide the court in cases of this kind, and we give them our unqualified support".

[124] Professor Macrory, (1999) 288 ENDS Report at p. 51.

[125] In her article, de Prez identifies culpability as one of two broad headings (the other being to trivialise the breach) under which the prevalent style of mitigation in environmental cases may be classified. Her observations from a study of 25 environmental prosecutions were that the strategy of denying culpability "took the form of blaming misfortune and third parties for the offence or asserting that, given that the offence was not deliberate, enforcement was an unreasonable restriction on the right to trade": see "Excuses, excuses: The ritual trivialisation of environmental prosecutions" (2000) 12 JEL 65 at p. 68.

unheeded warnings, or cavalier or lethargic behaviour in relation to the incident.

Although the Court of Appeal accepted the force of these arguments, it did however observe that:

> "...although the Port Authority is fully entitled to rely strongly on its relative lack of culpability – and its position would be very much more vulnerable if it were unable so to rely – it cannot reasonably hope to escape a very substantial financial penalty when its commission of an offence against the section has such serious results."[126]

With regard to counsel's second submission the Court of Appeal saw "no reason why the Port Authority should not be entitled to take full credit for its plea of guilty".[127] The Court of Appeal also accepted counsel's third submission, although it was anxious to stress that it did not amount to an immunity from criminal penalties for public bodies on account of their particular status.

The fourth submission, that Steel J had misunderstood the financial position of the Port Authority, raises interesting questions about a defendant's ability to pay and the information on which such an ability is assessed by a court. Whether or not judges ought to receive some form of expert guidance when assessing the financial position of a defendant is a moot point. As part of the consultation process which preceded the publication of its Advice to the Court of Appeal, the Sentencing Advisory Panel had sought views on the matter despite the fact that it was, strictly speaking, outside the scope of its remit. The responses which it received were, however, distinctly lukewarm. There was little support for the idea save in respect of complex Crown Court cases.[128] In the present appeal, the Court of Appeal received assistance from a detailed report prepared by an "eminent accountant". On the basis of that information, the Court reached the conclusion that Steel J had taken a "much too rosy view of the Port Authority's financial position and prospects".[129]

In conclusion, and in the light of the submissions put to them on behalf of the Port Authority, the Court of Appeal concluded that the fine imposed on the appellant's had been "manifestly excessive". A fine of £750,000 was therefore substituted for the original fine of £4 million. In the opinion of the Court of Appeal this revised sum accorded due recognition to the seriousness of the disaster, and the need for vigilance to present such disasters occurring, while at the same time avoiding danger of crippling the Port Authority's business and the blighting of the local economy.

---

[126] [2000] Env LR 632 at 644.
[127] At 645.
[128] See para. 24 of the Advice.
[129] [2000] Env LR 632 at 647.

The Court of Appeal in *Milford Haven* may be regarded as having declined to follow certain aspects of the Advice addressed to it by the Sentencing Advisory Panel. As such it is appropriate to have regard to the recent decision in *R* v *Anglian Water Services*[130] in order to assess where the Court of Appeal currently stands on the issue of sentencing for environmental offences.

The facts of *Anglian Water* were as follows. A member of the public, Mr Roy Hart, was walking along the banks of the river Crouch when he saw sewage and condoms floating on the surface of the water. He reported the matter to the Environment Agency and it subsequently became apparent that the pollution had been caused by a discharge from the Wickford Sewage Treatment Works which were run by the defendants, Anglian Water Services. A bolt operating one of the gates at the unmanned Treatment Works had become de-threaded and a computer had failed to recognise that the gate was not rising as it ought to. As a result, semi-treated sewage had been mixed with sediment in a ditch and then discharged into the river. In order to prevent a ditch becoming too contaminated, the Treatment Works had a monitor which would automatically divert the flow out onto a grass plot and sound an alarm. However, at the time that the offence was committed, the monitor had been sent to be repaired and no replacement had been installed. The discharge of sewage into the river Crouch caused the death of fish over a 2 km stretch and badly affected other wildlife, such as swans.

Mr Hart brought a private prosecution against Anglian Water Services alleging that they were guilty of the offence of causing sewage effluent to be discharged into controlled waters contrary to section 85(3) of the Water Resources Act 1991. The case was started in the Magistrates' Court but, following the defendant's entry of a guilty plea, it was remitted to the Crown Court for sentence on the basis that the statutory maximum fine for such an offence, £20,000, represented an inadequate penalty in the circumstances of the case. The Crown Court judge concluded that Anglian had been grossly irresponsible in two respects: (i) in failing to have a safety system in operation on the site; and (ii) in the absence of such a system, in not having the site manned in order to ensure that the gates were rising and closing properly. Several factors were pleaded in mitigation on behalf of Anglian. Attention was drawn to the fact that the company had pleaded guilty to the offence; that it had co-operated with the Environment Agency in respect of the pollution incident; that it had restored fish to the river the following day; and, that it had achieved an improvement in the way in which the Treatment Works were subsequently operated. Collectively these factors caused the judge to lessen the size of the fine that she would have otherwise imposed. Nevertheless, taking into account the defendant's previous record (64 convictions for sewage discharge), she set the level of that fine at £200,000 and ordered that Anglian pay the prosecutor's costs of £9,579.58. Anglian accordingly appealed.

---

[130] [2003] EWCA Crim 2243.

Several points emerge from the decision of the Court of Appeal which are worth noting. The first of these, which relates to the nature of the section 85(3) offence, will be returned to later in this book.[131] For present purposes it will suffice to note that whereas the courts have tended to regard water pollution offences as crimes which "are not criminal in any real sense, but are acts which in the public interest are prohibited under a penalty",[132] the Court of Appeal in *Anglian Water* opined:

> "We would not categorise breaches of section 85(3) of the nature that occurred in this case as being of a non-criminal character, albeit the offence is one of strict liability.

> The environment in which we live is a precious heritage and it is incumbent on the present generation to preserve it for the future. Rivers and watercourses are an important part of that environment and there is an increasing awareness of the necessity to preserve them from pollution. It is of note that the offence to which the appellant pleaded guilty carries an unlimited fine in the Crown Court and, if committed by an individual, imprisonment of up to 2 years."[133]

With regard to the issue of sentencing, the Court of Appeal's judgment is of interest on two counts: (i) in relation to the appropriateness of providing general guidance on the quantum of fines for environmental offences; and (ii) in terms of identifying the mitigating factors which a court may consider when determining sentence.

Three parties made submissions to the Court of Appeal in the present case. In addition to those of the appellant and Mr Hart (who appeared in person), the Court also heard submissions made on behalf of the Environment Agency. In these the attention of the Court was drawn to the fact that the absence of any "tariff" or scale of financial penalty for environmental offences made it difficult for both Magistrates' Courts and the Crown Court to set an appropriate fine in an individual case. The Court of Appeal was also shown a Circular issued by the Magistrates' Association[134] which it considered provided helpful advice and which it therefore endorsed. Nevertheless, despite being invited by counsel for the Agency to adopt a tariff based on the classification system for prosecuting offences which it had devised,[135] the Court of Appeal declined to do so. Instead, it reiterated its belief that "each case has to be decided in the light of its own facts" since "no two cases are likely to be identical". Accordingly, rather than establish a tariff, the Court of Appeal preferred an incremental approach in

---

[131] See Chapter 9.

[132] Per Wright J in *Sherras* v *De Rutzen* [1895] 1 QB 918 at 922. These words have subsequently been approved and applied to the causing offence in cases such as *Alphacell Ltd* v *Woodward* [1972] 2 All ER 475 and *Attorney-General's Reference (No.1 of 1994)* [1995] 2 All ER 1007.

[133] [2003] EWCA Crim 2243 at paras 13 and 14 of the judgment.

[134] *Fining of Companies for Environmental and Health and Safety Offences*, which was issued in September 2000 and revised in May 2001.

[135] This is the Common Incident Classification Scheme (CICS), discussed above at pp. 225-226.

which the decisions of the Court that "are likely to emerge with time ... will provide some kind of focal points".

With regard to the mitigating factors to be taken into account when setting a fine for an environmental offence, the Court of Appeal was referred to the earlier cases of *Milford Haven* and *Howe*. It was also referred to the case of *R* v *Yorkshire Water Services Ltd*,[136] where the water company had pleaded guilty to 17 offences of supplying water unfit for human consumption contrary to section 70(1) of the Water Industry Act 1991. Although it was noted by Scott Baker LJ (who gave the judgment of the Court) in *Anglian Water* that the *Yorkshire Water* case was concerned with a different statutory offence in respect of which there was a lower maximum fine (£5,000), it was nevertheless felt that "similar principles" applied to the two cases. In giving the judgment of the court in *Yorkshire Water*, Rougier J had observed:

> "We return to the facts which we consider certainly relevant in this case as follows. (1) The degree of culpability involved in the commission of what is in effect an offence of relatively strict though not absolute liability. (2) The damage done. This will include the spatial and temporal ambit of the effect of the offence, together with ill effects both physical and economical ... It seems to us that the above two are the most important, but also (3) The defendant's previous record, including any failure to heed specific warnings or recommendations will also be material ... (4) A balance may have to be struck between a fitting expression of censure, designed not only to punish but to stimulate improved performance on the one hand, and the counter productive effect of imposing too great a financial penalty on an already underfunded organisation on the other ... (5) The defendant's attitude and performance after the events, including their pleas ... (6) Finally it must be correct to determine what the penalty for any one incident should be rather than tot up the various manifestations of that incident as reflected in the counts in the indictment ..."[137]

Having regard to the facts of the case before it, the Court of Appeal in *Anglian Water* took the view that this was a "serious local case of pollution", although it was also noted that its "effect in time and space was fortunately limited". The river Crouch had, in the words of Scott Baker LJ, "recovered 24 hours later and this was due to the prompt remedial action taken by the appellant". With regard to the third factor identified by Rougier J in *Yorkshire Water*, a defendant's past record, the Court of Appeal in *Anglian Water* considered that the appellant's 64 previous convictions for sewage discharges was "not of great significance when seen in the light of the ambit of the appellant's operation" which covered something in the region of 20% of the land mass of England and Wales. Of

---

[136] [2001] EWCA Crim 2635.

[137] At para.17 of the judgment. The words omitted from this passage were specific to the facts of *Yorkshire Water* itself.

greater importance, however, was the appellant's guilty plea. The Court of Appeal felt that this was not significantly diminished by the fact that there had been a *Newton* hearing during the trial to determine the extent of the discharge of untreated sewage into the river Crouch.[138] Furthermore, the Court was of the view that this was a case where there was "no question of the appellant having deliberately cut corners to save cost".

Taking all these factors into account, the Court of Appeal concluded that the magistrates had not erred in declining jurisdiction despite the appellant's argument to the contrary. However, the Crown Court fine of £200,000 was held to be "manifestly excessive", especially when measured against the fine of £80,000 which had been imposed in *Yorkshire Water*.[139] Accordingly, the Court of Appeal substituted a fine of £60,000. This was considered to be at a level appropriate "to make some impact on the company and overcome any suggestion that it is cheaper to pay the fines than undertake the work that is necessary to prevent the offence in the first place."

A SPECIALIST ENVIRONMENTAL COURT OR TRIBUNAL?

In the fifth annual Garner Lecture, Sir Harry Woolf (as he then was) chose to address the question: "Are the judiciary environmentally myopic?"[140] In delivering that lecture, he referred to a growing area of law "which could properly be identified as being environmental law"[141] and noted that "a problem which should concern us all is whether our legal system is capable of adapting (as it did in the case of administrative law) so as to provide an effective means of protecting the environment".[142] The picture which he painted was of a complex area of law which required the courts to exercise either their civil,[143] criminal or judicial review jurisdictions, depending upon the circumstances of the case. After having considered the capacity of the judges and the High Court to provide redress in environmental cases, the lecture moved on to deal with statutory appeals and the criminal courts. With regard to the latter, Sir Harry Woolf opined:

---

[138] As a result of the hearing, the trial judge had concluded that approximately 200 tonnes of sewage had been discharged into the river.

[139] This was the sum which had been substituted on appeal. The original fine had been £119,000.

[140] The text of the lecture was subsequently published in the *Journal of Environmental Law*: see (1991) 4 JEL 1-14. The title was chosen to reflect the view that the judiciary might be "ignoring or at least giving limited attention" to environmental considerations in the discharge of their functions.

[141] At p. 1. Sir Harry Woolf had in mind the various planning Acts which were passed either in 1990 or 1991 and what he termed the "paramount" piece of legislation in the context of his lecture, the Environmental Protection Act 1990. He might also have referred to the consolidating water enactments which were passed in 1991, e.g. the Water Resources Act 1991.

[142] At p. 2.

[143] It was noted in this context that whilst "the English judiciary have of course been providing remedies for environmental interference with an occupier's enjoyment of land as long as Queens Bench Courts have existed ... the primary focus of environmental law is not on the protection of private rights but on the protection of the environment for the public in general" (at p. 4).

"... I do have reservations as to whether the criminal courts are the appropriate tribunal to determine some of the offences created by environmental legislation."[144]

And continued:

"I recognize the need for sanctions to enforce compliance with legislation designed to protect the environment. However I do question the appropriateness of the criminal courts having to deal with issues of this sort where all that is at stake is the imposition of a financial penalty."[145]

A possible alternative to the present arrangements was, therefore, the establishment of a specialist environmental tribunal.[146] In Sir Harry Woolf's opinion, that tribunal might have the following form and function:

"It is a multi-faceted, multi-skilled body which would combine the services provided by existing courts, tribunals and inspectors in the environmental field. It would be a 'one stop shop' which should lead to faster, cheaper and the more effective resolution of disputes in the environmental area. It would avoid increasing the load on already overburdened lay institutions by trying to compel them to resolve issues with which they are not designed to deal. It could be a forum in which judges could play a different role. A role which enabled them not to examine environmental problems with limited vision. It could however be based on our existing experience, combining the skills of the existing inspectorate, the Lands Tribunal and other administrative bodies."[147]

In the years since this lecture was delivered,[148] the debate about an environmental court or tribunal has not abated. The existence of specialist environmental tribunals in other jurisdictions[149] has provided support for

---

[144] At p. 10.

[145] At pp. 10-11. The notion that environmental offences are something less than "crimes" is implicit in the words used here. Later on in his lecture, Sir Harry Woolf commented that: "The Criminal Courts which have more than enough work already having to deal with quasi-criminal offences often giving rise to technical crimes which do not fit easily into the structure of a criminal trial" (at p. 12).

[146] The word "tribunal" may well have been deliberately used in order to impress upon his audience that he was making the case for something other than a court of law to act as a "multi-disciplined adjudicating panel" in the environmental field.

[147] At p. 14.

[148] It should be noted that prior to the 1991 Garner Lecture, Robert Carnwath QC (as he then was) produced a report (*Enforcing Planning Control* (1989)) for the Secretary of State in which he opined: "I can see a case for a form of Tribunal which is able to encompass the whole range of planning appeal and enforcement work, including the levying of penalties. Alternatively, there may be a case for reviewing the jurisdiction of the various Courts and Tribunals which at present deal with different aspects of what might be called 'environmental protection' (including planning), and seeking to combine them in a single jurisdiction". These conclusions were subsequently commended by Sir Harry Woolf, at p. 13. See also Carnwath, "Environmental Enforcement: the need for a Specialist Court" [1992] JPL 799.

[149] Australia, for example, has a number of specialist environmental and planning courts or tribunals in its various states and territories. Thus the Australian Capital Territory has a Land and

the view that there is a need for such bodies and that if established, they can provide an effective forum for the resolution of environmental disputes.[150] Accordingly in September 1999, Professor Malcolm Grant submitted a report commissioned by the then Department of the Environment, Transport and the Regions in which the concept of an environmental court was examined in order to gain a clearer understanding of what was being proposed. The study was also initiated in order to examine and evaluate the experience of environmental courts elsewhere and to test the applicability of the concept and its feasibility to England and Wales. A three stage approach was adopted in carrying out the study. Stage 1 entailed a desk study of planning and environmental decision-making in other jurisdictions.[151] The practical operation of the relevant provisions was tested against eight hypothetical factual scenarios.[152] Stage 2 consisted of a detailed study of four jurisdictions in which environmental courts were in operation: New Zealand, New South Wales,[153] Queensland and South Australia. The third stage was concerned with a detailed study of the planning and environmental decision-making process in England and Wales and an examination of the feasibility of introducing an environmental court in that jurisdiction.

As the Report notes, one of the features of the debate surrounding the establishment of an environmental court is that there is a "mix of aspirations" as to what form a court should take. In other words, whilst a number of commentators have been in broad agreement that there is a need for a specialist court or tribunal, they have differed in their visions as to the form of that body and the nature and extent of its jurisdiction.

Nevertheless, the Grant Report noted that an environmental court or tribunal ought to:

- be a specialist and exclusive jurisdiction;
- have power to determine environmental issues on their merits;

Planning Appeal Board established under the Land (Planning and Environment) Act 1991, Tasmania has a Resources Management and Planning Appeal Tribunal established under the 1993 Act of the same name, and Victoria has a Division of the Administrative Appeals Tribunal set up under the 1984 Act of the same name.

[150] In advancing the argument (based on her own research) that environmental prosecutions are routinely trivialised by English courts, de Prez makes the point that the establishment of a specialist environmental court may actually contribute to that trivialisation in that one might legitimately ask: "Why should these cases need a separate court structure, unless they are indeed distinct from traditional crimes?". Continuing on the same theme she remarks: "Whilst a change in venue may appear to be a sensible solution to the increasing complexity in both environmental law and science, it may compound existing problems of trivialisation by confirming environmental offences as different in nature from those crimes dealt with by a bench of magistrates, making prosecution a great deal more difficult": see "Excuses, excuses: The ritual trivialisation of environmental prosecutions" (2000) 12 JEL 65 at p. 77).

[151] These included: Denmark, Ireland, Sweden, New Zealand and several Australian states.

[152] In a review of the Grant Report, Tromans points out that the scenarios reflected "the widely divergent range of environmental 'cases' which may require determination ...": see (2001) 13 JEL 423 at p. 424.

[153] For a later discussion of the nature of the Land and Environment Court's jurisdiction and how it has performed since its establishment, see Ryan, "Court of Hope and False Expectations: Land and Environment Court 21 years on" (2002) 14 JEL 301.

- have an ability to adjudicate across the whole range of environmental regulation, both in terms of subject areas (e.g. land-use planning, controls over discharges to the environment, etc.) and types of suit (e.g. public law, civil action, enforcement, criminal prosecution);
- be independent of government;
- be politically unbiased and bear some of the hallmarks of a judicial approach to dispute resolution;
- have expertise in environmental issues from whatever disciplinary perspective;
- allow broad rights of access;
- apply comparatively informal procedures whereby the court itself takes a leading role in a more inquisitorial mode;
- possess an ability to overcome the problems of high costs associated with civil litigation; and
- be an innovative body capable of dealing with the different demands posed by environmental issues.

The Report identified five alternative models for an environmental court in England and Wales:

(i)   a planning appeal tribunal;
(ii) an environmental division of the High Court;
(iii) an environmental division of the High Court which incorporated the Lands Tribunal;
(iv) a separate Environmental Court, similar to the Employment Appeals Tribunal;
(v)   a separate two-tier Environmental Court, incorporating at the first tier the regulatory appeals jurisdiction of the Planning Inspectorate; or, the same two-tier model but incorporating also the jurisdiction of the Lands Tribunal.

Each of these options would require substantial changes to be made to present arrangements, some of those changes being rather more wide-ranging than others. For his part, Professor Grant favoured a two-tier Environmental Court operating as a new division of the High Court, with the lower (tribunal) tier dealing with appeals on their merits and the higher (court) tier having jurisdiction in respect of appeals on points of law. On the question of whether or not such a court should exercise both a civil and a criminal jurisdiction, the Grant Report came down in favour of confining the court's jurisdiction to civil matters. It was believed that if the court were to exercise both jurisdictions, it might create confusion due to the rather different natures of civil and criminal proceedings.[154]

---

[154] In making the case for the establishment of an environmental court, Day, Stein and Birtles take issue with the Grant Report on this point. In their opinion, the concerns about combining the civil and criminal cultures within a single structure were not well founded. Accordingly, they opined: "The fact that some companies see penalties imposed as a tax on their polluting activities, which they can bear, must be dealt with. In serious cases, where individual directors or other controlling individuals are clearly implicated in criminal activities, it is essential that they face serious penalties, including imprisonment. It would, therefore, seem very important that these matters are dealt with by a body (such as an Environmental Court) which is aware of the importance of the

The Government's response to the Grant Report can be gauged from a debate which took place in the House of Lords on 9th October 2000 in response to the question whether the government proposed to establish a specialist environmental court for England and Wales.[155] Speaking on behalf of the Government (and in particular on behalf of the Lord Chancellor), Lord Bach remarked that his "noble and learned friend does not believe that at present there is any consensus among the higher judiciary or elsewhere for the establishment of an environmental court".[156] Whilst Lord Bach refuted the suggestion that his words implied that such a lack of consensus meant that the Lord Chancellor was bound to do nothing about the matter, he did observe that "it would be strange if my noble and learned friend were not to take considerable notice of that fact in this particular instance."[157] Lord Bach then proceeded to identify further obstacles in the way of the establishment of an environmental court. He warned against a "knee-jerk reaction to proposals for change" and questioned whether there was a "readily definable body of environmental law".[158] He referred to the "disparate" nature of environmental claims and drew attention to the fact that such claims are currently heard in a variety of different courts, including the Chancery and Queens Bench Divisions of the High Court, the Administrative Court, the Technology and Construction Court, as well as the Magistrates' Courts and the Crown Courts in respect of environmental offences. In his Lordship's opinion:

> "Bundling them all together would inevitably affect the development of procedures to deal with them, particularly where civil and criminal remedies might be brought together. The creation of an apparently specialist jurisdiction, particularly where its definition is so uncertain, needs to be thought through with great care."[159]

Lord Bach also expressed concern that specialisation may have a corresponding detrimental impact on the quality of justice dispensed by the courts, in that judges would no longer be able to be generalists[160] in the way that they have been previously with the result that they would be ill-

---

issues at stake and experienced in hearing criminal cases on a regular basis": see "An Environmental Court – Part 2" (2001) New Law Journal at p. 697.

[155] The question was put by Lord Brennan.

[156] HL debates, 9th October 2000, vol. 617 at col. 98.

[157] *ibid.*

[158] *ibid* at col. 99. This question had previously been answered in the affirmative by the Grant Report. In that Report it was observed that: "For some observers, skepticism about the value of a new court or tribunal is founded on a reluctance to accept that environmental law is sufficiently distinct from other areas of law to warrant separate treatment. For lawyers, it is an area of specialist activity, but not a separate body of legal principle. It builds upon the conventional foundations of public law and the law of tort, contract, property and crime. But that is not to deny that it is capable of being identified as a separate area of law, any less than intellectual property or employment law. This perception that it is not has an old-fashioned ring to it. Some 15 years ago it might have been difficult to identify a separate corpus of environmental law, but that is hardly the case today" (at para. 13.4.4).

[159] HL debates, 9th October 2000, vol. 617 at col. 99.

[160] This traditional feature of the administration of justice in England and Wales was noted in the Grant Report, as was the more modern practice of both the Court of Appeal and the High Court to allocate cases to judges with particular expertise in the relevant area of law: see para. 13.4.2.

suited to determine cases beyond their own particular expertise. Although other specialist courts have been established when the need for them has become apparent,[161] Lord Bach was anxious to impress upon his audience, both in the chamber and beyond, that whilst the Government maintained an "open mind" on the matter, they were presently "not persuaded of the need for an environmental court".[162]

The Government's failure to have established an environmental court at the time of writing does not mean, however, that there might not be a change of policy in the near future. The UK is a signatory to the Convention on Access to Information, Public Participation in Decision-making and Access to Justice in Environmental Matters[163] which requires parties to guarantee certain such rights to members of the public in accordance with the provisions of the Convention.[164] For present purposes Article 9 is of particular interest. Paragraph 3 of this Article requires signatories to ensure that:

> "… members of the public have access to administrative or judicial procedures to challenge acts and omissions by private persons and public authorities which contravene provisions of its national law relating to the environment."

It is a moot point whether or not the UK's present arrangements for settling environmental disputes satisfy the requirements of this provision. The Government appears to be of the opinion that they do,[165] but it may be that this view of compliance is based more on the precise wording of the Convention than upon its spirit. If the Government were to be persuaded that its view regarding compliance is erroneous, the Convention may then have become a catalyst for change, with any subsequent reforms possibly including the establishment of an environmental court or tribunal. If the government were to want a less far-reaching institutional reform than that suggested in the Grant Report, it might have regard to the proposals made in a still more recent report, *Modernising Environmental Justice: Regulation and the Role of an Environmental tribunal.*[166]

---

[161] During the course of his speech in the debate on an environmental court, Lord Goldsmith referred to the establishment of the Commercial Court in March 1895 "as a direct result of pressure from the business community which had been outraged by the decision in *Rose* v *Bank of Australia* …" (at cols 89-90).

[162] At col. 100. It should also be noted that both the Auld Review of the criminal courts and the Leggatt Review of tribunals were ongoing at the time of the publication of the Grant Report and therefore the future structure of these bodies was in a state of uncertainty.

[163] The Aarhus Convention which was signed in Denmark in June 1998. At the time of writing, the Convention has yet to be ratified by the European Community.

[164] The aims of the Convention are set out in Article 1.

[165] In the House of Lords debate on the establishment of an environmental court, Lord Bach remarked that: "In the United Kingdom we already implement this requirement in a variety of ways under a range of different Acts relating to environmental protection, land use planning and environmental health."

[166] The report was commissioned by the Department of the Environment, Food and Rural Affairs and was published in June 2003. Its author is Professor Richard Macrory.

This Report stems from a recommendation made by the Royal Commission on Environmental Pollution in its twenty-third report, *Environmental Planning*.[167] In that Report, the Royal Commission considered, inter alia, the case for the establishment of environmental tribunals with the jurisdiction to hear appeals from planning and environmental decisions. The Royal Commission observed that:

> "What is needed is a system that commands public confidence, improves consistency, is effective at reaching decisions and is not unduly costly. Our main concern is with merits appeals. With the Administrative Court now established within the High Court, we are not convinced that there is a need for a specialist environmental court dealing with judicial review or statutory appeals on legal grounds. Criminal offences concerning planning or environmental matters are probably best left to the ordinary criminal courts, though there is a case for improved guidance on sentencing[168] and more training, especially for magistrates."[169]

In the light of these observations, the Royal Commission recommended the establishment of Environmental Tribunals "to handle appeals under environmental legislation other than the town and country planning system, including those now handled by planning inspectors".[170] It was envisaged that a number of tribunals could be established to cover England, Wales, Scotland and Northern Ireland. Each would have a legal chairperson and members with appropriate specialist expertise. The Tribunal's principal concern would be with appeals on a variety of subjects including contaminated land and statutory nuisance. The Royal Commission did not envisage, however, that the Tribunals would deal with civil litigation or criminal prosecutions. Such cases would continue to be heard by the civil and criminal courts.

Modernising Environmental Justice: Regulation and the Role of an Environmental Tribunal thus takes as its starting point the recommendation made by the Royal Commission on Environmental Pollution. As such the later Report is largely confined to considering the role of an Environmental Tribunal system in respect of the handling of environmental regulatory appeals. It therefore makes the case for a more modest form of institutional change than the "one-stop-shop" environmental court envisaged in the Grant Report. Under the model which it proposes, there would be no jurisdiction for the Tribunal to hear criminal environmental cases which would therefore remain with the ordinary criminal courts. Nevertheless, the Report does make several interesting observations in that regard.

---

[167] Cm 5459 (March 2002).

[168] It will be remembered that in *R v Milford Haven Port Authority* [2000] Env LR 632, the Court of Appeal declined to lay down sentencing guidelines for environmental offences along the lines of those proposed by the Sentencing Advisory Panel: see above at pp. 249-253.

[169] Paragraph 5.35.

[170] Paragraph 5.36.

Although it is noted that it was beyond the remit of the study to consider whether the Environmental Tribunal system which it proposes ought to be extended to include some form of criminal enforcement function, the Report does raise three areas for consideration: administrative or civil penalties; criminal enforcement; and, other judicial enforcement powers.[171]

With regard to the administrative or civil penalties, the Report notes that "there is growing interest in the possible value of the imposition of civil financial penalties as an additional enforcement tool to criminal prosecution".[172] It is further noted that whilst such penalties have not been used in an environmental context in the UK,[173] this is not true of other countries such as the United States and Germany.[174] The Report thus takes the view that "there appear to be attractions in using civil penalties" and the hope is expressed that the Government will consider the issue further.[175] If such a system were to be established, it would be likely to be complimentary to, rather than a substitute for, the present system of criminal sanctions since the Report expresses the view that:

> "Criminal sanctions could remain for the most serious environmental cases, but greater use of civil penalties might be a method for unravelling concerns about the low level of criminal fines currently imposed for many environmental offences, since the level of a civil penalty can be more directly related to economic advantages gained by non-compliance. The system could be uncoupled from the constraints clearly still felt in criminal courts … where magistrates and judges are conscious of the need to ensure that levels of fines are not totally out of step with those imposed for other criminal offences. Magistrates and judges may also sense that punitive sanctions are less appropriate for strict liability offences where no intention or recklessness is involved."[176]

As far as the second issue (criminal enforcement) is concerned, the Report does raise the possibility of extending the jurisdiction of its proposed Environmental Tribunal so as to cover designated criminal environmental offences. It is suggested, for example, that the jurisdiction may cover those offences currently tried in the Magistrates' Courts, with the more serious

---

[171] These powers are only touched upon in the Report and accordingly they are not considered further here.

[172] *Modernising Environmental Justice: Regulation and the Role of an Environmental Tribunal*, para. 16.3.

[173] The Report does comment, however, that in "British law, the use of civil penalties is more familiar in areas of fiscal regulation such as competition and tax" (at para. 16.4).

[174] It will be remembered that in making the case for civil penalties for environmental offences, Ogus and Abbot suggested that the German system of administrative offences (*Ordnungwidrigkeiten*) provided a model which could be adopted in the UK: see "Sanctions for Pollution: Do we have the right regime?" (2002) 14 JEL 283-298, considered above at fn. 23.

[175] It has been reported that DEFRA has commissioned Professor Macrory to investigate the potential role of civil penalties for environmental offences: see (2003) 341 ENDS Report at p. 4. At the time of writing the study is ongoing.

[176] Paragraph 16.6.

environmental offences being left as at present to be determined in the Crown Court. In the words of the Report:

> "A combined civil and criminal jurisdiction[177] would acknowledge that many of the distinctive characteristics of environmental law identified in this report are arguably also relevant to the application and interpretation of criminal environmental offences. The specialist Tribunal would bring a deeper appreciation of the environmental policy background and the significance of regulatory compliance than is often possible in ordinary criminal courts. It could also command greater confidence from those charged with enforcement responsibilities, as well as providing greater assurance to the majority of industries and individuals who comply with environmental requirements, that transgressors are being treated in an effective and consistent manner."[178]

These observations are, however, only tentative. It is expressly acknowledged in the Report that certain features of the criminal justice system, such as the greater procedural formality and the different evidential requirements, are such that it is debatable whether they could be handled by the tribunal system which it proposes.

It remains to be seen whether such an Environmental Tribunal system will prove to be more attractive to the Government than the models suggested to it by Professor Grant in his Report, and if it does, whether the jurisdiction of the tribunals will include any of the environmental offences currently tried in the Magistrates' Courts or Crown Courts.

---

[177] It will be remembered that the Grant Report was opposed to such an arrangement: see above at p. 260.
[178] Paragraph 16.10.

Chapter 8

PUBLIC NUISANCE

INTRODUCTION

Public nuisance[1] is a crime at common law,[2] triable summarily or on indictment.[3] In other words, in an extreme case a substantial penalty is within the capacity of the convicting court.[4] It is not, however, an offence which has been charged with any regularity in recent years, largely because other offences have appeared on the statute book which cover the kinds of conduct which were formerly the subject of prosecutions for the common law offence.[5] Nevertheless, as the case law illustrates, public nuisance is still an offence which is relied on by prosecutors in the absence of a more discreet statutory option.[6]

---

[1] At one time the courts and legal writers had occasion to talk of "common" nuisances to signify a nuisance committed against the community in general. However, with the passage of time, "common" was replaced by "public" to signify a nuisance of this kind – see J R Spencer, "Public Nuisance – A Critical Examination" [1989] 48 CLJ 55 at 58-59.

[2] Conspiracy to commit a public nuisance is also an offence, as is inciting others to commit a public nuisance: see *R* v *Soul* [1980] Crim LR 233 and *R* v *Clark* [1963] 3 All ER 884. In the former case, D appealed unsuccessfully against her conviction under s.1(1) of the Criminal Law Act 1977 for conspiring with another woman and a Broadmoor patient to try to effect the escape of the patient.

[3] Criminal Law Act 1977, s.16, Schedule 2; Magistrates' Courts Act 1980, s.17, Schedule 1.

[4] The penalty could, in theory, take the form of life imprisonment or an unlimited fine where the offence has been tried on indictment. In *R* v *Ong* [2001] 1 Cr App R(S) 404, the appellant had pleaded guilty at his trial to a charge of a conspiracy to commit a public nuisance where he and others had conspired to interfere with the course of a premiership football match between Charlton and Liverpool by extinguishing the floodlights. The underlying purpose was to recover large sums of money on bets struck in Malaysia where the practice of certain bookmakers was such that in the event of an abandonment, the scoreline at the time of the abandonment was treated as being the result of the match. The public nuisance would have taken the form of the annoyance caused to a large section of the public, i.e. the crowd whose entertainment would have been disturbed. In dismissing an argument that the sentence of *four years'* imprisonment had in the circumstances been manifestly excessive, Rougier J (delivering the judgment of the Court of Appeal) observed that: "we consider that the practice of interfering with such an important sporting fixture is something that should be actively discouraged by severe sentences". In *R* v *Harvey* [2003] EWCA Crim 112, the appellant's conviction for the offence of public nuisance where he had repeatedly followed groups of teenagers in his motor car, beeping his horn, waving, smiling and staring at them in such a manner as to cause them anxiety and stress, led the trial judge to impose a term of *life imprisonment* (the specified period being five years). In imposing such a sentence, the trial judge took into account the appellant's record which revealed that he had committed offences of this kind on a number of previous occasions. On appeal, however, the Court of Appeal reduced the sentence to *three years'* imprisonment on the basis that the criminality involved was not sufficiently serious to merit a life sentence.

[5] See the remarks of Rattee J in *R* v *Shorrock* [1993] 3 All ER 917 at 920.

[6] Note also how the concept of a public nuisance has recently been utilised by Parliament in the context of noisy premises. Where a police officer of the rank of inspector or above reasonably believes that "a public nuisance is being caused by noise coming from the premises and the closure of the premises is necessary to prevent that nuisance", he has the power to order the closure of the premises: see s. 161(1)(b) of the Licensing Act 2003.

For a defendant to be held criminally responsible for a public nuisance, it is necessary that he had the requisite *mens rea* at the material time. However, such a statement inevitably begs the question "what is the requisite *mens rea*?" In *R v Shorrock*,[7] this was the very issue raised on appeal. The Court of Appeal was faced with a choice between holding that it was sufficient that the appellant knew or ought to have known that his act[8] carried a real risk of causing a public nuisance, or holding that it had to be shown that the appellant had actual knowledge that such a nuisance would result. It concluded that actual knowledge of the public nuisance need not be established; it was enough that D knew or ought to have known that there was a real risk that the consequences of his actions would be the creation of the sort of nuisance that in fact occurred.[9]

The offence may be *prosecuted* by the public authorities or, by way of private prosecution, by an individual[10] or a group of individuals (for example, an amenity group).[11] However, an individual or a group of individuals may generally not seek, in the civil courts, to restrain a public nuisance by way of an injunction: this is the preserve of the Attorney-General, or a local authority (exercising powers under section 222 of the Local Government Act 1972[12]). An individual or a group of individuals

---

[7] [1993] 3 All ER 917.

[8] The act in question was the letting of a field for a weekend for the sum of £2,000. For a fuller discussion of the facts of this case, see below at p. 278.

[9] As Smith and Hogan point out, in effect this means that the offence is one of negligence: see *Criminal Law* (10th edn, (2002) Butterworths) at p.775.

[10] In *R v Holme* [1984] C.L.Y 2471, H was found guilty on a privately laid information of having committed a public nuisance and sentenced to 15 months' imprisonment, six of which were suspended to deter him from behaving in a way likely to be a public nuisance. The many activities in question which were found to constitute a public nuisance included: purposefully following people; banging on the roofs of cars; imitating an ape; persistently provoking dogs to bark in the early hours of the morning; having his backyard in an insanitary condition; playing one chord on the piano throughout the night; and playing a radio at top volume at all times of the day and night whilst it was suspended on a rope out of his bedroom window.

[11] It is worth noting that the delay by the Environment Agency in bringing a prosecution against the Milford Haven Port Authority for the running aground of the *Sea Empress* caused Friends of the Earth to issue a warning to the Agency that if it did not prosecute, then Friends of the Earth would. At the subsequent trial at the Cardiff Crown Court, the Port Authority pleaded guilty to the offence of causing water pollution contrary to s.85 of the Water Resources Act 1991. It pleaded not guilty to a second count, that it had committed a public nuisance, which was ordered to lay on the file by the trial judge, Steel J: see *Environment Agency v Milford Haven Port Authority* [1999] Lloyds Law Rep. 673.

[12] For the scope of a local authority's power to institute proceedings under this provision, see *Stoke-on-Trent City Council v B & Q (Retail) Ltd* [1984] 1 AC 754; [1984] 2 All ER 332. In the recent case of *Nottingham City Council v Zain* [2002] 1 WLR 607, where the local authority had relied upon s. 222 to obtain an interim injunction to prevent a public nuisance (drug dealing on a housing estate), Schiemann LJ remarked that: "...in my judgment it is within the proper sphere of a local authority's activities to try and put an end to all public nuisances in its area provided always that it considers that it is expedient for the promotion or protection of the interests of the inhabitants of its area to do so in a particular case. Certainly my experience over the last 40 years tells me that authorities regularly do this and so far as I know it has never attracted adverse judicial comment. I consider that an authority would not be acting beyond its powers if it spent time and money in trying to persuade those who were creating a public nuisance to desist". In the same case, Keene LJ observed that: "The position therefore is that where a local authority seeks an injunction in its own name to restrain a use or activity which is a breach of the criminal law but not a public nuisance, it may have to demonstrate that it has some particular responsibility for

may, however, seek to persuade the Attorney-General to bring such an action "on their relation": the *fiat* (consent) of the Attorney-General, if so obtained,[13] will avoid any difficulties arising as regards standing to seek injunctive relief. Where consent to such relator proceedings[14] has been obtained the proceedings, although brought in the name of the Attorney-General, are in substance brought by the private parties, who carry the burden and expense of the proceedings, together with contingent liability as regards costs if unsuccessful.

To the above statements a limited exception should be noted. In a case where a public nuisance gives rise to "special damage",[15] so that some of those affected by the public nuisance may argue that their private law rights have been infringed, those persons will have standing to seek injunctive relief instead of, or in addition to, any claim to damages they may pursue.

DEFINITION OF PUBLIC NUISANCE

What actions or activities may involve the commission of this offence? Certain definitions are commonly referred to. In *Stephen's Digest of the Criminal Law*, the offence is described as being:

> "an act not warranted by law or an omission to discharge a legal duty, which ... obstructs or causes inconvenience or damage to the public in the exercise of rights common to all Her Majesty's subjects."[16]

Blackstone in his *Commentaries* wrote that:

> " ... public nuisances ... are an annoyance to *all* the King's subjects; for which reason we must refer them to the class of public wrongs, or crimes ..."[17]

And in *Hawkins Pleas of the Crown*, what was termed a "common nuisance" was defined as:

> "an offence against the public, either by doing a thing which tends to the annoyance of all of the king's subjects, or by neglecting to do a thing which the common good requires."[18]

---

enforcement of that branch of the law. But where it seeks by injunction to restrain a public nuisance, it may do so in its own name... That is so even though it is seeking to prevent a breach of the criminal law, public nuisance being a criminal offence".

[13] The Attorney-General is under no duty to lend his or her name to such proceedings. Nor is his or her exercise of discretion in this matter subject to judicial review: see *Gouriet* v *Union of Post Office Workers* [1978] AC 435.

[14] For a discussion of the relator action in the context of public nuisance, see J R Spencer, "Public Nuisance – A Critical Examination" [1989] 48 CLJ 55 at 66-73. The author expresses the view that such an action "seems to be the parent of the modern rule that the Attorney-General may obtain an injunction to suppress any crime which cannot be suppressed by other legal means" (at 72).

[15] See the discussion of this concept in Chapter 5.

[16] Ninth edition (1950), at p. 179.

[17] 3 Bl Comm (1st edition, 1768), at p. 216.

These statements define public nuisance in a very broad manner.[19] They also reflect the fact that it is a little misleading to speak of "the offence" of public nuisance. In truth, as will become apparent from the examples discussed in this chapter, there are a whole host of activities which have been held by the courts to constitute a public nuisance.[20] Nevertheless, within the general scope of liability in public nuisance, cases arise of two principal kinds. Although both comprise the same offence – public nuisance – there may be some explanatory value in noting at this early stage the difference between the two categories.

On the one hand there are cases where a defendant's actions are of a kind similar to that which was characteristic of private nuisance cases – noise, smells, smoke, fumes, etc. Such conduct may constitute a public nuisance where the adverse experiences are suffered by a sufficient number of people to warrant taking the conduct beyond the confines of civil liability and to bring it within the realms of criminal responsibility. Within this class of public nuisance mention should be made also of certain kinds of behaviour which, whilst falling within the common understanding of the word "nuisance", have consequences of a kind which would not give rise to any civil liability in private nuisance. Private nuisance, it may be remembered, is fairly described as being a "property" tort: to be actionable the nuisance caused by the defendant must be to the condition of the plaintiff's property or to the plaintiff's use and enjoyment of that property. Public nuisance is not subject to such constraints: behaviour which inconveniences or annoys a sufficiently large number of persons will qualify as a public nuisance even though the nuisance may not relate in any way to the enjoyment of property.[21] Thus in *Butcher Robinson & Staples Ltd and others* v *London Regional Transport*,[22] where the claimant companies alleged that work carried out over a period of four years on extending the London Underground Jubilee Line gave rise to claims in private nuisance, negligence and public nuisance, it was held at the trial of a preliminary issue that none of the companies had sufficient proprietary

---

[18] Second edition (1724), at p. 197.

[19] J R Spencer has argued in relation to Hawkins' definition that it is "so wide that it can scarcely be called a definition at all". See "Public Nuisance – A Critical Examination" [1989] 48 CLJ 55 at 66.

[20] In *Jan de Nul* v *N V Royale Belge* [2000] 2 Lloyd's Rep 700, Moore-Bick J remarked that: "Public nuisance is a wide-ranging concept" (at 713). For a graphic illustration of the breadth of the offence of public nuisance, see the opening remarks of J R Spencer's "Public Nuisance – A Critical Examination", *ibid*. Markesinis and Deakin have criticised public nuisance as being "an amorphous and unsatisfactory area of the law covering an ill-assorted collection of wrongs". In their opinion (for which the authorities provide more than ample justification), public nuisance is an "intellectual mess" that "offends all contemporary notions of certainty and precedent in criminal law and must thus be regarded as dangerous": see *Tort Law* (4th edn, 1999) at pp. 450-454.

[21] For examples, see *R* v *Madden* [1975] 3 All ER 155: bomb hoaxer: but nuisance, on the facts, too limited in consequences to be a public nuisance; *Shillito* v *Thompson* (1875) 1 QBD 12. In *Commercial Radio Companies Association Ltd* v *Hatchings* (unreported), June 4, 2001, it was held that the carrying on of a private radio broadcast constituted a public nuisance because: (i) it interfered with the operation of the emergency services; and (ii) it interfered with the commercial operation of stations which were members of the Association.

[22] [1999] EGLR 63.

interest in any of the properties affected to maintain an action in private nuisance or negligence. However, the lack of a proprietary interest did not of itself defeat a claim in public nuisance and hence whether or not the claimants could sue under this head was a question which was left open by Judge Bowsher QC.

The second broad kind of case which will constitute a public nuisance comprises conduct which interferes, in the words of *Stephen's Digest*, with "the exercise of rights common to all His Majesty's subjects". A common example is the commission of a public nuisance by way of obstructing or interfering with the exercise of a public right of way, the use of the highway,[23] or a public right of navigation.[24]

The differences between these cases and those in the former category are as follows. First, the conduct in question may not in itself be intrinsically of a kind which would naturally be labelled a nuisance. One who locks a gate across a public right of way will, for example, fall within this category. Second, the numbers of persons *actually affected* in their exercise of their public rights will not be relevant to liability. Where there is interference with the *rights* possessed in common by all subjects it is the public nature of the rights affected rather than the number of persons actually inconvenienced which renders the matter a public nuisance. As Denning LJ explained in *Attorney-General (on the relation of Glamorgan County Council and Pontardawe Rural District Council)* v *PYA Quarries Ltd*:[25]

> "Take the blocking up of a public highway …: it may be a footpath very little used except by one or two householders; nevertheless the obstruction affects everyone indiscriminately who may wish to walk along it."[26]

This dictum was subsequently relied upon in *Jan de Nul* v *N V Royale Belge.*[27] Here the claimant, an English subsidiary of a Belgian company specialising in dredging operations, was employed by the operators of the

---

[23] In *East Hertfordshire District Council* v *Isabel Hospice Trading Ltd* [2001] JPL 597, for example, it was held that a 1100 litre wheeled bin which contained donated goods that could not be sold and which was situated at the rear of the shop in a corner formed by the protruding wall of the adjoining premises amounted to an obstruction and a public nuisance. In reaching such a conclusion, deputy judge Mr Jack Beatson QC rejected the contention that the obstruction was *de minimis*. The bin had obstructed that part of the highway on which it was situated and it did not matter that people could pass and repass by using other parts of the highway.

[24] See, for example, *Tate and Lyle Industries Ltd and another* v *GLC and another* [1983] 2 AC 509; [1983] 1 All ER 1159; [1983] 2 WLR 649.

[25] [1957] 1 All ER 894.

[26] At p 908. Contrast, however, *DPP* v *Jones* [1999] 2 AC 240, where a majority of the House of Lords (3:2) concluded that a peaceful, non-obstructive assembly of more than 20 persons did not exceed the public's right of user so as to constitute a trespassory assembly for the purposes of s.14A of the Public Order Act 1986. In the words of Lord Irvine LC: "Provided these activities are reasonable, do not involve the commission of a public or private nuisance, and do not amount to an obstruction of the highway unreasonably impeding the primary right of the general public to pass and repass, they should not constitute a trespass. Subject to these qualifications, therefore, there would be a public right of peaceful assembly on the public highway" (at 254).

[27] [2000] 2 Lloyd's Rep 700.

port of Southampton to increase the depth of the main navigation channel from the Solent to the container port and to straighten it at a specified point. The process involved is known as "capital dredging", i.e. the removal of previously undisturbed material from the bed of the channel. The claimants decided, in the light of tests which they had conducted, that the most appropriate way to deepen the channel would be to pre-cut the soil and then discharge it back onto the channel bed to await later collection by a suction hopper dredger. This method would inevitably result in a certain amount of material being held in suspension. However, the claimant's tests revealed that all the material would settle within the area of the channel from which it had been removed. In fact, this did not happen. Large amounts of material were carried away by the action of the tide and settled in other parts of the estuary. The consequent siltation affected commercial berths, the operators of wharves and yacht clubs. The operators of the port and Jan de Nul both carried out remedial dredging works in order to remove silt from various areas. Jan de Nul did so at a cost of approximately £2.5 million. They subsequently sought to recover this sum of money under an insurance policy with the defendants which insured them in respect of third party liabilities arising out of the works. For present purposes, it is that part of the judgment relating to public nuisance which is of interest.[28]

In the judgment of Moore-Bick J, it was common ground that there was a public right of navigation throughout the tidal waters of the estuary. Accordingly, applying the principle established in *Tate & Lyle Industries and another* v *Greater London Council and another*,[29] "any significant interference with the right of navigation caused by the deposit of silt would therefore constitute a public nuisance".[30] Of course, whether or not a state of affairs amounts to a public nuisance in law will depend upon the particular circumstances of the case. In the present litigation, counsel for the defendants sought to argue that the siltation did not sufficiently affect the public in order to constitute a public nuisance. However, Moore-Bick J was not prepared to accept such an argument. In his opinion:

> "The public had a right of navigation over the whole of the estuary and the passage in the judgment of Lord Justice Denning in *Attorney-General* v *P.Y.A. Quarries* to which I have referred,[31] as well as the decision of the House of Lords in *Tate & Lyle* v *G.L.C.*, makes it clear that where there is physical interference with a right of that kind the fact that it is actually exercised by very few members of the public does not prevent the obstruction from constituting a public nuisance... In the present case access to certain parts of the estuary

---

[28] With regard to that part of the judgment relating to the insurance policy, it should be noted that Moore-Bick J held that the insurers were liable under the policy. A subsequent appeal by the insurers on the issues to which eligible claims did the policy respond and what third parties had eligible claims was dismissed by the Court of Appeal: see *Jan De Nul (UK) Ltd* v *AXA Royale Belge SA* [2002] EWCA Civ 209; [2002] 1 All ER (Comm) 767.

[29] [1983] 2 AC 509; [1983] 1 All ER 1159; [1983] 2 WLR 649.

[30] [2000] Lloyd's Rep 700 at 713.

[31] Quoted above at p. 271.

was significantly affected by the deposit of silt and I am quite satisfied that there was in those areas a substantial interference with the public right of navigation."[32]

THE PUBLIC ELEMENT

Returning to the former of our two main kinds of public nuisance (i.e. involving conduct characteristic of a private nuisance), the critical question in relation to liability is likely to be whether a sufficient number of persons have been adversely affected to render the conduct of the defendant a public nuisance.

The courts have resisted the temptation to seek to go beyond quite general statements about what numbers of persons will, in this connection, suffice. The leading discussion is to be found in the *PYA Quarries* case. The issue raised on appeal was whether the dust and vibrations resulting from quarrying operations conducted by the defendants was having an adverse effect upon a sufficiently large number of persons to constitute a public nuisance. The Court of Appeal considered this to be more an issue of fact for lower court determination, than a matter of law for appellate reconsideration. Provided the trial judge had come to a not unreasonable conclusion based upon a correct general understanding of the applicable broad test, his decision must stand. What then was to be the broad principle?

Romer LJ began by making clear that the references, in the definitions referred to earlier, to *all* subjects of the Crown was not to be taken literally. As his Lordship explained:

" ... otherwise no public nuisance could ever be established at all."[33]

More positively, Romer LJ considered that the concept of "neighbourhood"[34] might be helpful in explaining what was necessary:

" ... any nuisance is 'public' which materially affects the reasonable comfort and convenience of life of a class of Her Majesty's subjects. The sphere of nuisance may be described as 'the neighbourhood'."[35]

Moreover, even within this class of subjects defined by reference to "neighbourhood", Romer LJ explained:

"It is not necessary ... to prove that every member of the class has been injuriously affected: it is sufficient to show that a representative cross-section of the class has been ... affected ..."[36]

---

[32] [2000] Lloyd's Rep 700 at 714.

[33] [1957] 1 All ER 894 at 900.

[34] See *Att-Gen* v *Keymer Brick and Tile Co Ltd* (1903) 67 JP 434; *Att-Gen* v *Stone* (1895) 60 JP 168; *Att-Gen* v *Corke* [1932] All ER 711.

[35] [1957] 1 All ER 894 at 902.

[36] *ibid.*

The issue was addressed, albeit in a rather different way, also by Denning LJ. His Lordship stated that:

" ... a public nuisance is a nuisance which is so widespread in its range or so indiscriminate in its effects that it would not be reasonable to expect one person to take proceedings on his own responsibility to put a stop to it, but that it should be taken on the responsibility of the community at large .... In such cases the Attorney-General can take proceedings for an injunction to restrain the nuisance: and when he does so he acts in defence of the public right, not for any sectional interest .... When ... the nuisance is so concentrated that only two or three property owners are affected by it[37]... then they ought to take proceedings on their own to stop it and not expect the community to do it for them."[38]

Beyond these moderately helpful general statements of guidance all that one may usefully do is to look at the decisions of the courts to see how, case by case, the judges have applied the general requirement that a *class of the public* has been affected.

We have already drawn attention to Denning LJ's oblique reference to *R* v *Lloyd*:[39] a nuisance affecting only two or three property owners is unlikely to qualify as a public nuisance. This case may, however, be contrasted with the Canadian case of *Attorney General of British Columbia ex rel. Eaton* v *Haney Speedways*.[40] Here seven neighbouring families brought an action seeking a declaration that motor racing speedway operated in a rural area on Sundays during the summer constituted a public nuisance, and an injunction to put a stop to the activity. In finding in favour of the plaintiffs, Brown J in the British Columbia Supreme Court applied the dictum of Romer LJ in the *PYA Quarries* case when reaching the conclusion that the families were a sufficient number of persons to amount to a class of the public for the purposes of public nuisance.

Reference may also be made to the bomb hoax case: *R* v *Madden*.[41] The defendant, by telephone, gave a hoax warning of a bomb on particular premises. The premises were cleared and searched over a period of about an hour. The Court of Appeal held that the range and number of persons affected by the hoax call was not, on the facts, sufficient to render the conduct a public nuisance. This was a case of inconvenience having been suffered by a *number of individuals* rather than what might be regarded as a more considerable number of persons comprising a *section of the public*. Other cases, however, show that using the public telephone system to make obscene or threatening calls may amount to a public nuisance even though

---

[37] Denning LJ's reference here was to the facts of *R* v *Lloyd* (1802) 4 Esp 200: noise produced by a tinman carrying on his trade which affected just three houses in Clifford's Inn was held by Lord Ellenborough not to be a *public* nuisance.
[38] [1957] 1 All ER 894 at 908.
[39] (1802) 4 Esp 200.
[40] (1963) 39 DLR (2d) 48.
[41] [1975] 3 All ER 155.

the number of persons directly affected may be relatively small. In *R* v *Millward*,[42] for example, the appellant made thousands of telephone calls to a single woman at a police station during a period of nearly two years. On one day, 636 calls were made. In determining his appeal against sentence, the Court of Appeal said nothing to suggest that a charge of committing a public nuisance had been inappropriate.[43] Similarly, in *R* v *Johnson*,[44] the Court of Appeal held that the appellant had been rightly convicted of committing a public nuisance where he had made hundreds of obscene telephone calls to at least 13 women living in the South Cumbria area over a period of five and a half years. In giving the judgment of the Court, Tucker J rejected the argument that each telephone call ought to be regarded as an isolated incident which might possibly be a private nuisance but which could not be a public nuisance. Instead, the Court felt that it was permissible to look at the cumulative effect of the calls in determining whether the appellant's conduct constituted a public nuisance. Whether there were a sufficient number of complaints of calls to amount to a public nuisance was a question of fact for the jury to decide.[45]

LOCALITY

A public nuisance may also be committed even though its effects are reasonably localised. In *R* v *Clifford*[46] a court in New South Wales had to consider whether the actions of prisoners who had climbed onto the roof of a gaol amounted to a public nuisance. On the facts it was held that their conduct was not of a *quality* such as to have been a nuisance. However, the court was satisfied that if inmates of a gaol were, as a group, discomforted by such behaviour, the test requiring a class of the public to have been affected could be satisfied. Reynolds JA commented:

> "A public nuisance can exist or be created ... in a gaol, notwithstanding the limited access thereto, just as much as it can be created in, for example, a cricket ground to which the public is not admitted except on payment of a fee. In both cases there can exist a class of persons who are affected."

---

[42] (1986) 8 Cr App R (S) 209.

[43] The consequences of the telephone calls were, of course, more widespread than they would have been had the appellant telephoned the woman's home address. By telephoning the police station, he was disrupting the work of the police and quite possibly preventing other members of the public from telephoning for assistance or to report the commission of a criminal offence. On appeal, the Court of Appeal upheld a sentence of 30 months' imprisonment.

[44] [1996] 2 Cr App R 434; [1996] Crim LR 828; (1996) 160 JP 605.

[45] It is apparent from the case of *R* v *Watson* [2000] 2 Cr App R(S) 301, that a public nuisance may also occur where a defendant offers a woman money for sex in a public place in front of her two young children, or where he makes indecent suggestions and gestures towards a woman who has just vacated a public telephone box. Given that these two offences were committed by a man with a long history of sexual misbehaviour, the Court of Appeal considered that "the public are entitled to a degree of protection from him and a prison sentence was entirely appropriate and justified". However, in the circumstances, the court decided to quash the sentence of two years' imprisonment for each offence and instead substitute periods of 18 months on each of the two counts to run concurrently.

[46] [1980] 1 NSWLR 314.

In *Shoreham-by-Sea UDC* v *Dolphin Canadian Proteins Ltd*,[47] the defendants owned a factory at which they produced feeding-stuffs, fertilizer and tallow from, among other things, chicken feathers, fats, bones and blood. The feathers were cooked and ground and then turned into a feeding-stuff meal. This process gave off hydrogen sulphide, a well-known smell comparable to that of bad eggs. The boiling or rendering of the fats gave off very fine particles of fat which were capable of clinging to clothing and which were described by Donaldson J as "nausea-making". Over a number of years, the local public health authority received many complaints from inhabitants of the area about the smells emanating from the factory. Accordingly, it brought an action for an injunction to restrain the defendants from creating a public nuisance. With regard to the question whether the smell created a public nuisance, Donaldson J observed that:

> "I have to remember that this is an industrial area. The local inhabitants are not entitled to expect to sit in a sweet-smelling orchard. They chose to build their houses or buy them, as the case may be, in an area where a tallow factory had been established for many years, where there are other factories. There has been a mushroom factory and a jam making factory... There was a chemical works across the river and there are the usual smells from a dock area. So this is certainly not an area where one should impose very tight and strict standards of smell. Furthermore, those who live in that area must accept that if a tallow factory or fertilizer factory of this kind is to carry on business at all there will, on occasion, be a mechanical breakdown or a human failure which will lead to an isolated smell of an offensive character. I do not, for my part, accept that the isolated occasion, by that I mean two or three times a year, perhaps not being of long duration, a matter of an hour or so, does constitute a nuisance in this locality. But that is not the situation as I see it at the moment. There is a frequent smell of a very unattractive and strong character such as, while it is in existence, to make the life of the local inhabitants intolerable."[48]

Given his finding that the smell did indeed constitute a public nuisance, Donaldson J went on to remark that the nuisance could be avoided if the factory owners: improved the factory flooring; improved the hooding over all possible sources of smell; and had greater supervisory control over the raw materials which they received from their suppliers. Nevertheless, Donaldson J did not make an order specifying the particular measures which the defendants should take. Instead, he considered a general order to be the more appropriate course of action although in the circumstances he accepted an undertaking from the defendants that the nuisance would be abated within a period of nine months.[49]

---

[47] (1973) 71 LGR 261.

[48] At 266-267.

[49] On the expiry of this period, the nuisance had still not been fully abated. Accordingly the council moved for leave to issue a writ of sequestration against the defendants for contempt of court by breach of their undertaking. This course of action was rejected by the court as being "too

Locality clearly played a part in the determination of whether there was a public nuisance in *Shoreham*.[50] Echoes of Thesiger LJ's remarks in *Sturges v Bridgman*[51] are evident in that part of Donaldson J's judgment which is quoted above. This serves to confirm a point made earlier in this chapter, namely that some public nuisances involve activities which are characteristic of private nuisance. In *Attorney General v Cole & Son*,[52] a case also concerned with the emanation of gases and smells from the premises of a fat-melter, Kekewich J remarked that the observation that what is a nuisance in one locality may not be so in another "does not carry us far". In his opinion, it was still necessary to return to the same question, namely "is what is complained of a nuisance?" On the facts of the case before him, Kekewich J concluded that the defendant had created a public nuisance and he therefore granted an injunction. The fact that the defendant conducted his business in a proper manner and took precautions to prevent it from being injurious to others in the neighbourhood did not absolve him from liability.

THE LANDOWNER'S RESPONSIBILITY

An owner's responsibility for a public nuisance on his land is evident in several nineteenth-century cases. Thus in *Attorney General v Tod Heatley*,[53] an injunction was sought to prevent the defendants from allowing their vacant land to remain in such a state as to constitute a public nuisance. The piece of land in question, at the corner of St Anne's Lane and Great Peter Street, Westminster, had been surrounded by a six foot hoarding. However, the hoarding had become dilapidated and all kinds of filth and rubbish, including dead dogs and cats, vegetable refuse, fish and offal, had been thrown or deposited upon the vacant ground. That the land constituted a public nuisance was beyond doubt.[54] The judgment in the case is of interest, however, for the reason that the Court of Appeal held

---

harsh" in that it would lead to the immediate closure of the business. Of the remaining alternatives, i.e. warning the defendants, issuing a writ of sequestration but ordering that it should not be operative for a short period of time or, fining the defendants, the court preferred the latter. Accordingly, the defendants were fined £1,000.

[50] Locality and the effect of a grant of planning permission upon that locality was central to the determination of whether the operation of a commercial port amounted to an actionable public nuisance in *Gillingham Borough Council v Medway (Chatham) Dock Co* [1992] 3 All ER 923; [1992] 1 Env LR 98. For an extended discussion of this case, see Chapter 2, pp. 54-56.

[51] (1879) 11 Ch D 852. See Chapter 2, pp. 46-47.

[52] [1901] 1 Ch 205.

[53] [1897] 1 Ch 560.

[54] Similar conclusions have been reached in other jurisdictions: see, for example, *Maynard v Carey Construction Co.* (1939) 19 NE (2d) 304 and *Bathurst City Council v Saban (No.2)* (unreported) 13 March 1986. In the latter case, the New South Wales Supreme Court granted injunctions in respect of a public nuisance caused by the accumulation of scrap metal and bottles piled over a metre high in the defendant's front and back yards. Although the council alleged, inter alia, that the defendant's land was unsightly, that it gave rise to a vermin problem, that it caused local inhabitants mental anguish and, that it had become something of a tourist attraction, none of these grounds formed the basis of the injunctions. Rather, injunctions were granted in respect of the fire risk presented by the state of the defendant's land and in respect of smoke and smell emitted from the land due to the combustion of material (principally plastic and rubber) by the defendant.

that the owner of a vacant piece of land was under a common law duty to prevent that land from becoming a public nuisance.[55] Moreover, where that land had become a public nuisance, the Court held that the common law imposed a further duty to prevent the land from continuing as a public nuisance, i.e. it imposed a duty to abate the nuisance.

In *R* v *Shorrock*[56] a jury convicted the organisers and the farmer landowner in relation to an "acid house party": the indictment read – "causing or permitting loud music to be played from a field off Broken Stone Lane, Blackburn, so interfering with the convenience and comfort of the people of the neighbourhood." Between 3000 and 5000 people attended the party. The event caused a very great deal of noise between 10.30 pm on a Saturday night and 1.20 pm the following afternoon. The local police received some 275 telephoned complaints from local residents in respect of the amplified music, some complaints coming from people living approximately four miles from the field being used for the event. On appeal, the farmer landowner accepted that the events of that night amounted to a public nuisance, an acceptance regarded by Rattee J as "not surprising".

The farmer's ground of appeal was that the trial judge had directed the jury incorrectly in relation to the farmer's responsibility for the events which had occurred. The farmer defendant claimed not to have been aware that the persons to whom he had let the field for the weekend had planned such an event, claiming that he had been told that their intention was a rather smaller event: some stalls and a disco to raise money for a wheelchair. The farmer, having let the field, went ahead with a planned weekend away with his wife; arriving back to discover the nature of what had occurred. The Court of Appeal held that the trial judge had correctly directed the jury that they should convict the defendant even if he was not actually aware of what the organisers intended if he *ought* to have known the consequences of letting the field to them. The rule, to similar effect, in private nuisance[57] applied also to the offence of public nuisance.[58]

In a more recent case, *London Borough of Wandsworth* v *Railtrack*,[59] the claimants contended, amongst other things, that a railway bridge owned by the defendants amounted to a public nuisance by reason of being infested with pigeons. The bridge in question carried trains over the Balham High Road in South London. Its underside, which consisted of a large number of horizontal girders, struts and ledges, had become a favoured roosting place for the local pigeon population. The attraction of the roost was enhanced by the ready availability of food from a large number of retail food outlets

---

[55] In the words of Lindley J: "It is no defence to say 'I did not put the filth on but somebody else did'. He must provide against this if he can. His business is to prevent his land from being a public nuisance" (at 566).

[56] [1993] 3 All ER 917. See above, p. 268.

[57] See the discussion of the *Sedleigh-Denfield* case, above pp. 87-89.

[58] See also, similarly, *R* v *Moore* (1832) 3 B & Ad 184: defendant responsible when it was foreseeable that his actions would lead others to obstruct the highway.

[59] [2001] 1 WLR 368; [2001] EHLR 54.

all within a short distance of the bridge. The consequences of the pigeons roosting under the bridge for pedestrians hardly require further comment, suffice it to say that droppings fell onto heads, clothing and bodies as well as onto the pavement. The slippery mess that resulted on the pavement meant that it had to be cleaned on a daily basis by the claimants using a modern machine and at an annual cost of £12,000. Meshing under the bridge which had previously proved to be an effective way of preventing the pigeons from roosting had been removed after a number of incidents involving dead pigeons. It was the contention of the claimants that the defendants were responsible for what amounted to a public nuisance. With regard to the question whether the pigeon infestation amounted to a public nuisance, Gibbs J had little difficulty in concluding that it did. He stated that:

> "As a matter of fact and degree I find that the pigeon infestation and the fouling caused by it amount to a nuisance. That is to say, they interfere substantially with the comfort and convenience of the public or a significant class of the public who use the footpath."[60]

This conclusion was based on a number of factors which included: the number of complaints and the number of complainants; the unpleasantness of the experience of the complainants; and the sheer amount of extra cleaning required of the pavement. The critical question, however, remained to be determined: was this a public nuisance for which the defendants were liable? Gibbs J concluded that they were liable. Although the public nuisance could not be said to be due to the defendant's own act or default, liability stemmed from their failure to remedy the nuisance "within a reasonable time or at all".[61] They had the means to control and even prevent roosting under their bridge, but they had failed to implement them.[62]

A subsequent appeal by Railtrack was rejected by the Court of Appeal.[63] In upholding the decision of Gibbs J, that Court stressed that where the cause of action is public nuisance, the decision in *Tod Heatley* still represents the law and that there is nothing in the later authorities[64] to suggest otherwise.

---

[60] At 72 of the latter report.

[61] At 73.

[62] Financial considerations clearly influenced Railtrack's decision not to pigeon-proof the bridge in question. Pigeon-proofing the bridge with mesh could have been achieved by a one-off capital cost of £9,000 at the time of the decision. This figure compared favourably with the annual cost of £12,000 for cleaning the pavement. However, given that there were in excess of 20,000 bridges throughout the country, the cost of pigeon-proofing all of them would have been astronomical. Nevertheless, as Gibbs J pointed out, it did not necessarily follow that all such bridges had problems with pigeons amounting to an actionable public nuisance. Whether or not a particular bridge amounted to a public nuisance would evidently depend upon the facts of the case. Thus, in the words of Gibbs J: "The cost of pigeon-proofing an individual bridge whilst not trivial is not in my judgment of an order to persuade me that it would be unreasonable to impose a duty on the defendants to meet the costs" (at 74).

[63] *Railtrack Plc* v *Mayor & Burgesses of London Borough of Wandsworth* [2002] EHLR 5.

[64] The Court of Appeal was here referring to the decisions in: *Slater* v *Worthington's Cash Stores (1930) Ltd* [1941] 1 KB 488; *Goldman* v *Hargrave* [1967] AC 645; *Leakey* v *National Trust for*

Thus it is evident that where there is a public nuisance on the defendant's land, liability is not dependent upon whether the nuisance was created by the defendant, a third party or by natural causes.[65] Instead, liability arises where the defendant was aware of the public nuisance; he had a reasonable opportunity and the means to abate it; and he failed to do so.

PUBLIC HEALTH

A line of public nuisance cases involves the exposure of members of the public to risks of infection, contagion or other illness.[66] In *R* v *Vantadillo*[67] the indictment charged the defendant with public nuisance in having carried her child along a highway, the child being infected with smallpox, thereby exposing members of the public to risk. In finding the defendant guilty of the offence, Le Blanc J observed:

> "... although the Court had not found upon its records any prosecution for this specific offence, yet there could be no doubt in point of law that if a person unlawfully, injuriously, and with full knowledge of the fact, exposes in a public highway a person infected with a contagious disorder, it is a common nuisance to all the subjects, and indictable as such."[68]

In *R* v *Henson*[69] the charge was that the defendant was in possession of a mare infected with a "contagious, dangerous and infectious disease called the glanders" and that the mare had been brought onto the highway with consequent danger of infecting members of the public. In *R* v *Stevenson*[70] the defendant was convicted and sentenced to six months' imprisonment for having committed a public nuisance by offering for sale meat which was not fit for human consumption. More recently, a surgeon pleaded guilty to a charge of causing a public nuisance where he had endangered the health of the public by carrying out invasive surgery knowing that he was a contagious carrier of hepatitis B.[71]

Places of Historic Interest or Natural Beauty [1980] I QB 485; and, *Holbeck Hall Hotel Ltd* v *Scarborough BC* [2000] 2 WLR 1396.

[65] A natural cause may take the form of, for example, an accumulation of snow: see *Slater* v *Worthington's Cash Stores (1930) Ltd* [1941] 1 KB 488, discussed in Chapter 5, at p. 167.

[66] See now the Public Health (Control of Diseases) Act 1984.

[67] (1815) 4 M & S 73; 105 ER 762.

[68] At 76-77 of the former report. In the later case of *Managers of the Metropolitan Asylum District* v *Hill* (1881) 6 App Cas 193, Lord Blackburn observed in relation to infectious diseases that "... there is a legal obligation on the sick person, and on those who have the custody of him, not to do anything that can be avoided which shall tend to spread the infection, and if either do so, as by bringing the infected person into a public thoroughfare, it is an indictable offence..." (at 204).

[69] (1852) Dears 24; 169 ER 621.

[70] (1862) 3 F & F 106; 176 ER 48, NP.

[71] See *Gaud* v *Leeds Health Authority* (1999) 49 BMLR 105 where the surgeon's conviction for the offence of public nuisance was referred to by the Court of Appeal in its explanation of the background to claims brought by the surgeon against the health authority. The two claims, that he had been negligently advised by the authority as to the areas in which he could practice following

VICARIOUS LIABILITY

The general principle of vicarious liability which originates from the law of tort (i.e. that an employer is responsible for the acts or omissions of his employees which are committed during the course of their employment) may have some limited application in the present context. Thus in *R v Stephens*,[72] it was held that the defendant, who owned a slate quarry, was liable on indictment for a public nuisance caused by the acts of his workmen in carrying out their quarrying activities. His workmen had cast and thrown slate stone and rubbish into a public river thereby obstructing the navigation of the river. Liability was held to have arisen even though the actions which caused the public nuisance were contrary to express orders given to the workmen by the defendant. Mellor J[73] sought to justify such a conclusion by observing that although the proceedings were criminal as a matter of form, in substance they were civil. In other words, what Blackburn J termed "the general rule that a principal is not criminally answerable for the act of his agent"[74] did not apply in the present case since the object of the proceedings was in truth to prevent a recurrence of the nuisance rather than to punish the defendant.[75]

The scope of the principle in *Stephens* is somewhat unclear. In the later case of *Chisholm v Doulton*,[76] where the question for the court was whether the owner of a pottery works was criminally liable for the negligence of the stoker of a furnace which had resulted in the emission of black smoke into the atmosphere, the general rule referred to by Blackburn J was applied. The owner had been charged with the offence of negligently using a furnace contrary to s.1(1) of the Smoke Nuisances (Metropolis) Act 1853. In the opinion of the court, however, since the use of the word "negligently"[77] imported the ingredient of *mens rea* into the offence, and since the owner was not personally guilty of any negligence whatsoever,[78] it followed that he could not be guilty of the offence. In arriving at such a conclusion, Field J stressed the criminal as opposed to the civil nature of

---

his diagnosis, and that the authority had failed to advise him as to his rights to benefit, were both rejected by the Court of Appeal.

[72] (1866) LR 1 QB 702.

[73] With whom Shee and Blackburn JJ agreed.

[74] (1866) LR 1 QB 702 at 710.

[75] Both Mellor and Shee JJ felt that "there may be nuisances of such a character that the rule… would not be applicable to them" (at 708) although they did not elaborate further on this point. Smith and Hogan citing Baty on *Vicarious Liability* have pointed to an important issue which arises in this context, i.e. who decides whether the proceedings are substantially civil or criminal where they relate to public nuisance. As the authors observe, proceedings for obstruction of the highway are often brought in order to punish the offenders: see *Criminal Law* (10th edn, (2002) Butterworths) at p. 776.

[76] (1889) 22 QB 736.

[77] Cave J who gave the other judgment in the case observed that: "If that word were not there, the owner would be responsible for the use of the furnace in such a way that the smoke was not consumed although the use was by his servants and not personally by himself" (at 742).

[78] The magistrate had found that the furnace had been properly constructed and that its owner had gone to great expense in taking precautions to ensure that smoke was not emitted from the furnace.

the proceedings. Moreover, in referring to the view taken by the judges in *R v Stephens* that those proceedings were civil, Field J observed:

> "Whether they were right or wrong in that view it is not necessary for me to express any opinion, but they carefully guarded themselves against being supposed to infringe on the general rule of law that a master is not criminally responsible for the acts of his servants. That case must be taken to stand upon its own facts. The case here being a criminal one I must apply the general rule, and by that rule the respondent must be acquitted."[79]

---

[79] (1889) 22 QB 736 at 740.

Chapter 9

OFFENCES IN THE CONTEXT OF WATER POLLUTION

INTRODUCTION

The principal statutory water pollution offences are to be found now in Chapter II of the Water Resources Act 1991. The scheme of this part of the Act is that the main offences are set out in section 85: the remaining sections (86-91) dealing with defences and ancillary matters. [1]

THE SECTION 85 OFFENCES

Section 85(1)

The most general, but also the most important, offence is that contained in section 85(1). This subsection provides:

> "A person contravenes this section if he *causes or knowingly permits* any *poisonous, noxious or polluting matter* or any *solid waste* to enter any *controlled waters*."

The apparent simplicity of this offence is deceptive. The section has generated a good deal of case law: cases in which the courts have been called upon to interpret and explain the meaning of each of the words and phrases to which emphasis has above been afforded.

Having set out this general offence in subsection (1), section 85 proceeds, in subsections (2)-(5), to define a number of rather more specific offences.

Section 85(2)

Section 85(2) provides:

> "A person contravenes this section if he causes or knowingly permits any matter, other than trade effluent or sewage effluent, to enter controlled waters by being discharged from a drain or sewer in contravention of a prohibition imposed under section 86 below."

---

[1] Note also the offences contained in s. 90 of the 1991 Act. Thus it is an offence to remove from any part of the bottom, channel or bed of any inland freshwaters a deposit which has accumulated there by reason of any dam, weir or sluice holding back the waters and cause the deposit to be carried away in suspension (subs. (1)(a) and (b). An ingredient of the offence is that the removal has taken place without the consent of the Environment Agency. No offence is committed, however, where the removal is in accordance with a statutory power relating to land drainage, flood prevention or navigation (s. 90(4)). By virtue of s. 90(2), it is an offence to cause or permit a substantial amount of vegetation to be cut or uprooted either in any inland freshwaters or so close to any such waters that it falls into them, and to fail to take reasonable steps to remove the vegetation. As with s. 90(1), in order to be an offence, the cutting or uprooting must have been carried out without the consent of the Environment Agency.

This offence is both wider and narrower in its terms than section 85(1). Subsection (2) applies not just to "poisonous, noxious or polluting matter" and "solid waste", but more generally to "any matter" – so long as that matter does not take the form of trade effluent or sewage effluent. However, subsection (2) is narrower in that whereas under section 85(1) it is *all*[2] entries of poisonous etc. matter caused or knowingly permitted by the defendant which attract liability; under subsection (2) it is only the entry of "any matter" which occurs:

- by discharge from a drain or sewer; and
- involves contravention of a section 86 prohibition.

Prohibitions under section 86 are in two forms. Section 86(2) imposes a general prohibition on the discharge of any effluent or other matter which:

> "(a) contains a prescribed substance or a prescribed concentration of such a substance; or
> (b) derives from a prescribed process or from a process involving the use of prescribed substances or the use of such substances in quantities which exceed the prescribed amounts."[3]

In addition to such section 86 prohibition by general regulation, section 86(1) provides for more specific prohibitions on discharges to be made by the Environment Agency. Thus, a discharge of effluent or other matter will involve a contravention of a section 86 prohibition where the Agency:

> "(a) ... has given that person notice prohibiting him from making or ... continuing the discharge; or
> (b) ... has given that person notice prohibiting him from making or ... continuing the discharge unless specified conditions are observed, and those conditions are not observed."

The drafting of section 86 has been subject to criticism in some quarters.[4] It has been suggested that it gives rise to difficulties on two counts. First, that since the giving of the notice by the Environment Agency constitutes the prohibition, if the notice is defective or not properly given it follows that there will not be a prohibition relating to the discharge in respect of which the defendant is being prosecuted. Secondly, there are difficulties in connection with the identity of the defendant. Section 86(1) refers to the Agency giving notice to "that person", but what if the person who causes or knowingly permits the discharge is someone other than the person to whom the notice was given? In these circumstances, once again, it would seem that no offence has been committed.

---

[2] Given the defences within s. 88(1) we should, strictly speaking, say "all non-consented" entries. Subs. (1) of s. 85 creates broad offences, subject to a "consent to discharge" defence; subs. (2) is defined in narrower terms, only applying to prohibited discharges.

[3] Substances, concentrations and processes will be prescribed for this purpose in ministerial regulations: see s. 221 of the Water Resources Act 1991. To date, however, no such regulations have been made.

[4] See *Encyclopedia of Environmental Law* (Sweet and Maxwell), Vol. V, at D24-181.

Section 85(3) and (4)

It was observed above that the offence under section 85(2) does not apply where the matter discharged takes the form of "trade effluent or sewage effluent". This form of pollutant is covered, however, by the specific terms of subsections (3) and (4) of section 85 although, it should be remembered, that in so far as such waste may fall within the ambit of the words "poisonous, noxious or polluting matter", the general offence under section 85(1) may also be applicable.

Section 85(3) provides:

> "A person contravenes this section if he causes or knowingly permits any trade effluent or sewage effluent to be discharged –
> (a)   into any controlled waters; or
> (b)   from land ... through a pipe into the sea outside the seaward limits of controlled waters."

And section 85(4) provides:

> "A person contravenes this section if he causes or knowingly permits any trade effluent to be discharged, in contravention of any prohibition under section 86 ... from a building or from any fixed plant –
> (a)   on to or into any land; or
> (b)   into any waters of a lake or pond which are not inland freshwaters."

It may be noted that subsection (3) applies to *all*[5] such discharges into, and by pipe beyond the seaward limits of, controlled waters; whereas subsection (4) is applicable to discharges to land and other waters in so far as such discharges may contravene, or be not in accordance with, a prohibition under section 86.[6]

Section 85(5)

The offence contained within section 85(5) differs from those described above in that it relates not to matter in water which has an intrinsic polluting potential, but rather to matter which has the potential to impede the flow of water, so rendering more serious any pollution which may have a quite different cause. Section 85(5) provides:

> "A person contravenes this section if he causes or knowingly permits any matter whatever to enter any inland freshwaters so as to tend (either directly or in combination with other matter which he or another person causes or permits to enter those waters) to impede the

---

[5] Subject, as with the s. 85(1) offence, to the "consented discharge" defence: see s. 88.

[6] It is also worth noting that the offence in subs.(4) is confined to a discharge of trade effluent from a building or fixed plant. If the discharge were from a mobile plant, e.g. a vehicle, no offence would have been committed under the subsection.

proper flow of the waters in a manner leading, or likely to lead, to a substantial aggravation of –
(a) pollution due to other causes; or
(b) the consequences of such pollution."

Section 85(6)

The final offence to be found in section 85 appears in subsection (6). It may be overlooked by the unwary in that the primary function of subsection (6) would appear to be determining the maximum level of penalty that may be imposed where the defendant has been convicted of an offence under section 85. However, the relevant part of section 85(6) provides:

> "Subject to the following provisions of this Chapter, a person who contravenes this section *or the conditions of any consent given under this Chapter for the purposes of this section* shall be guilty of an offence" (emphasis added).

Section 85(6) (or its statutory predecessor, section 107(6) of the Water Act 1989) has been considered by the appeal courts on several occasions. In *Taylor Woodrow Property Management Ltd* v *National Rivers Authority*,[7] the defendant company managed rather than owned or occupied an industrial estate in Southampton which was adjacent to the River Test. A consent to discharge had been granted to an associate company of the defendants by the Southern Water Authority, the predecessor of the National Rivers Authority. That consent contained four conditions. These related to: the construction of the outlet pipe; the use to which the outlet pipe was to be put; the nature and composition of the effluent; and, sampling point facilities to enable the authority's officers to determine compliance with the discharge consent. The key condition in terms of the present proceedings was the third condition. This required that the effluent discharged into the river waters should not contain any traces of oil or grease. It was alleged by the National Rivers Authority that the defendant company had breached the requirements of this condition on four separate occasions contrary to section 85(6) of the Water Resources Act 1991. On each occasion, a water quality officer employed by the Authority had visited the outfall and had observed oil emerging into the river from the outfall. It was argued on behalf of the defendants, however, that contrary to the reasoning of the Stipendiary Magistrate, the offence could only be made out if it could be shown that the defendant in fact made a discharge into controlled waters of matter to which the consent related. In short, it was submitted that Taylor Woodrow could only be found criminally liable under the Act if it was established that it had itself made a positive discharge into the river.

The Divisional Court which heard the appeal remained unconvinced by the argument. Having regard to the scheme of the legislation, in particular to sections 85, 88(2) and Schedule 10 to the 1991 Act, Steyn LJ (as he then was) considered it to be inherent that a failure to comply with positive

---

[7] 158 JP 1101.

obligations (or an omission to comply with such obligations) amounted to a contravention within the meaning of section 85(6). In these circumstances, it was unrealistic to argue that Taylor Woodrow were not criminally liable because they did not commit a positive act of discharge; they had failed to comply with a positive obligation contained in a condition which was lawfully applicable. Such a conclusion was supported by the fact that the word "contravention" is expressly defined by the statute to include a failure to comply,[8] which, in the words of Steyn LJ, "clearly imports the concept of omission to comply with positive obligations".

Thus the appeal in *Taylor Woodrow* was unsuccessful; the defendant company had been rightly convicted of the offences contrary to section 85(6). So much, therefore, for the argument that a failure to perform a positive act took the defendant outside the reach of a condition attached to a discharge consent. But, what would be the prospects of an even more fundamental defence: that a condition of a discharge consent which the defendant was alleged to have contravened was itself invalid?

Collateral challenge

In *R v Ettrick Trout Co Ltd and Baxter*,[9] the appellants sought to rely upon just such a collateral challenge. The first appellant was the owner and operator of a fish farm at Nursling Mill in Hampshire. The second appellant was the director of, and majority shareholder in, the company. Under the terms of a discharge consent granted to them by the Southern Water Authority, the appellants were permitted to discharge effluent into the River Test. However, that consent was subject to conditions relating to matters such as the nature and composition of the discharge. The consent was also subject to a condition as to the volume of the discharge. It stipulated that it was not to exceed 10 million gallons in any 24 hour period. Before the Crown Court at Southampton, the appellants had pleaded guilty to the offence of contravening this condition contrary to section 107(6) of the Water Act 1989.[10] That guilty plea had only been entered, however, after the Recorder had stated that the defence was not permitted to make a collateral challenge. The attempted collateral challenge had consisted of three strands: that the condition had not been imposed for a permitted purpose, i.e. pollution control, but for another purpose, namely in order to limit the volume of water that the appellants were permitted to extract; that the condition was unnecessary because the effluent from the fish farm had not caused a deterioration in the river quality downstream; and, that the condition was unreasonable in that its effect was to prohibit property rights. On appeal, therefore, the issue for the Court of Appeal was whether the appellants had been entitled to seek to rely upon a collateral challenge as a defence to the charge, or whether such a defence amounted to an abuse of the process of the court because it

---

[8] See s. 221(1) of the Water Resources Act 1991.

[9] [1994] Env LR 165.

[10] The predecessor of s. 85(6). Two further counts, that of causing trade effluent to be discharged into controlled water, and knowingly permitting trade effluent to be discharged into controlled water were ordered to remain on file by the Recorder.

was an attempt to by-pass normal judicial review procedures and the statutory appeal procedure.

Counsel for both parties relied upon a number of authorities to support their respective arguments.[11] In effect, the appellants sought to argue that since the courts had been prepared to accept the possibility of a collateral challenge where a defendant was being tried for the breach of a byelaw, that principle ought to be extended to cases such as the present, where it was alleged that a condition of a discharge consent was invalid. In giving the judgment of the Court of Appeal, McCowan LJ appeared to have some sympathy with this contention since he observed that:

> "This court finds itself unable to say that in no case could the validity of a condition be challenged by way of defence to a criminal prosecution. Each case may be looked at on its own particular facts. In our judgment it is not a simple question of whether what is under challenge is a by-law or a condition."[12]

However, in dismissing the appeal, the Court of Appeal was influenced by the decision in *Bugg* v *Director of Public Prosecutions*[13] and, in particular, by the analysis by Woolf LJ (as he then was) of the distinction between substantive and procedural invalidity. Given its influence upon the outcome in the present case, such a distinction must be examined a little further.

In *Bugg*, the defendant was prosecuted for the breach of a byelaw made under the Military Lands Act 1892. He claimed, however, that the byelaw was *ultra vires* on various grounds and the question for the Divisional Court was therefore whether he could attempt to rely upon such a defence before the magistrates. In giving judgment, Woolf LJ identified what he termed "substantive invalidity", where the byelaw:

> "...is on its face invalid because either it is outwith the power pursuant to which it was made because, for example, it seeks to deal with matters outside the scope of the enabling legislation, or it is patently unreasonable."[14]

Woolf LJ then went onto consider an alternative form of invalidity which he termed "procedural invalidity". This occurred where:

> "...there has been non-compliance with a procedural requirement with regard to the making of that by-law. This can be due to the

---

[11] Counsel for the appellants relied upon the following cases: *R* v *Reading Crown Court, ex p Hutchinson* [1988] 1 QB 384; *Attorney-General's Reference (No.2 of 1988)* [1989] 3 WLR 397; and *R* v *Oxford Crown Court, ex p Smith* [1990] 154 LG Rev 458. Counsel for the respondents principally relied upon *Quietlynn* v *Plymouth City Council* [1988] 1 QB 114 and *Bugg* v *Director of Public Prosecutions* [1993] 2 WLR 628.

[12] [1994] Env LR 165 at 171.

[13] [1993] 2 WLR 628.

[14] At 646.

manner in which the by-law was made; for example, if there was a failure to consult."[15]

The distinction between the two forms of invalidity was, it must be noted, of considerable practical importance for in Woolf LJ's analysis a collateral challenge allegation of substantive invalidity could be heard by a criminal court, whereas an allegation of procedural invalidity could not. His rationale for such a position was stated thus:

> "In the case of substantive invalidity, it is a matter of law whether, for example, a by-law is unreasonable in operation, or is outwith the authorising power. No evidence is required; the court can decide the issue by looking at the terms of the primary legislation and the subordinate legislation which is alleged to be invalid. The situation is different with procedural invalidity. Evidence will be required, for example, as to what happened during the course of the making of the by-law in order to see whether or not it had been validly made."[16]

In Woolf LJ's opinion, it was "not part of the jurisdiction of the criminal courts to carry out such an investigation and they are not properly equipped to do so."[17] Applying the distinction to the facts of the case before it, the Divisional Court in *R* v *Ettrick Trout Co Ltd and Baxter* concluded that the nature of the allegation was that the discharge consent condition was procedurally invalid. Accordingly, since such an allegation would require "evidence… as to what happened during the course of the decision to impose the condition",[18] it followed that the appropriate means of challenging the condition was by way of judicial review. Thus the Recorder had been right not to permit the defence to mount a collateral challenge since such a challenge would have amounted to an abuse of the process of the court.

Two points are worth noting about the decision in *Ettrick Trout*. First, despite the outcome of the appeal, it is clear from the words of McCowan LJ that the Court of Appeal was not prepared to close the door completely on the prospect of a collateral challenge made in respect of a condition attached to a discharge consent. Using the terminology employed by Woolf LJ in *Bugg*, it can be inferred from the decision in *Ettrick Trout* that if the challenge involved an allegation of substantive rather than procedural invalidity, then a criminal court would be in a position to determine the matter. The second point is connected to the first in that it also concerns the procedural/substantive invalidity distinction. Although cases such as *Ettrick Trout* and *R* v *Bovis Construction Ltd*[19] illustrate that distinction being applied, it is a distinction which was subsequently doubted by the

---

[15] *ibid.*
[16] At 647.
[17] At 651.
[18] [1994] Env LR 165 at 172.
[19] [1994] Crim LR 938.

House of Lords in *R* v *Wicks*[20] and then rejected by their Lordships in *Boddington* v *British Transport Police.*[21]

In the latter case the appellant, who had been convicted by a stipendiary magistrate of smoking a cigarette in a train carriage contrary to a byelaw,[22] sought to rely upon the alleged invalidity of the byelaw as a defence to the prosecution. Lord Irvine LC, who delivered the first speech in the House of Lords, sought to summarise the effect of the decision in *Bugg* v *DPP*. In his opinion, the Divisional Court had in that case established:

> "...a rule that by-laws which are on their face invalid or are patently unreasonable (termed 'substantive' invalidity) may be called in question by way of defence in criminal proceedings, whereas by-laws which are invalid because of some defect in the procedure by which they came to be made (termed 'procedural' invalidity) may not be called in question in such proceedings, so that a person might be convicted of an offence under them even if the by-laws were later quashed in other proceedings."[23]

Lord Irvine drew attention to the "strong reservations" which had been expressed about the decision in *Bugg* by the House of Lords in *R* v *Wicks*. In his opinion, "the time has come to hold that it [*Bugg*] was wrongly decided."[24]

Lord Irvine's concluded that *Bugg* should be overruled for the following reasons. As a starting point he took the view that the three authorities which had been cited in *Bugg* to support the view that except in a "flagrant" or "outrageous" case, a statutory order remained valid until

---

[20] [1998] AC 92; [1997] 2 WLR 876; [1997] 2 All ER 801. In this case, the appellant had been charged with failing to comply with the terms of an enforcement notice contrary to s. 179 of the Town and Country Planning Act 1990. At his trial, he sought to argue that in making the decision to serve the notice on him, the planning authority had acted in bad faith and had been motivated by immaterial considerations. The trial judge, however, accepted the prosecution's contentions that the matters raised by the appellant were matters of public law and that therefore they were more appropriately determined by an application for judicial review rather than during the course of a criminal trial. The Court of Appeal dismissed an appeal, as did the House of Lords. In so doing, their Lordships determined that the question whether or not a defendant in a criminal trial was entitled to make a collateral challenge against an order made under statute which it was alleged that he had breached depended upon the construction of the Act under which the prosecution had been brought. In the present case, the presence in the Town and Country Planning Act 1990 of detailed provisions regarding appeals indicated that the appropriate forum in which to challenge the procedural invalidity of an enforcement notice was the Divisional Court and not criminal proceedings arising from the alleged breach of the notice. A defendant who was being prosecuted for an offence contrary to s. 179(1) of the 1990 Act was not therefore entitled as a matter of right to rely upon the alleged invalidity of the enforcement notice as a defence. Such a notice was to be regarded as legally valid unless or until its vires had been successfully challenged in proceedings for judicial review.

[21] [1999] 2 AC 143; [1998] 2 All ER 203.

[22] The byelaw in question was Byelaw 20 of the British Railways Board's Byelaws, made under the authority of s. 67(1)(b) of the Transport Act 1962 (as amended).

[23] [1998] 2 All ER 203 at 212.

[24] *ibid.*

quashed, were not in fact authority for that proposition.[25] In his opinion, a careful reading of each of the relevant judgments demonstrated that they were authority for rather different propositions.[26] Moreover, Lord Irvine considered that by its suggestion that there were two classes of legal invalidity in the case of subordinate legislation, the Divisional Court in *Bugg* had also reasoned contrary to another decision of the House of Lords: *Anisminic Limited* v *Foreign Compensation Commission.*[27] In the words of Lord Irvine:

> "The *Anisminic* decision established, contrary to previous thinking that there might be error of law within jurisdiction, that there was a single category of errors of law, all of which rendered a decision ultra vires. No distinction is to be drawn between a patent (or substantive) error of law or a latent (or procedural) error of law. An ultra vires act or subordinate legislation is unlawful simpliciter and, if the presumption in favour of its legality is overcome by a litigant before a court of competent jurisdiction, is of no legal effect whatsoever."[28]

Lord Irvine identified several further reasons why the decision in *Bugg* should be overruled. In his opinion, the Divisional Court in that case had overlooked the fact that authority did exist to show that it was not improper for a criminal court to inquire into questions of what he termed "procedural irregularity".[29] Moreover, in his judgment the distinction between substantive and procedural invalidity was "not a practical distinction which is capable of being maintained in a principled way across the broad range of administrative action".[30] Finally there was:

> "… no rational ground for holding that a magistrates' court has jurisdiction to rule on the patent or substantive invalidity of subordinate legislation or an administrative act under it, but has no jurisdiction to rule on its latent or procedural invalidity, unless a statutory provision has that effect… If subordinate legislation is ultra vires on any basis, it is unlawful and of no effect in law. It follows that no citizen should be convicted and punished on the basis of it."[31]

---

[25] The authorities in question were three appeals determined by the House of Lords: *London and Clydeside Estates Ltd* v *Aberdeen District Council* [1979] 3 All ER 876; *Smith* v *East Elloe Rural District Council* [1956] 1 All ER 855; and, *Hoffmann-La Roche (F) & Co AG* v *Secretary of State for Trade and Industry* [1974] 2 All ER 1128.

[26] With regard to the decision in *Hoffman-La-Roche*, for example, Lord Irvine observed that the effect of Lord Diplock's speech in that appeal, when read as a whole, "makes it clear that subordinate legislation which is quashed is deprived of any legal effect at all, and that is so whether the invalidity arises from defects appearing on its face or in the procedure adopted in its promulgation" ([1998] 2 All ER 203 at 213).

[27] [1969] 2 AC 147; [1969] 1 All ER 208; [1969] 2 WLR 163.

[28] [1998] 2 All ER 203 at 213.

[29] Lord Irvine had in mind the decision of the House of Lords in *DPP* v *Head* [1958] 1 All ER 679.

[30] [1998] 2 All ER 203 at 214.

[31] *ibid.* at 215.

Lord Steyn, who also heard the appeal in *Boddington*, felt that there was one matter "above all", which "strikes at the root of the decision in *Bugg's* case". In his opinion:

> "[*Bugg*] contemplates that, despite the invalidity of a byelaw and the fact that consistently with *R* v *Wicks* such invalidity may in a given case afford a defence to a charge, a magistrates court may not rule on the defence. Instead the magistrates may convict a defendant under the byelaw and punish him. That is an unacceptable consequence in a democracy based on the rule of law. It is true that *Bugg's* case allows the defendant to challenge the byelaw in judicial review proceedings. The defendant may, however, be out of time before he becomes aware of the existence of the byelaw. He may lack the resources to defend his interest in two courts. He may not be able to obtain legal aid for an application for leave to apply for judicial review. Leave to apply for judicial review may be refused. At a substantive hearing his scope for demanding examination of witnesses in the Divisional Court may be restricted. He may be denied a remedy on a discretionary basis. The possibility of judicial review will, therefore, in no way compensate him for the loss of *the right* to defend himself by a defensive challenge to the byelaw in cases where the invalidity of the byelaw might afford him with a defence to the charge. My Lords, ... the consequences of *Bugg's* case are too austere and indeed too authoritarian to be compatible with the traditions of the common law."[32]

It is clear that in the light of the House of Lords decisions in *Wicks* and *Boddington*, the decision in *Ettrick Trout* must now be approached with caution. Although it was not cited in argument in either of the cases, its acceptance of the substantive/procedural distinction which was established in *Bugg* now appears to have been misplaced. In practice, however, whilst a collateral challenge may well now be possible where a defendant is being prosecuted for the breach of a condition attached to a discharge consent, the better course of action would be to have earlier utilised the appeals procedure in the Water Resources Act 1991.[33]

THE SECTION 85(1) OFFENCES

In the discussion which follows, we return to the general offence under section 85(1). In particular we shall be concerned to elaborate the key concepts which define the ambit of criminal liability under that subsection: "controlled waters", "poisonous, noxious and polluting matter" and "causing and knowingly permitting".

---

[32] *ibid.* at 227.
[33] See s. 91.

"Controlled waters"

This concept, for this purpose, is defined by section 104 of the Water Resources Act 1991 in broad terms. It comprises all waters within four categories:

territorial waters: the waters which extend seaward for three miles from the territorial sea baselines of England and Wales;

coastal waters: waters within the area landward of those baselines as far as –
• the limit of the highest tide,
• the freshwater limit of rivers and watercourses[34]

inland freshwaters: the waters of lakes and ponds,[35] and of rivers and watercourses above the freshwater limit

groundwaters: water contained in underground strata.

The concept is further extended by section 104(2):

> " … any reference to the waters of any lake or pond or any river or watercourse includes a reference to the bottom, channel or bed of any lake, pond , river or ... watercourse which is for the time being dry."

This subsection was significant to the decision of the Divisional Court in *National Rivers Authority* v *Biffa Waste Services Ltd*:[36] a case which also makes clear that the offence under section 85(1) is not committed by conduct which merely stirs up matter already within controlled waters.[37] The defendants had been engaged in works on the river Riddlesworth, clearing rubbish from the base of the river. To do this the company had driven tracked vehicles into the river and along the river bed. The effect of this was to have stirred up the mud and silt on the river bed. The material became suspended in the river water, significantly discolouring that water as it flowed downstream. Given the requirement of section 85(1) that matter must be caused or permitted to have *entered* controlled waters it was a critical question for the Divisional Court whether the bed of a river was, or was not, a part of the "controlled water"? If the bed formed a part of the controlled waters, nothing from outside would have "entered" those waters.

Understandably, attention focused on the wording of section 104(2) set out above. At first sight this subsection might seem to suggest that the bottom or bed of such waters is a part of the controlled waters in question *only* in

---

[34] But not a public sewer, or sewer or drain to a public sewer: s. 104(3).

[35] Including reservoirs of any description: but only lakes and ponds which discharge into a river or watercourse. Landlocked lakes and ponds are thus excluded from the general definition of 'controlled waters'. However, it is an offence to cause or knowingly permit the discharge of trade effluent into such waters: see s. 85(4).

[36] [1996] Env LR 227.

[37] Although in the appropriate circumstances, this will be an offence under s. 90(1) of the Water Resources Act 1991.

circumstances where the river (etc.) is dry. On this, literal, approach a conviction would have seemed appropriate.

However, the Divisional Court in *Biffa* took a contrary view. Staughton LJ explained:

> "It might be suggested that that means that the bottom, channel or bed is not part of the controlled waters when the watercourse is wet, rather than dry. That is not the conclusion which I would reach. It seems to me that the draftsman thought that the bottom, channel or bed was obviously part of the watercourse when there was water in it, but arguably not when there was no water in it; and therefore he put in subsection (2) to cover the latter case."[38]

Accordingly the Divisional Court upheld the approach taken by the magistrates in acquitting the defendants. A note of caution was, however, sounded. Rougier J, whilst accepting the correct application of the law to the facts of this particular case, commented:

> "It should not ... be assumed that such a decision gives to a contractor or plant operator *carte blanche* to disturb as much as he wishes of that which lies beneath any watercourse and to any depth. What is properly to be described as the bed of a river will vary according to the nature of the river and its subsoil. In certain circumstances it might turn out to be a very narrow stratum indeed."[39]

The broad scope of the section 104 definition of controlled waters is evidenced also by the decision of the Court of Appeal in *R v Dovermoss Ltd.*[40] The company appealed against its conviction in the Crown Court of having caused polluting matter (slurry) to have entered controlled waters at its farm in Carmarthenshire. Following complaints about the taste of supplied drinking water, Welsh Water discovered that ammonia levels at one source of spring water were substantially higher than normal. Pollution control officers of the National Rivers Authority visited the area from which the spring water supply derived. They discovered a field owned by the defendants upon which it appeared that dry slurry had been spread. The lower part of the field was waterlogged, with the result that the officers were required there to wade through some six inches depth of liquid slurry. They then found that a stream, whose normal course was to have run beside the field, had become obstructed, so that its present course was to overflow across the manured field, resulting in the slurry quagmire. Liquid from that quagmire appeared to have percolated through the ground and to have tainted the drinking water supply source.

---

[38] At 230.
[39] At 232. This interpretation was reinforced by s. 90(1) of the same Act: see above, p. 283. It was implicit in the establishment of this specific offence that the restrictive interpretation of liability under s. 85(1) adopted by Staughton LJ was correct.
[40] [1995] Env LR 258.

An issue raised on appeal was whether the water which had become diverted onto the defendant's field was, in law, "controlled water". The jury at the Crown Court had found, it seemed, that the defendants had caused the dry slurry to be spread on a known path of the diverted stream: but was such escaped water "controlled water"?

The Court of Appeal held that the definition in section 104 did indeed extend to water in such circumstances. Stuart-Smith LJ noted the inclusion of "inland freshwaters" within section 104(1); and that this concept itself included water of "watercourses" above the freshwater limit. "Watercourses" were further defined in section 221:

> "'watercourse' includes ... all rivers, streams, ditches, cuts, culverts, dykes, sluices and passages through which water flows, except mains and other pipes which –
> (a)   belong to the authority or a water undertaker."

His Lordship summarised defence contentions in the following words:

> "[Counsel for the defendant] contends that the water is only controlled water while it is flowing in the watercourse. If it had overflowed from it, or if the water had been diverted from its normal course so that it takes a different route and, as in this case, it meandered across the field until it eventually disappears into the ground, it is no longer controlled water. It may be controlled water again if it percolates through the ground to become underground water within section 104(1)(b), or if it finds its way back into the defined channel of the watercourse."[41]

These arguments were not, however, persuasive. To begin with it was a misconstruction of section 221 to consider that the words "through which water flows" qualifies all the preceding categories of watercourse: rather, these words are only applicable to the sewers and passages referred to. Those things are only watercourses in circumstances where water is flowing through them, whereas the other categories, in Stuart Smith LJ's words:

> "do not cease to be watercourses simply because they are dry at any particular time. Ditches are often dry for a part of the year. They do not cease to be watercourses."[42]

This conclusion was reinforced by a second feature of the statutory wording. Stuart Smith LJ noted that:

> " ...section 104(1)(a) refers to water *of* any watercourse. It does not say water in any watercourse .... In our judgment, water that

---

[41] *ibid.* at 262-263.
[42] *ibid.* at 263. This dictum was subsequently relied upon by Roch LJ in *Environment Agency* v *Brock plc* [1998] Env LR 607, discussed below.

overflows from a river, stream or ditch does not cease to be water of a watercourse."[43]

Moreover, this statutory language was in no way removed from ordinary usage:

> "In ordinary parlance one would say that the waters of the Rhine have overflowed into Coblenz."[44]

Given that the water diverted through the field remained controlled water, the issue for the jury had been properly summarised by the trial judge. The jury had been instructed that its verdict should depend on whether it believed the defence case (that the dry slurry had been put quite properly onto a dry field and that the stream had subsequently and unpredictably burst its banks so as to flow over that contaminant), or believed the prosecution case (that the stream had been blocked and diverted across the field for some time – and that the slurry had been spread in the known path of the diverted water).

The concept of "controlled water" was an issue also in *Environment Agency* v *Brock plc*.[45] The defendant company operated a landfill and, having extracted leachate, pumped that liquid through a hose to lagoons. The leachate leaked into a ditch, which connected with a river. However, the defendants had been able to block the ditch to prevent the escaped leachate entering the river. The issue was whether a charge could lie of having caused the polluting matter to enter the ditch? The Divisional Court held that the ditch did come within the concept of "controlled water", as defined in section 104. It was clear from the word "artificial" in section 104(3) that the concept of watercourse included a man-made channel; and it was clear from section 104(4) that the fact that the ditch dried out from time to time did not render it any less, even when dry, a watercourse.

One limit to the concept of "watercourse" was, however, noted. Section 221 makes clear that a *flow* of water is an essential of a watercourse. Accordingly, as Roch J explained:

> "… a man-made ditch will be a watercourse if it is a ditch through which water flows into another watercourse, lake or river which comes within the definition of 'controlled water' in the Act."

In contrast:

> " … a trench dug, for example, as part of a ha-ha which did not connect to any part of a system of controlled water, would not be a watercourse because water would not flow through it. The mere fact

---

[43] *ibid.*
[44] *ibid.*
[45] [1998] Env LR 607. For other aspects of this case, see, below, p. 323.

that in wet periods water may stand in the ditch for a time would not … make it a watercourse."[46]

On the facts of *Brock* the Divisional Court held that although it was true that there was very little flow of water in the man-made ditch, and that the ditch had been enlarged as a safety ditch to contain spillages, the fact that the ditch was connected so that water might flow into the river to which it connected via a brook, rendered the ditch "controlled water" within the legislation. The blocking of the ditch after the event which formed the basis of the criminal charge could not retrospectively alter the legal character of the ditch at the time those events occurred.

"Poisonous, noxious or polluting"

The meaning of the words "polluting matter" was considered, also, by the Court of Appeal in *R v Dovermoss Ltd.*[47] The facts of this case have already been described:[48] involving the spread of slurry onto a field across which it was known that water from a nearby stream was prone to overflow, following blockage of the ordinary course of that stream. The resultant slurry quagmire subsequently tainted the taste of water from a nearby spring, having increased its ammonia content. Counsel for the defendant contended that the trial judge had failed to explain to the jury that they must be satisfied that:

> "some harm has resulted to the water, such that it has a harmful effect on animal or plant life …. or [upon] those who use it."[49]

The Court of Appeal refused to accept such a narrow approach to the notion of "polluting matter":

> "We do not accept this submission. 'Pollute', 'pollutant' and 'pollution' are ordinary English words. The relevant definition of 'pollute' in the Oxford English Dictionary is: 'to make physically impure, foul or filthy; to dirty, stain, taint, befoul'. It is quite clear that it is intended to have a different meaning from 'poisonous or noxious matter', since those words appear in the section. 'Noxious' means harmful."[50]

Stuart Smith LJ explained that it was not appropriate for an appellate court to seek to provide a legal, as distinct from the ordinary, meaning for this concept:

> "We see no reason why the dictionary definition should not be adopted. It will, of course, be a question of fact and degree whether the matter does pollute the waters. Obviously, a very small quantity poured into a large watercourse may have no polluting effect at all. It

---

[46] *ibid.* at 615.
[47] [1995] Env LR 258.
[48] See, above, p. 294.
[49] [1995] Env LR 258 at 265.
[50] *ibid.*

is so diluted that it does not make it impure, foul or filthy. This is a question for the jury."[51]

This reminder that the issue is one of fact, or "fact and degree", rather than of law, is salutary. But appellate courts understandably find it hard to resist offering thoughts as to what might have been appropriate findings based upon the evidence brought to their attention. Indeed in *Dovermoss* itself, Stuart Smith LJ was at pains to make evident that, in his Lordship's view, the evidence would have supported a charge of having caused "noxious" matter to have entered controlled waters, quite apart from the more easily demonstrable "polluting matter" count. His Lordship observed, somewhat counter to the defence view of the evidence:[52]

> "It appears to us that the case could equally well have been charged as a noxious matter since it is obvious that it was likely to cause harm."[53]

Moreover, it was to be noted:

> "it is not necessary in such a case to establish actual harm. The likelihood or capability of causing harm to animal or farm life or to those who use the water is sufficient."[54]

The decision in *Dovermoss* stresses both the breadth of the concept of "polluting matter" and also that the judges will be reluctant to permit legal points to be taken as regards the scope of that broad concept. This means that certain important questions may be turned back by the appellate courts as being not questions upon which a definitive legal ruling can or should be given. One such question arises from one of the statements of Stuart Smith LJ extracted above. His Lordship explained that whether matter was "polluting matter" would need to be judged by reference to the impact (actual, or perhaps potential will suffice) of that matter on the waters into which it enters. Remember his Lordship's example of a small quantity of matter having, perhaps, little impact on a large volume of receiving water; whereas the same matter in larger proportion to the receiving waters might more likely be regarded as polluting matter. This seems entirely sensible. It does, however, lead us on to further, more difficult, questions.

It is one thing to say that the legally polluting or non-polluting effect of entry into controlled waters may depend on an overall assessment of the evidence as regards the nature of the matter entering the water, the volume and rate of such entry, and the volume and rate of flow of the receiving waters. This is to take a similar approach to whether matter is polluting matter as is taken, in the regulatory context, to the setting of the terms of consents to discharge into controlled waters.

---

[51] *ibid.*

[52] It seems that ammonia levels in the drinking water were sufficient to affect taste, but did not exceed levels prescribed as maxima by regulations.

[53] [1995] Env LR 258 at 265.

[54] *ibid.*

However, in any such assessment a further question arises: what may be the significance of the pre-existing quality of the water, be it good or bad, into which the matter has been caused or permitted to enter? May it be the case that a given impact on a body of receiving water may be regarded as polluting if that water was of hitherto pristine quality, but might not be regarded as polluting if that consequence was rather less noticeable because of the already tainted nature of the water?[55] To take an extreme position, might a stretch of water be already so badly polluted that only the worst additional matter might suffice to have any substantial further deleterious effect?

Should the courts be called upon to resolve such questions we should expect that little difficulty would be experienced ruling out such "defences" to criminal liability. One would expect the courts to stress that even polluted water may be further polluted[56] and that to keep water in a state of pollution which might otherwise have dissipated will involve pollution of that water.

"Causes or knowingly permits"

This expression appears in each of the first five subsections of section 85, providing alternative ways in which each of the offences within that section may be committed.[57]

The phraseology is not, however, unique to section 85. For example, as we shall see, it appears also in offences relating to waste[58] and it is fundamental also to certain important liability issues in the new legal

---

[55] There are clear parallels here between this discussion point and the effect of the doctrine of locality in determining liability for nuisance: see Chapter 3, above.

[56] Just as a person who has been depraved and corrupted by exposure to obscene material may be further depraved and corrupted by continued exposure to such material: see *DPP* v *Whyte* [1972] AC 849.

[57] Section 4(1) of the Salmon and Freshwater Fisheries Act 1975 is a further example of a statutory water pollution offence which has both a "causes" and a "knowingly permits" limb. It provides that: "... any person who causes or knowingly permits to flow, or puts or knowingly permits to be put, into any waters containing fish or into tributaries of waters containing fish, any liquid or solid matter to such an extent as to cause the waters to be poisonous or injurious to fish or the spawning grounds, spawn or food of fish, shall be guilty of an offence". It is quite common for a defendant to be charged with offences under both s. 4(1) and s. 85: see, for example, *F J H Wrothwell* v *Yorkshire Water Authority* [1984] Crim LR 45; *Wansford Trout Farm Ltd* v *Yorkshire Water Authority* (unreported) 23 July 1986; *Schulmans Incorporated Ltd* v *National Rivers Authority* [1993] Env LR D1; *National Rivers Authority* v *Welsh Development Agency* (1994) 158 JP 506; and *CPC (UK) Ltd* v *National Rivers Authority* [1994] Env LR 131. Proceedings under s. 4(1) can only be instituted by the Environment Agency or by a person who has first obtained a certificate from the Minister that he has a material interest in the waters alleged to be affected. This requirement may be satisfied by, for example, a group of anglers. Thus in *R* v *British Coal Corporation* (unreported) December 2, 1993, the Anglers' Cooperative Association brought unsuccessful proceedings against British Coal in respect of water pollution arising from ferruginous discharges from an abandoned mine working. It is a defence to a charge under s. 4(1) to show that the discharge was in accordance with a consent under Chapter II of Part III of the Water Resources Act 1991 or under Part II of the Control of Pollution Act 1974 (see the Water Consolidation (Consequential Provisions) Act 1991, Sched 1, para. 30(1)).

[58] Some formulae involve the word 'knowingly' qualifying also the word 'causing'. See further, below, p. 372.

regime as regards the identification and remediation of contaminated sites.[59]

Notwithstanding its apparent simplicity, and the attachment to it displayed by legislative draftsmen, the expression has engendered a good deal of case law, not all readily reconcilable. A degree of clarification, at least as regards the "causing" charge, was afforded by the House of Lords, in 1998, by its decision in *Empress Car Company (Abertillery) Ltd v National Rivers Authority.*[60] Nevertheless, significant issues remain, upon which the courts have not been called to offer guidance and upon which opinions may legitimately differ. It will be necessary to consider separately the concepts of *causing* and *knowingly permitting.*

"Causing"

Notwithstanding the guidance recently provided by *Empress Cars*, our discussion should begin with an earlier decision of the House of Lords: *Alphacell Ltd v Woodward,*[61] decided in 1972. The charge against Alphacell Ltd was of having caused polluting matter to have entered the River Irwell contrary to section 2(1)[62] of the Rivers (Prevention of Pollution) Act 1951. The defendants were manufacturers of manila paper fibres at their Mount Sion works. The process produced certain liquid effluents which were drained to two settling tanks situated beside the river, pending being either recirculated or taken away by tanker. The scheme was that liquid from the higher of the two tanks overflowed to the lower. A pumping system then removed liquid from the lower to a reservoir, from which it could be recirculated in the industrial process. One pump was ordinarily sufficient to remove the amount of water necessary to prevent the lower tank overflowing. In addition to this automatically primed pump, a second, manually operated, pump had been installed, in case of failure in the operation of the first. Should, for any reason, this pumping arrangement not operate effectively the consequence would be for overflowing effluent to pass through a channel and down into the river.

In due course such an event occurred, and on the very day that a river authority inspector came to view the site. Evidence was heard by the trial magistrates that a quantity of brambles, ferns and long leaves had been found wrapped around the impeller of each pump, so that even though both pumps were in operation they were ineffective in removing liquid from the lower settling tank. A variety of evidence was also heard as regards inspection practices, practice as regards cleaning out the pumping systems, previous experience as regards the presence of vegetation, and as regards inspection of water levels and pump efficiency in the period immediately prior to the overflow. The case stated was, however, equivocal as regards conclusions drawn by the magistrates from this evidence. Some evidence seemed to suggest no fault on the part of the defendant company: one

---

[59] See, below, Chapter 13.
[60] [1998] 1 All ER 481; [1998] Env LR 396.
[61] [1972] AC 824; [1972] 2 All ER 475.
[62] Identical in material terms to s. 85(1) of the Water Resources Act 1991.

witness, for example, had contended that the company had taken all reasonable steps to avoid such escape into the river. Equally, it did seem that previous experience had not indicated a propensity for such vegetation rapidly to build up around the impellers. On the other hand, evidence was presented that a foreman had been conscious that although the pumps were switched "on" they were not reducing the water level in the tank and yet had taken no action to prevent further ingress. In short, the case stated from the magistrates described a variety of evidence, from which they might have drawn a range of conclusions as regards the knowledge of the defendant company of the imminent overflow, and of its failure or otherwise to have taken reasonable care in the design and operation of the plant.

Notwithstanding this unsatisfactory situation, the House of Lords was able unanimously to uphold the magistrates' conviction of the defendant company. Their Lordships were able so to conclude because it was the clear view of the House that even on the basis that the magistrates might have been of the view that the defendant company were innocent of anything to which one might ascribe the label "blame" or "fault", nevertheless it was rightly convicted. There was a causal connection between Alphacell's activities and the entry of the polluting matter into the Irwell. This was all that the prosecution was required to prove. The offence was one of strict liability – a defendant was liable even though not aware of the entry or its likelihood, and even though not at fault in having failed to have taken reasonable care to have avoided the events which had occurred.

The view of the House of Lords, that when a charge is founded upon the first limb of what is now section 85(1), there is no requirement of proof of knowledge, intent or negligence on the part of the defendant, raises in stark profile as the critical issue the matter of *causality*. If all turns on whether a defendant "caused" the matter to enter the water in question, how is this key concept to be interpreted?

Lord Wilberforce emphasised the contrasting wording as between the two basic offences within, now, section 85(1):

> "The subsection evidently contemplates two things – *causing*, which must involve some active operation or chain of operations involving as a result the pollution of the stream; *knowingly permitting*, which involves a failure to prevent the pollution, which failure, must be accompanied by knowledge. I see no reason ... for reading back the word 'knowing' into the first limb... The first limb involves causing and this is what has to be interpreted."[63]

Lord Wilberforce eschewed the need for refined analysis of the concept of "causing":

---

[63] [1972] 2 All ER 475 at 479.

" ... 'causing' here must be given a common sense meaning and I
deprecate the introduction of refinements, such as *causa causans*,
effective cause or *novus actus*."[64]

And noting, percipiently, that other fact situations might give rise to more
difficulty "where acts of third persons or natural forces are concerned"
Lord Wilberforce continued:

" ... I find the present case comparatively simple. The appellants
abstract water, pass it through their works where it becomes polluted,
conduct it to a settling tank communicating directly with the stream,
into which the polluted water will inevitably overflow if the level
rises over the overflow point. They plan, however, to recycle the
water by pumping it back ... into their works; if the pumps work
properly this will happen and the level of the tank will remain below
the overflow point. It did not happen on the relevant occasion due to
some failure in the pumps.

In my opinion, this is a clear case of causing the polluted water to
enter the stream. The whole complex operation which might lead to
this result was an operation deliberately conducted ... and I fail to see
how a defect in one stage of it, even if we must assume that this
happened without their negligence, can enable [Alphacell Ltd] to say
they did not cause the pollution."[65]

Viscount Dilhorne adopted a similar, albeit slightly more sophisticated,
approach:

"... I propose to consider ... whether ... the act or acts of the
appellants caused the pollution. Its immediate cause was the blockage
of the impellers and the vats. The presence of the polluting liquid on
the bank of the river, and ... within a foot or so of the river, was due
to the acts of the appellants. The provision of the settling tanks with
an overflow channel ... leading directly to the river was directly due
to their acts. When the works were operating, there was, under the
system they instituted, bound to be an overflow into the river unless
the pumps provided were of sufficient capacity and working
efficiently to prevent this happening.

If they had not installed any pumps or only pumps of insufficient
capacity ... I do not think it could be suggested that their acts had not
caused the overflow and consequent pollution. Does it make any
difference if they had installed pumps of sufficient capacity and for
some reason the pumps had broken down ...? I think not. It was the
operation of the works which led to the flow of liquid to the tanks. It
was that operation which, with the system they had installed, led to
the liquid getting into the river. The roses at the end of the intake
pipes must have been fitted because it was realised that there was a

---

[64] *ibid.*
[65] *ibid.*

risk that without them debris would be sucked into and block the pumps. The fact that despite them debris was sucked in and prevented the pumps from working properly shows that that safeguard was insufficient and the result was the same as that which would have followed from the operation of the works if pumps of insufficient capacity had originally been installed. In these circumstances I see no escape from the conclusion that it was the acts of the appellants that caused the pollution. Without their acts there would not have been this pollution. It was their operation of their works that led to the liquid escaping into the tanks and their failure to ensure that the pumps were working properly that led to the liquid getting into the river."[66]

Viscount Dilhorne emphasised that this was a case where something had been done deliberately by the defendant – the operation of the works with its particular water circulation and storage system – with inevitable polluting consequences should certain eventualities occur. His Lordship stated:

"Here the acts done by the appellants were intentional. They were acts calculated to lead to the river being polluted if the acts done by the appellants, the installation and operation of the pumps, were ineffective to prevent it. Where a person intentionally does certain things which produce a certain result, then it can truly be said that he has caused that result, and here ... the acts done intentionally by the appellants caused the pollution."[67]

It will be seen that for Viscount Dilhorne the *intent* of the defendant has a relevance as regards the issue of causation. Indeed, his Lordship expressed the opinion that in a case where the pollution was not an unintended consequence of something deliberately done, but rather the unintended consequence of something not deliberately done the position might be different. His Lordship explained:

"We have not here to consider what the position would be if pollution was caused by an inadvertent and unintentional act without negligence. In such case it might be said that the doer of the act had not caused the pollution although the act had caused it."[68]

Precisely why Viscount Dilhorne seemed to consider it arguable that one does not cause a consequence where that consequence is a natural result of an act or action one does not intend (and which one did without negligence) was not explained. Indeed, this analysis would seem to

---

[66] At 482.

[67] At 483.

[68] *ibid.* Contrast the words of Lord Salmon: "It seems to me that, giving the word 'cause' its ordinary and natural meaning, anyone may cause something to happen, intentionally or negligently or inadvertently without negligence and without intention. For example, a man may deliberately smash a porcelain vase; he may handle it so negligently that he drops and smashes it; or he may without negligence slip or stumble against it and smash it. In each of these examples, no less in the last than in the other two, he has caused the destruction of the vase" (at 490).

undermine his Lordship's earlier recognition of the strict liability nature of the "causing" offence under section 85(1). Moreover, Viscount Dilhorne's comments may be regarded as inconsistent with the more robust approach which we have noted was taken by Lord Wilberforce and by their other Lordships.

So, for example, Lord Pearson explained:

> "I think that the justices ... were right in holding that the overflow was caused by the activities of the appellants. Those were positive activities and they directly brought about the overflow. What other cause was there? There was no intervening act of a trespasser and no act of God. There was not even any unusual weather or freak of nature. Autumn is the season of the year in which dead leaves ... may be expected to fall into water and sink below the surface and, if there is a pump, to be sucked up by it."[69]

Lord Cross, in his speech, gave an example which suggests that for him also the issue of fault and causation were not linked:

> "Suppose that the contractor whom the appellants had employed to install these works on the bank of the Irwell had provided a defective pump with the result that when the appellants operated their plant for the first time the tank overflowed – surely they could fairly be said to have 'caused' the pollution of the river even though they neither knew nor had any means of knowing that their act in setting the plant in operation would lead to that result?"[70]

However, Lord Cross did conclude with the words:

> "The appellants having started to operate their plant on that day could only escape being held to have caused polluted effluent to enter the river if they proved that the overflow of the tank had been brought about by some other event which could fairly be regarded as being beyond their ability to foresee or control."[71]

The final words "beyond their ability to foresee or control" indicate circumstances in which one whose actions would seem to form part of a chain of causation may be regarded, nevertheless, as not having caused the entry of the polluting matter for the purposes of the offence. The words ascribe this consequence to an unexpected and uncontrollable event which has caused one's actions to have a consequence they would not otherwise have had: a notion of *novus actus interveniens*.

---

[69] At 488.
[70] At 489. This example shares some similarities with the facts of *CPC (UK) Ltd* v *National Rivers Authority* [1994] Env LR 131, discussed below, p.324.
[71] *ibid.*

Lord Salmon also found no difficulty in holding the causation requirements to be satisfied. His Lordship contrasted the facts of the case with other possibilities:

> "What [Alphacell Ltd] did was something different in kind from the passive storing of effluent which could not discharge into the river save by an act of God, ..."

Rather:

> " ... the appellants caused the pollution by the active operation of their plant."[72]

We shall need to consider shortly the situations in which intervening circumstances or events, such as acts of a third party, may render it inappropriate to hold that a defendant caused matter to enter the controlled waters. Some such limit on the broad approach to causality was, as we have seen, acknowledged by their Lordships in *Alphacell*; but the ambit of that exception was not explored in any detail, the facts of the particular case not so requiring.

The decision of the House of Lords in *Alphacell* may be said to represent a broad purposive approach to the issue of causality. Lord Salmon's view was that the approach adopted by the House in its interpretation of the legislation was to achieve the only result which would produce an offence which would be readily prosecutable. His Lordship explained that:

> "It is of the utmost public importance that our rivers should not be polluted. The risk of pollution from the vast and increasing number of riparian industries, is very great. The offences created by the 1951 Act seem to me to be prototypes of offences which 'are not criminal in any real sense, but are acts which in the public interest are prohibited under a penalty': *Sherras* v *De Rutzen* [1895] 1 QB 918 at 920 per Wright J ... I can see no valid reason for reading the word 'intentionally', 'knowingly' or 'negligently' into s 2(1)(a) and a number of cogent reasons for not doing so. In the case of a minor pollution such as the present, when the justices find that there is no wrongful intention or negligence on the part of the defendant, a comparatively nominal fine will no doubt be imposed. This may be regarded as a not unfair hazard of carrying on a business which may cause pollution on the banks of a river. The present appellants were fined £20 and ordered to pay in all £24 costs ...
>
> If this appeal succeeded and it were held to be the law that no conviction could be obtained ... unless the prosecution could discharge the often impossible onus of proving the pollution was caused intentionally or negligently, a great deal of pollution would go unpunished and undeterred .... As a result, many rivers which are now filthy would become filthier still and many rivers which are now

---

[72] At 490.

clean would lose their cleanliness. The legislature no doubt
recognised that as a matter of public policy this would be most
unfortunate. Hence s 2(1)(a) which encourages riparian factory
owners not only to take reasonable steps to prevent pollution but to
do everything to ensure that they do not cause it."[73]

The guidance afforded by their Lordships in *Alphacell* makes clear that in
most cases defendants should not focus their attentions upon seeking to
defend themselves against conviction by raising arguments of causality or
absence of fault, but rather should concentrate upon the demonstration,
where possible, of mitigating circumstances which may be relevant as
regards sentence.

Nevertheless, and unsurprisingly, not all potential difficulties were
resolved by their Lordships' speeches. Their Lordships were, indeed, alert
to the fact that causality issues would arise in other, more complex,
situations: as we have seen, reference was made in particular to the issue of
the approach which should be taken in cases involving third party
interventions (for example, acts of trespassers) and acts of God.

A number of reported cases in the years following *Alphacell* sought to
grapple with these issues with, as will appear, only limited success. The
decisions were difficult to reconcile, and failed to produce clear principles
for courts to apply. In due course an opportunity arose, in *Empress Car Co
(Abertillery) Ltd* v *National Rivers Authority*,[74] for these decisions to be
reviewed and for further guidance to be offered.

Empress Cars

Empress Cars had been convicted by the justices of having caused
poisonous matter to enter the river Ebbw Fach beside their premises in
Abertillery. The matter in question was a large quantity of diesel oil which
had escaped from a tank on the defendant's premises; premises which
drained to the adjacent river. The evidence was that the tank was
surrounded by a bund – a walled area designed to retain the contents of the
tank in the event of leakage. However, the defendant company had
rendered ineffective this protective arrangement by having fixed a pipe to
the outlet of the tank so as to connect the tank to a drum outside the bund.
Oil was then drawn routinely from the drum rather than from the tank. The
outlet to the tank was governed by a tap, to which no locking mechanism
had been attached. That tap was opened one night and left so that the entire
contents of the tank overflowed the drum and passed from the defendant's
yard by drain into the river. The identity of the person who had opened the
tap was not known. The evidence was quite consistent with it having been
either an employee or a stranger.[75] The Crown Court, on appeal from the

---

[73] At 490-491.

[74] [1998] 1 All ER 481; [1998] Env LR 396.

[75] Note Lord Clyde's comment: "The tap had been turned on. It was not proven who had turned it
on. It could, and probably was a member of the appellant's staff, but it could have been an
intruder" (at 493 of the former report). As will become apparent, the case was decided on the

justices, held that whichever was the case, the company was guilty of the offence charged. Even if the tap had been opened by a stranger, the Crown Court considered that the defendant was guilty of having caused the oil to have entered the river. The reasoning was encapsulated in the following statement:

> "The appellant should have foreseen that interference with their plant and equipment was an ever-present possibility, and they failed to take the simple precaution of putting on a proper lock and a proper bund and this was a significant cause of the escape even if the major cause was third party interference."[76]

On appeal, the Divisional Court approached the matter similarly. It was true that the escape may have been caused by the acts of a stranger. This, however, did not prevent a finding, on the evidence, that the entry of the oil into the river had not been caused also by the defendant company. Nevertheless, the Divisional Court was uneasy at the existence of a variety of cases which in its opinion were not easy to reconcile, and so permitted appeal to the House of Lords.

Before the House argument centered on two points, reflecting the line of defence adopted by the company. First, the company argued that to be guilty it must have engaged in some positive act resulting in the escape and that mere storage of oil was not such an act. Second, even if this first requirement was not necessary for liability (or was satisfied), given the assumption that the escape had been a consequence of the acts of a stranger, the company should not be regarded, for that reason, as having caused the oil to have entered the river.

The leading speech was delivered by Lord Hoffmann, who dealt with each of these principal issues in turn.

Need for some positive act

Lord Hoffmann accepted the notion put forward by the defendant that some positive act causing the matter to enter controlled water is necessary where the charge is that of "causing" pollution under section 85(1). His Lordship explained:

> "Putting the matter shortly, if the charge is 'causing', the prosecution must prove the pollution was caused by something which the defendant did, rather than merely failed to prevent."[77]

In contrast, the "knowingly permitting" offence relates to those who may be said to have caused matter to have entered controlled waters by a knowing *omission* to have acted so as to have prevented that occurrence.

---

assumption that the events occurred because of the actions of a trespasser-vandal. The issue was whether, in such circumstances, the defendant would nevertheless be liable.

[76] Cited in the judgment of Lord Hoffmann at 484.

[77] At 485.

The concept of having caused the matter to have entered the water is an aspect of *both* charges – although explicit only in the language of the former. The crucial distinction is not between those who have caused and those who have not caused pollution, but between those who have caused pollution by some positive act and those who have caused pollution by an omission to have prevented that pollution. In Lord Hoffmann's words:

> " ... the structure of the subsection ... imposes liability under two separate heads: the first limb for doing something which causes the pollution and the second for knowingly failing to prevent the pollution. The notion of causing is present in both limbs: under the first limb, what the defendant did must have caused the pollution and under the second limb, his omission must have caused it .... Liability under the first limb, without proof of knowledge, therefore requires that the defendant must have done something."[78]

The critical question then becomes: what counts as a positive act on the part of the defendant, which may be considered to have caused the matter in question to have entered the controlled waters?

On this matter Lord Hoffmann considered that the judges had on occasions fallen into error by having asked themselves fundamentally the wrong questions on the issue of causality. Referring to reticence in some cases to hold that a defendant had, by having done something, caused the pollution in question, Lord Hoffmann commented:

> " ... these ... cases take far too restrictive a view of the requirement that the defendant must have done something. They seem to require that his positive act should have been in some sense the *immediate* cause of the escape. But the Act contains no such requirement. It only requires a finding that something which the defendant did caused the pollution."[79]

It may be helpful to examine the cases which, in Lord Hoffmann's view, took this too restrictive approach. The first was *Price v Cromack*.[80] The source of pollution of a tributary of the River Severn was traced to a farm owned by the defendant. Earlier that year two storage lagoons had been constructed on the defendant's land to contain abattoir and animal by-product effluent created by Ellesmere Animal Products Ltd at their nearby premises. An agreement as regards piping effluent to the lagoons had been reached two years earlier. A wall of one of the lagoons was found, on inspection, to contain a breach which had allowed effluent to escape and soak into surrounding land and this was followed by a breach in the wall dividing the lagoons. On the surrounding land becoming flooded by effluent, the pollutant made its way by ditch to the River Perry.

---

[78] *ibid.*

[79] *ibid.*

[80] [1975] 1 WLR 988; [1975] 2 All ER 113.

The justices convicted the defendant of having caused polluting matter to have entered the river. However, the Divisional Court allowed the defendant's appeal. Lord Widgery CJ referred with approval to the statement in *Alphacell* that:

"a man cannot be guilty of causing polluting matter to enter a stream unless at the least he does some positive act in the chain of acts and events leading to that result."[81]

What, then, was the required positive act in *Price v Cromack*?

Lord Widgery CJ noted the facts of the case:

"The effluent came on to [the defendant's] land by gravity and found its way into the stream by gravity with no act on his part whatever, if one thinks in terms of a physical act connected with the land or the owner."[82]

And concluded:

"I cannot myself find it possible to say that a causing of the entry of the polluting matter occurs merely because the land owner stands by and watches the polluting matter cross his land into the stream ..."[83]

Accordingly, the Divisional Court allowed the defendant's appeal. In *Empress Cars* Lord Hoffmann stated that it was an error for that court to have considered that the defendant in *Price* had not "done something" which could properly have founded a "causing" pollution charge. His Lordship commented:

"I do not see why the justices were not entitled to say that the pollution was caused by something which the defendants did. Maintaining lagoons of effluent ... is doing something."[84]

In other words, according to Lord Hoffmann's view of the facts, *Price v Cromack* was not a case of a defendant having merely permitted effluent to have entered his land. And nor was it a case where liability attached in respect of "mere storage". Rather, it was a case in which some, unexplained, failure in the maintenance of the lagoon walls had been the cause of the pollution.

The second case which had taken too restrictive an approach as regards liability was *Wychavon District Council v National Rivers Authority*.[85] The charge against the local authority was that it had caused sewage effluent to

---

[81] Approving statements of Bridge J at first instance: [1972] 2 QB 127 at 136.
[82] [1975] 2 All ER 113 at 118.
[83] *ibid.* Lord Widgery CJ expressly offered no opinion as to whether a "knowingly permitting" charge might have succeeded. Ashworth J, however, felt that such a charge would have been difficult to answer (at 119).
[84] [1998] 1 All ER 481 at 485-486.
[85] [1993] 1 WLR 125; [1993] 2 All ER 440.

have entered the River Avon via a storm outflow adjacent to Evesham Hospital. The sewage had proceeded through the storm outflow as a consequence of a blockage in the sewer pipe between the hospital and the river. The local authority, under an agency agreement, had undertaken to operate, maintain and repair sewers in the area. The sewer which had become blocked was gravity fed and had no history of problems: an explanation of the particular events was that it might have resulted from solid material emanating from the hospital's link sewer.

The local authority was convicted by the justices, who took the view that the word "cause" did not require any physical act on the part of the authority, but could include also a lack of effective preventive action. As the defendants had failed to discover the blockage so as to have prevented the pollution they could, by this failure, be regarded as having "caused" the pollution. Furthermore, the local authority could be regarded as having caused the pollution by their failure to have sufficiently maintained the sewage system.

The essential issue, on appeal to the Divisional Court, was whether by having failed to have acted properly to have discovered and have dealt with the blockage the local authority had, from that point on, been a "cause" of the sewage entering the river. Watkins LJ quoted extensively from Lord Widgery CJ's judgment in *Price*, and concluded:

> " … the facts … are not capable of establishing that the [defendants] caused the pollution …. There is nothing to point to the performance by [them] of either a positive or a deliberate act such as could properly be said to have brought about the flow of the sewage effluent into the River Avon. There are facts which, in my opinion, could point to inactivity amounting possibly to negligence. There are others which could amount to knowingly permitting sewage effluent to be discharged …, but the [defendants] are not charged with that."[86]

It followed, for the Divisional Court, that the justices' conviction of the local authority should be quashed. In *Empress Cars*, Lord Hoffmann expressed the view that the Divisional Court should have regarded "operating the municipal sewage system as doing something",[87] so that, one presumes, a conviction would have been appropriate.

Lord Hoffmann proceeded to apply this analysis to the facts of *Empress Cars*, stating that:

> "The … question was whether something which the defendant had done, whether immediately or antecedently, had caused the pollution."[88]

---

[86] At 137 of the former report.
[87] [1998] 1 All ER 481 at 486.
[88] *ibid.*

It was not necessary that the act done should have been the immediate cause of the pollution. On the facts:

> " ... the escape was caused by the way the company maintained its tank of diesel fuel. Maintaining a tank of diesel is doing something ..."[89]

The positive act requirement implicit in the 'causing' offence was, therefore, satisfied in *Empress Cars.*

Breaking the causal connection: subsequent acts of third parties and the effect of natural forces

Lord Hoffmann's general advice to justices was that they should begin by seeking to identify from the evidence what it was alleged by the prosecution that the defendant had done which was to be regarded as a cause of the pollution. If their conclusion, in spite of the broad approach described above, was that the defendant could not be said to have "done anything at all" which could be so characterised, the consequence was that a charge of "causing" pollution could not succeed.

As Lord Hoffmann put it, in such a situation:

> "the defendant may have 'knowingly permitted' pollution but cannot have caused it."[90]

Assuming, however, that the positive act requirement is satisfied, the next issue is whether what the defendant did should be regarded *in law as a cause* of the pollution. The indefinite article in this formulation is deliberate and significant. Lord Hoffmann was at pains to stress that it was all too easy for justices to fall into error by asking inappropriate questions. In particular, justices were prone to fall into error when they asked themselves "what" or "who" had caused the pollution in respect of which the prosecution had been brought . To ask such a question courted error. In cases where pollution may have resulted from the combined actions and activities of several parties, asking who had caused the pollution would tend to ascribe responsibility to, and only to, the party whose acts were the most immediate cause of the pollution: the actor who was last in time. But such a conclusion was unacceptable in two ways. It tended to suggest that in relation to an incident of pollution only one party could be regarded as having caused the offending matter to have entered the water; and it would ascribe such responsibility to later actors, tending thereby to absolve others.

This was, however, to produce wrong conclusions. If justices asked themselves not "who" or "what" caused the pollution, but "did the defendant cause the pollution", they were more likely, Lord Hoffmann felt, to come to their conclusions with a correct understanding that several

---

[89] *ibid.*
[90] At 492.

parties may each be regarded as persons whose acts have caused the pollution (and each, therefore, potentially subject to charges under section 85(1)).[91] They will also be more likely correctly to understand that the existence of a more immediate cause of the pollution (e.g. the act of a third party) is quite consistent with the precedent acts of the defendant also being regarded as *a* cause of the pollution.

In order to illustrate these basic points Lord Hoffmann referred with approval to the House of Lords decision in *National Rivers Authority* v *Yorkshire Water Services Ltd*.[92] This case arose out of an incident at the defendant's sewage treatment works at North Bierley. These works operated by gravity flow. Water flowed via sewers into the works, through the treatment processes and then also by gravity, following such treatment, into Hunsworth Beck and the River Spen. The defendant company had a statutory consent which authorised the discharge of treated sewage effluent into the beck but this did not cover sewage effluent containing iso-octanol. The defendant company regulated what was discharged by industry, for treatment at its sewage works, by way of the system of trade effluent consents. None of the consents granted permitted discharge to sewer of iso-octanol. One night an unidentified third party released a quantity of iso-octanol into the sewer. The treatment works were not appropriate to the treatment of this chemical, which passed in unaltered form through the works and into the beck and river. Furthermore, the chemical had the consequence of releasing grease from the settling tanks, which moved down to foul and render ineffective the lower settling bed stones. It was accepted that the release of the iso-octanol at night into the sewer was in order for the culprit to avoid detection; and that the defendants could not reasonably have been expected to have prevented that discharge into the sewer, or to have prevented it entering their works. Once within those works its eventual discharge to the controlled waters was inevitable.

One of the issues raised, on appeal to the House of Lords, was whether the defendant company had "caused" the polluting matter to have entered the river. In the leading speech Lord Mackay LC answered this question affirmatively. After referring to *Alphacell* his Lordship continued:

> "… it has to be remembered that what was being discharged by Yorkshire Water Services was not iso-octanol only but was iso-octanol along with other materials and it was of the whole discharge that the complaint is raised … I am of opinion that Yorkshire Water Services having set up a system for gathering effluent into their sewers and thence into their sewage works to be treated, with an arrangement deliberately intended to carry the results of that

---

[91] It is worth noting that in *Attorney-General's Reference (No.1 of 1994)* [1995] 2 All ER 1007, the Court of Appeal had held that the offence of causing water pollution could be committed by more than one person. This was so in the obvious case of a joint enterprise and also, where different defendants performed separate acts. Were it otherwise: "A jury faced with concurrent conduct by more than one party would experience difficulty and reluctance in 'choosing one culprit…'" (per Lord Taylor CJ at 1017-1018).

[92] [1995] 1 AC 444; [1995] 1 All ER 225.

treatment into controlled waters, the special circumstances surrounding the entry of iso-octanol into their sewers and works does not preclude the conclusion that Yorkshire Water Services caused the resulting poisonous, noxious and polluting matter to enter the controlled waters, notwithstanding that the constitution of the effluent so entering was affected by the presence of iso-octanol."[93]

In *Empress Cars*, Lord Hoffmann stressed that the *Yorkshire Water Services* decision provided a good example of a case where the activities of different parties might each be regarded as having "caused" the pollution. Whilst it could, the case demonstrated, be said that Yorkshire Water Services had caused the pollution, this did not mean that if a prosecution had been brought against the miscreant with the iso-octanol, that person might not equally have been found to have caused the pollution. And the characterisation of that person as a potential defendant did not render the Water Services Company any less a cause of the pollution.[94]

Having avoided the trap of asking such wrong questions, and remembering the potentiality that several parties might each by their acts be regarded as having caused the pollution, the justices should, Lord Hoffmann explained, be mindful of the fact that in certain circumstances the subsequent acts of third parties or subsequent natural events may be such as to render it inappropriate to regard those earlier acts as a cause of the pollution. The critical issue, upon which Lord Hoffmann sought to offer guidance, was the test which should apply to distinguish cases where third party action or natural events might have this effect, from cases where they will not.

Lord Hoffmann began:

" ... both the law and commonsense normally attach great significance to deliberate human acts and extraordinary natural events. A factory owner carelessly leaves a drum containing highly inflammable vapour in a place where it could easily be accidentally ignited. If a workman, thinking it is only an empty drum, throws a cigarette butt and causes an explosion, one would have no difficulty in saying that the negligence of the owner caused the explosion. On the other hand, if the workman knowing exactly what the drum contains, lights a match and ignites it, one would have equally little difficulty in saying that he had caused the explosion and that the carelessness of the owner had merely provided him with an occasion for what he did. One would probably say the same if the drum were struck by lightning. In both cases one would say that although the vapour-filled drum was a necessary condition for the explosion to happen, it was not caused by the owner's negligence."[95]

---

[93] At 231 of the latter report.
[94] Note, however, that the House ultimately allowed the defendant's appeal, holding that the special defence under, now, s. 87(2) of the 1991 Act had been satisfied (see further below).
[95] [1998] 1 All ER 481 at 488.

Now this example given by Lord Hoffmann needs to be approached with care. The purpose of the example was not to provide guidance as regards the approach to be taken in the particular legal context in question – the "causing" offence under section 85(1), but simply to illustrate more broadly that sometimes the law will excuse one person from liability on the grounds that that person's acts were followed by the deliberate acts of another. The word "sometimes" here is important. We have to be alert to this possibility but we should not assume such relief from liability in all cases. Indeed, we shall perhaps have cause to wonder whether the factory owner in Lord Hoffmann's example would be quit of liability under section 85, even in the deliberate arson context, if that arson led to chemical spillages and consequent pollution of water.

It was necessary, therefore, for Lord Hoffmann to proceed to consider the significance of third party acts and natural events in the specific context of liability under section 85. In this connection the purpose and objectives of the rule were of importance. Lord Hoffmann referred to the strict liability nature of the offence and noted that the offence was aimed at seeking effectively to protect controlled waters from pollution. The reasoning which, as we have seen, had supported the imposition of strict liability, Lord Hoffmann felt, also operated to justify a none-too-generous approach as regards occasions when such subsequent events or occurrences might relieve a defendant of liability. That the pollution-prevention policy objective of the Act had this twin consequence may be seen from his Lordship's statement that:

> "*National Rivers Authority* v *Yorkshire Water Services Ltd*[96] is a striking example of a case in which, in the context of a rule which did not apply strict liability, it would have been said that the defendant's operation of the sewage plant did not cause the pollution but merely provided the occasion for pollution to be caused by the third party who had discharged the iso-octanol."[97]

What principle should therefore govern this matter? Lord Hoffmann noted that a number of judges had considered that the critical issue was whether the act of the third party or the natural event was, or was not, foreseeable. His Lordship referred to the statement of Lord Salmon in *Alphacell* quoted above[98] and also to a similar comment of Buckley J in *National Rivers Authority* v *Wright Engineering Co Ltd*:[99]

> " ... foreseeability [of the third party actions] ... is one factor which the tribunal may properly consider in seeking to apply commonsense to the question: who or what caused the result ..."[100]

---

[96] [1995] 1 AC 444; [1995] 1 All ER 225.
[97] [1998] 1 All ER 481 at 489.
[98] See, above, p. 305.
[99] [1994] 4 All ER 281; [1994] Env LR 186.
[100] At 285 of the former report.

In Lord Hoffmann's view, however, the concept of "foreseeability" was not an appropriate test in this context. By importing an "unforeseeable act of third party" or "unforeseeable event" defence it seemed to undermine the strict liability which was the essence of the offence. By seeming to allow a "not reasonably foreseeable" defence into the issue of causation it provided a guiding principle which was likely to work unduly favourably. It introduced into the question of liability concepts relevant to liability based upon fault, but not relevant to strict liability. Where one's actions cause harm because of the not reasonably foreseeable actions of a third party one may not be culpable in one's behaviour, but that is not the same as saying that the lack of reasonable foreseeability should mean that one should be regarded as not having *caused* the harm in question. As Lord Hoffmann commented:

> "...foreseeability is not the criterion for deciding whether a person caused something or not. People often cause things which they could not have foreseen."[101]

If foreseeability goes to culpability rather than to causality, what test *should* apply to characterise or single out cases where subsequent third party acts or natural events will have broken the chain of causation? Lord Hoffmann advised as follows:

> "The true ... distinction is ... between acts and events which, although not necessarily foreseeable in the particular case, are in the generality a normal and familiar fact of life, and acts and events which are abnormal and extraordinary."[102]

And later:

> " ... the justices should consider whether [the] act or event should be regarded as a normal fact of life or something extraordinary. If it was in the general run of things a matter of ordinary occurrence, it will not negative the causal effect of the defendant's acts, even if it was not foreseeable that it would happen to that particular defendant or take that particular form. If it can be regarded as something extraordinary, it will be open to the justices to hold that the defendant did not cause the pollution."[103]

Applying this principle to the facts of *Empress Cars* itself, Lord Hoffmann considered there to be ample evidence upon which the trial court could quite properly have found that the defendant had caused the pollution. In other words, even if the immediate cause was the action of a trespassing vandal, and even if such an occurrence was not a foreseeable event in the particular circumstances, such an event could not be described as "extraordinary" but was rather an ordinary "fact of life". The company was engaged in a positive act – the maintenance of a fuel tank on its premises –

---

[101] [1998] 1 All ER 481 at 491.
[102] *ibid.*
[103] At 492-493.

and its performance of this act could, therefore, properly be regarded as having caused the oil to have entered the adjacent river.

Further illustrations of the operation of Lord Hoffmann's principle may be found in an example provided by his Lordship, and also by reference to his Lordship's comments and criticisms of certain earlier court decisions.

The example given by Lord Hoffmann provides a demonstration of what may be regarded as an extraordinary event breaking the chain of causation. Referring to the facts of *Price* v *Cromack*[104] his Lordship expressed the view that had the facts been that the walls of the effluent lagoon had been breached not by inadequate maintenance but by a bomb planted by terrorists, this would have sufficed to have rendered it no longer possible to take the view that the party maintaining the lagoon had caused the ensuing pollution.

This stark illustration repays closer analysis. For one thing it demonstrates the very great breadth of the notion of "causing", as understood by the judges in this context. Let us assume, in Lord Hoffmann's example, that there was nothing inadequate about the walls of the lagoon: that they failed only because of the force of the terrorist bomb. Let us assume also that a terrorist bomb is an extraordinary event and not an ordinary fact of life. On such facts one can readily understand the conclusion that the person maintaining the lagoon should bear no liability. Lord Hoffmann chose to explain this on the basis that the chain of causation has been breached. However, perhaps we should express some surprise at the analysis adopted in order to render the defendant not guilty. In a situation where a well maintained lagoon has been breached by the actions of the terrorists, might it not be a more natural analysis to say that the reason for the defendant not bearing liability is not so much a break in the chain of causation, but the absence of a chain of causation in the first place? For a chain of causation to exist one might think that there must be some act on the part of the defendant which may be regarded as having set in train the events which have led to the pollution. We know that to store effluent in a lagoon which, *without proper maintenance*, will result in leakage into controlled waters will suffice: see *Price*. We also know that to operate a plant where pollution of controlled waters will result if there is a *malfunction of operations* in which the defendant is engaged will suffice: see *Alphacell* and *Empress Cars*. But if we say that, as in Lord Hoffmann's example, there has to be an extraordinary intervening act or occurrence in order to exempt the defendant from liability in a case where that defendant has done no more than operate a well-maintained lagoon in a location adjacent to controlled water, we would seem to be reducing the "causality" requirement for liability to something close to nothing.

To give an example. I park my car beside controlled water and I leave the handbrake off (or because of a defect the handbrake fails). The car enters the river. We should here have little difficulty in holding that I have caused

---

[104] See, above, p. 308.

the car to enter the river. Equally, if the car not "in brake" has moved not by simple force of gravity, but by act of having been pushed by a third party, we may say that my having parked my car with inadequate brakes beside the water was a cause of its entry into the river. Liability would then very properly depend on whether the third party act broke the chain of causation. But what if the brakes of my car have been properly applied and work effectively, but my car has ended in the river simply by virtue of having been "bull-dozed" there by a third party's vehicle? To say that merely parking proximate to the river is a cause of the car's entry into the river seems to be an unnatural use of language; but nevertheless such would seem to be the reasoning implicit in Lord Hoffmann's example. For Lord Hoffmann, remember, the explanation of non-liability in the case of a terrorist breach of a well-maintained lagoon was the extraordinary nature of that event. It seems that those who are not only not at fault, but also have done no more to contribute to events than to have stationed potentially polluting matter in proximity to a river,[105] will bear liability for any entry of such matter into the river unless the explanation for such entry falls within the rather narrow confines of Lord Hoffmann's extraordinary act/event principle.

Perhaps, however, this is to read too much into what was, after all, merely an illustration given by Lord Hoffmann. In the cases under principal review, let us remember, there were features which took the situation of the defendant beyond that of one who had merely put matter into a position adjacent to controlled water. In each of *Alphacell*, *Price* and *Empress Cars* there was something further about the conduct or activities of the defendant which could be properly considered the commencement of a chain of causation: putting polluted water into a tank which would overflow if pumping arrangements failed, storing oil in a tank without proper utilisation of bund protection, and so on. Perhaps, however, the requirement of causality is not quite so easily satisfied as Lord Hoffmann's example might seem to suggest. This would seem a matter upon which further judicial consideration may, in due course, be necessary.

A further variation upon Lord Hoffmann's example may be presented. Suppose that the lagoon walls would have withheld the terrorist's bomb had they been properly maintained; but failed because of a lack of such maintenance. The lack of maintenance may either have been of such degree that a breach of the lagoon by the effluent was in any case imminent; or it may be that no such breach was likely in the near future simply as a result of the deterioration in the strength of the walls. How should we analyse each of these situations? Should we regard there as having been an extraordinary intervening event and therefore no liability? Or is some other analysis and conclusion appropriate? Given that the bomb would not have resulted in pollution but for the poorly maintained walls,

---

[105] The notion of proximity as a limiting factor to liability would seem implicit in Lord Hoffmann's statements. Those who position beside controlled waters matter which may pollute will be subject to the regime of liability described. The matter may be different where matter is taken by a third party, transported some distance, and then thrown into controlled waters.

should this not disentitle the custodian of those walls from evading liability? Perhaps in the case of the walls which were in imminent danger of giving way; but maybe not where the walls, although not of full strength, remained adequate for their particular effluent retention purposes. Confident conclusions are difficult: within the context of the notion of "causing" there may remain a variety of as yet unresolved issues to be explored.

In addition to the terrorist bomb example, Lord Hoffmann discussed the decision in *Impress (Worcester) Ltd* v *Rees*[106] and concluded that that decision was inconsistent with the principle which should apply, and so was wrongly decided.

Impress overruled by *Empress*

Impress involved a considerable quantity of fuel oil which had escaped from a fuel oil storage tank on the defendant's premises. The tank was enclosed by a brick retaining wall with two ground level outlets. Any liquid which escaped through those outlets was likely to make its way, via a storm water drain, into the River Severn. The defendants never locked the valve at the base of the tank, and were aware that one of the ground level outlets in the bund was not kept permanently closed. Their factory premises were not gated so as to prevent unauthorised entry and the tank was visible from the highway. No night-watchman was employed. One night the valve to the tank was opened and the oil flowed out, eventually polluting the Severn. It was a legitimate inference from the evidence that the valve was opened by an unauthorised trespasser for purposes unconnected with the defendant's business.

The Divisional Court allowed the defendant's appeal against conviction. Cooke J explained:

> "... can it be said ... that the [defendant] caused the oil to enter the river?
>
> Of course, in one sense the entry of the oil was the result of many causes, and it may be said that the mere fact that the [defendants] brought the oil on to their land was one of the causes. There were, however, a number of intervening causes, and in particular there was the opening of the valve by unauthorised persons .... On general principles of causation, the question ... was whether that intervening cause was of so powerful a nature that the conduct of the [defendants] was not a cause at all but was merely part of the surrounding circumstances. If the justices had asked themselves that question, it seems to me that it would have been susceptible of only one answer, namely that it was not the conduct of the [defendants] but the

---

[106] [1971] 2 All ER 357.

intervening act of the unauthorised person which caused the oil to enter the river."[107]

This reasoning did not, however, satisfy their Lordships in *Empress*. In Lord Hoffmann's view it was inconsistent with the clear and correct statement of Lord Wilberforce in *Alphacell*, that it was not:

"in every case [that] the act of a third party necessarily interrupts the chain of causation initiated by the person who owns or operates the plant or installation from which the flow took place."[108]

Lord Hoffmann considered that on the facts found by the justices the defendant had been rightly convicted. Although his Lordship was not explicit as regards the reasons supporting this conclusion, one can presume it was because had the justices asked themselves (a) whether the defendant had done something which was a cause of the pollution, and (b) whether vandalism by trespassers was an extraordinary event rather than a fact of life, the answers would have been (a) that the defendant had done something to cause the pollution, not just by storing the oil but by storing it with inadequate physical and other security, and (b) that such acts by trespassers were a fact of life rather than an extraordinary event. Accordingly, *Impress* should be considered to have been wrongly decided.

Lord Hoffmann took a similar view of the decision in *National Rivers Authority* v *Wright Engineering Co Ltd.*[109] Here the Rivers Authority had appealed against the dismissal by justices of charges that the defendant had caused polluting matter to enter Racecourse Brook, Stratford-upon-Avon. The defendants stored heating oil at the site of their light engineering company. The tank was adjacent to a surface water drain. The tank was equipped with a sight gauge and the flow of oil into that gauge was regulated by a tap, to which no lock had been fitted. At some time over a Christmas break the sight gauge had been vandalised causing the yard to become awash with oil, which then made its way down to the brook. In the light of previous occurrences it was found that the defendants were aware that their site was a potential target for vandalism but that they had not envisaged vandalism to the extent that had occurred on this particular occasion. However, this lack of foresight was reasonable: vandalism had never previously been a serious problem.

The Divisional Court considered that on this evidence the justices were entitled to have acquitted the defendants. Buckley J noted that liability did not depend upon the issue of foreseeability: the matter in issue was, rather, one of causation. Nevertheless:

"That does not mean that foreseeability is wholly irrelevant. It is one factor which a tribunal may properly consider in seeking to apply

---

[107] *ibid.* at 358.
[108] [1972] 2 All ER 475 at 479.
[109] [1994] 4 All ER 281; [1994] Env LR 186.

common sense to the question: who or what caused the result under consideration."[110]

In *Empress Cars* Lord Hoffmann expressed the view that the defendants in *Wright Engineering* should have been convicted. For reasons discussed earlier his Lordship was uneasy about Buckley J's even quite limited regard for foreseeability as a factor relevant to causality. Again, Lord Hoffmann was not explicit as regards his reasoning; but it is possible to understand his Lordship's conclusion in the light of his general statements of principle. The events which occurred were ones which were to be regarded as falling within the "ordinary facts of life" category rather than the "extraordinary event" class. As Lord Hoffmann put it:

> "The particular form of vandalism may not have been foreseeable ... but the precise details will never be foreseeable. In practical terms it was ordinary vandalism."[111]

As such, the events did not break the chain of causation. This conclusion seems entirely consistent with the application of this test in *Empress Cars* itself and with the approach which should have been taken in *Impress (Worcester)* v *Rees*. One point of reservation may, however, be sounded. Let us remember Lord Salmon's statement in *Alphacell* that, when one is determining what may qualify as a positive act of the defendant which may remain a cause of the pollution, something more is necessary than merely:

> "The passive storage of effluent which could not discharge into the river, save by an Act of God or ... by active intervention of a stranger ..."[112]

We are back to the proposition that if you throw something of mine into a river, you have polluted the river, not me. For me to have been also a cause of that pollution some positive contributory act over and beyond ownership or possession of that item must surely be shown. In *Alphacell* it was the design and installation of a pumping arrangement which involved some inevitable risk of overflow and pollution; in *Price* v *Cromack* it was the manner of having maintained lagoon walls; in *Impress (Worcester)* it was "operating" a fuel storage tank with inadequate security. One cannot be sure how one should characterise the "positive act" requirement in *Wright Engineering*, but one may speculate that Lord Hoffmann considered the evidence in relation to the robustness of the sight gauge as sufficient for the defendant's positive act to be characterised as poor security in relation to the tank. The evidence was that the sight gauge had been easy to remove and had been secured only by wire tightly wound around it by pliers.

The principles elaborated at some length by Lord Hoffmann in *Empress Cars* were expressly supported, but without separate speeches, by Lords Browne-Wilkinson, Lloyd and Nolan. Lord Clyde, however, chose to set

---

[110] At p 285 of the former report.
[111] [1998] 1 All ER 481 at 492.
[112] [1972] 2 All ER 475 at 490.

out, in a quite brief speech, his own statement of essentially the same principles. His Lordship's speech therefore is valuable in providing some alternative formulations of those principles. These passages deserve quotation.

Lord Clyde noted that:

> "['cause']... must involve some kind of active operation by the defendant, whereby, with or without the occurrence of other factors, the pollutant enters the controlled waters. If the defendant has simply stood back and not participated to any extent at all, although he may have been guilty of knowingly permitting it, ... he will not have caused the pollutant to enter the waters."[113]

Nevertheless:

> "I do not consider that [the requirement of 'active operation' as a judicial explanation of one component of the notion 'cause'] ... is to be regarded as anything more than a reminder that in the present context passivity is not enough to constitute a cause."[114]

This statement that it is only "absolute" passivity which may serve to make the "causing" pollution charge inappropriate was followed by a number of examples of conduct which may suffice:

> "The maintaining of a system, the carrying on of an enterprise, and the management of a going concern may each constitute causative factors. So also may the discontinuing of an enterprise or the closing down of a concern ..."[115]

Further, what linguistically may seem to amount to an omission rather than an act, may when more broadly analysed, seem more properly to be an aspect of the performance of some more general, "positive", activity.

> "In many cases an omission may be analysed as the provision or operation of an inadequate or deficient system. Thus a failure to take precautions in relation to a risk of the escape of a pollutant in the course of the management of premises ... may be seen as an active operation for the purposes of causation."[116]

Lord Clyde than turned to the circumstances in which the subsequent acts of a third party, or some natural event, may "entirely supersede" the positive acts of the defendant as a causative element. His Lordship agreed with Lord Hoffmann that "foreseeability" or "reasonable foreseeability" were not concepts relevant in this context. Rather, what was necessary was that the intervening event or occurrence should be of an:

---

[113] [1998] 1 All ER 481 at 493.
[114] At 494.
[115] *ibid.* Lord Clyde referred here to *Lockhart* v *National Coal Board* [1981] SLT 161.
[116] *ibid.*

"...unnatural, extraordinary or unusual character."[117]

And concluding that the justices had reached a decision which was open to them, in holding that the defendants had caused the oil to enter the Ebbw Fach, Lord Clyde noted:

> "...the provision [on the part of the defendants] of an exposed and unguarded tap in a situation where the premises were not secure against invasion, where on account of local opposition to the appellant's business the malicious or thoughtless intervention of a third party would not be something out of the ordinary course, ... where in the event of any escape of oil out of the tap onto the ground the layout was such as to carry such oil to the yard, to the storm drain and so to the river."[118]

In *Empress* it was the deficiently secure storage of the potential contaminant which constituted the sufficient "positive act" to found liability and to establish the necessary causal link with the pollution which had occurred; and the intervention of the third party was not an occurrence of a kind such as to break that chain of causation and to relieve the defendant from criminal liability.

One puzzle does, however, remain. When we ask whether an occurrence was "out of the ordinary course" or "unnatural" or "unusual" or "extraordinary" are we to judge this in the light of the circumstances of the particular case; or, more objectively, is the matter to be judged by reference to the general facts of life? We have noted that both Lords Hoffmann and Clyde stressed that "foreseeability" or "reasonable foreseeability" were not relevant to this question, and yet Lord Clyde expressly referred to the fact that:

> "...on account of the local opposition to the [defendant's] business the malicious or thoughtless intervention of a third party would not be something out of the ordinary course."[119]

This is language very close to that of foreseeability. Perhaps all that Lord Clyde intended was that something which, in the particular circumstances, was *not* unforeseeable could not be considered to be a sufficiently extraordinary event so as to break the chain of causation.[120] The question

---

[117] *ibid.*

[118] *ibid.*

[119] *ibid.*

[120] To return to Lord Hoffmann's terrorist example (above p. 316). Ordinarily we may regard this as an example of an *extraordinary event*, so quitting a defendant of responsibility. However, at certain times and in certain circumstances certain kinds of installation may be known to be vulnerable terrorist targets. A site operator who, in such circumstances, provides no site security against such attack might well not escape liability. This suggests that matters should be judged, to this extent at least, in the light of the particular circumstances of the case; and that the foreseeable events should not be considered extraordinary. The possibility must remain, however, if *Empress* is to have substance, that some unforeseeable actions or events will nevertheless fall within the category of being ordinary "facts of life".

we need to ask, however, is this: what if there had been no such local opposition, and no history of quite minor vandalism? Would the proper conclusion then have been that, in such circumstances, the incidents which occurred might have possessed the quality of being "extraordinary"; or do we here disregard the "personal equation" and simply say that, regardless of the particular context, vandalism is a "fact of life" and, however unforeseeable to the particular defendant, it cannot constitute a supervening act sufficient to quit the defendant of responsibility?

No easy or very confident answers may be given to these questions. Ultimately what is revealed, it seems, is that the notions of the ordinary and the extraordinary, and the foreseeable and the unforeseeable are not, perhaps, so very different. Indeed, is it not the case that we make conclusions about the former (ordinary/extraordinary) by reference to the latter (we foresee the ordinary – we do not foresee the extraordinary)?

Notwithstanding these misgivings the essential message from *Empress Cars* is clear. A defendant cannot seek to avoid liability simply by raising arguments that his or her precautionary measures were reasonable in the light of perceived risk from a third party or some natural event.

Empress applied

The principles explained and applied by the House of Lords in *Empress Cars* were afforded immediate application in *Environment Agency* v *Brock*.[121] The defendant company had been acquitted by magistrates on charges of having caused polluting matter, tip leachate, from their landfill site to have entered a ditch, a tributary of the River Dibbin, near Ellesmere Port. The site employed a system by which leachate was pumped from the landfill and then was passed by hose pipe to storage lagoons. On inspection by the Environment Agency a leak was found at a hose coupling point. The escaping leachate flowed to a ditch. An issue arose as to whether this ditch comprised "controlled water" for the purposes of the offence: this issue has been discussed earlier.[122] The other substantial question was whether if, as the defendants claimed, the entry of the leachate into the ditch was the result of a latent defect in the pipe and not down to any negligence on their part, this would render the defendants not guilty of the offence? The defendants had, on this issue, presented evidence that the hose and its couplings were only a couple of months old; had been inspected by an employee only shortly before the leak was discovered; and the seal with the latent defect had been immediately replaced upon discovery of the leakage.[123]

The Divisional Court found that defendant should nevertheless have been convicted. Applying the guidance of Lord Hoffmann in *Empress Cars*, decided only days earlier, the Divisional Court held:

---

[121] [1998] Env LR 607.

[122] See, above, p. 294.

[123] As noted earlier, by having taken actions also to block the ditch the leachate was prevented from entering the *river*.

(i) that there *were* positive acts done by the defendants. According to
     Roch LJ: "the [defendants] gathered the tip leachate ... and then
     from time to time ... pumped [it] into a lagoon ... [T]he pollutant
     would not have reached the ditch, but for the ... act of
     pumping."[124]

(ii) that the failure of the seal was an ordinary fact of life rather than
     something extraordinary. Roch LJ explained: "When such items
     are manufactured ... there are times when they are manufactured
     in a condition which makes them defective. That may not be
     detectable by the user of the seal. It is no doubt a rare occurrence,
     but it is an ordinary occurrence in my judgment."[125]

The defendants had argued before the magistrates that they were not to be
considered to have been at fault, since such seals "normally last twelve
months". For the Divisional Court this was to have misunderstood the
strictness of liability under section 85. Whether or not the defendants had
acted with reasonable care, or negligently, in relation to the perceptible risk
was not the issue. Maybe such seals do normally last for twelve months.
Maybe the likelihood of an earlier failure was small, and, given regular
inspection and a blockable ditch, maybe the defendants were not at fault in
the sense understood in civil law negligence liability. Nevertheless, given
that from time to time seals do fail earlier, such an earlier failure was to be
characterised as an "ordinary" rather than an "extraordinary" event. To
return to our earlier discussion of the connection between foreseeability
and the ordinary/extraordinary distinction, we might say that such failure
was foreseeable – albeit as something not very likely to occur. The case
was remitted to the magistrates with a direction to convict.

In *Brock* the Divisional Court noted the comparable decision in *CPC (UK)
Ltd* v *National Rivers Authority*,[126] a case which had been referred to with
approval by Lord Hoffmann in *Empress Cars*. In *CPC (UK) Ltd* the
charges followed pollution of the River Lyd, in Devon. The defendant
company owned a large dairy products factory beside the river. As part of
its operations the company stored and used cleaning liquids similar in
composition to caustic soda. From storage tanks the liquid was carried to
the factory premises along UPVC piping which ran along the outside of the
buildings at roof level. The pollution incident occurred following a
fracturing of this piping. The liquid had fallen to the ground and some 165
gallons proceeded to the river, via a stream. The fracture in the pipe was
accepted to be a consequence of the defective way in which that piping had
been installed – improper application of adhesive by the installation
contractors. That installation had occurred before the defendants had
become owners of the factory. At the time of that purchase a full survey
had not revealed this latent defect. The Court of Appeal upheld the Crown
Court conviction. The operation of the factory, with the latent defect, on

---

[124] [1998] Env LR 607 at 613.
[125] At 613-614.
[126] [1994] Env LR 131.

the day of the incident was a sufficient positive act and was capable of being found by the trial court to have been a cause of the pollutant having entered the river.

In his summing up, the learned recorder had explained to the jury:

> "Was the operation of the factory under [the defendants'] control that day? If the plant did not operate efficiently, would the effluent go into the river? Can it be said that without the defendant's act, there would not have been the pollution? And was it their operation of their works, and their failure to ensure that the pipes were sound that let the liquid ... get into the river? You are asked to ... determine causation, not fault or blameworthiness."[127]

The Court of Appeal upheld this direction. Evans LJ noted:

> "The fact that the [defendants] were unaware of the existence of the defect and could not be criticised for failing to discover it, meant that the defect was latent rather than patent ... but this was not relevant in law, because the statute does not require either knowledge or fault to be proved against them. If they did cause the pollution, ... it was equally irrelevant that some other person might ... have 'caused' it also."[128]

Empress applied also in *Express*

The decision in *Empress Cars* was also applied in *Express Ltd (trading as Express Dairies Distribution)* v *Environment Agency*.[129] Here a tanker containing milk was being driven southbound on the M5 by an employee of Express Ltd when it experienced a tyre blow-out. The blow-out caused part of the spray suppression system to become detached which in turn hit the under-run protection barrier. The barrier became detached and sheared the delivery pipe, causing approximately 4,000 litres of milk to escape from the forward compartment of the milk tank. The driver of the tanker had pulled over onto the hard shoulder. At the point at which he had stopped, two drains were situated approximately 100 metres apart. They fed into a culverted section of Battlefield Brook. The emergency services, including the Environment Agency, were alerted by the driver. The driver also contacted his depot for advice which led him to operate a foot valve on the tanker to stem the flow of milk. Express were subsequently convicted by West Mercia justices of causing any poisonous, noxious, or

---

[127] Cited in the judgment of Evans LJ at 137.

[128] At 137-138. If this case may seem to represent very much the extreme in terms of the application of strict liability and causality rules under s. 85 it may be valuable to note also that the Crown Court had, upon conviction, ordered the absolute discharge of the defendants. Their conduct *after* the event had, it appears, been exemplary – and their conduct prior to the event had, it seems, involved no culpability. Why, in such circumstances, it might be asked, the initiation of the prosecution? Perhaps to assuage public opinion, following a fish kill. Perhaps also as a way of recouping the costs – including the costs of investigating the incident – claimed by the Authority (although without evidence to support its calculations) to have been some £23,000.

[129] [2003] 2 All ER 778.

polluting matter to enter controlled waters contrary to section 85(1) and (6) of the Water Resources Act 1991 and fined £5,000. They subsequently appealed against that decision.[130]

The appellants in *Express* argued before the Divisional Court that the milk tanker's tyre blow-out amounted to an intervening act of such a powerful nature that it rather than anything which the appellants had done amounted to the cause of the pollution of the brook. To employ the terminology adopted by Lord Hoffmann in *Empress*, the argument was that the tyre blow-out amounted to an extraordinary act or event sufficient to break the chain of causation.

On the facts, the justices had concluded that although the tyre blow-out and the subsequent events were "unusual", they were nevertheless not extraordinary and they had not therefore broken the chain of causation. The Divisional Court had little difficulty in reaching the same conclusion on this issue. In delivering the leading judgment of the court, Hale LJ observed:

> "In this particular case, everything that happened flowed from the operation of this tanker on that road. That was obviously something which the appellants had done. Any vehicle's tyre may blow out. Blow outs, though thankfully rare, are certainly capable of being regarded as events in the *ordinary* run of things. Everything else that led to the escape of the milk from the tanker was part of the operation of that tanker on the road, and the entry of the escaped milk into the brook was finally caused by the driver pulling to the side of the road in that particular place."[131]

Her Ladyship continued:

> "In my judgment, in those circumstances, it is quite impossible to say that the chain of causation from start to finish was broken and that the principle adumbrated by Lord Hoffmann in the *Empress* case might operate .... This is a much stronger case than the *Empress* case, where there was indeed doubt about whether it was some act of a third party which led to the escape of the liquid."[132]

Accordingly, the Divisional Court determined the causation issue in favour of the Environment Agency. Whether or not the justices had been right to convict them, however, turned on whether the appellants were able to rely on the emergency defence as provided by section 89(1) of the 1991 Act (discussed below).

---

[130] In addition to the causation issue, the appellants also sought to rely upon the emergency defence provided for in s. 89(1) of the 1991 Act. See further on this aspect, below at p. 333.

[131] [2003] 2 All ER 778 at 782-783 (para. 15 of the judgment) (emphasis added).

[132] At 783 (para. 16).

Vicarious liability: "causing" by companies

In *National Rivers Authority* v *Alfred McAlpine Homes East Ltd*,[133] the question for the Divisional Court was whether a company could be vicariously liable for the commission of the "causing" offence where the offence was committed by an employee who was not exercising the "controlling mind and will" of the company. The facts of the case have already been noted.[134] For present purposes, it is sufficient to record that the Divisional Court held that vicarious liability had been established on the facts as found. In the words of Simon Brown LJ:

> "It accordingly seems to me nothing to the point that those in the company's head office here may well have had no direct part in determining the precise system of construction which allowed this cement to wash into the Ditton Stream. It is sufficient that those immediately responsible on site … were employees of the company and acting apparently within the course and scope of that employment."[135]

Similarly in the opinion of Morland J:

> "…to make the offence [section 85] an effective weapon in the defence of environmental protection, a company must by necessary implication be criminally liable for the acts or omissions of its servants or agents during activities being done for the company. I do not find that this offends our concept of a just and fair criminal legal system, having regard to the magnitude of environmental pollution, even though no due diligence defence was provided for."[136]

"Knowingly permitting"

We may treat the "knowingly permitting" offence more briefly. Although an offence of potential significance, it does appear that prosecutors have tended to confine prosecution to situations where the apparently simple "causing" charge can be made out; with considerably more reluctance as regards the greater challenge presented in substantiating this latter offence. A consequence is that whereas our discussion so far has benefited from much judicial explanation of the ambit of criminal liability, the scope of responsibility under the "knowingly permitting" limb remains very much more speculative.

We may begin with the words of Lord Wilberforce in *Alphacell* contrasting the two limbs of section 85:

> "The subsection evidently contemplates two things – *causing*, which must involve some active operation or chain of operations involving as a result the pollution of the stream; and *knowingly permitting*,

---

[133] [1994] 4 All ER 286.
[134] See above at p. 235.
[135] [1994] 4 All ER 286 at 294.
[136] *ibid.* at 298.

which involves a failure to prevent the pollution, which failure, however, must be accompanied by knowledge."[137]

The contrast was explained by Lord Hoffmann in *Empress Cars*, in the language of "causing by positive act" and "causing by omission to have acted so to prevent".

His Lordship stressed:

"The notion of causing is present in both limbs: under the first limb, what the defendant did must have caused the pollution and under the second limb, his omission must have caused it."[138]

As regards the "knowledge" element of the offence it seems that the prosecution must satisfy the court that the defendant had actual knowledge of the circumstances in relation to which he or she may be regarded as having permitted the polluting events to occur. Constructive notice will not suffice: that is, the situation where it seems that a person was not aware of something which, as a reasonable person, he or she should have appreciated to be the case. However, given that a tribunal of fact must, where the matter is disputed, resolve the issue of knowledge or no-knowledge by making its own judgment of what it believes the defendant did know, given the evidence presented by both sides, the absence of a constructive notice provision may not significantly narrow the scope of the offence. In practical terms the difference is perhaps between a court being able to say that it believes a defendant's protestations of ignorance, but that those protestations provide no defence – the defendant *should* have known; and a court having to conclude that the circumstantial evidence is such that it is simply not credible evidence on the part of the defendant that he or she was ignorant as to what seemed patent. Nevertheless, a distinction does exist between these things and a defendant who, perhaps against the odds, is able to persuade a court of absence of knowledge, will avoid conviction.

The scope of liability under the "knowingly permitting" offence was considered by the Divisional Court in *Schulmans Incorporated Ltd* v *National Rivers Authority*.[139] Fuel oil pollution of the River Ebbw was traced back via a brook and a drainage pipe connecting with the defendants' premises. It appeared that oil had spilled on the defendants' property, at or near a tank, and had made its way eventually to the river. The defendant was charged with having "knowingly permitted" poisonous matter to be discharged into the controlled waters.[140] The defendants were convicted by the magistrates, who found that although the spillage of the oil was brought to the defendants' attention at 10.00 am one morning,

---

[137] [1972] 2 All ER 475 at 479.
[138] [1998] 1 All ER 481 at 485.
[139] [1993] Env LR D1.
[140] Also, with having knowingly permitted to be put into waters containing fish, liquid matter so as to have caused those waters to be poisonous to fish: s. 4(1) Salmon and Freshwater Fisheries Act 1975.

"they ... shut their eyes to the obvious"

and did not arrange for the drainage system to be cleaned out until the next day. By that time the leaked or spilled oil had made its way to, and had polluted, the river.

The Divisional Court overturned the convictions on both charges. Legatt LJ noted a variety of essential questions which the magistrates had failed to ask themselves; and without having considered which, the conviction could not be allowed to stand. In particular, there were no precise findings by the magistrates that at any particular time the defendant was both aware of the fact that the spillage would find its way through the drainage system to the river prior to the time at which cleanup was proposed, and was able to have done something to have expedited that cleanup (or have taken other action to have prevented the pollution). In the absence of specific evidence on these particular issues, Legatt LJ considered that it had not been proven that the defendant "knowingly permitted" the oil to have entered the controlled waters. As his Lordship explained, there was:

> "nothing to show a recognition on the part of the [defendants] that the contents of the drainage system would ... find their way into the brook before the drainage system was due to be cleaned out the following day."

Moreover,

> "there was no finding and, as far as we can tell, no evidence that the [defendants] could have prevented the escape of fuel oil into the brook sooner than they did, or that there was an escape during any period when they could have prevented but failed to prevent it."

These statements from Legatt LJ serve to remind prosecutors of the need to produce evidence both as regards the defendant's state of knowledge, and also to demonstrate that in the light of that knowledge the defendant had failed to have done something which he or she could have done which would have prevented the occurrence which forms the basis of the offence charged: the pollution or poisoning of the water in question. It seems that specific evidence on these maters will be necessary: convictions on the basis merely of assumption as regards these matters will be overturned on appeal.

Certain questions do arise, however, from Legatt LJ's briefly noted judgment. The report indicates that his Lordship "confirmed that constructive knowledge of the escape by the fuel into the waters ... would satisfy" the knowledge requirement. It is not evident upon what basis his Lordship reached this interpretation of the statutory provision. In the absence of clear legislative guidance that it suffices for liability that a defendant ought reasonably to have been aware of something, this judicial extension of the scope of the statutory offence must be treated with some suspicion.

What seems likely is that his Lordship was not referring to liability based upon the principle that a defendant is deemed to know what he or she ought to have known but, rather, was alluding to the principles applied in cases such as *Berton* v *Alliance Economic Investment Co Ltd*[141] and *Westminster City Council* v *Croyalgrange*,[142] by virtue of which a defendant may not deliberately seek to escape liability under a "knowing" offence by the ploy of intentionally "shutting his or her ears" to the existence or non-existence of the matters in question. This may be a salutary principle and be applicable to this "knowingly permitting" offence. However, the principle is one which is quite limited in its scope of operation and is a narrower principle than that which would apply if a more general "constructive notice" approach were adopted.

In *Westminster City Council* v *Croyalgrange*, for example, the issue was whether a person had knowingly used, or knowingly caused or permitted the use of, certain premises as a sex establishment without a licence.[143] The particular facts need not here concern us. What is significant is that Lord Bridge took pains to allay prosecution fears that the requirement to prove knowledge would make the offences in question unenforceable. His Lordship alluded to the power of a tribunal of fact to make legitimate inference of knowledge from circumstantial evidence. His Lordship quoted from Lord Diplock in *Sweet* v *Parsley*:[144]

> "The jury is entitled to presume that the accused acted with knowledge of the facts, unless there is some evidence to the contrary originating from the accused who alone can know on what belief he acted ..."[145]

Moreover, the matter may go beyond such legitimate inference. Lord Bridge concluded his speech with the words:

> "... it is always open to the tribunal of fact, when knowledge on the part of the defendant is required to be proved, to base a finding of knowledge on evidence that the defendant had *deliberately shut his eyes to the obvious* or *refrained from inquiry because he suspected the truth but did not want to have his suspicion confirmed.*"[146]

This may involve some judicial enlargement of the concept of "knowing". However, to hold that one may infer that a person knows what they suspected and deliberately avoided making inquiries about, is substantially less an enlargement of the scope of liability than would be a general doctrine of constructive knowledge – that one knows all that a reasonable person in one's position would have known.

---

[141] [1922] 1 KB 742.

[142] [1986] 2 All ER 353.

[143] Paras. 6(1) and 20(1)(a) of Sch. 3 to the Local Government (Miscellaneous Provisions) Act 1982.

[144] [1970] AC 132.

[145] *ibid.* at 164.

[146] [1986] 2 All ER 353 at 359 (emphasis added).

A second issue which arises is this: it is clear that one does not "knowingly permit" something to happen, even if one knows what consequences will occur, if there is nothing one could have done which would have averted that consequence. Moreover, if there was nothing, objectively and viewed with the benefit of hindsight, that one could have done to have averted what occurred, it will presumably not matter that a defendant may in fact have made no attempt at what only later may have become appreciated to have been impossible.

These propositions would seem to follow from the very wording of the offence. What is less clear is the *standard* of liability imposed. According to Legatt LJ the evidence in *Schulmans* was deficient because, amongst other things, it did not show that the defendant "could have prevented" the occurrence. This only serves to require us to ask whether a defendant is liable simply because the prosecution can demonstrate the possibility that he or she could have prevented the occurrence (however demanding of the defendant that might have been). Or is it necessary for the prosecution to show that such action was reasonably to be expected of the defendant, or would not have imposed undue burdens upon the defendant? No firm view may be taken on this matter. However, should the latter possibility represent the correct statement of principle, it would, perhaps, require there to be conducted some form of judicial cost-benefit analysis: asking such questions as "what is the magnitude of the evil to be prevented"? and "what steps might one reasonably expect the defendant to have taken to have averted that evil"?

STATUTORY DEFENCES

Various defences to the section 85 offences are set out in the Water Resources Act 1991 itself. Thus by virtue of section 87(2):

> "A sewerage undertaker shall not be guilty of an offence under section 85 by reason only of the fact that a discharge from a sewer or works vested in the undertaker contravenes conditions of a consent relating to a discharge if—
> (a) the contravention is attributable to a discharge which another person caused or permitted to be made into the sewer or works;
> (b) the undertaker either was not bound to receive the discharge into the sewer or works or was bound to receive it there subject to conditions which were not observed; and
> (c) the undertaker could not reasonably have been expected to prevent the discharge into the sewer or works."

Patently, this statutory defence will only be available if each of the conditions in (a), (b) and (c) is satisfied. In *National Rivers Authority* v *Yorkshire Water Services Ltd*,[147] as has already been noted,[148] the House of

---

[147] [1995] 1 AC 444; [1995] 1 All ER 225.
[148] The facts of this case, which was the second of the three occasions on which the House of Lords had been required to consider the offence of causing water pollution, were set out above at p. 312.

Lords held that the defendants had caused the polluting matter (iso-octanol) to enter controlled waters since they had set up a system for the treatment of sewage which would involve the discharge of the results of that treatment into controlled waters. However, their Lordships allowed the water company's appeal against conviction on the basis that they were able to rely upon the defence provided by the predecessor to section 87(2), section 108(7) of the Water Act 1989.[149] In reaching this conclusion, Lord Mackay observed that:

> "In my view, the plain words of s. 108(7) show that it is intended to be available in respect of any allegation of an offence under s. 107[150] and I think it would be extremely unusual, if not unique, to enable the prosecutor by choice of allegation in a given state of facts to deprive an accused person of a defence which would be available if the prosecutor took another choice on the same set of facts."[151]

Authorised discharges

A person is not guilty of an offence under section 85 in respect of the entry or discharge of any matter into any waters if that entry or discharge is in accordance with the terms of a statutory consent or authorisation. For the purposes of section 88 of the 1991 Act, the relevant consents and authorisations are as follows:

- a discharge consent under the Water Resources Act 1991 or under Part II of the Control of Pollution Act 1974;[152]
- a permit granted under regulations made under section 2 of the Pollution Prevention and Control Act 1999;
- an authorisation for a prescribed process designated for central control under Part I of the Environmental Protection Act 1990;
- a waste management[153] or disposal licence;[154]
- a licence granted under Part II of the Food and Environmental Protection Act 1985;
- a discharge in accordance with section 163 of the Water Resources Act 1991 or section 165 of the Water Industry Act 1991;
- a discharge in accordance with any local statutory provision or order; or
- any prescribed enactment.

Since authorisations or consents are normally granted subject to conditions,[155] it follows that to take advantage of the section 88 defence,

---

[149] The Crown Court had upheld that the conditions in s. 108(7) were fulfilled and there was no challenge to that holding on appeal.

[150] Now s. 85 of the Water Resources Act 1991.

[151] [1995] 1 All ER 225 at 232.

[152] This makes corresponding provision for Scotland.

[153] Issued under Part II of the Environmental Protection Act 1990.

[154] Issued under s. 5 of the Control of Pollution Act 1974.

[155] In the case of an application for a discharge consent under the Water Resources Act 1991, the Environment Agency may respond in one of three ways: it may grant the consent unconditionally;

the entry or discharge must not exceed the terms of any such condition. Thus in *CPC (UK) Ltd* v *National Rivers Authority*,[156] the defendant was not able to rely upon a discharge consent[157] which permitted a maximum daily discharge of 150,000 gallons of trade effluent into the River Lyd, because the discharge in question raised the pH level of the water beyond the range 5-9 specified in a condition of the consent.

It should also be noted under this subheading that an additional defence to a charge under section 85 exists in respect of causing or permitting a discharge into a sewer where the undertaker was bound to receive the discharge either unconditionally or subject to conditions which were observed.[158] Patently the defence will not apply where the discharge was unconsented or where it has breached any of the consent conditions.

The emergency defence

Section 89(1) of the Water Resources Act 1991 affords what may be termed an "emergency defence" to a charge under section 85. In order to be able to rely on the defence, it will be necessary to show that:

- the entry was caused or permitted, or the discharge was made, in an emergency in order to avoid danger to life or health;
- that the defendant has taken all such steps as were reasonably practicable in the circumstances for minimising the extent of the entry or discharge and of its polluting effects; and
- particulars of the entry or discharge were furnished to the Environment Agency as soon as reasonably practicable after the entry occurred.

It would seem that a failure to satisfy any of these requirements will preclude a defendant from being able to take advantage of the defence. Given that the pollution incident might be of a serious nature involving, for example, a significant fish kill, it seems only right that even where an entry or discharge has occurred in an emergency situation, the defence should fail if either the second or third requirement is not satisfied. In such a case, the need to take action to limit the extent of the incident or to inform the Agency of the particulars of the entry or discharge so as to enable it to take effective action is self-evident. A defendant who fails to do these things should not escape criminal liability.

The Water Resources Act is silent as to the meaning of "emergency" in this or in any other context.[159] Accordingly, it is necessary to examine the

---

it may grant it subject to conditions; or, it may refuse it – see Sched.10, para. 3. For a discussion of how such consents are set and enforced, see [1994] 6 ELM 32.

[156] [1994] Env LR 131. Discussed above at p. 324.

[157] The consent had been issued under the Water Act 1989, the predecessor to the 1991 Act.

[158] See s. 87(3) of the Water Resources Act 1991.

[159] It is worth noting that in addition to failing to define what is meant by an "emergency", the Act does not state that it must have appeared to the defendant that there was an emergency or that he or she must have reasonably believed that there was an emergency in order to be able to rely upon the defence. In the absence of these or similar words it would seem that whether or not a state of affairs amounted to an emergency is a matter to be determined objectively on the basis of the facts of the case. Thus where a defendant believed that an emergency existed but the facts of the case

case law for guidance. In *National Rivers Authority* v *ICI Chemicals & Polymers*,[160] equipment failure at an ICI plant resulted in the escape of 45 cubic metres of chlorocarbon effluent[161] into the Western canal. Although the defendants were authorised to discharge a certain amount of such material, the volume in question exceeded that stated in the consent. The Widnes Justices convicted the defendant company of offences contrary to section 107(6) of the Water Act 1989[162] in respect of this incident and a subsequent pollution incident at the same plant. A further equipment failure at another plant the following month resulted in the discharge of one third of a tonne of ethylene chloride into the canal after storm drains had been washed out without being blocked off. The defendant company argued that the flushing out had been action taken in an emergency "in order to avoid danger to life or health". However, the defence did not succeed. Although the report of the case does not indicate why this was so, it would seem that equipment failure is unlikely to be accepted by the courts as the catalyst for an emergency situation.[163] Moreover, the defendant's failure to take what amounted to a basic precaution when flushing out the storm drains seems likely to have counted against it.

In *National Rivers Authority* v *North West Water*,[164] the defendant water company was authorised to discharge effluent from their sewage pumping station in the event of an emergency. A polluting discharge took place, but NRA officers found that it had been caused by a blockage of the sewage work's filters. Accordingly, the defendant was charged with causing or knowingly permitting the discharge of trade or sewage effluent contrary to section 107(1)(c) and (6) of the Water Act 1989. North West Water originally intended to rely upon the defence that the discharge had taken place in an emergency. In the event, however, a guilty plea was entered. Nevertheless, it would seem from the report of the case that as far as the NRA (now the Environment Agency) was concerned, a state of affairs has only become an emergency if it is beyond the control of the defendant. Thus equipment failure arising from poor maintenance is not likely to absolve a defendant from criminal liability. In the present case, the defendant's works records revealed that there had been a number of similar incidents during the course of the previous year. In these circumstances, it might be argued that North West Water ought to have sought to prevent a repetition by having its plant appropriately modified and properly maintained.

---

when viewed objectively indicated otherwise, the section 89(1) defence would not succeed, irrespective of the reasonableness of the defendant's belief.

[160] [1992] 4 LMELR 23.

[161] The material in question contained carbontetrachloride and perchloroethylene – "black list" substances for the purposes of the EC Dangerous Substances in Water Directive, 76/464.

[162] Now s. 85(6) of the Water Resources Act 1991.

[163] As we have already seen, equipment failure has not prevented the courts from concluding that a defendant has caused water pollution for the purposes of s. 85 of the Water Resources Act 1991: see, for example, *Alphacell Ltd* v *Woodward* [1972] AC 824 and *CPC (UK) Ltd* v *National Rivers Authority* [1994] Env LR 131, discussed above at pp. 300 and 324, respectively.

[164] [1992] 4 LMELR 131.

More recently, the emergency defence succeeded in the case of *Express Ltd (trading as Express Dairies Distribution)* v *Environment Agency.*[165] In that case, it will be remembered that a milk tanker had experienced a tyre blow-out whilst travelling southbound on the M5 motorway and that the driver of the tanker had pulled over onto the hard shoulder whilst thousands of litres of milk escaped from the tanker. In the opinion of both the justices and the Divisional Court, although a tyre blow-out was a rare event, it was not an extraordinary event and hence did not break the chain of causation between the appellants' acts and the pollution of the brook. Had that been the sole issue to determine on appeal, the appellants would clearly not have succeeded. However, the appeal also involved a second issue; whether the tanker driver's act of pulling onto the hard shoulder amounted to an act done in order to avoid danger to life or health.

It was argued on behalf of the Agency that there had to be a purposive connection between causing the entry of milk into the brook and the avoidance of danger to life or health in order for the section 89(1) defence to succeed in the present case. In other words, the entry had to be caused in order to save life or health. In rejecting this submission, Hale LJ observed:

> "The words 'in order to' clearly do import a purpose, but that begs the question: at which point in the chain of causation of entry does the question why a particular act was being done have to be asked? If it is to be asked at the beginning the chain, clearly the blowout was not caused in order to avoid danger to life or health. But the last element in the chain of causation, pulling into the side of the road where these drains into the brook happen to be, could well be said to have been for that very purpose."[166]

Although there was no evidence of the driver's intention, the Divisional Court was prepared to assume, as the justices had done before it, that that was why the driver had pulled onto the hard shoulder. Accordingly, on the facts of the case, the act which actually caused the entry of milk into the brook was done in an emergency in order to save life or health. Thus in the opinion of the Divisional Court, the various elements of the section 89(1) defence had been made out and the appeal was allowed on this issue.

Trade or sewage effluent from a vessel

Section 89(2) of the Water Resources Act 1991 provides that:

> "A person shall not be guilty of an offence under section 85 ... by reason of his causing or permitting any discharge of trade or sewage effluent from a vessel."

It is apparent from the wording of this provision that the scope of the defence is quite limited. The discharge in question must have been from a

---

[165] [2003] 2 All ER 778. For a fuller discussion of the facts of the case, see above at p. 325.
[166] At p. 784 (para. 22).

vessel.[167] Moreover, to be able to rely upon the defence, the discharge itself must have consisted of either trade or sewage effluent.[168] Accordingly, a defendant who caused or knowingly permitted any poisonous, noxious or polluting matter or any solid waste matter to enter controlled waters from a vessel would not have a defence under this subsection.[169]

Abandoned mines

Water pollution caused by abandoned mine workings is a recognised problem in areas where coal or tin mining formerly occurred. In March 1994, the National Rivers Authority published a Report[170] in which it described such pollution as "a rather specialized and local problem" the impact of which is "spectacular" where it occurs.[171] In one example mentioned in the Report, that of Wheal Jane (an abandoned metal mine in West Cornwall), it was stated that:

> "There is no doubt that the geology and hydrology of the area contributed to the development of acid conditions within the mine water, with consequent dissolution of metals from the ore bearing strata. The subsequent discharge from the mine therefore contained significant concentrations of heavy metals – particularly iron, zinc and cadmium – resulting in a major pollution incident in the Carrick Roads, not far from the discharge point. As with most mine water discharges, the most obvious impact was aesthetic. The discharge was probably one of the most visual pollution incidents ever recorded in the UK ... The visual impact extended over a large area, covering the Carnon Valley, Restronguet Creek, Carrick Roads, and Falmouth Bay."[172]

As a result of a survey which was carried out as part of a national project on abandoned coal mines, the NRA noted that:

> "Close to 100 discharges, mostly originating from underground workings, are currently causing considerable concern. Some 200 km of rivers, streams, or brooks are affected. Some also contain metal

---

[167] Defined in s. 221(1) of the 1991 Act to include a hovercraft under the Hovercraft Act 1968.

[168] Both "trade" and "sewage" effluent are defined in s. 221(1) of the 1991 Act. Under Sched. 25, para. 2 to the 1991 Act, the Environment Agency has the power to make byelaws for regulating the use of navigable rivers. The Agency's power to make byelaws "requiring the provision of such sanitary appliances as may be necessary for the purpose of preventing pollution" (Sched. 25, para. 2(4)) thus fills a gap (at least in terms of navigable rivers) which might otherwise have existed in the light of s. 89(2): see also para. 4(1)(b) of Sched. 25. For the position with regard to maritime pollution, see the International Convention for the Prevention of Pollution from Ships (1973) (MARPOL), Cmnd.5748.

[169] He or she may have a defence under s. 89(1), however, if it could be shown that the discharge from the vessel of such matter took place in an emergency and provided that the other requirements of the subsection were also satisfied (see above).

[170] *Abandoned Mines and the Water Environment*, Water Quality Series, No.14.

[171] See the Preface to the Report, p. iii.

[172] Page 31 of the Report.

deposits which contribute to the overall abandoned mine water pollution problem."[173]

Given the scale of the pollution problem, it is perhaps a little surprising that section 89(3) of the Water Resources Act 1991 provides that:

"A person shall not be guilty of an offence under section 85 above by reason only of his permitting water from an abandoned mine [or an abandoned part of a mine] to enter controlled waters."[174]

Several features of this statutory defence are worth noting. The first such feature to consider is the rationale underlying the defence. In short, why did Parliament see fit to legislate in this way? In order to answer this question, it is helpful to have regard to the following words uttered by the then Minister for Energy during the passage of the Coal Industry Act 1994. It was explained that:

"The legislation[175] is there in that form because when the Bill was introduced and the Act debated it was felt to be unreasonable to place an absolute obligation in respect of environmental damage on a landowner who may never have been responsible for mining at all and who may have bought the land without being aware that it was undermined."[176]

A further feature to note about the statutory defence is that it is restricted to water pollution emanating from an *abandoned* mine or an *abandoned part* of a mine. In other words, it would still be an offence to cause or knowingly permit water pollution from an *active* mine. Moreover, the defence only extends to *permitting* water from an abandoned mine to enter controlled waters. Thus an offence would be committed if a defendant were to *cause* water from an abandoned mine to enter such waters. There is also a temporal limitation on the operation of the defence. The defence only applies in respect of an abandoned mine or an abandoned part of a mine where the abandonment occurred prior to 31st December 1999.[177] Where an abandonment has taken place after this date, a mine operator will have to seek to rely upon an alternative defence if he is charged with the causing or knowingly permitting offence.[178]

---

[173] Page 13 of the Report.

[174] The words in square brackets were added by s. 60 of the Environment Act 1995.

[175] The Water Resources Act 1991 and in Scotland, the Control of Pollution Act 1974.

[176] *Hansard*, HC, March 22, 1994. Col.297 – quoted in *Encyclopedia of Environmental Law* at page D1080/6.

[177] See s. 89(3A) of the 1991 Act, as inserted by s. 60(2) of the Environment Act 1995.

[178] It should be noted that where a mine operator decides to abandon a mine, he is under a statutory duty to give the Agency at least six months' notice before the abandonment takes effect: see s. 91B(1) of the Water Resources Act 1991. The notice may give the operator's opinion as to the likely consequences of abandonment, and it is an offence to fail to comply with the notice requirement (unless the statutory defence applies): see s. 91B(2)-(4). It should also be noted, however, that there is no statutory duty on a mine operator to prepare a complete mine abandonment programme.

There has been little case law in respect of water pollution emanating from abandoned mines despite the potential problem which exists. In the Scottish case *Lockhart* v *National Coal Board*,[179] water containing polluting matter (oxidized pyrite) had welled up from the shaft of the Dalquharran mine and had found its way into the Quarrelhill Burn and the Water of Girvan. All working at the mine, including pumping operations, had previously ceased and the mine shaft had been sealed off after having been filled in with rubble. In the opinion of the High Court of Justiciary, and in accordance with the principles which had emerged from the decision of the House of Lords in *Alphacell Ltd* v *Woodward*,[180] the defendants could be said by their actions to have *caused* the pollution of the watercourses. Accordingly, the matter was remitted to the Sheriff with a direction that he should convict.

The only other decision in this context is the decision of the Cardiff Crown Court in *R* v *British Coal Corporation*.[181] Here the defendants were charged on an indictment with two counts: that over a period of about a year they did cause polluting matter – water containing iron – to enter controlled waters (the River Rhymney) contrary to section 85(1) of the Water Resources Act 1991; and that during the same period, they knowingly permitted liquid matter injurious to fish food and spawning grounds – water containing iron – to enter the River Rhymney thereby causing those waters to be injurious to the food of fish and the spawning grounds of fish, contrary to section 4(1) of the Salmon and Freshwater Fisheries Act 1975.[182] The defendants had carried out deep mining operations at Britannia and Pengam mines, both of which were upstream and within two kilometres of the discharges into the River Rhymney. There were also a number of old mine workings near the discharges which were nothing to do with the defendants. The cessation of pumping of water from the defendants' mines occurred in February 1990. Both of the shafts at Pengam and one of the two shafts at Britannia were then backfilled and capped. The second shaft at Britannia was not filled but it was capped. It was the defendants' intention that once pumping ceased, water would fill the mine workings, rise up the unfilled shaft and then discharge to a duct which had been constructed by the defendants for that purpose. It was the defendants' further intention that the water would be carried away by the duct into the River Rhymney at a discharge point close to the discharge point for the former pumping operations.

In giving judgment, Jones J paid full regard to a number of authorities, including *Alphacell*. In his opinion there had plainly been a positive act on the part of the defendants; they had turned off the pumps and ceased pumping. The effect of this act was to cause the water table to resume to its natural level. Once this happened, any rainwater which fell flowed down the valley and thence into the old mine workings. In other words, the

---

[179] 1981 SLT 161.
[180] [1972] AC 824. Discussed above at p. 230.
[181] 2nd December 1993 (unreported).
[182] This was a private prosecution brought by the Anglers Co-operative Association.

cessation of pumping allowed the rainwater to take the course that it would have taken naturally had the defendants not carried out their mining operations. Since these old workings contained pyrite, the water entering them became polluted and subsequently flowed into the River Rhymney. There was no evidence that the water discharging from the defendants' mines was anything other than clear. Accordingly, Jones J concluded that an intervening cause, i.e. the operation of natural forces, was "of so powerful a nature for it to be said that the Defendants switching off the pumps was not really a cause at all but simply part of the surrounding circumstances". The jury was therefore instructed to return a verdict of not guilty on both counts.[183]

The facts of *Lockhart* and *R v British Coal Corporation* are not dissimilar but the outcomes of the cases were rather different. How can this be explained? The answer to this question lies in a material distinction between the facts of the two cases. Although they share some similarities, most notably that water pollution had occurred after pumping had ceased at mines which had been abandoned by the defendants, in *Lockhart*, the polluting water actually came from the abandoned mine itself. It had been able to rise up the mine shaft due to the cessation of pumping and had discharged into the watercourses. In *R v British Coal Corporation*, however, the polluting water had come not from the defendants' abandoned mines but from old mine workings for which the defendants bore no responsibility. The cessation of pumping at their mines had simply allowed to happen that which would have occurred naturally many years previously had they not been mining in the vicinity.

Mine or quarry refuse

A person is not guilty of an offence under section 85 by reason of depositing the solid refuse of a mine or quarry on any land so that it falls or is carried into inland freshwaters.[184] The defence is only available, however, if three conditions have been fulfilled: that the deposit took place with the consent[185] of the Environment Agency; that no other site for the deposit was reasonably practicable; and that all reasonably practicable steps had been taken to prevent the refuse from entering the inland freshwaters. In *Jordan v Norfolk County Council*[186] it was held, albeit in the context of a mandatory order which required the council to remove a sewage pipe which had been laid through the plaintiff's land without his agreement and to reinstate the site to its former condition, that the phrase "reasonably practicable" was sufficiently general to embrace considerations beyond what was physically feasible and was apt to include financial considerations. Thus in the present context, in determining what was "reasonably practicable" in the circumstances, a court will have to

---

[183] The s. 4(1) charge was defeated on the basis that the evidence did not disclose knowledge (an essential ingredient of the offence) on the part of the defendant.

[184] See s. 89(4) of the Water Resources Act 1991.

[185] The procedure for applying for a consent is dealt with in s. 90A of the 1991 Act, as inserted by the Environment Act 1995, s. 120, Sched. 22, para. 142.

[186] [1994] 4 All ER 218.

balance the costs of preventive measures against the magnitude of risk involved. Where measures have been taken to prevent refuse from entering inland freshwaters but such an entry has nevertheless occurred, a defendant is likely to be able to rely upon section 89(4) if it can be shown that the costs of taking additional measures which would have prevented the entry were disproportionate to the risk involved.

The section 89(4) defence does not apply in respect of the entry into controlled waters of any poisonous, noxious or polluting matter. It does apply, however, in respect of the entry into such waters of solid waste matter[187] or the entry of any matter which impedes the proper flow of inland freshwaters.[188]

Highway authorities

Section 89(5) provides a specific defence for highway authorities (or other persons) who are entitled to keep open a drain by virtue of section 100 of the Highways Act 1980.[189] The defence applies in respect of the causing or permitting of any discharge from a drain kept open under that section unless the discharge is made in contravention of a prohibition imposed under section 86 of the 1991 Act.

PROSECUTING WATER POLLUTION OFFENCES

In England and Wales the responsibility for bringing criminal proceedings where a water pollution offence has been committed lies with the Environment Agency. However, as was noted previously,[190] there is a general rule at common law that everyone has the right to seek "to invoke the aid of courts of criminal jurisdiction for the enforcement of the criminal law".[191] Private prosecutions are therefore a possibility in the present context, although in practice the incidence of them is low.[192] Where they do succeed, however, a by-product of that success may be the embarrassment of the Agency. Thus at the conclusion of one recent case where the defendants, Anglian Water, pleaded guilty at Basildon Crown Court to causing sewage to enter the River Crouch contrary to section 85(1) of the 1991 Act and were fined £200,000, the views of the Agency and the individual who brought the proceedings appeared to differ quite considerably as to the Agency's role in the case. While the Agency was of

---

[187] Section 85(1) of the Water Resources Act 1991.

[188] Section 85(5) of the Water Resources Act 1991.

[189] This section provides, inter alia, that for the purpose of preventing surface water flowing into the highway, the highway authority may scour, cleanse and keep open all drains situated in the highway (s. 100(1)(c)). However, the highway authority is under a duty to compensate the owner or occupier of any land which suffers damage by reason of the exercise of this power (subs. (3)).

[190] See Chapter 6.

[191] Per Lord Diplock in *Gouriet* v *Union of Post Office Workers* [1977] 3 All ER 70 at 97.

[192] See, for example, *DA Wales* v *Thames Water Authority* (unreported) Aylesbury Magistrates' Court, May 1987, *R* v *British Coal Corporation* (unreported) December 2, 1993 (see above at pp 338-339) and *Greenpeace (Burton)* v *Allbright and Wilson* [1992] LMELR 56. All of these cases are cited in Howarth and McGillivray's *Water Pollution and Water Quality Law* (2001) Shaw & Sons, at para. 9.19.1.

the opinion that it had helped to bring the case, the private prosecutor considered that the regulator's involvement had amounted to a hindrance rather than a help.[193]

PENALTIES

Where a defendant is convicted of either causing or knowingly permitting water pollution, he is liable, on summary conviction, either to a term of imprisonment not exceeding three months or to a fine not exceeding £20,000, or to both.[194] Where the conviction is on indictment, the Crown Court may impose either a prison sentence of up to two years or a fine, or both.[195]

The level of fines imposed by magistrates for section 85 offences has been a matter of concern for the Environment Agency. In its *Water Pollution Incidents in England and Wales 1998*,[196] the Agency publicly stated that "the level of fines imposed for water pollution offences remains relatively low".[197] There is patently a feeling within that body that magistrates have tended not to use the full scope of their sentencing powers with the result that some polluters have come to regard a relatively small fine as a price worth paying. Indeed at its 1998 Annual General Meeting, the Agency's former Chief Executive drew attention to the fact that "fines of a few thousand pounds are no deterrent to multi-million pound companies". Moreover he went on to observe that the Agency wished to see the imposition of fines which "reflect the seriousness of the crime".[198]

The published figures seem to bear out the Agency's concerns. They reveal that the statutory maximum fine of £20,000 has only ever been imposed once, after Shell UK Ltd was found guilty of causing water pollution in respect of the escape of 140 tons of refined oil into the Manchester Ship Canal.[199] They also show that fines imposed by magistrates for water pollution incidents during 1998 fell within the range of 0-£12,000 for the eight Agency regions for England and Wales. In the case of the Welsh region, the range was £500-£1,000.[200]

The general perception that the level of fines imposed for environmental offences was too low, coupled with a growing awareness of the threat to the environment posed by pollution, provided the impetus for a direction from the Home Secretary to the Sentencing Advisory Panel (SAP)[201] to

---

[193] See (2002) 326 ENDS Report at p. 54.

[194] Water Resources Act 1991, s. 85(6)(a).

[195] Water Resources Act 1991, s. 85(6)(b).

[196] (1999).

[197] *ibid.* para. 8.4, p. 36.

[198] *ibid.*

[199] *ibid.* para. 7.7.3, p. 34.

[200] *ibid.* para. 7.6, Table 21, p. 33.

[201] The establishment of this independent advisory non-departmental public body sponsored by the Home Department is provided for under section 81 of the Crime and Disorder Act 1998. The Panel itself came into being on 1st July 1999.

consider five environmental offences[202] and to issue proposals to the Court of Appeal for the establishment of sentencing guidelines in respect of these offences. Following a period of consultation, the Panel published its advice to the Court of Appeal on 1st March 2000. The details of that advice have already been considered.[203] For present purposes, it should be noted that the appeal in *R* v *Milford Haven Port Authority*,[204] afforded the Court of Appeal its first opportunity to respond to the SAP's proposals.

The appeal arose from the decision of Steel J sitting in the Cardiff Crown Court in *Environment Agency* v *Milford Haven Port Authority*.[205] The case involved the prosecution of the Port Authority on two counts: that it caused the pollution of "controlled waters" contrary to section 85; and that it had committed a public nuisance. The incident in respect of which the prosecution was brought was the running aground of the *Sea Empress*. The ship was a segregated ballast tanker carrying a cargo of 130,994 tonnes of Forties light crude oil when it attempted to enter the port of Milford Haven on 15th February 1996. At 20.07 the ship struck mid-channel rocks and immediately lost 2,500 tonnes of crude oil. She subsequently ran aground and was not refloated and berthed until six days later. In the meantime, a further 69,300 tons of crude oil and 500 tons of fuel oil had escaped from the ship into the sea. At the time that the *Sea Empress* ran aground she was being piloted by a person supplied by the Port Authority under a compulsory scheme. The environmental impact of the oil spillage was significant,[206] although not as severe as originally forecast due to a combination of factors such as the weather and the efforts of those directly involved in the clean up operation. Nevertheless, between 5% and 7% of the oil was converted by the action of the sea into emulsion which was then washed ashore over 200 kilometres of coastline. Fishing in the area had to be banned for three months and a ban on lobster and crab harvesting lasted six months. Large numbers of sea birds died as a direct result of the oil spillage. The total cost of the clean up operation was estimated as being at least £60 million, although as Steel J remarked, the figure "does not reflect the financial impact on tourism or commercial fisheries measured in total in further tens of millions of pounds."[207]

---

[202] The relevant offences were: carrying on a prescribed process without, or in breach of an authorisation (s. 23 of the Environmental Protection Act 1990); depositing, recovering or disposing of controlled waste without a site licence or in breach of its conditions (s. 33 of the Environmental Protection Act 1990); polluting controlled waters (s. 85 of the Water Resources Act 1991); abstracting water illegally (s. 24 of the Water Resources Act 1991); and, failing to meet packaging, recycling and recovery obligations, or to register or to provide information (s. 93 of the Environment Act 1995 and the Producer Responsibility Obligations (Packaging Waste) Regulations 1997, SI No.648).

[203] See Chapter 6.

[204] [2000] Env LR 632.

[205] [1999] Lloyd's Rep 673.

[206] See the Friends of the Earth publication "Lost Treasure: The Long Term Environmental Impacts of the Sea Empress Oil Spill" (1996) ISBN 1 85750 267 0.

[207] *ibid.*, at p. 679. For unsuccessful civil claims by businesses which had lost profits under contracts in relation to the interrupted supply of whelks see *R.J Tilbury & Sons (Devon) Ltd* v *International Oil Pollution Fund* [2003] EWCA Civ 65, upholding the decision at first instance in *Alegrete Shipping Co Inc* v *International Oil Pollution Fund* [1999] 2 All ER (Comm) 416.

Before the Crown Court, the Port Authority pleaded guilty to having caused water pollution in the light of the strict liability nature of the offence and the House of Lords ruling in *Empress Car Company (Abertillery) Ltd* v *National Rivers Authority.*[208] Applying the principles which emerge from the judgment of Lord Hoffmann in that case to the facts of the case before him, Steel J fully appreciated why the Port Authority had entered a guilty plea. In his opinion:

> "… there is no difficulty in concluding that the port authority *did* something which *caused* pollution: (a) The authority operated the port. (b) It was compulsory for inward bound vessels such as *Sea Empress* to carry a pilot. (c) The port authority trained and supervised pilots. (d) A pilot was allocated to *Sea Empress* in accordance with the rota system. (e) The grounding, while attributable to the negligent navigation of the pilot, was a normal fact of life not something extraordinary. (f) The subsequent loss of further crude oil and fuel oil was attributable to bad weather and the general uncertainties of any salvage operation both of which factors are normal not extraordinary incidents of life."[209]

Whether or not the Port Authority was guilty was therefore not at issue in the case. The task for Steel J was to determine the size of the fine to be imposed. Having considered various arguments which had been put to him in mitigation relating to, for example, the plea of guilty, the financial impact of the accident and the means of the Authority, Steel J imposed a fine of £4 million.[210] The level of fine was welcomed in several quarters, including the Environment Agency. Its Chief Executive went on record as saying that the fine represented "an important landmark in environmental protection" which would "cause the businessmen who cynically calculate that a bit of environmental damage and the usual low fine are a cheaper and more acceptable alternative to operating their factories and equipment properly, to think again".[211] The Port Authority appealed against this penalty.

The wider implications of the Court of Appeal's decision in *Milford Haven* in terms of its general effect upon sentencing for environmental offences have already been considered.[212] For present purposes the significance of the decision lies in the Court of Appeal's reduction of the fine from what it termed the "manifestly excessive"[213] sum of £4 million imposed by Steel J to " an appropriate fine"[214] of £750,000. In reaching such a decision, the

---

[208] [1998] 1 All ER 481; [1998] Env LR 396.

[209] [1999] Lloyd's Rep 673 at 676.

[210] It will be remembered that the Crown Court has the power to impose an unlimited fine where a defendant is convicted of a s. 85 offence: subs. (6)(b).

[211] (1999) 288 ENDS Report, p.50. Prior to this decision, the largest fine imposed upon a defendant for a water pollution offence was £1 million imposed upon Shell UK Ltd in respect of an oil spill in the Mersey Estuary in 1990.

[212] See Chapter 6.

[213] [2000] Env LR 632 at 648.

[214] *ibid.*

Court of Appeal was clearly influenced by the submissions made on behalf of the Port Authority which may be summarised thus:

- that the trial judge gave inadequate recognition to the relative lack of culpability on the part of the Port Authority;
- that the trial judge was wrong to deny the Authority full credit for its guilty plea;
- that the status of the Authority as a public trust was relevant to the issue of assessing the appropriate level of fine; and
- that the judge misunderstood the financial position of the Authority.

Counsel for the Port Authority was anxious to impress upon the Court of Appeal that a plea of guilty had been entered in respect of a strict liability offence with no admission of fault on the part of the defendants. Moreover, attention was drawn to the absence of aggravating factors in the commission of the offence, e.g. there had been no corner-cutting on operational or safety measures in order to maximise profit or seek a competitive edge, and the defendants had neither a record of previous offending nor a history of non-compliance. These arguments weighed heavily upon the Court of Appeal which was of the opinion that:

> "The culpability of the Port Authority would have been very much greater had it pleaded not guilty or been convicted on any basis other than one of strict liability."[215]

ANTI-POLLUTION WORKS

The imposition of a fine where a defendant has been convicted of a section 85 offence is one way in which a polluter may be made to pay for the environmental damage for which he is responsible. However, since these fines are paid into the Treasury coffers, there is no guarantee that any of the money will be used for the purposes of environmental remediation. What solution, if any, to this problem does the law provide? In other words, how may a polluter be made to pay for the clean-up costs that have been incurred in removing poisonous, noxious or polluting matter from controlled waters or in restocking such waters with fish where there has been a fish kill? The answer is to be found in sections 161 and 161A-161D of the Water Resources Act 1991, considered below in Chapter 14.

---

[215] At 644.

Chapter 10

OFFENCES IN THE CONTEXT OF WASTE

INTRODUCTION

As with our treatment of water pollution offences in Chapter 9 our treatment in this chapter of waste offences will be quite selective, concentrating on those offences which may be regarded as of the most significance.

In the pages which follow[1] attention will focus on:

- the meaning of "waste" and the legal categories into which "waste" may fall;
- a general overview of the range and scope of criminal liability in relation to waste;
- the offences under section 33 of the Environmental Protection Act 1990 involving the unauthorised or harmful deposit, treatment or disposal of waste;
- the offences under section 34 of the 1990 Act: breach of the "duty of care" in the management of waste.

THE MEANING OF "WASTE"

The apparently simple concept of "waste" has, in fact, given rise to some considerable difficulties in terms of legal definition. Yet such definition is important in terms of the ambit of obligations related to the concept: in particular, the scope of regulatory controls attaching to activities involving waste, and the reach of criminal offences involving waste.

We should begin with section 75 of the Environmental Protection Act 1990. As originally enacted this provided that for the purposes of Part II of that Act – which includes the sections establishing the main offences to be considered below – the notion of "waste" included:

"(a) any substance which constitutes a scrap material or an effluent or other unwanted surplus substance arising from the application of any process; and

(b) any substance or article which requires to be disposed of as being broken, worn out, contaminated or otherwise spoiled."[2]

---

[1] For more comprehensive treatment of waste offences and the law relating to waste generally, see Laurence, *Waste Regulation Law* (1999), Butterworths, or Pocklington, *The Law of Waste Management* (1997), Shaw & Sons.

[2] Section 75(2). Substances which are explosives within the meaning of the Explosives Act 1875 were expressly stated not to be waste.

This basic definition has, however, been modified in order to secure more assured "harmonization" with waste obligations under EU law.[3] The Environment Act 1995, therefore, has provided a new subsection (2) to section 75 of the 1990 Act.[4] This provides:

> "(2) 'Waste' means any substance or object in the categories set out in Schedule 2B to this Act which the holder discards or intends or is required to discard ..."

For the purpose of the new subsection (2):

> "'holder' means the producer of the waste or the person who is in possession of it"; and,

> "'producer' means any person whose activities produce waste or any person who carries out pre-processing, mixing or other operations resulting in a change in the nature or composition of the waste."[5]

It will be seen that under the revised definition the critical questions will be:

Does the substance or object fall within one of the categories set out in Schedule 2B to the 1995 Act?

And if so:

Is it a substance or object which the holder has discarded or intends or is required to discard?

Accordingly we need to examine both the terms of Schedule 2B and the meaning to be attributed in this context to the word "discard".

The Schedule 2B list

Schedule 2B to the 1990 Act[6] seeks to assist the alignment of waste law in the United Kingdom with EU obligations by being in the same form as Annex I to the EU Waste Directive.[7] The Schedule and the Annex provide us, however, with rather less elucidation of the concept of "waste" than might perhaps have been expected. The reason is that after listing some fifteen descriptions of kinds of substance or object which, subject to the "discard" requirement, will have the quality of waste, the list is completed by the words:

---

[3] Subsection (11), added by the Environment Act 1995, provides that the revised definition in subs. (2) is "for the purpose of assigning to 'waste' ... the meaning it has in the Waste Directive", and that subs. (2) and Sched. 2 "shall be construed accordingly".

[4] 1995 Act, Sched. 22 para. 88

[5] The wording of the new s. 75(2) follows that of Article 1 of the EU Waste Directive 75/442 (as amended).

[6] As inserted by the Environment Act 1995, Sched.22 para.95.

[7] Directive 75/442 EEC, as amended.

"(16) Any materials, substances or products which are not contained in the above categories."[8]

In other words we may regard items (1) to (15) on the list as merely giving guidance as to the sorts of substances or materials which may perhaps most commonly be discarded so as to constitute waste, without that list being exhaustive of the kinds of material which *if* discarded will constitute waste. The list – items (1) to (15) – is illustrative rather than defining; and the key concept, by reference to which *any* material, substance or product may be adjudged to be waste, is therefore that of "discard".

Although illustrative only, the list in the Schedule/Annex may nevertheless be valuable in drawing to attention typical instances of products or substances which may be likely to become discarded, or be held in order to be discarded, so constituting waste. The list includes: production residues; off-specification products; products whose date for appropriate use has expired; materials spilled or having undergone mishap; materials contaminated as a result of mishap; substances which no longer perform satisfactorily; residues from pollution abatement processes; machining or finishing residues; and products for which the holder has no further use. In the words of one commentator, these categories are "not identified according to the level of damage they might inflict but rather according to the likelihood of their holders wishing to get rid of them".[9]

"Discard"

The key concept, as explained above, is that of "discard". This term is not further defined either in the EU directives or in domestic legislation.[10] Some substantial guidance exists, however, in several quite recent judgments of the European Court of Justice[11] and also in a number of judgments handed down by English courts.[12] The discussion which follows will therefore examine the relevant case law in chronological order and

---

[8] In *ARCO Chemie Nederland Limited*, joined cases C-418/97 and 419/97, the European Court of Justice described this category in Annex I to the EU Waste Directive as being a "residual category".

[9] See Cheyne, 'The Definition of Waste in EC Law' [2002] 14 JEL 61 at 64.

[10] Cheyne has argued that "Given the important role of the concept of 'discarding' in the Directive meaning of waste, it is surprising that the term is not defined": *ibid.* Accordingly, she is of the view that "... one is required to examine the ordinary meaning of the words, to glean any specialized meaning from other provisions, or be guided by the object and purpose of the Directive": *ibid.*, at 71.

[11] *Inter-Environnement* v *Region Wallonie*, Case C-129/96 [1998] Env LR 623, [1997] ECR I-7411; *Tombesi and others*, Cases C-304/94, C-342/94, and C-224/95, [1998] Env LR 59, [1997] ECR I-3561; *ARCO Chemie Nederland Limited*, Cases C-418/97 and C-419/97; *Palin Granit OY and Vehmassalon Kansanterveystyön Kuntayhtymän Hallitus* v *Lounais-Suomen Ympäristökeskus*, Case C-9/00 [2002] 2 CMLR 24; and *AvestaPolarit Chrome Oy*, Case C-114/01, ECJ, 11 September 2003.

[12] *Mayer Parry Recycling Ltd* v *Environment Agency* [1999] Env LR 489; *Castle Cement* v *Environment Agency* [2001] Env LR 813; and, *Attorney-General's Reference (No.5 of 2000)* [2002] Env LR 139.

will thus commence with the decision in *Mayer Parry Recycling Ltd* v *Environmental Agency*.[13]

Mayer Parry

In *Mayer Parry* the defendants' substantial business was that of scrap metal merchants. The case centred on the legal character – waste or not waste – of four categories of material with which the company dealt. The issue was whether the waste management licensing regime applied to their dealings with each of these kinds of material. The four categories, and the decision reached by Carnwath J as regards each, will be considered later in the discussion. For present purposes, attention will focus on what has been described judicially as "Carnwath J's fine exegesis of the law on this subject".[14]

In that part of his judgment which dealt with the meaning of "waste", Carnwath J began by drawing attention to the fact that some care needed to be taken as regards the word "discard", the critical term to be found in both the EU directives and the UK implementing legislation. It was to be remembered that EU legislation was to be interpreted in a purposive way. Moreover, it was relevant that community legislation is drafted in a number of languages, and that all the texts are equally authentic. Accordingly, it was not appropriate:

> "to attach too much weight to the specific connotations of the ordinary English usage of the word 'discard', without regard to the background and other language versions."[15]

In other words if the purpose of the community measures and the wording of other language texts suggested that "waste" should be afforded a legal meaning which involved what might involve a less than common usage of the word "discard", so be it.

Analysis of the language used in the several equally authoritative versions of the EU text did not, however, take matters further than to suggest that the word "discard" might have somewhat more negative characteristics than the terms used in, for example, the Italian and French texts. "Discard" would certainly suggest "getting rid of": but was it right to describe someone who has *sold* material (e.g. to a waste recycler) as having "discarded" that material? It might be that in such a situation the material could be said to have been "disposed of" by way of sale – but not "discarded". By contrast, the French and Italian language texts might be interpreted as more neutral as regards the means by which material has been "got rid of" by its producer. However, the matter was complicated by the fact that the usages "dispose" or "disposal" had indeed appeared in the

---

[13] [1999] Env LR 489.
[14] Per Stanley Burnton J in *Castle Cement* v *Environment Agency* [2001] Env LR 813; see below, at pp. 365-369. It is worth noting that although *Mayer Parry* involved what Carnwath J described as "an issue of pure European law", neither party to the proceedings had suggested that there ought to be an Article 177 (now Article 234) referral to the European Court of Justice.
[15] [1999] Env LR 489 at 499.

original draft of the proposed waste framework directive. The substitution of the word "discard" was, presumably, in order to narrow the scope of the concept – but by how far?

Carnwath J concluded that the word "discard" should be regarded, in the light of the other texts, as having a meaning:

> "somewhere between 'discard' and 'dispose of'."[16]

However where precisely the meaning should lie between these concepts could not be deduced from linguistic analysis and comparison alone. Rather, what was essential was to use these linguistic variations and uncertainties to place emphasis, as regards the interpretation and construction of the legislation, on matters of legislative context and purpose.

On this matter Carnwath J observed:

> "The general concept is reasonably clear. The term 'discard' is used in a broad sense equivalent to 'get rid of'; but it is coloured by the examples of waste given in Annex I ..., which indicate that it is concerned generally with materials which have ceased to be required for their original purpose, normally because they are unsuitable, unwanted or surplus to requirements."[17]

So, the concept of "waste" is, it seems, to be construed by reference to the common, underlying, features of the examples given in Annex I; and is not to be afforded a meaning distorted by the English word "discard" – a word somewhat, albeit elusively, narrower in scope that that found in other official language texts of the Directive.

However, this approach was itself to be limited by reference to context. The focus was to be on the notions "unsuitable", "unwanted" and "surplus to requirements", but the ambit of any such concepts was to be limited by reference to two broad considerations. First, it was clear that it was the intention of the EU legislation (and of national implementing measures) to subject what are commonly described as waste recovery operations to controls. It followed that the definition afforded to waste should be such that materials destined for, or supplied to, waste recoverers for such waste recovery should have the legal quality of waste and this, regardless of the economic value, or otherwise, of the "waste" so committed (sold as a valuable waste commodity, or given away, or taken away upon payment of a charge). Secondly, there was no reason why the concept of "waste" should be held to apply to material which is "got rid of" to a person who, without any waste recovery operations being required, may make some use of that material. As Carnwath J explained, the broad notion of "waste":

---

[16] *ibid.*
[17] *ibid.* at 505.

"is ... limited by the context, which shows that the purpose is to control disposal and recovery of such materials. Accordingly, materials which are to be re-used (rather than finally disposed of) but which do not require any recovery operation before being put to their new use, are not treated as waste. Similarly, materials which are made ready for re-use by a recovery operation, cease to be waste when the recovery operation is complete."[18]

Relating this general statement to the facts of the case itself, Carnwath J noted:

" ... all the materials referred to in the evidence are potentially within the definition of waste, in the sense that they are 'got rid of' by their original owners, because they are not wanted or needed for their original purpose ...

... the issue in this case turns on the scope of the term 'recovery'. In so far as the discarded materials do not require any recovery operation ... they are not to be treated as waste at all. In so far as they do require recovery operations, they remain waste until those recovery operations are complete."[19]

In so determining, Carnwath J was very much echoing the approach of Advocate-General Jacobs in the *Tombesi* case before the ECJ:

"It seems to me that little is to be gained by considering the normal meaning of the term 'discard'. It is clear from the provisions of the Directive ... that the term 'waste' and the regulatory system of the directive extend both to substances or objects which are disposed of and to those which are recovered. Thus the term 'discard' ... has a special meaning encompassing the disposal of waste and its consignment to a recovery operation. The scope of the term 'waste' therefore depends on what is meant by 'disposal operation' and 'recovery operation'."[20]

Returning to the facts of *Mayer Parry*, the four categories of material with which the company dealt, and the decision reached by Carnwath J as regards each, were:

---

[18] *ibid.*

[19] *ibid.*

[20] [1997] All ER (EC) 639; [1997] 3 CMLR 673; [1998] Env LR 59. Subsequently lawyers have referred to this passage as encompassing what has become known as the "Tombesi bypass". Essentially this constitutes an approach whereby the attention is focused on the act of consigning the relevant material to a recovery operation rather than considering when waste has been discarded. For a fuller discussion of the "bypass", see Van Calster, "The EC Definition of Waste: The Euro Tombesi Bypass and the Basel Relief Routes" [1997] European Business Law Review 137. Tromans has argued that the weakness in the "Tombesi bypass" is that while it "gets round the need to consider in detail when waste is discarded", it "really only shifts the problem to what in meant by 'recovery'": see "EC Waste Law: A Complete Mess?" (2001) 13 JEL 133 at 142.

Scrap metal which required no further processing prior to being used, by those to whom it was sold, as, for example, raw material for steel or other metal producers.

In respect of such material Carnwath J agreed with a concession by the Environment Agency that such material, bought and sold by the defendant company, did not have the legal quality of waste. In this respect the decision follows the guidance of Advocate-General Jacobs in *Tombesi*:

> "... what is entailed by 'recovery' is a process by which goods are restored to their previous state or transformed into a usable state or by which certain useable components are extracted or produced. It follows that ... goods which are transferred to another person and put to continued use in their existing form are not 'recovered' in the above sense."[21]

It was, however, a very different matter where:

> "objects or substances, even where they have a commercial value and are destined for further use ... must first undergo a recovery operation ..."

Scrap metal destined for treatment or processing – e.g. sorting, separating, cutting, shearing, crushing, fragmenting, compressing or baling – with a view to its later use as a raw material for smelting.

Scrap metal contaminated with oil and cutting fluids – so requiring, inter alia, special measures as regards its handling, storage or transport in order to protect public health or the environment.

Scrap containing small amounts of foreign matter – quantities of metal known to contain also small amounts of plastic, concrete, wood, soil, glass or rubber.

The Agency contended that recovery operations were necessary in respect of these three categories of material which had been "got rid of" to the defendants. Such recovery operations, the Agency argued, included the "special handling, storage and transport measures" referred to above; the process of separating potential furnace feed from the foreign matter – even where the potential raw material might itself require no further treatment; and any special procedures which an onward supplier might need to operate because of the pre-used nature of material purchased (for example, one particular category of material could be supplied without treatment by the defendant so long as the eventual smelter of the material was using a smelter equipped with an afterburner).

Carnwath J offered the following guidance as regards these various Agency contentions. In his opinion it was doubtful whether the mere fact that materials needed to be handled, stored and transported with special

---

[21] [1998] Env LR 59 at 74.

care involved such material having the character of waste. The same sort of care was necessary in relation to a variety of kinds of substances and materials and could not be the defining factor as regards their character as waste. To say that the need for special care in the matters referred to involved recovery operations was not a natural usage of that expression.

There was also a difficult distinction to be drawn between an industrial process which uses waste as a raw material and has to "recover" that waste prior to that industrial process, and an industrial process which simply requires to subject a raw material to some form of industrial treatment prior to its use. In the latter case it may well be that that treatment should be subject to environmental controls of various sorts. What was not the case is that the need for such "normal industrial treatment" of a raw material requires the characterisation of that material in all cases as "waste".

This distinction was not an easy one to define or to draw. Nevertheless, on balance, Carnwath J was prepared to accept Agency contentions that the "smelter afterburners" requirement as regards the use of the material contaminated with oil was such as to involve that material in a recovery process. Material so destined was, therefore, waste whilst being handled and transported by the defendants.

On the matter of whether "waste recovery" was involved in the mere separation of scrap metal from other, foreign, material, Carnwath J considered that he:

> "would agree with the Agency, that sorting ... to remove impurities is a recovery operation".[22]

ARCO and Epon

The general and specific guidance afforded by the Carnwath J in *Mayer Parry* appeared for a while to have clarified a number of important issues However, in the light of the decision of the European Court of Justice in the joined cases *ARCO Chemie Nederland Ltd and Epon*[23] and also in the light of later English cases,[24] it no longer may be regarded as representing the correct approach to the meaning of "waste".[25]

In *ARCO and Epon*, the Netherlands State Council referred several questions to the European Court of Justice for a preliminary ruling under the Article 177 (now Article 234) procedure. The questions, which arose in the context of appeals lodged against administrative decisions concerning

---

[22] [1999] Env LR 489 at 508.

[23] Cases C-418/97 and C-419/97.

[24] See *Castle Cement v Environment Agency* [2001] Env LR 813 and *Attorney-General's Reference (No.5 of 2000)* [2002] Env LR 139, both of which are discussed below.

[25] Further episodes in what has become the *Mayer Parry* saga occurred with the decisions in *R v Environment Agency, ex parte Mayer Parry Recycling Ltd (No.1)* [2001] Env LR 31 and *R (on the application of Mayer Parry Recycling Ltd)* v *Environment Agency* (C444/00) ECJ, 19 June 2003. See further, below, at p. 370.

substances[26] destined to be used as fuel in the cement industry or to produce electrical energy, essentially amounted to whether those substances constituted raw materials or waste for the purposes of the EU Waste Directive.[27]

In giving judgment, the European Court of Justice stressed that the scope of the term "waste" turned on the meaning of the term "discard". It also noted that that term must be interpreted in the light of the aim of the EU Waste Directive, and that the third recital in the preamble to that Directive states that:

> "the essential objective of all provisions relating to waste disposal must be the protection of human health and the environment against harmful effects caused by the collection, transport, treatment, storage and tipping of waste."

The Court further noted that Community environmental policy aims at a high level of protection and that it is based on the precautionary principle and the principle that preventive action should be taken. In the light of these considerations, it followed that the concept of waste could not be interpreted in a restrictive manner. Moreover, the Court considered that the effectiveness of the Treaty and the Directive would be undermined if Member State national legislatures were to use modes of proof (e.g. statutory presumptions) which had the effect of restricting the scope of the Directive and not covering materials, substances or products which correspond to the definition of "waste" within the meaning of the Directive.

In the light of these considerations, the Court set about answering the questions which had been referred to it. The first of these questions, which was the same for each of the joined cases, was stated as follows:

> "May it be inferred from the mere fact that LUWA bottoms/wood chips undergo an operation listed in Annex IIB to Directive 75/442/EEC that that substance has been discarded so as to enable it to be regarded as waste for the purposes of Directive 75/442/EEC?"

The Court was able to deal with the question quite briefly. All those who had submitted observations to the Court[28] had proposed that the question be answered in the negative. The Court agreed. Although Annexes IIA and IIB described methods of disposal and recovery of substances, it did not follow that all substances which were treated by such methods were

---

[26] The substances in question were "LUWA bottoms" and "wood chips". The former were a by-product of a manufacturing process used by Arco. They resulted from the distillation process, and were so-called because the "bottoms" were left at the bottom of the distillation column.

[27] 75/442 EEC, as amended.

[28] In addition to the parties, these included the Danish, German, Austrian and UK governments.

necessarily waste.[29] Some of the methods might be applied to raw materials which were not waste.[30]

Turning to the second question in both cases, the Court noted that it concerned the definition of the term 'discard' for the purpose of determining whether a particular substance was waste. However, it was a more complex question and could therefore be subdivided into three branches:

1. Whether, in order to determine whether the use of a substance constitutes discarding, it was necessary to take into account the fact that the substance was commonly regarded as waste *or* that it may be recovered in an environmentally responsible manner for use as fuel without substantial treatment *or* whether the use as a fuel amounted to a common method of waste recovery.

2. Whether, in order to determine whether the use of a substance constitutes discarding, it was necessary to consider whether the use relates to a main product or a by-product (a residue).

3. Whether, in order to determine whether the use of wood chips as a fuel constitutes discarding, it was necessary to consider whether the waste from the construction and demolition sector from which the chips were made had already undergone, prior to burning, operations which were to be regarded as a discarding of the waste, namely recycling operations, to render the waste suitable for re-use as fuel, and if so, whether the operation may be regarded as an operation for recovery of waste only if it was expressly mentioned in Annex IIB to the Directive or whether it may also be so regarded if it was analogous to an operation mentioned in that annex.

It was argued on behalf of ARCO that the fact that a substance was recovered in an environmentally responsible manner and without substantial treatment was a cogent argument that the substance in question was not waste. However, the Court rejected this argument and those put forward by Epon in respect of the first branch of question 2. In its judgment:

> "... for the purpose of determining whether the use of a substance such as LUWA-bottoms or wood chips as a fuel is to be regarded as constituting discarding, it is irrelevant that those substances may be recovered in an environmentally responsible manner for use as fuel without substantial treatment. The fact that that use as fuel is a common method of recovering waste and the fact that those substances are commonly regarded as waste may be taken as evidence that the holder has discarded those substances or intends or is

---

[29] By so holding, the Court appears not to have endorsed the "Tombesi bypass" (see above).

[30] By way of example, the Court noted that category R9 of Annex IIB, "Use principally as a fuel or other means to generate energy" could apply to fuel oil, gas or kerosene.

required to discard them within the meaning of Article 1(a) of the Directive. However, whether they are in fact waste within the meaning of the Directive must be determined in the light of all the circumstances, regard being had to the aim of the Directive and the need to ensure that its effectiveness is not undermined."[31]

With regard to the second branch of question 2, ARCO and Epon maintained that the use of a substance as a fuel could not be regarded as constituting discarding purely on the ground of its origin. As with the previous question, the Court also received submissions from a number of other parties. It was contended on behalf of the UK government, for example, that production residues which may constitute useful by-products, and may be used as a raw material without further processing, in the same way as any other raw material of non-waste origin, comprised part of the commercial cycle and did not therefore constitute waste. It was the Commission's contention, however, that the fact that a substance is a by-product of a production process whose purpose was to obtain a different product was an indication that the substance may constitute waste within the meaning of the Directive. It would seem that the European Court was more taken with the latter of these two arguments than by the former, since it concluded on this point:

> "... the fact that a substance used as fuel is the residue of the manufacturing process of another substance, that no use for that substance other than disposal can be envisaged, that the composition of the substance is not suitable for the use made of it or that special environmental precautions must be taken when it is used may be regarded as evidence that the holder has discarded that substance or intends or is required to discard it within the meaning of Article 1(a) of the Directive. However, whether it is in fact waste within the meaning of the Directive must be determined in the light of all the circumstances, regard being had to the aim of the Directive and the need to ensure that its effectiveness is not undermined."[32]

Turning to the third branch of question 2, which as has been noted above, related specifically to processes already undergone by the wood chips, Epon argued that a substance which had previously undergone a recycling operation must not be regarded as waste where it was used in an environmentally responsible manner (i.e. where its use was no more hazardous to human health or to the environment than the use of a primary raw material). With regard to the second part of the question, Epon pointed out that the list in Annex IIB to the Directive was not exhaustive, and that it must therefore be possible to take new recycling methods into consideration. On behalf of the governments and the Commission, it was argued that the fact that the waste at issue had undergone prior operations when it was sorted and transformed into chips was not sufficient for it to lose the character of waste. Such operations, it was contended, amounted

---

[31] Paragraphs 72 and 73 of the judgment.
[32] Paragraph 88 of the judgment.

to a simple pre-treatment of the waste rather than a recovery operation for the purposes of Annex IIB.

In determining this point the European Court first noted that:

> "… even where waste has undergone a complete recovery operation which has the consequence that the substance in question has acquired the same properties and characteristics as a raw material, that substance may nonetheless be regarded as waste if, in accordance with the definition in Article 1(a) of the Directive, its holder discards it or intends or is required to discard it."[33]

And continued:

> "The fact that the substance is the result of a complete recovery operation for the purposes of Annex IIB to the Directive is only one of the factors to be taken into consideration for the purpose of determining whether the substance constitutes waste and does not as such permit a definitive conclusion to be drawn in that regard. If a complete recovery operation does not necessarily deprive an object of its classification as waste, that applies a fortiori to an operation during which the objects concerned are merely sorted or pre-treated, such as when waste in the form of a wood impregnated with toxic substances is transformed into chips or those chips are reduced to wood powder, and which, since it does not purge the wood of the toxic substances which impregnate it, does not have the effect of transforming those objects into a product analogous to a raw material, with the same characteristics as that raw material and capable of being used in the same conditions of environmental protection."[34]

Thus whether a substance has undergone a recovery operation listed in Annex IIB to the Directive is a factor to be taken into account when determining whether or not that substance is "waste". However, as is evident from its answers to the other questions in *ARCO and Epon*, the European Court considered that the correct approach to adopt is to determine the question:

> "in the light of all the circumstances, by comparison with the definition set out in Article 1(a) of the Directive… regard being had to the aim of the Directive and the need to ensure that its effectiveness is not undermined."[35]

Such statements are not especially helpful. It is to be regretted that the European Court of Justice has responded to the challenge of defining "waste" by issuing general statements which offer little guidance to national courts and authorities. The identification of various factors which ought to be taken into account when determining whether or not a

---

[33] Paragraph(s) 94 of the judgment.

[34] Paragraph(s) 95 and 96 of the judgment.

[35] Paragraph(s) 97 of the judgment.

substance is waste is of little real assistance when those factors are self-evident.

Nevertheless, the decision in *ARCO and Epon* represents an authoritative pronouncement on the meaning of 'waste' which, as will be seen, has subsequently been applied at both the European and the domestic levels.

Palin Granit

The meaning of "waste" for the purposes of Directive 74/442/EEC was subsequently at issue in *Palin Granit Oy and Vehmassalon Kansanterveystyön Kuntayhtymän Hallitus* v *Lounais-Suomen Ympäristökeskus*,[36] a case referred to the European Court of Justice by the Finnish Supreme Court under Article 234 of the EC Treaty. The main issue for the Court to consider was whether left-over stone from quarrying which was stored on an adjacent site amounted to waste.[37] The issue was of practical importance for the Finnish environmental licensing system. Essentially, if the left-over stone was not waste, the municipal authority had been entitled to grant an environmental licence. If, however, it *was* waste, its storage amounted to a landfill and the competence to grant an environmental licence transferred from the municipal authority to the regional environment centre.

In addition to the main question identified above, four further sub-questions were referred to the Court. These were as follows:

- What relevance, in deciding the main question, does it have that the left-over stone is stored on a site adjoining the place of quarrying to await subsequent use? Is it relevant generally whether it is stored on the quarrying site, a site next to it, or further away?

- What relevance does it have that the left-over stone is the same as regards its composition as the basic rock from which it has been quarried, and that it does not change its composition regardless of how long it is kept or how it is kept?

- What relevance does it have that the left-over stone is harmless to human health and the environment?

- What relevance does it have that the intention is to transfer the left-over stone in whole or in part away from the storage site for use, for example for landfill or breakwaters, and that it could be recovered as such without processing or similar measures? To what extent in this connection should attention be paid to how definite the plans are which the holder of the left-over stone has for such use and to how

---

[36] Case C-9/00 [2002] 2 CMLR 560.

[37] The quantities of left-over stone were substantial. It amounted to approximately 50,000 cubic metres per annum, which represented between 65 and 80 per cent of the total stone quarried at the site. The adjacent site at which the left-over stone was to be stored had the capacity for 700,000 cubic metres of material.

soon after the left-over stone has been deposited on the storage site the use takes place?

In giving its judgment, the European Court of Justice approved the approach recommended to it by Advocate-General Jacobs in respect of the applicability of the EU concept of waste to quarrying operations. With regard to the main question, the Court noted that Annex I to Directive 75/442 and the European Waste Catalogue[38] clarify and illustrate the definition of "waste" in the Directive. However, the Court further noted that the lists are only intended to be guidance. The classification of a substance or an object as waste on one of the lists does not necessarily mean, therefore, that it is waste for the purposes of the Directive. What matters most are the holder's actions, in particular, whether or not the holder intends to *discard* the substance in question. Thus the Court, in *Palin Granit*, confirmed its previous position on this matter: that "the scope of the term 'waste' turns on the meaning of the term 'discard'".[39]

The term "discard" must, the Court felt, be interpreted in the light of the aims of the Waste Directive and Article 174(2) of the EC Treaty. Thus it must be interpreted in a way which seeks to protect human health and the environment against the harmful effects caused by the collection, transport, treatment, storage and tipping of waste,[40] and in a way which reflects that Community policy on the environment is based on the precautionary principle and the principle that preventive action should be taken. It followed, therefore, that "the concept of waste cannot be interpreted restrictively".[41]

The Court further noted that Directive 75/442 does not provide any criteria for determining the intention of a holder to discard a particular substance or object. Although a substance may undergo a disposal or recovery operation listed in Annex IIA or IIB to the Directive, once again, the Court felt that this does not of itself justify the classification of the substance as waste. Moreover, in response to the argument put on behalf of Palin Granit that the left-over stone was suitable for reuse,[42] the Court remarked that such an argument did not preclude the left-over stone being regarded as waste. In the joined cases *Criminal Proceedings against Vessoso and another*,[43] the Court had previously held that the concept of waste was sufficiently broad to encompass substances and objects which are capable of economic reutilisation.

---

[38] This was originally adopted by the Commission pursuant to Annex 1 of the Waste Directive by Decision 94/3/EC. That Decision has now been repealed and replaced by Commission Decision 2000/532, [2000] OJ L226/3.

[39] [2002] 2 CMLR 560 at 578.

[40] This aim is stated in the third recital to Directive 75/442.

[41] [2002] 2 CMLR 560 at 578.

[42] It was envisaged that it could be used in embankment work at the site of its storage or for building harbours and breakwaters.

[43] Cases C-206/88 and 207/88, [1990] ECR I – 1461.

Although it would seem that whether or not left-over stone has undergone an operation referred to in Directive 75/442 or, whether it is capable of reuse, are relevant considerations when determining whether or not it is waste for the purposes of the Directive, the Court was of the view in *Palin Granit* that there were "other considerations which are more decisive".[44] Essentially the decisive considerations were: (i) whether the substance was a *production residue*, i.e. a product not in itself sought for subsequent use, or a *by-product*; and (ii) the degree of likelihood that the substance will be reused, without any further processing prior to its reuse.

With regard to the former consideration, the Court noted that:

> "According to its ordinary meaning, waste is what falls away when one processes a material or an object and is not the end-product which the manufacturing process directly seeks to produce."[45]

In principle, therefore, it appeared that left-over stone from extraction processes, which was not the product primarily sought by the operator of a granite quarry, fell into the category of "residues from raw materials extraction and processing" under head Q11 of Annex I to Directive 75/442. However, the Court noted that such an analysis was subject to a counter-challenge: that goods, materials or raw materials resulting from a manufacturing or extraction process which was not undertaken with the primary aim of producing such items could nevertheless be regarded as a *by-product* of that process (rather than a residue) which the undertaking did not wish to "discard".

In the judgment of the Court:

> "Such an interpretation would not be incompatible with the aims of Directive 75/442. There is no reason to hold that the provisions of Directive 75/442 which are intended to regulate the disposal or recovery of waste apply to goods, materials or raw materials which have an economic value as products regardless of any form of processing and which, as such, are subject to the legislation applicable to those products."[46]

The Court went on to observe, however, that although a *by-product* may not therefore be "waste" for the purposes of Directive 75/442, regard had to be had to the obligation not to interpret the concept of "waste" in a restrictive manner. Thus it followed that:

> "... the reasoning applicable to by-products should be confined to situations in which the reuse of the goods, materials or raw materials is not a mere possibility but a certainty, without any further

---

[44] [2002] 2 CMLR 560 at 579.
[45] *ibid.*
[46] At 580.

processing prior to reuse and as an integral part of the production process."[47]

In the light of this passage from the judgment in *Palin Granit*, it is clear that a by-product of a process may not be waste for the purposes of Directive 75/442 provided that its reuse is a *certainty* without any further processing prior to its reuse. Thus much will turn upon the likelihood of the relevant substance being reused. This in turn will depend in large part upon whether the holder of a substance will derive financial benefit from that reuse. Where such a benefit will arise, the Court was of the opinion that the likelihood of reuse of the substance will be "high". In such circumstances, the Court considered that:

"... the substance in question must no longer be regarded as a burden which its holder seeks to 'discard', but as a genuine product."[48]

Applying this reasoning to the facts of the case before it, the European Court concluded that the leftover stone did *not* amount to a "by-product". In its judgment:

"... the only foreseeable reuses of leftover stone in its existing state, for example, in embankment work or in the construction of harbours and breakwaters, necessitate, in most cases, potentially long-term storage operations which constitute a burden to the holder and are also potentially the cause of precisely the environmental pollution which Directive 75/442 seeks to reduce. The reuse is therefore not certain and is only foreseeable in the longer term, with the result that the leftover stone can only be regarded as 'extraction residue' which its holder 'intends or is required to discard' within the meaning of Directive 75/442, and thus falls within the scope of head Q11 of Annex I to that Directive."[49]

Thus the answer to the main question referred to the European Court of Justice was that in all the circumstances of the case, the left-over stone was a *production residue* and hence "waste" within the meaning of Directive 75/442. This conclusion on the main question also provided the answer to the fourth sub-question raised by the referral (see above). With regard to the other three sub-questions, the Court concluded as regards sub-question (1) that the place of storage of the left-over stone was not relevant to its classification as waste. Similarly, the conditions under which the materials are kept and the length of time for which they are kept do not of themselves provide an indication of either their value to the undertaking or the advantages which the undertaking may derive from them. They do not reveal whether or not the holder intends to discard the materials.

With respect to sub-question (2), the Court noted that in the *ARCO* case, it had held that the fact that a substance is a *production residue* whose

---

[47] *ibid.*
[48] *ibid.*
[49] *ibid.*

composition is not suitable for the use made, or that special precautions must be taken when using it due to the environmentally hazardous nature of its composition, may amount to evidence that the holder has either discarded or intends to discard the substance within the meaning of Directive 75/442.

The argument that the composition and physical state of the left-over stone was the same as the quarried granite which was used in the construction industry would only be decisive if all the left-over stone were reused, which it was not. Moreover, the risk of environmental pollution[50] posed by unused left-over stone was not mitigated by the fact that its mineral composition was identical to the blocks of stone. In any event, the Court was of the opinion that:

> "... even where a substance undergoes a full recovery operation and thereby acquires the same properties and characteristics as a raw material, it may nevertheless be regarded as waste if, in accordance with the definition in Article 1(a) of Directive 75/442, its holder discards it, or intends or is required to discard it."[51]

Turning to sub-question (3), the Court was of the opinion that "the fact that the leftover stone does not pose any risk to public health or the environment also does not preclude its classification as waste".[52] Such a view could be supported on three grounds: (i) the fact that Directive 75/442 is supplemented by the Hazardous Waste Directive[53] implies that not all waste is hazardous; (ii) stockpiling left-over stone necessarily amounts to a source of harm to and pollution of the environment since the full reuse of the stone is neither immediate nor foreseeable; and (iii) the harmlessness of a substance is not necessarily decisive when determining what its holder intends to do with it.

The decision in *Palin Granit* casts further light on the meaning of "waste" in Directive 75/442. Clearly the critical issue in terms of whether something is to be characterised as waste is the intent of the holder of the material to discard that material. In this connection, such material may be regarded as discarded even if the holder has some contingent intention to make some commercial use of that discarded material.

AvestaPolarit Chrome Oy

The *Palin Granit* principles, described above, were applied most recently by the ECJ in *AvestaPolarit Chrome Oy*.[54] In this case AvestaPolarit, the operator of a chromium ore mine in northern Finland, had applied for an environmental licence in order to be able to continue mining activity at the site in question. Its mining activity involved the extraction of chromium

---

[50] The Court had in mind noise and dust pollution and the risk of "adversely affecting the countryside" within the meaning of Article 4 of Directive 75/442.

[51] [2002] 2 CMLR 560 at 581.

[52] *ibid.*

[53] 91/689/EEC.

[54] Case C-114/01, ECJ, 11th September 2003.

ore by a process of boring and blasting, followed by crushing, rough dressing and fine dressing. This process gave rise to quite substantial quantities of "left-over" rock. Each year some 1.1m tonnes of ore were extracted and left-over rock amounted to some eight million tonnes.

As a consequence of past mining activity there existed, stored around the mine, some 100m tonnes of left-over rock. According to the Court:

> "It is envisaged that after 70 to 100 years part will be used to fill in the underground parts of the mine, but ... the stacks will be landscaped before that. Part of the stacks could remain on the site indefinitely. Only a small proportion of the leftover rock, about 20%, will be processed into aggregates."[55]

An environmental licence was granted for continued operation of the mine, subject however to the issuing agency's opinion that the left-over rock was "waste" to which a separate regulatory regime was applicable. This conclusion resulted from its view that:

> "Since the residues and by-products resulting from the mine are not as such immediately reused or consumed, they are to be regarded as waste ... In so far as the residues and by-products to be discarded are recovered immediately as such (*inter alia* by returning them to the mine), they are not regarded as waste."[56]

AvestaPolarit appealed this decision to the Finnish Supreme Administrative Court, which referred the matter of whether the left-over rock was waste to the ECJ for a preliminary ruling.

The ECJ noted that the issue raised was substantially similar to that raised by *Palin Granit*. It summarised that earlier decision as having held that:

> "... the holder of leftover stone resulting from stone quarrying which is stored for an indefinite length of time to await possible use discards or intends to discard that leftover stone, which is accordingly to be classified as waste ..."

Moreover,

> "... the place of storage of leftover stone, its composition and the fact, even if proven, that the stone does not pose any real risk to human health or the environment are not relevant criteria for determining whether stone is to be regarded as waste."[57]

In *AvestaPolarit* the ECJ affirmed the statements in *Palin Granit* to the effect that there was a critical distinction to be drawn between "production residues" and by-products; and that, in an appropriate case, it could be argued that materials resulting from a manufacturing or extraction process,

---

[55] Paragraph 27 of the judgment.
[56] At para. 28.
[57] At para. 32.

the primary aim of which was not the production of those materials, could be regarded not as a production residue but as:

> " ... a by-product which the undertaking does not wish to discard ... but intends to exploit or market on terms which are advantageous to it, in a subsequent process, without any further processing prior to reuse."[58]

This "by-products exception" was, however, to be confined to situations where reuse of the materials was not a mere possibility but a certainty; and for such reuse to be a certainty the reuse must be "an integral part of the production process" of the undertaking.

Having stated these principles from the *Palin Granit* case, the court applied them to the facts of *AvestaPolarit* itself and came to the following conclusions.

In so far as non-primary quarried material was to be used, without any processing, for the infilling of underground galleries at the mine, such material was not to be regarded as having been discarded and so was not waste. This was because such material was:

> " ... being used ... as a material in the industrial mining process proper."[59]

The material was not to be regarded as having been discarded because the material was material which was needed for the principal activity of the undertaking. It followed that provided non-primary quarried material destined for such in-quarry use could be identified separately from other non-primary material, and provided that "sufficient guarantee" could be offered to regulators that it would be so used, such material should not be regarded as waste. In reaching a view on this matter in any particular instance, it was open to regulatory bodies to take into account the period of time during which residues said to be proposed for such use were likely to be stored prior to such eventual reuse. It will be remembered that in *AvestaPolarit* such storage was proposed for a period of some 70-100 years, and perhaps the ECJ was hinting to the Finnish Court that this might be regarded as undermining the claim that the material was not to be regarded as waste.

A very different approach applied, however, as regards the other non-primary material (i.e. that which was not necessary in the production process for filling underground galleries). The court stated that such materials "must ... be regarded in their entirety as waste".

In reaching this conclusion the Court adopted a narrow approach to the *Palin Granit* concept of non-waste by-product produced as an integral part of the production process. As explained above a proportion of the left-over

---

[58] At para. 34.
[59] At para. 37.

material was intended to be processed into aggregates. Such material was, however, according to the Court, properly to be characterised as waste. It could not be regarded as a non-waste by-product within *Palin Granit* because it required "processing" before such use was possible.

This decision in *AvestaPolarit* suggests that the concept of "non-waste by-product" may be of quite narrow practical application. However, a word of warning seems appropriate.

It is important that it is remembered that in every case what is crucial is the intent of the undertaking: whether the intent in relation to material is to discard, or whether the intention is something rather different. Care must therefore be taken not to regard decisions such as *Palin Granit* and *AvestaPolarit* as laying down *rules of law* about the legal quality of different categories of material.

To take an example, we may speculate that different operators of different types of quarry (perhaps in different countries and operating under different economic imperatives) might possess rather different mind-sets as regards the variety of materials which result from their quarrying operations. In *Palin Granit* and *AvestaPolarit* the Court approached the facts on the basis that the quarries in question were operated on the basis of there being a clear "primary" product, and that other material (even if it might be processed for sale) was therefore waste (subject to the limited exception for material used on-site, and without processing, for quarry-operations purposes).

No doubt these conclusions were correct interpretations of the evidence in each of those two cases. For the future, however, an open mind should be kept to the possibility that some other quarry operator might present credible evidence that his quarrying operations were motivated in a significantly different way. Take for example the case of a quarry where it might be accurate to say that it was operated not to produce a primary product, but rather was operated with a view to maximising revenue available from an integrated quarrying process through which a range of premium and lower value products were produced.

In such circumstances there would be no good reason for a court to assume that the quarry exists primarily to produce the premium product, or to assume that lower-grade materials are mere production residues. Indeed any such conclusions would be contrary to evidence. It could well be the case that the income derived from the large volume but lower-value material might exceed that from the lower-quantity premium product: but even this may not be essential in evidence. The key is that each product is regarded as an integral part of the economic rationale of the undertaking's business activities at the site.

In any case where this may be a genuine description of the way a quarry is exploited there would seem to be no cause to apply *Palin Granit* as it was applied in *AvestaPolarit*. Indeed in our hypothetical quarry it might be a perfectly legitimate conclusion to draw that aggregate produced alongside a premium product was produced as a main product of the quarry (and not as a by-product at all); or where the products of an aggregate quarry are different grades of aggregate, that low-grade aggregate was produced as a main product alongside premium-grade "main product" aggregate. In short, in such a hypothetical case, we are not concerned with the *Palin Granit* "non-waste by-product" at all. Rather we are concerned with a production process through which two products are produced which are each properly to be regarded as integral to the exploitation of the quarry, and neither should be regarded as a by-product of the other.

Castle Cement

Returning to domestic level a further opportunity to consider the meaning of "waste" arose in *Castle Cement* v *Environment Agency*.[60] The applicants were involved in the business of cement manufacture at sites in Ketton and Ribblesdale. As part of that process, the applicants used a substance known as Cemfuel[61] to fire its cement kilns. Since cement manufacture is a prescribed process for the purposes of Part I of the Environmental Protection Act 1990, the applicants held authorisations under section 6 of the 1990 Act, subject to conditions imposed by the Agency. The challenge in the present proceedings related to later decisions by the Agency to vary the terms of the authorisations. In particular, the Agency sought to vary the conditions of the authorisations in accordance with a direction given by the Secretary of State in 1998 so as to apply the terms of the Hazardous Waste Incineration Directive[62] to the use of Cemfuel at the plants. The varied conditions required reduced air emission limits and the increased monitoring of air emissions.

The issue to be determined by the Administrative Court was whether the burning of Cemfuel at the plants amounted to the burning of "hazardous waste" – as the Agency contended – or whether it was the burning of non-waste fuel – as Castle Cement contended. In argument, Castle Cement did not dispute that if Cemfuel was "waste", it was "hazardous waste" for the purposes of the Directive, or that the fuel was made from various waste streams. However, it contended that the process of recovery of fuel from those waste streams had ceased by the time that it had been produced and that accordingly, when Cemfuel arrived at Castle Cement's sites, it was a raw material akin to any other fuel. For its part, the Environment Agency contended that the burning of Cemfuel in the kilns was a part, indeed it was the end, of the recovery process and that therefore Cemfuel continued to be waste until it was burnt.

In commencing his judgment, Stanley Burnton J noted that the definition of "waste" for present purposes was to be found in the EU Waste Directive, as amended. He continued:

---

[60] [2001] Env LR 813.
[61] A substitute liquid fuel which was produced by an affiliated company of Castle Cement using mainly solvents and liquids derived from waste sources.
[62] 94/67.

"The question is not whether the Environment Agency could reasonably have determined that Cemfuel is waste for the purposes of the relevant legislation, but whether or not it is 'waste'. The question whether Cemfuel is waste for the purposes of the relevant legislation is a jurisdictional question: if Cemfuel is not 'waste', the Environment Agency had no power to issue the variations..."[63]

Stanley Burnton J also noted that in the light of the decision of the European Court of Justice in *ARCO and Epon*, neither party had asked him to refer the matter to that Court for a preliminary ruling under Article 234. In other words, the guidance given by the Court in that case made a reference unnecessary.

Turning to the substance of his judgment, it is worth drawing attention to several quite broad statements of opinion which Stanley Burnton J made prior to his examination of the decision in *ARCO and Epon* and its effect upon the present application. After having commented that it was accepted by both sides that the original constituent substances of Cemfuel were waste and that it was "obvious that material which is not waste can be recovered from waste", he continued:

"There are clearly difficulties in deciding whether a substance has ceased to be waste, and these difficulties are reflected in the jurisprudence. However, subject to the terms of the relevant legislative instruments and guidance from authority, I would expect the question whether a substance derived from waste remains waste to depend not only on the process involved in its production, but also on the nature of the substance itself. I should not regard the fact that the qualities of the substance are highly specified to affect this question. Used tyres remain waste tyres even if their specification is comprehensive and would exclude the very great majority of tyres. Furthermore, the removal of unwanted substances from the material would not of itself cause something to cease to be waste. Whether it does would normally be a question of fact and degree. For example... one would not expect a pure metal recovered from a production process and indistinguishable from the metal produced from natural ore to be regarded as waste."[64]

Stanley Burnton J also commented:

"It is in addition difficult if not impossible to base the classification of a material as 'waste' by comparing its characteristics with regard to the environment or to health with a 'natural' material. Coal may be an environmentally damaging fuel, but it is not waste; asbestos is a natural material which may be extremely damaging to health. Conversely, there may be harmless waste materials. Furthermore, if a comparison is to be made between a particular waste material and a

---

[63] [2001] Env LR 813 at 816-817.
[64] *ibid.* at 818.

non-waste material, the question has to be asked: what non-waste material is to be used for the comparison and what is the basis for the selection? In the case of a fuel, is it to be the most efficient and most environmentally-friendly non-waste fuel, or to the least efficient and least environmentally-friendly non-waste fuel, and why?"[65]

And:

"Furthermore, whether a material is "waste" cannot depend on whether any particular holder of it stores and uses it in an environmentally and otherwise safe manner. Its categorisation should depend on its qualities, not on the qualities of its storage or use. Otherwise, a material would be and cease to be waste, and come within and outside the controls on hazardous waste, as it passed from one holder to another. This would be inconsistent with any rational system of waste control."[66]

Several quite important propositions can be distilled from these passages. It is clear that for Stanley Burnton J, when determining whether a substance is "waste" for the purposes of the legislative regime, the process by which that substance is produced is important. However, it is not the single determining factor. Regard must also be had to the *nature* of the substance. There are other factors, however, which Stanley Burnton J identifies as *not* being helpful when determining whether a substance is "waste". Thus the effect of that substance on the environment or health is not determinative since raw materials can be equally if not more deleterious to both. Moreover, for Stanley Burnton J, the storage and use of the substance in an environmentally-friendly manner does not assist the process of categorisation.

With regard to the jurisprudence of the European Court of Justice on the meaning of "waste", Stanley Burnton J echoed the sentiments of lawyers and regulators alike when he remarked that the guidance given by that Court to the national courts had been "less than pellucid". In support of this observation, he cited the following passage from the judgment of the Court in *ARCO and Epon*:

"Whether (a substance resulting from a recovery operation) is waste must be determined in the light of all the circumstances, by comparison with the definition set out in Article 1(a) of the Directive, that is to say the discarding of the substance in question or the intention or requirement to discard it, regard being had to the aim of the Directive and the need to ensure that its effectiveness is not undermined."[67]

In the opinion of Stanley Burnton J, this amounted to a "Delphic utterance", a sentiment with which few would be inclined to disagree.

---

[65] *ibid.*

[66] *ibid.*

[67] Paragraph 97 of the judgment. Cited in *Castle Cement* at 819.

Later in the same judgment, following an extensive citing of passages from the judgment in *ARCO and Epon*, Stanley Burnton J levelled the same criticism when he remarked that:

> "I confess to finding important parts of the judgment of the European Court of Justice Delphic. However, it is clear that the carrying out of a 'complete' recovery operation, whatever that may be, does not necessarily result in a substance ceasing to be waste. To this extent, the judgment of Carnwath J in *Mayer Parry No.1* must be regarded as superseded."[68]

He concluded:

> "Looking at the issue more broadly, having 'regard... to the aim of the Directive and the need to ensure that its effectiveness is not undermined', I consider that the production process used for Cemfuel is not sufficient to cause its constituent parts to cease to be waste; and that Cemfuel is therefore waste for the purposes of the WFD [Waste Framework Directive] and the relevant controls."[69]

In seeking to explain this conclusion, Stanley Burnton J stated that:

> "... the fact that the specification of Cemfuel and its production processes are tightly controlled is of little assistance. The fact that different waste streams or materials are used in its manufacture is similarly barely relevant. The fact that it is necessary non-waste materials are used to increase the calorific value of the material does not cause it to cease to be waste, given the relative proportions of waste and non-waste materials, and that additives are rarely used ... The maceration of some materials does not change its constitution. What is waste in large pieces is likely to remain waste when reduced to small pieces or even to powder, or if dissolved in a liquid which itself is waste."[70]

It is clear from the decision in *Castle Cement* that the so-called "Tombesi-Bypass" is not the sole approach to be adopted when determining whether or not a substance is waste for the purposes of the EU Waste Directive. Whilst the "Tombesi-Bypass" had its attractions, they were essentially superficial. In terms of applying the law, it would have been convenient to by-pass the often difficult question of whether or not a substance had been discarded and instead focus on Annexes IIA and IIB to the Directive to see if the substance had undergone one of the processes described therein. It may be argued, however, that in matters such as the present, convenience ought not to be allowed to stand in the way of principle. Given that one of the operations mentioned in Annex IIB is "Storage of Waste pending any of the operations R 1 to R 12", the limitations of the "Tombesi-Bypass" approach were all too apparent. Thus, the fact that a substance has

---

[68] [2001] Env LR 813 at 828.
[69] *ibid.* at 829.
[70] *ibid.* at 830.

undergone a recovery operation listed in Annex IIB to the Directive does not necessarily mean that it is waste. As the European Court of Justice stated in *ARCO and Epon*, it is a factor which must be taken into account, but it is not the sole determining factor.[71]

Attorney-General's Reference (No. 5 of 2000)

The Court of Appeal had the opportunity to consider what was meant by the term "controlled waste" and hence to review the case law in this area in *Attorney-General's Reference (No.5 of 2000)*.[72] The reference to the Court arose from the determination of a preliminary issue in favour of a defendant relating to a prosecution for an offence under section 34(1)(a) of the Environmental Protection Act 1990.[73] The defendant in those proceedings operated an animal rendering company. During the process of rendering, a nitrogenous condensate was produced. The company claimed that it had value as a fertiliser, although this point was disputed. What was not in dispute, however, was that the condensate had been collected and spread on farm land owned by a person who was a director of the rendering company as well as being a director of the company which had collected and spread the condensate. All this was done outside the waste management licensing regime. In coming to a conclusion in favour of the defendant on the question of whether the condensate was capable of being "controlled waste", the trial judge had relied on the decision of Carnwath J in *Mayer Parry*:

> "Standing back from all those arguments I have got carefully to analyse whether at the end of the day this condensate can properly be regarded as 'controlled waste'. Bearing in mind the judgment in *Mayer Parry*, what does carry weight with me is that there is here, after the condensate leaves the defendants' rendering premises, no question of a recycling or recovery operation, it is simply placed upon the land, and that in my view is a powerful indication, reading the judgment of the Chancery Division and the opinion of the Advocate General in the European cases, that this is not waste."

The points of law referred[74] to the Court of Appeal by the Attorney-General for its opinion were as follows:

- Whether a substance may only be discarded (and thus become "controlled waste") if it is consigned to a recovery or disposal operation falling within Part 3 or 4 of Schedule 4 to the Waste Management Licensing Regulations 1994.

- Whether the fact that a substance was placed on land without first having been the subject of a recovery operation meant that it was not capable of being "controlled waste".

---

[71] See para. 97 of the judgment of the Court.
[72] [2002] Env LR 139.
[73] See below, at p. 399.
[74] The reference was made under s. 36 of the Criminal Justice Act 1972.

- Whether the fact that a substance is capable of resulting in a benefit to agriculture when applied to land means that it is not capable of being "controlled waste".

In a brief judgment, the Court of Appeal noted that Carnwath J's decision in *Mayer Parry* had been based on an approach which had been championed by Advocate-General Jacobs in *Euro Tombesi and others* and *Wallonie* v *Region Wallonne*, but which had not been endorsed by the European Court of Justice in either of those two cases or, for that matter, in *ARCO and Epon*. Accordingly, in delivering the opinion of the Court of Appeal, Lord Woolf CJ remarked:

"We consider that the approach of Stanley Burnton J [in *Castle Cement*] is correct. The approach of Carnwath J depends upon the references to recovery and disposal operations in Annex IIA and IIB of the Framework Directive. But the Annexes are not included in the definition of waste and so the restrictive approach of Carnwath J is not applicable."[75]

The judgment continues:

"Fortunately for the purposes of this reference it is not necessary for this court to define what is meant by waste or what is meant by discard. It is sufficient in order to give our opinion on the three points of law on which the Attorney-General seeks our opinion to acknowledge that recovery or disposal operations are not required before a substance can be 'controlled waste'. Accordingly we would answer each of the questions on which our opinion is sought in the negative."[76]

It is unfortunate though not surprising that the Court of Appeal confined itself in the present appeal to the questions which had been referred to it and did not therefore elaborate upon the meaning of "waste" or "discard". In the light of the jurisprudence which has emerged from the "waste" cases, it is clear that much turns on the intent of the holder of the material which is alleged to be waste. Moreover, given that this represents a significant subjective element in the meaning of waste, it follows that each case will turn upon its own particular facts.

R (on the application of Mayer Parry Recycling Ltd) v *Environment Agency*

These European Court of Justice proceedings[77] may be regarded as a sequel to the *Mayer Parry* case discussed earlier in this chapter.[78] The decision of the Court has shed some light on the difficult issue of when

---

[75] [2002] Env LR 139 at 144.
[76] *ibid.*
[77] Case C-444/00, ECJ, 19th June 2003.
[78] See above, p. 348.

waste material which has been subjected to a recycling or recovery operation may cease to continue to be "waste".

It will be remembered that in the earlier *Mayer Parry* case the company had challenged the Environment Agency's view as to when scrap metal dealt with at its metal recycling/recovery facilities ceased to be waste. In that case Carnwath J held, in a partial victory for Mayer Parry, that where scrap needed no further processing but was capable of being used as a raw material it was no longer waste.

On that basis[79] Mayer Parry took the view that certain of its operations in relation to packaging waste brought it within the definition of a "reprocessor" of packaging waste under the UK's Packaging Waste Regulations; entitling it to be so accredited with the Environment Agency and to generate income by selling packaging waste recovery notes to those requiring such notes to demonstrate compliance with packaging waste obligations.

In spite of the apparent logic of Mayer Parry's arguments the Agency turned down Mayer Parry's application and, in a challenge brought by Mayer Parry, the High Court referred a number of legal issues to the ECJ.[80]

The essential disagreement between the Agency and Mayer Parry was reasonably simple. Mayer Parry bought scrap metal, including packaging waste, from industrial sources.

It then inspected, sorted, cut, separated and shredded the material, producing so-called "Grade 3B material" which is in turn sold to steelmakers, who use it to produce ingots, sheets or coils of steel (from which, amongst other things, further packaging may be made).

The policy of the Environment Agency was to accredit as the "reprocessor" not those producing the Grade 3B material, but rather the steelmakers who produce the ingots, sheets or coils of steel from that Grade 3B material.

The ECJ heard complex arguments from a variety of interested parties, including steel companies and the Governments of the UK, Denmark, the Netherlands and Austria.

Ultimately the questions for the Court were: Does the concept of "recycling" include the reprocessing of metal packaging waste so as to transform it into a secondary raw material, such as Grade 3B material? Or is material only "recycled" when it has been processed further so as to have produced the ingots, sheets or coils of steel?

---

[79] Note that Carnwath J's views on this matter have been superceded by more recent pronouncements of the ECJ and the UK courts: see above, p. 352.

[80] See *R v Environment Agency, ex parte Mayer Parry Recycling Ltd (No.1)* [2001] Env LR 561.

It was clear that "recycling" was, within the relevant Directives,[81] a form of "recovery operation" and that an essential characteristic of a "waste recovery operation" was that the waste should serve a useful purpose in replacing other materials. It followed that waste must be transformed into its original state in order to be useable for a purpose identical to the original purpose of the material from which it was derived. In other words, metal packaging waste could be regarded as recycled, and hence no longer waste, only when it had undergone reprocessing so as to have produced new material which could be used for the production of metal packaging.

Applying this reasoning to the Grade 3B material the Court noted that the material produced was essentially a secondary raw material suitable for use in substitution for a primary raw material, such as iron ore. The production of Grade 3B material did not, however, involve the reprocessing of metal packaging waste so as to return it to its original state, namely steel, so as also to be reusable for its original purpose, namely the manufacture of metal packaging. Grade 3B material was a mixture which, apart from ferrous elements, contained a number of impurities which had to be removed if the material was to be used to produce steel. As the material could therefore not be used directly for the manufacture of new metal packaging it could not be said that the Grade 3B material had characteristics comparable to those of the material of which the metal packaging was composed, and could not be regarded as recycled packaging waste.

The Court then turned to the question whether, as the Agency believed, the use of Grade 3B material by the steel-manufacturers to produce ingots, sheets or coils of steel could be regarded as a packaging-waste recycling operation. This was found to be the case, since the production process in question resulted in the manufacture of new products (the ingots, etc.) which did possess characteristics comparable to those of the material of which the metal packaging waste incorporated in the Grade 3B material was initially composed, and which could themselves be used for a purpose identical to the original purpose of the material from which that waste was derived, namely the metal packaging.

OFFENCES UNDER SECTION 33 OF THE 1990 ACT: PROHIBITION ON THE UNAUTHORISED OR HARMFUL DEPOSIT, TREATMENT OR DISPOSAL OF WASTE

Section 33(1) provides that a person shall not:

"(a) deposit controlled waste, or knowingly cause or knowingly permit controlled waste to be deposited in or on any land unless a waste management licence authorising the deposit is in force and the deposit is in accordance with the licence;

---

[81] The Waste Framework Directive 75/442 and the Packaging Waste Directive 94/62.

(b) treat, keep or dispose of controlled waste, or knowingly cause or knowingly permit controlled waste to be treated, kept or disposed of

(i) in or on any land, or

(ii) by means of any mobile plant,

except under and in accordance with a waste management licence;

(c) treat, keep or dispose of controlled waste in a manner likely to cause pollution of the environment or harm to human health."[82]

Modification by regulations

The meaning of paragraphs (a) and (b) have been somewhat complicated by certain provisions of the Waste Management Licensing Regulations 1994[83] which have "modified" their meaning. By virtue of Schedule 4 paragraph 9(2) to the Regulations, the offence under section 33(1)(a) may be committed, amongst other ways, by any of the waste disposal operations listed within Schedule 4 Part III, or any of the waste recovery operations listed within Schedule 4 Part IV, so long as the operation in question involves a deposit of waste. This modification seems, however, not to involve a limitation upon the scope of liability under section 33 (1)(a). The offence covers, but is not restricted to, deposits of waste arising from the operations listed in Parts III and IV of Schedule 4.

In contrast Schedule 4 paragraph 9(3) of the 1994 Regulations does seem to modify the scope of criminal liability under section 33. It provides that the concepts, "treatment, keeping and disposal" of waste, as used in section 33 (1)(b) shall be taken to refer to submitting controlled waste to one of the operations listed in Parts III and IV of Schedule 4 to the Regulations, but do not include such an operation if it involves the *deposit* of waste.

The offences in paragraphs (a) and (b) of section 33 are designed to support the waste management licensing system established under sections 35-44 of the 1990 Act, superseding the waste disposal licensing system which had operated under the Control of Pollution Act 1974. The wording of paragraphs (a) and (b) is, however, potentially deceptive. Those paragraphs suggest that the licensing regime is applicable to *all* deposits of controlled waste and to *all* treatment, keeping and disposal of such waste: offences being committed, in certain circumstances, where these things are shown to have been done without, or otherwise than in accordance with, such a licence. In fact, the broad ambit of the waste management licensing regime is subject to significant limits or exceptions, contained in the Waste

---

[82] The offences under s. 33 may be tried summarily or on indictment. The maximum penalties differ depending upon whether the waste in question is, or is not, "special" waste (see ss. 62 and 75 and the Special Waste Regulations 1996, SI 1996/972). Where the offence under s. 33 involves waste which is not "special" waste a defendant may on summary conviction be sentenced to a term of imprisonment not exceeding six months, or a fine not exceeding £20,000, or both. On conviction on indictment a term of imprisonment not exceeding two years and/or an unlimited fine may be imposed. In cases involving "special" waste the potential custodial penalty on conviction on indictment is raised from two years to five: 1990 Act, s. 33(8)(9).

[83] SI 1994 No. 1056.

Management Licensing Regulations 1994. These Regulations accordingly limit also the scope of the offences established by paragraphs (a) and (b) of section 33.[84]

By virtue of section 75(4), "controlled waste" means household, industrial and commercial waste, and each of these expressions is further defined, in subsections (5), (6) and (7) respectively. The ambit of section 33 is therefore broad in terms of the forms of waste by reference to which the offences there contained may be committed. However, one limitation should be noted: section 33(1) does not apply in relation to "household waste from a domestic property which is treated, kept or disposed of within the curtilage of the dwelling by or with the permission of the occupier of the dwelling".[85]

In *Environment Agency* v *Short*,[86] it was necessary for the Divisional Court to consider, inter alia, whether all or any of a load of rubble and timber was "controlled waste" for the purposes of section 33(1) of the 1990 Act. The facts of this case were that the respondent had been carrying out demolition work at an address when he was approached by a landowner who requested that any hardcore be deposited at the piggery on his land. Since this amounted to a more convenient and less expensive disposal option than a trip to a licensed tip, the respondent agreed. Accordingly, a quantity of timber and rubble was taken to the land in question. The timber was thrown off the lorry near to a burning fire and the rubble was then tipped at a different part of the site. On completion of this task, the respondent handed the landowner a Controlled Waste Transfer Note in which the nature of the material that had been deposited was specified. The Note further stated that the person receiving the waste (the landowner) was exempt from the requirement to have a waste disposal or waste management licence since the land was being put to an agricultural use with full planning permission. The respondent failed to check with either the Environment Agency or the local council as to whether the land in question was a licensed site, which it was not. In respect of these events the respondent was charged with offences of having deposited controlled waste on land which did not have a waste management licence authorising such a deposit, contrary to section 33(1) and (6) of the 1990 Act, and with failing to take all such measures as were reasonable in the circumstances to secure that the transfer was only to an authorised person or to a person for authorised transport purposes, contrary to section 34(1)(c)(i) and (6) of the

---

[84] See s. 33(3) and (4) and Regs. 16 and 17 of the 1994 Regulations.

[85] Section 33(2). The occupier of a house who burns rubbish in his garden will not therefore commit an offence under s. 33. However, this example highlights that the scope of the exclusion is limited. The key feature of s. 33(2) is not the reference to "household waste" but the reference to "domestic property". The exclusion applies to the location where the household waste is treated, kept or disposed of rather than to the fact that it is household waste. Thus, no similar exclusion applies in respect of household waste from a caravan, a residential home, premises forming part of a University or School or other educational establishment, or, premises forming part of a hospital or nursing home: see s. 75(5) of the 1990 Act.

[86] [1999] EHLR 3.

1990 Act. The Justices dismissed the informations and the Environment Agency therefore appealed by way of case stated against that decision.

It was submitted on behalf of the Agency that in the light of the definition of "controlled waste" in section 75(4) of the 1990 Act and the terms of Regulation 5(2)(a) of the Controlled Waste Regulations 1992,[87] it followed that both the timber and the rubble came within the definition of waste to be treated as industrial waste since both arose from works of demolition, and that they were therefore controlled waste for the purposes of the 1990 Act. The Divisional Court accepted the force of this submission. However, it was further held by the Court that the rubble fell within the scope of the exemption provided for in Regulation 17 and paragraph 19 of Schedule 3 to the Waste Management Licensing Regulations 1994. In other words, the rubble amounted to waste arising from demolition or construction work which could be stored on the site since it was suitable for use in construction work on either a building, highway, railway, airport, dock or transport facility on that land. Thus the Justices had been entitled to conclude that the rubble satisfied all the requirements set out in the 1994 Regulations and therefore no offence had been committed in respect of its deposit. Such an exemption did not apply, however, in respect of the timber. Its deposit on the land in the absence of a waste management licence did, therefore, amount to an offence under the 1990 Act.

Whether or not waste deposits fell within the scope of exemptions set out in the Waste Management Licensing Regulations 1994 was also at issue in *Environment Agency* v *R Newcomb and Sons Ltd.*[88] Here the first respondent (the company) and the second respondent (one of the company's directors) owned a site which had been purchased with the intention of ultimately creating a football pitch and car park. Planning permission for such a development had been granted by the local authority. The respondents also carried out the screening of waste materials for the production of aggregates in their block-making plant at the site. This activity was entered on the Register of Exempt Activities under paragraph 13 of Schedule 3 to the 1994 Regulations. In any one month the company normally received in the region of 10,000-15,000 tons of pure inert material from the local authority. It had been agreed with the Environment Agency that this material was suitable for the purpose of forming the foundation of a football pitch. It had also been agreed that biodegradable waste was not suitable for such a purpose.

Following its observation of activities at the site and the contents of skips belonging to the company which had been situated outside various household and business premises, the Agency excavated ten trial pits at the site. Material which should not have been present was found in eight of those pits. Analysis of groundwater samples taken from the pits also

---

[87] This regulation provided that: "Waste arising from works of construction or demolition, including waste arising from work preparatory thereto … shall be treated as industrial waste for the purposes of Part II of the Act (except section 34(2)) …"

[88] [2003] EHLR 6.

revealed that they contained leachate. The Agency accordingly sent a letter to the respondent company in which it was made clear that unless the company complied with the terms of the 1994 Regulations, a waste management licence would become necessary for it to continue to carry out its activities. It was further stated in the letter that the exemption from the need for a waste management licence would only be permitted if 95 per cent of the wastes accepted at the site were used in the manufacture of aggregates, and that biodegradable waste was not considered suitable for the company's activities and therefore ought not to be accepted at the site. The company was later charged with offences contrary to section 33 of the Environmental Protection Act 1990.

Before the magistrates, it was accepted that the quantities of waste received at the site which fell outside the scope of the exceptions were within the five per cent working tolerance which the respondent had been led to believe would be acceptable. Accordingly, having reviewed all the evidence before them, the magistrates concluded that the prosecution had not proved its case and the company was therefore acquitted. The Environment Agency appealed by way of case stated.

The appeal raised two issues: the meaning and construction of the provisions which take an activity outside the ambit of the prohibition imposed by section 33; and, where the burden of proof lies in a case such as the present, where it is alleged that there has been a breach of a prohibition in respect of waste disposal activities.

Having regard to the first issue, Newman J considered the relevant legislative provisions and noted that the magistrates had obviously interpreted the Agency's letter to mean that so long as 95 per cent of the material deposited at the site was free from biodegradable waste, the exemption would apply. In his judgment, however, the magistrates had erred in their approach because:

> "The Agency had no power to alter the terms of the exemption created by the Regulations which govern each deposit and provide for no latitude or tolerance."[89]

In other words the magistrates had regarded an informal understanding between the parties as part of the waste management licensing regime itself. They had erred in doing so. Newman J did observe, however, that since he had heard no argument relating to the application of the *de minimis* principle, his judgment should not be taken to exclude the application of that principle. He continued:

> "The court readily understands that for practical purposes it may seem desirable for some form of pragmatic accommodation to be reached between the Agency and a depositor of controlled waste. Depositors may be very keen to achieve some tolerance in connection with deposits so as to relieve them from onerous sorting obligations. It is

---

[89] At para. 19 of the judgment.

not for this court to attempt to lay down the boundaries to be applied in reaching such an accommodation but the Agency should have in mind that subject to a *de minimis* consideration the provisions do not allow for derogation from strict requirements and as this case amply illustrates, if anything is agreed, needless to say it must be in writing, but when so reached great care must be taken in the drafting and it must be perfectly clear and lacking in ambiguity."[90]

Thus it is clear from this passage that, although accommodations between the Agency and those whom it regulates may be desirable, the Agency must be very careful that such accommodations do not later inhibit the effective operation of its enforcement function. It may be possible in some cases for a defendant charged with the unlawful deposit of controlled waste to contend that the deposit fell within the scope of a tolerance agreed to by the Agency. If a court accepts such an argument it may also take the view that the prosecution amounts to an abuse of process.

The second issue raised by the appeal, where the burden of proof lay in a case such as the present, was dealt with more briefly by Newman J. Having regard to the decisions in *R v Lambert*[91] and *Environment Agency v M E Foley (Contractors) Ltd*,[92] Newman J explained:

"… the effect of s.33 of the 1990 Act, so far as it confers a power on the Secretary of State to create exemptions to the general prohibition, is that a deposit of controlled waste falling within the exemption is not prohibited. It follows that if the prosecution allege that there has been a prohibited deposit it is for the prosecution to prove the facts which take the deposit outside the exemption and render it a prohibited deposit. In this appeal the prosecution had to prove that the deposit or deposits contained waste not suitable for the exempted purpose of being used for recreational purposes… It follows that it was not for the respondents to show on the balance of probabilities that the deposits were in relation to the carrying on of an exempt activity."[93]

It follows that where it is alleged that a deposit of waste has occurred in contravention of a permitted exemption to the waste management licensing

---

[90] At para. 20.

[91] [2001] 3 WLR 206.

[92] [2002] Env LR 27. In this case, the Administrative Court had been concerned with where the burden of proof lay where it was alleged that there had been unlawful deposits of special waste at two sites contrary to s. 33 of the 1990 Act. In the judgment of Auld LJ (with which Gage J agreed): "In the case of the first respondent … it was for the prosecution to prove that it had delivered special waste, namely contaminated soil, but not that it had done so without prior written approval. The latter, negative, averment was of a matter peculiarly within the first respondent's knowledge and it was for it to establish the requisite approval on a balance of probabilities if it sought to challenge the prosecution case in that respect. In the case of the first respondent … and for the second respondent when accepting deliveries to the site, it was for the prosecution to prove that the waste respectively delivered and accepted contained special waste, namely contaminated soil, thus taking it outside the exemption" (at paras.28 and 29 of the judgment).

[93] [2003] EHLR 6 at para. 28 of the judgment.

regime, the burden of proof is not thereby transferred to the defendant. In other words, it is not incumbent on the defendant to show, on the balance of probabilities, that the deposit occurred in relation to the carrying on of an exempt activity. Rather, the burden of proof remains with the prosecution and will be discharged only if it can be shown, beyond reasonable doubt, that the deposit in question has exceeded the permitted exception and therefore amounts to a prohibited deposit.

"Deposit"

A critical issue as regards an understanding of the scope of liability under section 33(1)(a) is the proper interpretation to be afforded to the word "deposit":[94] a matter upon which some division of judicial opinion has been evident.

It is convenient to begin with *R* v *Metropolitan Stipendiary Magistrate ex p London Waste Regulatory Authority; R* v *Berkshire County Council ex p Scott*.[95] The key facts and issues in each of these two cases were the same. In each case the defendant operated a waste transfer station – a place to which waste was taken not for permanent storage but pending transfer elsewhere. The issue raised in each case was whether there was in those circumstances a "deposit of controlled waste". In each case the magistrates had felt constrained by an earlier Divisional Court decision – *Leigh Land Reclamation* v *Walsall Metropolitan Borough Council*[96] – to hold that such temporary storage did *not* amount to the "deposit" of waste.[97]

In *Leigh* the reasoning of the Court was explained by Bingham LJ as follows:

> " ... the meaning of 'deposit' takes its colour from the context in which it is used. This statute [the Control of Pollution Act 1974] is concerned, primarily at least, with the manner in which waste is disposed of. Its provisions, and the conditions in the licence, are directed towards the mode of final disposal and not the intermediate processes. For the purposes of the Act, waste is, in my view, to be regarded as deposited when it is dumped on the site with no realistic prospect of further examination or inspection ..."[98]

The appeals in *ex p London Waste Regulation Authority* and *ex p Scott* clearly raised squarely the issue of the correctness of this interpretation of the word "deposit". The Divisional Court looked at certain other sections of the 1974 Act[99] (not referred to in the judgments in *Leigh*) and

---

[94] Important also as regards the ambit of waste management licensing.

[95] [1993] Env LR 417.

[96] [1993] Env LR 16. The case involved a prosecution in relation to the "deposit" of waste at a site prior to its final incorporation into that site: that is, at a time when further checks might have revealed the illegitimate nature of the waste, prior to its final deposit.

[97] The Control of Pollution Act 1974 applied to the "deposit" of waste but not, as does the 1990 Act, to the "keeping, treating, etc." of waste.

[98] [1993] Env LR 16 at 00.

[99] For example, the reference in s. 4(1) to "deposits which ... are of ... a temporary nature ...".

considered these to be suggestive that temporary storage of waste was indeed to be regarded as the "deposit" of waste. The Court also took the view that a purposive approach to the construction of the Act would favour a broader interpretation than was to be found in *Leigh*. In the words of Watkins LJ:

> " ... we feel compelled to conclude ... that section 3(1) is not concerned only with final deposits or disposals. To hold otherwise would, we think, involve an unnecessary erosion of the efficacy of the Act which, in our judgment, is as much concerned with the environmental damage that may be caused by a waste transfer station as with the effects created on or by a site where the waste reaches its 'final resting place'. Since we cannot escape the conclusion that the decision in *Leigh* was to the contrary, we are driven to hold, with respect, that it was wrongly decided."

Relationship between section 33(1) and 33(6)

Any person who contravenes section 33 subsection (1), or who contravenes a condition of a waste management licence, commits an offence.[100] The relationship between these two basic offences requires some explanation. In some cases an offence may be committed under subsection (1) without any breach of condition having occurred: for example, the deposit of waste in circumstances where no licence has been obtained. It may equally be the case that a licence condition has been breached without there having been any offence committed under subsection (1): for example, where required steps preparatory to use of the site have not been properly undertaken by the due date, but prior also to the first deposit of waste. In each of these situations no problem will exist as regards the appropriate charge, whether it be under subsection (1) or subsection (6).

What, though, of the situation where a deposit is said to be unlawful *because* it is in breach of a condition? Should the charge, in such a case, be brought under subsection (1) or under subsection (6)? Or may it be laid under either?

This matter was considered in *Thames Waste Management Ltd* v *Surrey County Council*.[101] The charge against the defendant was laid under section 33(1)(a): that the defendant had unlawfully deposited waste otherwise than in accordance with the conditions in their disposal licence – the waste in question not having been covered at the end of the day on which it had been deposited. On appeal the issue was whether it was proper to have charged the company under the unlawful depositing offence within subsection (1). For the defendants it was contended that at the time at which the material was deposited no illegality had occurred: that the wrongdoing on their part was their failure later in the day to have complied with the licence condition about the daily covering of such deposited waste.

---

[100] Section 33(6).
[101] [1997] Env LR 148.

The defendants contended that the case was comparable to *Leigh Land Reclamation Ltd* v *Walsall Metropolitan Borough Council*[102] which, notwithstanding its false guidance on the matter of the temporary deposit of waste,[103] was argued to remain good authority on this rather different point. In the course of his judgment in *Leigh*, Bingham LJ had said:

> "These deposits of plastic off-cuts, filter cakes, office waste and wood and vegetation, on which these informations were founded, were of authorised materials and no criticism was made of the manner in which they were deposited. To hold that those deposits were not made in accordance with the conditions of the licence because there was some improper deposit previously or because, to take the examples mentioned in argument, there was no sign board or no eating facilities in the site office would be to strain the language of this statute ..."

These arguments did not, however, persuade the Divisional Court in *Thames Waste Management Ltd*. Without doubting the words of Bingham LJ in *Leigh*, or the examples there given, the Divisional Court was of the view that it was open to the magistrates to have construed the notion "deposit" broadly and to have come to the view that, unlike in Bingham LJ's examples, this was a case where the conditions breached did refer to the manner of deposit of the waste. Accordingly, the waste could legitimately be regarded as having been deposited "not in accordance with" the terms of the licence: the offence under subsection (1).

Explaining this view, Rose LJ said:

> "Section 33(6) clearly envisages different kinds of offences, namely a contravention of either subsection (1) or of any condition of a waste management licence. It is apparent that in some cases there will be an overlap between the two subsections because subsection (1) expressly contemplates the possible breach of licence conditions as a result of the different kinds of activities identified in (a) and (b). Subsection (1) states that those two groups of activity must be carried out in accordance with licence conditions."[104]

And later:

> "Accordingly in the present case, as it seems to me, subsection (6) is apt to embrace both the activities in subsection (1) which breach the licence conditions and other breaches not arising from those identified activities. It follows ... that the justices were entitled to conclude that the facts found by them would have justified a charge under both section 33(1)(a) and section 33(6). The fact that failure to cover gave rise to a breach of licence condition under section 33(6) did not preclude a finding that, because of the failure to cover, the

---

[102] [1993] Env LR 16.
[103] See, above, p. 378.
[104] [1997] Env LR 148 at 000.

deposit had not been in accordance with the licence under section 33(1)."

The offence under section 33(1)(c)

The offence under section 33(1)(c) is of rather broader scope than those under paragraphs (a) and (b), in that this offence is not limited to the ambit of the waste management licensing regime. It applies a quite general prohibition:

> "a person shall not treat, keep or dispose of controlled waste in a manner likely to cause pollution of the environment or harm to human health."

Certain words within this offence are given further definition within section 29 of the 1990 Act; although the practical value of this further definition may be doubted, perhaps doing little more than to emphasise the substantial breadth of potential liability. Thus the word "environment" is stated to:

> "consist of all, or any, of the following media, namely, land water and air."

"Pollution of the environment" means:

> "pollution of the environment due to the release or escape (into any environmental medium) from –
> (a)   the land on which the waste is treated,
> (b)   the land on which the waste is kept,
> (c)   the land in or on which controlled waste is deposited,
> (d)   fixed plant by means of which controlled waste is treated, kept or disposed of,
> of substances or articles constituting or resulting from the waste and capable (by reason of the quantity or concentrations involved) of causing harm to man or any living organisms supported by the environment."

In other words it constitutes "pollution of the environment" to release into an environmental medium substances from waste with a *capability* of causing harm. It seems not essential to prove that such harm has actually occurred.

For the purposes of the definition of "pollution of the environment" the word "harm" means:

> "harm to the health of living organisms or other interference with the ecological systems of which they form part and in the case of man includes offence to any of his sense or harm to his property ..."

"Knowingly"?

It will be noted that section 33 creates certain offences in respect of which the prosecution must prove that the defendant acted "knowingly"; but that this requirement of knowledge is not expressly made applicable to all the methods by which the offences may be committed. Thus, to take the offence set out in section 33(1)(a) by way of example, there may be seen to be no express requirement of "knowing" in relation to the first formulation of the offence "depositing controlled waste other than in accordance with a licence": but, in contrast, it is provided expressly that "knowledge" must be proven where it is alleged that a defendant has committed the offence either by "causing" or "permitting" controlled waste so to be deposited.[105]

The distinction between "causing" and "permitting" has been considered earlier, in the context of water pollution offences.[106] In that context the distinction is significant because "knowingly" is a requirement only in relation to the "permitting" charge:[107] the "causing" offence being one of strict liability. In the waste context the position is rather different: "knowledge" must be demonstrated by the prosecution whether the charge, under whichever limb of section 33, is of "causing" or "permitting".

The possibility arises however that a rather different distinction may be critical in relation to criminal liability in the context of waste; "knowledge" not apparently being an essential component of liability where it is alleged that the defendant has actually "done" the things which comprise the offence in question (depositing, treating, keeping or disposing of the waste) rather than with having "caused" or "permitted" those things to have been done or to have occurred.

The above paragraph has been phrased with some caution. This is for two principal reasons. First, the precise distinction between "depositing", "causing" to be deposited and "permitting" to be deposited raises some problematic issues. In the context of water pollution offences we noted that very extensive criminal liability exists by reference to just the second and third of these two categories. Moreover, given the very broad interpretation there afforded to the concept of "causing", one is bound to wonder what separate substance may exist as regards the additional method of committing the offence to be found in these provisions on waste. And secondly, one may wonder whether, notwithstanding the contrasting language used by the draftsman – appending "knowingly" to some but not

---

[105] The distinction between the offences in s. 33(1)(a) is discussed further below, at pp. 383-385.

[106] See, above pp. 299-331.

[107] It should be noted, however, that in *Alphacell Ltd* v *Woodward* [1972] 2 All ER 475, some doubt was expressed about the inclusion of the word "knowingly" before the word "permits". Viscount Dilhorne observed that: "Whether the inclusion of that word [knowingly] before 'permits' makes any difference to the meaning of 'permits', is, I think, open to doubt ..." (at 483). In support of this view, Viscount Dilhorne drew attention to the words of Lord Goddard CJ in *Lomas* v *Peek* [1947] 2 All ER 574, where the latter had opined: "If a man permits a thing to be done, it means that he gives permission for it to be done, and if a man gives permission for a thing to be done, he knows what it is to be done or is being done ..." (at 575 of the latter report). Returning to *Alphacell*, Lord Salmon thought that the inclusion of the word "knowingly" before the word "permits" was "probably otiose" (at 491).

all possible formulations of the offences – the courts would interpret "mere" depositing as involving strict liability.

Some, but not all, of these issues have been explored by the courts in the cases to be described in the sections which immediately follow. We shall need to consider:

- the distinction between (e.g.) depositing controlled waste and causing the deposit of controlled waste;
- the provision of "due diligence", etc. defences, even where liability is strict;
- the scope of the requirement of knowledge: knowledge of what?

DEPOSITING CONTROLLED WASTE AND *CAUSING* THE DEPOSIT OF CONTROLLED WASTE

It is clear in the light of the decision of the Court of Appeal in *R v Leighton and Town and Country Refuse Collection Ltd*[108] that section 33(1)(a) of the 1990 Act creates a single waste offence which may be committed in one of several ways. Thus a defendant will have committed the offence under this section where he: deposits controlled waste in or on land; knowingly causes controlled waste to be so deposited; or knowingly permits the deposit of such waste. In each case, the deposit is required to have taken place otherwise than in accordance with a waste management licence. For present purposes, however, the issue which needs to be considered is whether there is any significance in the absence of the word "knowingly" from the first formulation of the section 33(1)(a) offence. In other words, does the different formulation of words mean that a different offence is contemplated?

The first part of this question can be answered in a relatively straightforward manner. As a matter of English law, there is a general presumption that where a statute creates an offence, *mens rea* is a necessary ingredient of that offence. In *Sherras v De Rutzen*,[109] Wright J explained the position thus:

> "There is a general presumption that mens rea, an evil intention, or a knowledge of the wrongfulness of the act, is an essential ingredient in every offence; but that presumption is liable to be displaced either by the words of the statute creating the offence or by the subject-matter with which it deals, and both must be considered."[110]

The absence of the word "knowingly" from the first formulation of the section 33(1)(a) offence, as contrasted with its presence in the second and third formulations in that subsection, thus suggests that the offence may be committed without *mens rea* needing to be established, whereas the other formulations of the offence require proof of *mens rea* to secure a

---

[108] [1997] Env LR 411.
[109] [1895] 1 QB 918.
[110] *ibid.* at 921.

conviction. In other words, the offence gives rise to strict liability in its first formulation, but not in respect of its other two formulations.

In support of this view it is appropriate to have regard to the Divisional Court decision in *Shanks and McEwan (Teesside) Ltd* v *Environment Agency*, the facts of which are discussed below.[111] For present purposes, it is sufficient to note that in giving judgment in that case, Mance J observed:

> "So far as it is necessary to seek any explanation for the insertion of the word 'knowingly' before 'cause' in the 1990 Act, when it did not appear in the 1974 Act,[112] one likely explanation is that it was considered appropriate to assimilate the operation of s 33(1) in cases of permission and causation, where the person responsible for the deposit may be less immediately involved than the person actually undertaking the deposit. On this basis, s 33(1)(a) makes clear that in both cases a defendant must know that controlled waste is to be deposited in or on any land. Once he knows this, the strict obligation imported by the rest of s 33(1)(a) comes into play. The initial case of a person actually depositing controlled waste in or on any land remains free of any expressed requirement of knowledge. Normally, no doubt, such a person would know what he was doing. Even if he was, for some reason, under a misapprehension, he could in appropriate circumstances establish a defence under s 33(7)(a)."[113]

In this passage, Mance J acknowledges the distinction that we have already drawn between the first formulation of the offence in section 33(1)(a) and the second and third formulations of the offence in that subsection in respect of the requirement of knowledge. Perhaps more important, however, is the recognition that the first formulation of the offence is directed at the person who actually deposited the controlled waste on the land, or as one commentator has put it, "persons who are inevitably located in close proximity to the offence".[114] In practice, this person is likely to be an employee who has, for example, driven a consignment of waste to a site and has there deposited it on the land. However, need this necessarily be the case? In other words, is the first formulation of the of section 33(1)(a) confined to employees, or might it also cover the conduct of an employer?

In answering this question, regard may usefully be had to the remarks of Laurence in *Waste Regulation Law*. In that book, the author states:

> "From the face of s 33(1)(a) of the EPA 1990, it is not clear whether or not a driver *and* an employer can be convicted of *depositing* waste, or whether it should be alleged that the driver is 'depositing' waste and the employer is either 'knowingly causing' (or even 'knowingly permitting') the deposit. However, if it is held that only the driver 'deposits' waste, then this does not appear to fall in line with the

---

[111] [1997] 2 All ER 332; [1997] Env LR 305; see p. 396.
[112] The Control of Pollution Act 1974.
[113] [1997] 2 All ER 332 at 340.
[114] Laurence, *Waste Regulation Law*, para. 7.117.

construction and purpose of s 33(1)(b). No driver is ever likely to 'treat' or 'keep' waste – this is likely to be the function of the organisation as a whole."[115]

There appears to be much force in these submissions. In support of the argument, the author draws a parallel between section 33(1)(a) (and section 33(1)(b)) and road traffic law.[116] As Laurence points out, offences in the latter legislation which refer to the "user" of the vehicle as well as to persons who "cause or permit" the vehicle's use have not been accorded a narrow construction by the courts. In other words, it has been held that the scope of an employer's liability is not confined to causing or permitting the vehicle's use; an employer may be said to use the vehicle where an employee is driving it on the employer's business.[117] If section 33(1)(a) is sufficiently wide to cover an employer as well as an employee, there are clear advantages for the prosecution in this state of affairs. In effect it would mean that the prosecution would have a lesser evidential burden to discharge than if they were compelled to rely upon the other formulations of the offence in subsection (1)(a), both of which, as we have already seen, require proof of knowledge on the part of the defendant.

Deposit from motor vehicles

Section 33(5) makes special provision in respect of the deposit of waste from motor vehicles. It provides:

> "Where controlled waste is carried in and deposited from a motor vehicle, the person who controls or is in a position to control the use of the vehicle shall for the purposes of subsection (1)(a) above be treated as knowingly causing the waste to be deposited whether or not he gave any instructions for this to be done."

The purpose behind this provision would appear to be to make it easier for the Environment Agency to secure a conviction in the case of fly tipping. In such cases, the exact circumstances leading up to the commission of the offence will often be obscure. Two facts may, however, be known: that tipping has taken place; and the identity of the vehicle from which the waste was deposited. Section 33(5) therefore eases the task of the prosecution by deeming that the person who controls or is in a position to control the vehicle shall be treated as having knowingly caused the waste to be deposited irrespective of whether or not he gave instructions for this to be done. In other words, *prima facie* guilt for the unlawful deposit of waste is established by reason of a defendant's control of the relevant vehicle at the material time.

---

[115] At para. 7.136.

[116] A parallel which, as he acknowledges, was alluded to by the Court of Appeal in *R v Leighton and Town and Country Refuse Ltd* [1997] Env LR 411 at 416.

[117] See, for example, the following cases to which Laurence refers (at para. 7.137): *James & Son Ltd v Smee* [1954] 3 All ER 273; *Ross Hillman v Bond* [1974] RTR 279; and, *Hallett Silberman v Cheshire County Council* [1993] RTR 32.

In *Environment Agency* v *Melland*,[118] a motor vehicle had been observed driving onto an industrial estate on three separate occasions and depositing, by means of a skip, controlled waste consisting of garden waste, window frames and general household waste. The respondent was not the driver of the vehicle at the material times, and the registered keeper of the vehicle at the Driver Vehicle Licensing Agency was Melland Skip Hire. The Environment Agency served a statutory notice on the respondent pursuant to section 71 of the Environmental Protection Act 1990 requiring him to state whether or not he was the owner or keeper of the vehicle on the relevant dates. The respondent replied that he was. Since he was not the holder of a waste management licence authorising the disposal of controlled waste on the relevant dates, he was therefore charged with knowingly depositing controlled waste on land contrary to section 33(1)(a) and (6) of the 1990 Act.

At his trial before the justices, it was submitted on behalf of the respondent that there was no case to answer. The submission was based on the terms of section 33(5). It was argued that the mere fact that he was the owner or keeper of the vehicle at the material times was insufficient evidence to show that he was in control of it or in a position to control its use on the dates in question. The justices accepted the force of that submission and accordingly dismissed the informations laid against him. The Environment Agency appealed against that decision by way of case stated.

The question for the opinion of the Administrative Court was stated as follows:

> "Were we correct in law in our decision to dismiss the informations upon a submission of no case to answer on the basis that the appellant had failed to produce sufficient evidence tending to show that the respondent was a person in control or in a position to control the use of the vehicle on the days in question for the purposes of section 33(1)(a) and 33(5) Environmental Protection Act 1990?"

On behalf of the Agency, it was submitted that this question ought to be answered in the negative. Whether or not a person controls, or is in a position to control a vehicle at the relevant time was, it was submitted, essentially a question of fact and common sense. It was further submitted, therefore, that once it has been established that a defendant was the owner or keeper of the vehicle at the relevant time, that amounted to sufficient evidence that he controlled, or was in a position to control, the vehicle.

Harrison J, who heard the appeal, accepted the force of the Agency's argument and therefore held that:

---

[118] [2002] Env LR 29.

"... evidence of ownership of a vehicle is capable of amounting to prima facie evidence that the owner controls, or is in a position to control, the vehicle."[119]

His Lordship then sought to clarify these remarks as follows:

"I stress the words 'is capable of' amounting to prima facie evidence because there may be evidence before the court that, at the material time, the vehicle had been stolen or that it had been loaned to another or that it was a hired vehicle. If, for instance, the owner was Hertz or Avis or some other well known hire company, the court would be entitled to decline to draw the inference that ownership carried with it the ability to control the vehicle."[120]

Thus it is evident that in each particular case, whether or not a defendant was the person who was in control, or was in a position to control, the relevant vehicle at the time of the commission of an offence contrary to section 33(1), will be a matter to be determined according to the facts of that case. On the facts in *Melland*, Harrison J had little difficulty in concluding that the respondent, who traded as Melland Skip Hire, was the owner or keeper of the vehicle at the material times and that it could be inferred, therefore, that he also controlled, or was in a position to control, the vehicle at those times. In the opinion of Harrison J such a conclusion did not involve any transfer of the legal burden of proof:

"The burden of proof remains on the prosecution. Once the prosecution had adduced evidence amounting to a prima facie case, it is, as in all criminal cases, up to the defendant to decide whether or not to give or call evidence or to rely on submissions."[121]

The fact that a defendant was in control of, or in a position to control, a vehicle at the time of the commission of a section 33(1) offence does not mean, however, that a conviction will inevitably follow. It may be that the facts of the case are such that he will seek to rely upon one of the statutory defences set out in section 33(7) of the 1990 Act. Accordingly in the discussion which follows, the nature and scope of those defences will be considered.

DUE DILIGENCE, ETC. DEFENCES

Section 33(7) provides certain general defences to liability under subsection (1) and the breach of condition offence under subsection (6).

Thus, it is a defence for a defendant so charged to prove:

(a) that he took all reasonable precautions and exercised all due diligence to avoid the commission of the offence; or

---

[119] At para. 16 of the judgment.
[120] *ibid.*
[121] At para. 20.

(b) that he acted under instructions from his employer and neither knew nor had reason to suppose that the acts done by him constituted a contravention of subsection (1) above, or

(c) that the acts alleged to constitute the contravention were done in an emergency in order to avoid danger to human health in a case where –

    (i) he took all such steps as were reasonably practicable in the circumstances for minimising pollution of the environment and harm to human health; and

    (ii) particulars of the acts were furnished to the waste regulation authority as soon as reasonably practicable after they were done.

The onus of proof in respect of each of these statutory defences will rest firmly with the defendant. This is entirely reasonable given that knowledge of the facts which constitute the defence will often lie exclusively with the defendant. By providing for statutory defences, the drafters of the 1990 Act have reinforced the point that the section 33 offences are not absolute. In other words, although Parliament wished to create various offences in respect of the deposit etc. of controlled waste, it did not wish liability to attach to a defendant regardless of blameworthiness.

Due diligence

The key feature of this defence is the need for the defendant to show that he took all reasonable precautions and that he exercised all due diligence. In this context, the word "reasonable" would seem to have the meaning ascribed to it in *Austin Rover Group* v *HM Inspector of Factories*.[122] In that case, which concerned a prosecution for an alleged breach of duty under section 4(2) of the Health and Safety at Work etc. Act 1974 that had resulted in a fatal accident, Lord Jauncey of Tullichettle observed in the context of the statutory duty that:

> "…'reasonable' relates to the person and not to the measures. The question is not whether there are measures, which themselves are reasonable which could be taken to ensure safety and the absence of risk to health but whether it is reasonable for a person in the position of the accused to take measures with these aims. The emphasis is on the position of the accused."[123]

Thus it would seem that the word "reasonable" in the context of section 33(7)(a) imports a subjective element into the defence. Accordingly, provided that a defendant can show that the precautions which he took to avoid the commission of a waste offence were reasonable with regard to his own particular position, it would not matter that there were some other reasonable precautions which could have been taken.

---

[122] [1989] 3 WLR 520.

[123] *ibid.* at 534.

Guidance as to the meaning of "due diligence" can also be obtained from the decision in *Riverstone Meat Co* v *Lancashire Shipping Co*.[124] The facts of this case are not important in the present context, suffice it to say that damage had been caused to a ship's cargo where sea water entered the hold during a voyage as a consequence of a fitter's failure properly to secure nuts on two inspection covers. The cargo owners claimed damages against the shipowners on the ground that they had failed in their duty to exercise due diligence to make the ship seaworthy as required by the Hague Rules. The Court of Appeal held that the shipowners were not liable[125] to pay damages for a number of reasons, which included that the fitter was not the servant of the shipowners but of independent contractors. For present purposes, however, we need only note the words of Willmer LJ who observed that:

> "An obligation to exercise due diligence is to my mind indistinguishable from an obligation to exercise reasonable care – a concept not unfamiliar in English law, and one to be sharply distinguished from the obligation, to which certain relationships give rise, to see that care is taken."[126]

Assuming that "due diligence" and "reasonable care" are indeed synonymous, as Willmer LJ suggested, it follows that due diligence is an elastic concept. In other words, whether a defendant has acted with all due diligence will depend upon the particular circumstances of the case which include the prevailing standards of the day. What may have been a diligent way to have acted to avoid the commission of a waste offence 20 or 30 years ago may not be so today.

The due diligence defence in subsection (7)(a) exists in similar form also in other statutory contexts. Thus, for example, a defendant who is charged with engaging in street trading in a prohibited area or of contravening any of the principal terms of a street trading licence may seek to rely on the defence that he took all reasonable precautions and exercised all due diligence to avoid the commission of the offence.[127] In *South Tyneside Metropolitan Borough Council* v *Jackson*,[128] the respondent was charged with engaging in street trading in a prohibited area contrary to paragraph 10(1)(a) of the Local Government (Miscellaneous Provisions) Act 1982. He performed music on the streets from a wheeled unit which he was able to move as he continued to play. At the material times, the respondent had a pedlar's certificate granted under the Pedlars Act 1871. The significance of being a pedlar was that such persons were exempt from the prohibition on street trading. In order to ensure that he was able to rely upon this exemption, the respondent had studied the law relating to pedlars and had designed his unit to conform with his understanding of the legal definition

---

[124] [1960] 1 All ER 193.

[125] This decision was reversed on appeal by the House of Lords: see [1961] 1 All ER 495.

[126] [1960] 1 All ER 193 at 219.

[127] See the Local Government (Miscellaneous Provisions) Act 1982, s. 3 and Sched. 4, para. 10(2).

[128] [1998] EHLR 249.

of "pedlar" in section 3 of the 1871 Act. Moreover, the respondent had sought the advice of the relevant Police Authority as to what was required to fall within the definition and he had taken counsel's opinion on the point. Thus on the occasions when the offences were alleged to have been committed, the respondent was acting in a manner which he believed to be legal and in accordance with his pedlar's certificate. Before the magistrates, the two informations laid against him were dismissed. However, the prosecutor's appeal against that decision succeeded. In the opinion of the Divisional Court, based on the relevant authorities,[129] what the respondent did was not peddling within the meaning of the 1871 Act and therefore he was not exempt from the street trading regime under the 1982 Act. With regard to the due diligence defence, the Divisional Court noted the lengths that the respondent had gone in order to avoid transgressing the law, although as Kennedy LJ accepted:

> "... he did not consult the local authority, so I suppose it could be argued that he had not taken 'all' reasonable precautions, but he may well have thought that it would be the police rather than the local authority who would be seeking to enforce the law."[130]

Despite those efforts, however, the defence of due diligence failed because:

> "Generally speaking ignorance of the law, even on the part of the defendant who has made inquiries, is no defence."[131]

In an earlier case, *Stevenage Borough Council* v *Wright*,[132] magistrates had accepted that the due diligence defence had been made out by a defendant who had been able to show that the past acceptance of his pedlar's certificate by the police and by local authority officials in other areas caused him to believe that he was entitled to trade as he had been doing at the time of the commission of the alleged offence. On appeal, however, the Divisional Court rejected this finding. In the words of Leggatt LJ, such a finding amounted to:

> "...an assertion that a person who, for no better reason than that proceedings have not previously been taken against him, erroneously believes that lawfully he is entitled to do what he has in fact done, has

---

[129] In his judgment, Kennedy LJ referred to *Watson* v *Malloy* [1988] 1 WLR 1026, *Norman* v *Alexander* (1994) SLT 274, *Shepway District Council* v *Vincent* (unreported) 29th March 1994, *Tunbridge Wells Borough Council* v *Dunn* (unreported) 19th March 1996 and *Stevenage Borough Council* v *Wright* (1997) 161 JP 13. For a discussion of these and other cases in this area, see Parpworth and Thompson, "To be or not to be a pedlar: That is the question" (1998) 17 Tr. Law 201-212.

[130] [1998] EHLR 249 at 256.

[131] *ibid.* In support of this proposition, Kennedy LJ cited a passage from Smith and Hogan's *Criminal Law* (8th edition), Butterworths, at pp. 83-84.

[132] (1997) 161 JP 13.

taken all reasonable precautions and exercised all due diligence to avoid breaking the law."[133]

It is apparent from both of these authorities that whether or not a defence of due diligence will succeed depends very much upon the particular facts of the case. In *Environment Agency v Short*,[134] the facts of which were discussed above,[135] it will be remembered that after tipping rubble and timber at a site, the respondent had been handed a Controlled Waste Transfer Note in which it was stated that the person receiving the waste (Mr. James) was exempt from the requirement to have a waste disposal or waste management licence because the land was being put to an agricultural use with full planning permission. It was also found as a matter of fact that the respondent did not check with either the Environment Agency or the local council whether the site in question was a licensed landfill site. Nevertheless, the magistrates held that in respect of the deposit of timber, the respondent was entitled to rely on the section 33(7)(a) defence. However, on appeal, the Divisional Court rejected such a finding. In the words of Bell J:

> "One is always very reluctant to interfere with a decision of Justices on the question of whether a section 33(7) defence has been made out … In my view, however, the Justices could not legitimately come to the decision which they did, for the simple reason that what was in Mr. Short's mind as excusing the deposit of the timber on Mr. James' land was the fact of an agricultural user carrying with it permission for construction of the road without planning permission. That clearly could not, in this case, apply to the timber which, however late in the day, he chose to leave behind at Mr. James' site for burning, and thereby deposit … The inquiries which Mr. Short made of Mr. James and the answers which he elicited from Mr. James could not offer any good reason for being allowed to leave the wood where Mr. Short did in the circumstances where Mr. James did not have the appropriate licence."[136]

In *Durham County Council v Peter Connors Industrial Services*[137] an information was laid against the respondent alleging that it had committed an offence contrary to section 3 of the Control of Pollution Act 1974. The facts as found by the justices were that the respondent carried on the business of transporting industrial waste from factories to waste disposal sites. Under one contract, it was required to collect controlled waste (but not special waste) from the site of a founder of metal castings. The arrangement was that the founder would leave the waste in a skip provided by the respondent at the founder's premises. One of the respondent's drivers would then collect the waste, after checking as far as possible that toxic materials were not included in the consignment, and take it to a waste

---

[133] *ibid.* at 15.
[134] [1999] EHLR 3.
[135] See p. 374.
[136] [1999] EHLR 3 at 10.
[137] [1993] Env LR 197.

disposal site. On the day in question, the consignment which had been collected and then deposited had contained a number of drums marked as containing or having contained hazardous chemicals. One such drum was found to contain special waste. Before the justices, the information was dismissed. The court held that the respondent had been entitled to rely upon the defence in section 3(4) of the 1974 Act. This provided that:

> "It shall be a defence for a person charged with an offence under this section to prove
> (a)   that he—
> > (i)   took care to inform himself, from persons who were in a position to provide the information, as to whether the deposit or use to which the charge relates would be in contravention of subsection (1) of this section, and
> > (ii)   did not know and had no reason to suppose that the information given to him was false or misleading and that the deposit or use might be in contravention of that subsection."

The prosecutor's appeal to the Queen's Bench Division was, however, successful. That court concluded that on the facts as found by the justices, they could not have determined that the statutory defence was properly made out. In the words of Beldam LJ:

> "The requirement of the section is clear. It requires a person to receive information about the specific deposit or use to which the charge relates and a system which merely relies on a general provision of a skip into which the producer of the waste can put material without being required to give any information to the person who is going to deposit the load is clearly one which is not sufficient to fulfil the requirement to take care to inform himself whether the deposit would be in contravention of section 1."[138]

Although the defence in section 3(4) of the 1974 Act was different to the statutory defences which now appear in the 1990 Act, the decision in *Durham County Council* v *Peter Connors Industrial Services* does shed some light on the due diligence defence. Were the same facts to occur now, it would seem highly unlikely that a defendant who acted in the manner that the respondent did in that case would be able successfully to argue that he had taken all reasonable precautions and exercised all due diligence to avoid the commission of a section 33 offence. A visual inspection of a consignment of waste is a precaution of sorts, but in practice it will not satisfy the high standard of care which is implicit in the due diligence defence. As will become apparent later in this chapter,[139] the Code of Practice in respect of the section 34 Duty of Care in the Management of

---

[138] *ibid.* at 200.
[139] See below, at pp. 399-414.

Waste requires a waste producer to give rather more information[140] to the person to whom he transfers the waste than was given in *Peter Connors*.

Acting under instructions from an employer

The defence in section 33(7)(b) applies in respect of an employee who is acting under orders from his employer. The defence will only apply, however, where the defendant is able to show that he neither knew nor had reason to suppose that the acts done by him constituted a section 33(1) offence. It has been suggested that the defence is "principally aimed at persons who are drivers of waste delivery vehicles or lowly plant operatives".[141]

Some guidance as to the meaning of "suppose" was offered in *Kent County Council v Rackham*,[142] albeit in the context of section 3(4)(a)(ii) of the Control of Pollution Act 1974. In applying one of the main canons of construction, that in the absence of a statutory definition, words in an Act of Parliament should be accorded their ordinary and natural meaning, French J remarked that:

> "I would attribute to 'suppose' a meaning closer to 'suspect' than to 'believe'... Regarding the meaning of 'suppose', the Shorter Oxford English Dictionary contains among the definitions of the word 'suppose' the following: 'to have in mind or as an object of thought or speculation; to think of, conceive, imagine, contextually to suspect'. In my judgment, that supports the construction ... which I would favour."[143]

The emergency defence

We have already seen that section 89(1) of the Water Resources Act 1991 provides for an emergency defence to a charge of causing or knowingly permitting the pollution of controlled waters contrary to section 85 of the 1991 Act.[144] The defence in section 33(7)(c) is expressed in broadly similar terms. Two distinctions can, however, be made. The 1991 Act justifies an entry or discharge on the basis that it was done "in order to avoid danger to

---

[140] Essentially, this will entail an identification and description of the waste which is to be transferred.

[141] See Laurence, *Waste Regulation Law*, para. 7.152.

[142] (unreported) 4th February 1991, cited in Laurence, *ibid.* In giving judgment, the High Court upheld an appeal by the County Council against the decision of the Crown Court. That Court had accepted the respondent's argument that the statutory defence under s. 3(4)(a)(ii) had been made out. However, the High Court considered that it was an "absurd and vain hope" for the respondent to think that he could rely on the defence. The facts as found by the Crown Court, which indicated that council officials were of the opinion that a licence was required for the collecting and disposal of abandoned vehicles and that the respondent was well aware of this view, meant that "no court could possibly accept that the respondent was able to establish that he had no reason to suppose that he might be in breach of the law" (per Watkins LJ).

[143] Watkins LJ, who gave the other, briefer judgment in the case, remarked that: "The words 'might' and 'suppose' are much used English words. Their meaning in my view is plain. A jury might require some assistance as to their meaning but surely not Justices, and certainly not a judge in the Crown Court."

[144] See Chapter 9, at p. 333.

life or health" whereas the 1990 Act refers to the acts being done "in order to avoid danger to human health". In truth, however, there is little significance in the different wording.

The other distinction which can be drawn between the two provisions concerns the taking of all such steps as were reasonably practicable to minimise the effect of the defendant's acts. In the case of the 1991 Act, those steps relate to minimising the extent of the entry or discharge into a watercourse and of its polluting effects. In the 1990 Act, however, the steps relate to minimising the pollution of the environment *and* harm to human health. Unless the phrase "polluting effects" encompasses "harm to human health", which seems unlikely, the 1990 Act therefore imposes an additional burden on a defendant seeking to rely upon the emergency defence.

The meaning of "emergency" was considered in *Waste Incineration Services and another* v *Dudley Metropolitan Borough Council*.[145] Here the first appellants were the operators of a waste incineration plant in the Dudley area. They held a waste disposal licence which was subject to a number of conditions. One such condition provided that, save in an emergency, the receipt and/or removal of waste outside of specified hours[146] or on a Sunday or bank holiday was prohibited, unless it was with the prior approval of the waste disposal authority. Another condition stipulated that waste should not be allowed to accumulate at the site unnecessarily, and that clinical waste should be disposed of on the day of receipt. A nearby hospital was unable for a variety of reasons to incinerate all of its waste on site. Accordingly, it entered into an arrangement with the first appellants whereby they would collect and dispose of the waste. On the occasion in question, the first appellants collected waste (1,600 bags) which had accumulated over a weekend and incinerated it on the Easter Bank Holiday Monday without the prior approval of the waste disposal authority.[147] They were duly charged and convicted before the justices of having failed to dispose of controlled waste in accordance with the conditions of a site licence contrary to sections 3(1)(b) and 3(2) of the Control of Pollution Act 1974. The second appellant, the managing director of the first appellant, was also found guilty on the basis that the offence had been committed with his consent or connivance or was attributable to his neglect,[148] contrary to sections 3(1)(b), 3(2) and 87(1) of the 1974 Act.[149]

---

[145] [1993] Env LR 29.

[146] The hours in question were 07.30 to 17.30, Mondays to Saturdays.

[147] It was accepted that had the waste remained on the hospital site, no offence would have been committed, or the hospital would have been covered by Crown immunity: see [1993] Env LR 29 at 32.

[148] For a general discussion of the criminal liability of a director of a body corporate where an environmental offence has been committed, see Chapter 7.

[149] It was found as a matter of fact by the justices that the managing director had given instructions to carry out the incineration on the Easter Bank Holiday Monday.

On appeal, the High Court was required to consider a number of questions. The first of these related to where the onus of proof lay in establishing whether or not an emergency existed. Did it lie with the prosecution beyond reasonable doubt? Or with the defence on the balance of probabilities? In giving the judgment of the court, Nolan LJ dealt with this point quite briefly, In his opinion:

> "… the burden rests upon the defence to bring itself within the exception for emergencies, no matter whether it does so by way of a direct answer to the charge under section 3(1)(b) or by way of reliance upon the statutory defence in subsection (4)(d)."[150]

Turning to the second question, whether when determining if an emergency existed it was appropriate for the justices to have regard to the appellants site only or to the hospital as well, Nolan LJ remarked:

> "As to that, the parties agree, and so do I, that the appropriate course for the justices was to look at all the relevant circumstances, including the situations existing both at the plant and at the hospital."[151]

The third question raised by the appeal was the most significant for the appellants in that it was concerned with whether the justices had been correct in their finding that on the evidence before them, no emergency had existed as defined by the condition of the waste disposal licence. In answering this question, the High Court noted that the absence of a definition of "emergency" in the licence condition meant that the word must bear its ordinary meaning. Having regard to the dictionary, the court further noted that:

> "'emergency' means a state of things unexpectedly arising and urgently demanding immediate attention."[152]

Whether or not an emergency situation had existed at the material time was a question of fact to be determined according to the evidence. For the appellants, it was argued that the incineration of the waste had been justified on a number of grounds: that the accumulation of clinical waste in a hospital courtyard which was accessible to the public and animals amounted to a public health hazard; that no other incineration facilities other than those of the appellants were available; that given reasonable notice, the first appellant could have provided the hospital with lockable containers for temporary storage of the waste, but that no such notice was given; and that the need to comply with the licence condition required waste to be disposed of by the first appellant on the day of receipt. On behalf of the respondents, it was accepted that on the day in question, the hospital had no disposal outlet available other than the first appellant. However, it was argued that the hospital would have sought temporary

---

[150] [1993] Env LR 29 at 33.
[151] *ibid.*
[152] *ibid.*

storage facilities on its own site had it been aware of the licence condition. Moreover, attention was drawn to the justices' finding that neither the first nor the second appellants had made any effort to obtain permission from the disposal authority for incineration on the Bank Holiday, despite the fact that such permission could have easily been sought.

The High Court preferred the respondent's arguments and accordingly dismissed the appeal. In the words of Nolan LJ:

> "The most important single factor, in my judgment, was the failure of the appellants to seek approval from the Authority for the Bank Holiday incineration ... The plain purpose of the Condition is that the Authority should retain control over incineration outside the permitted periods, save only in an emergency which calls for incineration without their approval. This is sensible purpose because in many cases, if not the present case, the Authority might be able to provide a solution for the problem other than immediate incineration. The exception for emergencies is designed to provide for cases in which it is impracticable for approval to be sought. This was not such a case."[153]

It is clear from the decision in *Waste Incineration Services* that determining whether or not an emergency situation existed at the material time will depend upon an objective assessment of all the relevant circumstances. Since this is a question of fact for a court of first instance to determine, it is unlikely that its decision will be overturned on appeal unless the evidence suggests that the conclusion was not reasonable in the circumstances. In the present case, the "emergency" was partly of the appellants' own making. The waste did not have to be removed from the hospital site; it could have been left in secure containers until after the Bank Holiday when it could have been incinerated in accordance with the appellants' licence. By removing the waste and then incinerating it on the Bank Holiday, the appellants had breached one condition of the licence in order to satisfy another, i.e. disposal of clinical waste on the day of receipt.

THE REQUIREMENT OF KNOWLEDGE: KNOWLEDGE OF WHAT?

The leading judicial discussion of this issue is to be found in *Shanks and McEwan (Teeside) Ltd* v *Environment Agency*.[154] The case involved operations at the defendant's waste disposal site in Hartlepool. The company was charged with having knowingly caused controlled waste to have been deposited at its site, which deposit was not in accordance with a condition of its waste management licence: the condition in question being that an Advice Note should issue in relation to each tanker, indicating the location of the tank into which that vehicle should discharge its load. The facts involved a tanker, which had received instructions and an Advice

---

[153] *ibid.* at 35.
[154] [1997] Env LR 305.

Note on arrival at the site, subsequently being instructed, by a less senior employee of the defendant company, to discharge other than to the tank referred to in the Note, and with no new Note having been prepared and issued. An argument raised by the defendant centred on the proposition that it was essential for the prosecution to prove that the company knew not only of the waste being deposited, but also to prove that it knew that the deposit was in breach of the site licence condition. Such knowledge was to be attributed to the company only if known by persons more senior than the employee who had given the revised instruction. Accordingly, the defendant company contended, it should not be considered to have known of the deposit in breach of the condition, and therefore should not bear liability.

The Divisional Court rejected these arguments. It took a quite broad view of the "knowledge" which could be attributed to a company, not accepting that a company knew only what was known to those employees who might constitute its "directing mind and will".[155] However, even on the basis that knowledge on the part of senior management *was* necessary, what knowledge was it that was necessary?

We may begin by noting the conclusion drawn by Mance J:

> "The issue of principle before us is simply whether a company may under section 33(1)(a) be said to have knowingly caused a deposit by operating a business inviting such deposits to be made in or on its land. The answer to this … is that, if section 33(1)(a) does require knowing causation of the deposit in or on land at Tafts Road West on July 31, 1995 on the part of senior management, then it is sufficient that the appellant company's senior management knowingly operated and held out the site … for the reception and deposit in and on it of just such controlled waste. It is unnecessary to show more specific knowledge regarding particular loads on the part of senior management …"[156]

The process of reasoning which led to this conclusion was founded upon the proper construction of section 33(1). The issue was whether the word "knowingly" qualified only the words "deposit", "treat", "keep" or "dispose": or whether knowledge was also required that such deposit (etc.) was a deposit which was not in accordance with a licence condition. The former interpretation was preferred by the court. Mance J explained:

> "I take first the issue whether the knowledge required … goes to the breach of condition as well as to the deposit … The structure of the section is that the word 'knowingly' qualifies on its face two (out of three) of the cases identified in its first part;[157] and the exception beginning 'unless a waste management licence' appears as a separate

---

[155] See further, above, p. 227.
[156] [1997] 2 All ER 332 at 341.
[157] [ed.] That is, "causing" and "permitting".

factual qualification in all three cases, not involving any requirement of knowledge ..."[158]

This conclusion followed the view taken in an earlier decision of the Divisional Court, *Ashcroft* v *Cambro Ltd*,[159] upon the substantially similar wording within the earlier Control of Pollution Act 1974.[160] In that case, the justices had found as a matter of fact that the defendant company's director with overall responsibility for the relevant site had no knowledge that the conditions of a waste disposal licence had been contravened. The site foreman, who did know of the contravention, was responsible for the practical operation of the site, but he had not had any of the functions of management delegated to him. The justices dismissed the informations. On appeal, the issue for the Divisional Court was whether it was necessary for the prosecution to show not only that the respondents had knowingly permitted the deposit of waste but also that any person concerned with the management of the company had knowingly permitted a breach of the conditions of the licence. The Court concluded that it was not necessary. To have held otherwise would have been to insert a further requirement into the offence which in turn would make it more difficult for the prosecution to secure a conviction.

An important issue in the present context is whether it can be inferred from the facts of a case that a defendant had the requisite knowledge even where it is submitted on his behalf that he had no knowledge that the illegal deposit of waste had taken place. This was the issue which the Divisional Court had to consider in *Kent County Council* v *Beaney*.[161] The facts of this case were as follows. The respondent was the owner and occupier of a farm in Herne Bay, Kent. An enforcement officer in the employ of the appellant council had visited the farm on one occasion and had observed two large fires burning. Whilst he was present, he witnessed the arrival and departure of three lorry-mounted skips each bearing a different commercial sign. Each lorry tipped a full load of material, e.g. hedge cuttings and chip board, timber, wooden doors and garden waste, onto one of the fires prior to departing the farm. On a subsequent occasion, the same enforcement officer witnessed the contents of two lorry-mounted skips being deposited onto the respondent's land. The waste in question consisted of subsoil, polythene sheeting and cardboard. The enforcement officer went to the farmhouse on this occasion and interviewed the respondent. The respondent was asked if it was his land upon which the waste had been deposited and whether he had a waste disposal licence. The first question was answered in the affirmative; the second in the negative. The enforcement officer accordingly advised the respondent that he considered that offences had been committed in contravention of section 3 of the Control of Pollution Act 1974 and that he intended to report him for the offences. The officer did not, however, ask the respondent whether he had

---

[158] [1997] 2 All ER 332 at 337-338.
[159] [1981] 1 WLR 1349.
[160] Section 3(1).
[161] [1993] Env LR 225.

given permission or had been aware of the waste disposal since his farmhouse was only 50 yards from the fires across a road. At his subsequent trial before the Justices on five informations, it was submitted on his behalf at the conclusion of the prosecution case that there was no case to answer on any of the informations. That submission was accepted by the Justices and the council accordingly appealed. The sole question which arose on appeal was whether the facts as described above disclosed sufficient material for there to be a case to answer.

In what was a brief judgment, Mann LJ commenced by observing that the law applicable to this question was "clear" and could be found in cases such as *Galbraith*.[162] In short, the position was that provided that the material contained the necessary minimum to establish the alleged crime, then there would be a case to answer. On the facts of the present case, the Divisional Court was in no doubt that there was adequate material to show that the section 3 offences had been committed. Although it was "unfortunate" that the enforcement officer had not asked the respondent directly whether he knew what was going on and whether he had permitted it, a provisional inference[163] could be drawn from the facts that he did indeed have the requisite knowledge. In the words of Mann LJ:

> "The case is not one of casual fly-tipping at a remote place. Here we have, as facts, the proximity of the deposits to the respondent's farmhouse, a frequency of deposit and the medium of lorry-mounted skips bearing commercial signs. These are facts which in my judgment must give rise to the inference that Mr. Beaney both knew what was occurring and that he was permitting it to occur."[164]

THE DUTY OF CARE IN THE MANAGEMENT OF WASTE

Notwithstanding the typically civil law connotations of the expression "duty of care", in the discussion which follows we are concerned with a quite broadly defined *criminal* offence: to be found in section 34 of the Environmental Protection Act 1990.

The key provision is in subsection (1): failure to comply with the terms of which may result in prosecution, which may be summary or on indictment. No custodial sentence may be imposed for this offence, although, following conviction on indictment, an unlimited fine may be ordered.[165]

Section 34(1) provides:

---

[162] (1981) 73 Cr App R 124.

[163] The expression "provisional inference" was chosen carefully by Mann LJ to signify that it was an inference which may be capable of being displaced by evidence called on behalf of the defendant at the resumed hearing before the Justices.

[164] [1993] Env LR 225 at 228. When originally interviewed by the enforcement officer the respondent had stated that he had been advised by a lady at the council that he could raise the level of his land with hardcore by 20 feet. In the opinion of Mann LJ, this reinforced the inference as to permission since it "would seem to have been a pointless anecdote if the tipping had been nothing to do with him".

[165] 1990 Act, s. 34(6).

"it shall be the duty of any person who imports, produces, carries, keeps, treats or disposes of controlled waste or, as a broker, has control of such waste, to take all such measures applicable to him in that capacity as are reasonable in the circumstances –

(a)   to prevent any contravention of section 33 above;[166]
(b)   to prevent the escape of the waste from his control or that of any other person; and
(c)   on transfer of the waste, to secure –
    (i)   that the transfer is only to an authorised person or to a person for authorised transport purposes; and
    (ii)   that there is transferred such a written description of the waste as will enable other persons to avoid a contravention of that section and to comply with the duty under this subsection as respects the escape of waste."

The duty is expressly stated not to apply to occupiers of domestic property as regards the household waste produced on that property.[167] The concepts of "authorised persons", "authorised transport purposes" and "transfer of waste" are further defined or explained in subsections (3)(4) and (4A) respectively. By virtue of section 75(4) of the 1990 Act: "controlled waste" means household, industrial and commercial waste;[168]and each of these forms of waste is further defined, in subsections (5)(6) and (7) respectively.

Reasonable in the circumstances? – the Code of Practice

It will be apparent that this duty of care in the management of waste involves criminal liability of very broad scope. It imposes obligations on a wide range of categories of persons (those who import, produce, carry, keep, etc. waste) and in relation to their actions in the management of a wide range of kinds of waste.

The most significant limiting factor as regards the scope of criminal liability is that the duty imposed by section 34 is to take all such measures "as are reasonable in the circumstances" to seek to prevent the occurrences stated in section 34(1)(a) and (b), and to seek to secure that the provisions of section 34(1)(c) are met.

The critical issue as regards liability in any case may, therefore, be to assess the reasonableness of the measures which may have been taken by the defendant to have sought to have avoided the occurrence of those things. On this issue lawyers and judges, as well as those directly involved with waste who may wish to understand their responsibilities, are all assisted by the provision made in section 34(7) for the preparation and

---

[166] That is, to seek to prevent any other person committing the offences of depositing, treating, keeping, or disposing of controlled waste except in accordance with a waste management licence; or treating, keeping or disposing of controlled waste in a manner likely to cause pollution of the environment or harm to human health. See further, above, p. 372.

[167] Section 34(2).

[168] Note that "controlled" waste includes "special" waste: ss. 75(9) and 62.

issuance of a Code of Practice: to provide practical guidance on how to discharge the duty imposed by subsection (1).

As is typically the case the Code so provided for does not in itself have the status of law. However, according to section 34(10) it:

> "shall be admissible in evidence and if any provision of such a code appears to the court to be relevant to any question arising in the proceedings it shall be taken into account in determining that question."

A first Code of Practice was issued in December 1991 and became operational on the introduction into force of section 34 in April 1992. A revised, and current, Code of Practice superseded the original in 1996.

The substantive provisions of the Code are preceded by an *Introduction*, containing some valuable statements about the policy underlying this aspect of the law on the management of waste. The Introduction begins by explaining the essential features of the "duty of care" scheme as follows:

> "The duty of care is designed to be an essentially self-regulating system which is based on good business practice."

In the light of the substantial concern which exists in many quarters as regards the issue of the enforcement (or rather the lack of enforcement) of environmental laws,[169] the concept of a self-enforcing scheme of regulation is one which must provoke interest – and maybe also some scepticism. What is the nature of such self-enforcement? How is such a scheme to work? Can such a scheme prove effective so as to secure results without the need for substantial resources being provided to the enforcement agencies: a need unlikely in reality to be met? Some answers to these questions will emerge during the discussion which follows.

And what of the expression: "based on good business practice"? This seems to suggest that the standard to be set as "reasonable" may be that exemplified by what we might describe as "model" good business practice, rather than any (perhaps lower) standard based upon the hypothetical reasonable behaviour of the "business on the Clapham omnibus".

The Introduction explains the nature of the Code which is to follow. Its purpose is to "recommend … steps which should normally be enough to meet the … duty" imposed by section 34. The words "recommend" and "normally" seem particularly well-chosen in view of the legal status of the code; but the expression "series of steps" is also significant. It provides a pointer to the fact that:

> "the purpose of the Code is to provide practical advice for waste holders and brokers subject to the duty of care."

---

[169] See generally Chapter 7.

The Code itself is divided into seven sections of "Step by Step Guidance", and these sections are followed by a summary check-list: some attention seems certainly to have been paid to the idea of user-friendliness. It may help to list at the outset the titles of the seven section of guidance; titles which, in themselves, give a clear idea of the "style" of the document.

The seven sections are labelled:

- Identify and Describe the Controlled Waste;
- Keep the Waste Safely;
- Transfer to the Right Person;
- Receiving the Waste;
- Checking Up;
- Expert Help and Guidance;
- The Duty of Care and Scrap Metal.

Identifying and describing controlled waste

Section 1 of the Code begins by emphasising the importance, for all those subject to the duty of care (as holders of waste or as waste brokers) of:

- identifying whether the matter is "controlled waste" in respect of which the section 34 duty is applicable (or other waste to which the duty may not apply);

- identifying the physical characteristics of waste which is controlled waste;

- giving thought to the problems which might be caused by waste with such characteristics if not properly managed.

The importance which, as will be seen, the Code attaches to proper identification and description of waste is a reflection of the duty of care requirement, under section 34(1)(a) to "take all such measures ... as are reasonable in the circumstances – (a) to prevent any contravention by any other person of [the various offences under section 33]." One of the principal ways in which one person in the waste chain may take measures which may help to avoid others committing such offences will be to secure that those subsequent holders of the waste know what it is they are dealing with; and are properly alerted, where appropriate, to the need for special care[170]or for disposal at an appropriately licensed site.[171]

On the general issue of the problems which may arise as regards waste the following significant statement appears:

> "Waste cannot be simply divided between the safe and the hazardous. There are safe ways of dealing with any waste. Equally any waste can

---

[170] See s. 33(1((c).
[171] See s. 33(1)(a).

be hazardous to human health or the environment if it is wrongly managed."[172]

In order to allow subsequent holders of waste to be able to make appropriate decisions as regards their management of that waste it is of importance that they should know sufficiently the nature of that waste. The onus, therefore, is upon the producer (or importer) of waste to identify and provide a description of that waste which is adequate to enable subsequent holders to manage the waste properly.

Accordingly, the starting-point as regards safe waste management involves ensuring that subsequent holders know the nature of the waste, both in terms of its identity and in terms of any particular requirements which may need to be met as regards the safe handling, treatment, storage and disposal of that waste. For this reason the Code of Practice provides a useful check-list reminder of questions which any holder of waste will need to consider in order to seek to ensure that no problems occur with that waste:

- Is it necessary to put the waste into some form of container in order to prevent escape or to protect the waste?
- Can the waste safely be mixed with any other wastes, or are there wastes with which it should not be mixed?
- Can it safely be crushed, or incinerated, or disposed of to landfill along with other waste?
- Is it likely to change its physical state during storage or transport?[173]

The Code adverts to problems sometimes caused when waste contains substances which are out of anticipated proportion. It explains:

> "Anything unusual in waste can pose a problem. So can anything which is out of proportion. Ordinary business waste from shops and offices, often contains small amounts of potentially hazardous substances. This may not matter if they are mixed in large quantities of other waste. What should be identified as potential problems in the assignment of waste, are significant quantities of an unexpected substance, or unusual amounts of an expected substance."[174]

The requirement that the producer/importer of waste should adequately describe that waste is linked to obligations under the Environmental Protection (Duty of Care) Regulations 1991[175] that where waste is to be transferred a transfer note must be completed, signed and kept by the parties involved in that transfer. The transfer note is required, inter alia, to indicate:

- the quantity of waste transferred: usually by weight;
- how it is to be packed – loose or contained;

---

[172] Paragraph 1.3.
[173] Paragraph 1.4.
[174] Paragraph 1.5.
[175] SI 1991 No. 2839.

- the kind of container, if not loose;
- a description of the waste (as part of the transfer document or by separate document).[176]

The description should, the Code stresses, always mention any special problems associated with the waste. The amount of detail necessary in a description will vary depending on the nature of the waste. The key is that:

> "the description must provide enough information to enable subsequent holders to avoid mismanaging the waste."[177]

For many wastes a quite simple description may suffice for this purpose – the description "household waste", for example. However, in other cases this may not be adequate sufficiently to inform subsequent holders of what they need to know. It may then be necessary to provide more specific information about the source of the waste, the process or processes from which the waste is derived, and perhaps a chemical or physical analysis of the waste.[178]

A "source of waste" description may well suffice where the kinds of businesses referred to as the source of the waste:

> "produce a mixture of wastes none of which has special handing or disposal requirements; or where there are no special handling or disposal requirements which cannot be identified from such a simple description."[179]

However, a "source of waste" description will not suffice if the proportions of different wastes are not as might be expected from that source, and if that atypical nature of the waste may lead to unheralded storage or disposal problems.[180]

Where a quantity of waste is a single material or a simple mixture of materials it may be that it can best be described not by source but by simple description, not necessarily involving the use of scientific chemical terms.

For most industrial, and some commercial, wastes the Code indicates that the description should make reference to the *process* by which the waste was produced. In other words it may commonly be necessary, as regards such waste, for subsequent holders to be aware of the materials used in that process, the equipment used and the treatment and changes which resulted in the waste products. This might require those whose processes produce waste to make inquiries of their own suppliers of raw materials and equipment, in order that an adequate description of ensuing waste may be provided.

---

[176] It is also "good practice" to append a description of the waste physically to drums and other closed containers.

[177] Paragraph 1.9.

[178] Paragraph 1.8 and 1.9.

[179] Paragraph 1.12.

[180] Paragraph 1.12.

In some cases waste may be held without knowledge of its source or the processes by which it came into being. Or it may be known to involve a mixture of wastes from different sources. Or it may not be known what the physical or chemical characteristics of waste from a particular source may be. The Code stresses that in this situation there may be no alternative than to conduct an analysis of the chemical and physical properties of the waste. However, before so doing it may be worthwhile discussing with persons who will subsequently manage the waste – its transport, storage, treatment or disposal – to seek to identify the issues as regards potential content of the waste which may be significant so that the waste may be dealt with safely.[181] So, for example, if such persons will, in any case, take steps suited to relatively toxic wastes it may not be necessary to conduct a detailed analysis of the waste.

Keeping waste safely

The next section of the Code provides practical guidance as regards what may be necessary in order to comply with section 34(1)(b): the obligation upon persons to take "all ... measures as are reasonable in the circumstances ... (b) to prevent the escape of waste from his control or from that of any other person".

The Code's advice begins quite generally:

> "All waste holders must act to keep waste safe against –
> (a) corrosion or wear of waste containers;
> (b) accidental spilling or leaking or inadvertent leaching from waste unprotected from rainfall;
> (c) accident or weather breaking contained waste open and allowing it to escape;
> (d) waste blowing away or falling while stored or being transported;
> (e) scavenging of waste by vandals, thieves, children, trespassers or animals."[182]

Moreover reasonable care should be taken not only to ensure that waste is secure whilst in the individual's own possession: consideration should be given also to its future security. The Code explains:

> "Waste should reach not only its next holder but a licensed facility or other appropriate destination without escape. Where waste is to be mixed immediately, for example in a transfer station, a civic amenity site or a municipal collection vehicle, it only needs to be packed well enough to reach that immediate destination. Preventing its escape after that stage is up to the next holder."[183]

However, warns the Code:

---

[181] Paragraph 1.17.
[182] Paragraph 2.1.
[183] *ibid.*

"there are wastes that may need to reach a disposal or treatment site in their original containers. For example, drummed waste. In such cases, holders will need to know through how many subsequent hands; under what conditions; for how long; and to what ultimate treatment their waste will go in order to satisfy themselves that it is packed securely enough to reach its final destination intact."[184]

In other words the Code makes clear that such consideration, and the making of inquiries, may be necessary if a holder of waste is not to risk having been found not to have taken reasonable care to have prevented the escape of waste from a person later in possession of that waste. Or to put the matter another way: where waste *has* escaped it may be that investigation as regards its previous holders and their actions as regards containment of that waste may reveal breaches of this duty on their part.

Transfer to the right person

The next section of the Code covers the obligation under section 34 (1)(c) to take reasonable measures to secure (i) that waste which is transferred is transferred only to an authorised person, or to a person for an authorised transport purpose; and (ii) that the transfer is accompanied by an adequate description of the waste.

The aim here of the duty of care seems evident. "Unauthorised" persons should find it harder to continue illicit involvement in the waste industry if those who use their services may, for so doing, find themselves in breach of the duty of care under section 34. In this way the duty of care under section 34 can be regarded as a mechanism by which enhanced compliance with other provisions of waste management law may be secured – requirements, for example, as regards registration of waste carriers and the licensing of those who deposit, keep, treat, store or dispose of waste. Those who might seek to engage in such activities without such registration, or without having become properly licensed, should find that section 34 has provided a strong disincentive for holders of waste to use their services.

Where a waste carrier is used to send waste for disposal, treatment or recovery the consignor should, before using any carrier for the first time, check with the Environment Agency that the proposed carrier's registration (under section 2 of the Control of Pollution (Amendment) Act 1989) is valid. Where a carrier claims exemption from the requirements for registration the holder of the waste should seek that the carrier provide evidence as to that exemption. On subsequent use of a carrier the consignor should check the carrier's certificate of registration, although this obligation may not apply in full in the case of a carrier used for repeated transfers of waste.[185]

---

[184] *ibid.*
[185] Paragraphs 3.8, 3.11, 3.23 and 3.24.

In a situation where waste is to be sent for disposal, treatment or recovery – to a person referred to in the Code as a "waste manager" – the holder of the waste is advised to:

- check that the waste manager has a waste management licence; and
- check that that licence authorises the manager to take the type and quantity of waste in question.

Such a' check should involve an examination of the waste manager's licence: mere inquiry of the waste manager should not be considered sufficient. If the holder is unsure whether the waste falls within descriptions within the licence, inquiry should be made with the Environment Agency.

Where the waste manager claims that his or her activities are such as not to require a waste management licence – by virtue of falling within the ambit of an exemption within Regulation 16 or 17 and Schedule 3 of the Waste Management Licensing Regulations 1994 – the holder should call upon the waste manager to state the exemptions with some particularity and explain the grounds upon which he or she falls within that exemption. Exemptions are limited to specific circumstances and specific kinds of waste. The holder is to be expected, having been informed of the grounds of exemption relied upon, to check that the waste in question falls within that exemption.

These various provisions impose obligations upon producers/importers of waste, carriers, and other holders of waste to check the credentials, in terms of being appropriately registered or licensed, of those to whom they may wish to transfer waste. The provisions of the next part of the Code – section 4: Receiving Waste – look the other way: imposing obligations upon those who *receive* waste.

Receiving waste

The practical advice provided by the Code on this matter is certainly of a salutary and sensible nature. However, here it is of particular importance to remember that non-compliance with the Code is not itself an offence; the Code simply seeks to provide guidance as regards practice which should lead persons towards compliance with their more general legal obligations within section 34. It has been quite easy to see the link between the Code and the requirements of section 34 in the situations discussed so far: the requirement to describe waste adequately (see section 34 (1)(a)) and to transfer waste only to appropriate persons (see section 34(1)(b)). A little more difficulty arises when it comes to the advice offered by the Code about *receiving waste*: one needs to ask – in what ways may failure to comply with obligations there stated involve a failure to have taken reasonable measures in relation to the specific matters with paragraphs (a)(b) and (c) of section 34(1)?

The Code stressed its view that:

"Checking is not only in one direction. No-one should accept waste from a source that seems to be in breach of the duty of care. Waste may only come either from the person who first produces it or imports it or from someone who has received it. The person who receives it must be one of the persons entitled to receive waste – that is, an authorised person or a person for authorised transport purposes."[186]

This paragraph presents certain difficulties. Certainly, a person who has received waste, and now seeks to pass it on, must be a person entitled to receive the waste or transport the waste. If that person is not such a person he or she will have committed offences under the waste management licensing legislation or the waste carriers legislation. It may equally be the case that the person who transferred waste to that person will be in breach of the duty of care under section 34 (as considered above). What is by no means so clear is how it may be a breach of section 34 to "receive" waste from such an improper person. As indicated earlier an offence under section 34 is not committed simply because the Code contains the bold statement:

"No-one should accept waste from a source that seems to be in breach of the duty of care."

The Code may provide persuasive evidence of what may be reasonable or not reasonable conduct in relation to the prevention or securement of the particular matters referred to in section 34(1)(a)(b) and (c). To go beyond this and to suggest it is a breach of the duty of care simply to have engaged in dealings with another person who is in breach of the duty of care seems to be to go beyond the legitimate interpretation of section 34. Dealings with such persons will not involve a breach of the duty of care *per se*. They will do so only if, and in so far as, the dealings have occurred in circumstances which can be brought within the broad, but not unlimited, terms of section 34(1)(a)(b) or (c).

Indeed this seems acknowledged by the Code itself: suggesting that some admonishments in the Code relate to what may or may not be "good practice"; whereas other admonishments relate more closely to criminal liability under section 34. That such a distinction exists seems to be evidenced by the Code's discussion as regards those who may receive waste from an *unregistered* carrier. The Code acknowledges:

"There is no explicit requirement for a person receiving waste from a waste carrier to check on whether or not the carrier is registered. In the Department's view, it is not an offence under section 34(1) of the 1990 Act for a recipient to accept waste from an unregistered carrier."[187]

---

[186] Paragraph 4.2.
[187] Paragraph 4.3.

This seems to be correct but some potential confusion may result from the statement in the Code which immediately follows:

> "However, the first time a carrier delivers waste, the recipient should satisfy himself that he is dealing with someone who is properly registered to transport the waste."[188]

Given the admission in the previous quotation, as regards the scope of criminal liability under section 34, the word "should" must here be taken not to refer to the avoidance of such liability, but rather to good practice which goes somewhat beyond the principal object of the Code: good practice in seeking to avoid the occurrences within section 34(1)(a)(b) and (c).

Although some caution should therefore be adopted as regards statements in the Code as regards obligations borne by *recipients* of waste, this is not to say that such persons owe no duties under this duty of care. Indeed there are clear situations in which a recipient of waste may properly be regarded as in breach of the duty.

Two such situations are referred to expressly by the Code of Practice. Thus it is stated:

> "Before receiving any waste, a holder should establish that it is contained in a manner suitable for its subsequent handling and final deposit or recovery"

Also:

> "The recipient should also look at the description and seek more information from the previous holder if this is necessary in order to manage the waste."[189]

The link between this advice and the terms of section 34 is evident. To receive waste without having adequately ascertained its characteristics or the condition of its containment may well involve having failed to have taken reasonable measures to seek to have prevented, for example, escape of that waste (now or later), or to have prevented offences under section 33 being committed by the recipient or by persons to whom the recipient may have transferred the waste.

Checking up

Section 5 of the Code deals with what it describes as "Checking Up". It begins with a short statement about checks which it considers should be made *after transfer* by persons who have previously held waste.

---

[188] Paragraph 4.4.
[189] Paragraphs 4.5 and 4.6.

The advice begins by acknowledging that the duty of care does not result in any all-embracing, "cradle to grave", channelling of legal responsibility to waste producers. Thus, it is noted:

> "A person is under no specific duty to audit his waste's final destination."[190]

Nevertheless, a producer who fails to take any interest in what happens to the waste which he or she has consigned once it has been consigned to an appropriate person may be in breach of the duty of care in a variety of ways.

For one thing, as we noted earlier, it may only be by having made such inquiries that it may have been possible for the producer to have taken measures so as to have *contained* the waste appropriately. Equally, it may be that such inquiry is necessary in order to judge what reasonable measures are necessary as regards description of the waste in question. And, further, it may be that a producer of waste may be in a position to exert some influence over the actions of those who may subsequently deal with the waste. This may most likely be the case where there is an ongoing contractual link between a producer and a waste manager. If such influence – so as to prevent breaches of section 33 for example – is a practical possibility it will be important for the producer of the waste not to have failed to have taken reasonable measures to have exerted that influence. In such circumstances a failure to have shown concern over the fate of the producer's waste may well seem to show absence of such reasonable measures.

It is, therefore, no surprise to find the following advice in the Code. Having acknowledged the absence of a specific duty upon a producer to audit his waste's final destination, the paragraph quoted earlier continues:

> "However, undertaking such an audit and subsequent periodic site visits would be a prudent means of protecting his position by being able to demonstrate the steps he had taken to prevent illegal treatment of his waste."[191]

The Code continues by indicating a particular situation where the obligation may be rather more extensive although, it may be noted, without explaining why this should be the case:

> "One exception is where a holder makes arrangements with more than one party. For example, a producer arranges two contracts, one for disposal and another for transport to the disposal site. In that case the producer should establish that he not only handed the waste to the carrier but that it reached the disposer ..."[192]

---

[190] Paragraph 5.2.
[191] Paragraph 5.2.
[192] Paragraph 5.3.

It is not easy to see why, in terms of compliance with the specific requirements of section 34, it makes a crucial difference whether there may be such a contractual link between the producer and the eventual disposer of the waste. The critical issue is one of the likely "influence" which the former may be capable of bringing to bear upon the latter. This may well be more extensive where a contractual relationship between the two exists;[193] but to elevate the contractual nexus into the acid test of legal duty upon waste producers to monitor their waste through to its final disposal would seem to be to focus on "form" rather than "substance": upon legal relationship rather than likely influence as regards disposal operations. Here again, we may conclude that the Code adopts language which does not at all times make transparent whether its statements of obligation ("should") are based upon likely breach of the section 34 duty of care if not complied with, or simply represent an official statement of what may, undeniably, be a feature of "good industry practice".

Once waste has been received, the holder of that waste has what the Code describes as a "strong practical interest in the description being correct and containing adequate information".[194] Accordingly:

> "Anyone receiving waste should make at least a quick visual check that it appears to match the description. For a waste manager it would be good practice to go beyond this by fully checking the composition of samples of waste received."[195]

The Code cautions waste holders to be alert for evidence which suggests that the duty of care is not being complied with or that illegal waste handling is taking place. Obvious causes for concern are listed as follows:

"(a)   waste that is wrongly or inadequately described being delivered to a waste management site;

(b)   waste being delivered or taken away without proper packing so that it is likely to escape;

(c)   failure of the person delivering or taking waste to complete a transfer note properly, or an apparent falsehood on the transfer note;

(d)   an unsupported claim of exemption from licensing[196] or registration as a carrier;

(e)   failure of waste consigned via a carrier to arrive at a destination with whom the transferring holder has an arrangement; or

(f)   damage to, or interference with containers."[197]

If a waste holder suspects that that his waste is not being dealt with properly, the Code counsels against hasty action. It suggests that the holder

---

[193] And here the terms of that contract may be significant.

[194] Paragraph 5.4.

[195] *ibid.*

[196] In *Environment Agency* v *Short* [1999] EHLR 3, this is an issue to which the respondent failed to be alert: see above at p. 374.

[197] Paragraph 5.5.

should first check all the facts, which may involve requesting that further details be added to the waste description or that more information is provided as to the status of the holder for the purposes of waste management licensing or carrier registration. If the holder is not satisfied with the responses that he receives, the Code recommends that "his first action should normally be to refuse to transfer or accept further consignments of the waste in question to or from that person, unless or until the problem is remedied."[198] The fact that this is what ought *normally* to happen is significant. The Code recognises that in some circumstances, it simply may not be practicable to adopt such a course of action, such as where a breach of contract would be involved. However, the Code suggests that a way round "such inflexibility" would be "for new waste contracts to provide for termination if a breach of the duty occurs and a notice to rectify is not complied with".[199]

Policing the waste management regime is not, however, the responsibility of a waste holder; it is the responsibility of the Environment Agency (and SEPA in Scotland). Accordingly, the Code states that a waste holder should inform the Agency where they know or suspect that:

"(a) there is a breach of the duty of care; or
(b) waste is carried by an unregistered carrier not entitled to exemption; or
(c) waste is stored, disposed of, treated or recovered:
(i) without a licence or in a way not permitted by the licence;
(ii) contrary to the terms or conditions of a licence exemption..."[200]

Expert help and guidance

The sixth section of the Code commences with the acknowledgement that "a waste holder may not always have the knowledge or expertise to discharge his duty of care".[201] If this is the case, the Code counsels the holder to seek the advice of experts, although it points out that even in such an event he retains the responsibility for discharging his own duty of care. In other words, consulting an expert does not cause the burden of responsibility to transfer from the waste holder to the expert. Thus if a waste holder were to use an analytical laboratory in order to establish the nature of an unknown waste which he needs to describe, a consultant or laboratory is acting in an advisory capacity only. The position is different, however, if a consultant arranges the transfer of waste. In these circumstances, he will have become a broker and as such "shares responsibility with the two holders directly involved for the proper transfer of the waste".[202]

---

[198] Paragraph 5.8.
[199] *ibid.*
[200] Paragraph 5.12.
[201] Paragraph 6.1.
[202] Paragraph 6.3.

As might be expected, the Code draws attention to the fact that the Environment Agency has expertise in the management of all types of controlled waste. However, it warns that although the Agency will try to provide help wherever it can, it is "not in a position to offer advice to every waste holder on how he should deal with the waste".[203] The Code then proceeds to list the various types of information on waste which the Agency is required to hold and which is available on request. This includes: the register under section 64 of the Environmental Protection Act 1990, as amended; the register under Regulation 18 of the Waste Management Licensing Regulations (establishments or undertakings carrying on exempt activities involving the recovery or disposal of waste); and the register of waste carriers under Regulation 3 of the Controlled Waste (Registration of Carriers and Seizure of Vehicles) Regulations 1991.

The Code also draws attention to a series of Waste Management Papers issued by the departments and published by HMSO. These papers cover a number of topics, including the handling, disposal, treatment and recovery of particular wastes, as well as waste management licensing.

The duty of care and scrap metal

The seventh and final section of the Code relates to scrap metal, which became a controlled waste for the purposes of the duty of care as from 1 October 1995.[204] Although the guidance provided in the Code therefore applies to the holders of scrap metal as it does to other types of controlled waste, section 7 seeks to provide additional guidance which takes account of the "distinctive features of scrap metal and the circumstances in which it is recovered".[205]

The Code notes that operators of metal recycling sites are well placed to meet the requirements of the 1991 Regulations because of the records which they are required to keep under the Scrap Metal Dealers Act 1964. Section 2 of that Act imposes a duty on every scrap metal dealer to keep, at each place occupied by him as a scrap metal store, a book in which he must record all scrap metal received, processed or dispatched from that place together with certain specified particulars of the scrap metal, e.g. a description of it and its weight. The Code then proceeds to set out further provisions of the 1964 Act, which will not be replicated here.

With regard to the transfer and receipt of scrap metal, it is noted that the guidance provided in sections 3 and 4[206] of the Code applies to anyone subject to the duty of care, including the operators of metal recycling sites. However, the Code recognises a distinctive feature of the scrap metal industry, i.e. that it receives metal from diverse sources and that "it could take considerable time to verify carriers' or suppliers' credentials at a site which undertakes a great number of transactions each day". Accordingly,

---

[203] Paragraph 6.6.
[204] See the Waste Management Licensing (Amendment etc.) Regulations 1995, SI No. 288.
[205] Paragraph 7.1.
[206] See above at pp. 406-409.

the Code "is not intended to place dealers in the position where they have to seek excessive verification from their suppliers to an extent that in time, discourages them from transferring scrap metal for recovery".[207]

---

[207] Paragraph 7.18.

Part III

ADMINISTRATIVE LIABILITIES

Chapter 11

STATUTORY NUISANCE: THE SUBSTANTIVE LAW

INTRODUCTION

Earlier in this book the tort of private nuisance was described, and potential remedies in the form of damages and injunctions were discussed.[1] This civil law concept of "nuisance" has, however, a significance which goes beyond the law of tort. It is a concept which was utilised by Parliament, in public health legislation dating back to the nineteenth century, [2] to provide one of the statutory preconditions necessary for the exercise of important local authority administrative procedures in the public health-environment context.

The law relating to statutory nuisance[3] is now to be found principally[4] in Part III of the Environmental Protection Act 1990. Section 79(1) of that Act lists a variety of matters which shall constitute statutory nuisances for the purposes of triggering local authority duties as regards the exercise of the statutory procedures provided for under that Part of the Act.

Simple, and less simple, cases

Statutory nuisance procedures often provide a relatively simple and inexpensive means by which a local authority or an aggrieved individual may seek to deal with an environmental problem of local significance. It would be wrong, however, to think that the procedures are only applicable to such cases. In instances where it is the manner of operation of a substantial business which is in issue much may turn financially upon the outcome of proceedings. In such a case it may very well be that the proceedings will be strongly contested, that expert testimony will be adduced by both sides on crucial issues,[5] and that close attention will be paid by the lawyers to all possible arguments of law. Such cases may very well involve magistrates in several days of hearing of evidence (where an appeal is lodged against an abatement notice); and substantial costs being

---

[1] See above pp. 25-158.

[2] See, for example, the temporary Act of 1846 (9 & 10 Vict c.96) "for the more speedy removal of certain nuisances", the Nuisances Removal and Diseases Prevention Act 1848 and, the Nuisances Removal Act 1855.

[3] Note also McCracken, Jones, Pereira and Payne, *Statutory Nuisance* (2001, Butterworths) and Malcolm and Pointing, *Statutory Nuisance: Law and Practice* (2002 OUP).

[4] Certain other enactments also provide for the existence of statutory nuisances. See, for example, s. 259 of the Public Health Act 1936 which makes provision for statutory nuisances in connection with watercourses, ditches, ponds etc., which are "so foul or in such a state as to be prejudicial to health or a nuisance".

[5] For example, as to the health or nuisance impacts; and, in appropriate cases (see below, p. 477) as regards the defence of "best practicable means".

incurred by the parties, the costs issue may become a significant one at the conclusion of the hearing.

A good illustration is *R* v *Southend Stipendiary Magistrates ex parte Rochford DC*.[6] The district council had formed the view that a family-run mushroom farm business was being conducted in a way which, owing to odour nuisances, warranted the service of abatement notices. This course of action was potentially very serious for the business. Judge J explained:

> "The operation ... was substantial. Their business involved some sixty employees. The annual turnover approached £1 million. The allegations, if successful, would have severely damaged, if not altogether destroyed the business."[7]

The recipients of the abatement notice appealed against that notice to the Magistrates' Court. They prepared a detailed defence which involved not only legal arguments but also technical reports. The appeal hearing before the stipendiary lasted eight days. The decision of the court was to allow the appeal and to set aside the abatement notice.

The successful appellants sought an award of costs.[8] Counsel supported the costs application by handing over an eight-page itemised list of expenses incurred. On the basis of this informal list a sum of £94,655 plus VAT was sought. In response, counsel for the local authority expressed concern at the "rates and hours" presented in the list, commented on what he referred to as the "unnecessary drawing out" of the hearing and noted the fact that the local authority had itself incurred rather more modest sums in the preparation of its own case. The local authority, it seemed, regarded expenditure by the appellant of £38,000 plus VAT as justifiable, but not more. Without giving reasons for his decision the magistrate awarded the appellants £64,000 plus VAT by way of costs. In an affidavit in the subsequent judicial review proceedings the court explained its decision as founded on its conclusion, contrary to view of the local authority, that the hearing had not been unnecessarily protracted and the expert evidence had been properly ventilated before the court.

The local authority brought judicial review proceedings to challenge the manner and substance of this exercise of statutory discretion by the Magistrates' Court. Judge J explained the nature of the power conferred on the magistrates in the following words:

> "The court which heard the proceedings is responsible for the quantification of the figure for costs. Although his advice may be sought, the question is not adjourned for a decision by the clerk to the justices, and the procedure is not a formal taxation of costs, as understood in the High Court or County Court. The issue is argued

---

[6] [1995] Env LR 1.

[7] *ibid.* at 3.

[8] Under s. 64 of the Magistrates' Courts Act 1980: power to make such order as the court thinks "just and reasonable".

and the decision announced in open court. The jurisdiction frequently involves fairly modest amounts, but it can, as here, concern very substantial sums indeed, to be dealt with in summary fashion without pleadings, or any formal bill of costs, or referral to a Taxing Officer of the court. Section 64 itself suggests that formal procedures are not anticipated."[9]

And later, Judge J continued:

"To achieve a 'just and reasonable' decision, the court is entitled to exercise all the procedural powers which are normally available to it. For example, it may adjourn the hearing .... The court may hear or require formal evidence. It may invite the parties to consider specific issues on which the court may seek assistance ..."[10]

Notwithstanding that the stipendiary magistrate had not taken advantage of these various procedural options, the reviewing court felt unable to conclude that his manner of dealing with the matter was flawed in any way. Nor was his failure to have offered reasons to support his decision something which could be regarded as undermining its validity. Judge J explained:

"... there is ... no general duty on the Magistrates' Court to give judgments or reasons for their decisions when delivering them, although there is, of course, nothing to prevent them doing so if they think it appropriate."[11]

The final argument in the judicial review challenge was that, quite apart from any procedural failings on the part of the magistrate, the figure of costs awarded was so far in excess of what any reasonable court would have awarded as to render the award *Wednesbury* unreasonable. Judge J noted that in considering this issue it was necessary to confine attention to evidence available to the magistrate at the time of the decision: the issue was whether his decision was, or was not, unreasonable on the evidence then available. Accordingly, expert opinion from law costs draftsmen, obtained after the Magistrates' Court decision and for the purposes of the judicial review, was not admissible.[12]

Confining his attention to the material before the Magistrates' Court, Judge J considered the original sum claimed (nearly £100,000) to be "... an alarming figure even allowing for the importance of the issues ... and the careful preparation and analysis which the defence case involved."[13] In his opinion:

---

[9] [1995] Env LR 1 at 5.

[10] *ibid.* at 6.

[11] *ibid.*

[12] It is not clear why such information should not help the reviewing court to reach an assessment of the reasonableness or otherwise of the decision under review, so long as the "expert evidence" is itself based, and based only, on matters of which the initial costs decision-maker was aware.

[13] *ibid.* at 7.

"Not surprisingly the magistrates reduced that figure by £30,000. His affidavit omits reference to [the] specific elements ... which he rejected. There is, therefore, no way of knowing where the cuts were made. Another possibility is that no specific cuts were made when he prepared his calculation, but he decided that an across-the-board percentage would be appropriate ..."[14]

Judge J expressed regret that the magistrate had not been invited to swear a further affidavit explaining more particularly his conclusions as regards the sums claimed as costs. Nevertheless, in the absence of such evidence the reviewing judge formed his own conclusions, commenting:

"I remain unable to comprehend how the preparation of the appeal against this abatement notice required nearly 300 hours work by a partner with the consequent mark up ..."[15]

As regards attendance of the partner throughout the hearing, it was "extremely doubtful" that such attendance produced costs which it was "just and reasonable" that the local authority should bear. Moreover, the use of two counsel in the proceedings was not justifiable: the presence of junior counsel was not necessary to have ensured proper legal representation.

Accordingly:

"The conclusion is inescapable that the amount claimed in the itemised list was unreasonable."[16]

The magistrate had, therefore, been right to have decided upon a substantial reduction. The issue, however, for the present reviewing court was whether the sum ordered remained unreasonable even after that substantial reduction. Judge J indicated that his own assessment of "just and reasonable" costs would have been less generous, but explained that his own view of the matter was not of significance unless it was such as to require him to view the magistrate's decision as *Wednesbury* unreasonable. Although expressing continuing concern at the amount of costs awarded, the magistrate's decision was not one with which, on that basis, the reviewing court felt it could interfere.

KINDS OF STATUTORY NUISANCE: THE SECTION 79 LIST

The list in section 79(1) comprises a broad and diverse catalogue of matters which may qualify as statutory nuisances, the somewhat quaint language of the nineteenth-century legislation having been retained in the modern law. It provides that:

---

[14] *ibid.*
[15] *ibid.* at 8-9.
[16] *ibid.* at 9.

"...the following matters constitute 'statutory nuisances' for the purpose of this Part, that is to say:

(a) any premises in such a state as to be prejudicial to health or a nuisance;

(b) smoke emitted from premises so as to be prejudicial to health or a nuisance;

(c) fumes or gases emitted from premises so as to be prejudicial to health or a nuisance;

(d) any dust, steam, smell or other effluvia arising on industrial, trade or business premises and being prejudicial to health or a nuisance;

(e) any accumulation or deposit which is prejudicial to health or a nuisance;

(f) any animal kept in such a place or manner as to be prejudicial to health or a nuisance;

(g) noise emitted from premises so as to be prejudicial to health or a nuisance;

(ga) noise that is prejudicial to health or a nuisance and is emitted from or caused by a vehicle, machinery or equipment in a street;[17]

(h) any other matter declared by any enactment to be a statutory nuisance."[18]

"PREJUDICIAL TO HEALTH OR A NUISANCE"

It will be noted that it is standard formula, within section 79(1), for the matters there listed to amount to a statutory nuisance only where they are such as to be "prejudicial to health or a nuisance". It follows that it is a feature of the list that circumstances *may* amount to a statutory nuisance notwithstanding that they may not meet the requirements of being a legal nuisance provided that the other, alternative condition – "prejudicial to health" – is satisfied.

"Prejudicial to health"

What, then, is meant by "prejudicial to health"? A definition is provided in section 79(7), which states the meaning to be:

"injurious, or likely to cause injury, to health."

---

[17] Added by s. 2 of the Noise and Statutory Nuisances Act 1993.

[18] The list is expressly not comprehensive in its listing of what may be statutory nuisances. Note also that the breadth of the list presented above is limited by a number of provisions later in s. 79. Thus, to give just one example, if an apparent statutory nuisance comprises, or is caused by, land in a "contaminated state" the statutory nuisance provisions of Part III of the 1990 Act shall not be applicable: the matter will be governed by the special regime for the identification and remediation of contaminated sites to be found in Part II A (added to the 1990 Act by s. 54 Environment Act 1995).

Ex p Everett

The meaning of the expression was considered by the High Court, and also the Court of Appeal, in *R* v *Bristol City Council ex p Everett.*[19] The case concerned a steep internal staircase within a nineteenth-century house which had for some years been let to tenants. Some time earlier the local authority had served on the landlord an abatement notice, on the basis that the steepness of the staircase was such as to have presented a risk of personal injury: the view being taken that occupants were at risk of falling as they descended the stairs. The notice had required works to be undertaken in order to abate the nuisance, involving the construction of a new and less steep staircase. Given the physical configuration of the house this was no simple matter and, in due course, the landlord came to an understanding with the local authority in order to avoid having to undertake that work. The basis of the understanding was that as the premises had become unoccupied there were no current occupants for whom the staircase presented a risk and so the premises should not be regarded as a statutory nuisance. The local authority agreed, in those circumstances, not to take further proceedings to enforce the abatement notice. The local authority also agreed that no statutory nuisance would arise if the premises were to be let only to able-bodied adults: such persons not being persons for whom the steep staircase presented a particular risk of injury. However, the local authority indicated that it would take a different view were the premises to be let to persons with mobility difficulties or to a family with small children. Subsequently the property was let to a tenant who suffered from a back injury and who, accordingly, experienced some difficulty negotiating the staircase. The new tenant complained to the local authority, but the local authority now declined to enforce the abatement notice. The local authority had changed its view on whether the steep staircase could involve a statutory nuisance. It now considered that its steepness should not be regarded as something which could be regarded as inherently detrimental to health and so should not be regarded as "prejudicial to health". Rather than enforce the earlier abatement notice, it chose instead to withdraw that notice, as having been inappropriately served.

By way of judicial review the tenant sought to challenge this interpretation of the phrase "prejudicial to health". During the course of the proceedings the local authority further modified its stance. Whereas in earlier discussions it had accepted that a dangerously steep staircase *could* be "prejudicial to health" (but that in the circumstances which existed this one did not fall within that category), the authority now argued that a hazard of *accidental personal injury by falling* was not a kind of harm which could, as a matter of principle, fall within the statutory phrase "prejudicial to health".

The High Court accepted this argument. In so doing the court was much assisted by the legislative history of statutory nuisance provisions. Richards J noted:

---

[19] [1999] Env LR 256; [1999] Env LR 587 (CA).

"The relevant statutory language can be traced back to the mid-nineteenth century. In a temporary Act of 1846, 'for the more speedy Removal of certain Nuisances', provision was made for certain public officers to lay a complaint before justices of the peace upon receipt of a complaint in writing, in prescribed form and signed by two medical practitioners, regarding 'the filthy and unwholesome Condition of any Dwelling House or other Building, or the Accumulation of any offensive or noxious Matter refuse, Dung, or Offal, or the existence of any foul or offensive Drain, Privy, or Cesspool'. The prescribed form of certificate required the medical practitioners to certify that such a condition existed 'and that the same is likely to be *prejudicial to the Health* of the Occupiers, or the Persons whose Habitations are in the Neighbourhood of the above-mentioned Premises'"[20] (emphasis added).

This early language was continued, with only very minor modifications, through a series of subsequent legislative measures, appearing in its modern form in the consolidating Public Health Act of 1936 (including there also, the current statutory definition of "prejudicial to health" as involving something which is "injurious, or likely to cause injury, to health").

In addition to the statutory history, the respondent in *Everett* relied strongly on earlier court decisions and, in particular, *Coventry City Council* v *Cartwright*.[21] That case concerned a vacant site in a residential district upon which the local authority had permitted the tipping of quantities of rubble and other inert builders' waste. A local resident was successful in persuading the magistrates that the site constituted an "accumulation or deposit which is prejudicial to health or a nuisance": on the basis that people who went onto the site, particularly children, might hurt themselves because of the broken glass, old tin cans and the general physical nature of the site. The risk of injury by way of cuts and the like was sufficient, the magistrates concluded, to render the site "prejudicial to health". The Divisional Court in *Cartwright* ruled that, in so holding, the magistrates had erred in law. Lord Widgery CJ accepted that the phrase "prejudicial to health" should be broadly construed, but was of the view that the magistrates had extended its meaning too far. His Lordship explained:

"I think that the underlying conception of the section is that that which is struck at is an accumulation of something which produces a threat to health in the sense of a threat of disease, vermin or the like."[22]

Given that the evidence presented to the magistrates in *Cartwright* had related solely to the physical dangers present and not also to the presence

---

[20] [1999] Env LR 256 at 263.
[21] [1975] 1 WLR 845.
[22] *ibid.* at 849.

of any additional features such as vermin or smells, their decision could not stand.

In *Everett* the High Court was persuaded by these arguments, and held, in the words of Richards J, that the statutory nuisance regime:

> "is not intended to apply in cases where the whole concern is that, by reason of the state of the premises, there is a likelihood of an accident causing personal injury."[23]

Furthermore:

> "When powers to take action against premises that were 'prejudicial to health' or 'injurious to health' were conferred by the mid-nineteenth century statutes, the object of concern was plainly the direct effect on people's health of filthy or unwholesome premises and the like: in particular the risk of disease or illness. There is nothing to suggest that the powers were intended to protect against the danger of accidental injury."[24]

Moreover, there was nothing in the later version of the enactments which justified a conclusion that the scope of the powers had subsequently been enlarged.

On appeal the Court of Appeal upheld this reasoning, notwithstanding strong argument on the part of the appellant that to do so would be to uphold a judgment which had reversed a settled understanding amongst environmental health officers as to the rather broader scope of the concept "prejudicial to health". The result, it was argued, would be to leave a variety of potentially lethal defects in buildings not subject to the procedures under Part III of the 1990 Act. Counsel for the appellant referred to the consequent non-applicability of statutory nuisance procedures as regards such matters as "defective wiring presenting a risk of electrocution, fire or smoke; defective gas installations with a risk of poisoning, fire or smoke; exposed hot pipes with a risk of burning; lack of adequate means of escape in the event of fire; weak, brittle or broken glass in a vulnerable location; slippery and dangerous surfaces; lack of handrails to stairs, landings or balconies, with risk of falling; and unsafe kitchen layouts carrying risks of accidental injury, fire or smoke."[25]

The Court of Appeal eschewed any notion that its task was, in the words of Mummery LJ, to "construct a fresh, comprehensive and rational system for protecting public welfare".[26] Rather, its task was to give effect to legislative provisions whose historical scope and meaning had been correctly understood by Richards J, and the phraseology of which

---

[23] [1999] Env LR 256 at 268.
[24] *ibid.* at 269.
[25] As summarised by Mummery LJ, [1999] Env LR 587 at 593.
[26] *ibid.* at 595.

Parliament seemed deliberately to have retained in its more modern re-enactments.

In one respect, however, the Court of Appeal went further than had Richards J. In the High Court it had been accepted that as a simple matter of ordinary understanding of the English language it was possible for accidental injury to fall within the notion "injury to health". It was the history of the legislation and its interpretation in the case-law which militated ultimately against that being the correct legal interpretation.

In the Court of Appeal a different view was taken as regards the ordinary meaning of these expressions. Buxton LJ[27] stated:

> "It is very unnatural to describe a physical accident as causing injury to health. First such accidents as a broken ankle or a sprained wrist are in ordinary usage not described as interfering with the victim's health, as opposed to affecting or injuring his body. Secondly, once the concept of injury is introduced into the definition, the specific limitation to injury to health underlines the fact that 'injury' here is not used in its normal sense of bodily injury."[28]

Birmingham City Council v Oakley

The meaning of the expression "injurious, or likely to cause injury, to health" received further consideration, on this occasion by the House of Lords, in *Birmingham City Council v Oakley.*[29] The case concerned a property owned by the council which was occupied by a tenant and his wife and four children (18, 9, 4 and a grandchild of 17 months). The ground floor of the house included a bathroom with a wash basin, next to a kitchen which had a sink. On the side of the kitchen opposite the bathroom was a door which led into the lavatory. There was no washbasin in the lavatory and the room itself was too small for one to be installed. Anyone who wished to wash their hands after using the lavatory was required to do so in the kitchen sink or to go through the kitchen to the bathroom. The tenant brought proceedings claiming that this state of affairs amounted to a statutory nuisance for which the council was responsible. The magistrates agreed. In their opinion it was unacceptable in the interests of hygiene that persons who had used the lavatory in the house were required to wash their hands in the kitchen sink, or cross through the kitchen in order to use the washbasin in the bathroom. Accordingly, they ordered that the lavatory be moved into the bathroom with an extractor fan, and that the door to the bathroom be re-sited. On appeal by way of case stated, the Divisional Court upheld the magistrates' decision although "not ... without hesitation".[30] In the words of Simon Brown LJ (with whom Astill J agreed):

---

[27] With whose judgment their other Lordships expressed agreement.
[28] [1999] Env LR 587 at 601.
[29] [2001] 1 All ER 385; [2001] EHLR 128.
[30] See *Birmingham City Council v Oakley* [1999] EHLR 209.

"... in cases like this the way the premises are used is the direct result of their layout, and if, as it was found here, that use is predictably so unhygienic as to create a health risk, then it is the state of the premises which is injurious to health."[31]

The local authority appealed to the House of Lords. Their Lordships decision is of interest for a number of reasons, not least because it was decided by a majority of 3:2 that the appeal should be allowed. A majority of the House of Lords was of the opinion that as long as there was nothing in the premises themselves which was prejudicial to health, then the premises could not be in such a state as to be prejudicial to health and hence a statutory nuisance. The mere layout of premises was insufficient to render them a statutory nuisance.[32]

Lord Slynn, who was in the majority, delivered the first speech in the appeal, and remarked that:

"The facts are simple and homely but the question is important to the individual family and to the local authority. Your Lordships have been told that there are throughout the country, tens of thousands of homes (and 20,000 in the council's area alone) where the separate lavatory has no washbasin and that the decision of the justices and the Divisional Court will cause great financial problems and interfere with the planned upgrading of older houses."[33]

Lord Slynn then proceeded to consider the history of the legislation, the purpose for which it was enacted and previous decisions of the courts in order to help determine the meaning of the words in the 1990 Act. With regard to the history, he noted that the story began with an Act of 1846 which had been passed "for the more speedy removal of certain nuisances".[34] This had been followed by the Nuisance Removal and Diseases Prevention Act 1848,[35] the Nuisances Removal Act 1855[36] and the Public Health Act 1875.[37] Whereas the former two enactments had referred to the "condition" of dwelling houses, the latter Acts had opted instead to refer to the "state" of the premises. Lord Slynn also noted that whilst there were other enactments which dealt with matters in issue in the present case,[38] and whilst "they may be some indication as to the scope of

---

[31] *ibid.* at 215.

[32] In the Scottish case *Robb* v *Dundee City Council* [2003] EHLR 9, it was noted that this narrow construction contrasted with the broader view taken by the minority of their Lordships in *Oakley*. However, the Court of Session (Inner House) was bound by the view of the majority: see the remarks of Lord Johnston at para. 9 of his judgment.

[33] [2001] 1 All ER 385 at 388.

[34] 9 and 10 Vict. c.96.

[35] 11 and 12 Vict. c.123.

[36] 18 and 19 Vict. c.121.

[37] 38 and 39 Vict. c.55.

[38] The legislation in question was: s. 604 of the Housing Act 1985 (house not fit for habitation if it does not have a suitably located WC); s. 64(1) of the Building Act 1984 (WC to be provided if the closets in a building are "in such a state as to be prejudicial to health or a nuisance"); s. 1(1) of

the provisions in the 1990 Act", they were in "no way" conclusive "that the facts of the present case cannot fall within s 79(1)(a)."[39]

With regard to previous decisions of the courts, Lord Slynn referred to nineteenth and twentieth-century statutory nuisance cases where the words of the various statutes had been interpreted by the courts. Thus he noted, for example, that in *R v Parlby*[40] the court had stated in relation to the phrase "premises in such a state as to be a nuisance" in the Public Health Act 1875:

"... we do not attempt to define every class of case to which the first head applies [i.e. a nuisance], but we think it is confined to cases in which the premises themselves are decayed, dilapidated, dirty, or out of order, as, for instance, where houses have been inhabited by tenants whose habits and ways of life have rendered them filthy or impregnated with disease, or where foul matter has been allowed to soak into walls or floors, or where they are so dilapidated as to be a source of danger to life and limb."[41]

Turning to the context in which the statutory words appeared, Lord Slynn was prepared to accept that the meaning of the words could change with the passage of time. In his opinion:

"If in this case 'the state of the premises' could include the arrangement of the rooms or the lack of a washbasin in the lavatory it would be nothing to the point that in 1846, perhaps even in 1920 or 1940 most people would not have regarded this as being prejudicial to health. Standards and attitudes change and the contemporary insistence on 'now wash your hands' would make the position clear as the justices found."[42]

However, what influenced Lord Slynn was:

"... the fact that the earlier statutes were dealing with a 'filthy and unwholesome condition' of a house or the collection of noxious matter or a foul or offensive drain or privy. All of these were in themselves prejudicial to health because of germs or smells and the risk of disease. When the words 'in such a condition' or 'such a state' were added they are to be read as seeking to achieve the same objective. They are directed to the presence in the house of some feature which in itself is prejudicial to health in that it is a source of possible infection or disease or illness such as dampness, mould, dirt

---

the same Act (power of the Secretary of State to make regulations in respect of the design and construction of buildings); and the Building Regulations 1991, SI 1991/2768.

[39] [2001] 1 All ER 385 at 390.

[40] (1889) 22 QBD 520.

[41] *ibid.* at 525.

[42] [2001] 1 All ER 385 at 392.

or evil smelling accumulations or the presence of rats. The state of the house must in itself have been prejudicial to health."[43]

Having regard to the more recent legislation, Lord Slynn noted that:

"… the premises are not limited to dwelling houses but the matters listed in s 79 of the 1990 Act are still in themselves capable of being prejudicial to health – smoke or gases, dust or an accumulation or deposit. Subsection (1)(a) of course is not limited to the specific terms listed in the other parts of the subsection but the other items do give an indication of the essential feature of the statutory nuisance which is being dealt with. There must be a factor which in itself is prejudicial to health."[44]

And concluded:

"I do not think that the arrangement of the rooms otherwise not in themselves insanitary so as to be prejudicial to health falls within s 79(1)(a)."[45]

Had there been a defect in the lavatory, drain or washbasin in the respondent's house, then this might have made the premises prejudicial to health. However, there were no such defects and therefore there was "nothing in the premises themselves which is prejudicial to health". In Lord Slynn's opinion:

"It is not sufficient to render the house itself 'in such a state' as to be prejudicial to health that the lavatory and washbasin are in separate rooms or that to get from one to the other it is necessary to pass through the kitchen where food is prepared. The prejudice to health results from the failure to wash hands or the use of the sink or basin after access through the kitchen. Undesirable though this arrangement is, it does not seem to me that it is permissible to give an extended meaning to the words in s 79(1)(a), however socially or hygienically desirable this might be."[46]

The other Law Lords in the majority were Lords Hoffmann and Millett. Lord Hoffmann regarded the case as one of "great constitutional importance". The issue could be stated as:

"When it comes to the expenditure of large sums of public and private money, who should make the decision? If the statute is clear, then of course Parliament has already made the decision and the courts merely enforce it. But when the statute is doubtful,[47] should

---

[43] *ibid.*

[44] *ibid.*

[45] *ibid.*

[46] *ibid.*

[47] Lord Hoffmann had already described the statute as being "ambiguous": *ibid.* at 393.

judges decide? Or should they leave the decision to democratically elected councillors or members of Parliament?"[48]

As Lord Slynn had done previously, Lord Hoffmann noted the statutory predecessors to section 79 of the 1990 Act and commented:

"... the statutory origins of s. 79(1)(a), together with the separate statutory code dealing with the toilet facilities required to be provided in dwelling houses,[49] throw a clear light on what Parliament meant by the premises being 'in such a state as to be prejudicial to health'. The section contemplates a case in which the premises as they stand present a threat to the health of the occupiers or neighbours which requires summary removal."[50]

Moreover, Lord Hoffmann observed:

"... the facts found by the justices in the present case are consistent with the premises being in the highest state of disinfected cleanliness. What they lack is a facility which, if used, would make it more convenient for the occupants to avoid the risk that they might transmit infection from their own urine or faeces to the food which they or other members of the household eat."[51]

As to the argument that section 79(1) of the 1990 Act should be construed in the light of modern conditions, Lord Hoffmann remarked:

"I quite agree that when a statute employs a concept which may change in content with advancing knowledge, technology or social standards, it should be interpreted as it would currently be understood. The content may change but the concept remains the same. The meaning of the statutory language remains unaltered."[52]

However:

"This doctrine does not however mean that one can construe the language of an old statute to mean something conceptually different from what the contemporary evidence shows that Parliament must have intended."[53]

---

[48] *ibid.*

[49] Dating back to the Public Health Act 1848.

[50] [2001] 1 All ER 385 at 395.

[51] *ibid.* at 395-396.

[52] *ibid.* at 396.

[53] *ibid.* To illustrate the point Lord Hoffmann referred to the House of Lords' decision in *Goodes* v *East Sussex County Council*. In that case, the issue for their Lordships was whether a highway authority's duty to maintain the highway under s. 41(1) of the Highways Act 1980 included preventing the formation of ice on the road. Their Lordships held unanimously that it did not. Although it was felt that "as a matter of ordinary language 'maintain' is wide enough to include the taking of preventive steps and to include steps to keep the road safe for ordinary use by motor cars", the duty could not be regarded in isolation. It had to be seen in the light of the statutory

For Lord Hoffmann the question of "great constitutional importance" was to be answered as follows:

> "I am entirely in favour of giving the 1990 Act a sensible modern interpretation. But I do not think that it is either sensible or in accordance with modern notions of democracy to hold that when Parliament re-enacted language going back to the nineteenth century, it authorised the courts to impose upon local authorities and others a huge burden of capital expenditure to which the statutory language had never been held to apply.[54] In my opinion the decision as to whether or not to take such a step should be made by the elected representatives of the people and not by the courts."[55]

Lord Millett summarised the majority's approach in the following passage:

> "... the Public Health Acts are concerned with the *state* of the premises, not with their *layout* or with the facilities which ought to be installed in them. In the present case the risk to health can variously be ascribed to the layout of the premises (because the lavatory was poorly sited) or to the absence of a desirable facility (a washbasin in reasonable proximity to the lavatory). But it does not derive from the *state* of the premises."[56]

Before we consider the dissenting judgments of Lord Steyn and Lord Clyde, one further aspect of the majority view should be noted: the effect of the House of Lords' decision on the earlier case of *Southwark London Borough v Ince*.[57]

The *Southwark* case involved proceedings brought by two tenants against the local authority under section 99 of the Public Health Act 1936.[58] It was alleged on their behalf that the noise and vibration from road and rail traffic near the building in which they lived was such as to be prejudicial to their health and hence a statutory nuisance. The magistrates had found that when the building had been converted by the local authority to flats no adequate sound insulation measures had been taken. This failure had resulted in the flats suffering from severe noise penetration which was capable of causing, and which was found to have caused, injury to the health of the tenants. Accordingly, the magistrates made an order requiring the local authority to sound insulate the building. On appeal, the Divisional Court upheld the magistrates' decision.

---

antecedents of s. 41 which suggested that the scope of the duty was confined to keeping the fabric of the road in good repair.

[54] Lord Hoffmann had earlier drawn attention to the absence of any case law in which it had been held that an absence of a facility in a house, such as a toilet, which would enable the occupants to avoid a risk to health, had been held in itself to make the state of the premises prejudicial to health: see 396.

[55] [2001] 1 All ER 385 at 397.

[56] *ibid.* at 401.

[57] (1989) 21 HLR 504.

[58] The forerunner of s. 82 of the Environmental Protection Act 1990.

Saville J, who gave the first judgment, noted that the building in question was neither a public nuisance[59] nor a private nuisance.[60] In his opinion:

> "Under section 92(1)(a),[61] the question is not whether the noise itself is a statutory nuisance but whether the premises are in such a state as to be prejudicial to health. That may be the case for a whole variety of external factors, be they weather, noise, the incursion of sewage, or indeed anything else. To my mind, the fact that there is legislation dealing with those responsible for some of those external factors does not begin to suggest that the Public Health Act is inappropriate to premises which are in such a state as to be prejudicial to health by reason of the external factors for which others may be responsible."[62]

A similar point was made by Woolf LJ (as he then was), who observed:

> "The important feature to note with regard to section 92(1)(a) is that it is the premises which have to be in such a state as to be prejudicial to health or a nuisance."[63]

And continued:

> "... the interpretation which this court has now adopted in relation to section 92(1)(a) is not to the effect that noise in itself amounts to a statutory nuisance but to the effect that if premises are in such a state that they unreasonably allow the emission of noise then in that situation they can amount to a statutory nuisance if they can be regarded as being prejudicial to health ..."[64]

In the House of Lords in *Oakley*, Lord Hoffmann observed that whilst *Southwark London Borough* v *Ince* was not directly in point, he would nevertheless "wish to reserve" his "position on whether it was correctly decided".[65] A similar sentiment was expressed by Lord Millett, who considered that the decision in that case "may require reconsideration".[66] The reason for such doubt was the parallel which can be drawn between the absence of the washbasin in *Oakley* and the absence of sound insulation in *Ince*. If the absence of the former is insufficient to render premises in such a state as to be prejudicial to health, as the majority of their Lordships held in *Oakley*, the same might be argued of the latter.

---

[59] The reasoning underpinning this conclusion was that the tenants in the building could not be described as a class of Her Majesty's subjects: (1989) 21 HLR 504 at 506. On this issue generally, see Chapter 8.

[60] This conclusion was reached on the basis that "there is no interference by one owner or occupier with the use and enjoyment of other property".

[61] Now s. 79(1)(a) of the 1990 Act.

[62] (1989) 21 HLR 504 at 506.

[63] *ibid.* at 510.

[64] *ibid.* at 510-511.

[65] [2001] 1 All ER 385 at 396.

[66] *ibid.* at 402. The other Law Lord who was in the majority, Lord Slynn, referred to *Ince* on two separate occasions during the course of his judgment: see 390 and 392, respectively. However, on neither occasion did he cast doubt on the correctness of the decision in that case.

Moreover, in *Oakley*, the majority made it clear that the words in section 79(1)(a) were "directed to the presence in the house of some feature which in itself is prejudicial to health in that it is a source of possible infection or disease or illness such as dampness, mould, dirt or evil smelling accumulations or the presence of rats".[67] On the facts of *Ince*, there was nothing in the building which of itself was prejudicial to health: the noise was an external factor over which neither side had any control.

Whether or not *Ince* is readily distinguishable from *Oakley* is, therefore, a matter of some doubt. The better view may, however, be that both decisions are supportable in terms of basic principle. Certainly there is a clear similarity between a building which lets in the rain (with adverse health effects) and a building which lets in an unnecessary amount of external noise (with adverse health effects). If statutory nuisance may apply to landlord obligations in the former case there seems no reason why it should not apply also in the latter. The situation in *Oakley* was rather different, the cause of the risk to health being the hygiene standards of the occupants rather than anything intrinsically deficient about the premises.

The dissenting judgments in *Oakley* are of interest in this context. Lord Steyn opined:

> "... I take the view that, in the context of s. 79(1)(a) of the Environmental Protection Act 1990, the positioning of facilities, or the lack of a facility, may depending on the circumstances cause the premises to be in 'such a state as to be prejudicial to health' and therefore a statutory nuisance. The appeal to Victorian social history, and legislative history going back more than a 150 years, is in my view not appropriate to the context. The 1990 Act must be given a sensible interpretation in the modern world. The distinction between layout and state of the premises is not to be found in the statute, and it is certainly not indicated by the language of the provision or the context. It is on analysis no more than a verbal technique to cut down the generality of the wording of the modern statute."[68]

And Lord Clyde commented that:

> "... the broad view is to be preferred. It is important ... to take into account the purpose and intent of the legislation. One of the principal purposes of the public health legislation from the nineteenth century onwards has been to secure the prevention of illness and disease ... The concept of the 'statutory nuisance' is designed to identify the situations where risks to health may occur and the machinery provided in the successive enactments is designed to effect a simple and swift remedy wherever such a risk may be found to exist. The definition of what may be 'prejudicial to health' is formulated in wide terms ... I find nothing in the 1990 Act which supports the adoption

---

[67] [2001] 1 All ER 385, per Lord Slynn at 392.
[68] *ibid.* at 393.

of a narrow construction of the word 'state' and the whole purpose of the legislation seems to me to point to a broad construction in the interests of the good health of the public. A narrow construction which would exclude consideration of a layout which was injurious to health, or the absence of a facility without which a risk to health would be likely to arise, seems to me to run counter to the intent and purpose of the past and the present legislation."[69]

Lord Clyde was not persuaded that the decided cases justified the narrow construction which they favoured. In his opinion, cases from the nineteenth century[70] and more recently[71] supported the view:

"... that a failure to provide adequate washing facilities for use with a WC, or the failure so to site the WC as to enable the user to have proper access to a hand basin are within what has always been recognised to be the scope of the statutory provision and a proper subject matter for an order by the justices."[72]

Accordingly, Lord Clyde opined:

"In the ordinary use of language it seems to me that the state of premises may include a deficiency due to the absence of a facility or a particular positioning of the facilities. In the present case the use of one or other of the washing facilities in the kitchen or bathroom was inevitable so far as anyone using the WC was concerned. Thus there was clearly something inadequate with the premises themselves so far as health and hygiene were concerned. The remedy was to do something to the premises."[73]

Objective or subjective approach to risk of prejudice to health?

An issue arose in *Cunningham* v *Birmingham City Council*[74] as to whether the "prejudicial to health" requirement within section 79 was to be interpreted objectively or subjectively. To put the matter another way: was it the health of particular individuals (perhaps with unusual sensitivities and susceptibilities) which mattered, or was the matter to be judged by reference to the perceived likely health impact upon "average" or "normal" people?

The tenant's arguments in *Cunningham* centered around the special health impact which the design and layout of the premises were said to have in

---

[69] *ibid.* at 399.

[70] Lord Clyde referred to *R* v *Wheatley, ex p Cowburn* (1885) 16 QBD 34 and *Ex p Saunders* (1883) 11 QBD 191: see [2001] 1 All ER 385 at 399.

[71] Into this category fell *Greater London Council* v *London Borough of Tower Hamlets* (1983) 15 HLR 54, *Birmingham DC* v *Kelly* (1985) 17 HLR 572 and, *Southwark London Borough* v *Ince* (1989) 21 HLR 504: see [2001] 1 All ER 385 at 400-401.

[72] *ibid.* at 400.

[73] *ibid.* at 401.

[74] [1998] Env LR 1. See also *London Borough of Southwark* v *Simpson* [1999] Env LR 553 at 560 per Lord Bingham CJ (as he then was).

respect of her ten-year-old son. The boy suffered from autistic-spectrum syndrome – a condition which resulted in his possessing severe behavioural problems. In particular, he did not understand danger, was a hazard in a confined space, had a fascination with doors and became aggressive very easily. In the circumstances, argued the tenant, the premises amounted to a statutory nuisance because, having regard to the boy's condition, they were too small and were of a dangerous layout (four doorways leading in and out of the kitchen). The tenant sought abatement of the alleged nuisance by means of construction of a new bathroom/WC at the rear of the property and the enlargement of the present kitchen by removal of the wall between it and the present bathroom.

The existing arrangement was evidently in no way prejudicial to the health of an "average" or "ordinary" tenant. Nevertheless, the magistrate hearing the complaint took the view that a subjective test applied. What mattered was not what effect the premises might have on some hypothetical ordinary/average person. If there was evidence of prejudice to the health of an actual, albeit atypical, person then the statutory requirement under section 79(1)(a) was satisfied.

On appeal, the Divisional Court held that the magistrate had been wrong to apply this subjective test. The proper approach was to apply an *objective* test.[75] The state of premises should be judged according to their likely effects on the health of the average person, disregarding the "abnormal sensitiveness of particular occupiers". Premises should meet a standard which is independent of the particular characteristics of the persons ordinarily resident there.[76]

In the opinion of the court the tenant's contentions would have imposed on owners of premises unduly high demands. Referring to the context of local authority lettings, Pill LJ commented:

"The extent of obligations upon local authorities would be enormous if they had to meet the reasonable but individual health requirements of prospective occupiers."[77]

The principles stated in *Cunningham* are, no doubt, correct. The issue, however, which remains for the courts to work out – case by case – is this: what *are* the health characteristics of the ordinary person? Established case-law would seem to make clear that average persons may be adversely affected in their health by conditions of premises involving dampness and

---

[75] This test had been applied in *Hall v Manchester Corporation* (1915) 84 LJ Ch 732 which related to fitness for habitation under earlier public health legislation. In that case, Lord Parker had observed that the test was that of "the ordinary reasonable man", i.e. an objective test.

[76] Implicit support for this view can be found in *Birmingham City Council v Oakley* [2001] 1 All ER 385, where Lord Clyde observed: "It is to the state of the premises themselves that attention is required to be paid and in approaching the matter of the state of the premises it is clear that an objective viewpoint is required. One should not be looking to the particular requirements of a particular occupier" (at 398).

[77] *ibid.*

mould.[78] But will premises fall within the category "prejudicial to health" in circumstances where only those with asthmatic susceptibilities may become unwell. The tenant's son in *Cunningham* may be regarded as having possessed highly unusual sensitivities. It remains to be seen whether susceptibility to substantially more common health conditions, such as asthmatic or bronchial problems, is to be regarded as a propensity to illness possessed by the ordinary person, or by persons only with abnormal susceptibility.

Basis for magistrates' decision: expert evidence or judicial notice?

Upon what basis should magistrates come to conclusions as regards whether the evidentially demonstrated condition of premises is such as to be likely to have a prejudicial effect on the health of ordinary occupants? This matter was considered in *London Borough of Southwark* v *Simpson*.[79]

The complaint in this case related to premises in which there was dampness, mould growth on internal and external walls, and condensation. It was alleged that the premises were "in such a state as to be prejudicial to health". The magistrates heard evidence about the state of the premises from the complainant, other witnesses, and also a chartered surveyor. The surveyor gave evidence principally as regards the causes of the defects. No expert witnesses were called as regards the likely health consequences of the condition of the premises. However, questions about this were put to the chartered surveyor, who stressed that he had no medical expertise but had read articles which indicated that there was such a likely connection. The surveyor was not, however, able to offer the court any details as to the literature to which he alluded.

The court heard evidence that the complainant and her three children (17, 3 and 3 months) were obliged to sleep in their living room due to the severity of the mould and damp problems in the bedroom, and that the two younger children had continuing respiratory problems – in the case of the three year old, problems which were quite severe. The magistrates, on the evidence presented to them, drew the conclusion that the premises were prejudicial to health. On appeal the Divisional Court held that, following *Patel* v *Mehtab*,[80] it was necessary for the court to be informed by expert evidence about the likely health effects following from the condition of premises.[81] This was not a matter upon which magistrates were entitled to draw

---

[78] See, for example, *Greater London Council* v *London Borough of Tower Hamlets* (1983) 15 HLR 54. Dampness and condensation associated mould growth will not, however, amount to a statutory nuisance where it has been caused by an occupant's lifestyle and a failure to take measures, e.g. not using a heating system due to cost, to combat it: *Dover District Council* v *Farrar and others* (1980) 12 HLR 32; *Pike* v *Sefton Metropolitan Borough Council* [2000] EHLR 273.

[79] [1999] Env LR 553.

[80] (1980) 5 HLR 78.

[81] In that case, Donaldson LJ (as he then was) had observed that: "In deciding some questions of fact magistrates are entitled to draw on their own personal experience ... But when it comes to deciding whether the condition of premises is or is not liable or likely to be injurious to health, one is moving outside the field where the tribunal is entitled to draw on its own experience. That is a matter upon which the tribunal needs informed expert evidence": *ibid.* at 82.

conclusions from their own personal knowledge and experience. It was, according to Collins J, "not for untutored laymen [so] to decide".[82] In particular, the mere fact that it might be quite common knowledge that in some circumstances a particular state of premises (e.g. those which are damp) might cause health problems should not be allowed to prejudge whether in the "given case the actual dampness and mould was such as was likely to be injurious to health".[83]

Having indicated the need for the expert evidence the court acknowledged that it was not necessary for such expert evidence to come from persons who were medically qualified. In the *Patel* case the evidence and conclusions as regards prejudice to health had been presented by environmental health officers. Such persons would, typically, have an appropriate degree of experience or expertise so as appropriately to inform the magistrates. A surveyor might also be an appropriate expert witness on this matter. This might be the case where, in the words of Collins J:

> "he had in the course of his duties as a surveyor taken the trouble to consider and deal with the relationship between damp and mould and injury to health."[84]

Furthermore, and following *R* v *Abadom*,[85] there was no objection even where such an expert had acquired that expertise, and could evidence that expertise, only by "hearsay" reference to the findings of other experts.

In *Simpson* itself, however, the chartered surveyor had expressly denied possessing any experience or expertise on these health effects matters. He should, therefore, have been regarded in this respect as a *non-expert* making reference to the views of others: and such evidence should have been excluded as hearsay.

In practice, environmental health officers will often be able to assist magistrates in determining whether or not premises were "prejudicial to health or a nuisance" for the purposes of section 79 of the 1990 Act. Comments to this effect in *London Borough of Southwark* v *Simpson* were subsequently followed and applied in *O'Toole* v *Knowsley Metropolitan Borough Council*,[86] where the High Court held, inter alia, that magistrates had erred in refusing to accept evidence from environmental health officers as to whether premises affected by dampness were prejudicial to health or a nuisance. In the opinion of Dyson J:

> "... it was not necessary for the environmental health officers to possess medical qualifications in order to express an opinion as to whether or not the premises were prejudicial to health as defined by section 79(1)(a) of the Act... The environmental health officers

---

[82] [1999] Env LR 553 at 559.
[83] *ibid.* at 560.
[84] [1999] Env LR 553 at 559.
[85] [1983] 1 ALL ER 364.
[86] [1999] EHLR 420.

possessed appropriate knowledge and expertise which the Justices did not have. By refusing to accept the evidence of those witnesses, the Justices substituted their own view on this issue which they were not entitled to do ..."[87]

"Nuisance"

The 1990 Act does not define what is meant by "nuisance" in the context of Part III of the Act. Accordingly, it would seem that "nuisance" must be accorded the meaning that it has at common law. This was the approach adopted in *National Coal Board* v *Thorne*,[88] where it was alleged that the Coal Board were the owners of premises which constituted a statutory nuisance by reason of being in a state of disrepair.[89] The Divisional Court applied notions of nuisance at common law and held that:

> "... a nuisance cannot arise if what has taken place affects only the person or persons occupying the premises where the nuisance is said to have taken place. A nuisance coming within the meaning of the Public Health Act 1936 must be either a private or public nuisance as understood by common law."[90]

The effect of the decision in *Thorne* is, therefore, that nuisance presupposes an intrusion from off-site. This adoption of the common law meaning of "nuisance" in *Thorne* has subsequently been endorsed by the decisions in *Murdoch* v *Glacier Metal Co*[91] and *Godfrey* v *Conwy County Borough Council*.[92] In the words of Rose LJ in the latter case, it is now clear that "the test for a statutory nuisance is the Common Law test ...".[93]

THE SECTION 79(1) LIST

"Any premises in such a state as to be prejudicial to health or a nuisance": section 79(1)(a)

It has recently been noted judicially that the word "premises" appears on "no less than fourteen occasions in section 79".[94] The meaning of this expression is therefore of some significance. In the nineteenth-century case of *R* v *Parlby*,[95] Wills J construed the term as it appeared in section 91 of the Public Health Act 1875 in such a way as to exclude sewage works from the scope of the provision. In arriving at such a construction his Lordship was influenced by the policy considerations which were considered to

---

[87] *ibid.* at 424.

[88] [1976] 1 WLR 543.

[89] There were two defective windows, no stop end for a rainwater gutter and there was a defective skirting board.

[90] Per Watkins J, [1976] 1 WLR 543 at 547-548.

[91] [1998] EHLR 198; [1998] Env LR 732.

[92] [2001] EHLR 160.

[93] *ibid.* at 167.

[94] Per Scott Baker LJ in *London Borough of Hounslow* v *Thames Water Utilities Ltd* [2003] EWHC Admin 1197 at para. 58.

[95] (1889) 22 QBD 520.

underlie the scheme of the Act. These suggested that Parliament had not intended when legislating to allow an individual to bring a major public sewage works to a halt by establishing before the courts that the works had created a nuisance. In such a case a complainant should instead seek an alternative means of redress to statutory nuisance proceedings, by seeking to enlist the support of the Attorney General to obtain an injunction in proceedings for public nuisance.[96]

The decision in *Parlby* was subsequently explained by Lord Goddard in *R v Epping (Waltham Abbey) Justices, ex parte Burlinson*[97] as follows:

> "That case [*Parlby*] seems to me to decide no more than this, that a nuisance alleged to arise from the construction of a sewage system is not one of the statutory nuisances within the sections of the Public Health Act, and that is really the whole of the decision in that case. No doubt there was an offensive smell arising from it, but the court would not hold that main sewers and sewage works of that description fell within the words of the section; they would not hold that it was one of these statutory nuisances in respect of which alone the justices had power to make an abatement order, and they said the case must be decided by the High Court."[98]

The application of the statutory nuisance regime to sewerage was in issue more recently in *East Riding of Yorkshire Council v Yorkshire Water Services Ltd.*[99] The respondent water company had been served with an abatement notice pursuant to section 80 of the 1990 Act in respect of an alleged statutory nuisance caused by a defect to or a blockage of a sewer. The question for the determination of the court was whether a public sewer could be "premises" for the purposes of section 79(1)(a). The Deputy Stipendiary Magistrate, in an appeal against the abatement notice, had concluded in the light of the existing authorities[100] that a public sewer was not "premises" within the meaning of that section. Notwithstanding "sophisticated submissions" made by counsel on behalf of the council, Maurice Kay J observed:

> "It seems to me that it is beyond dispute that the line of cases, beginning with *Parlby* and culminating in what Lord Goddard said in *ex p. Burlinson*, is indeed authority for the proposition that a public sewer is not premises in the sense in which that word was used in the 1875 Act."[101]

---

[96] For a discussion of the relator action in public nuisance proceedings, see Chapter 8.

[97] [1948] 1 KB 79.

[98] *ibid.* at 87. The distinction here is between the powers of the magistrates under the statutory nuisance procedure, and the more general power of the High Court to issue an injunction in relation to public and private nuisances at common law.

[99] [2001] Env LR 7.

[100] *R v Parlby* (1889) 22 QBD 520 and *Fulham Vestry v London City Council* [1897] 2 QB 76.

[101] [2001] Env LR 7 at para. 23 of the judgment.

The question remained, however, whether the interpretation accorded to "premises" in the 1875 Public Health Act by Wills J in *Parlby* applied also to that word as it appeared in the same provision as re-enacted in an Act passed in 1990. In other words, had the interpretation of 1889 survived the repeal and re-enactment of the provision in respect of which it arose? In answering this question in the affirmative, Maurice Kay J had regard to the presumption that where an identical word has been carried forward from one Act to another, that word shall bear the same meaning in the later Act as it had been afforded by the courts interpreting the earlier Act. The presumption was rebuttable, but the circumstances of the present case did not warrant such rebuttal. Accordingly, a public sewer did not amount to "premises" for the purposes of section 79(1)(a) of the 1990 Act.

A common meaning?

It was noted earlier that in the various paragraphs which comprise section 79(1), the word "premises" appears on 14 occasions. The meaning of that word as used in section 79 (1) (a) has been authoritatively determined in the line of cases culminating in *East Riding*. It might be expected though that the word "premises" would bear the same meaning wherever it appears within section 79(1). However, to so assume would run counter to guidance to be found in the recent decision of *London Borough of Hounslow v Thames Water Utilities Ltd.*[102]

Thames Water were the owners of Mogden Sewage Treatment Works in Isleworth, Middlesex. They had been served with an abatement notice by the council pursuant to section 80 of the Environmental Protection Act 1990. The notice stated that the Council was of the opinion that an odour amounting to a statutory nuisance had occurred at the premises by reason of the release of malodourous gases, such as Hydrogen Sulphide, in the process and treatment of sewage. It further stated that Thames Water was required, as the person responsible for the nuisance, to abate it within 60 days of the service of the notice and to prevent its recurrence. On appeal against the notice Thames Water argued, inter alia, that the sewage treatment works did not constitute premises within the meaning of section 79(1)(d) of the 1990 Act. At a preliminary hearing before District Judge Day, these submissions were accepted and the abatement notice was duly quashed. The Council accordingly appealed. The issue for the Divisional Court to determine was whether the District Judge had been right to hold that the sewage works were excluded from the operation of section 79(1)(d) of the 1990 Act.

Had the matter been free from authority, it is clear that both Pitchford J and Scott Baker LJ would have had little difficulty in concluding that a sewage works could amount to "premises" for the purposes of section 79(1)(d). In the words of Pitchford J:

"Applying ordinary English usage to section 79(1)(d) and (7) it would appear beyond question that the Respondents were carrying on an

---

[102] [2003] EWHC Admin 1197.

industrial process on premises. On the face of it the Respondents qualified for the service of an abatement notice."[103]

The matter was not nearly so straightforward, however, given the existence of the decision in *Parlby*. In *Hounslow*, it was noted that *Parlby* was authority for the proposition that sewage works were not "premises" for the purposes of section 79(1)(a) of the Environmental Protection Act 1990. The question for the Divisional Court was whether a similar construction should be placed on "premises" as it appears in section 79(1)(d) of the 1990 Act?

In answering this question, the Divisional Court, and in particular Pitchford J, had regard to the legislative history of the statutory nuisance provisions. His Lordship also examined the decision in *Parlby* "with some care". However, things had moved on since 1889. In the words of Scott Baker LJ, "life has moved on over the last century, not least in the relationship between local authorities, public utilities and the expectations of the public".[104] Accordingly, since none of the policy considerations identified in 1889 applied to the interpretation of section 79(1) in 2003, it followed that the Divisional Court was not bound by the authority of *Parlby*. The word "premises" in section 79(1)(d) of the Environmental Protection Act 1990 could therefore be construed free from the influence of *Parlby*. In the words of Scott Baker LJ:

> "In my judgment the effect of *Parlby* is relevant only to section 79(1)(a) of the 1990 Act. It should not be allowed to spill over into other provisions where the word 'premises' is used and which on its natural interpretation must include sewage treatment works."[105]

"Smoke emitted from premises so as to be prejudicial to health or a nuisance": section 79(1)(b)

For the purposes of this second category of statutory nuisance, "smoke":

> "includes soot, ash, grit and gritty particles emitted in smoke."[106]

In *Griffiths* v *Pembrokeshire County Council*[107] the appellant occupied a property in Pembrokeshire at which he kept a pack of hounds. The hounds were fed on animal carcasses and from time to time, bones and other residues from the carcasses were burnt, along with the hounds' bedding, in the rear yard of the premises. His neighbours complained to the council. Being satisfied that this amounted to a statutory nuisance under section 79(1)(b) of the 1990 Act, the council served an abatement notice. That notice identified the statutory nuisance as arising from:

---

[103] [2003] EWHC Admin 1197, at para. 11 of the judgment.
[104] *ibid.* at para. 56 of the judgment.
[105] *ibid.* at para. 70 of the judgment.
[106] Section 79(7) of the Environmental Protection Act 1990.
[107] [2000] EHLR 359.

"The periodic burning of animal carcase remains within the rear yard ... giving rise to a smoke nuisance, to the occupants of the neighbouring property."

The notice required the abatement of the nuisance and the prohibition of its recurrence. In the schedule of works to the notice, the appellant was required either to cease burning carcasses "unless reasonable and adequate steps can be taken to have due regard to wind direction and direct supervision at all times of the fire whilst lit"; or to make suitable alternative arrangements for the final disposal of the carcasses, e.g. collection by an approved renderer. It was alleged by the council that on three separate occasions, the appellant had either contravened or failed to comply with the terms of the abatement notice. He was convicted by magistrates of the three offences and fined £300 in respect of each. In subsequent proceedings before the Divisional Court an argument was raised that the magistrates had applied a wrong definition of "smoke".

It was argued by the appellant that any smoke which had passed over the neighbouring property was at too high a level to cause a nuisance. It was further argued that although there may have been a smell, the nuisance identified in the abatement notice as being a "smoke nuisance" rather than a nuisance arising from smell.[108]

The judgment of the Divisional Court was delivered by Kennedy LJ, who drew attention to dictionary definition of "smoke":

"the visible volatile product given off by a burning or smouldering substance."

However, as Kennedy LJ pointed out, "smoke" also had a meaning in "common parlance". In such parlance, "smoke" he observed, can "also be applied to the smell of smoke".[109] Thus in his judgment, the Crown Court had been entitled to accept evidence that "it was possible to detect the smell of smoke when nothing can be seen with the naked eye".[110] For this reason the argument that the abatement notice should have been framed by reference to section 79(1)(c) or (d) rather than (b) had no substance.

"Fumes or gases emitted from premises so as to be prejudicial to health or a nuisance": section 79(1)(c)

"Fumes" are defined by section 79(7) of the 1990 Act to mean:

"any airborne solid matter smaller than dust."

That subsection further provides that "gas":

---

[108] "Smell" which arises on industrial, trade or business premises and which is prejudicial to health or a nuisance is, as we have seen, a statutory nuisance in its own right: see s. 79(1)(d) of the 1990 Act.

[109] [2000] EHLR 359 at 363.

[110] *ibid.* at 363-364.

"includes vapour and moisture precipitated from vapour."

It should be noted that for the purposes of section 79(1)(c) the word "premises" is accorded a narrower meaning than it has elsewhere in Part III of the 1990 Act. In this present context it is confined to private dwellings.[111] The emission of fumes or gases from industrial or commercial purposes does not therefore fall within the scope of this provision, although it may be caught by section 79(1)(d).[112]

It will be remembered that in *Griffiths* v *Pembrokeshire County Council*[113] the appellant argued, inter alia, that the abatement notice served upon him had been wrongly framed in that it should have referred to a statutory nuisance under section 79(1)(c) or (d) rather than (b). As we saw this argument failed given the wide meaning that the Divisional Court was prepared to accord to "smoke". On the facts, however, it would seem that it would not have been inappropriate to have referred to section 79(1)(c) in the abatement notice. "Fumes" may well be a word which is broad enough to encompass "smell". If this were the case, the issue would then have been whether the property occupied by the appellant was a private dwelling.

"Any dust, steam, smell or other effluvia arising on industrial, trade or business premises and being prejudicial to health or a nuisance": section 79(1)(d)

For the purposes of this provision, "dust":

> "does not include dust emitted from a chimney as an ingredient of smoke."[114]

"Industrial, trade or business premises" means:

> "premises used for any industrial, trade or business purposes or premises not so used on which matter is burnt in connection with any industrial, trade or business process, and premises are used for industrial processes where they are used for the purposes of any treatment or process as well as where they are used for the purposes of manufacturing."[115]

Of all the categories of statutory nuisance listed in section 79(1) this is the only category which is expressly confined to "industrial, trade or business premises" as being the source of the nuisance.

The 1990 Act only partly defines the terms referred to above. The definition of "dust", for example, is rather limited. In truth its purpose is to state what is not "dust" for the purposes of section 79(1)(d) rather than to positively define what that word does mean in the present context.

---

[111] Section 79(4) of the 1990 Act.
[112] See further below.
[113] [2000] EHLR 359.
[114] Section 79(7) of the 1990 Act.
[115] *ibid.*

Some limitation to the scope of application of this category of statutory nuisance was indicated in *Wivenhoe Port* v *Colchester Borough Council*,[116] where it was alleged that dust from the handling of soya meal constituted a statutory nuisance. Butler J remarked:

> "To be within the spirit of the Act [section 92(1)(a) of the Public Health Act 1936] a nuisance to be a statutory nuisance has to be one interfering materially with the personal comfort of the residents, in the sense that it materially affects their well-being although it may not be prejudicial to their health. Thus, dust falling on motor cars might cause inconvenience to their owners, it might even diminish the value of their motor cars, but it will not be a statutory nuisance. In the same way, dust falling on gardens or trees, or on stock held in a shop will not be a statutory nuisance. But dust in eyes or hair, even if not shown to be prejudicial to health, will be so as an interference with personal comfort."[117]

In respect of the meaning of some of the other terms in section 79(1)(d), the Act is silent. Thus "steam", "smell" and "effluvia" are not defined. Nor, for that matter, is any light shed upon what is meant by "industrial", "trade" or "business".

"Steam" and "smell" may perhaps be regarded as sufficiently well understood terms as not to require further consideration, save to say that the former term does not apply to steam emitted from a railway locomotive engine.[118]

The meaning of "effluvia" is not perhaps quite so obvious. It is the plural of "effluvium", which is defined by the *Compact Oxford English Dictionary* as follows:

> "a flowing out, an issuing forth."

In *Malton Board of Health* v *Malton Manure Co*,[119] the effluvium which was said to amount to a nuisance resulted from the processing or manufacturing of artificial manures. It had been blown or carried into the homes of residents living some 200 yards away from the respondents' works and in one or two cases, had been claimed to have caused nausea and vomiting. In the words of Kelly CB:

> "I am clearly of opinion that any effluvium such as that complained of, which had the effect of causing any person who is ill to become worse, is within the Act."[120]

---

[116] [1985] JPL 175.
[117] At 178. Butler J's decision was later affirmed by the Court of Appeal: [1985] JPL 396.
[118] Section 79(5).
[119] (1879) 4 Ex D 302.
[120] *ibid.* at 305.

"Any accumulation or deposit which is prejudicial to health or a nuisance": section 79(1)(e)

This provision has existed in broadly similar terms in public health legislation since the Nuisances Removal Act 1855. Under that Act it was held, for example, that an accumulation of sheep droppings on a pavement amounted to a nuisance,[121] as did an accumulation of seaweed in a harbour.[122] Other examples of accumulations or deposits amounting to a nuisance include: a pile of garden manure which gave off smells and attracted large numbers of flies;[123] an accumulation of cinders and ashes which emitted offensive smells;[124] and an accumulation of soil on the defendant's land which was put there to raise the surface but which resulted in rainwater seeping through the defendant's wall and into the plaintiff's house.[125]

More recently, it will be remembered that in *Coventry City Council* v *Cartwright*,[126] the Divisional Court considered that the provision was aimed at "an accumulation of something which produces a threat to health in the sense of a threat of disease, vermin[127] or the like".[128] Accordingly, in that case it was held that quantities of rubble and other inert builders' waste did not constitute a statutory nuisance.

"Any animal kept in such a place or manner as to be prejudicial to health or a nuisance": section 79(1)(f)

There is a degree of overlap between this category of statutory nuisance and the power that local authorities have under section 235 of the Local Government Act 1972 to make byelaws for good rule and government and the suppression of nuisances.[129] In *Galer* v *Morrissey*,[130] Kent County Council had made a byelaw pursuant to section 249(1) of the Local Government Act 1933[131] which provided that:

---

[121] *Draper* v *Sperring* (1861) 10 CB (NS) 113.

[122] *Margate Pier and Harbour Co* v *Margate Town Council* (1869) 33 JP 437.

[123] *Bland* v *Yates* (1914) 58 SJ 612.

[124] *Bishop Auckland Local Board* v *Bishop Auckland Iron & Steel Co* (1882) 10 QBD 138.

[125] *Hardman* v *North Eastern Rly* (1878) 3 CPD 168.

[126] [1975] 1 WLR 845. See above, at p. 423.

[127] Where it is necessary to keep land free from rats or mice or to destroy those which are present on the land local authorities have the power to issue a notice to the owner or occupier of the land requiring them to take such reasonable steps as are necessary for either of these purposes: see s. 4(1) of the Prevention of Damage by Pests Act 1949, *Albion* v *Railtrack Plc* [1998] EHLR 83 and, *Leeds City Council* v *Spencer* [1999] EHLR 394.

[128] Per Lord Widgery CJ, [1975] 1 WLR 845 at 849.

[129] The model byelaw provides that: "no person shall keep within any … premises any noisy animal which shall be or cause a serious nuisance to residents of the neighbourhood". For the meaning of "serious nuisance", see *Phillips* v *Crawford* (1984) 72 LGR 199. In *Galer* v *Morrisey* [1955] 1 All ER 380, Lord Goddard CJ opined: "I think the word 'serious' may give rise to a great deal of dispute. If a nuisance is proved, it is a nuisance whether it is or is not serious".

[130] [1955] 1 All ER 380.

[131] The power conferred by this section was expressed in much the same terms as the power later enacted in s. 235 of the Local Government Act 1972.

"No person shall keep within any house, building, or premises any noisy animal which shall be or cause a serious nuisance to residents in the neighbourhood."

The respondent, the owner of a number greyhound dogs who barked and made a noise, was convicted and fined for having breached this byelaw at his premises. He appealed against that conviction, however, on the basis that the byelaw was ultra vires and unreasonable. It was contended that the byelaw was bad because its subject matter was already dealt with by section 92(1)(b) of the Public Health Act 1936.[132] In due course the Divisional Court held that the byelaw was good. Lord Goddard CJ observed:

"In my opinion it is clear that this byelaw does not deal with the same matter as the statute… The conditions under which the animal is kept may create a nuisance and an abatement notice can be served, but the subsection [section 92(1)(b)] does not deal with a noisy animal. A noisy animal may be kept in the most sanitary conditions and yet still be a nuisance."[133]

Lord Goddard CJ continued:

"What puts the matter beyond doubt is that you find this provision in Part III of the Public Health Act, 1936, which is headed 'Nuisances and offensive trades' and there is a fasciculus of sections, all of which deal with factories, houses unfit for human habitation and smoke nuisance — all matters which come from insanitary or defective premises. It is clear, to my mind, that s. 92(1) is dealing with cases where, for example, pigs are kept so near to other houses as to cause a nuisance from effluvia."[134]

Galer v *Morrissey* would appear to be authority for the proposition that section 79(1)(f) of the 1990 Act is not sufficiently wide to cover a nuisance caused by a noisy animal: it being confined to instances where, for example, a nuisance is caused by the smell of an animal. However, in *Coventry City Council* v *Cartwright*[135] Lord Widgey CJ doubted this distinction. His Lordship observed:

"I would have thought for my own part that a noisy animal could as much be prejudicial to health as a smelly animal …"[136]

---

[132] This provision was expressed in the same terms as s. 79(1)(f) of the Environmental Protection Act 1990.

[133] [1955] 1 All ER 380 at 380.

[134] *ibid.* Lord Goddard CJ also noted how counsel for the appellant had drawn the court's attention to the fact that several local Acts gave express powers to deal with noisy animals in pursuance of s. 92(1). Lord Goddard accepted that this constituted a "recognition by Parliament that noisy animals do not come within s. 92(1)(b)" although he went on to observe that the appeal was being allowed "on a matter of construction of the sub-section": *ibid* at 381.

[135] [1975] 1 WLR 845.

[136] *ibid.* at 850.

Faced with this inconsistency between the reported authorities it may be helpful to have regard to an unreported authority in order to determine which is the better view. In *Myatt* v *Teignbridge District Council*,[137] the appellant lived in a house (and had the opportunity to occupy the next door house) along with 17 dogs. The dogs were the subject of complaints made by neighbours to the local council. The appellant was subsequently served with an abatement notice in respect of each of the two houses. The first notice informed the appellant that she was to "cease the keeping of dogs" and the second notice instructed her to "reduce the number of dogs kept at the premises to no more than two and to take such steps as are necessary in the housing, welfare and management of the dogs to ensure that they do not cause a nuisance". The appellant failed to exercise her statutory right of appeal against the notices and the magistrates went on to find that the matters were proved. On appeal, the issue for the Divisional Court to consider was whether or not the notices were set out with sufficient particularity.

It was argued on behalf of the appellant that whilst she knew from the abatement notices what she had to do to put matters right, it was not obvious from either notice what in fact was wrong. In other words since the keeping of dogs does not in itself amount to a statutory nuisance the abatement notices should have stated the nature of the alleged statutory nuisance.

In giving the judgment of the Court, Butler-Sloss LJ was prepared to accept that the drafting of the abatement notice displayed a lack of care on the part of the council. However, in Her Ladyship's opinion:

> "... where you have a person who is keeping 17 dogs in one or two presumably quite small properties and which has been the subject of criticism from neighbours, it really requires one to have an exceptionally technical approach to say that they would not know when complaint is made what it is that people are complaining about. The only two possibilities would be noise and/or smell.... Anybody who keeps 17 dogs must know when they get an abatement notice in respect of a statutory nuisance where the sections of the Environmental Protection Act 1990 is dealt with, and the only subsection which is relevant is (f), subject to noise in general coming under (g), but noise comes in my view under (f), that it is to be animals, because it is the keeping of dogs, and the keeping of 17 dogs in the circumstances in which [the appellant] kept them, it must have been absolutely clear to her what was objectionable."[138]

In this not entirely clear passage we find some support for the proposition that a noisy animal can come within the terms of section 79(1)(f) even though noise nuisances from premises are also caught by section

---

[137] [1995] Env LR 78.
[138] *ibid.* at 81.

79(1)(g).[139] In later cases where the barking or howling of dogs has been alleged to amount to a statutory nuisance, the relevant local authorities have opted to serve abatement notices under section 79(1)(g) rather than section 79(1)(f).[140] This reflects Butler-Sloss LJ's observations about the general nature of that subsection. However, it does not necessarily rule out the possibility of the service of an abatement notice under section 79(1)(f). Moreover, since in neither of the later cases were the courts referred to either *Galer* or *Cartwright*, the inconsistency between those two cases remains.[141] It would seem, therefore, that a noisy animal may amount to a statutory nuisance contrary to section 79(1)(f).

"Noise emitted from premises so as to be prejudicial to health or a nuisance": section 79(1)(g)

Noise is an insidious environmental problem[142] and this category of statutory nuisance is invoked on a regular basis by local authorities, reflecting the high incidence of noise complaints that they receive from members of the public.

For the purposes of section 79(1)(g), "noise" is defined to include vibration.[143] However, noise emanating from premises occupied for naval, military or air force purposes or for the purposes of a visiting force is excluded from the ambit of this provision,[144] as is noise caused by aircraft other than model aircraft.[145]

When determining whether or not "noise" amounts to a statutory nuisance for the purposes of the 1990 Act, the test to be applied is that derived from the common law.[146] In other words, whether the noise constitutes an unreasonable interference with the use and enjoyment of land, judged by the standard of the reasonable man and taking into account the nature of the area.

In *Godfrey* v *Conwy County Borough Council*,[147] the appellant owned a house with outbuildings, one of which had been converted into a music studio where rock bands practised. The house and outbuildings were situated in an extremely quiet rural location where the only source of noise was agriculture, wildlife, a river and the weather. The appellants' neighbours, who lived some 180 metres away, complained to the council

---

[139] See further below.

[140] See *Budd* v *Colchester Borough Council* [1997] Env LR 128 (DC) and [1999] Env LR 739 (CA) and *Manley and Manley* v *New Forest District Council* [2000] EHLR 113.

[141] It should be noted also that the remarks of Butler-Sloss LJ in *Myatt* v *Teignbridge District Council* were made without reference to either *Galer* or *Cartwright*.

[142] Note also that other public law controls exist in respect of noise from raves and noise from dwellings at night: see the Criminal Justice and Public Order Act 1994 and the Noise Act 1996, respectively.

[143] Section 79(7) of the 1990 Act.

[144] Section 79(2)(a) and (b). But note that such nuisance may be actionable at common law.

[145] Section 79(6).

[146] *Murdoch* v *Glacier Metal Co Ltd* [1998] EHLR 198.

[147] [2001] EHLR 160.

about the noise made by the playing of drums and amplified music. A council officer investigated the complaint, visiting the area on three separate occasions. On the third occasion she tried to take readings using a noise meter but was unable to do so due to the sound of haymaking in a nearby field. However, she formed the view that the sound of the drums and bass could be heard clearly notwithstanding the tractor noise, and that the noise would affect the enjoyment of the neighbouring property.

The appellant was served with an abatement notice pursuant to section 80 of the 1990 Act. In the Divisional Court it was contended by the appellant that in order for there to be a statutory nuisance there must be something more than a nuisance at common law: it was necessary also for the noise to give rise to a health hazard. Moreover, the appellant sought also to argue that there could only be a statutory nuisance if a particular decibel level was reached, since this was a way of determining that the noise level was capable of causing injury to health. The appellant referred the Court to statement in a number of cases, including *R* v *Bristol City Council, ex p Everett*[148] and *National Coal Board* v *Thorne*.[149] In the latter case, Watkins J referred to an argument to the effect that:

> "Not only must a statutory nuisance be either of a private or a public kind at common law, but the act of nuisance itself must be such as comes within the spirit of the Public Health Act 1936, by which I assume [counsel] to be saying that whatever is complained about must in some way be directed to the health of the person who claims to be or who has been affected by the nuisance. I find that proposition to be an attractive one although I foresee difficulties, assuming it to be right, in the application of it in certain circumstances."[150]

Counsel for the respondent drew attention to the repeated appearance of "prejudicial to health or a nuisance" in section 79(1)(a)-(ga) in support of the argument that Parliament could not have intended to equate nuisance with prejudice to health. Had Parliament so intended, the word "nuisance" would have been otiose. Moreover, the nineteenth-century authorities did not support the submissions made by counsel for the appellant. Rather, they demonstrated that even then, injury to health was not a necessary requirement of nuisance. Thus in *Bishop Auckland Local Board* v *Bishop Auckland Iron and Steel Co Ltd*,[151] it was held:

> "That an accumulation or deposit of cinders and ashes was a nuisance if it emitted offensive smells which interfered with the personal comfort of persons living in the neighbourhood, but did not cause injury to health."[152]

---

[148] [1999] Env LR 587. For a discussion of this case, see above at p. 421.
[149] [1976] 1 WLR 543.
[150] *ibid.* at 548.
[151] (1882) 10 QBD 138.
[152] See headnote, *ibid.*

In giving the judgment of the Divisional Court, Rose LJ accepted the respondent's submissions. In his opinion (with which Moses J agreed):

> "... it is, on the statutory provisions to which I have referred, impossible to contend either that a decibel level, or noise above the naturally occurring ambient level, must be demonstrated before a statutory nuisance can be shown. The test for a statutory nuisance is the common law test..."[153]

Acoustic evidence

In practice where it is alleged that a noise nuisance has breached the terms of an abatement notice such an allegation will generally be supported by acoustic measurement evidence. However, it is clear from the decision in *Lewisham LBC* v *Hall*[154] that the production of such evidence is not a precondition of conviction. Justices are therefore entitled to convict in the absence of acoustic evidence, relying instead on the evidence of an environmental health officer or lay witness. Whether or not they are satisfied to the required standard of proof that a noise nuisance has breached the terms of an abatement notice in the absence of acoustic evidence is, however, a matter for the justices to determine on a case by case basis.

"Noise that is prejudicial to health or a nuisance and is emitted from or caused by a vehicle, machinery or equipment in a street": section 79(1)(ga)

This category of statutory nuisance was added to section 79 by the Noise and Statutory Nuisance Act 1993.[155] It does not apply, however, to noise made by traffic, any naval, military or air force[156] or by a political demonstration or a demonstration supporting or opposing a cause or campaign.[157] For the purposes of section 79(1)(ga), "street":

> "means a highway and any other road, footway, square[158] or court that is for the time being open to the public."

In *London Borough of Harringey* v *Jowett*,[159] the Divisional Court acknowledged that section 79 as originally enacted made no provision for traffic noise but that in the light of observations made in *Southwark*

---

[153] [2001] EHLR 160 at 167.

[154] [2003] Env LR 4.

[155] Section 2.

[156] The exception applies to such forces of the Crown and to a visiting force for the purposes of the Visiting Forces Act 1952: see s. 79(2) and (6A).

[157] Section 79(6A).

[158] In *Tower Hamlets London Borough Council* v *Creitzman* (1985) 83 LGR 72, it was held that whether or not a particular place could properly be described as a court or square was essentially a question of fact for the justices. In the absence of a legal definition of "square", it ought to be given its ordinary and natural meaning. In the circumstances of the case and considering the object of the Control of Pollution Act 1974, it was held that an open space beneath a building could properly be described as a "square".

[159] [1999] EHLR 410.

London Borough v *Ince*,[160] it was wide enough to embrace such noise. However, *Ince* had been decided prior to the addition of subsection (1)(ga). In the opinion of Kennedy LJ (with which Mitchell J agreed), since that provision came into force:

> "section 79(1)(a) must be read together with, and in the light of, the additional provisions [subsections (1)(ga) and (6A)] which now form part of section 79."[161]

Accordingly:

> "...since 1994 the ambit of section 79(1)(a) must be regarded as restricted so as to exclude traffic noise from vehicles, machinery and equipment in the street."[162]

Thus it would seem that traffic noise falls outside the scope of the statutory nuisance provisions in section 79 of the 1990 Act.

"Any other matter declared by an enactment to be a statutory nuisance": section 79(1)(h)

Section 79(1)(h) brings into one final, miscellaneous category, all those other nuisances which are declared by other statutes to be statutory nuisances. The key statute in this context is the Public Health Act 1936.[163] It states, for example, that:

> "Any well, tank, cistern, or water-butt used for the supply of water for domestic purposes which is so placed, constructed or kept as to render the water therein liable to contamination and to be prejudicial to health, shall be a statutory nuisance ..."[164]

With regard to nuisances in connection with watercourses etc., the 1936 Act provides that the following are statutory nuisances:

> "any pond, pool, ditch, gutter or watercourse which is so foul or in such a state as to be prejudicial to health or a nuisance;[165] any part of a watercourse, not being a part ordinarily navigated by vessels employed in the carriage of goods by water, which is so choked or silted up as to obstruct or impede the proper flow of water and thereby to cause a nuisance, or give rise to conditions prejudicial to health."[166]

The 1936 Act further provides that a tent, van, shed or similar structure used for human habitation is a statutory nuisance where it, "is in such a

---

[160] (1989) 21 HLR 504.

[161] [1999] EHLR 410 at 415.

[162] *ibid.*

[163] However, see also s. 151 of the Mines and Quarries Act 1954.

[164] Section 141 of the 1936 Act.

[165] Section 259(1)(a). See *R* v *Falmouth and Truro Port Health Authority, ex p South West Water Ltd* [2000] 3 All ER 306, discussed below at pp. 455-460.

[166] Section 259(1)(b).

state, or so overcrowded, as to be prejudicial to the health of the inmates",[167] or where:

> "the use of which, by reason of the absence of proper sanitary accommodation or otherwise, gives rise, whether on the site or on other land, to a nuisance or to conditions prejudicial to health ..."[168]

---

[167] Section 268(2)(a).
[168] Section 268(2)(b).

Chapter 12

STATUTORY NUISANCE: PROCEDURAL
MATTERS

INTRODUCTION

In this chapter we move from the substantive law of statutory nuisance to describe the procedures associated with statutory nuisance proceedings (initiated by local authorities or by individuals), criminal penalties, rights of appeal, and the rules which apply as regards costs.

LOCAL AUTHORITY PROCEEDINGS

Inspection

Local authorities[1] are under a "duty ... to cause their areas to be inspected from time to time" to detect any nuisances "which ought to be dealt with" under the Act. Moreover, where a complaint of a statutory nuisance is made to such a local authority by a person living within its area the authority is under a duty to take such steps as are reasonably practicable to investigate that complaint.[2]

Duty to serve abatement notice

Where, upon such inspection or investigation, a local authority is satisfied that a statutory nuisance exists, or is likely to occur or recur, the local authority is required by section 80 to serve an abatement notice.[3]

That section 80 is couched in terms of duty rather than discretion was emphasised by the Divisional Court in *R* v *Carrick District Council ex parte Shelley.*[4] The case arose out of pollution problems experienced at the Cornish beach of Porthtowan[5] as a consequence of sewage-related debris becoming washed up onto the shore. Evidence suggested that amongst a volume of some 20 to 40 bags of ordinary litter collected from the beach each day during the summer season there would be included about one

---

[1] As defined in the Environmental Protection Act 1990, s. 79(7). In England the functions are vested in the London Boroughs and the district councils.

[2] Section 79(1).

[3] As far as the drafting, form and content of an abatement notice is concerned, Malcolm has commented that: "Normally, the notice is drafted by the officer investigating the case and will be signed by an authorising officer. At this stage it is unlikely, in most authorities, that a lawyer will be consulted. There is no statutory form of notice and the notices which are habitually used are pro formas. These have space to be completed which indicate the name of the alleged perpetrator, the source of the nuisance and the period of time allowed for compliance. In addition the notice will contain a requirement to abate the nuisance and/or to prevent its recurrence": see "Statutory Nuisance: The Validity of Abatement Notices" [2000] JPL 894 at 894-895.

[4] [1996] Env LR 273.

[5] Described by the judge as "an attractive bay and sandy beach ... apparently good for surfing".

kilogramme (net weight) of sewage-related debris – in the form principally of sanitary towels and condoms. The sources of this debris were two sewage outfalls (serving Redruth and Camborne). Both outfalls had been granted modified discharge consents by the National Rivers Authority in late 1992. However, these consents, requiring screening at both outfalls, were not complied with by the Water Authority to which they were addressed, pending the outcome of appeals to the Secretary of State. These appeals were still pending at the date of hearing and judgment in the statutory nuisance proceedings under discussion – April 1996 – a circumstance which the trial judge considered to be "quite extraordinary".

Local pressure against this unpleasantness was led by "Surfers Against Sewage". This group called upon the local district council to take statutory nuisance proceedings in respect of the matter. The issue was regarded as sufficiently important to be referred, within the district council, to the Environmental and Community Services Committee, rather than (as is more typically the case) being determined by an environmental health officer acting under delegated authority. The committee decided against the initiation of immediate statutory nuisance proceedings. It had before it a report from its Chief Environmental Health Officer, which had expressed the view that "there are grounds for considering that the accumulation of sewage-derived material could, under extreme circumstances, be considered as being a statutory nuisance". The report warned, however, that "action under the Environmental Protection Act 1990 could be difficult to sustain, given the information currently available". The report recommended no immediate statutory nuisance proceedings, but rather a combination of further monitoring and evidence gathering, together with lobbying and complaint in appropriate quarters.

The committee adopted a similar approach. The minute of its decision referred to a lengthy debate on the matter and a resolution that further beach monitoring should occur, that the Committee Chairman should write to the Minister calling upon the Minister to reject the Water Authority's appeals against the screening requirements, and that further work should be done to study dispersal routes from the suspect outfalls. The resolution concluded:

> "... upon due consideration of the evidence available to the council, ... service of [a] notice under the provisions of the Environmental Protection Act 1990 is not considered appropriate and therefore shall not be pursued at the current time."

The applicants argued that the minute indicated that the Committee had come to an improper conclusion as a consequence of having misdirected itself, or had simply misunderstood its legal responsibilities. The committee had asked itself whether as a matter of political strategy it was appropriate to initiate statutory nuisance procedures. This, it was contended, was to have adopted a wrong approach. In the words of Carnwath J, summarising the argument of counsel for the applicants:

"... it is not a question of appropriateness, which imports considerations of expediency and discretion."[6]

Rather, it was:

"... a question of fact; is there an accumulation or deposit which materially affects the personal comfort of the people using the beach? If so, who is responsible? If those questions are answered so as to result in a decision that there is a statutory nuisance and someone is identified as responsible, then action follows."[7]

The question for the court, accepting this argument that in such a situation the initiation of proceedings was a matter of duty and not discretion, was, accordingly, one of fact: in the words of section 80 – was the committee satisfied that a statutory nuisance existed? Carnwath J reviewed closely the wording of the minute of the committee's decision, and also regarded two other documents as potentially relevant to his finding of fact on this matter: the report to the committee from the CEHO (which was somewhat equivocal as to whether a statutory nuisance existed) and the letter subsequently written to the Minister by the committee's chairman, in part implementation of the terms of the resolution. Carnwath J was satisfied, on the totality of this evidence, that the committee had opted not to take proceedings notwithstanding its opinion that a statutory nuisance *did* exist and that the Water Authority was responsible for that nuisance. In so resolving, the committee had failed in its duties under section 80 and a declaration to that effect was granted.

Consultation prior to service of an abatement notice

Where a local authority has satisfied itself that a statutory nuisance exists and it is accordingly under a duty to serve an abatement notice pursuant to section 80, must it first consult the alleged perpetrator of the nuisance? In other words, is the duty to serve an abatement notice preceded by a corresponding duty (either under statute or at common law) to consult as part of the investigative process?

This issue was considered by both the High Court and the Court of Appeal in *R v Falmouth and Truro Port Health Authority, ex p South West Water Ltd*.[8] In this case South West Water was under a statutory duty pursuant to section 94 of the Water Industry Act 1991 to deal with the contents of sewers within its area. Pursuant to that duty South West Water provided a sewerage outfall as an interim phase of a larger scheme. This involved laying a pipe 760 metres offshore to the outfall point where sewage was to be fine-screened and then discharged at particular times in the tidal cycle. The interim phase had been undertaken in order that the UK could meet its obligations under the EC Bathing Waters Directive.[9] The second phase of

---

[6] [1996] Env LR 273 at 282.
[7] *ibid.*
[8] [1999] EHLR 358 (QBD); [2000] 3 All ER 306 (CA).
[9] EC 76/160.

the scheme, which was to involve the biological treatment of the sewage at the outfall, was for the purposes of compliance with the EC Urban Waste Water Treatment Directive.[10]

In order to discharge sewage into the sea as part of the first phase South West Water required a consent from the Environment Agency under Part III of the Water Resources Act 1991. A discharge consent was duly granted, subject to conditions relating to, inter alia, the discharge times relative to the tides. Subsequently, Falmouth and Truro Port Health Authority received complaints about the outfall operation. These were brought to the attention of South West Water in a letter sent by a deputy port health authority officer in which it was stated that early indications suggested that they were not without foundation. That letter invited South West Water to contact the Authority if it had any observations to make regarding the complaints. South West Water replied the same day. In that reply it requested to view any medical or scientific evidence which the Authority had in its possession relating to the matter. At a meeting held on the same day as the receipt of the reply, the Authority considered the interim sewage scheme and resolved that, subject to a favourable opinion being obtained from counsel, it would serve an abatement notice on South West Water pursuant to section 80 of the 1990 Act. That notice was duly served after having taken advice from the Environment Agency as to how long it might take to make changes to the interim scheme and following the receipt of water quality sampling results. It stated that the Authority was satisfied that a statutory nuisance existed under section 79(1)(h) of the 1990 Act, the relevant enactment being section 259(1)(a) of the Public Health Act 1936. The notice required that the discharge of sewage from the outfall should cease within a period three months. Moreover, it stated that in accordance with regulation 3(3)(b) of the Statutory Nuisance (Appeals) Regulations 1995,[11] the notice would not be suspended pending any appeal to the magistrates' court.

South West Water appealed to the magistrates' court against the abatement notice. However, given the effect of regulation 3(3)(b), it also sought leave to apply for judicial review. Following a contested hearing, leave was duly granted by Collins J who also granted a stay of the abatement notice and a stay of the appeal to the magistrates' court pending the determination of the substantive judicial review application. Before Harrison J a number of issues relating to consultation arose for determination.

On behalf of applicants it was argued that the Authority had been under a duty to consult South West Water as part of the statutory scheme. That duty arose as part of the duty under section 79(1) of the 1990 Act to investigate complaints of a statutory nuisance. It was argued that consultation, by which it was meant giving the applicant an adequate opportunity and sufficient information to enable it to comment on the complaints – whether the sewage outfall gave rise to prejudice to health or

---

[10] EC 91/271.
[11] SI 1995/2644.

a nuisance and, what the applicant could reasonably be expected to do to address the complaints within the timescale – was a necessary part of the investigative process.[12] South West Water acknowledged that the duty to consult was not absolute: there might, for example, be cases, such as an emergency or where the alleged perpetrator was physically absent, where consultation would not be possible. Arguing in the alternative, counsel contended that if such a duty did not exist under the statutory scheme, then it arose under the common law as a supplement to that scheme. In support of this argument counsel relied on the words of Lord Bridge in *Lloyd* v *McMahon*,[13] where his Lordship had observed:

> "…it is well established that when a statute has conferred on anybody the power to make decisions affecting individuals, the court will not only require the procedure prescribed by the statute to be followed, but will readily imply so much and no more to be introduced by way of additional procedural safeguards as will ensure the attainment of fairness."[14]

It was further submitted that the duty to consult could be implied in all cases where an abatement notice was served, and that it was especially appropriate where the notice was not suspended pending an appeal. Moreover, counsel for the applicant contended that it was unfair that an alleged perpetrator of a statutory nuisance could have an abatement notice served on him without any advance warning or an opportunity to comment upon what it proposed. This was inimical to good administration.

Counsel for the Authority's submissions had four main strands. First, it was contended that there was nothing in the duty to investigate complaints under section 79(1) which imported a general duty to consult prior to the service of an abatement notice. Moreover, it was argued that such a requirement would be defeated by the effect of the immediate duty under section 80(1) once an enforcing authority was satisfied that a statutory nuisance existed.[15] Secondly, it was argued by way of analogy with the suspension notice regime under the Consumer Protection Act 1987 and the decision of the Court of Appeal in *R* v *Birmingham City Council, ex p Ferrero*[16] in respect of that regime, that a duty to consult would frustrate

---

[12] The arguments as to the essentials of consultation reflect the views expressed by Webster J in *R* v *Secretary of State for Social Services, ex p Association of Metropolitan Authorities* [1986] 1 WLR 1, where it was observed that: "… in any context the essence of consultation is the communication of a genuine invitation to give advice and a genuine receipt of that advice … to achieve consultation sufficient information must be supplied by the consulting to the consulted party to enable it to tender helpful advice. Sufficient time must be given by the consulting to the consulted party to enable it to do that, and sufficient time must be available for such advice to be considered by the consulting party" (at 4).

[13] [1987] AC 625.

[14] *ibid.* at 702.

[15] See further below.

[16] [1993] 1 All ER 530. In this case, the Court of Appeal had concluded that an implied duty to consult a trader prior to serving him with a suspension notice would frustrate the purpose of the 1987 Act which was to achieve consumer safety by enabling the immediate withdrawal from sale of unsafe or dangerous goods.

the purpose of the statute, i.e. to ensure that immediate steps were taken to protect the public against injury or threat to health. Thirdly, attention was drawn to section 266(1) of the Public Health Act of 1936 which provides that:

"The powers conferred by the foregoing provisions[17] of this Part[18] of this Act shall not be exercised—
(i)   with respect to any stream, watercourse, ditch or culvert within the jurisdiction of a land drainage authority, except after consultation with that authority... *provided that nothing in this subsection shall apply in relation to the taking of proceedings in respect of a statutory nuisance.*"[19]

It was argued by the Authority that although this section provided for consultation, that consultation was expressly excluded in the context of a statutory nuisance. Finally, it was pointed out that there would be policy implications if a duty to consult was applied to all the section 79 categories of statutory nuisance, such as nuisances involving anti-social neighbours.[20]

Having considered the various competing arguments, Harrison J reached the conclusion, "after some hesitation", that:

"...there is no duty on the enforcing authority to consult the alleged perpetrator before serving the abatement notice, either as part of the statutory scheme or by implication in order to achieve fairness."[21]

Harrison J continued:

"I do not accept that the statutory duty under section 79 of the 1990 Act to investigate complaints of a statutory nuisance necessarily includes a duty to consult the alleged perpetrator. In the vast majority of cases, consultation with the alleged perpetrator by the enforcing authority would form both a sensible and an appropriate part of the investigative process, but that arises at the enforcing authority's discretion, not as part of a statutory duty. The investigation of

---

[17] These relate to matters such as: the power of a parish council or local authority to deal with any pond, pool etc. which is likely to be prejudicial to health (s. 260); and, the power of a local authority to require culverting of watercourses and ditches where building operations are in prospect (s. 262).

[18] Part XI.

[19] Emphasis added.

[20] In addition or as an alternative to bringing statutory nuisance proceedings, local authorities (or the police) are entitled to make such individuals the subject of anti-social behaviour orders on application by complaint to the magistrates' court: see s. 1 of the Crime and Disorder Act 1998. It should be noted that there is a statutory duty to consult "each other relevant authority" prior to making such an application: s. 1(2) of the 1998 Act. Furthermore, local authorities may seek an injunction from either the High Court or the county court under ss. 152-158 of the Housing Act 1996 to protect council tenants from anti-social behaviour. Such an injunction will prohibit a defendant from, inter alia, "engaging in, or threatening to engage in, conduct causing or likely to cause, a *nuisance* or annoyance for a person residing in, visiting or otherwise engaging in a lawful activity in residential premises, to which this section applies, or in the locality of such premises": see s. 152(1)(a) (emphasis added).

[21] [1999] EHLR 358 at 370.

complaints of statutory nuisances arises in a myriad of different circumstances and there will be situations where the enforcing authority could quite properly conclude that it would not be appropriate to consult the alleged perpetrator, whether for reasons relating to the nature of the alleged perpetrator, the need for urgent action or for any other reason. If a lack of consultation thereby leads to service of an abatement notice when it should not have been issued, the alleged perpetrator can appeal to the magistrates' court under section 80(3) of the Act on any of the grounds set out in regulation 2(2) of the 1995 Regulations.[22]

There will be many situations when fairness may suggest that the enforcing authority should consult with the alleged perpetrator, particularly in cases like the present one, where the notice is not suspended pending appeal because the nuisance is injurious to health, but the very fact that the statute has provided for non-suspension of the notice in those circumstances indicates the more draconian nature of the power given to the enforcing authority where injury to health is involved. The more serious the alleged injury to health, the more urgent is the need for action by the enforcing authority. The more urgent the need for action, the greater the likelihood that it may not be possible or appropriate to consult the alleged perpetrator.

In view of the fact that there will be cases where consultation with the alleged perpetrator is not possible or is inappropriate, it would be wrong to hold that such a duty of consultation exists before an abatement notice is served...."[23]

Harrison J then considered whether, despite his finding on the issue of a general duty to consult, the Authority ought to have consulted South West Water in the particular circumstances of the case. In other words, did the water undertaker have in this particular case a legitimate expectation of being consulted? Harrison J concluded that in the circumstances, it would have "as a matter of common sense and good administration"[24] been appropriate for the Authority to have exercised its discretion and have consulted South West Water prior to serving the abatement notice. Moreover, he further concluded that the Authority's letter to South West Water "gave rise to a legitimate expectation of a genuine consultation exercise which never took place due to the respondent's decision... to serve the abatement notice".[25] Accordingly, he held that on this basis, the decision to serve the abatement notice should be quashed.[26]

---

[22] See below, at p. 475.

[23] [1999] EHLR 358 at 370-371.

[24] *ibid.* at 371.

[25] *ibid.* at 377.

[26] For a discussion of Harrison J's decisions in respect of other issues raised in this case, see below at p. 482.

The Authority's appeal against Harrison J's ruling was heard by a Court of Appeal consisting of Simon Brown, Pill and Hale LJJ. The leading judgment was delivered by Simon Brown LJ.

On the issue of whether a general duty to consult arose under the statute or at common law Simon Brown LJ commented:

> "... I, like the judge below, would reject this contention for the reasons he gave (although in my case without 'some hesitation'). I would furthermore respectfully question the judge's view that 'in the vast majority of cases, consultation with the alleged perpetrator by the enforcing authority would form both a sensible and appropriate part of the investigative process' in the exercise of the enforcing authority's discretion. That seems to me to go altogether too far. Often, certainly, it will be appropriate to consult the alleged perpetrator, at least on some aspect of the matter, before serving an abatement notice, but the enforcing authority should be wary of being drawn too deeply and lengthily into scientific or technical debate, and warier still of unintentionally finding itself fixed with all the obligations of a formal consultation process."[27]

Thus the decision in *Falmouth* is clear authority for the proposition that an enforcing authority is not under a duty to consult an alleged perpetrator of a statutory nuisance prior to serving an abatement notice.

The Court of Appeal was also unimpressed by the arguments which had underlain Harrison J's finding on the issue of legitimate expectation. In a case where consultation was not required by law the Court of Appeal considered that "only the clearest of assurances can give rise to its legitimate expectation", and in this case the letter in question did not contain such a clear assurance.

Requirements of the notice

An abatement notice may impose, by a specified time or times:

> "... all or any of the following requirements:
> (a)   requiring abatement of the nuisance or prohibiting or restricting its occurrence or recurrence;
> (b)   requiring the execution of such works, and the taking of such steps, as may be necessary for any of those purposes ..."[28]

A number of separate, but related, questions have arisen as regards the nature and scope of these obligations, revealing that what may be required of a local authority may differ depending on: (i) the nature of the statutory nuisance in question; and (ii) the ways in which the respondent may be able to cause the statutory nuisance to discontinue.

---

[27] *ibid.*
[28] Section 80(1) of the 1990 Act.

To begin with we may take the situation where a statutory nuisance is of a kind which may be abated without there being any necessity to undertake any "works" or "take any steps". In such a case a local authority may simply require that the nuisance be abated, without being required in the notice to be more specific as regards how this result is to be achieved, and without being required to indicate what degree of improvement of the situation will suffice in order to have abated the nuisance. Support for these propositions can be found in *Budd* v *Colchester Borough Council*,[29] as explained and approved in *Surrey Free Inns plc* v *Gosport Borough Council.* [30]

In *Budd* the local authority had served an abatement notice on an owner of premises in respect of a noise nuisance arising from the barking of his dogs.[31] A challenge was lodged, contending that the notice was defective in the following ways: it did not specify with precision the levels of noise and times of barking which were said to have amounted to a nuisance; nor did it specify with precision what had to be done in order to comply with the notice. The Divisional Court held the notice to be valid. Schiemann LJ explained:

> "... the local authority [may] ... require a result ... [I]n a case such as the present, dealing with barking dogs, there is no necessity, either in setting out the nuisance to indicate the levels of barking which the dogs have exhibited so as to constitute a nuisance, or the precise times when they have been barking so as to constitute a nuisance, or in requiring the abatement of the nuisance, ... to specify precisely what has to be done about the nuisance."[32]

The Court of Appeal upheld this approach. Swinton Thomas LJ giving the judgment of the Court, explained:

> "In the ordinary way a local authority is entitled ... to serve a notice simply requiring the recipient to abate the nuisance. It was a wholly appropriate course for the ... Borough council to take in this case."[33]

It was "wholly appropriate" because, in so doing, it preserved opportunities for the recipient to make his own choice as regards the way in which the nuisance would be abated, rather than a particular course of action being imposed prescriptively by the local authority.

Swinton Thomas LJ continued:

> "There were many ways in which the appellant might abate the nuisance. The most extreme would be to get rid of all six greyhounds,

---

[29] [1997] Env LR 128 (DC) and [1999] Env LR 739 (CA).

[30] [1999] Env LR 1 (DC) and [1999] Env LR 750 (CA). The approach followed in these cases had been previously advocated in *Millard* v *Wastell* [1989] 1 QB 342.

[31] The local authority had acted in response to neighbour complaints about the early morning barking of six greyhounds, three kept indoors and three outside.

[32] [1997] Env LR 128 at 133.

[33] [1999] Env LR 739 at 747.

but that might well be an unreasonable requirement. A reduction in the number of dogs might abate the nuisance. Insulation of part of the house might be sufficient. It might be possible to send the dogs to an animal training centre to cure the problem. However, it might well not be reasonable for the local authority to require the appellant, for example, to take that course, because he might not be able to afford to do so. It is quite sufficient for the local authority to require the appellant himself to abate the nuisance in a manner which is the least inconvenient or expensive and the most acceptable to him."[34]

A similar approach was adopted in the *Surrey Free Inns* case. As in *Budd* the situation was one in which there was no necessity for any works to be undertaken in order to discontinue the nuisance (although – as will appear – the undertaking of works was a *possible* way in which the respondent might have sought to abate the nuisance). It was held that the local authority could, as in *Budd*, simply direct in the abatement notice that the nuisance should cease, without any further elaboration.

The *Surrey Free Inns* case involved the commission of a noise nuisance by the playing of loud amplified live music from within a licensed bar. The abatement notice simply required the prohibition of any recurrence of the nuisance by ceasing the "playing of amplified music at levels which cause a nuisance at neighbouring premises". The notice did not state what levels of noise at those premises had constituted a nuisance; nor did it specify a level to which such noise was required to be reduced.

This abatement notice was upheld by the Divisional Court. Mann LJ commented that the notice:

"… left it open to the appellant to abate the nuisance in any number of ways, not all of which would involve any works or other positive steps … For example, the appellant could cease playing amplified music at all, or cease doing so on warm days when the doors/windows were open; or it could give instructions or introduce restrictions to reduce the volume of music; or it could undertake works, such as it in fact chose to do, involving new doors, double-glazing and air-conditioning. The notice is neither defective nor in error in leaving it to the appellant to abate in any way it chose."[35]

The decision and reasoning of the Divisional Court was subsequently upheld, without further elaboration, by the Court of Appeal.[36]

A further illustration of this approach may be found in *Lowe and Watson* v *South Hams District Council*.[37] In this case an appeal was brought against an abatement notice which had been served in respect of a noise nuisance caused by the alleged crowing of cockerels and the chorus of waterfowl, at

---

[34] *ibid.* at 747-748.
[35] [1999] Env LR 1 at 9.
[36] [1999] Env LR 750 – the appeal focusing on a rather different issue.
[37] [1998] Env LR 143.

night and in the early morning. The abatement notice did, in fact, state with some particularity what was required of the recipient: "provide dark housing ... or take other no less effective measures to prevent, so far as is reasonably practicable, the crowing of cockerels and the chorus of waterfowl between the hours of 10 o'clock at night and 6 o'clock the following morning." What was not stated in the abatement notice was whether the noise of the poultry and ducks was alleged to be a statutory nuisance because it was a "nuisance" or because it was "prejudicial to health" (or whether, perhaps it could be regarded as falling under either head). In the opinion of the Divisional Court the abatement notice displayed no legal deficiency. Gage J noted that:

> "none of the statutory requirements provide for a notice to set out precisely whether the nuisance alleged is one which is prejudicial to health or is a common law nuisance or both."[38]

Nevertheless, some reassurance was provided for appellants:

> "In my judgment, what is important in the notice is the requirement that the acts which constitute the statutory nuisance are sufficiently alleged so that a person served with such a notice knows what he is required to do to abate."[39]

In other words a recipient of a notice should be made aware what matters constitute a statutory nuisance, in the view of the local authority, even though it is not essential for the authority to state whether the "prejudicial to health" or "nuisance" limb is being relied upon. Nevertheless, the words of Gage J may, perhaps, be thought to go too far. It is certainly true that the requirement to identify in the notice what matters are alleged to be involve a statutory nuisance will inform the recipient "what he is required to ... abate". However, the words used by Gage J suggest more: that the notice will inform the recipient "what he is required *to do* to abate" the statutory nuisance. This may, however, not be the case. The obligation, to take an example, may be to identify the noise which it is alleged amounts to a statutory nuisance. The recipient will know, therefore, the noise which is in question. It is not, however, necessary, as has been seen, to explain why the noise involves a statutory nuisance; nor is it necessary to identify what degree of moderation of the noise (less noise, shorter duration, more infrequent) might be considered no longer to involve a statutory nuisance. Only if a recipient were required to be informed of these maters would it be true to say that an abatement notice will inform its recipient as regards "what he is required to do to abate" the statutory nuisance.

Budd and *Surrey Free Inns* and more recently *Lowe and Watson* indicate the approach taken in cases where it was not *necessary* for works to be undertaken or positive steps to be taken in order to abate a nuisance.[40]

---

[38] *ibid.* at 148.

[39] *ibid.*

[40] The courts have also been willing to accept that where an abatement notice made a reference to the "carrying out of works" which was, in the circumstances, superfluous, the notice was not

What, however, of cases where the only way in which a nuisance may be abated is by such works or steps? Is it essential to the validity of an abatement notice, in a situation such as this, that the works or steps be described in the notice? And if so, with what degree of particularly must those works or steps be described?

These issues have come before the courts in several recent cases: *Sterling Homes* v *Birmingham City Council*;[41] *Kirklees Metropolitan Borough Council* v *Field*;[42] and *Network Housing Association* v *Westminster City Council*.[43] More recently still these cases have been reviewed by the Court of Appeal in *R* v *Falmouth and Truro Port Health Authority, ex p South West Water Ltd*.[44] Although *Falmouth* represents the present state of the law it is best understood by reference to the earlier decisions.

In *Sterling Homes* the abatement notice related to a nuisance caused by noise and vibrations. The notice was not, however, served on the industrial operator whose mammoth press was the source of the noise and vibrations. Rather, the notice was served on the landlord/owner of a residential block, whose tenants were adversely affected by the noise and vibrations. The terms of the notice were as follows:

> "... Require you to abate the said nuisance within 56 days ..., and for that purpose require you to carry out such works as may be necessary to ensure that the noise and vibration does not cause prejudice to health or a nuisance ..."

The Divisional Court held that this notice was defective. In the words of Mance J in *Surrey Free Inns*, explaining the *Sterling* case:

> "If the *only way* in which the nuisance can be abated is by works or steps, then the notice must specify them. That was ... plainly ... the situation in *Sterling*. Sterling were not owners or occupiers or operators of the press on the neighbouring industrial premises. All that they could do to prevent the nuisance to their tenants was to undertake works on their own residential block."[45]

Since in the *Sterling* case the terms of the notice only required that "works" be undertaken, without specifying what works were required, the notice was held to be invalid.

The same approach may be seen also in *Network Housing*. Here the local authority served an abatement notice upon the freehold owners of let premises in relation to an external noise source which it was not within the power of those owners to prevent or reduce. The noise was, in fact,

thereby rendered invalid: see *Brighton and Hove Council* v *Ocean Coachworks (Brighton) Ltd* [2000] EHLR 279.
[41] [1996] Env LR 121.
[42] [1998] Env LR 337. Now overruled by the *Falmouth* case, below.
[43] [1995] Env LR 176.
[44] [2000] 3 All ER 306.
[45] [1999] Env LR 1 at 8.

perfectly ordinary external noise: the noise of "normal everyday living". It amounted to a statutory nuisance owing to structural (noise insulation) deficiencies of the tenanted property. It was evident that to abate the nuisance the provision of noise insulation was necessary. Expert opinion differed as to where the noise insulation should be installed (on the floor, within the ceiling void or under the ceiling), and yet the abatement notice failed to inform the owner which of these was to be adopted. The decision was explained by Mance J, in the *Surrey Free Inns* case, as follows:

> "The notice failed to address or resolve a question, contentious between experts, whether the works should be in the void or under the ceiling or on the floor. The notice was held invalid because of this lack of precision in relation to the necessary works."[46]

A further illustration may be found in the *Kirklees* case. Here the nuisance comprised a rockface and wall which was in imminent danger of collapse onto some cottages. The situation, being one in which works were *necessary* in order to prevent continuation of the nuisance, it was held to be deficient of an abatement notice simply to have required abatement of the nuisance: works were necessary in order to abate the nuisance and those works should have been specified in sufficient detail to allow the person to whom the notice has been addressed to know what was required of him.

These three cases demonstrate the contrasting approach which came to be adopted by the courts in the two broad situations discussed. In a case where, in principle, a nuisance might be remedied without "works" being necessary there might be some uncertainty confronting the party served with the notice as regards the extent to which he or she must modify his or her conduct (or its effects) in order no longer to transgress the somewhat ill-defined boundaries of nuisance/prejudice to health. Whether or not that boundary continued to be transgressed by the notice recipient, even following some change in behaviour, might, ultimately, become a matter for the magistrates to resolve, should criminal proceedings be initiated for such alleged failure to have complied with the abatement notice.

In a case, however, where "works" were necessary in order to abate a nuisance, a notice would only be valid if those works were described with some precision. Failure to have undertaken those prescribed works involved, in itself, the commission of a criminal offence;[47] and since criminal liability flowed automatically from not having complied with the terms of such requirements it seemed appropriate, as an elementary aspect of criminal justice, that those requirements of the notice be reasonably clear and precise.[48] The view that the courts have taken here was, perhaps,

---

[46] *ibid.*

[47] Assuming, of course, that any appeal against the terms of the notice had not succeeded. See, further, below, p. 475.

[48] The need for clarity in an abatement notice was emphasised, for example, in *Brighton and Hove Council v Ocean Coachworks (Brighton) Ltd* [2000] EHLR 279 where Astill J observed: "A

inevitable. In proceedings alleging failure to have complied with works/steps required in an abatement notice it would seem an essential of criminal liability that the obligation imposed by the notice be capable of reasonably precise definition.[49]

These various cases and distinctions were recently fully reviewed in *R v Falmouth and Truro Port Health Authority, ex p South West Water Ltd.*[50] It will be remembered that the abatement notice in *Falmouth* required South West Water to cease to discharge sewage from the outfall within three months of the date of receipt of the notice. The notice was silent as to the specification of the works or steps necessary to abate the nuisance. Before Harrison J it had been argued by the Authority that the failure to specify the works or steps necessary was due to the fact that none were needed. Abatement could be achieved by the simple expedient of switching off the pumps. Any consequential works carried out by the Authority related to the performance of its statutory functions elsewhere rather than the abatement of the nuisance. South West Water argued, however, that the switching off of the pumps and such other works could not be so easily separated. In fact, it was contended, they were inextricably linked. Moreover, it was argued that the abatement notice did envisage that some works would be required because: (i) the three month time limit for compliance was not necessary if all that was required was the switching off of the pumps; and (ii) the notice dealt with its own non-suspension under regulation 3 of the Statutory Nuisance (Appeals) Regulations 1995 which presupposed that expenditure on works was necessary.

Harrison J briefly set out the legal position as distilled from the cases of *Kirklees*, *Sterling Homes* and *Surrey Free Inns*. He then continued:

> "Whilst [counsel's] submission that all that is required is to switch off the pumps is academically attractive, it is, in my view, unrealistic. Switching off the pumps without making any alternative arrangement for disposing of Falmouth's sewage is plainly quite out of the question and could not be contemplated by any rational public health authority. It follows that alternative arrangements have to be made before the pumps can be switched off. The works required for such an alternative arrangement are therefore necessary works to enable compliance with the requirement of the notice to cease the discharge.

---

notice must be clear for the recipient, not least because of the criminal sanctions that might follow a breach" (at 283).

[49] A parallel may be drawn here between an abatement notice and a binding-over order where an individual is said to have acted *contra bones mores,* i.e. in a way which is wrong in the judgment of a majority of contemporary fellow citizens. In *Hashman and Harrap v UK* (2000) 30 EHRR 241, the European Court of Human Rights held that such an order was too imprecise to amount to a valid restriction (under Article 10(2) of the Convention) on the right to freedom of expression. The order itself needed to state with greater clarity the nature of the conduct which its subject should refrain from carrying out.

[50] [2000] 3 All ER 306.

In those circumstances … the notice should have specified the works, but it did not do so."[51]

Thus in Harrison J's opinion, the failure of the abatement notice to specify the works or steps required to abate the nuisance where such works or steps were in fact necessary meant that the notice was thereby invalid.

On appeal, it was necessary for the Court of Appeal also to consider this issue. The leading judgment on this issue was delivered by Simon Brown LJ. In considering whether an abatement notice must specify the works or steps required in "any and every case", his Lordship noted that:

> "One's starting point must be s 80(1) itself: '… the local authority shall serve a notice … imposing *all or any* of the following requirements' (my emphasis). That provision, unlike s 93(1) of the 1936 Act[52] (and its predecessors), on its face gives the local authority a discretion in the matter: it can, if it wishes, in addition to requiring abatement, require the execution of the necessary works."[53]

Simon Brown LJ dealt with the earlier caselaw, and noted a number of inconsistencies which it was necessary for the Court of Appeal now to resolve. Explaining his view of the law Simon Brown LJ said:

> "If, as [counsel for South West Water] accepts, there is no duty to specify works in those cases where the nuisance can be abated in a number of ways, not all of which require the execution of works, then I can see no good reason why the position should be any different merely because in a particular case some works *are* essential to abate the nuisance. If, as the Court of Appeal held in *Budd* v *Colchester BC* '…It is quite sufficient for the local authority to require the occupier himself to abate the nuisance in a manner which is the least inconvenient or expensive and the most acceptable to him', why should this be any the less sufficient in a case like the present where, although some works are required, there is a clear choice between various options? Why should the local authority have to make that choice rather than leave it to the owner? For my part, I find McCullough J's reasoning in the *Sterling* case – in favour of leaving the choice to the owner – more persuasive than the court's reasoning in the *Kirklees* case that, because of the criminal sanctions attending non-abatement, the specification must be made by the local authority. I would, therefore, overrule the *Kirklees* case and hold that in *all cases* the local authority can if it wishes leave the choice of means of abatement to the perpetrator of the nuisance. If, however, the means of abatement *are* required by the local authority, then they must be specified; the *Network* case and the *Sterling* case remain good law.

---

[51] [1999] EHLR 358 at 384.

[52] This had provided that: "…a local authority … shall serve a notice … requiring [the person served] to abate the nuisance *and* to execute such works and take such steps as may be necessary for that purpose".

[53] [2000] 3 All ER 306 at 322.

> Even if I was prepared (like the Court of Appeal in *Budd*'s case, strictly obiter as I think) to recognise a class of case where it was irrational for the local authority not to use its discretion to require specific works for the abatement of the nuisance, the present case would not fall within it. On the contrary, there were compelling reasons here for leaving the decision as to how the nuisance should be abated to the water undertaker..."[54]

In the light of these statements Simon Brown LJ was of the view that Harrison J had erred on this point in the High Court. In other words, the notice in the present case was not invalid for failing to have specified the works or steps required to abate the nuisance.

The decision in *Falmouth* clarifies the law relating to the specification of works or steps in an abatement notice. It is now clear, therefore, that where an enforcing authority serves an abatement notice it has a choice open to it. If it so wishes, it may simply require that the nuisance is abated and say nothing whatsoever as to how such abatement is to be achieved.[55] Where this is the chosen course of action, it will be incumbent upon the recipient to abate the nuisance undertaking whatever works or steps it considers necessary for that purpose. If, however, an enforcing authority chooses to require that works or steps are carried out, then it is obliged to specify them with sufficient clarity.[56]

The general principle established in *Falmouth* would seem to hold good even for cases where the abatement of a nuisance must clearly involve the execution of works or the taking of steps. In other words, since *Kirklees* has been overruled, it is probable that works or steps do not have to be required by an abatement notice even where the need for them is obvious. This conclusion must, however, be subject to a few words of caution. As Simon Brown LJ acknowledged in *Falmouth*, such a conclusion is contrary to what the Court of Appeal in *Budd* concluded on this point. In that case Swinton Thomas LJ observed:

> "I accept that it is not difficult to envisage facts where it would be wholly unreasonable for a local authority to serve a notice merely requiring the recipient to abate the nuisance without stating the works or steps which the local authority required to be taken for that purpose, or where it is clear on the face of the notice that the notice itself required such works or steps to be taken."[57]

Moreover, the conclusion has been doubted in the post-*Falmouth* case of *Sevenoaks District Council* v *Brands Hatch Leisure Group Ltd.*[58] In this

---

[54] *ibid.* at 328-329.

[55] In practice, this would be a means of insulating the abatement notice against an appeal by its recipient.

[56] See the summary of the effect of the decision in *Falmouth* by Langley J in *Lambie and Minter* v *Thanet District Council* [2001] EHLR 44 at 49.

[57] [1999] Env LR 739 at 747.

[58] [2001] EHLR 114.

case Laws LJ cited the concluding remarks of Simon Brown LJ in *Falmouth* and then remarked:

> "With very great deference to Simon Brown LJ, I venture to think that there may well be some utility in recognising a class of case, as he puts it, where it may be irrational for the local authority not to specify works ..."[59]

The remarks of both Swinton Thomas LJ and Laws LJ were obiter, and it may be unwise to make too much of what may be termed the "irrational" category of case.

One further point should be noted. In decisions post-*Falmouth* the courts have been willing to hold that where an abatement notice refers to "works" or "steps" but does not specify the nature of such works or steps the notice is not for that reason to be regarded as invalid.[60] What matters is whether, when read as a whole, the notice makes it clear to the recipient what is required of him. If this is clear, and if no injustice will be done to the recipient by adopting this approach, then the courts are prepared to treat erroneous references to "works" or "steps" as superfluous and of no significance as regards the validity of the notice.

Time requirements

Section 80 of the Environmental Protection Act 1990 concludes with the words: "and the notice shall specify the time or times within which the requirements of the notice are to be complied with". Notwithstanding the quite broad compass of this requirement, the courts have held that a notice need impose no time limit in cases where what is required is a prohibition of a statutory nuisance which the local authority is satisfied is merely *likely to occur*. Since, in such cases, the prohibition relates to a nuisance not presently occurring (at the time of the service of the notice) it is quite appropriate for the notice to be silent as regards time for compliance: in other words, for the prohibitions to be of *immediate* effect.

The position is different when it comes to obligations in abatement notices to discontinue or modify an activity which *is giving rise* to a statutory nuisance, and where the obligations within a notice include the "execution of works" or "the taking of steps". Such matters cannot, in their very nature, be subject to immediate obligation (on pain of criminal penalty): such obligations must of necessity come into operation only following a clearly stated period (or periods) of time for compliance.

Authority for these propositions may be found in *R* v *Tunbridge Wells Justices ex parte Tunbridge Wells Borough Council*.[61] The local authority served an abatement notice requiring its recipient to prohibit the

---

[59] *ibid.* at 120.

[60] See, for example, *Brighton and Hove Council* v *Ocean Coachworks (Brighton) Ltd* [2000] EHLR 279, *Sevenoaks District Council* v *Brands Hatch Leisure Group Ltd* [2001] EHLR 114 and, *Cambridge City Council* v *Douglas* [2001] EHLR 150.

[61] [1996] Env LR 88.

occurrence or recurrence of an alleged nuisance involving amplified music and other anti-social activity. The local authority, being of the view that the nuisance had recurred later on the same day that the abatement notice had been served (and on the following day), commenced criminal proceedings before the magistrates. In due course those proceedings terminated in favour of the defendant, the magistrates accepting the defence contention that the abatement notice was defective owing to its failure to have set a time or times at which its obligations would take effect. In judicial review proceedings the Divisional Court found the magistrates to have erred in this conclusion. Their decision had been reached in ignorance of the clear decision in *R* v *Clerk to the Birmingham City Justices ex parte Guppy*.[62] In that case Bingham LJ (as he then was) had explained:

"It does not, however, seem to me that the time limit provision can, with any ease, be applied to the prohibition on recurrence."[63]

His Lordship was willing, therefore, to regard a notice containing no reference to time as requiring noise to cease immediately, and that from that time indefinitely onwards there should be no recurrence.

The approach adopted by Bingham LJ in *ex parte Guppy* was followed by Simon Brown LJ in *ex parte Tunbridge Wells Borough Council.* The nuisance in that case was not occurring at the time of service of the notice. The only requirement in the notice was to avoid recurrence, and this requirement required no works or steps to be undertaken in order for there to be compliance.[64]

Service of abatement notices

Abatement notices should be served, in the first instance, on the person "responsible for the nuisance".[65] The concept of responsibility for the nuisance is defined in section 79(7) of the 1990 Act. This provides that in the context of a statutory nuisance, the "person responsible":

"means the person to whose act, default or sufferance the nuisance is attributable."

If the person responsible for the nuisance "cannot be found", or where the nuisance has not yet occurred but is likely to occur, the notice should be

---

[62] (1988) 152 JP 159.

[63] *ibid.* at 162.

[64] In a case where a nuisance may be *discontinued* without any need for "works" or "steps" (i.e. by mere cessation or modification of conduct involving the commission of a nuisance) it would seem that a date must be set for such discontinuance. However, it would seem that the reasoning behind *Guppy* may apply equally here also, there being no necessity for time to be afforded during which "works" or "steps" to secure discontinuance may be taken. Thus in *Brighton and Hove Council* v *Ocean Coachworks (Brighton) Ltd* [2000] EHLR 279, where a noise nuisance at a vehicle repairs premises could be abated by closing the doors when it was not necessary to have them open for genuine business reasons, it was held, inter alia, that the fact that the notice served on the owners required the abatement of the nuisance "forthwith", i.e. at once, did not thereby render the notice invalid.

[65] Section 80(2)(a).

served on the "owner or occupier" of the premises;[66] and the owner or occupier is also the appropriate person to be served the notice in cases where the nuisance arises from any property defect of a structural character.[67]

In *London Borough of Camden* v *Gunby*,[68] the Divisional Court was required to consider what Rose LJ described as "an interesting and ultimately short point of interpretation",[69] namely the meaning of "owner" within section 80(2)(b) of the 1990 Act. In particular, it was necessary for the Court to determine whether a managing owner who received rack rent as an agent or trustee constituted an "owner" for the purposes of the service of an abatement notice.

The facts can be briefly stated. Mr Gunby was a partner in a firm of surveyors which acted as managing agents for the freehold owners of premises in London. He was served with an abatement notice pursuant to section 80 of the 1990 Act in which it was alleged that the premises had structural defects which amounted to a statutory nuisance. Mr Gunby appealed against the notice on a number of grounds, including that it should have been served on the freehold owners of the premises rather than himself. The Stipendiary Magistrate dismissed the complaint and Mr Gunby accordingly appealed to the Crown Court. In finding in his favour, the Crown Court noted that prior to the service of the abatement notice, requests for information pursuant to section 16 of the Local Government (Miscellaneous Provisions) Act 1976[70] had been made of both him and the freehold owners. The responses which were received indicated that abatement notices were to be served on the managing agent. Nevertheless, the Crown Court was of the opinion that a managing agent could not be an "owner" for the purposes of section 80(2)(b). The local authority appealed.

Before the Divisional Court, counsel for the local authority contended that the Crown Court had reached an erroneous conclusion for a number of

---

[66] Section 80(2)(c).

[67] Section 80(2)(b). Special rules apply where the nuisance falls within category (ga) and the nuisance has either not yet occurred or arises from noise emitted from or caused by an unattended vehicle or machinery or equipment. In such circumstances the notice should be served, where the person responsible for the vehicle can be found, on that person. Where that person cannot be found the notice should be served by it being fixed to the vehicle, machinery or equipment. A local authority may determine that service by fixing to the vehicle (etc.) shall in its area be the normal method of service of notices. However, even where this is so, in any case where the person responsible for the vehicle (etc.) "can be found and served with a copy of the notice within an hour of the notice being fixed" a copy of the notice must be served on that person – 1990 Act, s. 80A.

[68] [2000] EHLR 33.

[69] *ibid.* at 34.

[70] This section confers a general power on local authorities to obtain particulars of persons interested in land where such information is necessary in order to enable the authority to perform any of its statutory functions. Where a notice is served under s. 16, a local authority is required to name the Act which is the source of the function that it is performing. It is not required, however, to set out the relevant sections: see *Barry Stanley* v *Ealing London Borough Council* [2000] EHLR 172. In that case, the Divisional Court also held that for a s. 16 notice to be valid, it must specify the function or functions conferred on the authority by the Act for which the information is required.

reasons. The main thrust of the argument was that in a whole series of statutes[71] dealing with statutory nuisances dating back to the Public Health Act 1848, "owner" had been defined to mean: "... the person for the time being receiving the rack rent of the premises in connection with which the word is used, whether on his own account or as agent or trustee for any other person."[72] Counsel for the local authority argued, therefore, that this was the definition which should be applied to "owner". However, an objection could be raised to this argument. Although section 80(2) of the 1990 Act is silent as to the meaning of "owner", section 81A(9) of the same Act states that "owner":

> "in relation to any premises, means a person (other than a mortgagee not in possession) who, whether in his own right or as trustee for any other person, is entitled to receive the rack rent of the premises or, where the premises are not let at a rack rent, would be so entitled if they were so let ..."

Thus there was an argument that if the section 81A(9) definition was not applied to "owner" in section 80(2), there would be a potential ambiguity in that the word could be defined in two different ways within Part III of the 1990 Act. However, counsel for the local authority did not "shrink"[73] from this consequence. He argued that in conformity with the approach adopted by the Court of Appeal in *R* v *Bristol City Council, ex p Everett*[74] to the interpretation of "injury to health" in section 79, the interpretation of "owner" ought to be historically based. Moreover, he pointed to the fact that the definition in section 81A(9) was stated by the Act to be for the purposes of that section. In other words, it did not apply generally to "owner" wherever that word appeared in Part III of the Act. Counsel for the local authority further submitted that a managing agent would not suffer injustice as a consequence of being held to be an "owner" for the purposes of section 80(2). Several points were made in support of this submission. First, it was contended that enforcement proceedings could only be taken against a true managing agent.[75] Secondly, it was pointed out that a managing agent has a right of appeal against an abatement notice under the Statutory Nuisance (Appeals) Regulations 1995.[76] Thirdly,

---

[71] In addition to the 1848 Act, the other enactments referred to were: the Nuisances Removal and Diseases Prevention Act 1855; the Public Health Act 1875; the Public Health Act 1936; the Public Health Act 1961; the Control of Pollution Act 1974; the Local Government (Miscellaneous Provisions) Act 1976; and the Clean Air Act 1993.

[72] See, for example, s. 64(1) of the Clean Air Act 1993.

[73] Per Rose LJ, [2000] EHLR 33 at 39.

[74] [1999] Env LR 587. See above, at p. 421.

[75] The authorities for this proposition are *Bottomley* v *Harrison* [1952] 1 All ER 368 and *Midland Bank Ltd* v *Conway Corporation* [1965] 1 WLR 1165. In the former case, it was held that a person who received rent in the form of a cheque on behalf of an owner during his absence from the country was not an "owner" for the purposes of the service of an abatement notice under s. 93 of the Public Health Act 1936. Rather, such a person was a "conduit pipe" between the tenant and the owner. The situation may have been different, however, had the rent been paid in cash rather than as a cheque. In the latter case, it was held that a bank branch which received rent from a tenant on behalf of an absent landlord and which paid the rates on the property was not a managing agent and hence not the "owner" of the property.

[76] See regulation 2(2)(h)(iii) of the 1995 Regulations, below at p. 476.

counsel noted that although failure to comply with an abatement notice is a criminal offence, a managing agent could seek to rely on the 'defence' of reasonable excuse in section 80(4).[77] Finally, it was pointed out that a managing agent could recover any expenses that it had incurred by making deductions from the rent that it had collected on behalf of the landlord.

Counsel for the managing agent sought to counter these submissions by arguing, inter alia, that the penal nature of the 1990 Act required that the Court should not widen the meaning of "owner". However, the Divisional Court found in favour of the local authority and held that a managing agent could be an "owner" for the purposes of section 80(2)(b) of the 1990 Act. In giving judgment, Rose LJ (with whom Smedley J agreed) observed:

> "It seems, to my mind, that the reference in section 81A(9) to 'this section' immediately poses a question mark or ambiguity as to the meaning of owner, where it appears undefined in section 80(2). That being so, a judge is entitled to resolve that ambiguity by recourse to the overwhelming legislative history … a legislative history which, it is to be noted, not only precedes this Act by 150 years but also succeeds it in the terms of the Clean Air Act 1993 section 64. That being so, the answer to the question imposed by the case stated, as to whether the Crown Court was correct in concluding that the respondent was not the owner of the premises within the meaning of section 80(2)(b) is 'no'."[78]

Accompanying letters

When serving an abatement notice on a person responsible for a statutory nuisance, it is by no means an uncommon practice for local authorities to send an accompanying letter. Provided that the letter does no more than merely introduce the abatement notice, there would appear to be no problem. Where, however, the letter seeks to explain and expand upon the terms of the abatement notice, problems may arise. In such circumstances, a court may conclude that the letter has itself become part of the abatement notice and that it should therefore be taken into account where the validity of the notice is in issue. This is what happened in *London Borough of Camden* v *Easynet Ltd*.[79] Here the Council had served an abatement notice on Easynet Ltd relating to an alleged noise nuisance caused by the operation of equipment, machinery and plant at premises which it owned. The notice itself was expressed in clear and unequivocal terms. It was accompanied by a letter written by a member of the Council's pollution control team. In that letter, reference was made to the general background to the service of the abatement notice and the view was expressed that it was appropriate to require the recipient to "expedite works to abate the statutory nuisance within 40 days from service". In subsequent proceedings before a District Judge, it was held that the abatement notice was invalid. In reaching such a conclusion the District Judge had regard to the contents

---

[77] For a fuller consideration of what is not, strictly speaking, a defence, see below at p. 490.

[78] [2000] EHLR 33 at 41.

[79] [2003] EHLR 5.

of the accompanying letter. In his judgment, since the content of the letter was such as to require that works be carried out, the notice was invalid because it failed to specify the nature of those works. The Council appealed.

In dismissing the appeal, Stanley Burnton J noted that the test to be applied when construing documents of the kind at issue in the present case was that which had been stated by Lord Steyn in *Mannai Investment Co Ltd v Eagle Star Life Assurance Co Ltd*.[80] In that case, which had concerned the construction of notices given by a tenant to a landlord under the terms of a lease, Lord Steyn had stated:

> "The issue is how a reasonable recipient would have understood the notices. And in considering this question the notices must be construed taking into account the relevant objective contextual scene."[81]

Applying this test to the facts of the present case, Stanley Burnton J had little option but to construe the Council's accompanying letter as something more than a mere courtesy letter introducing the enclosed abatement notice. Rather, in his Lordship's opinion:

> "A reasonable person reading that letter, having regard to the fact that there had been discussions relating to such works and then turning to the notice itself, would, in my judgment, understand the notice as a notice requiring him to abate the nuisance by the carrying out of works. If that is the proper way of reading the notice, the works are unspecified and the notice falls."[82]

His Lordship continued:

> "I reach that conclusion with some regret, having regard to the fact that the notice was in clear terms. Nonetheless, it seems to me that, particularly in an area attended by possible criminal sanctions, a local authority should be held to its word and the reader of such a letter should be entitled to accept its contents as an accurate description of the more formal document which it encloses."[83]

In practice, it would be advisable for a local authority to ensure that the wording of an accompanying letter is confined to the formalities of introducing the abatement notice. An even safer though less acceptable option from the standpoint of its dealings with members of the public would be for a local authority to serve abatement notices unaccompanied by any other documents.

---

[80] [1997] AC 749.

[81] *ibid.* at 767.

[82] [2003] EHLR 5 at para.21 of the judgment.

[83] *ibid.* at para.22.

APPEALS

A person upon whom an abatement notice has been served may appeal against that notice within 21 days to a Magistrates' Court.[84] The grounds upon which such an appeal may be argued, and the appeal procedures, are as provided in the Statutory Nuisance (Appeals) Regulations 1995.[85]

The grounds of appeal comprise:

(a) that the abatement notice is not justified by section 80 ...;

(b) that there has been some informality, defect or error in, or in connection with, the abatement notice ...;

(c) that the authority have refused unreasonably to accept compliance with alternative requirements, or that the requirements of the abatement notice are otherwise unreasonable in character or extent, or are unnecessary;

(d) that the time, or where more than one time is specified, any of the times, within which the requirements of the abatement notice are to be complied with is not reasonably sufficient for the purpose;

(e) where the nuisance to which the notice relates –

   (i) is a nuisance falling within section 79(1)(a), (d), (e), (f) or (g) of the 1990 Act and arises on industrial, trade or business premises;

   (ii) is a nuisance falling within section 79(1)(b) of the 1990 Act and the smoke is emitted from a chimney; or

   (iii) is a nuisance falling within section 79(1)(ga) of the 1990 Act and is noise emitted from or caused by a vehicle, machinery or equipment being used for industrial, trade or business premises,

   that the best practicable means were used to prevent, or to counteract the effects of, the nuisance.[86]

(f) that, in the case of a nuisance under section 79(1)(g) or (ga) of the 1990 Act (noise emitted from premises) the requirements imposed by the abatement notice by virtue of section 80(1)(a) of the Act are more onerous than the requirements for the time being in force, in relation to the noise to which the notice relates, of –

   (i) any notice served under section 60 or 66 of the 1974 Act[87] (control of noise on construction sites and from certain premises), or

   (ii) any consent under section 61 or 65 of the 1974 Act (consent for work on construction sites and consent for noise to exceed registered level in a noise abatement zone), or

   (iii) any determination made under section 67 of the 1974 Act (noise control of new buildings);

(g) that, in the case of a nuisance under section 79(1)(ga) of the 1990 Act (noise emitted from or caused by vehicles, machinery or

---

[84] Section 80(3) of the 1990 Act.

[85] SI 1995/2644.

[86] See further, below, p. 477.

[87] The Control of Pollution Act 1974.

equipment), the requirements imposed by the abatement notice by virtue of section 80(1)(a) of the Act are more onerous than the requirements for the time being in force, in relation to the noise to which the notice relates, of any condition of a consent given under paragraph 1 of Schedule 2 to the 1993 Act[88] (loudspeakers in streets and roads);

(h) that the abatement notice should have been served on some person other than the appellant, being –
  (i)   the person responsible for the nuisance;
  (ii) the person responsible for the vehicle, machinery or equipment, or
  (iii) in the case of a nuisance arising from any defect of a structural character, the owner of the premises, or
  (iv) in the case where the person responsible for the nuisance cannot be found or the nuisance has not yet occurred, the owner or occupier of the premises;

(i) that the abatement notice might lawfully have been served on some person instead of the appellant being –
  (i)   in the case where the appellant is the owner of the premises, the occupier of the premises, or
  (ii) in the case where the appellant is the occupier of the premises, the owner of the premises,
  and that it would have been equitable for it to have been so served;

(j) that the abatement notice might lawfully have been served on some person in addition to the appellant, being –
  (i)   a person also responsible for the nuisance, or
  (ii) a person who is also owner of the premises, or
  (iii) a person who is also an occupier of the premises, or
  (iv) a person who is also the person responsible for the vehicle, machinery or equipment,
  and that it would have been equitable for it to have been so served.[89]

Where, and in so far as, an appeal is based on the ground of some informality, defect or error in, or in connection with, the abatement notice the court is required to dismiss the appeal if it is satisfied that the informality, defect or error is not a material one.[90]

In any other case the court hearing the appeal may:

(a) quash the abatement notice, or
(b) vary the notice in favour of the appellant in such manner as it thinks fit,[91] or

---

[88] The Noise and Statutory Nuisance Act 1993.

[89] Regulation 2(2).

[90] Regulation 2(3).

[91] In *Lambie and Minter* v *Thanet District Council* [2001] EHLR 44, Langley J described the power of the Court to vary thus: "The discretion to vary an abatement notice is in very broad terms. Plainly a notice can only be varied when service of it in principle is valid. So the power assumes that there was a statutory nuisance when the notice was served. On ordinary principles it

(c) dismiss the appeal.[92]

Moreover, the court hearing the appeal has wide powers to make orders relating to the appealed abatement notice. It may make:

"such order as it thinks fit –
(a) with respect to the person by whom any work is to be executed and the contribution to be made by any persons towards the cost of the work, or
(b) as to the proportions in which any expenses which may become recoverable by the authority under Part III of the 1990 Act are to be borne by the appellant and any other person."[93]

Best practicable means

The 1990 Act provides[94] that it shall be a defence in any criminal proceedings for contravention of an abatement notice for the defendant to prove that the best practicable means were used to prevent or to counteract the effects of the nuisance. The generality of this statement is, however, limited in significant ways.[95] Thus, the defence is not applicable at all in relation to nuisances within categories (c) and (h) on the list given above.[96] Where the nuisance is of the types described at (a), (d), (f) or (g) on that list the defence applies only where the offence occurred on industrial, trade or business premises. Where it is a (ga)-type nuisance the defence is only applicable where the noise was emitted from or was caused by a vehicle, machinery or equipment being used for industrial, trade or business purposes. Where the nuisance is of type (b) the defence only operates where the smoke is emitted from a chimney.

What is meant by "best practicable means"? The Act offers the following guidance.[97] So, for example, it is stated that in assessing what is "practicable" consideration should be given to what is reasonably practicable having regard amongst other things to "local conditions and circumstances", to the "current state of technical knowledge" and to

---

seems to me that, in exercising the discretion, the court should have in mind the extent of any defects in the notice which it may be asked to cure and whether the substance of what the notice requires remains valid and appropriate or is itself tainted by valid objections" (at 52). In applying this approach to the facts of the case before him, Langley J held that the substance of the abatement notice was to be found in the first and second paragraphs of a three paragraph schedule of works. Accordingly, it lay within the court's discretion to vary the notice by: (i) making an amendment to the second paragraph for the sake of clarity; and (ii) deleting the whole of the third paragraph.

[92] Regulation 2(5).
[93] Regulation 2(6). In the exercise of its powers under regulation 2(6) the court must "have regard as between an owner and an occupier, to the terms and conditions … of any relevant tenancy and to the nature of the works required"; and must be satisfied, before imposing any requirement on any person other than the appellant, that that person … received a copy of the notice of appeal", as required under regulation 2(4).
[94] 1990 Act, s. 80(7).
[95] 1990 Act, s. 80(8).
[96] See p. 421.
[97] 1990 Act, s. 79(9).

"financial circumstances". As regards "means" to be employed, this is stated to be a broad concept embracing such matters as the "design, installation, maintenance and manner and periods of operation of plant and machinery, and the design and maintenance of buildings and structures".

The meaning of this concept was discussed recently in *Manley and Manley* v *New Forest District Council*.[98] In this case the appellants were served with an abatement notice by the respondent council in respect of a noise nuisance caused by the howling of a pack of 24 Siberian Huskies which they bred commercially and which were housed in kennels in the appellants' back garden. The appellants exercised their right of appeal to the Magistrates' Court under section 80(3) of the 1990 Act, but their appeal was dismissed. Before the Crown Court they submitted that the abatement notice was not justified (regulation 2(2)(a) of the 1995 Regulations) and that the best practicable means had been used to prevent or counteract the effects of the nuisance (regulation 2(2)(e)). Both submissions were rejected by the Crown Court. With regard to the latter submission, the Court held that "'best practicable means' includes moving the kennels to a non-residential location". The appellants further appealed to the Divisional Court. In giving the judgment of that Court, Newman J remarked that an important feature of the "doctrine or concept" of "best practicable means" "has always been that it allowed for flexibility to cater for local and individual circumstances." Its deployment in the context of environmental pollution control (which dated back to 1842) "reflected a conciliatory and co-operational approach, so that the method of enforcement would not place an undue burden on the manufacturing industry and on businesses." By holding in the present context that "best practicable means" could include relocating the kennels to a non-residential location, the Crown Court judge's interpretation of the concept had, in the opinion of Newman J, defeated the "very intention of Parliament, which was to provide the business operator with a defence to the nuisance his business created, so long as the best practicable means had been employed." Accordingly, the appeal was allowed.

Suspensory effect of appeals?

The position here is quite complex.[99] In certain, limited, situations the bringing of an appeal against an abatement notice will have the effect of suspending the operation of that notice until the appeal has been either abandoned or decided by the court. This applies, however, only where the following requirements are met. It must be the case that *either*:

---

[98] [2000] EHLR 113

[99] It has been suggested that the regulation 3 provisions are "somewhat convoluted": per Harrison J in *R* v *Falmouth and Truro Port Health Authority, ex p South West Water Ltd* [1999] EHLR 358 at 366.

"(i)   compliance with the abatement notice would involve any person in expenditure on the carrying out of works[100] before the hearing of the appeal, *or*

(ii)   in the case of a nuisance under section 79(1)(g) or (ga) of the 1990 Act, the noise to which the abatement notice relates is noise necessarily caused in the course of the performance of some duty imposed by law on the appellant ..."[101]

However, even here, the process of appeal will not suspend the abatement notice where certain further conditions apply. This will be the case where *either*:

(a)   the nuisance to which the abatement notice relates –
   (i)   is injurious to health; *or*
   (ii)   is likely to be of limited duration such that suspension of the notice would render the notice of no practical effect, *or*
(b)   the expenditure which would be incurred by any person in the carrying out of works in compliance with the abatement notice before any appeal has been decided would not be disproportionate to the public benefit to be expected in that period from such compliance."[102]

In such cases a notice will not be suspended pending appeal except where this intent is specifically stated within the abatement notice itself (and also, that the abatement notice specifies which of the grounds above should require non-suspension of the effect of the notice pending the appeal).[103]

The appeal decision

As we have already seen, there are a number of grounds under the 1995 Regulations on which the recipient of an abatement notice may seek to bring an appeal against that notice[104] and a court hearing such an appeal has a wide measure of discretion as to how the matter will be determined.[105] Where several grounds of appeal are advanced by an appellant and the appeal is ultimately successful, one would normally expect the judgment of the court to make it clear on what basis the appeal has been upheld. What would be the position, however, if the judgment of the court fails to state conclusions on certain of the grounds of appeal?

---

[100] In *Cambridge City Council* v *Douglas* [2001] EHLR 150, Sir Edwin Jowitt observed: "Whether or not compliance would involve the cost of any works is a question of fact whose resolution has to be approached with common sense and fairness" (at 154).

[101] Regulation 3(1)(b).

[102] Regulation 3(2).

[103] Regulation 3(3). As we have already seen, in *R* v *Falmouth and Truro Port Health Authority, ex p South West Water Ltd* [2000] 3 All ER 306, the abatement notice which the Authority served on South West Water contained a statement (in accordance with regulation 3(3)(b)) to the effect that it would not be suspended pending an appeal because the nuisance to which it related was injurious to health: see above, at p. 455.

[104] See above, at p. 475.

[105] See above, at p. 476.

This was in essence what occurred in *R (on the application of East Devon District Council) v Farr*.[106]

The respondent carried on a metal polishing business at an industrial estate in Exmouth. Following the receipt of complaints from nearby residents relating to the noise emanating from the respondent's unit, an officer from the claimant authority visited the site and measured the noise. In the light of her readings,[107] she decided to serve an abatement notice. The notice obliged the respondent to ensure that the windows and doors were kept closed when the machinery was in use at the unit.[108] The respondent exercised his right of appeal, and contended before the justices that the notice should be quashed under regulations 2(2)(a), (c) and (e).[109] The justices accepted the force of the respondent's submissions and accordingly quashed the abatement notice. The District Council appealed by way of case stated.

On behalf of the appellant it was argued that the magistrates had failed to give a properly and adequately reasoned decision in that their judgment failed to inform the parties in broad terms why the decision had been reached; clear conclusions in relation to regulations 2(2)(a) and (c) were not evident in the judgment. Elias J accepted these submissions. In relation to regulation 2(2)(c), for example, it was:

> "... not altogether clear whether they came to the conclusion that the requirements of the abatement notice were unreasonable in character or extent. Again it may be that they formed no concluded view on that matter."[110]

However, the position was "rather different" with regard to the third ground of appeal, regulation 2(2)(e). Although the justices had not in their judgment expressly referred to the terms of this provision, they had reached the conclusion that the respondent had taken all reasonable and practicable steps to reduce the effect of the noise.[111] On this basis, therefore, the justices' determination was valid.

Patently it amounts to good practice for justices hearing an appeal against an abatement notice to state clearly their conclusions on each of the grounds for appeal in giving judgment. The decision in *Farr* demonstrates,

---

[106] [2002] EHLR DG5.

[107] The noise in question was measured at 57 decibels when the respondent's machinery was in use and at between 45-47 decibels when the noisiest machinery was not in use.

[108] This was despite the fact that the unit had no windows, only sliding double doors.

[109] For the wording of these provisions, see above at p. 475.

[110] At para. 24 of the judgment.

[111] Paragaphs 6(c) and (d) of the case stated contained the following conclusions which had been reached by the justices: "(c) Since the problem was first brought to the attention of the respondent he had taken all reasonable and practicable steps to reduce the effect of the noise. (d) The respondent had explored various options such as extraction and air conditioning, but the noise level of the extraction equipment could be greater. The efficiency of air conditioning was questionable because of the fine dust particles. The cost of either equipment could be prohibitive" (at para. 17 of Elias J's judgment).

however, that a failure to do so will not necessarily invalidate a decision provided that the reasoning of the court makes clear at least on sound basis upon which the justices have upheld the appeal.

Appeals vs judicial review

An important issue is whether the recipient of an abatement notice who wishes to challenge that notice must always do so via the statutory appeal mechanism; or are there circumstances in which the recipient may challenge that notice by way of judicial review?

The courts have generally taken the view that where a statutory appeals mechanism is in place, a person aggrieved by a decision to which that mechanism applies should first exhaust that remedy before seeking to pursue another. Thus in *R v Hillingdon London Borough Council, ex p Royco Homes Ltd*[112] the applicants sought an order of certiorari[113] to quash a grant of planning permission on the grounds that four conditions attached to it were ultra vires. On the issue of the availability of judicial review Lord Widgery CJ (with whom Melford Stevenson and Bridge JJ agreed) observed:

"... it has always been a principle that certiorari will go only where there is no other equally effective and convenient remedy. In the planning field there are very often, if not in an almost overwhelming number of cases, equally effective and convenient remedies. As is well known, there is now... a comprehensive system of appeals from decisions of local planning authorities. In the instant case the applicants could, had they wished, have gone to the Secretary of State for the Environment in the form of a statutory appeal under the Act instead of coming to this court. There would, if they had taken that course, have been open to them a further appeal to this court on a point of law following on the decision of the Secretary of State."[114]

Lord Widgery CJ continued:

"It seems to me that in a very large number of instances it will be found that the statutory system of appeals is more effective and convenient than an application for certiorari, and the principal reason why it may prove itself to be more convenient and more effective is that an appeal to the Secretary of State on all issues arising between the parties can be disposed of at one hearing. Whether the issue between them is a matter of law or fact, or policy or opinion, or a combination of some or all of those, one hearing before the Minister has jurisdiction to deal with them all, whereas of course an application for certiorari is limited to cases where the issue is a matter

---

[112] [1974] 2 All ER 643.
[113] Now known as a quashing order in the light of the reforms made to the judicial review procedure by the Civil Procedure Rules: see Part 54 of the Rules.
[114] [1974] 2 All ER 643 at 647.

of law and then only when it is a matter of law appearing on the face of the order."[115]

Thus although the statutory appeal system was, generally speaking, the appropriate procedure to follow on account of it being "more effective and convenient", this did not mean that certiorari would always be inappropriate. There may be cases, for example where a matter of law was concerned, where an application for judicial review would be the appropriate way to proceed.[116]

Whether or not a statutory appeal procedure can be by-passed in a given case is, therefore, a matter of discretion for the court. In *R v Birmingham City Council, ex p Ferrero Ltd*,[117] the Court of Appeal was required to consider, inter alia, whether the respondents should have been granted judicial review or whether they ought to have pursued their statutory right of appeal under section 15 of the Consumer Protection Act 1987 where one of its products had been made the subject of a suspension order by the local council.[118] In giving the judgment of the Court of Appeal (with which Russell and Fox LJJ agreed), Taylor LJ (as he then was) noted that "there is much authority on the approach of this court to judicial review where a statutory appeal procedure has not been exhausted".[119] Such authority included *R v Epping and Harlow General Commissioners, ex p Goldstraw*,[120] where Sir John Donaldson MR had stated:

> "But it is a cardinal principle that, save in the most exceptional circumstances, that jurisdiction [judicial review] will not be exercised where other remedies were available and have not been used."[121]

Returning to this issue in the later case of *R v Chief Constable of the Merseyside Police, ex p Calveley*,[122] Sir John Donaldson MR cited the above passage and continued:

> "This, like other judicial pronouncements on the interrelationship between remedies by way of judicial review on the one hand and appeal procedures on the other, is not to be regarded or construed as a statute. It does not support the proposition that judicial review is not available where there is an alternative remedy by way of an appeal. It

---

[115] *ibid.* at 647-648.

[116] In *ex parte Royco* itself the Divisional Court held that the applicants were entitled to the order. They did so on the basis, inter alia, that although the relevant legislation gave the local authority wide powers to impose such conditions as they though fit, two of the four conditions were so unreasonable as to go beyond anything that Parliament could have intended, or any reasonable authority could have imposed, and the remaining conditions although not ultra vires themselves could not be severed from those that were. These were matters suited to judicial review.

[117] [1993] 1 All ER 530.

[118] The order had been made after a little girl had died from asphyxiation after accidentally swallowing part of a plastic toy which was found in a chocolate egg manufactured by the respondents.

[119] [1993] 1 All ER 530 at 535.

[120] [1983] 3 All ER 257.

[121] *ibid.* at 262.

[122] [1986] 1 All ER 257.

asserts simply that the court, in the exercise of its discretion, will very rarely make this remedy available in these circumstances."[123]

In the opinion of Taylor LJ in *Ferrero*, authorities such as these emphasised:

> "... that where there is an alternative remedy and especially where Parliament has provided a statutory appeal procedure it is only exceptionally that judicial review should be granted. It is therefore necessary, where the exception is invoked, to look carefully at the suitability of the statutory appeal in the context of the particular case."[124]

Having regard to the particular facts of the case before the Court of Appeal, Taylor LJ concluded that this was not an instance where the discretion of the court should have been exercised in favour of granting review. Rather, the statutory appeals procedure under section 15 of the 1987 Act ought to have been utilised.

The decision in *Ferrero* was central to the arguments advanced on this point in *R v Falmouth and Truro Port Health Authority, ex p South West Water Ltd.*[125] In the judicial review proceedings it was contended that the issues raised in those proceedings before the High Court and the Court of Appeal ought instead to have been raised by way of an appeal to the magistrates' court under section 80(3) of the 1990 Act.

Before Harrison J the Port Authority submitted, inter alia, that the dicta of Taylor LJ in *Ferrero* applied to the present case which, since it was not exceptional, ought to have been determined via the statutory appeal procedure. In support of this argument, it was pointed out that the first five issues in the application could have been raised under regulation 2(2)(a) of the 1995 Regulations,[126] whereas the sixth issue could have been dealt with under regulation 2(2)(b) of the same regulations.[127] Counsel for the water undertaker argued, on the other hand, that the present case and *Ferrero* were sufficiently distinguishable that an application for judicial review had been an appropriate way for South West Water to proceed.

In determining this issue Harrison J accepted that *Ferrero* could indeed be distinguished on the basis that the statutory regime and the real issues to be determined in that case "were materially different from the present case". In his Lordship's judgment:

> "... the real issues involved in the present case are, firstly, the consultation issues and, secondly, the legal issues relating to the validity of the notice, in particular the meaning of the word

---

[123] *ibid.* at 261.

[124] [1993] 1 All ER 530 at 536.

[125] [2000] 3 All ER 306.

[126] SI 1995/2644.

[127] The issues raised in the application were listed above, at p. 455.

"watercourse". I doubt very much whether the consultation issues could have been raised under ground (a) of regulation 2(2) of the 1995 Regulations because that ground relates to the question whether the notice is justified by section 80, whereas the consultation issues were mainly directed to the investigation stage under section 79 of the Act. However, whether that is so or not, I take the view that the issues of consultation and legitimate expectation are issues which are particularly suitable for decision by judicial review. Furthermore, the resolution of the legal issue as to the meaning of the word "watercourse" is more conveniently dealt with by way of judicial review in the circumstances of this case."[128]

In the light of the above, Harrison J concluded that:

"... this is a case which is an exception to the general rule, where judicial review is a more convenient and suitable remedy than the alternative appeal procedure for resolution of the real issues involved in the case."[129]

On appeal, the issue was further considered by the Court of Appeal.. Simon Brown LJ observed:

"I have not found this an altogether easy issue to decide. It is complicated, moreover, by a recognition that there were two stages at which the court had to exercise a discretion, the permission/stay stage and then the substantive hearing. Perhaps the most important decision was taken by Collins J... just three weeks after the abatement notice was served.[130] The hearing before Harrison J was some nine months later by when different considerations were in play. Of course Harrison J could simply have ruled that the water undertaker should be left to its statutory right of appeal and lifted the stay (expressing no views on the substantive issues), but really that would not have been very helpful given the time, effort and expense spent in preparing for, and holding, a five-day hearing. The real question seems to me to be whether permission to move and a stay ought ever to have been granted in the first place."[131]

In seeking to answer the "real question" which he had identified, Simon Brown LJ cited an observation of his own in *R v Devon County Council, ex p Baker, R v Durham County Council, ex p Curtis.*[132] These two appeals were concerned with the questions whether a local authority was under a duty to consult the residents of a home for old people which it proposed to

---

[128] [1999] EHLR 358 at 390.

[129] *ibid.*

[130] This was the decision to grant leave to apply for judicial review and to stay the abatement notice and the appeal to the magistrates' court pending the determination of the substantive judicial review application.

[131] [2000] 3 All ER 306 at 331.

[132] [1995] 1 All ER 73.

close and whether the availability of an alternative remedy[133] prevented the court from granting judicial review. With regard to the second question, Simon Brown LJ had observed:

> "Which of the two available remedies, or perhaps more accurately, avenues of redress, is to be preferred will depend ultimately upon which is the more convenient, expeditious and effective. Where ... what is required is the authoritative resolution of a legal issue ... I would regard judicial review as the more convenient alternative remedy."[134]

In *Falmouth*, Simon Brown LJ sought to distinguish *ex p Baker* from *ex p Ferrero* and the present appeal on the basis that the alternative remedies to judicial review were in each of the various cases different; a ministerial default power in the former and statutory appeal processes in the latter two cases. Moreover, Simon Brown LJ remarked that:

> "... in cases like *Ex p Ferrero* and the present appeal, the need to safeguard the public, even sometimes at the expense of the other party, is likely to be the paramount consideration. In deciding whether, exceptionally, to allow an application for judicial review, the judge should never lose sight of this. Questions of convenience, expedition and effectiveness should be assessed accordingly. If, for example, in this case, as ultimately in *Ex p Ferrero*, the enforcing authority had defeated all grounds of challenge, then the decision to allow a judicial review would have delayed abatement, quite possibly with damaging public health consequences. This should be recognised."[135]

With these thoughts in mind, Simon Brown LJ concluded that in the present case:

> "... it was inappropriate for permission and a stay to have been granted here on so wide-ranging a basis. In particular, I do not share Harrison J's 'view that the issues of consultation and legitimate expectation [were] particularly suitable for decision by judicial review'. I acknowledge that in *Ex p Baker* these were precisely the issues which I suggested could conveniently be decided by judicial review but, as I have sought to explain, that was in a very different context. Here it was imperative that if any judicial review challenge was to go ahead it should be dealt with expeditiously and the stay kept as short as possible. Given the volume of evidence required for the consultation issues it is unsurprising that the hearing was delayed.

---

[133] The remedy in question was an application to the Secretary of State pursuant to s. 7D of the Local Authority Social Services Act 1970. This provided that: "(1) If the Secretary of State is satisfied that any local authority have failed, without reasonable excuse, to comply with any of their duties which are social service functions ... he may make an order declaring that authority to be in default with respect to the duty in question ...".

[134] [1995] 1 All ER 73 at 92.

[135] [2000] 3 All ER 306 at 331.

In any event … non-consultation might well have been thought an inappropriate basis upon which to quash an abatement notice in a public health case."[136]

With regard to the other issues (the specification of works or steps in the abatement notice and the meaning of 'watercourse'), however, Simon Brown LJ reached a different conclusion. In his opinion:

"The resolution of these issues needed no evidence whatever, merely the notice itself and a map. These issues, moreover, if decided in the water undertaker's favour, would inevitably have been decisive of the case. I see no reason why an expedited judicial review hearing could not have resolved them within a very short time."[137]

His Lordship continued:

"Given (a) that the water undertaker's appeal did not operate to suspend the notice, (b) that it might well not be heard before (and at best would be heard only shortly before) the three months period for compliance expired (bearing in mind that the appeal would be heard on all issues and involve extensive oral evidence), (c) that to avoid the risk of committing an offence the water undertaker would have to start work on an alternative sewage scheme before its appeal could be heard, (d) that it would not be compensated for its work even if its appeal succeeded, and (e) that if its appeal failed, it would almost certainly wish to appeal by case stated to the Divisional Court, I think that a limited judicial review along the lines I have indicated could properly have been permitted."[138]

The conclusion on the issue of alternative remedies for the purposes of the present appeal was, therefore, that judicial review was an appropriate means of redress in respect of *some* rather than *all* the issues as Harrison J had held. On a more general level, however, Simon Brown LJ suggested that there was a "lesson to be learned" for the future. In his opinion:

"The critical decision in an alternative remedy case, certainly one which requires a stay, is that taken at the grant of permission stage. If the applicant has a statutory right of appeal, permission should only exceptionally be given; rarer still will permission be appropriate in a case concerning public safety. The judge should, however, have regard to all relevant circumstances which typically will include, besides any public health consideration, the comparative speed, expense and finality of the alternative process, the need and scope for fact-finding, the desirability of an authoritative ruling on any point of

---

[136] *ibid.* at 331-332.
[137] *ibid.* at 332.
[138] *ibid.*

law arising, and (perhaps) the apparent strength of the applicant's substantive challenge."[139]

Of the other two judges who heard the appeal in *Falmouth*, Pill LJ also considered the issue of alternative remedies. After having expressed his approval for the remarks of Simon Brown LJ, Pill LJ commented:

> "Given the public health context and the provision of a statutory remedy, I question whether matters of convenience and expedition should be allowed to permit proceedings by way of judicial review the effect of which is to circumvent ... or subvert a detailed statutory procedure. If the statutory intention is to provide that any appeal is to be to the magistrates' court, the aim must be to make that remedy effective rather than to surmise that it is so ineffective that judicial review is permitted."[140]

Pill LJ continued:

> "The emphasis should in my judgment be upon making the statutory procedures effective rather than assuming ineffectiveness and treating judicial review as a default procedure. There is in my view a very high burden on a party claiming, in the context of public health, that the statutory remedy will be ineffective before he can expect permission to apply to be granted. The grant has the effect of deferring the resolution of factual issues and, in this case, rendering ineffective by passage of time the operation of a notice which the statutory scheme contemplates should, subject to the powers of the magistrates, be effective."[141]

And concluded:

> "There may be cases where a grant of permission to apply for judicial review is appropriate. They will be rare. The fact that a legal point arises on the wording of the notice does not of itself in my view justify the intervention of the High Court by way of judicial review."[142]

OFFENCES

It is an offence triable summarily for a person upon whom an abatement notice has been served, without reasonable excuse to contravene or fail to comply with any requirement or prohibition imposed by that notice.[143]

---

[139] *ibid.*

[140] *ibid.* at 336.

[141] *ibid.*

[142] *ibid.*

[143] Section 80(4). Note that the maximum fine may depend on the kind of location where the offence is committed. Where the offence is committed on "industrial trade or business premises" the maximum fine which may be imposed is £20,000, as compared with a lower maximum (level 5 on the standard scale – currently £5,000) where the offence is committed elsewhere. However,

In serious offence cases an alternative procedure is available to local authorities. Section 81(5) provides that if a local authority is of the opinion that ordinary criminal proceedings would afford an inadequate remedy in the case of any statutory nuisance it may take proceedings in the High Court to secure the abatement, prohibition or restriction of the nuisance. Such proceedings are to secure a High Court injunction.[144] Any failure then to comply with the terms of such an injunction would bring into operation a range of orders associated with civil contempt of court (which might include custodial orders and financial penalties at the discretion of the court).

This procedure was considered in *Vale of White Horse District Council* v *Allen and Partners*.[145] In this case, which concerned alleged statutory and common law nuisances arising out of intensive pig husbandry, the local authority had commenced High Court proceedings for an injunction as an alternative to the more standard procedures involving recourse to the Magistrates' Court. As we have seen, section 81(5) provides for High Court injunctive relief to be an option where the local authority forms the opinion that summary proceedings for an offence would "afford an inadequate remedy". In the *Vale of White Horse* case this requirement was described as involving a situation where the respondents were:

> "deliberately or flagrantly flouting the law"

and

> "where only an injunction will stop their illegal or potentially illegal activities."[146]

The possibility of an injunction having greater influence on the future behaviour of a respondent stems, of course, from the more serious sanctions which may follow from non-compliance with the terms of a High Court injunction as compared with the level of criminal penalty which may be imposed by a summary court.

The legal issue which arose for determination in *Vale of White Horse* was this: there appeared to have been a failure on the part of the district council to have formally formed the view required by section 81(5), that criminal proceedings would "afford an inadequate remedy". The council meeting at which the matter had been considered certainly took the view that High Court proceedings for an injunction would conveniently lead to a solution

---

where the "level 5" maximum applies there is also provision for further proceedings and a further fine "equal to one-tenth of that level" for each day on which the offence continues after the conviction. It is not clear whether the "one-tenth" relates to the level of the original fine or to the maximum penalty provided for in level 5. It would seem that the former is the more sensible interpretation.

[144] It is explicitly stated in the Act that such proceedings shall be maintainable notwithstanding that the local authority has itself suffered no damage from the nuisance.

[145] [1997] Env LR 212.

[146] *ibid.* at 214.

of the problem and that such proceedings should be preferred, as more appropriate, than summary proceedings. However, as Bell J commented:

> "that is not the opinion required for valid High Court proceedings pursuant to section 81(5)."[147]

Given that the local authority had, it seemed, not formed the requisite opinion which was a necessary precondition of the power to bring High Court proceedings the question arose whether those proceedings could nevertheless be regarded as valid by virtue of section 222 of the Local Government Act 1972. This section provides:

> "Where a local authority considers it expedient for the promotion or protection of the interests of the inhabitants of their area –
> (a)   they may prosecute or defend or appear in any legal proceedings and, in the case of civil proceedings, may initiate them in their own name ..."

The council resolution authorising officers to commence High Court proceedings referred to it being considered "expedient for the protection of the interests of the inhabitants of the area to institute those proceedings". The council contended, accordingly, that section 222 was a sufficient and separate legal base upon which the intended recourse to the High Court could be justified.

The Divisional Court, for a variety of reasons, rejected this argument. In particular, the court ruled that:

> "...if the district council's contention is correct it would be entitled to bring High Court proceedings under section 222(1), even though summary proceedings for an offence ... would afford an adequate remedy."[148]

Bell J would not accept this proposition, explaining that:

> "...Part III of the 1990 Act, and the regulations made under it, amount to a statutory code for dealing with statutory nuisances and section 81(5) makes it clear that High Court proceedings are only to be used when the local authority is of the opinion that the statutory code will be ineffective."[149]

And elsewhere Bell J noted:

> "Section 222 of the 1972 Act does not provide a separate entitlement to restrain a perceived statutory nuisance."[150]

---

[147] *ibid.* at 224.

[148] *ibid.* at 221.

[149] *ibid.*

[150] *ibid.* at 223. This statement is, it would seem, rather too broad. The limitation upon s. 222 would seem to apply only where the recourse to the High Court is for a remedy in relation to

Without reasonable excuse

The offence under section 80(4) includes within its terms the requirement that the contravention of, or the failure to have complied with any requirement or prohibition imposed by, an abatement notice shall be "without reasonable excuse". Although sometimes loosely referred to as a defence to liability, this provision is more properly to be regarded as a component of the offence itself, with significant consequences as regards the matter of burden of proof.

This point was emphasised in *Polychronakis* v *Richards and Jerom Ltd*,[151] where it was explained that the proper approach was that the matter – "without reasonable excuse" – was one in respect of which the prosecution is required to satisfy the court, at the usual criminal standard of proof – "beyond reasonable doubt".

The prosecution will not be required to prove this negative in every case. Nevertheless, in any case where the defence produces some evidence which it contends may amount to a reasonable excuse the burden then shifts to the prosecution, in the words of Brooke LJ:

> "to satisfy the court to the criminal standard that the excuse is not a reasonable one."[152]

In *Polychronakis* the Divisional Court explained that its decision involved no more than the application of ordinary principles of criminal law and evidence. It referred, with approval, to *R* v *Clarke*.[153] In that case, in a rather different legal context (drink-driving) it had been held that once some evidence of a reasonable excuse for failing to have provided a specimen had been offered to the court by the defendant it was "for the prosecution to eliminate the existence of such a defence to the satisfaction of the jury".[154]

Some comment is appropriate as regards the use of the expression "burden of proof" and "beyond reasonable doubt" in this connection. These expressions are relevant to the proof of primary fact: in other words, to the establishment, to the appropriate degree of likelihood, of "what happened". Now, such evidence may well be crucially important. The argument between the complainant and the defendant may well principally be as regards whether or not certain events occurred, or whether or not certain circumstances prevailed. In such a situation it may well be very important

---

failure to have complied with an abatement notice which has earlier been served. There would seem to be no reason why a local authority may not choose, *instead of serving such a notice*, to seek an injunction (under s. 222) in relation to conduct which may be properly regarded equally as, for example, a public nuisance.

[151] [1998] Env LR 346.

[152] *ibid.* at 351.

[153] [1969] 1 WLR 1109.

[154] Per Brooke LJ at 350. The court also approved *Saddleworth Urban District Council* v *Aggregate and Sand Ltd* (1970) 69 LGR 103.

whether the onus of proof lies with one side or with the other (and as regards the required standard of such proof).

However, even after the primary facts have been established there may remain contention as regards whether it is a correct inference, for the court to draw, that the defendant's proven conduct in those proven circumstances should be categorised as providing a "reasonable excuse" for the nuisance caused. This will certainly provide opportunity for forensic argument: each side seeking to produce persuasive arguments as regards the inference which the court should draw. However, it would not seem appropriate to speak here of *burdens* or *standards* of proof. Once the primary facts have been found by the tribunal of fact, the inferences which follow (in terms here of whether the evidence gives rise to what should be regarded as a reasonable excuse) will be matters of "secondary fact", in relation to which the notions of standard or burden of proof are not apposite. The matter becomes apparent when one seeks to ask, for example, whether, on the basis of primary facts found, it is "more likely than not" or whether it is "beyond reasonable doubt" that there was a "reasonable excuse". The questions so asked make no sense. We are in the realm here of "judgment" upon the evidence, rather than of demonstration by evidence of some further layer of fact: the realm of forensic persuasion rather than judicial proof.

One further aspect of the decision in *Polychronakis* warrants discussion. The prosecutor had relied upon the terms of section 101 of the Magistrates' Courts Act 1980. This provides:

> "Where the defendant to an information ... relies for his defence on any ... excuse, whether or not it accompanies the description ... in the enactment creating the offence ..., the burden of proving the ... excuse shall be on him, and this notwithstanding that the information ... contains an allegation negativing the ... excuse."

At first sight this provision might seem to provide support for the prosecution's contentions as regards the burden of proof under section 80(4) of the 1990 Act. However, the court in *Polychronakis* noted that this provision had been subject to a restrictive interpretation by the Court of Appeal in *R v Edwards*.[155] In that case the Court of Appeal had ruled that section 101 provides an exception to the "fundamental rule of our criminal law that the prosecution must prove every element of the offence charged".[156] It was, for that reason, appropriate to regard this "reverse-burden" as:

> "limited to offences arising under enactments which prohibit the doing of an act save in specified circumstances or by persons of

---

[155] [1975] 1 QB 27.
[156] *ibid.* at 40.

specified classes or with specified qualifications or with the licence or permission of specified authorities."[157]

In the later case, *R v Hunt*,[158] Lord Griffiths approved this statement and noted that there would rarely be occasions where a statutory provision not falling within that description would come within the rule in section 101. In *Polychronakis* the court took the view that the "reasonable excuse" provision within section 80(4) was not of a kind similar to the matters described in the quotation given above. Absence of reasonable excuse was, it concluded, different from matters by way of defence such as the possession of a licence or permit, or that the defendant fell within a specified class of exempted person.

Whereas those who may be exempt from criminal liability in the ways described within the above quotation may be required to prove to the court that they fall within those statutorily exempt categories, section 101 of the 1980 Act will not be regarded as applicable to more *substantive* limitations upon criminal liability.

COMPENSATION ORDERS

In addition to recourse to statutory nuisance procedures for the purpose of nuisance abatement and the imposition of a fine, a conviction by the magistrates will also bring into play the powers of the magistrates to make a compensation order.

The matter is governed by section 130(1) of the Powers of Criminal Courts (Sentencing) Act 2000.[159] This provides;

> "... a court by or before which a person is convicted of an offence, instead of or in addition to dealing with him in any other way, may, on application or otherwise, make an order (in this Act referred to as a "compensation order") requiring him—
>
> (a) to pay compensation for any personal injury, loss or damage resulting from that offence or any other offence which is taken into consideration by the court in determining sentence; ..."

The amount of compensation which may be ordered is subject to a statutory limit:[160] currently £5000.

Certain points about section 130 warrant immediate comment. To begin with it applies only in proceedings where a person is convicted of an *offence*. In the context of statutory nuisance this would apply to proceedings for the offence of having failed to comply with an abatement

---

[157] *ibid.*

[158] [1987] AC 352.

[159] This Act consolidated various enactments relating to the powers of courts to deal with offenders and defaulters, including the Powers of Criminal Courts Act 1973, s. 35 of which provided for the making of compensation orders.

[160] Section 131(1) of the 2000 Act. Formerly the statutory limit was to be found in s. 40(1) of the Magistrates' Courts Act 1980.

notice served by a local authority; and also proceedings brought under section 82 by an aggrieved individual alleging the existence of a statutory nuisance.[161] In either case, if the summary court convicts, the power to award compensation comes into operation.

Secondly, it should be noted that the section confers a *power* to award compensation: not a duty. We shall consider shortly the circumstances in which it may, or may not, be appropriate for magistrates to make an award. Any determination *not* to make an award must, however, be reached on the basis of the principles to be described, and reasons for so determining must be given. This follows from section 130, which states that:

> "A court shall give reasons, on passing sentence, if it does not make a compensation order in a case where this section empowers it to do so."[162]

Thirdly, the compensation awarded under section 130(1)(a) relates, and may relate only, to the following matters: "personal injury, loss or damage". The courts have interpreted these words somewhat restrictively. Furthermore, the compensation awarded may relate only to injury, loss or damage *resulting from the offence* (or from others taken into consideration). This, as we shall see, may be a substantial limiting factor. In each case it may need to be considered whether an item of injury, loss or damage for which recovery of compensation is sought has resulted from the particular offence for which the defendant has been convicted, or from some other conduct on the part of the defendant.

The basis upon which magistrates should exercise their discretion whether or not to make a compensation order was considered in *Davenport* v *Walsall Metropolitan Borough Council.*[163] The local authority had pleaded guilty before the magistrates to a statutory nuisance complaint brought by a tenant of a property which it owned. The circumstances involved substantial misrepair and quite serious damp, mould and condensation. An order was made by the magistrates that works to abate the nuisance should be undertaken, and completed, within eight weeks. The magistrates reached no immediate decision as regards any fine, costs, or the award of any compensation. They adjourned the proceedings for some three months. When the proceedings resumed the issue of compensation was considered. The complainant sought compensation under two headings: *special* damages in relation to harm which had resulted to items such as carpets and curtains; and *general* damages in relation to the unpleasantness, anxiety and distress associated with having lived in premises in conditions so prejudicial to health. The local authority disputed these categories, and also the amounts of damages claimed.

---

[161] See *Herbert* v *London Borough of Lambeth* (1982) 24 HLR 299; *Botros* v *Hammersmith London Borough Council* (unreported, October 21, 1994). See further, on the s. 82 procedure, below at p. 497.

[162] Section 130(3) of the 2000 Act.

[163] [1997] Env LR 24.

Having listened to argument the magistrates decided against making a compensation order. It was their view that the damages were not easily quantifiable and that the "correct venue" for determining the amount of civil recovery was via a separate civil action in the county court.

In the Divisional Court, on appeal, Keene J noted that the courts had given clear guidance as regards the unsuitability of criminal compensation machinery for dealing with complicated issues. He referred, with approval, to the following words of Woolf LJ (as he then was) in *Herbert* v *London Borough of Lambeth*,[164] quoting from *Stones Justices Manual*:

> "The machinery of a compensation order under this Act is intended for clear and simple cases. It must also be remembered that the civil rights of the victim remain, although the power to make a compensation order is not confined to cases where there is civil liability. A compensation order made by a court of trial can be extremely beneficial as long as it is confined to simple straightforward cases, and generally cases where no great amount is at stake."[165]

Keene J also referred to the statement by Eveleigh LJ in *R* v *Donovan*,[166] that:

> "a compensation order is designed for the simple, straightforward case where the amount of compensation can be readily and easily ascertained."[167]

Further, in *R* v *Kneeshaw*[168] Lord Widgery CJ had made quite clear that magistrates should decline this jurisdiction in any case where to assess the quantum of compensation would involve them embarking upon what might prove to be a complicated investigation.

An issue arose in *Davenport*, whether the magistrates had based their judgment as regards the not easily quantifiable nature of the damages in that case on sufficient evidence: the complainant contending that they had been wrong to so decide without having first heard the evidence which was to be presented on the matter. Keene J sided with the magistrates on this issue:

> "Clearly the justices cannot decide whether or not it is an appropriate case for a compensation order without having some information put before them about the nature of the alleged loss or damage, and whether or not there is any dispute between the parties. They may, however, be able to obtain enough information to be able to form a

---

[164] (1992) 24 HLR 299.

[165] *ibid.* at 304-305.

[166] (1981) 3 Cr App R (S) 192.

[167] *ibid.* In this case discretion was exercised appropriately not to make an award of compensation for the loss of use of a motor car for four and a half months.

[168] [1975] QB 57.

judgment on that aspect from what is said by and put to them by the advocates .... In the present case, the justices were addressed at length by the advocates on this matter. I can see no reason why the justices in this case could not have reached their conclusion that the damages were not easily quantifiable on the documents with which they were provided, together with what they heard from the advocates during their lengthy submissions.

It will be remembered that the difficulty in quantifying the claims was only an aspect of the broader reasoning of the magistrates. The full statement of reasons referred to their view that 'the correct venue for deciding the amount of compensation ... is the county court'."[169]

In argument before the magistrates it had been contended by the complainant that, since there was quite probably no remedy in civil law available to her as regards losses resulting from the condensation,[170] it was an improper exercise of discretion effectively to deny such compensation entirely by refusing to make a compensation order in the criminal proceedings. In other words, in the sort of case adverted to in the quotation from Woolf LJ above, in which a compensation order may extend compensation beyond what is recoverable at civil law, there was argued to be a duty to make such an award.

Keene J rejected this argument. He put the matter as follows:

"The absence of, or the difficulty of obtaining, a civil remedy in the courts in respect of some or all of the loss suffered is ... a relevant factor which the magistrates should take into account .... But it cannot be an overriding consideration, forcing magistrates' courts to embark on complex investigations."[171]

On examination of the magistrates' hearing there was no reason to think that the justices had failed to take proper account of this factor in coming to their decision.

A final argument on the part of the complainant was that the magistrates had reached a perverse decision – one to which no reasonable bench could have come – in reaching its decision that the damages were not easily quantifiable and that the case was not a suitable one for a compensation order. The Divisional Court was unwilling to accept that the decision of the magistrates' court could be so characterised. It was open to the bench to have arrived at the decision they reached without that decision having the character of being legally perverse. Nevertheless, Keene J was anxious that the decision should not encourage magistrates to opt over-often for the simple solution of denying compensation. He noted:

---

[169] [1997] Env LR 24 at 32.
[170] A view deriving from *Quick* v *Taff-Ely Borough Council* [1986] 1 QB 809.
[171] [1997] Env LR 24 at 35.

"It is a virtue of compensation order proceedings in the magistrates' court that they do provide a relatively simple and inexpensive way of obtaining redress ... I ... would be reluctant to say anything which would discourage justices from using [the] power ... Nor would I wish it to be thought that justices can avoid performing their duty under the 1973 Act[172] by an over-eager resort to assertions of complexity."

Abatement by the local authority

Where an abatement notice has not been complied with the local authority may take action itself to abate the nuisance.[173] This power exists whether or not proceedings are commenced for the offence of having contravened the notice.

Any expenses which are reasonably incurred by the local authority in so abating, or preventing the recurrence of, a statutory nuisance may be recovered by the authority from the person "by whose act or default the nuisance was caused".[174]

It would appear form the wording of the Act that although a person who has a liability to abate a nuisance *qua* owner or occupier[175] may incur criminal liability for failing to comply with such notice, such an owner or occupier seems not to be a permitted target for local authority recoupment of its costs where the authority has abated at its own expense. Such an "innocent" owner or occupier, not being a person "by whose act or default the nuisance was caused", would not fall within the category of persons referred to above upon whom such reimbursement liability may fall. However, the Act provides further that if the person by whose act or default the nuisance was caused is the owner of the premises, costs may be recouped "from any person who is for the time being the owner thereof". This would appear to render an "innocent" owner subject to such cost recoupment in the limited situation where that person shares ownership with a person by whose act or default the nuisance was caused.

Proceedings for recoupment are by way of civil debt action. Given that it is only "expenses reasonably incurred" which may be recovered it would seem that argument on this matter may form the substance of a defence to the action.

The civil court has power to apportion expenses as between persons by whose acts or defaults the nuisance was caused: such apportionment to be made on the basis of the court's assessment of what is "fair and reasonable".

---

[172] Now the Powers of Criminal Courts (Sentencing) Act 2000.
[173] 1990 Act, s. 81(3).
[174] 1990 Act, s. 81(4).
[175] See above, p. 471.

In cases where expenses are recoverable from an owner of the premises a notice may be served[176] upon that person,[177] which will have a dual effect. It will render the expenses claimed subject to interest charges between the date of service of the notice and the date of full payment,[178] and will also result in the expenses and the accrued interest becoming a charge on the premises. An appeal may be lodged against such a notice. The appeal is to the county court and must be lodged within 21 days of the date of service. The court may confirm the notice, order that it shall be of no effect,[179] or substitute a different sum of money as due. This last option would seem to permit argument to be raised as regards the reasonableness of expenses incurred by the local authority in its abatement actions.

PROCEEDINGS BY PERSONS AGGRIEVED: SECTION 82 PROCEEDINGS

The provisions discussed above describe procedures which apply in cases where, as is the typical case, statutory nuisance proceedings are taken by a local authority. The 1990 Act provides also for proceedings to be initiated by individuals, provided they fall within the category of persons aggrieved by a statutory nuisance.

The matter is governed by section 82. The starting-point is that before commencing court proceedings by complaint to the magistrates' court the person aggrieved is required to give the potential defendant notice in writing of his intention to bring those proceedings. This "warning" notice must specify the matter complained of, and the notice must be given not less than 21 days before proceedings are commenced.[180]

To whom should such notice be given? The answer is – the potential defendant, and this will generally be the person responsible for the nuisance. Where the person responsible "cannot be found" the notice and subsequent proceedings will fall at the lap of the "owner or occupier" of the premises. Where a nuisance arises from a structural defect in premises it will be the owner who should receive such notice; and where the matter relates to noise from a vehicle, machinery or equipment the appropriate person will be the person responsible for the item making the noise.[181]

Address for service?

Section 82(6) of the 1990 Act provides, as we have seen, for notice in writing of intention to bring proceedings to be given to the proposed defendant. In the proceedings which follow an argument may arise as to

---

[176] Under 1990 Act, s. 81A.

[177] A copy must be served also on all other persons who, to the knowledge of the authority, have a proprietary interest in the premises: s. 81A(3).

[178] Interest at such reasonable rate as the local authority shall determine: subs. (1)(a).

[179] For example, where it is successfully argued that the recipient of the notice is not a person from whom expenses are recoverable, or is not an owner of the premises.

[180] 1990 Act, s. 82(6). In the case of noise nuisances (categories (g) and (ga)) the notice period is shorter: not less than three days' notice (s. 82(7)).

[181] 1990 Act, s. 82(4).

whether such written notice was addressed appropriately. A good illustration may be found in *Leeds* v *London Borough of Islington*:[182] a case which demonstrates that judicial willingness to relax some technicalities in favour of individual complainants under section 82 must not be permitted to go so far as to undermine procedural safeguards established to protect the interests of defendants.

A local authority tenant had sought to bring proceedings against his landlord local authority – as responsible for the statutory nuisance in question, in its capacity as owner of the premises. The tenant sent a notice of intention to bring proceedings, not to the principal office of the local authority but to an office referred to on the rentcard which he possessed in relation to his tenancy. That document contained a statement which indicated that notices served under section 48 of the Landlord and Tenant Act 1987 should be served to a particular address given. The tenant, presumably considering that that office would deal with all issues relating to the condition of council property, addressed his statutory nuisance notice to that address.

In the proceedings which followed, the local authority took issue on this point. Attention focused on section 160 of the 1990 Act. This provides, so far as is relevant, that:

> "(a) in the case of a body corporate, notices should be addressed to the secretary or clerk of that body;
> (b) in the case of a body corporate the proper address for service shall be the address of its registered or principal office."[183]

No point was, in fact, taken by the local authority that the person addressed was not the "secretary" or "clerk" to the local authority, but rather, the Senior Estate Manager. Nevertheless, Schiemann LJ expressed the view that to have taken such objection might have been legitimate. He commented:

> "If the notice is merely addressed to 'the authority' that arguably would not suffice. The notice should have been addressed to the clerk who would be in a position to secure that action was taken with all appropriate speed. But if the notice is addressed to someone other than the clerk – say the librarian – that does not seem to me to be good enough. In the present case it was addressed to the Senior Estate Manager at Canonbury Neighbourhood, Canonbury West Office. That does not seem to me to comply with section 160(3)."[184]

In other words the starting point was that the notice should have been served at, or posted to, the authority's principal office and have been addressed to its clerk. It was, however, contended by the tenant that the local authority had itself indicated a different address for receipt of notices

---

[182] [1998] Env LR 655.
[183] Section 160(3).
[184] [1998] Env LR 655 at 658.

(the Canonbury address); and that, by virtue of section 160(4), in such circumstances that different address was equally a proper address for service. Schiemann LJ concluded that this argument could not succeed. The statement on the rentcard could not properly be interpreted as applying to the service of notices other than those under the Landlord and Tenant Act 1987.

Content of notices under section 82

The scope of "warning notice" obligations was discussed in two cases decided in late 1998: *East Staffordshire BC* v *Fairless*[185] and *Pearshouse* v *Birmingham City Council.*[186]

In the *Fairless* case, solicitors for the tenant of a council property wrote to the landlord council giving by letter 21 days notice of intention to bring proceedings under section 82. The letter indicated the view that the premises, about which repeated complaints had been made to the council's Housing Officer, were in a state which was prejudicial to the health of the tenant and his family. The letter enclosed a lengthy inspection report by an independent housing consultant/surveyor. The letter stressed that the report, which dealt with disrepair, dampness and mould growth, was not an exhaustive catalogue of matters which might be regarded as prejudicial to health. Some six months later the tenant initiated formal proceedings, by laying an information, complaining to the magistrates about the alleged statutory nuisance. A summons was issued to the local authority, and the magistrates heard the case seven months later. It was admitted by the local authority that the premises amounted to a statutory nuisance on the date that the legal proceedings were initiated. It was also admitted by the parties that the premises were no longer a nuisance at the date when the case came to trial. Given this second admission the case was dismissed by the magistrates: the substantial issue at this stage having become the matter of liability to costs under section 82(12).

Ordinarily, where a nuisance is found to have existed when, following a warning notice, proceedings were initiated under section 82(1), the court is under a duty to award costs against the respondent, even where the nuisance has subsequently been remedied. In the *Fairless* case, however, it was argued that such liability to costs did not arise because the "warning notice" given did not satisfy the requirements of section 82(6). It was contended that it failed to do so in that it did not specify sufficiently the matters complained of. The letter from the tenant's solicitors expressly stated that the matters referred to were not an exhaustive list of matters alleged to constitute a nuisance. The local authority argued that in the absence of any complete list having been prepared and communicated by the tenant, it was not in a position to know precisely what was required to be rectified.

---

[185] [1999] Env LR 525.
[186] [1999] Env LR 536.

The magistrates rejected this argument, holding that the letter and the independent report, read together, constituted a valid warning notice under section 82(6). On appeal the Divisional Court affirmed this approach. In his judgment Sullivan J stressed the significance of the matter in issue. A great many section 82 complaints are made against local authorities. In each case the local authority will incur a liability to pay costs if it is not able to demonstrate that a nuisance which may have existed at the date of the warning notice had been remedied by the date proceedings were initiated. The argument of the local authority was that given such a financial "penalty" for not having put matters right following such notice (and within a period which might be as short as three weeks from first notice) it was appropriate that the matters to be remedied should be required to be identified exhaustively and with some precision.

The Divisional Court approached the matter rather differently. To begin with, it noted that there were significant differences between abatement notices and warning notices in terms of their legal effects: accordingly it might be that a different approach was appropriate to each case. In the words of Sullivan J:

> "... the effect of a section 82(6) notice and an abatement notice are fairly described as comparable. But the analogy ... should not be pushed too far .... [T]he recipient of an abatement notice must either appeal against it or comply with it. If he does not, he may be fined. Understandably the requirements of such a notice should be spelt out with some particularity. By way of contrast the recipient of a notice under section 82(2) need do nothing. He can wait to see if the complaint is made and, if it is, he can then contest the making of an order."[187]

On this basis the court saw no reason to interpret section 82(2) as imposing requirements beyond its bare terms: to "specify the matters complained of". This was not to be interpreted as requiring the *works to be undertaken* to be itemised. In particular:

> "It is ... important that ordinary members of the public, such as tenants, are not deterred from pursuing complaints ... by over-technical procedural requirements. The complainant may know very well what it is he is complaining about, but find it difficult to set out at that stage precisely what should be done to remedy it. By way of contrast, local authorities ... have access to legal and technical advice. It is understandable that greater particularity should be required in [an abatement notice] served by a public body, with penal consequences, if it is not complied with or appealed against."[188]

A similar approach was adopted in the *Pearshouse* case. Here the magistrates had accepted the contention of the local authority that a

---

[187] [1999] Env LR 525 at 533.
[188] *ibid.* at 534.

warning notice was inadequate, and so had dismissed the proceedings. The warning notice, like that in *Fairless*, comprised a surveyor's report on the condition of the tenant's premises. It contained a substantial list of defects, room by room. Some appeared to be such as might constitute a nuisance or be prejudicial to health. Other defects did not seem to have this likely character. Some defects which were listed were such as not presently to be prejudicial to health, although they might become so if not remedied. In this last context the court noted that whereas an abatement notice under *section 80* might be served whether an alleged statutory nuisance existed *or was likely to occur or recur*, the procedure under section 82 applied only in relation to nuisances which *existed at the time proceedings before the magistrates were commenced.* It was therefore argued by the local authority that the warning notice served upon them was faulty: that not only did it not distinguish between defects which could, in principle, be characterised as a nuisance and those of a different and lesser nature, it also did not distinguish between items which were currently giving rise to a nuisance and those which merely had such future potential.

The Divisional Court allowed the complainant's appeal from the magistrates' dismissal of his case. The court stressed, as in *Fairless*, the significant differences in the legal significance of abatement and warning notices. However, in accepting this difference and acknowledging lesser burdens on complainants in relation to section 82(6) warning notices, the court was not willing to go so far as to accede to an argument that all that was necessary was to indicate which kind of statutory nuisance, within the list contained in section 79, was alleged. Collins J indicated:

> "It ... is difficult to see that merely to specify the relevant subsection is sufficient to specify the matter complained of. Those words suggest that Parliament was thinking of something more. What is necessary, in my judgment is for the tenant (or whoever) to indicate very broadly the nature of the complaint. For example, if the tenant is concerned about dampness ... he need say no more than: 'The premises are damp and that is damaging my health". Or if there is a leaking roof, reference can be made to that. Nor does it matter, ... that the tenant is wrong in identifying particular defects which do not amount to a statutory nuisance and omits ... defects which in the end do amount to a statutory nuisance."[189]

Collins J then continued:

> "I am far from saying that a list of defects should not be given. It is clearly desirable that as much information is given ... as is reasonably possible. But, ... any errors or indications that the notice may not be exhaustive cannot conceivably invalidate it."[190]

---

[189] [1999] Env LR 536 at 549-550.
[190] *ibid.* at 550.

In coming to the same conclusion, that the warning notice was valid within section 82(6), Lord Bingham CJ (as he then was) explained:

> "Section 82 is intended to provide a simple procedure for a private citizen to obtain redress ... It would frustrate the clear intention of Parliament if the procedure provided ... were to become bogged down in unnecessary technicality or undue literalism. It is important that the system should be operable by people who may be neither very sophisticated nor very articulate, and who may not ... have the benefit of specialised and high quality advice."[191]

Lord Bingham noted that the purpose of the warning notice was to enable the local authority to make an inspection and make its own assessment of the practical and effective steps necessary to eliminate the nuisances. In other words itemisation of matters requiring attention and the diagnosis of the causes of the nuisances complained about, could be regarded more as a task for the local authority at this inspection stage than as a task imposed by virtue of section 82(6) upon the complainant. Furthermore, the burden imposed by section 82(6) – slight as it is – may vary depending on the nature and extent of any earlier correspondence between the complainant and the person to be served the notice. As Lord Bingham put it:

> "If there has been a long preceding correspondence, very little by way of elaboration may be called for. But even in the absence of any preceding correspondence a brief reference to damp, or broken windows, or draughts, or lack of ventilation or the presence of mould will be enough."[192]

Concern that the system under section 82 ought not to be allowed to become overly technical or legally complex is evident in two further cases:[193] *Hall* v *Kingston Upon Hull City Council*;[194] and *Hewlings* v *McLean Homes East Anglia Ltd.*[195] In each case, the appellants had served section 82(6) notices on their local authority landlords at addresses which had been specified by the landlords.[196] In each case, however, the specified address was not the same as the council's "proper address", i.e. its principal office. Subsequently the appellants had commenced proceedings against the council, but the information had been dismissed by magistrates on the basis that they had not been properly served in accordance with section 160 of the 1990 Act. In allowing their appeals, Mitchell J (who delivered the judgment of the court) described the section 82 procedure thus:

---

[191] *ibid.* at 551.

[192] *ibid.* at 552.

[193] See also the Scottish case of *Adams* v *Glasgow City Council* [2000] Hous. LR 3.

[194] [1999] 2 All ER 609. There were in fact three appeals before the Divisional Court, the other two being *Ireland* v *Birmingham City Council* and *Baker* v *Birmingham City Council*.

[195] [2001] EHLR 34.

[196] In *Hall*, the notice had been sent to the council's housing department in accordance with a direction given to that effect in a letter sent by the council to the appellant. In *Ireland* and *Baker*, the notices were sent to the local neighbourhood housing team in accordance with the council's terms and conditions.

"It is a simple procedure for a private citizen to obtain redress when he or she suffers a s 79(1) statutory nuisance. Thus the system should be operable by people who may be neither very sophisticated nor very articulate and who may not in some cases have the benefit of legal advice. The notice should be such as will reasonably alert the recipient to matters complained of so that the recipient may take timely and effective steps to put right such matters as he accepts need to be put right. Thus the hallmarks of the statutory remedy can be summarised in two words: 'simple' and 'speedy'."[197]

Turning to consider the effect of section 160 of the 1990 Act, Mitchell J noted that in each case the respondent council had taken the point that as section 160(2) to (4) had not been complied with, the section 82(6) notice had not been served and the court therefore lacked jurisdiction. On behalf of the appellants, however, it had been argued that the notice had been properly served in accordance with section 160(5) since in each case, the council had specified an alternative address for the service of such notices. The substantial issue was "who within a local authority has power to specify a different address for service than that prescribed under the legislation?". The appellants argued that this was not limited to the "secretary" or "clerk". In finding in favour of the appellants, Mitchell J observed:

"In our judgment the person to be served and accordingly, the person who has to specify for the purpose of s. 160(5), is the body corporate – here the city council. What must be specified is an address other than '*his* proper address within the meaning of subsection (4)' – in other words an address other than the city council's proper address. In our judgment s. 160(3)(a) and s. 160(4)(a) do no more than make provision, where the person to be served is a body corporate, for the means by which that end is to be achieved. Whether s. 160(3)(a) is mandatory or directory is an entirely different question. Regardless of the answer to that question, where the person to be served is a body corporate s. 160(3)(a) provides that service 'may' be achieved by service on the secretary or clerk to that body. We see no reason to interpret s. 160(5) in such cases as these as confining (on the basis of s. 160(3)), the category of persons who can specify an alternative address, to the persons who are (or equivalent to) the secretary or the clerk. The 'person to be served' for the purposes of the Act is the person responsible for the nuisance or, s. 82(4) apart, the owner of the premises (see s. 82(4) and (6)). Here the relevant person is the landlord, namely the local authority. It is, in our judgment, the local authority which has, under s. 160(5), the power to specify. The 'secretary' or 'clerk' (or the equivalent) are simply vehicles by which the 'person to be served' may be served. In our judgment the Act does not identify the class of persons who can, on behalf of a body corporate, 'specify' for the purposes of s. 160(5). That omission does not create a problem because in the vast majority of cases (if not all)

---

[197] [1999] 2 All ER 609 at 618.

and whether or not the case involves a local authority, it will be perfectly clear whether the specification of an alternative address for the purposes of s. 160(5) has been made on behalf of the relevant body corporate. In our judgment what matters in the circumstances currently under review is the reality of the situation. Where it is the local authority which ostensibly has specified what is said to be an alternative address for the purposes of s. 160(5) it matters not that the precise communicator of that information either cannot be identified or is not someone who can be classed as the secretary or clerk (or the equivalent) of the relevant body corporate."[198]

Thus the Divisional Court held that the section 82(6) notices had been properly served on the councils in accordance with section 160 of the 1990 Act. In the opinion of Mitchell J, the lesson to be learned for the future was:

"If in any particular authority area there is uncertainty on the part of either the local authority's tenants or their legal advisers as to where and to whom s. 82(6) notices should be sent in order (a) to constitute proper service and (b) to set in train, as speedily as possible, any appropriate remedy it seems to us that it is in everyone's interests for the local authority to inform its tenants precisely how to proceed. That, as we have found, is what happened in each of these cases. If a local authority appears to have informed its tenants and/or legal advisers how to proceed it cannot thereafter expect a sympathetic hearing of a claim that in spite of that appearance it was not in fact intending to do any such thing."[199]

In *Hewlings v McLean Homes East Anglia Ltd*,[200] where the Divisional Court similarly upheld an appeal against the decision of the magistrates that a section 82(6) notice had not been properly served, Rafferty J (with whom Rose LJ agreed) observed:

"The provisions contained within section 160 of the Act seem to me to be clearly on their face permissive as is demonstrated by the explicit use of the word 'may' in contrast to the selected word 'must' in other parts of the statute."[201]

Moreover, Rafferty J observed that a failure to comply with the section 160 provisions was "amenable to correction"[202] and that with regard to the section 82 remedy generally:

"*Hall* and *Hull* epitomises the proper approach to Parliament's intention, that is to provide a straightforward remedy to ordinary folk;

---

[198] *ibid.* at 620-621.
[199] *ibid.* at 624.
[200] [2001] EHLR 34.
[201] *ibid.* at 40.
[202] *ibid.* at 41.

it should not be frustrated by the introduction of any technical obstacle."[203]

Initiation of proceedings under section 82

Following the giving of a section 82(6) notice, the person aggrieved by an alleged statutory nuisance may commence proceedings against the person responsible for that nuisance. If a magistrates' court is satisfied that the alleged nuisance exists (or that an abated nuisance is likely to recur on the same premises) it is required to make an order requiring either or both of the following:

- that the defendant should abate the nuisance within a time specified in the order, and execute any works necessary for that purpose;
- prohibition of a recurrence of the nuisance, and requiring the execution within a time period specified of any works necessary to prevent such recurrence.[204]

A magistrates' court also has the power to impose an immediate fine on the person responsible for the statutory nuisance.[205] In addition to the possibility of the imposition of this immediate fine, a further offence is committed where the person against whom such a court order has been made contravenes, without reasonable excuse, any requirement or prohibition there imposed.[206]

In relation to the offence of contravention of the magistrates' order a "best practicable means" defence may be raised. The defence is subject to the same limits as regards its scope of operation as were described above,[207] with the additional provision in these "person aggrieved" proceedings that the defence shall not operate in cases of nuisances which are such as to render the premises unfit for human habitation.[208] Where a magistrates' court is satisfied that a statutory nuisance does exist, and that it is such as to render the premises unfit for human habitation, a section 82(2) order may additionally prohibit the use of the premises for human habitation until such time as the court is satisfied that the premises have been rendered fit for that purpose.[209]

It was noted, when local authority proceedings were being described,[210] that those bodies possess powers to take direct action to abate nuisances (and seek recoupment of costs incurred) where an abatement notice has not

---

[203] *ibid.* at 42.

[204] 1990 Act, s. 82(2)(a) and (b).

[205] Not exceeding level 5 on the standard scale – currently £5,000.

[206] 1990 Act, s. 82(8). The fine may not exceed the level 5 maximum and there is provision for a further fine of an amount equal to one-tenth of that level for each day on which the offence continues after conviction. See further above, fn. 143.

[207] See p. 477.

[208] 1990 Act, s. 82(10)(d). Note, in this connection the value of the "person aggrieved" procedure in the context of local authority housing.

[209] 1990 Act, s. 82(3).

[210] See above, p. 496.

been complied with. In the context of "person aggrieved" proceedings, rather than provide that that individual should have such extensive powers of direct action, the Act provides certain powers by which the court may impose such obligations upon a *local authority*.

In the first place it is provided that where a person is convicted of having contravened a magistrates' notice under this section, the court may direct the local authority to do anything which the person convicted was required to have done under that order. Such a direction to the local authority must be preceded by the provision of an opportunity for the local authority to be heard before the court.[211]

A second situation in which the court may impose such an obligation upon a local authority arises where a person aggrieved by a nuisance brings section 82 proceedings but no person responsible for the nuisance and no owner or occupier of premises can be found. In such a situation the court may, after giving the local authority an opportunity to be heard, direct the authority to do anything which the court would have ordered such a person (if found) to have done.[212]

COSTS

The duty imposed by section 82(12) as regards the award of costs in favour of complainants is of self-evident importance in terms of the practical value of the "aggrieved individual" procedure provided for under that section.[213] Such costs may indemnify complainants in respect of their legal expenses and also other expense which may have been incurred in preparing and presenting their case of nuisance (for example, expert evidence).[214]

In this respect the decision of the Divisional Court in *R v Dudley Magistrates Court ex p Hollis*[215] deserves examination. It indicates the unwillingness of the court to accept contentions which would have quite substantially undermined the apparent benefit conferred by subsection (12). However, it also has brought to light certain limitations as regards the ambit of such cost recovery.

---

[211] 1990 Act, s. 82(11).

[212] 1990 Act, s. 82(13). It is not entirely clear how such proceedings may arise. Upon whom would the "warning notice" under s. 82(6) be served; and against whom should the complaint to the magistrates' court be addressed?

[213] The summary procedure under s. 99 of the Public Health Act 1936 made no provision for costs. Such costs were, accordingly, at the discretion of the court: see *Sandwell Metropolitan Borough Council v Bujok* [1990] 3 All ER 385.

[214] It has been held that where a complainant has a solicitor acting on his or her behalf in s. 82 proceedings, it is reasonable to assume that the complainant will be personally liable to pay the solicitor's costs. If, however, there is a genuine issue as to whether a complainant has properly incurred costs, that person may be required to adduce evidence to show that the costs have in fact been incurred: see *Hazlett v Sefton Borough Council* [2000] Env LR 416.

[215] [1998] EHLR 42.

In relation to proceedings by individuals under section 82 three dates are of particular significance: (i) the date of service of the notice of intention to bring proceedings; (ii) the date upon which those proceedings were instituted; and (iii) the date of the eventual hearing.

In terms of the imposition of a fine and/or the making of an abatement order the critical date is the date of the proceedings before the magistrates. If the nuisance does not exist at that date no such notice or fine may be made or imposed. There may, however, be an obligation to pay costs under section 82(12). The critical date as regards the existence of the statutory nuisance here is the date of the making of the complaint to the magistrates (i.e. date (ii) above). In other words, in a case where a nuisance is put right between the date of complaint and the date set for the court hearing, the sole purpose of those proceedings continuing to the magistrates will be to secure an award of costs. The issue raised for the court in *Hollis* was whether, in a case where proceedings are continued notwithstanding that it appears that the defendant is well on his way to dealing expeditiously with the nuisance in question, the magistrates had acted properly in denying costs, on the basis that for the complainant to have continued the proceedings in those circumstances was to involve a claim for costs not "properly incurred" (as required by section 82(12)). The issue was whether "properly incurred" had a meaning beyond that relating to the disallowance of surplus or excessive expenditure, to include also a power to disallow costs incurred where, in terms solely of securing an end to the nuisance (as distinct from obtaining costs), the proceedings need not have been brought to the court.

The Divisional Court condemned the approach of the magistrates in having denied costs to the complainant. Far from proceedings for "costs only" being an improper course of action on the part of the complainant, this could be regarded as something expressly contemplated by Parliament. In the words of Moses J:

> "... Parliament specifically contemplated proceedings being brought at which the only issue is whether the statutory nuisance existed at the date of the making of the complaint, in other words in circumstances where it is plain that the nuisance has been abated at the time of the hearing and is not likely to recur. The only forum in which the statutory pre-condition for an award of costs can be proved, namely that the alleged nuisance existed at the date of the making of the complaint, is on the hearing of proceedings identified in subsection (12) as "proceedings for an order under subsection (2)."[216]

Having noted and upheld a complainant's absolute right to costs in the circumstances where a nuisance has been proven to have existed at the date of the complaint, the court contrasted the less favourable position where a nuisance which may have existed at the time of the giving of notice of intention to bring proceedings (date (i) above) has been remedied before

---

[216] *ibid.* at 49.

such legal proceedings are commenced (date (ii)). At first sight, the denial of costs to a complainant who institutes proceedings after a nuisance has been abated may seem perfectly sensible. It is one thing to allow proceedings already commenced to continue to court solely on the issue of costs: it is another to adopt the same approach where the matter in dispute has been satisfactorily resolved at a time before formal legal proceedings have been initiated. Nevertheless, this apparently sensible rule about recovery of costs may well operate in a way which may provide a disincentive to complainants as regards the use of section 82 procedures.

The matter was explained by Moses J in the following words:

> "However lax the conduct of those responsible for the nuisance ..., however great the justification for the aggrieved person issuing the notice, those responsible will escape not only criminal liability but also liability for costs, provided they abate the nuisance in a way which will prevent its recurrence before the notice has expired. A person aggrieved by a statutory nuisance is likely to incur substantial expenditure when he takes steps to have the nuisance from which he is suffering abated. He may well have to retain an expert in order to specify his complaint in the statutory notice under section 82(6)."[217]

Moses J noted that at that early time a complainant could not know whether abatement work will be undertaken "voluntarily" or only following the initiation of formal legal proceedings and, in the latter case, whether the abatement will occur before the court hearing or following the issuance by a court of a formal abatement order. For this reason it is understandable for a complainant to prepare for the worst, and to incur expenses in preparation for having, perhaps, subsequently to prove the nuisance to the satisfaction of a court. Yet, as Moses J emphasised, the position of a complainant is, in fact, somewhat precarious:

> "... if the work is completed by the time the period of notice expires [the complainant] will recover nothing, not even his costs."[218]

The point made by Moses J is a good one. Indeed, a stronger example could have been given demonstrating the potential disadvantage as regards complainants. Certainly, a responsible party who puts right a nuisance within the 21-day notice period (for noise – three days) will incur no potential liability to costs. The same will apply to a responsible party who takes longer than that 21 days, so long as formal legal complaint to the magistrates has not yet been lodged. In other words a complainant who may be persuaded to give the party responsible "just a little longer" to put right the nuisance before commencing proceedings, may in so doing fail to protect his or her right to costs. It will be evident that from the point of view of protection of the right to costs it is important for proceedings to be

---

[217] *ibid.* at 48.
[218] *ibid.*

commenced promptly once the 21-day time period within the notice has expired.

What practical advice may be offered to complainants in order to minimise the risks referred to above? It will be remembered from the *Fairless* case[219] that notices of intention to commence legal proceedings do not need to be written with any high degree of technical precision. It may, therefore, be appropriate to delay the commissioning of expert evidence until it has become apparent, from the expiration of the 21-day period without abatement having occurred (or seeming imminent), that such expert evidence will be necessary. At that stage the complainant may feel safe to commission expert evidence and to commence the legal proceedings more or less contemporaneously.

Hughes: pro bono work?

An issue of some importance in relation to costs arose in *Hughes* v *Kingston-upon-Hull City Council*.[220] A firm of solicitors had acted on behalf of a section 82 complainant on a tacit understanding, the magistrate hearing the nuisance proceedings found, that its costs would not be sought from the complainant should the proceedings fail. This was regarded by the magistrate, and on appeal by the Divisional Court, as an unlawful and unenforceable arrangement in the context of *criminal* proceedings. Its unlawfulness related both to it being contrary to public policy, and also a breach of the Solicitors' Practice Rules.

The significance of these findings and conclusions in terms of an order under section 82(12) was as follows. Costs operate on an indemnity principle. They relate to items of expenditure incurred or in respect of which a liability to payment exists. Given the unlawful and unenforceable nature of the champertous "retainer" arrangement with the complainant's solicitors there were no costs which could be enforced against the complainant by that firm. It followed that since there was no liability to legal costs in respect of which a costs order under section 82(12) could provide indemnity, no such order could be made. This case demonstrates some clear difficulties as regards the development of "pro bono" legal work in this criminal prosecution context.

---

[219] See above, p. 499.
[220] [1999] Env LR 579.

Chapter 13

WATER POLLUTION: ANTI-POLLUTION WORKS NOTICES

INTRODUCTION

The Water Resources Act 1991, as amended and supplemented by provisions in the Environment Act 1995, provides valuable powers under which the Environment Agency may, in the context of actual or threatened pollution of controlled waters, *either* take action itself and subsequently recoup its costs incurred, *or* serve a works notice requiring such action to be taken by another person, on pain of criminal penalty in the event of default.

The power to take "direct action" is contained in section 161 and derives from earlier water legislation. The "works notice" procedure has been available only since 1999. Since that time the direct action procedure has become available only in situations where the "works notice" procedure is inapposite: either because the Agency considers that it is necessary for the works to be undertaken "forthwith", or because, after reasonable inquiry, no person can be found on whom to serve such a notice. In other words in non-emergency situations where a candidate upon whom to serve a works notice can be found, the works notice procedure, rather than the direct action approach, is mandatory.[1]

Notwithstanding the fact that the direct action procedure is now the exception rather than the norm it is with this procedure that we should begin.

SECTION 161

Where direct action under section 161 continues to be available to the Agency the scope of the power is as follows. Where it appears to the Agency that:

> "any poisonous, noxious or polluting matter or any solid waste matter is likely to enter, or to be or to have been present in any controlled waters"

the Agency may undertake the following works and operations:

> (a) …where the matter appears likely to enter any controlled waters, works and operations for the purpose of preventing it from so doing; or

---

[1] Section 161(1A).

(b) in a case where the matter appears to be or to have been present in any controlled waters, works or operations for the purpose –
 (i) of removing or disposing of the matter;
 (ii) of remedying or mitigating any pollution caused by its presence in the waters; or
 (iii) so far as it is reasonably practicable to do so, of restoring the waters, including any flora and fauna dependent on the aquatic environment of the waters, to their state immediately before the matter became present in the waters.

The Agency is also empowered, in either such situation:

"to carry out investigations for the purpose of establishing the source of the matter and the identity of the person who has caused or knowingly permitted it to be present in controlled waters or at a place from which it is likely ... to enter controlled waters."

This power of investigation is significant in that it permits expense to be incurred not just in the preventive or remedial works or operations, but also as regards the identification of persons who may bear cost recoupment liabilities under subsection (3) of the section.[2]

Subsection (3) provides that where the Agency carries out works, operations or investigations, as described above:

"it shall ... be entitled to recover the expenses[3] reasonably incurred in doing so ..."

Such recovery to be from:

"any person who, as the case may be –
(a) caused or knowingly permitted the matter in question to be present at the place from which it was likely ... to enter any controlled waters; or
(b) caused or knowingly permitted the matter in question to be present in any controlled waters."[4]

The decision in *Bruton and the National Rivers Authority* v *Clarke*[5] provides a useful illustration of the recovery of clean-up costs in civil proceedings. The case also sheds some light on how a court may calculate the level of costs to be awarded.

---

[2] Or, as will be seen later, to identify persons who may be served a works notice: s. 161A(11).

[3] The word "expenses" is expressly stated to include "costs": see s. 161(6).

[4] Section 161(4) excludes the operation of subs. (3) as regards recoverability of expenses in relation to works, operations or investigations in relation to waters from abandoned mines. Thus any anti-pollution works etc. carried out by the Environment Agency in respect of an abandoned mine would be at its own expense, unless they were carried out in respect of a mine abandoned after December 31, 1999: see s. 161(4A) and (4B).

[5] July 23, 1993 (unreported). See [1995] Env Liability CS13-14.

The defendant, a pig farmer, had constructed a number of slurry lagoons on his land. During a period of prolonged heavy rainfall, a bank of one of the lagoons burst with the result that three million gallons of ammonia-saturated slurry were discharged into a stream which eventually flowed into the River Sappiston in Suffolk. The effect on the river's fish stock was catastrophic.

Mr Bruton (suing on behalf of the Bury St Edmunds Angling Association) and the NRA subsequently instituted civil proceedings. The Anglers sought general damages for the loss of amenity caused by the effect of the pollution on the river's fish stocks. The NRA, for its part, sued to recover the costs that it had incurred under section 46(4) of the Control of Pollution Act 1974[6] in carrying out operations to remedy or mitigate the effects of the pollution. For present purposes it is the latter claim which is of interest.[7] It consisted of the following elements: the costs of various surveys which the NRA had undertaken following the pollution incident; the scientific costs that it had incurred in terms of the hours spent by scientists on investigative work; and the costs of restocking the river with mature fish and fry. In giving judgment, Mellor J was anxious to ensure that any award of costs should reflect what the NRA had spent on clean-up and not what it had spent on work which was not directly related to the pollution incident. Thus, in the case of the surveying work, he concluded that some surveys had not been a necessary corollary of the incident and therefore the NRA were not allowed to recover for them. Moreover, with regard to the scientific work, a distinction was drawn between that which had contributed to the general body of scientific knowledge and that which had been necessary in order to enable both the judge and jury properly to comprehend the issues before the court. In the event, Mellor J awarded the NRA approximately £90,000 to cover all the costs raised by its claim.[8]

Practical difficulties

The power under section 161 to prevent or to remediate water pollution was found, over the years, to be less valuable to the authorities than might have been expected. The problem lay in the shortage of financial resources available to the authorities which possessed the powers. Expense had first to be incurred by the public authority. It might be that some person appeared to fall within the "causing or knowingly permitting" description against whom costs recoupment might later be sought. However, recoupment of costs expended could never be a certainty. It might be that

---

[6] Now s. 161(3) of the Water Resources Act 1991.

[7] The Anglers were ultimately awarded the sum of £8,489 in damages and £8,400 in legal costs. The former sum took into account the harm that they had suffered by not being able to get the type of fishing for which they had paid a subscription coupled with their inability to purchase an alternative fishing right. This was balanced against the existence of parts of the river which were not affected by the pollution and which could therefore be fished.

[8] In practice, a company may seek to insure itself against the carrying out of emergency work in order to remediate environmental pollution. Whether or not the company or its insurers will be liable to pay a claim made by the Environment Agency under s. 161(3) will, however, depend upon the terms of the relevant insurance policy: see *Yorkshire Water Services Ltd v Sun Alliance & London Insurance plc & others* [1998] Env LR 204.

proof of causing or knowingly permitting would fail. Alternatively, that person might prove to have a rather smaller financial capacity than had been believed to be the case. In any event the sequence of "incur expense – seek recoupment" proved to be problematic in simple cash flow terms for public authorities operating on modest budgets which might have made inadequate provision for the carrying out of pollution prevention or remediation works.[9]

WORKS NOTICES

Given the practical difficulties associated with section 161 anti-pollution works, it is not surprising that the Environment Act 1995 added new sections to the Water Resources Act in the hope of introducing more effective procedures. Rather than the conferment of powers on public authorities to take action (supported by cost recoupment provisions) these new provisions provide for administrative directions to be given to certain categories of persons requiring that they should perform certain actions on pain of criminal penalty should they default.[10]

The procedure involves the service by the Environment Agency of a works notice under section 161A. The circumstances in which such a notice may be served echo the terms of section 161:

"… where it appears to the Agency that any poisonous, noxious or polluting matter or any solid waste matter is likely to enter, or to be or to have been present in, any controlled waters the Agency shall be entitled to serve a works notice …"

Such a notice may be served[11] upon:

"… any person who, as the case may be, –

---

[9] In one reported instance, the NRA opted to pursue ordinary civil proceedings against a polluter in order to establish the firm's liability for removing dioxin-contaminated sediment from two Yorkshire rivers at an estimated cost of approximately £1million. The Agency was able to take such proceedings because in its role as flood defence authority, it was a riparian owner of the parts of the rivers affected by the pollution. Proceedings under s. 161 were considered to be a less attractive option due to the risks involved in recovering the costs of cleaning up the rivers after the work had been done: see (1992) ENDS Report 213, at pp. 5-6.

[10] On the coming into force of the Anti-Pollution Works Regulations 1999 (SI 1999/1006) it was reported that the Environment Agency considered that the works notice provisions would be particularly useful in combating pollution caused by the construction industry. The temporary nature of building sites was seen as a key reason why companies had generally been reluctant to spend money on precautions such as bunded fuel tanks to prevent the escape of oil: see (1999) ENDS Report 291, at p. 42. Regulations enabling the Scottish Environmental Protection Agency (SEPA) to serve anti-pollution works notices did not come into force until April 1 2003: see The Anti-Pollution Works (Scotland) Regulations 2003, SSI No.168.

[11] Before serving such a notice on any person the Agency is required to take reasonable steps to endeavour to consult such persons about the works or operations to be required: s. 161A(4). However, failure to comply with such consultation requirements is expressly stated not to render invalid any ensuing notice: subs. (6).

(a) caused or knowingly permitted the matter in question to be present at the place from which it is likely, in the opinion of the Agency, to enter any controlled waters; or

(b) caused or knowingly permitted the matter in question to be present in any controlled waters."[12]

The concept of a "works notice" is explained in section 161A(2). It may require the person upon whom it has been served to carry out any or all of the following kinds of works or operations as may be specified in the notice:

"(a) in a case were the matter in question appears likely to enter any controlled waters, works or operations for the purpose of preventing it from doing so;

(b) in a case where the matter appears to be or to have been present in any controlled waters, works or operations for the purpose –
(i) of removing or disposing of the matter;
(ii) of remedying or mitigating any pollution caused by its presence in the waters; or
(iii) so far as is reasonably practicable to do so, of restoring the waters, including any flora and fauna dependent on the aquatic environment of the waters, to their state immediately before the matter became present in the waters."

Unsurprisingly, a works notice must specify the period within which the person upon whom it has been served is required to do each of the things specified in the notice.[13] The Agency is not permitted, however, to require the carrying out of works or operations which would impede or prevent the making of a discharge in pursuance of a consent granted under Chapter II of Part III of the 1991 Act.[14] Nor is it permitted to serve a works notice on any person in respect of water from an abandoned mine or an abandoned part of a mine which he has permitted to be at a place from which it is likely to enter controlled waters, or which he has permitted to enter controlled waters.[15]

Further provisions about the content of works notices are to be found in the Anti-Pollution Works Regulations 1999.[16] Where a notice relates to a potential pollution incident the notice must describe the nature of the risk to controlled waters, must identify the controlled waters which may be affected and must specify the place from which the matter in question is

---

[12] Section 161A(1).

[13] Section 161A(3).

[14] Section 161A(7). This provision mirrors s. 161(2) which applies where the Agency carries out the works or operations itself: see above.

[15] Section 161A(8). This exception only applies in respect of a mine or part of a mine which was abandoned before 31st December 1999: see s. 161A(9). See further on abandoned mines and water pollution, above, Chapter 9.

[16] SI 1999/1006.

considered likely to enter those waters.[17] Where it relates to an actual pollution incident the notice served must describe the nature and extent of the pollution and identify the controlled waters affected.[18] In addition to specifying the works or operations required of the person served, the notice must give the Agency's reasons for serving the notice on that person and its reasons for requiring those works or operations to be carried out.[19] Further, the notice must indicate the rights of appeal available to the person served,[20] and indicate the various consequences which may follow should the person served not comply with the notice.[21]

Before a works notice may be served it may be necessary for the Agency to have carried out certain investigations as regards the physical state of controlled waters, the threat posed by substances adjacent to such waters, and the persons whose actions or omissions may render them subject to the works notice procedure. We noted earlier that such investigations may be undertaken under section 161(1). Where those investigations are followed by the service of a works notice in relation to the matter to which the investigation related, the expenses reasonably incurred in that investigation may be recovered from the person upon whom the notice has been served.[22]

Rights of entry and compensation

It will be apparent that there is no necessary coincidence between the current ownership or occupation of land or water and the identity of the person who may be served a works notice as being a person falling within the "caused or knowingly permitted" liability criteria referred to above. It may, therefore, follow that the necessary works or operations should take place on land or water to which the recipient of the notice has no right of access. The legislation provides rights to enable persons served with a works notice lawfully to fulfill its requirements, whilst at the same time providing rights to compensation for owners and occupiers adversely affected by those activities.

Section 161B makes clear that:

> "A works notice may require a person to carry out works or operations in relation to any land or waters notwithstanding that he is not entitled to carry out those works or operations."[23]

This is followed by an obligation that:

---

[17] Regulation 2(a).

[18] Regulation 2(b).

[19] Regulation 2(d).

[20] See below, pp. 518-520.

[21] See below, pp. 520-521.

[22] Section 161A(11). This provision does not apply if the works notice is subsequently quashed or withdrawn after having been served.

[23] Section 161B(1).

"Any person whose consent is required before any works or operations required by a works notice may be carried out, shall grant, or join in granting, such rights in relation to any land or waters as will enable the person on whom the works notice is served to comply with any requirements imposed by the works notice."[24]

Compensation is governed by subsection (5). A person who has granted, or joined in granting, any rights under the compulsion provided by section 161B(2):

"shall be entitled ... to be paid [compensation] by the person on whom the works notice in question is served ...."

The claim to compensation is dealt with in the Schedule to the Anti-Pollution Works Regulations 1999.[25] This states that an application for compensation must be made:

"within the period beginning with the date of the grant of the rights in respect of which compensation is claimed and ending on whichever is the latest of the following dates –

(a)   12 months after the date of the grant of those rights;
(b)   where there is an appeal against the works notice which imposed the requirements in relation to which those rights were granted, 12 months after the date on which the appeal is determined or withdrawn; or
(c)   six months after the date on which the rights were first exercised."[26]

Applications for compensation must be in writing and addressed to the last known address for correspondence of the person to whom the right was granted (i.e. the person upon whom a works notice has been served). The application must indicate the amount of compensation sought and must indicate how the aggregate sum has been calculated (by reference to the provisions of paragraph 4, below).[27]

For what loss or damage is compensation payable? Paragraph 4 of the Schedule to the Regulations provides:

"Compensation shall be payable for loss and damage of the following descriptions –
(a)   any depreciation in the value of any relevant interest to which the grantor is entitled which results from the grant of the right;
(b)   loss or damage, in relation to any relevant interest to which he is entitled, which –

---

[24] Section 161B(2). Subs. (3) requires the Agency, before serving a works notice, to consult any person who appears to be the owner or occupier of relevant land as regards the rights which that person might be required to grant to the person on whom the notice has been served.

[25] SI 1999/1006. Made under s. 161B(5).

[26] Schedule, para. 2.

[27] Schedule, para. 3(2)(c).

(i)   is attributable to the grant of the right or the exercise of it;

(ii)   does not consist of depreciation in the value of that interest; and

(iii) is loss or damage for which he would have been entitled to compensation by way of compensation for disturbance, if that interest had been acquired compulsorily under the Acquisition of Land Act 1981, in pursuance of a notice to treat served on the date on which the grant of the right was made;

(c)   damage to, or injurious affection of, any interest in land to which the grantor is entitled which is not a relevant interest and which results from the grant of the right or from the exercise of it;

(d)   any loss or damage sustained by the grantor, other than in relation to any interest in land to which he is entitled, which is attributable to the grant of the right or the exercise of it; and

(e)   the amount of any valuation and legal expenses reasonably incurred by the grantor in granting the right and in the preparation of the application for and the negotiation of the amount of compensation."

As regards the basis upon which compensation for such loss or damage should be assessed, the Schedule provides that this shall be done in a way which is equivalent to how compensation for the compulsory acquisition of land is assessed under section 5 of the Land Compensation Act 1961.[28] Disputes about compensation fall within the jurisdiction of the Lands Tribunal.[29]

Appeals against works notices[30]

A person on whom a works notice has been served may, within a period of 21 days beginning with the day on which the notice is served, appeal against that notice. The appeal lies to the Secretary of State.[31]

---

[28] Schedule, para. 5(1): "so far as applicable and subject to any necessary modifications". Para. 5(2) makes provision where the interest in respect of which compensation is to be assessed is subject to a mortgage. In such a case the compensation shall be payable to the mortgagee as if it were proceeds of sale.

[29] Schedule, para. 6(1).

[30] The availability of an appeal in respect of a works notice issued under s. 161(3) of the 1991 Act has been contrasted with the position under the Animal Byproducts Order 1999, where there is no right of appeal in respect of a remedial notice served under article 5(2) of the Order: see *R (on the application of Langton and Allen)* v *Department for the Environment, Food and Rural Affairs and Derbyshire County Council* [2002] Env LR 463.

[31] Section 161C(1). Note that the appeal lies against a works notice: no such appeal operates in relation to cost recoupment under s. 161. In the very nature of such cost recoupment there is no room for an appeal mechanism. The claim to recoupment of costs is a claim to a statutory debt, recoverable by way of civil action provided all the statutory requirements are satisfied. There is no order or decision against which a right of appeal might apply: the option for a person seeking to resist recoupment being not to appeal, but to resist any civil action brought to recover the debt. Given the evidential issues which may be presented it seems unlikely that a person who may fear that cost recoupment may be sought will be allowed, by way of judicial review, to initiate proceedings for a declaration that (e.g.) he or she is not a person against whom such costs are

The Secretary of State must quash the notice if it appears to contain a material defect. In any other case the Secretary of State has a discretion to confirm the notice as it stands, to confirm it subject to modifications, or to quash the notice.[32]

Further provisions as regards appeals are contained in the Anti-Pollution Works Regulations 1999.[33] The notice of appeal must state the grounds upon which the appeal is being lodged and also whether the appellant wishes the appeal to be determined by written representations or by way of a hearing.[34] There must accompany the notice of appeal any documents which are relevant to the appeal (e.g. copies of any correspondence or any relevant notices or decisions).[35] Notice of appeal and such accompanying documents must also be sent by the appellant to the Environment Agency; and, if the ground of appeal is that the notice might have been served upon some other person, the notice and documents must be served on that person also.[36]

Neither section 161C nor the Regulations offer much in the way of guidance as to the grounds on which an appeal may be brought. This omission was the subject of criticism by the Joint Committee on Statutory Instruments. In its opinion:

> "… Parliament included in section 161C the power to prescribe grounds of appeal so that persons served with works notices would know where they stood as regards appealing."[37]

In a Memorandum submitted to the Committee by the DETR, it was argued that the lack of specification of grounds of appeal in either the Act or the Regulations allowed for the possibility of an appeal on any grounds. However, the Memorandum went on to identify a number of potential grounds for appeal, although the list is by no means exhaustive.[38] The six grounds were as follows:

- the Agency had not complied with the regulations prescribing the content of works notices or to specify the period in which the works must be completed;
- insufficient time had been allowed to do the works specified in the notice;
- the works specified in the notice would not remedy the problem or are not the most cost effective way of remedying the problem;

---

recoverable, or against the reasonableness of the expenses incurred and in respect of which recoupment is anticipated. These are issues which a court of review is likely to consider more appropriate for determination by the civil court hearing a debt action on its merits.

[32] Section 161C(2).

[33] SI 1999/1006.

[34] Regulation 3(2).

[35] Regulation 3(3).

[36] Regulation 4(b).

[37] See the Committee's Nineteenth Report, session 1998-99, 18th May 1999.

[38] These were in addition to the ground that there is a material defect in the works notice.

- the person on whom the notice was served did not cause or knowingly permit the matter to be present at the place which poses the risk of pollution or did not cause or knowingly permit the matter in question to be present in controlled waters;
- there is no pollution risk or pollution did not occur; or
- it would be unfair for the appellant to be made responsible for the remedial work in all the circumstances of the case.

Despite the articulation of these potential grounds of appeal, the Joint Committee still reported the Regulations for failing to contain provisions stating grounds of appeal. It is not uncommon for environmental legislation to make provision with regard to grounds of appeal,[39] and there is no good reason why such grounds cannot be illustrative rather than exhaustive.

An appeal will, on the request of any party to the appeal or if the Secretary of State so decides, take the form of a hearing; otherwise it will be disposed of by way of written representations.[40] Any hearing which is held may, at the decision of the person holding the hearing, take place wholly or to some extent in private. All parties to an appeal have the right to be heard at the hearing, and permission to be heard may not unreasonably be refused to any other persons.[41] Following the hearing the person appointed to hear the appeal makes a report to the Secretary of State containing his or her conclusions and recommendations.[42] The position is different, however, where the person appointed to hear the appeal has also been conferred powers of *decision* in the matter.[43]

Consequences of not complying with a works notice

An offence is committed by any person upon whom a works notice has been served who fails to comply with any of the requirements of that notice.[44] Trial may be summary or on indictment. In the latter case a fine (unlimited) and/or a term of imprisonment not exceeding two years may be imposed. On summary conviction, the maximum custodial penalty is three months and the maximum fine is £20,000.[45] Provision is made in

---

[39] See, for example, the Statutory Nuisance (Appeals) Regulations 1995, SI 1995/2644, which set out in Reg. 2 the grounds on which the recipient of an abatement notice may appeal against that notice: for a discussion of these grounds, see Chapter 11.

[40] Regulation 5(1).

[41] Regulation 5(6) and (7).

[42] Regulation 5(8). If recommendations are not made the reasons for this must be explained.

[43] Under the Environment Act 1995, s. 114(1)(a).

[44] Section 161D(1).

[45] Section 161D(2). The first successful prosecution under this provision occurred on 23rd March 2000, when Okehampton magistrates fined a defendant £2,000 for failing to comply with a works notice. As the owner of a residential home in Beaworthy, Devon, he had been served with a notice after the Agency had discovered an illegal sewage discharge from a septic tank into a nearby stream. The notice required him to carry out works to prevent future pollution. A subsequent visit by Agency officers revealed that no attempt had been made to comply with the notice. In addition to the fine in respect of the works notice the defendant was found guilty of polluting controlled waters contrary to s. 85(1) and (6) of the Water Resources Act 1991 and ordered to pay a fine of £1,000: see (2000) ENDS Report 302, at p. 48. Subsequent successful prosecutions for offences contrary to s. 161D(2) have resulted in justices fining defendants £8,000 and £1,500, respectively: see (2001) ENDS Report 323, at p. 56 and (2002) ENDS Report 326, at p. 58.

subsection (4) for High Court proceedings (for an injunction) in any case where the Agency is of the opinion that proceedings for an offence may afford an ineffectual remedy against a person who has failed to comply with the requirements of a works notice.[46]

It may be noted that the offence is defined in terms simply of having failed to comply. There is no requirement on the prosecution to show that the failure was unreasonable; nor any defence that reasonable attempts had been made to comply, or that a reasonable excuse for non-compliance may have existed.[47] Such matters, in this context, seem to go more to mitigation than to liability.

In the event that any of a works notice's provisions are not complied with the Environment Agency may undertake those tasks itself, and may then recover from the person in default the costs it has reasonably incurred in doing those things.[48]

Policy and guidance on the use of anti-pollution works notices

The Environment Agency has published a policy statement setting out the principles which underpin its approach to the use of anti-pollution works notices.[49] The purpose of the statement is to:

> "...provide both Agency staff and those on whom a works notice may be served with a clear understanding of the way in which the Agency will proceed and of the sorts of cases of pollution or potential pollution for which the Agency considers works notices to be the appropriate enforcement mechanism."[50]

Since anti-pollution works notices are part of the Agency's enforcement regime their use will reflect the principles set out in its *Enforcement and Prosecution Policy Statement.*[51] In other words, the use of such notices should be: proportionate; consistent; transparent; and targeted.

In determining whether or not to serve a works notice, the Agency will adopt a risk-based approach. A risk assessment will be carried out relating to, inter alia, "the nature and quantity of the matter in question, the likelihood of it entering the waters and the state of the waters". It is further

---

[46] A similar provision in the context of statutory nuisance allows a local authority to bring proceedings in the High Court where it considers that proceedings for breaching or failing to comply with an abatement notice would afford an inadequate remedy: see s. 81(5) of the Environmental Protection Act 1990, discussed above in Chapter 12.

[47] This may be contrasted with the position under the contaminated land regime where it is a defence to show that there was a reasonable excuse for failing to comply with any of the requirements of a remediation notice: see s. 78M(1) of the Environmental Protection Act 1990.

[48] Section 161D(3).

[49] See Sweet and Maxwell, *Encyclopedia of Environmental Law*, Volume VI, F30/31-F30/40.

[50] Paragraph 1.3 of the Statement.

[51] Discussed in Chapter 7: see above, at pp. 222-226.

stated that risk assessment procedures may include those to be found in the Agency's *Pollution Prevention Manual*.[52]

As we saw in Chapter 12 the specification of works or steps in an abatement notice has been an issue over which there has been much litigation in the context of statutory nuisance. In the present context, the Statement notes:

"Where a works notice is served in order to prevent pollution of controlled waters, the works specified in the notice will be appropriate to preventing matter from entering the water. Where matter is, or has been, present in controlled waters, works specified in a works notice to remove the matter or remedy or mitigate pollution will be appropriate to those purposes. The Agency will consider all practicable measures and specify the most cost-effective option to prevent entry, remove matter or remedy pollution."[53]

In respect of restoration the Statement observes:

"... the Agency may specify works for the purpose, so far as it is reasonably practicable to do so, of restoring the waters to their state immediately before the matter became present in them.... [T]he Agency will examine the practicable works or operations and require those which are most cost-effective to be carried out."[54]

A reasonable inference to draw from the service of a works notice under the Water Resources Act 1991 is that this level of coercion is necessary in order to secure that the recipient shall carry out the necessary works or operations. Wherever possible, however, the Agency prefers voluntary action to the service of a works notice.[55] In order to enable this to happen, the Statement notes that "the Agency must reasonably endeavour to consult the person on whom it is considering serving a notice about the works or operations which would be specified in the notice."[56]

---

[52] See para. 2.1 of the Statement.

[53] Paragraph 2.3.

[54] Paragraph 2.4.

[55] Note also the facts of *Eastern Counties Leather plc* v *Eastern Counties Leather Group plc* [2002] EWHC Ch 494 confirming the Agency's focus on seeking a voluntary solution. For an example of a similar situation where the role of the Agency has been to broker a clean-up plan to be put into effect by a consortium of companies which have previously been involved at the site of a tar distillation plant, see (2002) ENDS Report 328, at p. 14.

[56] Paragraph 2.5. The requirement to consult is to be found in s. 161A(4) of the 1991 Act. This can be contrasted with the position of a local authority when it is considering whether or not to serve an abatement notice under Part III of the Environmental Protection Act 1990: see, above, pp. 455-460. There is also a duty under s. 161B(3) to consult the owner or occupier of any relevant land or any other person who is in a position to grant rights in respect of that land which enable the recipient of a works notice to carry out the requirements imposed by the notice.

The third section of the Statement discusses the relationship between works notices and the contaminated land regime under Part IIA of the Environmental Protection Act 1990.[57] It observes:

"After Part IIA has come into force,[58] there may be cases in which remediation of historic pollution of controlled waters cannot be addressed through the contaminated land regime. This could be where the entry of pollutants from the land has already taken place but is not ongoing and there is no longer a linkage between pollutants in the land and the waters. In these cases, the use of works notices may be the most appropriate mechanism for securing any necessary remediation of the waters."[59]

Sections Four and Five of the Statement are concerned with the persons on whom a works notice may be served and the content of such a notice. Once again, these paragraphs broadly reflect the position under the Act and, in the case of Section Five, under the Anti-Pollution Works Regulations 1999.[60]

The sixth section of the Statement is concerned with the procedure for using works notices. Prior to the service of a works notice, the Agency will:

"Where possible ... give a written warning and explanation of its intention to serve a works notice. However, where the pollution or potential pollution requires urgent action, but in the Agency's opinion it is reasonable to expect the person on whom the notice is to be served to carry out the necessary works in the available time, the Agency may serve a works notice without prior warning. In these circumstances, it will endeavour to provide a written explanation of the reasons as soon as practicable after the event."[61]

Section Eight of the Statement deals with the enforcement of works notices. In respect of the section 161D offence, it is worth noting that even where all the features of the offence are present, it does not automatically follow that the Environment Agency will prosecute. Its initial response will be to seek an explanation from the recipient of the notice as to why he or she has failed to comply with all or any of its requirements. In the words of the Statement:

"If the failure is due to circumstances beyond the control of the person on whom the notice was served, the Agency will, in exceptional circumstances, consider withdrawing the notice and

---

[57] Discussed in Chapter 14: see below, at pp. 624-625.

[58] As we will shortly see, the contaminated land regime came into force in England on 1st April 2000: see below, at p. 540.

[59] Paragraph 3.5 of the Statement.

[60] SI 1999/1006.

[61] Paragraph 6.7.

serving a new one specifying a longer period of time for the works to be carried out or amending the works to be performed."[62]

Where this is the case:

"The Agency will send an accompanying letter explaining why the extra time has been allowed and setting out the consequences of failure to comply with the extended period."[63]

The relationship between section 161 and a prosecution under section 85 of the 1991 Act was discussed earlier.[64] For present purposes, it should be noted that the Agency's view is that:

"Prosecution for failure to comply with a works notice does not preclude prosecution by the Agency under section 85 of the Water Resources Act 1991 for pollution of controlled waters."[65]

Prosecutions for these offences are not, therefore, mutually exclusive. A polluter could be charged with and convicted of both offences. However, if he were acquitted of the section 85 offence, it might be thought wise not to prosecute for the section 161D offence where the acquittal was on the basis that he did not cause or knowingly permit the matter in question to be present in controlled waters.[66] If, however, the acquittal was on the basis that the polluter had made out the defence in section 89(1) of the 1991 Act, a later failure to comply with a works notice could well result in a further prosecution.[67]

Anti-pollution works notices in practice

In the 20 months from April 1999 to mid-December 2000, the Agency issued 26 works notices under section 161A of the 1991 Act.[68] The most common pollution threats were: illegal sewage discharges; inappropriate disposal or storage of waste materials; and inadequate bunding of oil tanks. The majority of the recipients of the notices tended to be small businesses[69]

---

[62] Paragraph 8.2.

[63] *ibid.*

[64] See above, at p. 344.

[65] Paragraph 8.4 of the Statement.

[66] Since the service of the works notice is upon the person who "caused or knowingly permitted" the matter in question to be present in controlled waters (or to be at the place from which it is likely, in the opinion of the Agency, to enter controlled waters), it would seem highly unlikely that a court hearing the subsequent s. 161D prosecution would be prepared to depart from an earlier ruling that the defendant did not, *beyond reasonable doubt*, cause or knowingly permit polluting matter to enter controlled waters contrary to s. 85 of the 1991 Act. This can be contrasted with the position under s. 161, where, as has been noted already, the proceedings are civil in nature and hence the burden of proof is *on the balance of probabilities*. The prospects of the Agency succeeding in such proceedings even where the defendant has already been acquitted of the s. 85 offence are therefore not quite so slim given the reduced burden of proof.

[67] The defence under s. 89(1) does not negate causation. Rather, it provides that the entry of polluting matter into controlled waters which was either caused or knowingly permitted by the defendant was justified due to the emergency nature of the situation.

[68] See (2001) ENDS Report 312, at p. 10.

[69] For example, construction/development companies, residential homes and service stations.

and farms,[70] although it should also be noted that three private homes and three golf courses received section 161A notices.

Several prosecutions for failing to comply with an anti-pollution works notice have culminated in the conviction of the defendant. The fines imposed by justices have, however, been well below the statutory maximum of £20,000. While it may be the case that each fine was entirely appropriate given the particular circumstances of the case, it should not be forgotten that concerns have been expressed in some quarters about the magistracy's seeming reluctance to use the full scope of its sentencing powers in the context of environmental crime.[71]

---

[70] Seven of the 26 notices which were served during the relevant period were served on farms.

[71] For a fuller discussion of this issue, see Chapter 7.

Chapter 14

CONTAMINATED LAND: IDENTIFICATION AND REMEDIATION

INTRODUCTION

Range and variety of liabilities: scope of chapter

This chapter is concerned with liabilities in connection with contaminated land.[1] It is, however, important to point out that it does not seek to discuss contaminated land liabilities in a comprehensive way. The chapter is concerned, as is appropriate in this Part of this book, only with the "administrative liabilities" in relation to contaminated land which may arise under Part IIA of the Environmental Protection Act 1990. Detailed and complex as the picture to be presented of such administrative liability will of necessity be, it should be emphasised that contaminated land may give rise to liabilities over and beyond those which may flow from this particular legislation.

The provisions of the 1990 Act provide English lawyers for the first time with a body of rules tailor-made to seek to deal with the identification and remediation of contaminated sites;[2] but it would be quite wrong to think that prior to the coming into operation of this legislation there existed no liability implications associated with, or flowing from, the contaminated condition of land. Quite the contrary. There has long been, and even with the entry into force of Part IIA there remains, substantial scope for the operation, in this context, of a wide variety of rules of civil and criminal environmental liability – rules which have been considered earlier in this book, in Parts I and II above.

There has been, and will remain, for example, the possibility of utilising the ordinary rules of *tort liability* (for example, actions in negligence, nuisance or the *strict liability* rule in *Rylands* v *Fletcher*) where the action of one person contaminates property belonging to another, or where the condition of a site causes the spoiling of another person's enjoyment of his or her property.[3]

---

[1] For a more comprehensive discussion of the contaminated land regime, readers are advised to have regard to *Contaminated Land: The New Regime* (2000) (London: Sweet and Maxwell), by Tromans and Turrall-Clarke.

[2] Lawyers advising in relation to sites in Scotland and Wales will also need to take the provisions of Part IIA of the 1990 Act into account. Following devolution, the implementation of Part IIA in these countries has been in accordance with decisions taken by the Scottish Executive and the National Assembly for Wales: see The Contaminated Land (Scotland) Regulations 2000, SSI 2000/178 and The Contaminated Land (Wales) Regulations 2001, SI 2001/2197 (W.157), respectively. In order to avoid undue complexity the discussion which follows in this chapter focuses solely on the manner of implementation of Part IIA in England.

[3] See further, above, Chapter 1.

Equally, there has been, and there remains a variety of well-established *criminal offences* which may be committed by those who contaminate sites (or, in some cases, by those who are responsible for contaminated sites). For example, in instances where the condition of a site may be causing further contamination of adjacent or subterranean water, the offences of "causing or knowingly permitting" poisonous, noxious or polluting matter to enter controlled water may be applicable;[4] and a reminder is appropriate here of the important "waste" offence contained in section 33(1)(c) of the Environmental Protection Act 1990: "a person shall not ... treat, keep or dispose of waste in a manner likely to cause pollution of the environment or harm to human health".[5]

These rules of tortious and criminal liability may be of considerable significance; and the new legislation, valuable as it may be as regards the particular matters to which it relates (principally, contaminated site *identification* and *remediation*), is unlikely to diminish their importance. The new rules will supplement rather than supersede such civil and criminal liabilities.

The new, administrative liability, provisions of Part IIA of the 1990 Act fall short, therefore, of comprising anything in the form of a complete "Code" of rules on the subject of contaminated land. That the legislation does not seek any such comprehensive treatment of the subject was a matter of deliberate policy on the part of Government. The official documents which preceded the publication in 1994 of the first draft of the new legislation made clear the official view that the new rules should concentrate on what one might describe as the "public law of contaminated land": that is, the powers and duties of public bodies in achieving a general strategy of site remediation, together with associated powers to subject individuals to administrative orders and administrative liabilities. Issues of purely civil liability were stated already to have been worked out in a broadly satisfactory manner by decisions of the courts, involving a balance having been struck between principles of strict liability and liability based upon fault;[6] and a similar view seems implicit as regards the operation of the general environmental offences referred to above.

Contractual (and similar) liabilities

In addition to the continuing operation, alongside the new legislation, of such basic rules of *criminal* and *civil* liability there should be referred to here also a further range of liabilities which may arise from the contaminated condition of land: these are liabilities which may arise under property or commercial transactional documents associated with a site

---

[4] Water Resources Act 1991, s. 85. For the most recent authoritative interpretation of the wide breadth of this offence, see the decision of the House of Lords in *Empress Car Company (Abertillery) Ltd* v *National Rivers Authority* [1998] 1 All ER 481 (discussed above at pp. 306-323).

[5] See further, above, pp. 381-382.

[6] See, for example, *Paying for Our Past* (DOE/Welsh Office Consultation Paper, March 1994) Preliminary Conclusion 4D.9 (p. 29).

which may have become discovered to be contaminated. Such transactional documents may relate to transfers of interests in the land itself, or may relate to interests in companies which may be closely associated with the land or its contamination. The liabilities will be of an essentially contractual nature. They will reflect agreements which may have been negotiated during property transactions or corporate mergers/acquisitions, whereby warranties and indemnities may have made some provision as regards where and in what sums, by process of contractual recourse, financial costs associated with the cleanup of contaminated sites should ultimately be borne.

Connection between private and public law liabilities

In general, such arrangements may be thought to be of a "private" or "private law" nature; their content depending fundamentally on the bargaining strengths of the parties. They may be said to add a further dimension, a further layer of complexity, to the law relevant to any situation of land contamination. However, private law and administrative liability law do not here operate in perfect isolation from each other. As we shall see below, when the "administrative/public law" provisions of Part IIA of the Environmental Protection Act 1990 (and associated statutory guidance) is considered, the *private* arrangements which may have been agreed between parties connected with a contaminated site may have a bearing on the way in which *public law liabilities* will, under the terms of that legislation and statutory guidance, be distributed by the enforcing authorities.

The effect of the quite recent bringing into force of the provisions of Part IIA of the 1990 Act is, therefore, to have introduced an additional layer of quite complex and sophisticated public law powers and duties to sit alongside these other, more established, fields of law. Certainly the working concerns of practising lawyers will continue to encompass this whole field of contractual, tortious, criminal and public law.

OUTLINE OF CHAPTER

Complexity and sophistication of new legal regime

A review even only of the administrative liabilities associated with the contaminated condition of land will, the reader is warned, involve a quite substantial volume of material of quite considerable legal complexity. It may, therefore, be helpful to indicate in outline the structure of the discussion which is to follow. This may be seen from a list of the main headings and sub-headings under which the material will be organised:

- Nature and magnitude of contaminated land problems;
- Development of policy, and overview of the new regime;
- Definition of "contaminated land";
- Site identification and characterisation;
- Site notification: remediation notices;

- Service of notices;
- Appeals;
- Urgent remedial action;
- Remediation by agreement;
- Meaning of "remediation";
- Standard of remediation;
- Remedial Liability;
- "Appropriate persons";
- Allocation of burdens as between "appropriate persons": exclusion and apportionment;
- Remediation by the enforcing authorities: cost recovery provisions;
- Compensation provisions: grant of rights over land to secure remediation;
- Register provisions;
- Inter-relationship between Part IIA and other statutory remediation regimes;
- The experience to date.

NATURE AND MAGNITUDE OF CONTAMINATED LAND PROBLEMS

Indeterminate magnitude

Precise information about the number, area and nature of contaminated sites in England and Wales cannot readily be provided. The reasons for this may be simply explained. On the one hand the physical, chemical, biological and other qualities and characteristics (clean or contaminated) of much land is simply not known with any real certainty. Moreover, speculative assumptions may often prove unfounded. Present-day green field sites may, historically,[7] have been put to a contaminative use, and so may present risks which are not readily apparent; and "suspect" sites, known to have had a past industrial usage, may have – against all odds – avoided contamination.

Significance of definitions

Quite apart from this lack of hard data, the task of cataloguing and quantifying contaminated sites is one which, even where data exists, depends fundamentally on definitions and understandings of the basic concept: *contamination.* As will be evident from what follows, this is a concept which may well have a quite different meaning to each category of persons who may use the term – scientists, environmentalists, lawyers and others. Depending on the definition adopted the number of sites and the aggregate area of contaminated land may shrink or enlarge. For this reason great care needs to be taken as regards the assumptions upon which any published estimates have been made: international comparisons are, for this reason, especially problematic.

---

[7] For example, heavy metal soil contamination may be present as a consequence of mineral workings many centuries ago; or as a result of small-scale industrial operations in the early industrial period (e.g. tanneries) of which no current evidence is visible.

Best estimates

Nevertheless, some statement as regards the nature and scale of the problem in England and Wales may be expected. An idea of the possible extent of the problem may be gleaned from a Department of the Environment consultation document issued in 1994.[8] This included a statement that:

> "the *number of sites* might ... be as high as ... 100,000... The *area* might be as much as ... 200,000 hectares... But higher or lower estimates can result from different assumptions."

More recently the estimates have tended to suggest that the scope of the problem is somewhat greater than was originally thought. Thus the Environment Agency has estimated that some 300,000 hectares of land in the United Kingdom may be affected by contaminating substances, whereas research carried out by consultants W. S. Atkins for the Department of the Environment put the figure at 360,000 hectares.[9] Not all of these *sites* may, however, pose immediate threats. The present Government's approach, set out in its Circular on *Contaminated Land* (April 2000) is to stress that:

> "international experience suggested that only a small proportion of potentially contaminated sites posed an immediate threat to human health and the environment."[10]

Nevertheless, there is no room for a complacent approach. The same Circular proceeds to describe the overall task of remediation, even of only the more problematic sites, in terms which do not make light of the exercise:

> "... we have to deal with a substantial legacy of land which [has been] ... contaminated."[11]

Cost estimates

If it is no easy task to quantify the *physical scale and nature* of the problem, it is even more difficult to assess the likely *cost* of tackling land contamination. Here additional assumptions may be necessary before any guesses may begin to be made. For example, what will be the scale and intensity of the site survey and investigation work necessary? Where sites are cleaned up, what will be the standard of cleanup required? Over what period of time may these costs be incurred? Spreading costs effectively reduces costs and as new techniques and new technologies are developed and become practically tested, site remediation is, in some contexts, becoming less expensive in real terms.

---

[8] *Paying for Our Past* (DOE/Welsh Office, March 1994): the estimates were based on figures contained in a report on *Contaminated Land* published by the Parliamentary Office of Science and Technology in 1993.

[9] See (2000) ENDS Report 305, at pp. 4-5.

[10] DETR Circular 02/00 Annex 1, para. 5.

[11] Circular, para. 4.

Notwithstanding these difficulties there may, again, be a wish for some monetary figure to be assigned to the task of remediation. The 1994 consultation document, *Paying for our Past*, referred, without dissent, to a then recent estimate that even on the basis of only moderate cleanup requirements the total costs involved might amount to some £20 billion. This figure actually exceeds a more recent estimate by consultants W. S. Atkins in the research carried out on behalf of the Department of the Environment, referred to above. They put the cost of the investigation and remediation of contaminated land at £15.2 billion, although they consider that the actual figure may well prove somewhat lower.[12]

DEVELOPMENT OF POLICY AND OVERVIEW OF THE NEW REGIME

Scope of provisions

Section 57 of the Environment Act 1995 contains a set of provisions which have added a new Part, Part IIA, to the Environmental Protection Act 1990. Brought into operation in year 2000 these provisions, for the first time in the United Kingdom, establish a discrete body of law designed with specific reference to the problem of contaminated land, comprising a complex set of substantive rules and associated procedures.

The scope of the new legal regime is quite broad.[13] However, as a start it may be noted that it encompasses the following matters of prime significance:

- *a definition of the critical concept – contaminated land*: thereby indicating the nature of the sites to which the new legal provisions apply. Moreover, the definition of contaminated land which has been adopted has, as we shall see, inevitable and important implications as regards the standard of remediation to be required;

- the *conferment of various duties and powers on public bodies* as regards the tasks of site identification, the investigation of contaminated sites, and the initiation of procedures for the securement of site remediation;

- the *establishment of responsibility amongst "appropriate persons" for site remediation*; including, in default, provisions permitting *cost recoupment by public bodies* in instances where those public bodies may have themselves undertaken works in relation to contaminated sites.

---

[12] See (2000) ENDS Report 305, at pp. 4-5.
[13] In *X* v *A, B and C* [2000] Env LR 104, Arden J remarked that Part IIA "imposes a new and far-reaching liability regime on owners of land and others for cleaning up land" (at 105).

Development of the new measures

The contaminated land provisions of the Environment Act 1995 followed a quite extensive period of governmental consideration, consultation and review.

The more recent history may perhaps be said to date from an influential report of the House of Commons Select Committee on the Environment, entitled *Contaminated Land*,[14] which was published in January 1990 and drew attention to problems not at that time commonly appreciated, and the pressing need for governmental action. An immediate effect of this Report was the addition in the Environmental Protection Bill, then before Parliament, of what became section 143 to the Environmental Protection Act 1990. Broadly, under this section, duties would be imposed upon local authorities to make investigations[15] and to compile public registers which would indicate parcels of land which had been subject in the past to potentially contaminating uses. It should be noted that inclusion on such a public register would, of itself have indicated nothing about the *actual* historical (let alone the present) condition of land. Land which may have in the past have been subject to any of a quite substantial number of potentially contaminating uses might, in fact, have escaped such contamination. Moreover, even if it *had been* contaminated it might subsequently have been cleaned up. In either case, according to the legislation, the site should nevertheless appear upon the register. Equally sites which might well be contaminated, and be known to be such, would not appear on the register if they had not historically been subject to any of the uses comprised in the "official" list of the (more) potentially contaminating land uses. The document was intended merely as a historical record relating to past land use, which would alert would-be purchasers and developers to the need for careful investigation of the present condition of a site.

These provisions, which could not be brought into operation immediately for logistical reasons – local authorities needing time to prepare – provoked much controversy. Quite apart from the burdens upon local authorities in producing the registers, there were fears expressed about the effect on property values which would follow from a site being included within a register. Moreover, it became evident that such sites would not exclusively be ones with a present industrial or commercial usage. A good many listed sites would be sites with a past industrial history (perhaps small scale and long past) but which had more recently been developed for residential use. The spectre of ordinary householders discovering their homes depreciating in value, or at least in ready saleability, as they might become placed on registers which were commonly described, albeit of course inaccurately, as "Registers of Contaminated Land", caused the Conservative Government to reconsider its position. In due course, that Government announced, in March 1993, that it had decided against the implementation of the register arrangements provided for in section 143.

---

[14] House of Commons Environment Committee, First Report Session 1989-90.

[15] Principally envisaged to be "desk audits".

At the same time the Government noted that there remained a substantial deficiency in the law relating to contaminated land. In the words of the then Secretary of State for the Environment:

> "when sites are identified as actually contaminated it remains unclear in some cases what action should be taken, what remediation measures should be carried out and by whom, which regulatory bodies should be involved, and, where the liability for the cost of remediation should fall."[16]

Inter-departmental review: cost-benefit approach

It was therefore decided that an inter-departmental group of officials should conduct a wide-ranging review. The group was asked:

> "to review the powers and duties of public authorities which relate to the identification, assessment and appropriate treatment and control of land that could cause pollution of the environment or harm to human health ..."

This provided a quite broad remit. However, an immediate guiding limitation was placed upon the committee in its deliberations and eventual proposals. Its terms of reference continued with the statement that it should consider these questions:

> "having regard to the need to minimise the costs which existing and new regulatory burdens place on the private sector."

The inter-departmental committee spent a year in a process of *informal* discussion and consultation, prior to releasing, in March 1994, a formal Department of the Environment/Welsh Office consultative document: *Paying for Our Past*. This document sought to draw attention to what the committee regarded as the principal questions which needed to be considered in developing a legal and regulatory framework for the identification and remediation of contaminated land. Whilst it presented its own "Preliminary Conclusions" as regards a number of such issues, it stressed that it welcomed further views on each of the numerous matters high-lighted.

Environment Bill

This consultation process sought responses by May 1994. The Government's response to the consultation followed in November 1994, involving the contemporaneous publication not only of a document indicating the basics of Government policy (*Framework for Contaminated Land*), but also an Environment Bill containing within it a set of quite complex legislative provisions designed to support and implement that stated policy.

---

[16] House of Commons, Written Answers, cols 633-634, 24th March 1993.

The following brief extracts from a section of *Framework for Contaminated Land* entitled "Policy and Priorities" provide a fairly succinct summary of the Conservative Government's general approach.

The document stated:

"2.1 The Government is committed to sustainable development and to the polluter pays principle...

2.3 The Government is also committed to the 'suitable for use' approach to the control and treatment of existing contamination. This supports sustainable development both by reducing damage from past activities and by permitting contaminated land to be kept in, or returned to, beneficial use wherever practicable – minimising avoidable pressures for new development to take place on greenfield sites.

2.4 This approach requires remedial action only where:
  • the contamination poses unacceptable actual or potential risks to health or the environment; and
  • there are appropriate and cost-effective means available to do so, taking into account the actual or intended use of the site.

2.6 It would be neither feasible nor sensible to try to deal with all land contaminated by past activities at once: the wealth-creating sectors of the economy could not afford to do so. The urgent and real problems should be dealt with, but in an orderly and controlled fashion with which the economy at large and individual businesses and land-owners can cope."

This general approach produced a broad range of reactions. Some regarded the expression of commitment to dealing with what they felt to be a substantial environmental problem as somewhat half-hearted; others welcomed what they characterised as a sensibly measured balance between environmental zeal and economic and administrative practicality – a policy driven by pragmatism rather than environmental fundamentalism. And some expressed a degree of alarm at the proposals, notwithstanding the quite moderate language used in the policy statements.

The truth may perhaps be said to lie somewhere in between these extremes. Certainly the approach put forward was substantially less demanding than that which was understood to be applicable under the laws in certain other legal jurisdictions.[17] Nevertheless, it could be said in support of the proposals that the fundamentals of the legislative "liability" scheme were derived, albeit without any very substantial discussion or debate, from that

---

[17] The most common comparative references being to CERCLA in the USA and to the Dutch "multi-functionality cleanup" arrangements as they existed at this time.

set of laudable dogma we may label "general principles of environmental policy"; and in particular, the "polluter pays" principle.[18]

The clauses of the Environment Bill containing the proposed primary legislation setting up the framework of the new legal regime, provoked a good deal of discussion during the Bill's Parliamentary committee stages. They became quite substantially supplemented and amended: this part of the Bill nearly doubling in length. Nevertheless, notwithstanding such detailed modification of the Bill the *essential features* of the scheme proposed by the Government in its original Bill may be regarded as having remained intact.

Form of the legislation

The drafting technique adopted in this part of the 1995 Act was to secure, by one lengthy section (section 57) the addition of some 26 new sections to the Environmental Protection Act 1990. These take the form of a new Part to that earlier Act: Part IIA; and comprise new sections 78A to 78YC. The new provisions, it may be noted, immediately precede Part III of the 1990 Act, dealing with statutory nuisances, a matter in relation to which there are at least some procedural similarities with the new arrangements for contaminated land.[19]

Skeletal legislation – the statutory guidance

Notwithstanding that the provisions contained in the primary legislation possess a fair measure of complexity, the provisions do not provide answers to all the questions which require legal definition before any such legal regime may come into operation. The approach adopted was to provide an essential structure within the primary legislation, and for this to be amplified and clarified by further "statutory guidance" from the Environment ministry.

In principle this approach is unexceptionable. It is familiar practice for primary legislation to contain the skeletal framework of a scheme, with the detail to be "fleshed out" and maybe subsequently amended in the light of experience or changed circumstances, by ministerial rules. Indeed, in principle, this approach may be welcomed. It can do much to allow debate in Parliament to focus on essentials rather than upon minutiae.

Nevertheless, in relation to the measures currently under discussion some concern should be expressed. What will shortly become apparent is that a range of matters which are quite fundamental to the operation of any legal regime in relation to contaminated land were not set out in detail (or, in

---

[18] Note, in this connection, the fundamental policy choice that the *actual polluter* should be the primarily responsible party as regards the imposition of remediation responsibilities. See below, p. 573.

[19] See above, Chapter 12. For the view that these similarities should not be overstated, see the chapter by one of the present authors on *Environmental Competences* in *Environmental Law in the United Kingdom and Belgium from a Comparative Perspective* (eds Kurt Deketelaere and Michael Faure, Intersentia, 1999).

some instances, at all) in the primary legislation. In other words one may study the primary legislation very closely without being able to find answers to very important questions.

If all these important (as well as the less important) matters of detail could have been found in documents to be consulted, contemporaneously, alongside the principal Bill there would be little of substance about which to complain. Indeed, the Government, at the time of the Bill going through Parliament, seemed aware that it should provide some answers to the important questions unanswered within the Bill itself. It therefore issued, on 10th May 1995, a draft of its proposed guidance on the definition and identification of contaminated land: matters which, it acknowledged, formed a "key element" in the provisions of the Bill, then before a House of Commons Committee.

This draft guidance was certainly helpful in seeking to gain a fuller and more detailed understanding of the regime which would, in due course, enter into force. However, the guidance was only in draft form: it was not issued, alongside the Bill, in final form for Parliamentary approval, amendment or rejection of the legislative package as a whole. Moreover, the draft guidance constituted only the first part of a rather more substantial tranche of such guidance which would be required from the Department of the Environment, clarifying very significant aspects of the primary legislation and indicating, as authorised by that legislation, how numerous powers and duties conferred upon public agencies were to be exercised. The whole debate, within and outside Parliament, on the complex, yet also merely skeletal, scheme set out in the Bill was, therefore, conducted in the absence of clear guidance, even in draft form, on quite critically important matters.

We may take just one such matter by way of example. The Bill, now the Act, contains provisions which define the categories of persons who are to be subject to remediation obligations under the new law. What is not clear from the primary legislation is how burdens will be divided or allocated as between those who fall within the stated categories. The primary law states that this will be determined in accordance with governmental guidance; but that guidance was not available even in a preliminary or draft form, at the time the Bill was being discussed by Parliament (nor, as it transpired, for several years thereafter).

Delays

The Bill which became the Environment Act 1995 received Royal Assent on 19 July 1995. Substantial parts of the Act, including the ones under present discussion, did not, however, come immediately into operation. Delay was necessary in order to allow the Department of the Environment to continue its work on the development of the various items of statutory guidance and other secondary regulations. Indeed it was not until

September 1996 that even the first tranche of guidance documents on contaminated land were issued in draft form for consultation.[20]

Mandatory and other guidance

It is important in considering the statutory guidance issued under the 1995 Act to note that the Act provides for guidance in two forms. Certain provisions of the Act provide that Government shall issue guidance, and that enforcing authorities shall "have regard to" that guidance in the exercise of their functions. The effect of such a provision is that although the enforcing authority must consider the terms of the guidance before acting in a particular matter, the guidance is not binding upon that authority. In the words of one case, the authority need not "slavishly adhere"[21] to the guidance.

In contrast, certain important provisions of the Act provide for "guidance" which will have a legal effect which will go rather beyond the normal meaning of that word. In these cases the Act provides that authorities shall be *required* to act, or shall be *required* to determine questions, in accordance with the guidance to be issued. Whereas the first kind of guidance will no doubt be of some importance to lawyers in assisting their prediction of how authorities are likely to operate the new legislation, the second kind (what we may legitimately call *mandatory* guidance) will be of even greater significance, indicating how authorities *must* interpret and apply aspects of the legislation. In view of the often substantial financial implications of many decisions which will be taken in the exercise of the functions to be described, it may be expected that opportunities presented here for judicial review may be closely monitored by those affected.

No consensus

The Draft Guidance issued in September 1996 demonstrated clearly the complexity and significance of important matters upon which the Act itself was either quite silent, or offered only a broad idea of how the new regime would apply. Inevitably, the content of the guidance produced no immediate consensus, and it was a matter of little surprise, also with a General Election looming, to find that even once the consultation period had concluded on 18th December 1996, no immediate final draft of the guidance emerged from Government.

The General Election of May 1997 brought a new administration to power. Word soon issued from the renamed central ministry, the Department of the Environment, Transport and the Regions (DETR),[22] that the new Government proposed to undertake its own review of the guidance to be

---

[20] *Consultation on Draft Statutory Guidance on Contaminated Land* (September 1996: two vols) Prior to this date there had been some degree of *informal* consultation on the basis of documents which were expressly stated to be no more than "working drafts" (for example, the document issued in May 1995 referred to in the text above and another document issued in February 1996).
[21] See *Simpson* v *Edinburgh Corpn.* 1960 SC 313.
[22] Now of course the renamed Department of the Environment, Food and Rural Affairs (DEFRA) following the General Election of June 2001.

issued under this part of the 1995 Act. In particular, it was evident from an early stage that the new Minister wished to consult and reflect on two important issues. First, whether a "completion certificate" arrangement should be introduced, whereby those who had undertaken remediation of a site to the satisfaction of the enforcing authority might thereby become exonerated from any further liabilities in relation to the contamination to which such a certificate related. And secondly, whether the liability scheme under the Act should be moderated by the introduction of some kind of "foreseeability" requirement: whether those whose actions may have polluted land should escape remediation responsibilities in instances where it could be demonstrated that the harm in question could not have been foreseen.[23]

In addition to a period of delay associated with the consideration of these issues relating to the *substance* of the implementation of this part of the 1995 Act, it soon became evident that there were other factors which would mean that introduction of the new legal regime would not be imminent. The new Labour Government acknowledged something which had substantially been denied by its predecessor: that imposition of the Act's various contaminated land responsibilities upon the designated enforcing agencies, and in particular the burdens to be imposed upon local authorities, could not be unaccompanied by additional central exchequer financial support.[24] Given that the new Government was committed to not exceeding the short and medium term public expenditure plans which had been set by the outgoing Conservative administration, it seemed to follow that funding of the new administrative burdens would not be possible until at least 1998. An announcement to this effect came from the DETR in December 1997.

Even this new anticipated commencement time was to prove over-optimistic. It was only in October 1998 that the "new" Government circulated to a relatively select group of informal consultees its revised proposals as regards the necessary statutory guidance. The circulation of this document was accompanied by an announcement that the Government intended that the new legal regime would come into operation in July 1999.

As things transpired this revised and long delayed target could not be met. In due course the DETR issued a draft *Circular on Contaminated Land* in October 1999. The circular explained Government policy generally on contaminated land issues, and explained Government understanding of the

---

[23] Such a change might, it was felt, produce a closer alignment than seemed to exist under the bare provisions of the 1995 Act between principles of civil liability at common law (as evidenced in the relatively recent decision of the House of Lords in *Cambridge Water Co Ltd v Eastern Counties Leather plc* [1994] 2 AC 264) and the new statutory burdens.

[24] The Explanatory and Financial Memorandum to the Bill which became the 1995 Act had stated that the Part IIA regime would have no manpower or financial implications as it "largely restated existing functions of local authorities". The DETR Circular 02/00 notes, however, that following consultation and further reflection, a sum of £50 million would be provided over three years to "help local authorities develop inspection strategies, carry out site investigations and take forward enforcement action". (Circular para. 10.)

provisions of the 1995 Act with which we shall be concerned. It also contained a number of Annexes, containing the (draft) statutory guidance, issued in further revised form for final consultation.

Following this consultation exercise the final statutory guidance was issued in the DETR Circular 02/00, *Contaminated Land*, and the new regime came into operation on 1st April 2000.

Differences of emphasis as between the Act and the statutory guidance

The delays which have been described, and to some degree explained, may be regarded as an unfortunate consequence of the original Bill being steered through Parliament without policy on a number of quite critically important matters having been determined. Indeed, this episode of law-making can be held up as a model of what should be avoided. In terms of the role of Parliament in discussing and reviewing Government Bills we may comment that Parliament was presented in 1994/5 with only a part of the overall legislative package. Any sensible assessment of the new legal regime must be based upon a consideration of both the terms of the Act and also the associated final ministerial guidance. This point will be seen to have particular force when it is noted that on numerous important points the terms of the statutory guidance documents have the effect of *moderating* the apparent scope of burdens and responsibilities described in the Act itself.

Retrospective liabilities

One further unfortunate consequence of the delay may also be noted. It will become evident in the discussion which follows that the new legal regime operates in a way which may be described as imposing responsibilities retrospectively. For example, under the new regime it is a task of the enforcing authorities to look back in time to seek to discover whose actions or activities may have resulted in the substances being present on land which now render the land contaminated and appropriate for remediation under the new provisions. It may well be that such a person or persons may bear remediation liabilities, under this new regime, which did not exist, or at least did not clearly exist, hitherto. Whether this is acceptable or unacceptable in terms of legal policy, and what purely pragmatic issues may arise as regards the sheer practicability of operating a policy of targeting the "historic polluter" are important questions later to be explored. For the moment, it will suffice to note that over the years, since at least the time the Environment Bill was published, lawyers were required in offering advice to take account of the fact that such retrospective liability (albeit of uncertain detailed scope) was in the legislative pipeline.

Essential objectives

Before beginning to consider the details of the new legal regime it may be useful to refer briefly to statements which have issued from Government explaining its essential policy objectives: statements which suggest that, notwithstanding a change in Government in 1997, the *essentials* did not alter significantly over the period during which the detailed guidance was developed.

The principal objectives of Government in respect of contaminated sites are summarised in the Circular on *Contaminated Land* to be:

"(a) to identify and remove unacceptable risks to human health and the environment;

(b) to seek to bring damaged land back into beneficial use; and

(c) to seek to ensure that the cost burdens faced by individuals, companies and society as a whole are proportionate, manageable and economically sustainable."

These objectives "underlie the 'suitable for use' approach to the remediation of contaminated land, which the Government considers the most appropriate approach to achieving sustainable development in this field."[25]

A number of aspects of this broad statement of objectives will be discussed more fully in due course. For the moment it will suffice to note that Government objectives in relation to contaminated land involve an amalgam of environmental aims tempered with economic and practical realism; the objective, quite sensibly, being to seek a strategy of cleanup of sites which takes account of environmental considerations, but which also balances such considerations with factors of cost, economic affordability and practical manageability.

"Suitable for use"

The Circular also provides some valuable insights into the thinking which underlies the "suitable for use" approach to the standard of cleanup to be required for contaminated sites. As we shall see, this policy approach has had a very marked influence on the drafting of the provisions of the primary legislation and on the content of the associated statutory guidance. The Circular explains:

"9. The 'suitable for use' approach focuses on the risks caused by land contamination. The approach recognises that the risks presented by any given level of contamination will vary greatly according to the use of the land and a wide variety of other factors, such as the underlying geology of the site. Risks therefore need to be assessed on a site-by-site basis.

10. The 'suitable for use' approach … consists of three elements:

(a) *ensuring that land is suitable for its current use* – in other words, identifying any land where contamination is causing unacceptable risks to human health and the

---

[25] Circular, Annex I paras 7 and 8.

environment, assessed on the basis of the current use and circumstances of the land, and returning such land to a condition where such risks no longer arise...;

(b) *ensuring that land is made suitable for any new use, as official permission is given for that new use* – in other words, assessing the potential risks from contamination, on the basis of the proposed future use and circumstances, before official permission is given for the development and, where necessary to avoid unacceptable risks to human health and the environment, remediating the land before the new use commences;

(c) *limiting requirements for remediation to the work necessary to prevent unacceptable risks to human health or the environment in relation to the current use or the officially-permitted future use of the land* – in other words, recognising that the risks from contaminated land can be satisfactorily assessed only in the context of specific uses of the land, and that any attempt to guess what might be needed at some time in the future for other uses is likely to result either in premature work (thereby risking distorting social, economic and environmental priorities) or in unnecessary work (thereby wasting resources)...

12. Regulatory action may be needed to make sure that necessary remediation is carried out. However, limiting remediation costs to what is needed to avoid unacceptable risks will mean that we will be able to recycle more previously-developed land than would otherwise be the case, increasing our ability to make beneficial use of the land. This helps to increase the social, economic and environmental benefits from regeneration projects and to reduce development pressures on greenfield sites.

13. The 'suitable for use' approach provides the best means of reconciling our various environmental, social and economic needs in relation to contaminated land. Taken together with tough action to prevent new contamination, and wider initiatives to promote the reclamation of previously-developed land, it will also help to bring about progressive improvements in the condition of the land which we pass on to future generations...

15. The one exception to the 'suitable for use' approach to regulatory action applies where contamination has resulted from a specific breach of an environmental licence or permit. In such circumstances, the Government considers that it is generally appropriate that the polluter is required to remove the contamination completely. To do otherwise would be to undermine the regulatory regimes aimed at preventing new contamination."

The Circular proceeds to explain how the administrative liability provisions, discussed in the remainder of this chapter, form an essential part of Governmental policy as regards achieving the "recycling" of contaminated sites for future beneficial use. It notes:

> "17. The Government is determined to limit the unnecessary development of greenfield areas, and has in particular set a target for 60% of new housing to be built on previously-developed land...
>
> 19. There are very few cases where land cannot be restored to some beneficial use. However, the actual or potential existence of contamination on a site can inhibit the willingness or ability of a developer to do so. The Government is acting in three specific ways to overcome the potential obstacles to the redevelopment of land affected by contamination:
>
> (a) *by providing public subsidy* – substantial funding is made available through the Single Regeneration Budget, English Partnerships and the regional development agencies to support site redevelopment costs for projects aimed at particular social and economic objectives;
>
> (b) *by promoting research and development* – ...to improve scientific understanding and the availability and take-up of improved methods of risk assessment and remediation; and
>
> (c) *by providing an appropriate policy and legal framework* – the "suitable for use" approach ensures that remediation requirements are reasonable and tailored to the needs of individual sites; a significant objective underlying the new contaminated land regime is to improve the clarity and certainty of potential regulatory action, thereby assisting developers to make informed investment appraisals."

THE DEFINITION OF "CONTAMINATED LAND"

Introduction

The new statutory provisions confer very significant powers and duties on public authorities in relation to contaminated land, and require the imposition of remediation responsibilities on defined categories of persons. The notion "contaminated land" requires careful definition if there is to be any hope that an acceptable measure of legal certainty as regards liabilities may be achieved. Moreover, as will become apparent, there is inevitably a close connection between any definition of contaminated land and the substance of remediation requirements which may be imposed. A measure of understanding of the former concept seems necessary before the latter issue can sensibly be broached.

The basic definition of contaminated land is to be found in new section 78A(2) of the Environmental Protection Act 1990. In slightly abridged, and rearranged, form this provides as follows:

Contaminated land is –

"any land which ..., by reason of substances in, on or under that land, ... is in such condition that:
(a)		significant harm is being caused or there is a significant possibility of such harm being caused; or
(b)		pollution of controlled waters is being, or is likely to be caused."[26]

The Act then proceeds to provide further definition of certain of the above terms. Thus, it is made clear that "substances" may be solid, liquid or gaseous; and that by "pollution of controlled waters" is meant the "entry into controlled waters of any poisonous, noxious or polluting matter".[27] Furthermore, "controlled waters"[28] is widely defined so as to include most instances of surface water and also, and importantly in this context of land contamination, to include groundwater.

"Harm"

The Act explains also the meaning of the expression "harm".[29] It states that "harm" means:

"harm to the health of living organisms or other interference with ecological systems of which they form part and, in the case of man, includes harm to his property."[30]

Radioactivity exclusion

The Act provides, limiting the scope of its operation, that "harm" or "pollution of controlled waters" which is attributable to any radioactivity possessed by any substance shall not render the land contaminated for the purposes of Part IIA.[31] However, power is conferred upon the Secretary of

---

[26] The Water Act 2003 (c.37) has amended the definition of "contaminated land" in relation to water pollution. It substitutes the following for subsection 78A(2)(b): "(b) significant pollution of controlled waters is being caused or there is a significant possibility of such pollution being caused" (see section 86(2)(a) of the 2003 Act). The purpose behind the amendment would appear to be to ensure that the requirements of the regime are not applied to minor cases of water pollution caused by contaminated land. It will come into force on a date to be appointed: see section 106 of the 2003 Act.

[27] This trilogy of adjectives derives from early water pollution legislation, and may now be found within the principal water pollution offence: s. 85 of the Water Resources Act 1991: extending none too perfect legislative phraseology from one context into another. See, further, above pp. 297-299.

[28] Again, a quite familiar concept within UK water legislation. See above, pp. 293-297.

[29] Note that harm, as so defined, must be "significant"; and, if only a possibility, must be a "significant" possibility.

[30] 1990 Act, s. 78A(4). This definition is broadly similar to that found in s. 1(4) of the 1990 Act, save for the fact that "harm" there is also stated to include "offence caused to any of his senses."

[31] Section 78YC.

State to make regulations applying the new regime – with modifications if appropriate – to instances of radioactive contamination. The Government began consultation on the content of such regulations in February 1998.[32]

Implications of definition of contaminated land

An initial quite general comment on the definition of contaminated land may be helpful. Anyone setting out to devise a legislative scheme on this subject has a choice between two broad approaches. Either, as is the case with the Act under review, he or she may define the principal concept by reference to the consequences, actual or anticipated, of the presence of contaminating substances on the land ("significant harm", "pollution of water");[33] or, alternatively, the notion of "contaminated land" may be defined simply by reference to officially ordained scientific/technical soil quality standards or thresholds.[34] Both approaches will require information as regards the nature and degree of contamination of the site in question. Under the latter, "quality standard", approach such information will generally suffice for a judgment to be reached as regards whether the land is "contaminated" in the legal sense, and will generally suffice to determine whether remediation is to be required, and the level and degree of such remediation. However, under the former approach, as evidenced in the new British legislation, information about the nature and degree of contamination of a site will not, by itself, be sufficient for a judgment to be reached as regards whether that site is "contaminated" for the purposes of the legislation. Additional site-specific information will be necessary before the vital decision may be made as to whether such levels of the contaminants which have been discovered on the site in question, with its particular configuration and in its particular location, have given rise or are likely to give rise to the "harm" or to the "pollution of water" which the legislation requires.

The implications of this fundamental policy choice may be illustrated by a simple example. Imagine a site upon which there has been a spillage of toxic chemicals. Let us assume that the chemicals are such as would in a typical case render a site in need of remediation. However, suppose also that the site in question is somewhat unusual in its qualities. It is, itself, of quite negligible ecological quality;[35] its physical and hydro-geological characteristics are such that there are no concerns as regards the chemical

---

[32] See *Control and Remediation of Radioactively Contaminated Land.*

[33] Requiring, as will be seen, site specific assessment of "pollution pathways" and "pollution receptors".

[34] The difference deserves note but should not, perhaps, be exaggerated. Quality standards are likely to have been set on the basis of harm typically caused by such levels and kind of contamination. The real difference may be between systems where likelihood of harm is *presumed* and systems where this matter must be demonstrable *site by site.*

[35] It is quite possible that any ecological value which may be ascribed to the site is a *consequence* of its chemical contamination, and so may itself be destroyed upon remediation. This is the case with "spoil" heaps at a number of ancient mining sites in the United Kingdom. Metal contaminants within the "spoil" may continue to this day to prevent ordinary vegetative growth, thereby allowing to flourish certain tolerant species which otherwise would be over-run.

contamination of adjacent or underground water;[36] and let us suppose that members of the general public may be kept safe by the simple and effective method of their being fenced out. In respect of such a site – admittedly a rather unusual one – the fundamental policy issue will arise: should the site be required to be remediated on the basis that its soil quality fails to meet quality standards which may have been prescribed, or should the site be not regarded as "contaminated" so far, at any rate, as concerns the applicability of such remediation obligations? From what has been described above, it will be apparent that it is the latter approach which may be said to characterise law and policy in the United Kingdom.

The approach adopted in the United Kingdom will be a matter of no surprise given the basic "suitable for use" policy stance which government has consistently supported as regards the standard to be set in situations where remediation is required. The definition afforded to the concept "contaminated land" is, after all, likely to reflect closely the chosen policy as regards standards of remediation. The definitions described above may, accordingly, be regarded as naturally following from the United Kingdom Government's attachment to the "suitable for use" approach to cleanup,[37] as compared with the alternative approach based upon the objective of securing potential for "multifunctionality".

Subjective aspects of definition

It is a matter of inevitability that a country which opts for the "suitable for use" approach, based upon a consideration of a broad range of site specific circumstances,[38] will not be able to define "contaminated land" for legal purposes in a way which would seem to secure much in the way of legal

---

[36] The reader might like to think of the site as the natural equivalent of a skillfully engineered modern landfill site.

[37] This broad approach has been noted earlier. The documents which contained what was the draft statutory guidance explained that "the condition of land is to be assessed in relation to the *current* use of the land or of any other land which may be affected…". Where it is proposed to change the use made of land this will generally bring into operation a requirement to obtain planning permission from the local planning authority (usually the district council); and if building work is necessary there will be a need for building control requirements to be satisfied. Such permissions and approvals will require assessment of the physical condition of the land, and also the impact which may flow from the proposed development. Land which may not have the legal quality of being "contaminated" when the land usage is industrial may become so (and remediation be required) should its use be proposed for residential development. Equally, attention must be paid to the possibility that the conduct of building or engineering activities on land may have the consequence of releasing contaminants so as to render a site "contaminated" within the terms of the statutory definition: for example, where work undertaken may result in the release of polluting substances to adjacent water or to groundwater.

[38] Assessed by reference to what the statutory guidance documents issued by the DoE/DETR refer to as "pollution linkages": the linkage being between the "source", the "pathway" and the "receptor". This is, perhaps, a rather complex terminology for describing something quite simple: that one should judge a site only once one has worked out the *actual* harm/pollution of water, or *actual potential* for harm/pollution of water, resulting from *those* substances being present on *this* land, given its particular *situation* and *characteristics*. The language of the statutory guidance is that the "definition of contaminated land embodies the concept of risk assessment". Further, "risk" is defined as a combination of (a) the probability, or frequency of occurrence of a defined hazard…; and (b) the magnitude…of the consequences": see Statutory Guidance, Annex 3, Chapter A, Part 2, para. A9.

precision or certainty. Nevertheless, attention should be drawn to certain particular features of the definition of "contaminated land" as contained in the new legislation on the grounds that they secure rather less objectivity in the determination of the questions which have to be addressed than might be thought desirable.

The general definition of "contaminated land", as set out above, was deliberately presented in a somewhat simplified way. A more precise statement of the Act's definition of "contaminated land" would explain that the concept applies not to land which, *objectively* considered, meets the description given above; but rather, it applies to any land which "appears to the local authority" to have those harmful or polluting characteristics.

What will be critical, therefore, will be not so much the actual condition, and harmful or polluting potential of the land, as the local authority's perception of those things.[39] For alert lawyers, mindful of possibilities in terms of judicial review, such differences in formulation may be quite significant.

When the Environment Bill was before Parliament, concerns were expressed that differing approaches might be taken by the enforcing authorities in different areas and that in consequence there might be as many laws on contaminated land as there were authorities applying the new laws. To seek to meet such concerns the Act, as enacted, contains a provision which states that:

"in determining whether any land appears to be [contaminated] a local authority shall...act in accordance with guidance issued by the Secretary of State..."[40]

Moreover, the Act provides that:

"The questions –

(a) what harm is to be regarded as 'significant',
(b) whether the possibility of significant harm being caused is 'significant',
(c) whether pollution of controlled waters is being, or is likely to be caused,

shall be determined in accordance with guidance issued ... by the Secretary of State..."[41]

---

[39] For a brief discussion of the scope of judicial review of discretionary powers couched in terms of subjective belief, see Garner and Jones, *Garner's Administrative Law* (8th edn. 1996). The courts do not limit themselves to asking whether such belief was actually held; they will uphold a challenge where they may be persuaded that a belief held was unreasonable (in the sense that no reasonable person or body *could* have formed that belief (what is called, after a leading case – unreasonableness in the *Wednesbury* sense).

[40] 1990 Act, s. 78A(2)(b).

[41] 1990 Act, s. 78A(5). The Water Act 2003 has amended this subsection in order to make the provision clearer. Under the amended subsection, the Part IIA regime only applies where the

What guidance has been afforded to such authorities in their consideration of these matters?

Here the statutory guidance documents make interesting reading. The messages signalled are somewhat different from those which would seem to appear from the terms of the principal Act itself. When the *Act* is studied what is evident is the quite broadly defined notion of contaminated land, and the quite extensive powers to require various categories of persons to remediate such land. When, instead, one focuses attention on the *guidance documents* a rather different picture emerges. The "headlines" which may have greeted the enactment of the original legislation are belied by the more cautious approach displayed by Government as regards its implementation.

"Significant harm"

Some illustration of these very general statements is appropriate. We may begin by looking at the statements in the statutory guidance which explain the approach which local authorities are required to adopt as regards the issue whether "harm" should be regarded as "significant" for the purpose of the definition of "contaminated land".

The guidance begins by noting that for the harm in question to be "significant" it must be harm to one of a limited range of "receptors" and must, for each receptor, be harm of a particular description.[42] Here the guidance may be said simply to be reminding authorities of the terms of the Act: the Act itself, it may be remembered, limits the concept of "harm" by restricting consideration to harm to "man" (including his property), other "living organisms", and "ecological systems" of which such living organisms form part. However, when we consider the detail of the guidance we see that the qualifying receptors are defined somewhat more narrowly than the primary legislation might have suggested, and that what may be considered to constitute "significant harm" in the case of each receptor is none too broadly drawn.

In the case of harm to "human beings"[43] a quite substantial variety of kinds of harm are listed and are stated "to be regarded as significant". These

---

pollution of controlled waters is "significant" or that there is a significant possibility of it being so. Accordingly, section 86(2)(b)(iii) of the 2003 Act repeals section 78A(5)(c), and section 86(2)(b)(i) and (ii) amend subss. (5)(a) and (b) as follows: "(a) what harm *or pollution of controlled waters* is to be regarded as significant; (b) whether the possibility of significant harm *or of significant pollution of controlled waters* being caused is significant" (the words in italics are inserted by the Water Act 2003 and will come into force on a date to be appointed).

[42] The type of receptor and the description of the harm for that particular receptor are specified in tabular form in Annex 3 to Circular 02/00: see Part 3, Table A.

[43] In order to assist local authorities in assessing risks to human health posed by contaminated land, the Environment Agency has produced a contaminated land exposure assessment (CLEA) model which replaces guidance note 59/83, drawn up by the former Inter-departmental Committee on the Redevelopment of Contaminated Land. The CLEA guidance is based on soil guideline values (SGVs) which, it argues, "represent a combination of authoritative science tempered with policy judgements". To date SGVs have been drawn up for seven contaminants – arsenic, cadmium, chromium, inorganic mercury, nickel, selenium and lead – although the intention is that

include intrinsically serious matters such as "death" and "serious injury", "genetic mutation", "birth defects" and "impairment of reproductive functions". The list of categories of harm to be regarded as significant also includes "disease", and this is defined as "an unhealthy condition of the body or part of it". This may seem an appropriately broad range of kinds of impact on human beings: it should, of course, be a principal function of any law on contaminated land to protect the health and well-being of people. This part of the mandatory guidance goes on, however, to rule out "mental illness" as qualifying within the term "disease", "except insofar as it is attributable to the effect of a pollutant on the body of the person concerned".

When attention is turned to harm to living organisms or ecological systems one is struck immediately by an important limitation. The organism and the ecological system which is the receptor (the thing harmed) must be in a location which falls within a list of the principal nature conservation designations under United Kingdom,[44] EU[45] and other protective regimes.[46] In other words harm done to organisms and ecosystems outside these most prized sites will not qualify.

When we look to the *kind* of harm within such sites which may qualify as "significant" we see that the harm noted or anticipated must involve an "irreversible adverse change, or some other substantial adverse change in the functioning of the ecological system within any substantial part of that location".

The Act, it may be remembered, extends the notion of "harm" to harm to man's *property*. The guidance imposes limitations on the kinds of property in respect of which harm being done, or anticipated, will lead to land being regarded as contaminated. The notion of "property" extends to crops (including timber), to home-grown or allotment produce, to livestock and other owned or domesticated animals, to wild animals which are the subject of shooting or fishing rights, and to buildings.

What is to be regarded as "significant" harm to these things? In the case of crops the guidance refers to the need for "substantial diminution in yield or other substantial loss in value resulting from death, disease or other physical damage". As regards other property of the kinds listed above, the equivalent reference is to "substantial loss in its value" attributable to

---

a rolling programme of 55 contaminants will be included in the model. For each substance, an SGV is determined according to whether the land use is residential, allotment, or commercial/industrial. Ten exposure pathways are identified in the model, including ingestion of soils and dust, consumption of vegetables, skin contact with soils and dust and inhalation of dust and vapours. Although the SGVs are not binding, they are intended to assist in the determination of whether there is a need to intervene to prevent unacceptable risks. For a fuller discussion of the CLEA model, see (2002) ENDS Report 326 at pp. 45-46, and Hobley and McCann, "Contaminated land in the UK – the current position" ELM 15 [2003] 79 at p. 80.

[44] e.g. Sites of special scientific interest, nature reserves, and marine nature reserves, designated under ss 28, 35 and 36 respectively of the Wildlife and Countryside Act 1981.

[45] e.g. Areas of Special Protection for Birds, Special Areas of Conservation.

[46] e.g. Ramsar sites.

similar reasons: although, for domestic pets loss of value is not relevant, the requirements being death, serious disease or serious physical damage only. It can be seen that "significant" has here been re-defined in terms of "substantial" loss of yield or "substantial loss" of property value. What, then, is meant by "substantial"? Table A states that a local authority should regard:

> "a substantial loss in value as occurring only when a substantial proportion of the animals or crops are dead or otherwise no longer fit for their intended purpose ... A 20% diminution or loss should be regarded as a benchmark for what constitutes a substantial diminution or loss."

In terms of harm to buildings the guidance defines "significant" harm as involving "structural failure", "substantial damage" or "substantial interference with any right of occupation"; and "substantial damage" or "substantial interference" will arise only where "any part of the building ceases to be capable of being used for the purpose for which it is or was intended".[47] Cosmetic rather than functional damage would not seem to qualify.[48]

"Significant possibility" of significant harm?

So much for the mandatory guidance on whether a local authority should regard a kind of harm as "significant". It will be remembered that in instances where significant harm is merely anticipated there must be a "significant possibility" of such harm occurring. Again, this is a matter for mandatory guidance to local authorities. The guidance explains that account must be taken of (a) the nature and degree of harm anticipated; (b) the susceptibility of the receptors to such harm; and (c) the timescale within which the harm might occur.[49]

The inclusion of the first of these three factors may seem strange: matters of "nature and degree" would seem more an aspect of judgment of the *seriousness* of harm anticipated than its *likelihood*. Here we must note that the guidance seems to interpret the wording of the Act ("significant possibility of such harm being caused") as not relating simply to the matter of likelihood, but also involving judgment as regards how serious the matter would be should the possibility occur. In other words a low

---

[47] Special provision is made as regards harm to, or threatened in respect of, scheduled ancient monuments. The test relates to significant impairment of the monument's historical, architectural, traditional, artistic or archaeological interest by reason of which the monument was scheduled.

[48] It is important to remember that the fact that actual or anticipated harm may not suffice to lead a local authority properly to the conclusion that the land from which the harm or risk emanates is in law "contaminated" does not rule out a civil action for compensation (for example, in negligence, nuisance or under the principle in *Rylands* v *Fletcher*) on the part of the owner of the property.

[49] Annex 3, Chapter A, Part 3, para. A28. The significance of (c) would seem to be that if a use of land involving a susceptible receptor is likely to be discontinued before the risk of harm is likely to materialise, the risk of harm may not be a significant possibility.

possibility may be a *significant* possibility if the consequence of that occurrence is a serious one.

This expansive interpretation of the expression "significant possibility" is to be commended. Were the expression to be interpreted as relating only to the *degree of likelihood* of harm occurring one would be confronted by the conclusion that land could not be regarded as, in law, "contaminated" if there was only a quite small chance of some catastrophic harm occurring as a result of its condition.

The guidance proceeds to present, in tabular form, a statement of the conditions which it requires should be satisfied in relation to each category of significant harm[50] before it will be appropriate for a local authority to regard the risk of such harm as a "significant possibility". In relation to harm to ecological systems, and animals and crops the requirement is that the local authority shall make an informed judgment[51] and shall regard a risk of harm as a significant possibility if "significant harm is more likely than not to result from the pollution linkage in question". In relation to buildings also this "more likely than not" approach applies, although here the judgment must be made in relation to such harm resulting "during the expected economic life of the building".[52]

Slightly more complex language is used to describe the conditions applicable in relation to an assessment of the "significant possibility" of significant human health effects. Again the judgment must be informed by relevant, authoritative and scientifically-based information; and the requirement as regards the "significance" of the possibility discovered is that it should be considered one which is "unacceptable". The assessment which is made must take account of the total intake, or exposure, of persons to the pollutant in question *from all sources*, as well as the relative contribution of the pollution linkage under scrutiny to that overall exposure. This seems designed to avoid onerous remediation requirements being imposed in instances where remediation of a site may, because of exposure to other sources of the pollutant, have an insignificant overall beneficial effect on the human health risks in question.

"Pollution of controlled waters"

It will be remembered that quite apart from the "significant harm" criteria, a second way in which a site may fall into the category of "contaminated land" is where "pollution of controlled waters is being, or is likely to be caused".[53] Further, the Act defines "pollution of controlled waters" as the

---

[50] For example, "human health effects", "ecological system effects", "animal and crop effects".

[51] Having taken into account "the relevant appropriate, authoritative and scientifically based information" for the type of pollution linkage in question "particularly in relation to the ecotoxicological effects of the pollutant".

[52] In relation to scheduled ancient monuments the prescribed timescale is stated to be the "foreseeable future".

[53] Section 78(2)(b). It will be remembered (see fn. 26 above) that the Water Act 2003 has amended this provision so that, from a date to be appointed, a site will be contaminated land

"entry into controlled waters of any poisonous, noxious or polluting matter or any solid waste matter".[54] Local authorities are required to act in accordance with the statutory guidance in determining whether pollution of controlled waters is being, or is likely to be, caused.[55] The guidance provides:

> "Before determining that pollution of controlled waters is being, or is likely to be caused, the local authority should be satisfied that a substance is continuing to enter controlled waters or is likely to enter controlled waters. For this purpose, the local authority should regard something as being 'likely' when they judge it more likely than not to occur."[56]

The idea that the Part IIA regime does not apply where contaminants are no longer entering controlled waters from the land in question is then reinforced:

> "Land should not be designated as contaminated where:
> (a)   a substance is already present in controlled waters;
> (b)   entry into controlled waters of that substance from land has ceased; and
> (c)   it is not likely that further entry will take place."[57]

As regards "entry", the Guidance states:

> "Substances should be regarded as having entered controlled waters where:
> (a)   they are dissolved or suspended in those waters; or
> (b)   if they are immiscible with water, they have direct contact with those waters on or beneath the surface of the water."[58]

It will be evident that there is a quite marked contrast between the "harm" and the "water pollution" limbs of the definition of contaminated land. As regards the former the Act goes to great pains, as we have seen, to confine the concept to instances where the land is giving, or is likely to give, rise to harm which is significant. By contrast *any* actual or likely pollution of *controlled water* will suffice to render land contaminated. Moreover, the Circular notes:

> "There is no power to issue guidance on what constitutes the pollution of controlled waters."[59]

---

where: "(b) significant pollution of controlled waters is being caused or there is a significant possibility of such pollution being caused" (section 86(2)(a) of the 2003 Act).
[54] Section 78A(9).
[55] Section 78A(5)(c). From a date to be appointed, local authorities will be required to determine whether the possibility of significant pollution of controlled waters being caused is significant: see section 86(2)(b)(ii) of the Water Act 2003.
[56] Guidance, Chapter A, Part 4, para. A36.
[57] Paragraph A38.
[58] Paragraph A39.

The matter is governed by the very broad definition in the Act itself, as set out above, and there is no power, by guidance, to *narrow* the scope of the concept. The consequences of this would seem to be that more land will fall within this contaminated land category than perhaps was intended by Government. Certainly the present Government has made evident in its Circular to local authorities that where pollution of controlled water is not serious it may well be that when the Guidance on *remediation requirements* is applied the consequence will be that no remediation of the not seriously problematic contaminated site will be adjudged necessary. The Circular explains:

> "If there is only a very low level of contamination on any land, which gives rise to only a low degree of seriousness of pollution of controlled waters, it will be reasonable to incur only a correspondingly low level of expenditure in attempting to remediate the land."[60]

This may provide some solace for those who may have been responsible for the contamination of the site. Nevertheless, it has been recognised by Government that for such sites to bear the label "contaminated", and for local authorities to be obliged to go through the procedures shortly to be described, is not ideal. For this reason the Circular notes:

> "The Government has indicated its intention of reviewing the wording of the legislation ... and of seeking amendments to the primary legislation."[61]

Meanwhile, however, the label "contaminated" will attach, even if remediation notices served will acknowledge no liability to remediate on the part of appropriate persons. In order, for the present, to minimise for owners of such land the adverse impacts of this unsatisfactory state of affairs the Circular advises:

> "... It is therefore important that the circumstances of such cases are clearly entered on the Register kept by the enforcing authority. If remediation is not carried out because it would not be reasonable, a remediation declaration needs to be published by the enforcing authority (section 78H(6)) and entered on the Register (section 78R(1)(c)). In this way, a public record is created explaining that no

---

[59] Circular, para. 2.9.

[60] Circular, para. 6.31.

[61] Circular, para. 2.10. The review of the wording of the legislation has resulted in the amendments made by the Water Act 2003: see fn. 26 and fn. 41, above. The effect of the amendments is that, from a date to be appointed, this category of contaminated land will have been narrowed by the added requirement that the pollution of controlled waters will have to have been "significant". Presumably, since there is no power to issue guidance on what constitutes the pollution of controlled waters (para. 2.9 of the Circular), there will also be no power to issue guidance on what constitutes the *significant* pollution of such waters.

remediation is required under Part IIA, even though the land has been formally identified as contaminated land."[62]

SITE IDENTIFICATION AND CHARACTERISATION

Having looked in some detail at the way in which the Act and the statutory guidance define the land which is subject to the substantive provisions of the Act, we can now begin to describe the various powers and duties which are conferred upon the enforcing agencies, and also explain the burdens and liabilities which may result from the exercise of those powers and duties.

Site identification

The Act imposes what, at first sight, would seem to be quite substantial site identification responsibilities upon local authorities.[63] Adopting long-familiar language taken from legislation on the matter of statutory nuisances, section 78B(1) of the 1990 Act provides:

> "Every local authority shall cause its area to be inspected from time to time for the purpose–
> (a) of identifying contaminated land; ..."

How extensive is the inspection obligation created by this section? The answer may be found not within the Act itself, but, once again, within the terms of the statutory guidance issued by Government. In this context, as with the very definition of "contaminated land", the statutory guidance is of a mandatory rather than merely recommendatory nature.

The guidance begins by explaining that "in carrying out its inspection duty ... the local authority should take a strategic approach to the identification of land which merits detailed individual inspection."[64] This sentence makes clear that local authorities must be proactive in site identification. They may not merely respond to concerns which may be expressed to them about the condition of sites. Nevertheless, it is also clear that local authorities are not to be expected mindlessly to subject to inspection all land within their areas: the proactive, strategic, approach is intended to produce a targeting and prioritising of sites which may warrant closer investigation.

The strategy to be devised by each local authority is required, amongst other things, to be "rational, ordered and efficient", to be "proportionate to the seriousness of any actual or potential risk", should "seek to ensure that the most pressing and serious problems are located first" and must "ensure that resources are concentrated on investigating areas where the authority is most likely to identify contaminated land".[65] The strategy devised by

---

[62] Circular, para. 6.32.

[63] Generally, *district* councils: of which there exist, in England and Wales, several hundred.

[64] Guidance, Chapter B, Part 3, para. B9.

[65] *ibid.* More than 18 months after the establishment of the new contaminated land regime, it was noted that local authorities faced "two big challenges" before they could commence the systematic

each local authority must be set out in the form of a written document, which should be formally adopted by the authority and published.[66]

It will be evident that the burdens upon individual local authorities as regards this inspection function will vary considerably. Some authorities will have responsibilities in respect of regions where substantial land contamination problems are known, or may be perceived as likely, to exist. Others may operate in areas where much less substantial land contamination problems may be thought to present themselves.[67]

Site inspection

In the implementation of its site investigation strategy each local authority will identify particular areas of land where it is possible that a "pollutant linkage" exists, such that the site may prove to be "contaminated" within the meaning discussed above. In relation to such sites the local authority is required by the guidance to undertake a detailed inspection to allow it to determine whether indeed the land does seem to fall within that legal description.

This may very likely require a visit to the site for the purpose of a visual inspection and limited sampling. This is permissible when, and only when, it is "a reasonable possibility" that a pollutant linkage exists. There may also be required some more intrusive investigation. This is appropriate, and permitted, where there is a "reasonable possibility" that each element of the necessary pollutant linkage will be discovered.[68] It will be seen that the

---

inspection of land in their areas: "First they need to gather all the available data – preferably in a geographical information system (GIS), although by no means all councils possess such software … Next they need to screen the sites on the basis of risk so as to prepare a list of sites for inspection": see (2001) ENDS Report 322 at p. 20.

[66] Guidance, Chapter B, Part 3, para. B12. This had to be done with some expedition: within 15 months of the issuance of the statutory guidance (i.e. autumn 2002). Once adopted each Strategy should periodically be reviewed. At the end of October 2001, it was reported that only 235 of the 353 local authorities in England had published finalized strategies. This figure had increased to 333 (94% of the 353 authorities) by the end of July 2002: see *Dealing with Contaminated Land in England: Progress in 2002 with implementing the Part IIA Regime*, figure 4.1, a report published by the Environment Agency. Although many of the strategies were available on council websites, a recent survey carried out by the National Society for Clean Air (July 2003) revealed, inter alia, that of the 109 local authorities who responded, 40 had not placed their strategies on their websites: see (2003) ENDS Report 342 at p. 11. It has been suggested that a "quick trawl" through the strategies revealed a "wide variation in approaches and in quality": see (2001) ENDS Report 322 at p. 19. Whilst acknowledging that there were variations in strategies according to local circumstances, the Agency reported that "most local authorities have followed a broadly common approach in developing and presenting their strategies" (para.4.2). The common elements included: presenting strategic objectives; preparing a strategic overview; identifying priority areas for inspection; evaluating areas; identifying key activities and dates for progress; dealing with urgent sites, local-authority owned sites and others outside the general prioritisation programme; and, setting a date or triggers for review of the strategy.

[67] In some cases, of course, there is likely to have been a significant discrepancy between perception and reality. An employee of Portsmouth City Council was reported as saying, for example, that: "One rural authority near here thought it didn't have a problem with contaminated land – but it turned out to have 1,200 sites to consider": see (2001) ENDS Report 322 at p. 20.

[68] Guidance, Chapter B, Part 3, B22. Extensive powers of entry and inspection are provided in the Environment Act 1995, s. 108.

legislation and guidance seems to be at pains both to impose obligations upon local authorities as regards site entry and inspection (visual and intrusive), whilst at the same time providing safeguards in the interests of site owners and occupiers. It is clear that purely speculative inspections are not authorised. In this connection it is appropriate also to note the statement in the guidance that a local authority should not carry out an intrusive investigation of a site if a person offers to, and does, provide within a reasonable time detailed information on the condition of the site, such that the local authority may make its determination as to whether the site is contaminated.[69]

"Special sites"

On a local authority becoming alert to the fact that a site may be contaminated it is under a duty to consider whether the site should receive ministerial designation as a "special site".[70] The Act envisages two broad categories of contaminated sites: (a) "special sites"; and (b) other sites. Behind this distinction will lie the choice of agency given responsibility for the exercise of the Act's site "remediation notice" powers. If a site is an "ordinary" contaminated site these functions will be exercised by the district council.[71] If, however, a site is designated as a "special site" the district council's functions will end once the site has been determined by it to be "contaminated". Once designated as a "special site" the exercise of the various new powers and duties attach to the Environment Agency.

What criteria are to be used by district councils in determining whether a site should be referred for such ministerial designation? The Act provides that the criteria shall be prescribed in regulations to be made by the Secretary of State. The Act indicates that the Secretary may, in delimiting the scope of this category, have regard to whether land of a particular description is likely to be contaminated in such a way that *serious*[72] harm or *serious* pollution of water[73] may be caused; and whether the Environment Agency is likely to have special expertise in dealing with the kind of significant harm or pollution associated with the particular kind of contaminated land in question.

The Secretary of State has issued, for this purpose, the Contaminated Land (England) Regulations 2000.[74] The circumstances in which a site must be designated as "special" are listed in regulations 2 and 3, read together with Schedule I. Although the designation of a site as a "special" site may only occur after investigation has demonstrated the site to be, in law, contaminated, the Circular contemplates that:

---

[69] Guidance, Chapter B, Part 3, B23.

[70] 1990 Act, s. 78B(1)(b).

[71] Where the two-tier pattern, of district and county councils, remains.

[72] Not just "significant".

[73] Not just "pollution of water".

[74] SI 2000/227. The National Assembly for Wales has made broadly similar provision for Wales: see the Contaminated Land (Wales) Regulations 2001, SI 2001/2197 (W.157).

"detailed investigation of any *potential* special site [should be] carried out by the Environment Agency, acting on behalf of the local authority."[75]

The Guidance provides an example. Noting that in some instances a site may be "special" by reference to a particular former use which has been made of the land, the Guidance explains:

"This might occur ... where the ... description of land in the Regulations relates to its current or former use, such as land on which a process designated for central control under the Integrated Pollution Control regime has been carried out, or land which is occupied by the Ministry of Defence."[76]

In its first report on the implementation of the Part IIA regime,[77] the Environment Agency noted that by 31st March 2002, 33 sites in England had been determined as contaminated. Of these, 11 had been designated as "special sites".[78] A recent update on the implementation of the Part IIA regime revealed that by 17th June 2003, 58 sites in England had been determined as falling within the statutory definition of contaminated land. Of these, 14 had subsequently been designated as "special sites".[79] In the Agency's report, it was stated that the designation of the 11 special sites occurred in each case "because controlled waters are being, or are likely to be, polluted".[80] Both this report and the figures supplied by the Government reveal, however, that there are a number of potential special sites over which the Agency may subsequently assume regulatory control.[81] Although it is noted that there may be more than one cause of contamination at each of these sites, former contaminative uses include: MOD activities on land; disposal of waste acid tars; chemical weapons; explosives manufacture or processing; and biological weapons. The vast majority, however, are uses which have affected water quality or drinking water supply, or where listed substances have migrated into defined aquifers.[82] Current land use on potential special sites[83] includes: derelict; agriculture; industrial premises; housing; park and recreational; and forestry.[84]

---

[75] Circular, para. 3.14; and Guidance, Chapter B, Part 3, para. B29 (emphasis added).

[76] Guidance, Chapter B, Part 3, para. B28.

[77] *Dealing with Contaminated Land in England: Progress in 2002 with implementing the Part IIA regime.*

[78] Paragraph 5.1.

[79] The figures were supplied by the Environment Minister, Elliot Morley MP, in response to a written question: see (2003) ENDS Report 342 at p. 40.

[80] Paragraph 5.2.

[81] The Agency has agreed to inspect 63 sites at the request of local authorities as potential special sites: see (2003) ENDS Report 342 at p. 40.

[82] See *Dealing with Contaminated Land in England: Progress in 2002 with implementing the Part IIA regime*, figure 5.5.

[83] As with multiple contaminative causes, there may be more than one use to which the land is currently being put.

[84] See the Agency report, at figure 5.6.

SITE NOTIFICATION: REMEDIATION NOTICES

Upon identification[85] of a site as contaminated the local authority is required to give notice of that fact to a variety of parties,[86] including the "owner" of the land, apparent "occupiers", and persons who appear to the authority to be "appropriate" persons within the meaning of the Act.[87] This last category – "appropriate persons" – is defined as persons who, in accordance with Section 78F, may "bear responsibility for any thing which is to be done by way of remediation in any particular case".

The issuance of notices to the categories of persons described above brings into operation a process of consultation as regards the remediation which may be appropriate, and by whom. These important statutory provisions, which seek to promote and provide encouragement for what we may call "voluntary" remediation on the basis of such consultation, are described below under the heading "Remediation by agreement".[88]

Service of notices

Should such purely voluntary action not appear likely to be forthcoming, or appear not to be likely to be adequate, the next stage in the procedures is for the district council (or, if a "special site" the Environment Agency) to prepare a "remediation notice" and to serve that notice on "each person who is an appropriate person" to bear responsibility for remediation.[89] Such remediation notices are required by the Act to specify what each recipient is required to do by way of remediation; and to indicate the dates by which each is required to do each of the things specified.[90]

The required content of remediation notices is further elaborated by regulation 4 of the Contaminated Land (England) Regulations 2000. This provides additionally, inter alia, that notices shall state:

- the name and address of the addressee;
- the location and extent of the contaminated land to which it relates;

---

[85] In terms of the *cogency* of evidence required (of the matters described in detail above) the Circular refers, generally, to the authority being satisfied on the "balance of probabilities". This is the standard of proof in the civil courts in England and Wales. It posits that something is the case if the evidence suggests that this is more likely than not. This is a rather lower standard of proof than that required in the criminal courts: "proof beyond reasonable doubt": Circular, para. 3.23.

[86] Section 78B(3). For precedents relating to notices served pursuant to s. 78B(3) and (4), see Appendix A to *Contaminated Land: The New Regime*, by Tromans and Turrall-Clarke.

[87] Section 78A(9).

[88] See below, pp. 564-565.

[89] Section 78E(1). For a suggested form of a remediation notice served pursuant to this section, see precedent 8 in Appendix A to *Contaminated Land: The New Regime*.

[90] Remediation may need to be planned in accordance with a phased programme. In such circumstances it may not be possible for all remediation requirements to be stated within the initial remediation notice. Further notices may, in due course, be necessary. To date, the use of remediation notices has been extremely limited with only two such notices having been served: see (2001) ENDS Report 323, at pp. 11-12. A survey of 109 local authorities in England carried out by the National Society for Clean Air revealed, inter alia, that none of the authorities had reported serving a notice. In a summary of the NSCA's findings, it has been suggested that this indicates that "councils are wary of getting involved in complex litigation": see (2003) ENDS Report 342 at p. 11.

- the date of any notice given under section 78B, identifying the land as contaminated;
- the capacity in which the person served with the notice is considered to be an "appropriate person": polluter, owner or occupier?
- the significant harm or pollution of controlled waters by reason of which the land is considered to be contaminated;
- the substances by reference to which the land is regarded as contaminated;
- where substances have escaped from other land, the location of that other land;
- the reasons for the enforcing authority's decisions as regards what is required by way of remediation, including indication of how it has applied the statutory guidance on standard of remediation and associated reasonableness requirements;
- where two or more persons are appropriate persons in relation to the contaminated land: the identity and address of each such person, and what each is required to do by way of remediation;
- the reasons for the enforcing authority's decision as regards whether any persons who might otherwise be appropriate persons should not be so regarded in the light of statutory guidance issued under section 78F(6);[91]
- where the remediation notice apportions costs as between appropriate persons, the proportion of costs which each such person is required to bear and the reasons for having reached such apportionment;
- where known to the enforcing authority the name and address of the owner or occupier of the contaminated land;
- where known to the enforcing authority the name and address of any person whose consent is required before any thing required by the notice may be done;
- the penalties which may apply upon conviction[92] for failure, without reasonable excuse, to comply with any of the requirements of the notice;
- that there is a right of appeal against the notice;[93] the grounds upon which such an appeal may be lodged; and the fact that where an appeal is duly made, the notice is suspended pending the final determination or abandonment of the appeal.

It will be evident that an enforcing authority may serve different remediation notices, requiring the doing of different things, on different persons, where this is appropriate in the light of the presence of different substances on the land.[94]

It is also evident that it is a function of the remediation notice, where applicable, to apportion cost responsibilities as between "appropriate persons". Section 78E(3) provides:

---

[91] See below, p. 573.
[92] Under s. 78M(1).
[93] Under s. 78L.
[94] Section 78E(2).

"Where two or more persons are appropriate persons in relation to any particular thing which is to be done by way of remediation, the remediation notice served on each of them shall state the proportion ... of the cost of doing that thing which each of them respectively is liable to bear."

In making such apportionment the enforcing authority is required to act in accordance with the provisions of section 78F(7) and statutory guidance on this crucially important matter. The details of the guidance are considered later in this chapter.

APPEALS

Any person upon whom a remediation notice has been served has 21 days within which to lodge an appeal against that notice.[95] Where the notice has been served by a local authority the appeal lies to the magistrates' court; where the notice has been served by the Environment Agency, in relation to a special site, the appeal lies to the Secretary of State.[96]

On an appeal the appellate authority must quash the notice if it is satisfied that there is a material defect in the notice. In cases other than where a material defect is disclosed the appellate authority may confirm the notice (with or without modification), or may quash the notice.[97] Where a notice is confirmed the appellate authority may extend the period of time specified within the notice for doing what is required by the notice.[98] In any case where an appellate authority intends to modify a notice in a way which is less favourable to the appellant the provisions of regulation 12 of the Contaminated Land (England) Regulations 2000 apply. This requires that the appellant should be given notice of this intention and be afforded an opportunity to be heard. If this opportunity is taken up, certain other interested parties must be afforded a similar opportunity. It is also provided that an appellate authority may, once such notice of proposed modification has been afforded, refuse to permit the appeal subsequently to be withdrawn.

---

[95] Section 78L(1).

[96] From the magistrates' court there may lie a further appeal to the High Court. Appeal may be lodged by the original appellant, the enforcing authority or any other "appropriate person" named in the notice or who exercised their right to appear at the appeal hearing (regulation 13). This appeal does not appear to be limited, as is commonly the case, to points of law. No right of appeal, in contrast, lies following an appeal decision by the Secretary of State: the Circular warns that "once a decision letter has been issued, the decision is final, and the Secretary of State and the inspector can no longer consider any representations or make any further comments on the merits or otherwise of the case". The Circular does, however, acknowledge that in certain circumstances a decision of the Secretary of State may be challengable by way of judicial review (Circular, Annex 4, para. 75) or be the subject of a complaint of maladministration made to the Parliamentary Commissioner for Administration via an MP.

[97] Section 78L(2).

[98] Section 78L(3).

The grounds for any such appeal are laid down in regulation 7 of the Contaminated Land (England) Regulations 2000.[99] This regulation lists some 19 grounds, including:

- that in determining that the land in question is contaminated land the enforcing authority has failed to act in accordance with the statutory guidance on the definition and identification of contaminated land, or has "unreasonably identified" all or any of the land as contaminated;

- that in determining a requirement of the notice the enforcing authority has failed to have had regard to the statutory guidance on the remediation of contaminated land, or has "unreasonably required" the appellant to do any thing by way of remediation;

- that the enforcing authority has unreasonably determined the appellant to be the appropriate person to bear responsibility for any thing required by the notice to be done by way of remediation;

- that the enforcing authority unreasonably failed to determine that some person in addition to the appellant is an appropriate person in relation to any thing required to be done by way of remediation;[100]

- that the appellant should have been regarded as excluded from liability in relation to any thing required by the notice, following the statutory guidance issued on the exclusion of liability of appropriate persons;

- that the proportion of costs to be borne by the appellant has not been assessed properly in accordance with the statutory guidance on the apportionment of costs as between appropriate persons;

- that the enforcing authority has issued an immediate notice on the grounds of imminent danger of serious harm or serious pollution of controlled waters in circumstances where the authority could not reasonably have come to the conclusion that the land was in such a condition that such imminent danger exists;

---

[99] SI 2000/227.

[100] Note in this connection the terms of regulation 7(2): a person who claims not to be an appropriate person on the basis that he or she did not cause or knowingly permit the substances to be on the land may only benefit from this ground of appeal if he "claims to have found some other person who is an appropriate person" by reason of having so behaved. Mere innocence will not found a successful appeal – the appellant has to be able to point to the real culprit. However, "claims to have found" may mean something less than "has found someone who may reasonably be thought": but perhaps an absurd "claim" will not be considered a real claim. A person served with a notice who seeks to contest that he or she caused or knowingly permitted substances (etc.), but who cannot claim to have found a more appropriate recipient of the notice, may fare better by way of judicial review than under this restricted ground of appeal. In similar vein, a person may claim not to be an appropriate person because he or she has been served as an owner or occupier for the time being of the contaminated land and that no owner or occupier may be an appropriate person because of the existence (or possible existence were reasonable inquiry to have been made) of an appropriate person within the "caused or knowingly permitted" category. For such a person to satisfy this ground of appeal, however, he or she must "claim to have found" some such other person.

- that the enforcing authority has unreasonably failed to be satisfied that appropriate remediation will take place without service of a remediation notice;

- that the enforcing authority should have decided that the appellant should have benefited from the hardship provisions of section 78N(3)(e), so that the authority itself had power to carry out the remediation and was precluded from serving such notice on the appellant;

- that a period specified in the notice within which the appellant is required to do any thing is not reasonably sufficient for the purpose;

- that the notice seeks to make an insolvency practitioner, an official receiver or other receiver or manager personally liable in breach of the limits on such liability under section 78X(3)(a) and (4);

- that the notice contravenes section 78YB as regards the interaction between Part IIA and other regimes under which cleanup of pollution may be ordered under the integrated pollution control provisions of Part I of the Environmental Protection Act 1990 and the waste management licensing provisions of Part II of that Act.

The procedures for appeals are prescribed in regulations 8 and 9: the former applying to appeals to the magistrates' court, the latter to appeals to the Secretary of State. Where appeal lies to the magistrates' court it is anticipated that cases will ordinarily be heard by stipendiary magistrates.[101] Where appeal lies to the Secretary of State most cases will be decided by inspectors.[102] In some cases, however, decisions will be "recovered" by the Secretary of State who will reach his or her decision in the light of a written report from an inspector.

The standard procedure on appeals to the Secretary of State will involve an assessment of the appeal on the basis of written representations.[103] However, a hearing will be arranged if either the appellant or the Environment Agency so requests, or the Secretary of State considers a hearing desirable. Such hearings will ordinarily take place in public. Exceptionally, however, the inspector conducting the hearing may decide that a hearing be held, or be held to some extent, in private. This may be appropriate, for example, in cases where pleas for privacy are warranted on grounds of commercial confidentiality or national security.[104] In addition to appeals being dealt with by written representations or hearings, it is provided that the Secretary of State may order that an appeal involve the convening of a public local inquiry where this is in his or her view

---

[101] Circular, Annex 4, para. 48.
[102] Section 78L(6) and Circular, Annex 4, para. 60.
[103] The normal procedure is summarised in the Circular at Annex 4, para. 65. It includes a site visit by the inspector, accompanied by relevant parties.
[104] Circular, Annex 4, para. 69.

desirable.[105] This is anticipated to be appropriate for "particularly complex or locally controversial cases".[106]

Where an appeal is lodged against a remediation notice this has the effect of suspending that notice until the final determination of the appeal or the abandonment of the appeal.[107]

Costs may be awarded by the magistrates' court in accordance with section 64 of the Magistrates Courts Act 1980: power to award costs where just and reasonable. Where the appeal is to the Secretary of State costs may be awarded only in cases where there has been a hearing or a public local inquiry. Where, as will be most common, the matter is dealt with on the basis of written representations each party must meet his or her own costs. The principles upon which costs may be expected to be awarded following a hearing or a public local inquiry are set out in DoE Circular 8/93, describing the principles applicable in the planning appeals context. The principles there described seem less generous than in the magistrates' court. The starting-point would seem to be the same as with written representations: each party should bear his or her own costs, unless there can be shown to have been unreasonable behaviour leading to unnecessary expense.

URGENT REMEDIAL ACTION

Immediate notices

In any case where it may appear to the enforcing authority that there is an imminent danger of serious harm or serious pollution of controlled waters being caused by an identified pollution linkage the authority may need to ensure that some remediation action is taken as a matter of urgency.

The Circular explains:

> "It is likely that any remediation action carried out on an urgent basis will be only a part of the total remediation scheme for the relevant land or waters as not all the remediation actions will need to be carried out urgently."[108]

Where need arises for such urgent remediation action the enforcing authority may, in respect of those actions, proceed without having engaged in the consultations and allowed to elapse the three months interval

---

[105] Regulation 14(1). There have not been provided any procedural rules specific to this kind of public local inquiry. However, the Circular, Annex 4, para. 70 states that the inquiries will be "conducted in accordance with the spirit of the Town and Country Planning (Inquiries Procedures) Rules".

[106] Circular, Annex 4, para. 70.

[107] Regulation 14. The suspension of the notice may make it necessary for the enforcing authority to consider whether it is necessary for it to take urgent remediation action of its own. Its power to recoup the costs of such action from the appellant may then depend on the outcome of that appeal: for example, in a situation where the appeal is on the grounds that the party served is not an "appropriate person".

[108] Circular, Annex 2, para. 5.2.

between notification of appropriate persons that land is contaminated and the service of the remediation notice – that is, the three months consultation period which seeks to promote voluntary cleanup. Instead, the enforcing authority may serve a remediation notice on an urgent basis. The rules, to be described below, about the persons upon whom such a notice may be served, and the rules about "exclusion" and "apportionment" apply nevertheless in the normal way.

Action by the enforcing authority

The procedure described above simply by-passes the three months period during which, following service of notice that land is contaminated, an enforcing authority may not serve a remediation notice. It does not follow, of course, that it may be *practicable* for there to be immediate service of a remediation notice. For example, the enforcing authority may be aware of an urgent situation in terms of continuing harm or pollution of water but not yet have the information it needs in order to be confident about the persons who should be regarded as the "appropriate persons" upon whom to serve such a remediation notice. Moreover, even where an enforcing authority is able to serve a remediation notice promptly it does not follow that remedial action will follow immediately upon the service of a remediation notice. For example, an appeal may be lodged against the notice, and the requirements of the notice may thereby be suspended pending the outcome of that appeal. In such circumstances as these it may be that the enforcing authority takes the view that the matter is of such urgency that it should undertake remedial action itself. The provisions about costs recovery where such action has been taken are considered later in this chapter.[109]

REMEDIATION BY AGREEMENT

Before it may serve a remediation notice in respect of any site, an enforcing authority is required to "reasonably endeavour" to consult a variety of persons: principally persons upon whom such a notice may be served and also the site's owners and occupiers.[110]

The purpose of this requirement would seem to be to provide a full opportunity to those persons with closest knowledge of the site, and with the most interest in there being chosen a cost-effective and minimally disruptive set of remedial measures, to contribute in a constructive way to remediation decisions.

The policy of Government is clear. The Circular states:

---

[109] See below, p. 606.

[110] Even where not subject to liabilities in this situation (Class A persons having been found) the site's owners and occupiers will understandably have an interest in knowing from an early time that remedial actions may be imminent.

"It is the Government's intention that, wherever practicable, remediation should proceed by agreement rather than by formal action by the enforcing authority."[111]

The consultation requirement referred to above is supplemented and supported by a provision that there may be no service of a remediation notice during this consultation period.[112] Furthermore, the Act provides that an enforcing authority "shall not serve a remediation notice on a party if and so long as ... the authority is satisfied that appropriate things are being, or will be, done by way of remediation without the service of a remediation notice on that person".[113]

It will be evident that clear opportunity is provided for persons who might shoulder remedial liabilities under the Act to be proactive in the development of remedial solutions, and to avoid the operation of formal statutory procedures by providing credible assurances as regards their proposed remedial operations.

In cases where remediation is "voluntary" there are provisions which will secure some transparency as regards what might otherwise have seemed likely to be an all too private "deal" between the remediating party and the enforcing authority. The enforcing authority is under a duty to prepare and publish a reasoned document which will indicate what remediation would have been required under a remediation notice. The document must also indicate the reasons why the authority is satisfied that it is precluded from serving the statutory notice (that is, the reasons why it considers that appropriate remediation will occur without the service of that notice).[114]

MEANING OF "REMEDIATION"?

The Act defines this concept quite broadly.[115] It includes not only the process of actual cleanup of a site,[116] but also extends to:

---

[111] Circular, Annex 2, para. 6.6.

[112] The provision is a little complex, but broadly provides for a three-month period during which such discussion may take place. Special provision is made, however, for urgent situations.

[113] Section 78H(5).

[114] Section 78H(6). The document is a "remediation declaration". The legislation also provides for the making of a "remediation statement" by the party engaging in "voluntary" cleanup. This will describe, amongst other things, the measures to be undertaken and the expected completion times (s. 78H(7)). Recent figures from DEFRA reveal that since the Part IIA regime came into force, remediation statements have been made in 24 cases: see (2003) ENDS Report 342 at p. 40.

All these various documents appear on the statutory registers maintained by local authorities under section 78R (discussed below at pp. 616-618). These registers contain a variety of entries indicating what statutory procedures have been performed in relation to a site – for example, the notifications and notices described above. They do *not*, however, purport to indicate authoritatively the contaminated or other state of the land.

[115] Section 78A(7). It has been noted that "among his many other achievements", the draftsman of the Environmental Protection Act 1990 and the Environment Act 1995 "managed to invent several words and expressions not known to the Editor of the Shorter Oxford Dictionary", including the word "remediation": see D. Woolley's "Contaminated Land: The Real World" [2002] JPL 5 at p. 6.

(i) pre-cleanup assessment of the condition of the land in question, controlled waters affected by that land, and land adjoining or adjacent to that land; and

(ii) inspections of the site from time to time, after the cleanup has been completed, for the purpose of keeping under review the condition of the land or adjacent waters.

The statutory guidance confirms the Act's approach, stressing that a distinction must be drawn between investigation and assessment which is necessary *in order to characterise the land as contaminated*, and investigation and assessment which may subsequently be necessary *in order to determine the appropriate remedial actions.* Investigation and assessment in the latter situation will be an aspect of the remediation of the site.

The implication is clear. The matter is well explained in the statutory guidance:

> "The overall process of remediation on any land or waters may require a phased approach, with different remediation actions being carried out in sequence. For example, the local authority may have obtained sufficient information about relevant land or waters to enable it to identify the land as falling within the definition of contaminated land, but that information may not be sufficient information for the enforcing authority to be able to specify any particular remedial treatment action as being appropriate. Further assessment actions may be needed in any case of this kind as part of the remediation scheme ...

> Where it is necessary for the remediation scheme as a whole to be phased, a single remediation notice may not be able to include all of the remediation actions which could eventually be needed. ... In due course the authority may need to serve further remediation notices ...

> However, before serving any further remediation notice, the enforcing authority must be satisfied that the contaminated land which was originally identified still appears to it to meet the definition [of contaminated land] ..."[117]

An important consequence of the extended definition of remediation will be evident. It shifts a part of the investigatory burdens from the enforcing authorities onto the "appropriate persons" with remediation responsibilities. Once sufficient evidence has been gleaned (at public expense) to characterise the land as contaminated, the cost of further investigatory work shifts from the public purse to that of the "appropriate" persons with remediation responsibilities.

---

[116] Which may include or involve measures designed simply to prevent substances causing harm or pollution of water (without the removal or treatment of those substances).

[117] Statutory Guidance, Annex 3, Chapter C, paras C12–15.

STANDARD OF REMEDIATION

Cost-benefit considerations

We have already referred to the clear policy of Government that remediation should be based upon the "suitable for use" principle, rather than on notions of "multi-functionality". Moreover, both the Act and the associated statutory guidance temper even this relatively relaxed standard of remediation by reference to cost-benefit considerations.

In this connection the Act contains some potentially important limiting provisions which express clear concern lest the Act's provisions might impose undue economic burdens. So, it is provided in section 78E(4):

> "The only things by way of remediation which the enforcing authority may ... require to be done ... are things which it considers reasonable, having regard to –
> (a)   the cost which is likely to be involved; and
> (b)   the seriousness of the harm, or pollution of controlled waters, in question."

Section 78E(5) provides that in determining what is or is not to be regarded as reasonable for this purpose an enforcing authority shall "have regard to" statutory guidance. The contexts in which an enforcing authority may have to have regard to the guidance for this purpose are:

- when determining what remediation action it should specify in a remediation notice;[118]
- when satisfying itself that appropriate remediation is being, or will be , carried out without service of a notice;[119]
- when deciding what remediation action it should carry out itself.[120]

In order to comply with the guidance the enforcing authority will need to prepare an assessment of costs likely to be involved and a statement of the benefits likely to result. The guidance provides:

> "The enforcing authority should regard a remediation action as being reasonable for the purpose of section 78E(4) if an assessment of the costs likely to be involved and of the resulting benefits shows that those benefits justify incurring those costs. Such an assessment should include the preparation of an estimate of the costs likely to be involved and of a statement of the benefits likely to result. This latter statement need not necessarily attempt to ascribe a financial value to these benefits."[121]

---

[118] Section 78E(1).

[119] Section 78H(5)(b). The Circular indicates that an enforcing authority should be satisfied of this: "that remediation would remediate the relevant land or waters to an equivalent, or better, standard than would be achieved by the remediation action ... the authority could ... otherwise specify in a remediation notice". Circular, Annex 3, Chapter C, para. C11.

[120] Section 78N.

[121] Statutory Guidance, Annex 3, Chapter C, para. C30.

The guidance includes significant statements, in this connection, about the "timing of expenditure" and the "realisation of benefits". It states that:

> "In assessing the reasonableness of any remediation, the enforcing authority should make due allowance for the fact that the timing of expenditure and the realisation of benefits is relevant to the balance of costs and benefits. In particular, the assessment should recognise that:
>
> (a) expenditure which is delayed to a future date will have a lesser impact on the person defraying it than would an equivalent cash sum to be spent immediately;
>
> (b) there may be a gain from achieving benefits earlier but this may also involve extra expenditure: the authority should consider whether the gain justifies the extra costs. This applies, in particular, where natural processes, managed or otherwise, would over time bring about remediation; and
>
> (c) there may be evidence that the same benefits will be achievable in the foreseeable future at a significantly lower cost, for example, through the development of new techniques or as part of a wider scheme of development or redevelopment."[122]

However, at this stage in its deliberations, the issue of reasonable costs should not be assessed by the enforcing authority in the light of what, in other contexts, is sometimes termed the "personal equation":

> "The identity or financial standing of any person who may be required to pay for any remediation are not relevant factors in the determination of whether the costs of that action are, or are not, reasonable …"[123]

When assessing, for this balancing purpose, the costs likely to be involved in remediation the enforcing authority will need to keep in mind the extensive meaning of remediation (considered above). The costs to be considered will comprise:

> "…
>
> (a) all initial costs (including tax payable) of carrying out the remediation action, including feasibility studies, design, specification and management, as well as works and operations, and making good afterwards;
>
> (b) any on-going costs of managing and maintaining the remedial action; and

---

[122] Paragraph C32.

[123] Paragraph C33. Although not relevant to the assessment of whether the remediation action is reasonable, the "personal equation" factors referred to may be relevant to subsequent questions about whether the enforcing authority can impose the cost of such remediation on that person, either by way of remediation notice or by costs recoupment where the remedial action is taken by the enforcing authority itself. See, further, below, pp. 572-582 and 606-614.

(c)   any relevant disruption costs."[124]

For this purpose the expression "relevant disruption costs" is explained as:

"… depreciation in the value of land or other interest, or other loss or damage, which is likely to result from the carrying out of the remediation action in question …"[125]

In assessing reasonableness of cost the guidance states that "it shall be a necessary condition of an action being reasonable that … there is no alternative scheme which would achieve the same standard of remediation for a lower overall cost."[126]

In this way there may be achieved some protection for "appropriate persons" against being called upon to remediate in an unnecessarily expensive way; together with some potential for more in the way of remediation legitimately to be required. Given that enforcing authorities should, in accordance with this guidance, have made themselves (or be made) aware of the cheapest effective options which may secure each level of potential remediation, it may feel it may reasonably require a higher level of remediation to be attained than would otherwise have been the case.

So much for the "cost" side of the equation: what about the "benefits" which may result from any proposed remediation. The statutory guidance states that for the purpose of assessing the reasonableness of a proposed remediation there should be considered, inter alia, the "context in which the effects" (i.e. the pollution-linkage) are occurring or may occur.[127] The significance of this would seem to be that it requires that there be consideration given to questions such as whether the receptor or the controlled waters have already been harmed or polluted by other means, and whether further harm or pollution *from the contaminated site* will materially affect its condition? The converse of this formulation may seem equally significant: will removal of this pollution-linkage produce material benefits to the harmed receptor or the polluted water? If the answer is "no" it will be difficult for an enforcing authority to conclude that the cost of a remedial action, producing little by way of benefit, would be reasonable. In a case where the harm or the pollution of water is a result of impacts from a number of sites, this principle would seem to make difficult any action

---

[124] Statutory Guidance, Chapter C, para. C34. Costs should be included "even where they would not result in payments to others by the person carrying out the remediation. For example, a company may choose to use its own staff or equipment to carry out the remediation…" (Chapter C, para. C36).

[125] Paragraph C35. The costs are to be assessed by reference to the compensation payable under s. 78G(5) – compensation which might actually be payable if the appropriate person is not the owner of the land and must exercise a statutory right of entry onto the land for remediation purposes; or, where the appropriate person *is* the owner of the land, the amount of compensation which would have been payable had this not been the case and such a right of entry been necessary. See further, on compensation under section 78G(5), below p. 614.

[126] Statutory Guidance, Chapter C, para. C37(a).

[127] Paras C39 and 41.

being taken except in a co-ordinated and collective way against those with responsibilities in respect of each, or most, of those sites.

Best practicable techniques

The statutory guidance provides some further elaboration of the characteristics of the remediation requirements to be imposed. It provides that:

> "In deciding what represents the best practicable technique for any particular remediation, the enforcing authority should look for the method of achieving the desired results which, in the light of the nature and volume of the significant pollutant concerned and the timescale within which remediation is required:
>
> (a) is reasonable, taking account of the guidance ...; and
> (b) represents the best combination of the following qualities:
>   (i)   practicability ...
>   (ii) effectiveness ...
>   (iii) durability in maintaining that effectiveness over the timescale within which the significant harm or pollution of controlled waters may occur."[128]

In terms of practicability,[129] effectiveness[130] and durability[131] the enforcing authority is required to base its judgments on "authoritative scientific and technical advice".[132] Given that the techniques for remediating contaminated sites are developing rapidly, with innovative techniques being promoted and supported by "manufacturer" claims to achieve objectives ever more effectively and cheaply, an issue must arise as regards the circumstances in which such innovative – and therefore not yet tried and tested – techniques should be required by enforcing authorities. The guidance states:

> "In some instances, there may be little firm information on which to assess particular remediation actions, packages or schemes. For example, a particular technology or technique may not have been subject previously to field-scale pilot testing in circumstances comparable to those to be found on the contaminated land in question. Where this is the case, the enforcing authority should consider the effectiveness and durability which it appears likely that any such action would achieve, and the practicability of its use, on the

---

[128] Statutory Guidance, Chapter C, para. C19.
[129] Further explained at paras C48-50. Note that some remediation techniques may themselves require regulatory approvals. Time taken to obtain such approvals may be relevant to the practicability of a particular technique.
[130] Further explained at paras C58-60. In some instances a balance may need to be drawn between the most effective solutions (which may take a little time) and more speedy solutions (which may be less effective).
[131] Further explained at paras C61-63.
[132] Paragraph C21.

basis of information it does have at that time (for example information derived from laboratory or other ... testing)."[133]

In other words, although some caution should be observed, the absence of a tested record for innovative techniques should not rule out the specification of such techniques where there may be good reason to think they may satisfy requirements of practicability, effectiveness and durability.

Where a new technique may be cheaper than other more familiar approaches to remediation it may well be the "appropriate person" who may propose that that technique be specified. Some reassurance is offered to enforcing authorities who might, on the evidence, have been reluctant to adhere to such a request:

> "If the person who will be carrying out the remediation proposes the use of an innovative approach to remediation, the enforcing authority should be prepared to agree to that approach being used ... notwithstanding the fact that there is little available information on the basis of which the authority can assess its likely effectiveness. If the approach to remediation proves to be ineffective, further remediation actions may be required, for which the person proposing the innovative approach will be liable."[134]

While we are considering techniques for remediation it ought to be recalled that the statutory concept of *remediation* and the colloquial expression *site cleanup* do not have an identical meaning. The difference is most apparent in the situation where a site may be contaminated (in law) because of its potential to do harm or to pollute controlled water. Remediation will involve any action which may remove that potential to cause harm or to pollute water. One way of so doing will be to clean up the site – to remove or to render harmless the contaminating substances on that site. However, alternative strategies, not involving site cleanup may also achieve this objective. A site which threatens the quality of adjacent controlled waters may be remediated by the introduction of a physical barrier to prevent the contaminants from entering that water. Another example may be offered. It may be that a site is to be regarded as contaminated by reference to the possibility of harm to a receptor (e.g. children playing on the land). In this situation, in keeping with the "suitable for use" approach, one potential remedial action may be to remove the receptor from the site: to bar entry to the site and to support this by the provision of fencing and other security devices for such time as the contamination may be likely to present risk. These examples illustrate how remediation sufficient to render land no longer legally contaminated may involve actions which are quite different from, and which do not involve, actual cleanup of the contamination in question.

---

[133] Paragraph C45.
[134] Paragraph C46.

REMEDIAL LIABILITY

Probably the most critically significant issue in the design of a legal regime for the remediation of contamination is the determination of where the costs involved in securing that remediation shall fall.

The problem is somewhat intractable. The difficulties do not, however, stem from the breadth of variety of basic choices. Indeed the number of different candidate categories for the imposition of cleanup financial responsibilities is really quite small, the choice being broadly between those whose conduct may have given rise in some way to the contamination, owners and occupiers (present and/or past), and the State (in any of its manifestations – central, regional, local government). Given the unlikelihood, in current times, of any Government proposing a regime in which the burdens fall upon its own purse, the range of potential parties to bear such financial burdens becomes still smaller.

Of course, the range of possibilities becomes larger when it is appreciated that cost burdens may be spread across more than one of these potential categories. Moreover, even within each of the categories there may be more than one candidate to bear the financial burden. In such instances, there will then arise an issue of whether, and how, the law should seek to determine how the overall cost burden should be shared as between the different categories of responsible party, or between the several responsible parties within any one category.

The *equity* of any proposed solution is likely, given the substantial sums of money commonly involved, to give rise to a good deal of controversy. Perhaps prospects of progress lie more in concentration on more *pragmatic* issues, in asking what arrangements or schemes are the most likely to be workable in practice, to impose costs on parties with an ability to bear the costs involved and to produce the most legal certainty as regards these environmental liabilities? What solutions to these questions are to be found within the English legislation?

Once again, the primary legislation does not provide all the answers. The new Part IIA contains some quite complex provisions on this matter, but the critically important detail has been left to the statutory guidance.

The Act approaches the matter of the identification of parties upon whom burdens may fall by way of its indication of the persons upon whom an enforcing authority is required to serve a remediation notice. Such persons are referred to in the legislation as "appropriate persons". Remediation notices should be served on *all* persons ("each person") whom the enforcing authority considers, in the circumstances, to fall within this statutory category.[135]

---

[135] Section 78E(1).

"Appropriate persons"

The concept of "appropriate person" comprises two broad categories. The first category are persons who may be said to possess primary liability under the new legislation. The second category are persons with a secondary liability, a liability which will only be triggered in certain statutorily defined circumstances. These secondary liable parties may be thought of as bearing a "reserve", or "contingent", liability. The statutory guidance refers to the first of these two categories as "Class A persons"; the second, as "Class B persons".

Class A appropriate persons

The definition of those with *primary* liability is as follows:

> "... any person, or any of the persons, who caused or knowingly permitted the substances, or any of the substances, by reason of which the contaminated land is such to be in, on or under that land ..."[136]

The persons upon whom the Act imposes primary responsibility to remediate a site are, therefore, those whose conduct has *caused* the contamination and those who have *knowingly permitted* the contamination of the land. In other words principal liability will attach to those whom we might label, broadly, the "polluter(s)" of the land.

The choice of such persons as parties with principal responsibility reflects a governmental wish to act in accordance with the "polluter pays principle" of environmental policy. This seems to have been regarded by government as almost an inevitable, or given, feature of any new scheme; a basic feature upon which little discussion, debate, justification or assessment of practicalities seems to have occurred. This is, of course, in itself, neither to condemn nor to support the substance of this policy choice: it is simply a reflection of the influence which this broad general principle of environmental policy may, on occasions at least, possess.

The choice by the draftsman of the words "causing" and "knowingly permitting" to describe the necessary link between an individual and the land contamination involves utilisation of concepts which, to adopt the language of the Circular, have "been used as a basis for establishing liability in environmental legislation for more than 100 years".[137] In particular these concepts have for long formed the test for criminal liability under the principal water pollution legislation.[138] The concepts have been

---

[136] Section 78F(2).

[137] Circular, Annex 2, para 9.8. Lawrence and Lee argue, however, that although this may be so, "it is only comparatively recently that these tests have been the subject of judicial scrutiny by the higher courts": see "Permitting Uncertainty: Owners, Occupiers and Responsibility for Remediation" (2003) 66 MLR 261 at p. 263.

[138] See, now, Water Resources Act 1991, s. 85. Whilst recognising that this has been the case in the context of water pollution and waste-related offences, Lawrence and Lee nevertheless make the valid point that: "the exact ambit of its meaning ['knowingly permitting'] in the context of the contaminated land provision of Part IIA EPA '90 has yet to be determined by the courts": *ibid.*

discussed fully earlier in this book.[139] It will be remembered from that discussion that whereas the notions of "knowledge" and "capacity to prevent" introduce some measure of fault liability into the "knowingly permitted" category, those who may be "appropriate persons" under the "causing" part of the definition will bear a strict liability. If their operations, broadly regarded, may be said to have caused the contamination of the land they will not escape being characterised as "appropriate persons" by virtue only of the fact that the contamination may thereby have been caused without their knowledge, and without any carelessness on their part. Even demonstration of all due diligence will avail them nothing.[140]

As regards the "causing" requirement the statutory guidance notes that there will need to have been some involvement on the part of the person concerned "in some active operation, or series of operations, to which the presence of the pollutant is attributable".[141] However, as was seen in our earlier discussion of the interpretation of "causing" under the water pollution legislation,[142] the cause of the presence of a substance may be equally attributable to a failure to have acted as to a positive act on the part of the potential appropriate person.[143]

As regards the meaning of "knowingly permit" the Circular draws attention to the following words used by Lord Ferrers whilst steering the Environment Bill through the House of Lords:[144]

> "The test of "knowingly permit" would require both knowledge that the substances in question were in, on or under the land and possession of the power to prevent such a substance being there."[145]

Perhaps, in the particular context under discussion the final phrase in this quotation would better have been expressed as:

> "power to have prevented the substance becoming present on the land or power to have secured the removal of that substance from the land."

That a person may become a Class A "appropriate party" on the basis of having failed to have removed a substance put on land by a third party

---

[139] See above, pp. 299-331.

[140] See, for example, *CPC (UK) Ltd* v *National Rivers Authority* [1995] Env. LR 388.

[141] Circular, Annex A, para. 9.9.

[142] See above, p. 300.

[143] See for example, *Alphacell* v *Woodward* [1972] 2 All ER 475 (requirement of involvement in active operation satisfied by fact that the defendant operated an industrial plant from which the pollutants entered controlled waters: not relevant that the reason for the entry was an omission to have cleared vegetation and debris so as to have permitted continued effective operation of pumping arrangements).

[144] House of Lords Hansard (11th July 1995, col. 1497).

[145] Lawrence and Lee have argued that: "The use of the word *prevent* implies taking advance measures against the presence of the substances and seems to align with the reasoning of Lord Hoffmann in the *Empress Cars* case in the sense that a failure to prevent involves an element of causation": see (2003) 66 MLR 261 at p. 267.

seems evident. The issue in such a case will be to determine when a person who has acquired knowledge of the presence of such a substance may be regarded, through inaction or inadequate action, as having permitted its continued presence? On this matter the Circular offers some degree of reassurance. It considers the situation of a person who has been informed of the presence of a pollutant on his or her land: a pollutant which it cannot be shown that that person caused to be there. In such a case, that person would only be characterised as having knowingly permitted its continued presence:

> "...where the person had the ability to take steps to … remove that presence and had a reasonable opportunity to do so."[146]

It is not entirely clear what is meant here by "ability": is it "legal power", or is it "technical ability", or is it "financial or other capacity"? The key concept would seem likely, however, to be that of "reasonable opportunity" to have prevented the presence of, or have removed, the substance; raising the question, unanswered by the Act or the guidance, whether this should be judged *objectively*, or *subjectively* (i.e. with or without reference to the particular circumstances of the particular person under consideration).

The Circular provides some reassurance also to banks and lenders in cases where their clients may have caused or knowingly permitted the presence of pollutants on land. Again, the words Earl Ferrers used during Parliamentary debate are quoted:

> "I am advised that there is no judicial decision which supports the contention that a lender, by virtue of the act of lending money only, could be said to have "knowingly permitted" the substances to be in, on or under the land such that it is contaminated land.[147] This would be the case if for no other reason than the lender, irrespective of any covenants it may have required from the polluter as to its environmental behaviour, would have no permissive rights over the land in question to prevent contamination occurring or continuing."[148]

The act of lending money will of itself, therefore, not suffice to amount to "knowingly permitting" the presence of a contaminating substance, even, it would appear, where the money lent is closely connected with the activities which have resulted in that presence of those substances on the land. Being the source of the monetary fuel which has made possible a borrower's polluting activities is not intended, it seems, to be sufficient. Nevertheless,

---

[146] Circular, Annex A, para. 9.12. Accordingly, *mere* knowledge of the presence of a pollutant on land does not transform a mere owner/occupier (potential Class B party) into a knowing permitter Class A party. See also, Circular, Annex A, para. 9.13.

[147] Lawrence and Lee have argued in relation to these words that: "Of course, it would be extraordinary if there were such cases given that the law was in the process of introduction". Accordingly, they rightly assume, it is submitted, "that Earl Ferrers meant that there were no cases in which lenders, by virtue of powers over a borrower, had been found to have knowingly permitted any environmental offence": see (2003) 66 MLR 261 at p. 264.

[148] House of Lords Hansard (11th July 1995, col. 1497).

a lender which has become more closely involved in a borrower's affairs than simply having lent money – perhaps becoming a joint venturer in the success of a funded project – cannot be so certain of not falling within the concept under consideration.

In addition to involving, at any rate for those within the "causing" category, *strict* liability, the liability to remediate which the Act imposes upon such Class A persons may also be characterised as *retrospective*: a present day liability existing irrespective of the legality or illegality of the behaviour in question at the time when it occurred. Even where the past behaviour may have involved the commission of some illegality (e.g. an offence in relation to the deposit of waste on land) the new liabilities may be retrospective in the sense of being of a different kind and magnitude to the liabilities which existed contemporaneously with those actions.

Where the present contamination relates to substances whose harmful potential may have become appreciated only in the years since their initial deposit, this marks a policy approach to environmental liability which, it may be noted, is rather different from that adopted quite recently by the House of Lords in the context of *tortious civil liability*.[149]

Scope of Class A remedial liability

The scope of the remedial liability imposed by the new legal regime upon persons who have "caused or knowingly permitted" contamination is restricted by the following important provision:

> "A person shall only be an appropriate person ... in relation to things which are to be done by way of remediation which are ... referable to substances which he caused or knowingly permitted to be present, in on or under the contaminated land in question."[150]

This provides some protection in situations where a "polluter" may have contaminated only a part of a site (remedial responsibility relating to that part only) or where the remediation necessary in relation to the substances for which that person is responsible is of a different kind from that which is required as a consequence of the presence also of other pollutants.

Such "severability" between remediation referable to the substances deposited by different polluters may, however, in many situations prove to be practically unachievable. It seems likely that the more typical case will be one in which the various pollutants have intermixed across a site, in such a way that it will not be practically possible to identify parts only of

---

[149] See *Cambridge Water Co Ltd* v *Eastern Counties Leather plc* [1994] 2 WLR 53: liability in nuisance and under the strict liability rule in *Rylands* v *Fletcher* is tempered by a limitation that the strict liability only applies to kinds of harm (albeit quite broadly categorised) which were foreseeable at the time the defendant's actions occurred. See, further, above pp. 187-198.
[150] Section 78F(3).

an overall remediation strategy which are referable to the presence of particular substances put there by identifiable parties.[151]

No Class A polluter(s) found?

It will be remembered that in addition to the primarily responsible persons (Class A), described above, the Act defines a further group of persons who may bear a contingent or secondary liability (Class B) . It is necessary therefore to indicate the *circumstances* in which this contingent liability may come into operation, and the *persons* who may fall within this category.[152]

The matter is governed by section 78F(4), which provides:

> "(4) If no person has, after reasonable inquiry, been found who is ... an appropriate person [with primary liability, as described above] to bear responsibility for the things which are to be done by way of remediation, the owner or occupier for the time being of the land in question is an appropriate person."

In other words the Class B category may be described as *current owners and occupiers*,[153] and their contingent liability comes into being where no Class A appropriate person to bear responsibility, after reasonable inquiry, *has been found.*[154]

Given that the fact of just a single Class A party having been "found" will rule out liability on the part of any potential Class B party[155] it will clearly

---

[151] In such a case an appropriate person will not benefit from section 78F(3). However, the enforcing authority will have to determine appropriate apportionment of the cost of remediation. This will be determined in accordance with the guidance discussed below at pp. 602-606.

[152] It may also be noted that the liability of these secondary parties is not as extensive as that of Class A parties. It extends to liability to cleanup contamination which is causing or threatening "significant harm". It does, not, however, extend to liability to cleanup contamination where the purpose of the remediation is to clean up or protect *controlled water* (for example, rivers, streams or groundwater): see s. 78J.

[153] These persons will, by definition, be persons who will have had no close involvement in the events by which the site became contaminated; nor will they be persons who may be characterised as having knowingly permitted the site to remain contaminated (see above). Were either of these things to be the case they would have qualified as Class A parties.

[154] Note the important limit to Class B liability contained in s. 78J(2). Where land is contaminated by reference to actual or likely pollution of *controlled waters* (for this reason alone, or in addition to the "harm" criterion) a Class B appropriate party may not be served a remediation notice in respect of remediation associated with that pollution of controlled waters (as distinct from remediation, if any, which may be associated with the "harm" condition). The aim here is to produce an equivalence between liability under Part IIA and liabilities under the Water Resources Act 1991, ss 161 and 161A.

[155] There is one exception to this statement which should be mentioned. In a situation where a person who has caused or knowingly permitted contamination has been able to limit his or her remediation responsibility to remediation which is referable to the substances for which (s)he is responsible, and no other person can be found as a primary appropriate person in relation to the contamination by other substances, the owner or occupier will be the appropriate person as regards the cleanup of that remaining contamination: see s. 78F(5).

be a matter of some importance to gain an understanding of the meaning to be attributed to that rather imprecise expression.[156]

It might have been hoped that legislative intentions might have been made clear by there having been included within the Act some definition or explanation of the meaning of the word "found", as used in this context. Such hopes, regrettably, are not fulfilled by an examination of the Act. Rather than government having determined its policy as regards what should be the particular contingencies which should trigger Class B liability, and then having written that policy clearly into the legislation, the technique has been simply to have copied somewhat ambiguous language from other statutory contexts and then to seem to deny any further responsibility in the matter. The Circular notes, correctly, that "it is ultimately for the courts to decide whether, in any case, it can be said that no Class A person has been found".[157] This is true – but fails to acknowledge the fact that the heart of the uncertainty lies not in the fact that the judges have not yet been called upon to give rulings on this matter, but in the fact that the primary legislation has failed to use language which would have disclosed whatever may have been its proponents' intentions with precision and clarity. It is as if the legislating Government felt for some reason constrained to have used past legislative language, even though uncertain as to precisely what it meant, rather than giving a clear lead to the judges as to what the law on this matter should be.[158]

What policy might one have expected to govern this matter? One quite likely answer would be that owners and occupiers might have been expected to bear responsibility in any case where their contribution is necessary in order to ensure that the full funding of necessary remediation is secured without recourse having to be made to public funds. Such an approach, however, would require legislation which would allow owners and occupiers to be served remediation notices in a wider variety of situations than we seem to find under the new Act. It would require such parties to bear potential liability either: (a) where it is not known who caused or knowingly permitted the contamination of the site; or (b) where the funding which can be generated by recourse to Class A persons alone will not suffice to cover all necessary remediation.

Such a policy might be thought reasonably justifiable. Indeed there were numerous unofficial statements, describing the legislative proposals contained in the 1994 Bill, which described the new scheme very much in such terms. Nevertheless, the language of the Act would seem to be such as to achieve not this, but a rather different and significantly more limited,

---

[156] The use of the expression follows from the draftsman's attachment to phraseology with a "respectable history": in this case the legislative provisions relating to statutory nuisances – upon which, see further, below, Chapters 11 and 12.

[157] Circular, Annex 2, para. 9.17.

[158] Given that government only worked out it policies on "exclusion" and "apportionment" some substantial while *after* the enactment of the 1995 Act, it may be fair to speculate that the draftsman took sanctuary in the "tried" but "little tested" formula as a consequence of an absence of clear drafting instructions.

contingency as regards the introduction of liability on the part of any Class B party. The formulation "no appropriate [Class A person] has been found" seems rather different from alternatives which might readily have been chosen: different, for example, from "where *all* persons responsible for site contamination cannot be identified and found ..."; or "where those responsible for site contamination have, collectively, inadequate financial means reasonably to bear the cost of remediation ...".

In the absence of such alternative formulae what may one expect of enforcing authorities in their interpretation and application of this Class B liability threshold test?

Critically important questions such as the following will need to be answered:

- Does the notion "not been found" include situations where the identity of the polluters (or at least one) is known but none of those persons can be located in order to serve remediation notices? One would imagine that a positive answer should be given to this question: the notions of "identifying" and "finding" being not the same.

- Does the notion extend to the situation where a corporate polluter can be identified but is no longer an existent corporate entity (for example, because it has been dissolved or wound up)? The wording of the Act would not seem to permit a confident answer. Is to have made such identification to have "found" the polluter, or can a now non-existent entity not be capable of being found?

- Does the notion cover the situation where the polluters can be identified but are discovered to have (individually and collectively) insufficient financial resources to bear the cost of the required remediation? It would seem rather difficult to regard the wording of the legislation as applying to this, all too likely, situation. Moreover, remember, should a *single* Class A party be found, however impecunious, the liability of those in Class B cannot arise.

These issues will, no doubt, need eventually to be resolved by the courts. However, for the moment the official guidance may be expected to influence the decisions taken by enforcing authorities.

After cautioning that it will be for the courts to rule on the meaning of the statutory language, the Circular offers the following view as to the meaning of the undefined word "found":

"In the Government's view, the context in which the word is used in Part IIA implies that a person must be in existence in order to be found. Section 78F(4) provides that the owner or occupier shall bear responsibility only 'if no person has, after reasonable inquiry, been found who is an appropriate person to bear responsibility for the things which are to be done by way of remediation'. A person who is no longer in existence cannot meet that description. Under section 78E(1), the responsibility of an appropriate person for remediation is established by the service of a remediation notice. Service implies the existence of the person on whom the notice is served. In general, therefore, this means that a natural person would have to be alive and a legal person such as a company must not have been dissolved. However, it may be possible in some circumstances for the authority to act against the estate of a deceased person or to apply to a court for an order to annul the dissolution of a company."[159]

Owners and occupiers

Over and above this element of uncertainty which may exist as regards the precise contingency which may *trigger* Class B liability, there may be further difficulties as regards the persons who may fall within Class B: this results from some lack of precision as regards the meaning of each of the expressions "owner" and "occupier".

As regards the term "owner", the Act provides some helpful guidance by stating, by way of partial exclusion, that the term excludes the property interest possessed under English law by a mortgagee not in possession (i.e. a lending institution which has lent money on the basis of a security interest in the land).[160] A secured lender not in possession is not, therefore, by virtue only of its property interest in the land to be regarded for this purpose as an owner of the land. However, it must be remembered that a main purpose of taking a security interest in the land is that if the borrower should default on repayment of the loan the secured creditor may then realise the security by, amongst other things, going into possession of the land (perhaps as a preliminary to its sale). In such a way a lender may become an "occupier" and hence a potential Class B party.[161] On this matter, as will in due course be seen, the statutory guidance contains provisions as regards the remediation burdens which it is appropriate should attach to this category of Class B party.[162]

Beyond this the Act provides that "owner" means:

> " a person ... who, whether in his own right or as trustee for any other person, is entitled to receive the rack rent of the land or, where the land is not let at a rack rent, would be so entitled if it were so let."[163]

---

[159] Circular, Annex 2, para. 9.17.

[160] Section 78A(9).

[161] Lenders are, it may be remembered, also exempted from being regarded as *Class A* parties solely by virtue of their having lent money to enable activities to take place which may have resulted in contamination. However, a lender who may become involved in the decision-making processes of a company to which it has lent money may not be so immune.

[162] See below, pp. 605-606.

[163] Section 78A(9). The definition of "owner" here discussed relates to the owner of any land in England or Wales. The Act adopts a different definition of "owner" where the land in question is in Scotland: see s. 78A(9).

No definition appears in the Act of the word "occupier". Accordingly, this word should be regarded as bearing its ordinary meaning, said by the Circular to mean, by no means astonishingly, "the person in occupation", and that "in many cases that will be the tenant or licensee of the premises".[164]

It should not be thought that the presence of a person in occupation different from the owner will render the owner not an appropriate party. It is both categories of persons who comprise Class B appropriate persons. We shall see later how, where Class B parties bear responsibility, the enforcing authority should apportion responsibility between such Class B appropriate persons.[165]

More complex situations: migration of contamination from one site to another

The discussion so far has proceeded on the basis that the site upon which substances have been deposited and the site to be remediated are one and the same (site X). It may, however, be the case that substances may have migrated from site X and have caused site Y to become contaminated so as to require cleanup. The principles which will apply in this situation differ somewhat from those considered above.

The matter is governed by the rather complex provisions of section 78K. The starting point is that the person (P) who caused or knowingly permitted the contamination of site X is regarded also as the contaminator of site Y. Accordingly, assuming this person can be found he or she is an appropriate person for the service of a remediation notice in respect of the cleanup of site Y.

This follows the pattern, described above, of imposing liability principally on those whose acts or omissions have given rise to the need for remediation. The difference, between this situation and situations where only one site is involved, may be seen in cases where no person who was the cause of, or who knowingly permitted, the contamination of site X can be found. In such a situation can the owner or occupier of site X (let us call this person OX) be made responsible for the cleanup of site Y? Does the owner or occupier of site X bear secondary liability as regards cleanup of site Y in the same way as that party will bear secondary liability in relation to site X itself? The Act provides that such an owner or occupier[166] will *not* bear such secondary liability.

What, though, of the owner or occupier of site Y? Assuming that party P (the polluter of site X, from which the contaminants have migrated to site Y) cannot be found, the owners and occupiers of site Y will bear secondary

---

[164] Circular, Annex A, para. 9.21.

[165] See below, pp. 605-606.

[166] At any rate not liability *qua* owner or occupier. If the evidence is that such a person has knowingly permitted contamination, caused by a third party, to escape to site X, then such an owner or occupier of site Y will have a primary liability, as described above, as having knowingly permitted the substances to have contaminated site Y.

liability in respect of the cleanup of that site. This may be regarded as following the essential principles underpinning secondary liability under the Act: that where the actual polluter cannot be found the burdens should fall on those with an economic interest in the condition and value of the land.

In situations where the ground conditions, or more usually *groundwater* conditions, are such that contamination has migrated from site X to site Y, there is a strong likelihood that it may have migrated also through site Y to site Z (and beyond). Who may be appropriate persons as regards the remediation of, and beyond, site Z?

The answer to be given is quite consistent with the principles just described. In cases where the polluter (P) of the initially contaminated site (site X) can be found the remediation notice should be served upon that person. In cases where that person cannot be found, the owners and occupiers of sites X and Y will bear no liability (in their capacity as owners and occupiers[167]) to remediate site Z: the responsibility in respect of site Z will fall upon that site's appropriate secondary liability parties – *its* own owners and occupiers.

DISTRIBUTION OF BURDENS BETWEEN SEVERAL APPROPRIATE PERSONS: EXCLUSION AND APPORTIONMENT

Introduction

A simple instance of contaminated land may involve only one "appropriate person" and one remediation action. The task of the enforcing authority will here be relatively straightforward and the appropriate person will be required by the remediation notice to undertake, within a given timescale, remediation to the appropriate "suitable for use" standard specified in that notice.

Such simplicity may, however, prove to be atypical. A more common situation may require the exercise of these statutory powers in relation to sites with a rather more complex history: sites in respect of which a variety of contributors may have precipitated a present-day "cocktail" of contamination, giving rise to a range of kinds of harm or instances of pollution of water, via numerous pollution linkages. As the statutory guidance explains:

> "… a succession of different occupiers or of different industries, or a variety of substances may all have contributed to the problems which have made the land 'contaminated land.'"

Moreover, in terms of efficient and effective remediation action:

---

[167] Again, it should be noted that such persons (OX and OY) may bear a primary liability in any situation where they may be regarded as having knowingly permitted contamination (albeit caused by another) to have spread from their land.

"Numerous separate remediation actions may be required, which may not correlate neatly with those who are to bear responsibility for the costs."

Accordingly:

"The degree of responsibility for the state of the land may vary widely. Determining liability for the costs of each remediation can be correspondingly complex."[168]

The fundamental question arises: what principles should apply as regards the distribution of such burdens as between the various "appropriate persons" defined by the legislation? This is another of the fundamental liability issues which one might have expected to have been addressed with some care, and in some detail, at the time of the legislative passage of the 1995 Act. Perhaps it was understandable for the detailed principles applicable to be contained in documents outside the main Act. Nevertheless, those principles should have been available for consideration, discussion and debate at that time, being such an important feature of the overall regime. Indeed it would be no exaggeration to suggest that this is the single most important feature of any system of rules about the remediation of contaminated land. It is surely at least as significant as the *definition* of contaminated land and the *standard of remediation* to be required. Moreover, it is probably rather more controversial than these other questions; although, of course, the view which any individual takes about standard of cleanup may well depend upon whether that person (or someone else) may have responsibility for that cleanup (and the extent of that potential responsibility).

In the discussion which follows we shall begin by noting certain general principles which the statutory guidance states shall be applicable to the application of its more detailed provisions about exclusion from liability and apportionment of liabilities. We shall then discuss the broad contexts in which issues of apportionment of liabilities may arise. Finally we shall examine the detailed rules about exclusion and apportionment which are set out in the statutory guidance.

General principles governing exclusion and apportionment

The statutory guidance provides that as a general principle:

"the financial circumstances of those concerned should have no bearing on the application of the procedures for exclusion [and] apportionment.."[169]

---

[168] Statutory Guidance, Annex 3, Chapter D, para. D7.

[169] Guidance, Annex 3, Chapter D, para. D35 (word in square brackets added by the authors). An exception, acknowledged by the guidance, is where cost recovery under s. 78P(2) is under consideration: see below, p. 608.

It also states that enforcing authorities should take note of and seek to give effect to any agreements which parties may themselves have made as regards the division of cost responsibilities. Thus:

> "In any case where:
>
> (a)   two or more persons are responsible for all or part of the costs of a remediation action;
>
> (b)   they agree, or have agreed, the basis on which they wish to divide that responsibility; and
>
> (c)   a copy of that agreement is provided to the enforcing authority and none of the parties to the agreement informs the authority that it challenges the application of the agreement;
>
> the enforcing authority should generally make such determinations on exclusion, apportionment and attribution as are needed to give effect to this agreement, and should not apply the remainder of this guidance ... However the enforcing authority should apply the guidance to determine any exclusions, apportionments and attributions between any or all of the parties and any other appropriate persons who are not parties to the agreement."[170]

This provision, allowing parties to determine for themselves what their respective burdens should be, and to crystallise that burden so as to reduce uncertainties, provides substantial opportunities for lawyers to afford assistance to clients – particularly at the time of property or corporate transactions – which may obviate the exercise against them of the statutory provisions presently under consideration.

The policy of respecting arrangements which appropriate persons may have made voluntarily *inter se* as regards their respective responsibilities for remediation may be regarded as fully consistent with the support for voluntary remediation which was considered earlier.[171] Respect for such agreements must, however come at a price: it is an inevitable feature of such an approach that the agreement reached may allocate responsibilities differently from the way in which the enforcing authority, applying the statutory guidance to be considered shortly, would have decided. Respect only for agreements which produce results equal to the application of such guidance is to pay no more than lip-service to support for such agreements. Nevertheless, there needs to be some limit to the degree to which arrangements agreed between the parties may be allowed to deny the protections afforded to certain persons in certain contexts by the principles we are about to consider. The statutory guidance therefore provides:

> "... where giving effect to such an agreement would increase the share of the costs theoretically to be borne by a person who would

---

[170] Guidance, Annex 3, Chapter D, para. D38.
[171] See above, pp. 564-565.

benefit from a limitation on recovery of remediation costs under the provision on hardship in section 78P(2)(a) or under the guidance on cost recovery issued under section 78P(2)(b), the enforcing authority should disregard the agreement."[172]

The contexts in which issues of apportionment and exclusion arise

Before we begin to consider in detail the statutory guidance which has been issued on the matter of the distribution of remedial burdens in relation to multi-contaminated sites, it may be helpful:

(i) to define more clearly the situations of multi-contamination to which the guidance on distribution of burdens may be applicable; and

(ii) to explain more fully the inevitably complex nature of the task which the guidance addresses.

Let us begin by considering the variety of kinds of sites we may need to have in mind. Some examples may help:

Site 1: A site containing several contaminating substances and several pollution pathways. However, there is just one Class A appropriate person or, such a person not having been found, just one single Class B person. Notwithstanding the complex contamination this is not a site to which the following discussion is applicable.

Site 2: This site is similar to site 1 except that it is found that the substances were caused or knowingly permitted to be on the site by several different Class A parties. Assume, however, that each substance renders the site contaminated via a different pollution linkage. For example, imagine two different substances on quite different parts of a site, one causing "harm" and the other causing pollution of controlled water. Here also, it may well be that there is no reason for the enforcing authority to do anything other than treat each instance of contamination separately, both in terms of remedial requirements and in terms of allocation of remedial burdens.

Site 3: Similar to site 1, except that the substances on site, as a consequence of actions of several Class A appropriate persons, have become mixed within the site and separate remedial action is, therefore, not practicable, or even possible, in relation to each separate substance. Some form of combined remediation action will be necessary. This will be a situation where there will need to be some rules about the division of the costs of such remediation between the several Class A parties.

We shall need to look at further examples of potential multi-polluted sites. However, the examples given are sufficient for the moment to help us to

---

[172] Guidance, Annex 3, Chapter D, para. D39. See further, below, at pp. 608–609.

distinguish such sites where issues of apportionment between appropriate persons may arise, and cases where notwithstanding there being several appropriate persons in relation to substances on a single physical site, the matter may nevertheless – subject to exceptions described below – be approached by the enforcing authority as if the site were, in fact, several separate sites.

It is important to have noted these distinctions because they may seem unnatural ones from the vantage point or perspective of those whose focus is the design of a remediation programme rather than the issue of who should pay for each aspect of that programme, or how the overall costs should be apportioned between appropriate persons.

From the perspective of persons who are focusing more on activities necessary on a site in order to render it no longer (legally) contaminated the task in hand may perhaps be described in the following broad terms. From this perspective the task of the enforcing authority might seem to involve simply:

- identification of the contamination problems associated with the site: what harm or pollution of controlled water is being, or is likely to be, caused;

- assessment of the most effective range of remediation measures, for the site as a whole, in order most effectively and efficiently to prevent such harm or pollution continuing, or remaining a likelihood;

- to divide the overall cost of those measures in some appropriate way (in accordance with guidance) between all those who have been identified, in accordance with the rules we have considered, as Class A or as Class B appropriate persons.

From a perspective of securing effective and efficient site remediation this might seem a satisfactory way of approaching the issue of distribution of remedial burdens. However, a little thought will reveal that the process so described will be somewhat inadequate.

The procedure described above involves a risk that insufficient attention will be focused upon the particular individual legal responsibilities of each of the several appropriate persons who may have been identified as Class A, or as Class B, appropriate persons in relation to a site.

To illustrate this, let us return to the distinctions drawn in our earlier site examples. Let us assume that three persons have separately released different contaminants onto different parts of a site. Each is giving rise to a different pollution-pathway hazard, and each requires a different remedial procedure. The proper approach should, we might expect, be not to aggregate the costs and divide the total, equally or otherwise, between the parties. Here we have separate liabilities with separate remedial actions. We should expect this kind of case not to involve the amalgamation of costs, necessitating rules for distribution of the aggregate burden between the several parties. It is a case for individual assessment of individual remedial responsibilities.

The warning would seem to be: be careful before making assumptions that just because several persons have caused a site to have become legally contaminated the situation will be one in which the guidance under review in this section will be applicable. To avoid this danger, it is important to think always in terms of substances, pollution pathways and receptors. Even a site contaminated over a good many years, in a good many ways, and by a number of different entities, may involve no more liability complexity than a situation involving a number of separate remedial actions on adjacent/separate sites – different actions being required of each party in relation to the pollution pathway resulting from the substances for which each is responsible.

But this point leads us on to an important necessary qualifying point addressed by the guidance. Imagine a site of the kind just described where, in principle, it might seem that each instance of contamination should be separately remediated, with costs readily attributable to particular appropriate persons. It may well be the case that to address remediation in this way would be technically feasible but would, taken overall, produce site remediation at a greater cost than a scheme of remedial action designed not with primary reference to each *individual* pollution pathway, but with reference to the most cost-effective remediation of the site *as a whole*. To take an extreme example: perhaps a single remedial action may be appropriate to deal with the separate contaminating actions of the several parties. Such overall cost savings may be envisaged in various ways. For example, it may be cheaper overall to extend the ambit of one kind of necessary remedial action on the site to cover also "lesser" forms of contamination than ordinarily might require that form of remedial action, than to commission different forms of remedial action each tailored to a particular substance and pollution pathway. Alternatively, we should remember that one way in which a site may be remediated is not to clean up the contamination but to take steps to prevent the contamination coming into contact with the receptor by reference to which the site has the quality in law of being contaminated. It may be that judged by reference to each individual substance and each individual appropriate person, the cost of cleanup is less than the cost of engineering a barrier between the substance and the receptor. When the cost of cleanup of the substances is aggregated, however, it may be that the erection of a barrier which may block the pollution pathways in respect of each and all the substances may become a cheaper overall site solution.

In situations such as these it may well be in the interests of each and all of the appropriate parties for an "individualised remediation" approach to the separate pollution pathways to be departed from, and for the site problems to be addressed more strategically, and thereby more cheaply. Such a process will, however, necessitate a process of division of the overall cost burden of this remedial action as between the several appropriate persons.

These introductory words should suffice to give some idea of why the guidance which we shall shortly describe possesses, as a matter of inevitably, a good deal of complexity: inevitability resulting from a wish to preserve individual responsibilities where there is no good reason for there to be a process of amalgamation of costs, but to provide for such a process where there would otherwise be a failure to remediate a site in a cost efficient way.

The statutory guidance

The statutory guidance sets out procedures – in five stages for the more complex cases – which enforcing authorities should follow in order to determine "which appropriate persons should bear what responsibility for each remediation action".[173]

The first stage in this process will be to identify potential "appropriate persons": to identify the persons amongst whom liabilities may need to be apportioned. The simplicity or otherwise of this task may depend, as we have seen, upon whether there is, in respect of the site, a single pollution linkage, or two or more such pollution linkages.

Where there is a single pollution linkage in relation to the site the enforcing authority should begin by identifying all the persons who appear to be "appropriate persons" to pay for any remediation action which is referable to the pollutant which forms part of that pollution linkage. These persons collectively comprise what the guidance calls the "liability group" in respect of that pollution linkage. This will require the enforcing authority to make reasonable inquiries to find all persons who fall within the Class A category of appropriate persons described above. If no such persons can be found the enforcing authority will need to consider whether the pollution linkage of which the pollutant forms a part relates solely to the pollution of controlled waters. In such a case there will be no question of any persons who are current owners or occupiers bearing any responsibility: Class B liability, it may be remembered,[174] only applies where the site is (in law) contaminated because it is causing or threatening "significant harm" (not pollution of water). In a case where there can be found no Class A parties, and Class B liability is inapplicable, the site will be what the guidance characterises as one involving an "orphan linkage".[175] If no Class A parties can be found and the pollution linkage relates not solely to pollution of controlled waters, the enforcing authority will need to identify all current owners and occupiers of the site. These persons will comprise the Class B liability group.

---

[173] Guidance, Annex 3, Chapter D, para. D8.
[174] See above, p. 577.
[175] See further on "orphan linkages", below, p. 592.

Where in relation to a site there is more than one pollution linkage, the enforcing authority should go through the process described in the above paragraph so as to establish the persons who comprise the liability group in relation to each of the several pollution linkages.[176]

Whether the site involves just one, or more than one pollution linkage, the next step will be for the enforcing authority to consider whether any persons within the liability group(s) so established is a person who may be able to claim *exemption* from liability under the provisions of Part IIA.

On the matter of such exemption under Part IIA the guidance explains:

"This could apply where:

(a) a person who would otherwise be a Class A person is exempted from liability arising with respect to water pollution from an abandoned mine (see section 78J(3);

(b) a Class B person is exempted from liability arising from the escape of a pollutant from one piece of land to other land (see section 78K);[177] or

(c) a person is exempted from liability by virtue of his being a person 'acting in a relevant capacity' (such as acting as an insolvency practitioner), as defined in section 78X(4)."[178]

If all the members of any liability group benefit from one or more of these exemptions, the enforcing authority will be obliged to treat the pollutant linkage in question as an "orphan linkage".[179]

Once an enforcing authority has established the membership of the liability group in relation to each pollution linkage it will be in a position to begin to apply the statutory guidance as regards the apportionment of costs as between those members.[180]

In relation to a site where there may exist more than one pollution linkage it will be necessary for the enforcing authority to go through a process of characterising each remedial action, which is to take place in relation to the site, in terms of its referability to one or more of those pollution linkages.

---

[176] Guidance paras. D10-14.

[177] See above, pp. 581-582.

[178] Paragraph D16.

[179] See below, p. 592.

[180] Given that Class B persons may only bear responsibilities where no class A person has been found in relation to a pollution linkage, the issue of distribution of burdens *between the membership of the two Classes* does not (ordinarily) arise. The word "ordinarily" has been included in the last sentence because the guidance does, in fact, deal with situations where there should *be combined remediation of several separate pollution linkages* within a site. If each linkage is regarded as giving rise to a separate liability it may be the case that in respect of one a Class A party can be found; whereas in respect of another, Class B parties may bear responsibilities. If the remediation package is best designed as a whole, as discussed in the text above, there may then be a need to divide the costs between the Class A and Class B parties.

In other words, for the purpose of the process of determining the cost burden of each person within the site's several liability groups, it is necessary to attribute remedial actions to particular pollution linkages so that the sum of the costs to be borne by each liability group (and then to be apportioned within its members) can be known. Where a remedial action has the intended effect of dealing with more than one pollution linkage its cost should be allocated across and between those linkages' liability groups.[181] The share of responsibility to be borne by each liability group in this situation will be decided in accordance with Part 9 of the Chapter D statutory guidance.[182]

This Part 9 of the guidance begins by explaining that it applies:

> "where one remediation action is referable to two or more significant pollution linkages."

Such a remedial action is designated a "shared action". Such shared remedial actions may occur:

> "either where both linkages require the same action ... or where a particular action is part of the best combined remediation scheme for two or more linkages ..."

Action in the former of these situations is called a "common action"; action in the latter is called a "collective action".[183]

Common actions

The guidance requires enforcing authorities to attribute responsibility for the costs of common actions, between the liability groups for the pollution linkages involved, on the following basis:

- where there is a single Class A liability group the full cost of carrying out the common action should fall on that group – and no cost should fall upon any Class B liability group;[184]

---

[181] Guidance, Annex 3, Chapter D, para. D21.

[182] Paragraphs D98-102.

[183] These concepts are further explained in Statutory Guidance, Annex 3, Chapter D, para. D22. A "common action" is an action which addresses together all of the significant pollutant linkages to which it is referable, and which would have been part of the remediation package for each of those linkages if each of them had been addressed separately. A "collective action" is an action which addresses together all of the significant pollution linkages to which it is referable, but which would not have been part of the remediation package for every one of those linkages if each of them had been addressed separately, because: (i) the action would not have been appropriate in that form for one or more of the linkages (since some different solution would have been appropriate); (ii) the action would not have been needed to the same extent for one or more of the linkages (since a less far-reaching version of that type of action would have sufficed): (iii) the action represents a more economic way of addressing the linkages together which would not be possible if they were addressed separately.

[184] Accordingly, where a common action secures remediation in relation to a linkage where Class A persons have been found as well as in relation to linkages where no such Class A persons can be found, the former Class A persons shall bear the whole cost of that action, and the

- where there are two or more Class A liability groups, an equal share of the cost of the common action should fall on each of the groups – and no cost should fall upon any Class B group;[185]

- where there is no Class A liability group and there are two or more Class B liability groups,[186] the enforcing authority should treat those liability groups as if they formed a single liability group.

Collective actions

The guidance about attribution of responsibility for the cost of collective actions amongst the liability groups for the pollution linkages to which the collective action is referable begins by stating that the principles, described above, for common actions, should be followed:

"except that where the costs fall to be divided among several Class A groups, instead of being divided equally, they should be attributed on the following basis:

(a) having estimated the costs of the collective action, the enforcing authority should estimate the hypothetical cost for each of the liability groups of carrying out the actions which are subsumed by the collective action and which would be necessary if the significant pollution linkage for which the liability group is responsible were to be addressed separately …;

(b) the enforcing authority should then attribute responsibility for the cost of the collective action between the liability groups in the proportions which the hypothetical estimates of each liability group bear to the aggregate of the hypothetical estimates of all the groups."[187]

The guidance summarised above is, however, subject to acknowledgment that in "very exceptional" cases it may result in disproportionate burdens being imposed upon a liability group. It is, therefore, provided that where any member of any liability group is able to satisfy an enforcing authority that the principles set out above would result in his or her liability group bearing disproportionate and unjust liability (taking into account overall relative responsibilities for the condition of the land), the enforcing authority should "reconsider" the attribution. There is not, however, provided any more constructive guidance, as regards such reconsideration, than the statement that it should:

---

owners/occupiers who would otherwise have been called upon to remediate in the latter situation are relieved of liability.

[185] There will be more than one Class A group where there is more than one pollution linkage and each has a different person or persons who have caused or knowingly permitted the substances to be present which give rise to the linkage in question.

[186] For example, where as regards part of a site there may be an occupier and an owner and as regards another part of the site an owner-occupier.

[187] Statutory Guidance, Annex 3, Chapter D, para. D100. In other words, they will each benefit, from the overall saving achieved, in proportion relative to the costs that each would otherwise have incurred.

"adjust the attribution between the liability groups so that it is just and fair in the light of all the circumstances."[188]

"ORPHAN" LINKAGES

The statutory guidance acknowledges that it may occur that even after reasonable inquiry on the part of an enforcing authority no Class A or Class B person may be found. In other words it may be the case that (i) in relation to a pollution linkage it is not possible to ascertain who may have caused or knowingly permitted the substance within the linkage to be on the land, (ii) there may be no person in occupation and (iii) the ownership of the land may not be reasonably ascertainable.[189] Equally, it may be the case, that although persons within the Class A or Class B category have been found, they may all be able to claim exemption from liability under guidance provisions to be considered below. In any such cases as these, the statutory guidance states the approach which an enforcing authority should adopt.[190]

The guidance provides that where the case is one involving a single pollution linkage, the enforcing authority must normally bear the cost of remedial action in relation to that linkage. However, where a shared action may remediate the "orphan" linkage, the consequence is that the Class A liability group in relation to the other linkage benefited should carry the full cost of that action. Where there is more than one such Class A liability group (i.e. the shared action relates to more than one pollution linkage other than the orphan linkage) the entire cost will be shared between these Class A groups, as if the orphan linkage did not exist. This division will depend upon whether the shared action is a common action or a collective action: equal division of the whole costs in the former case and in proportion to the hypothetical cost of the action which would otherwise be required, in the latter case.

Where there is (i) an orphan linkage, (ii) a shared action which will secure remediation of that orphan linkage, and (iii) a Class B liability group in relation to another linkage benefited by the shared action, the position is that if the shared action is a common action, the enforcing authority is to attribute all the cost of remediation to the Class B liability group. Where, alternatively, a shared action which is not a common but a collective action will secure orphan linkage remediation, and there is a Class B liability group in relation to another linkage remediated by the shared action, the enforcing authority should limit costs to that Class B group to the hypothetical cost of remediation of that group's linkage alone. The remainder of the cost of the collective shared action will be borne by the enforcing authority.

---

[188] Statutory Guidance, Annex 3, Chapter D, para. D101.
[189] Or Class B liability may be inapplicable because the contaminated relates not to "harm" but to "pollution of controlled waters": see above, p. 577.
[190] Statutory Guidance, Annex 3, Chapter D, para. D103.

THE DETAILED PROVISIONS AS REGARDS EXCLUSION OF PERSONS FROM WITHIN CLASS A AND CLASS B LIABILITY GROUPS

Introduction

The guidance sets out the principles by which the enforcing authority shall determine whether any member of a Class A liability group should be excluded from liability on the ground that, in relation to other members of that group it is fair that (s)he should be quit of such responsibility.[191] The principles are set out as a number of tests, each of which is summarised below.

The guidance makes clear that the tests to be described must not be applied so as to exclude all the members of the group. The tests are to be applied in the sequence set out in the guidance. Should all but one within a group become excluded, that last remaining member of the group may not take advantage of any subsequent exclusionary test even if it would seem, otherwise, to be applicable to his or her situation.[192] If the result of applying a test would be to exclude all the members of the liability group who remain after any exclusions resulting from previous tests, that test should not be applied.[193]

The effects of applying the tests, to be described below, as regards exclusion, are of two kinds, depending upon the test which is being applied. The simplest situation is where a member of a liability group falls within the ambit of Tests 1, 4, 5 or 6. Here the consequence is that that person is removed completely from any liability that would have arisen as a member of that liability group;[194] and that apportionment within the liability group should occur as if

> "the excluded person had never been a member of the liability group."

Where, however, it is Tests 2 or 3 (below) which the member of the liability group satisfies the process is somewhat different. These tests also

---

[191] Note also that there is a general provision that "related companies" should be treated as a single economic unit so as to prevent companies evading their proper liabilities by structuring themselves so that liabilities fall on subsidiaries with insufficient assets to meet those burdens. "Related companies" are those which are members of a group of companies consisting of a "holding company" and its "subsidiaries": those expressions having the same meaning as in s. 736 of the Companies Act 1985. Where two or more companies within a liability group are related companies (at the time the enforcing authority first served notice that the land is contaminated) then for the purpose of applying the exclusion tests (to be described below) the enforcing authority should regard the related companies as if they were a single person. Guidance, Annex 3, Chapter D, paras. D44-46.

[192] Guidance, Annex 3, Chapter D, para. D41(a) and (b).

[193] Guidance, Annex 3, Chapter D, para. D41(c).

[194] That person may, of course, be also a member of another liability group relating to another pollution linkage upon the same site. Exclusion from one liability group does not exclude from all such liability groups. The tests must be applied, as appropriate, in relation to each group of which the person is a member in order to assess that person's overall position. See Guidance, Annex 3, Chapter D, para. D41(a).

quit the beneficiary of all liability as a member of the liability group. However, the effect of this on other members of the group is not the same as for Tests 1, 4, 5 and 6. Tests 2 and 3 apply to situations where the excluded person is quit of liability for a reason which means that his or her share of liability should not be borne equally by other members of the group but should be taken over by one or more particular members of the group. That other person:

> "should bear the liability of the person excluded ... in addition to any liability which he is to bear in respect of his own acts or omissions."

To achieve this consequence the enforcing authority must apply each of the exclusion tests in turn in order to determine the ultimate liability group within which to apportion costs. It should then apportion liability within that group on the basis that the person excluded by Test 2 or 3 is still a member of the group. It should then add the sum apportioned to the excluded person to the sum apportioned to the person who is to bear this added share.[195]

Exclusion tests for Class A persons

Test 1: *Excluded activities*

Where a person has caused or knowingly permitted land to be contaminated solely by virtue of having performed one or more of a listed range of activities that person should be excluded from the category.

The guidance explains:

> " The activities are ones which, in the Government's view, carry such limited responsibility, if any, that exclusion would be justified even where the activity is held to amount to 'causing or knowingly permitting' under Part IIA."[196]

Indeed the list of excluded activities which is contained in the guidance comprises a range of activities which one might not at first sight have thought to be likely to render a person liable within this Class A category: that is, not activities which might be likely to characterise the person so engaged as a person who has caused or knowingly permitted the contamination. As such the purpose of this provision would seem primarily to be to resolve any doubts, should they exist, as regards the non-liability of such persons. The guidance seems to acknowledge this. It provides that the fact that such activities are excluded activities:

---

[195] Guidance, Annex 3, Chapter D, para. D43. It seems that such a person will bear this added share even if his or her own liability would be nil, because a beneficiary of one of the other exclusion tests – see Guidance, Chapter D, para. D 43 (b) final phrase: "this should be done even if the payee or buyer would otherwise have been excluded from any liability group by one of the other exclusion tests."

[196] Guidance, Annex 3, Chapter D, para. D47.

"… does not imply that the carrying out of such activities necessarily amounts to 'causing or knowingly permitting'."[197]

The "excluded activities" are listed in sub-paragraphs (a) to (k) of paragraph D48 of the statutory guidance. It is not appropriate here to set out this list in full. However, the points made immediately above may be illustrated by reference to one or two of the excluded activities. So, for example, we see in subparagraph (a):

"…providing financial assistance to another person, in the form of any one or more of the following:
(i)   making a grant,
(ii)   making a loan or providing any other form of credit …,
(iii)   guaranteeing the performance of a person's obligations,
(iv)   indemnifying a person in respect of any loss, liability or damage,
(v)   investing in the undertaking of a body corporate,
(vi)   providing a person with any other financial benefit …"

Subparagraph (b) covers:

"withholding financial assistance of any of the forms identified in subparagraph (a) above."

Subparagraph (d) is of some interest. It excludes those whose sole reason for being included as a Class A person may have been their:

"consigning as waste, to another person the substance which is now a significant pollutant, under a contract under which that other person knowingly took over responsibility for its proper disposal or other management on a site not under the control of the person seeking to be excluded from liability."

And (e) and (f) comprise:

"creating at any time a tenancy over the land in favour of another person who has subsequently caused or knowingly permitted the presence of the significant pollution linkage in question (whether or not the tenant can now be found)."

and

"as owner of the land, licensing at any time its occupation by another person who has subsequently caused or knowingly permitted the presence of the significant pollutant in question …"[198]

---

[197] It has been contended by Lawrence and Lee that: "All that is being said in relation to the exclusion is that, in so far as the wide range of activities referred to in Test 1 might amount in certain unspecified circumstances to these parties positively permitting contaminants under their control to be on the land, there is an available exclusion in their favour": see (2003) 66 MLR 261 at p. 269.

Subparagraph (i) will provide some reassurance to those providing certain professional services:

> "providing legal, financial, engineering, scientific or technical advice to (or design, contract management or works management services for) another person (the 'client'):
> (i)　in relation to an action or omission … by reason of which the client has been held to have caused or knowingly permitted …,
> (ii)　for the purpose of assessing the condition of the land, for example whether it might be contaminated, or
> (iii)　for the purpose of establishing what might be done to the land by way of remediation."

And paragraph (j) applies to exclude those whose only reason for being within a Class A group is their having "carr[ied] out any intrusive investigation in respect of the land in question" in the course of preparing advice, or providing services, in the circumstances set out in the preceding subparagraph.

However, exclusion will not apply under subparagraph (j):

> "where the investigation is itself a cause of the existence, nature or continuance of the significant pollution linkage in question."

In relation to all of the activities referred to in paragraph D48 of the guidance it must be remembered that exclusion form Class A only applies where the person is within a Class A liability group solely by reason of having carried out such an activity. Anyone who may have carried out such an activity, but who is properly to be characterised as a Class A party for some reason beyond the mere fact of having engaged in one of the listed activities will not be excluded under this test.

Test 2: *Payments made for remediation*

This test will exclude from liability certain persons who may be regarded as having already met their responsibilities, by having previously made certain kinds of payments to some other member of the liability group.

The test is designed to take appropriate account of the situation where payments have been made by one member of the group to another for the purpose of remediation; and which, had they been spent on appropriate and effective remedial measures would have sufficed to have resolved the land contamination problem. In such circumstances it is appropriate that the party which has incurred such expenditure should be excluded from the group. It is also appropriate that the party which has received such payments but has not put the land to right should, vis-à-vis the remaining members of the group, bear a relatively higher burden. The guidance so

---

[198] The subparagraph continues: "… this test does not apply in a case where the person granting the licence operated the land as a site for the disposal or storage of waste at the time of the grant of the licence".

provides, by requiring that party, in effect, to take over the burdens which under the various tests would have attached to the excluded party had that party not been so excluded.

The enforcing authority should, however, only regard payments of the following kinds as qualifying:

> "(a) a payment made voluntarily, or to meet a contractual obligation, in response to a claim for the cost of the particular remediation;
>
> (b) a payment made in the course of a civil legal action, or arbitration, mediation or dispute resolution procedure, covering the cost of the particular remediation, whether paid as an out of court settlement, or paid under the terms of a court order; or
>
> (c) a payment as part of a contract ... for the transfer of ownership of the land in question which is either specifically provided for in the contract to meet the cost of carrying out the particular remediation or which consists of a reduction in the contract price explicitly stated in the contract to be for that purpose."[199]

There then follows what may be considered to be a potentially important limitation upon this exclusion test. No payment should be taken into account in a situation where:

> "the person making the payment retained any control after the date of the payment over the condition of the land in question (that is, over whether or not the substances by reason of which the land is regarded as contaminated land were permitted to be in, on or under the land)."[200]

It is made clear, however, that neither of the following shall suffice to amount to "retaining control" over the condition of land:

> "(a) holding contractual rights to ensure the proper carrying out of the remediation ...; nor
> (b) holding an interest or right of any of the following kinds:
> > (i) easements for the benefit of other land, where the contaminated land is the servient tenement, and statutory rights of an equivalent nature;
> > (ii) rights of statutory undertakers to carry out works ...;
> > (iii) reversions upon the expiry or termination of a long lease; or
> > (iv) the benefit of restrictive covenants or equivalent statutory agreement."[201]

---

[199] Guidance, Chapter D, para. D53. Payment may however include consideration in any form.
[200] Guidance, Annex 3, Chapter D, para. D54.
[201] Guidance, Annex 3, Chapter D, para. D55.

Test 3: *Sold with information*

The aim of this important provision is to exclude from liability those who on having sold land, or having let land on a long lease, have ensured that the purchaser or lessee had information as to the presence of the pollutants on the land and thereby, it may be presumed, agreed a price on the basis of that knowledge.[202] As with the previous test the effect of this exclusion is intended not to have a consequentially adverse effect on the burdens which will attach to others within the group: the purchaser/lessee will shoulder the burdens which would otherwise have attached to the now excluded party.

The requirements of this test are as follows:

(a) One member of the liability group has sold the land in question to another member of the group. The expression "sold" covers, here, a transfer of the freehold or the grant or assignment of a long lease.[203]

(b) The sale took place at arm's length (that is, on terms which could be expected in a sale on the open market between a willing seller and a willing buyer). Where the sale is a part of a group of transactions or a wider agreement (such as the sale of a company or business), a sale at arm's length should be taken to include any case where the person seeking to be excluded can show that "the net effect of the group of transactions or the agreement as a whole was a sale at arm's length".

(c) Before the sale became binding the buyer had information that would "reasonably allow that particular person to be aware of the presence on the land of the pollution identified in the significant pollution linkage in question, and the broad measure of that presence". Moreover, the seller must be able to show that he or she "did nothing material to misrepresent the implications of that presence".

(d) After the date of the sale, the seller did not retain any interest in the land in question or any rights[204] to occupy or use that land.[205]

In terms of the information which the buyer must possess under item (c) above, it should be emphasised that:

"in transactions since the beginning of 1990 where the buyer is a large commercial organisation or public body[206] permission from the

---

[202] The sale must be one which took place on the open market between a willing seller and a willing buyer.

[203] For this purpose, a long lease means a lease (or sub-lease) granted for a period of more than 21 years and under which the lessee satisfies the definition of "owner" under s. 78A(9) (definition in terms of entitlement to receive the "rack-rent").

[204] Certain retained rights should be disregarded: as listed above, p. 597.

[205] Guidance, Annex 3, Chapter D, paras D58 and 59.

[206] Lawrence and Lee have drawn attention to the fact that the provision is restricted to such organisations and bodies. In their opinion, this amounts to an attempt by the statutory guidance to

seller for the buyer to carry out his own investigations of the condition of the land should normally be taken as sufficient indication that the buyer had the information referred to [in that subparagraph]."[207]

Test 4: *Changes to substances*

This test is designed to exclude persons who have been responsible for the presence of substances which would not have contributed to the land being contaminated were it not for the effect upon those substances (by interaction) of other substances *later* introduced to the land by other members of the liability group.

The requirements of this test comprise:

> "(a) the substance forming part of the significant pollution linkage in question is present, or has become a significant pollutant, only as a result of a chemical reaction, biological process or other change (the "intervening change") involving:
>> (i)   both a substance (the "earlier substance") which would not have formed part of the significant pollution linkage if the intervening change had not occurred, and
>> (ii) one or more other substances (the "later substances");
> (b) the intervening change would not have occurred in the absence of the later substances;
> (c) a person (the "first person") is a member of the liability group because he caused or knowingly permitted the presence...of the earlier substance, but he did not cause [etc.] the presence of any of the later substances;
> (d) one or more other persons are members of the liability group because they caused [etc.] the later substances to be in, on or under the land;
> (e) before the date when the later substances started to be introduced ... the first person:
>> (i)   could not reasonably have foreseen that the later substances would be introduced onto the land,
>> (ii) could not reasonably have foreseen that, if they were, the intervening change would be likely to happen, or
>> (iii) took what, at that date, were reasonable precautions to prevent the introduction of the later substances or the

---

"shift the risk to those with the capacity and resources to deal with the problem". They argue, however, that the test "needs to be applied with great care if it is to achieve a fair allocation of responsibility". As they rightly point out: "There may... be issues about the extent of investigations that would have been needed to arrive at a detailed understanding of the contamination, its measure and whether, in fact, the seller had afforded the buyer with an adequate opportunity for such investigations to be carried out": see (2003) 66 MLR 261 at p. 272.

[207] Guidance, Annex 3, Chapter D, para. D59(d). The words in square brackets have been added by the authors. This has been a matter of standard practice in such sales since that date, so benefiting a substantial number of Class A property sellers and lessors (subject, of course, to whatever indemnities may have been agreed within the sale or similar contract).

occurrence of the intervening change, even though those precautions have, in the event, proved inadequate; and

(f)   after that date the first person did not:

    (i)   cause or knowingly permit any more of the earlier substance to be in, on or under the land …;

    (ii)   do anything which has contributed to the conditions that brought about the intervening change; or

    (iii) fail to do something which he could reasonably have been expected to do to prevent the intervening change happening."[208]

Test 5: *Escaped substances*

Where land has become contaminated solely as a result of the escape of substances from *other* land certain special rules as regards liability have been seen to apply. The purpose of this test is to exclude one Class A party from liability where it can be shown that another Class A person was responsible for the *actual escape* of contaminants from one site to the other.

The requirements for this test to be satisfied are that:

"(a)   a significant pollutant is present in, on or under the contaminated land … wholly or partly as a result of its escape from other land;

(b)   a member of the liability group for the significant pollutant linkage of which the pollutant forms a part:

    (i)   caused or knowingly permitted the pollution to be present in, on or under that other land (that is, he is a member of that liability group by reason of section 78K(1));[209] and

    (ii)   is a member of that liability group solely for that reason; and

(c)   one or more other members of that liability group caused or knowingly permitted the significant pollutant to escape from that other land and its escape would not have happened but for their actions or omissions."[210]

Test 6: *Introduction of pathways or receptors*

The intention here is to exclude from liability those who may have caused or knowingly permitted substances to be present on land, in contexts in which those substances would not have caused any harm or water pollution had it not been for the acts of some other persons within the liability group in subsequently introducing a relevant pathway[211] or receptor.

The requirements for the test to be satisfied are:

---

[208] Guidance, Annex 3, Chapter D, para. D63.
[209] For which see above, pp. 581–582.
[210] Guidance, Annex 3, Chapter D, para. D66.
[211] A route by which the contaminant may do harm or pollute water.

"(a) that one or more members of the liability group have carried out a 'relevant action' and/or made a 'relevant omission'[212] (the 'later actions'), either:

(i) as part of the series of actions and/or omissions which amount to their having caused or knowingly permitted the presence of the pollutant in a significant pollutant linkage, or

(ii) in addition to that series of actions and/or omissions;

(b) the effect of the later actions has been to introduce the pathway or the receptor which forms part of the significant pollution linkage in question;

(c) if those later actions had not been carried out or made, the significant pollutant linkage would either not have existed, or would not have been a significant pollutant linkage, because of the absence of a pathway or a receptor; and

(d) a person is a member of the liability group in question solely by reason of his carrying out other actions or making other omissions ('the earlier actions') which were completed before any of the later actions were carried out or made."

Exclusion from Class B

The statutory guidance sets out a *single* test to determine whether any members of a Class B liability group – that is, persons liable to meet remediation costs solely by reason of their current ownership or occupation of the land in question – should be excluded from that group. The rationale behind the test is to exclude those who, notwithstanding their ownership or occupation, do not have an interest in the capital value of the land. The aim would appear to be to cast Class B remedial burdens upon those who may benefit from the enhanced market value which may attach to the remediated land.

The guidance states that the Class B exclusion test applies where two or more persons have been identified as Class B persons for a significant pollutant linkage.[213] Where this is the case:

"the enforcing authority should exclude any Class B person who either:

---

[212] Relevant actions and omissions are defined in para. D70, and must take place on the contaminated land itself (para. D71). A relevant action involves (i) the carrying out at any time of building, engineering, mining or other operations in, on, over or under the land in question, and/or (ii) the making of any material change of use of the land in question for which a specific application for planning permission was required to be made ... at the time when the change of use was made. Relevant omission means: (i) in the course of a relevant action, failing to take a step which would have ensured that a significant pollution linkage was not brought into existence as a result of that action, and/or (ii) unreasonably failing to maintain or operate a system installed for the purpose of reducing or managing the risk associated with the presence on the land in question of the significant pollutant in the significant pollution linkage in question.

[213] Guidance, Annex 3, Chapter D, para. D88.

(a)   occupies the land under a licence, or other agreement, of a kind which has no marketable value or which he is not legally able to assign or transfer to another person (for these purposes the actual marketable value, or the fact that a particular licence or agreement may not actually attract a buyer in the market, are irrelevant) or

(b)   is liable to pay a rent which is equivalent to the rack rent for such of the land in question as he occupies and holds no beneficial interest in that land other than any tenancy to which such rent relates; where the rent is subject to periodic review, the rent should be considered to be equivalent to the rack rent if, at the latest review, it was set at the full market rent at that date."[214]

Apportionment between members of any single liability group

The tests we have considered for exclusion from Class A and Class B liability groups will have the effect of determining the persons amongst whom remediation liabilities shall be apportioned. It is now time to consider the guidance as regards the principles which should be applied by enforcing authorities when it comes to such apportionment. The guidance deals separately with apportionment within a Class A liability group, and apportionment within a Class B liability group.

Apportionment within a Class A group

The guidance begins with a note of warning:

"The history and circumstances of different areas of contaminated land, and the nature of the responsibility of each of the members of any Class A liability group for a significant pollution linkage, are likely to vary greatly. It is therefore not possible to prescribe detailed rules for the apportionment of liability between those members which would be fair and appropriate in all cases."[215]

The general principle to be adopted, however, is stated to be as follows:

"...the enforcing authority should follow the general principle that liability should be apportioned to reflect the relative responsibility of each of those members for creating or continuing the risk now being caused by the significant pollution linkage in question..."[216]

---

[214] Paragraph D89. Para. D90 reiterates the general principle applicable to exclusion tests under the guidance: "the test should not be applied, and consequently no exclusion should be made, if it would result in the exclusion of all the members of the liability group".

[215] Guidance, Annex 3, Chapter D, para. D74. Where a company and one or more of its relevant officers are included within a Class A liability group the general principle stated in the text should be applied taking into account "the responsibilities of the company and its relevant officers as a whole, in comparison with the responsibilities of other members of the liability group": Guidance, Annex 3, Chapter D, para. D85(a).

[216] Paragraph D75.

The application of this principle might, however, require there to be elicited information not presently or readily available to the enforcing authority. In order to limit the burdens upon the enforcing authority it is provided by the guidance that if appropriate information is not available for such an estimation of relative responsibility to be made, and if such information cannot reasonably be obtained,[217] the enforcing authority should apportion liability in equal shares between the members of the liability group.[218]

The general principle, referred to above, is supplemented in the guidance by what are described as "specific approaches", to be adopted in particular contexts or as regards particular issues, in order to help guide the process of determining relative responsibility.

The first such approach involves some favour being afforded to any persons who may have been able to go some way to having demonstrated that one of the Class A exclusion tests applied to them, but ultimately were not able to satisfy any of those tests fully. The guidance provides:

> "If for any member of the liability group, the circumstances set out in any of the exclusion tests … apply to some extent, but not sufficiently to mean that … exclusion should be made, the enforcing authority should assess that person's degree of responsibility as being reduced to the extent which is appropriate in the light of all the circumstances and the purpose of the test in question."[219]

By way of illustration an example is offered of a person who may have failed to have satisfied Test 2[220] because the sum paid towards remediation may have fallen short of the full amount necessary for that purpose. Nevertheless, if what was paid was sufficient to have paid for a proportion of the remediation, the responsibility which that person should bear when it comes to apportionment should be reduced accordingly.[221]

---

[217] Note here also the general statement in para. D36: enforcing authorities "should seek to obtain only such information as it is reasonable to seek, having regard to: (a) how the information might be obtained; (b) the cost of obtaining the information for all parties involved; and (c) the potential significance of the information for any decision".

[218] On the matter of "equal shares" the guidance states that for *this* purpose certain connected members of the liability group may be treated as one, thereby bearing only one such equal share: for example, a company and one or more of its "relevant officers" (i.e. directors, managers, secretaries or other similar officers: or persons purporting to act in that capacity). This share should then itself be apportioned by the enforcing authority in the notice served: this apportionment taking into account the degree of personal responsibility of the officers and the relative levels of resources available to the officers and the company to meet the liabilities. Guidance, Annex 3, Chapter D, para. D85.

[219] Guidance, Annex 3, Chapter D, para. D77.

[220] See above, pp. 596-597.

[221] The guidance says that if the sum paid would have paid for half the remediation the enforcing authority should reduce that person's liability burden by a half. It may be noted that this produces results which are not quite the same as had the exclusion test been satisfied. Remember that, as regards Test 2, the burden arising out of having excluded the payer falls not amongst the rest of the group as a whole, but upon the payee (who failed to use the money for remediation, or for effective remediation notwithstanding that the sum was sufficient for that purpose).

The second "specific approach" to the apportionment of relative responsibility relates to the responsibilities of those who have caused or knowingly permitted the entry of a pollutant into, onto or under land ("first persons"), as compared with persons who may have knowingly permitted its continued presence there ("second persons").

In this connection it is provided:

> "... the enforcing authority should consider the extent to which the second person had the means and a reasonable opportunity to deal with the presence of the pollutant in question or to reduce the seriousness of the implications of that presence ..."

Having so considered:

> "The authority should then assess the relative responsibilities on the following basis:
> (a) if the second person had the necessary means and opportunity, he should bear the same responsibility as the first person;
> (b) if the second person did not have the means and opportunity, his responsibility relative to that of the first person should be substantially reduced; and
> (c) if the second person had some, but insufficient, means or opportunity, his responsibility relative to that of the first person should be reduced to an appropriate extent."[222]

The third category of "specific guidance" applies where the enforcing authority is considering the relative responsibilities attaching to different persons who may have caused or knowingly permitted the entry of the significant pollutant into, onto or under the land.

The guidance begins with the simplest situation:

> "If the nature of the remediation action points clearly to different members of the liability group being responsible for particular circumstances at which the action is aimed, the enforcing authority should apportion responsibility in accordance with that indication. In particular, where different persons were in control of different areas of the land in question, and there is no interrelationship between those areas, the enforcing authority should regard the persons in control of the different areas as being separately responsible for the

---

[222] Guidance, Annex 3, Chapter D, para. D78. This guidance may prove disappointing to Class A persons who may hope to benefit from subparagraph (b). Persons who did not have the means or opportunity to deal with the continued presence of the pollutant or to deal with the seriousness of its implications would not seem to fall within Class A at all: see above, pp. 574-576 on the meaning to be attributed to "knowingly permitted". Any person who has properly been characterised as a Class A person will, therefore, find it hard to satisfy the requirements of subpara. (b).

events which make necessary the remediation actions or parts of actions referable to those areas of land."[223]

Where this approach is, on the facts, inapplicable it may nevertheless be an appropriate indication of relative responsibility to consider the relative amounts of the significant pollutant whose entry is referable to the various Class A persons. This may be appropriate where the quantity of the pollutant is a major factor in the cost of the remediation which is necessary.[224]

It may be no easy task to assess with accuracy the volume of the pollutant referable to the activities of each of the Class A parties. Where direct evidence is not available, the guidance calls upon enforcing authorities to ask whether estimates may be made on the basis of what it refers to as "surrogate" measures of such pollution. It continues:

"Such surrogate measures can include:
(a) the relative periods during which the different persons carried out broadly equivalent operations on the land;
(b) the relative scale of such operations carried out on the land by the different persons (a measure of such scale may be the quantities of a product that were produced);
(c) the relative areas of land on which different persons carried out their operations;
(d) combinations of the foregoing measures."[225]

The fourth "specific approach" relates to the determination of relative responsibilities as between persons who have knowingly permitted the continued presence of a significant pollutant in, on or under land. Apportionment here should be:

"in proportion to:
(a) the length of time during which each person controlled the land;
(b) the area of land which each person controlled;
(c) the extent to which each person had the means and a reasonable opportunity to deal with the presence of the pollutant in question or to reduce the seriousness of the implications of that presence; or
(d) a combination of the foregoing factors."[226]

Apportionment within a Class B group

In general terms the statutory guidance on apportionment within this Class follows the basic logic of the Class B exclusionary test, described above: that those Class B persons who may benefit in terms of capital value

---

[223] Guidance, Annex 3, Chapter D, para. D80.
[224] Paragraph D81.
[225] Paragraph D82.
[226] Paragraph D84.

enhancement following the remediation of land should bear the costs of that remediation.

The guidance begins with the situation where the whole or a part of a remediation action for which a Class B group is responsible clearly relates to a particular area within the wider contaminated site, and that area is owned or occupied by some but not all of the members of the Class B group. In this situation the cost of that remedial action, or that part of the remedial action, should be apportioned among those who own or occupy that part.[227]

Where it is not possible to relate the costs of remediation to ownership or occupation of particular portions of the site the enforcing authority should apportion liability amongst all the members of the liability group.[228] This apportionment should be in proportion to the capital values[229] of the interests in the land in question. Furthermore:

> "(a) where different members of the liability group own or occupy different areas of land, each such member should bear responsibility in the proportion that the capital value of his area of land bears to the aggregate of the capital values of all the areas of land;
>
> (b) where different members of the liability group have an interest in the same area of land, each such member should bear responsibility in the proportion which the capital value of his interest bears to the aggregate of the capital values of all those interests; and
>
> (c) where both the ownership or occupation of different areas of land and the holding of different interests come into the question, the overall liability should first be apportioned between the different areas of land and then between the interests within each of those areas of land, in each case in accordance with the last two subparagraphs."[230]

Where appropriate information is not available to enable the enforcing authority to make an assessment of relative capital values the enforcing authority should apportion liability in equal shares among all members of the Class B liability group.[231]

---

[227] Paragraph D92.

[228] Paragraph D93.

[229] Assessed on the basis of the available information, "disregarding the existence of any contamination": para. D95.

[230] Paragraph D94.

[231] Paragraph D97.

REMEDIATION BY THE ENFORCING AUTHORITY: COST RECOVERY PROVISIONS

The main thrust of the new measures in Part IIA of the 1990 Act is to confer on local authorities and the Environment Agency powers by virtue of which remediation may be required to be undertaken by the statutorily defined appropriate persons.

In certain contexts, however, the enforcing authority is given power to take steps to undertake some or all of the remediation actions itself. These situations are set out in section 78N.

The section begins with two provisions which limit its general scope. They provide no surprises. First, and as might be expected, the land in question must be land which has been identified as a contaminated site or designated as a special site.[232] Secondly, the power does not exist in a situation where the service of a remediation notice would, in the particular case, have been precluded by section 78YB.[233] Section 78YB precludes the service of a remediation notice under Part IIA in certain situations where other statutory procedures are applicable (e.g. in relation to IPC or waste licensing).

Provided the general provisions described above are not applicable the power of an enforcing authority to carry out remediation will apply in each of the circumstances listed in section 78N(3):

"(a) where the enforcing authority considers it necessary to do anything itself by way of remediation for the purpose of preventing the occurrence of any serious harm, or serious pollution of controlled waters, of which there is imminent danger;

(b) where an appropriate person has entered into a written agreement with the enforcing authority for that authority to do, at the cost of that person, that which he would otherwise be required to do under this Part by way of remediation;

(c) where a person on whom the enforcing authority serves a remediation notice fails to comply with any of the requirements of the notice;

(d) where the enforcing authority is precluded by section 78J or 78K[234] ... from including something by way of remediation in a remediation notice;

---

[232] Section 78N(1).

[233] Section 78N(2).

[234] Section 78J places certain restrictions on liability where contamination includes pollution of controlled waters – see below, p. 577, fn. 152; s. 78K deals with liabilities where contaminating substances have escaped to other land – see above, pp. 581-582.

(e)   where the enforcing authority considers that, were it to do some
      particular thing by way of remediation, it would decide, by
      virtue of subsection (2) of section 78P ... or any guidance
      issued under that subsection –

    (i)   not to seek to recover under subsection (1) of that section
       any of the reasonable cost incurred by it in doing that
       thing; or

    (ii)   to seek so to recover only a portion of that cost;

(f)   where no person has, after reasonable inquiry, been found who
      is an appropriate person in relation to any particular thing."[235]

Cost recovery

Cost recovery in respect of such public sector works is governed by section
78P and the associated statutory guidance. Section 78P(1) provides:

> "Where, by virtue of section 78N(3) (a), (c), (e) or (f) ... the
> enforcing authority does any particular thing by way of remediation,
> it shall be entitled, subject to sections 78J(7) and 78K(6) ... to
> recover the reasonable cost incurred in doing it from the appropriate
> person or, if there are two or more appropriate persons in relation to
> the thing in question, from those persons in proportions determined
> pursuant to section 78F(7) ..."

In deciding whether to recover such costs, and if so, how much of those
costs, the enforcing authority is required to have regard to the statutory
guidance which has been issued, and also:

> "to any hardship which the recovery may cause to the person from
> whom the cost is recoverable."[236]

In coming to decisions as regards the matter of cost recovery the enforcing
authority should have regard to a number of general and more specific
considerations set out in the statutory guidance. The guidance makes clear,
however, that:

> "In view of the wide variation in situations which are likely to arise
> ... the statutory guidance ... sets out principles and approaches,
> rather than detailed rules. The enforcing authority will need to have
> regard to the circumstances of each individual case."[237]

Nevertheless, certain principles of general application are stated:

---

[235] Section 78N(3).

[236] Section 78P(2)(a). For the linkage between hardship precluding the service of a remediation
notice and hardship conferring power on enforcing authorities to undertake action itself, see
s. 78H(5) and above pp. 567.

[237] Guidance, Annex 3, Chapter E, para. E10.

"In making any cost recovery decision, the enforcing authority should have regard to the following general principles:

(a)   the authority should aim for an overall result which is as fair and equitable as possible to all who may have to meet the costs of remediation, including national and local taxpayers;

(b)   the 'polluter pays' principle, by virtue of which the costs of remediating pollution are to be borne by the polluter; the authority should therefore consider the degree and nature of responsibility of the appropriate person for the creation, or continued existence, of the circumstances which led to the land in question being identified as contaminated land."[238]

The guidance makes clear that:

"In general this will mean that the enforcing authority should seek to recover in full its reasonable costs."[239]

However:

"... the authority should waive or reduce the recovery of costs to the extent that the authority considers this appropriate and reasonable, either:

(a)   to avoid any hardship which the recovery may cause to the appropriate persons; or

(b)   to reflect one or more of the specific considerations set out in the statutory guidance ..."

Moreover:

"When deciding how much of its costs it should recover in any case, the enforcing authority should consider whether it could recover more of its costs by deferring recovery and securing them by a charge on the land ... Such deferral may lead to payment from the appropriate person either in instalments ... or when the land is next sold."[240]

The more specific guidance on the matter of cost recovery is divided into three parts: (i) considerations applicable to both Class A and Class B persons; (ii) considerations specific to Class A persons; and (iii) considerations specific to Class B persons.

---

[238] Paragraph E11.

[239] Paragraph E12.

[240] Paragraph E13.

Cost recovery considerations applicable to both Class A and Class B persons

The guidance exhorts enforcing authorities, as a starting point, to adopt the same approach to all types of commercial or industrial enterprises which have been identified as appropriate persons. This applies whether the appropriate person is a public corporation, a limited company, a partnership or an individual operating as a sole trader.[241]

Some distinction is, however, drawn between large enterprises and those which are small or medium-sized.[242] The guidance states that where an appropriate person is a small or medium-sized enterprise:

> "the enforcing authority should consider whether recovery of the full cost attributable to that person would mean that the enterprise is likely to become insolvent and thus cease to exist."

The enforcing authority should here take into account somewhat broader economic considerations:

> "Where the cost of closure appears to be greater than the costs of remediation which the enforcing authority would have to bear themselves, the authority should consider waiving or reducing its costs recovery to the extent needed to avoid making the enterprise insolvent."[243]

An important limit to the application of this consideration is emphasised:

> "... the authority should not waive or reduce its costs recovery where it is clear that an enterprise has deliberately arranged matters so as to avoid responsibility for the costs of remediation."[244]

There are provisions in the guidance in relation to "trusts" which mirror the approach described above as regards small and medium-sized enterprises. Where the appropriate persons include persons acting as trustees, the enforcing authority:

> "should assume that such trustees will exercise all the powers which they have, or may reasonably obtain, to make funds available from the trust, or from borrowing that can be made on behalf of the trust, for the purpose of paying for remediation."

The authority should, nevertheless, consider waiving or reducing its costs recovery:

---

[241] Paragraph E20.

[242] The categorisation follows that which is familiar in the context of EU State Aid – see OJ C213 1996, item 4. A small or medium-sized enterprise is an independent enterprise with fewer than 250 employees and either an annual turnover not exceeding 40 million Euro, or an annual balance sheet total not exceeding 27 million Euro.

[243] Paragraph E22.

[244] Paragraph E23(a).

"... to the extent that the costs of remediation to be recovered from the trustees would otherwise exceed the amount that can be made available from the trust to cover those costs."[245]

Again, there are exceptions to such beneficence. The authority should not waive or reduce its costs recovery where it is clear that the trust was formed for the purpose of avoiding paying the costs of remediation, or to the extent that trustees may benefit, or may have benefited personally, from the trust.

In similar vein, an enforcing authority should consider waiving or reducing its costs recovery where the appropriate person in question has charitable status. Such waiver or reduction may be considered the proper course of action where otherwise costs recovery:

"would jeopardise that charity's ability to continue to provide a benefit or amenity which is in the public interest."[246]

Waiver or reduction of costs recovery should also be considered where such action might cause financial difficulties for social housing landlords, which would not serve the public interest. The guidance refers to "persons eligible for registration as a social housing landlord under section 2 of the Housing Act 1996".[247] The liability of that landlord must relate to land used for social housing, and it must be considered that:

"full cost recovery would lead to financial difficulties for the appropriate person, such that the provision or upkeep of the social housing would be jeopardised."[248]

In such a case it may be felt appropriate to reduce or waive costs recovery so far as is necessary to avoid the stated consequences.

Cost recovery considerations applicable to Class A persons only

Where an appropriate person is a Class A person certain additional considerations should be taken into account when an enforcing authority is considering costs recovery. In reaching its decision, applying the approach shortly to be described, the enforcing authority:

"should be less willing to waive or reduce its costs recovery where it was in the course of carrying on a business that the Class A person caused or knowingly permitted the presence of the significant pollutants, than where [the Class A person] was not carrying on a business."[249]

---

[245] Paragraph E27.

[246] Paragraph E29.

[247] Paragraph E30(a). For example, a housing association.

[248] Paragraph E30(c).

[249] Paragraph E33.

The rationale behind this general approach is stated to be that the appropriate person "is likely to have earned profits from the activity which created or permitted the presence of those pollutants".

What, then, are the specific considerations which should be applied according to this general approach?

The guidance begins by positing a situation where in addition to a Class A person who *has* been found, some other person has been identified who would have been a Class A appropriate person *had that person been found.* In what circumstances may a party be "identified" but not "found"? The guidance, consistent with its earlier discussion of the notion "found",[250] refers to the example of companies which have been dissolved.

The guidance states that the authority should consider waiving or reducing its costs recovery from a Class A person where:

> "(a) another identified person, who cannot now be found, also caused or knowingly permitted the significant pollutant to be in, on or under the land; and
>
> (b) if that other person could be found, the Class A person seeking the waiver or reduction of the authority's costs recovery would either:
>
> (i) be excluded from liability by virtue of one or more of the exclusion tests [for members of a Class A liability group], or
>
> (ii) the proportion of the cost of remediation which the appropriate person has to bear would have been significantly less, by virtue of the guidance on apportionment [as between members of a Class A liability group]."[251]

Cost recovery considerations applicable to Class B persons only

Where an appropriate person is a Class B person certain additional considerations apply to an enforcing authority's costs recovery decision-making.

The guidance begins by noting that in some cases the costs of remediation may exceed the value which the land will have after the required remediation (related to its current use) has been carried out. It advises:

> "The enforcing authority should consider waiving or reducing its costs recovery from a Class B person if that person demonstrates to the satisfaction of the authority that the costs of remediation are likely to exceed the value of the land."[252]

---

[250] See above, pp. 577-580.

[251] Paragraph E35. The words in square brackets are those of the authors.

[252] Paragraph E39. "Value" should be taken to be "the value that the remediated land would have on the open market disregarding any possible blight arising from the contamination".

The extent of the waiver or reduction should be sufficient to ensure that the costs borne by the Class B party do not exceed the value of the land. However, the enforcing authority should "seek to recover more of its costs to the extent that the remediation would result in an increase in the value of any other land from which the Class B person would benefit".[253]

The guidance next draws a distinction between cases where a Class B appropriate person may have been reckless as to the possibility that land which he acquired was contaminated, and cases where such a person may have taken precautions in order to have tried to avoid such an acquisition. The guidance states:

"The authority should consider reducing its costs recovery where a Class B person who is the owner of the land demonstrates to the satisfaction of the authority that:

(a)   he took such steps prior to acquiring the freehold, or accepting the grant [or] assignment of a leasehold, as would have been reasonable[254] at that time to establish the presence of any pollutants;

(b)   when he acquired the land, or accepted the grant [or] assignment of the leasehold, he was nonetheless unaware of the presence of the significant pollutant now identified and could not reasonably have been expected to have been aware of their presence; and

(c)   it would be fair and reasonable, taking into account the interests of national and local taxpayers, that he should not bear the whole cost of remediation."[255]

Where a Class B person is an owner-occupier of a dwelling on the contaminated land, it may be appropriate for there to be a waiver or reduction of costs recovery where:

"that person satisfies the authority that, at the time he purchased the dwelling, he did not know, and could not reasonably have been expected to have known, that the land was adversely affected by presence of a pollutant."[256]

Any such waiver or reduction should be to the extent necessary to ensure that that Class B person:

---

[253] Paragraph E40.

[254] Paragraph E43 provides reassurance, that "the enforcing authority should bear in mind that the safeguards which might reasonably be expected to be taken will be different in different types of transaction (for example, acquisition of recreational land as compared with commercial land transactions) and as between buyers of different types (for example, private individuals as compared with major commercial undertakings)".

[255] Paragraph E42.

[256] Paragraph E44.

"bears no more of the cost of remediation than it appears reasonable to impose, having regard to his income, capital and outgoings."[257]

This waiver or reduction principle will apply only as regards remediation relating to the dwelling and its curtilage. If the Class B person owns a more extensive area of land, which requires remediation beyond the area of the dwelling and its curtilage, ordinary cost recovery principles should apply in relation to remediation of that wider area.[258]

COMPENSATION PROVISIONS: GRANT OF RIGHTS OVER LAND TO SECURE REMEDIATION

It is possible that a remediation notice may require an appropriate person to undertake remedial action notwithstanding that he is *not entitled* to do those things. In such circumstances, section 78G(2) of the 1990 Act provides that:

"Any person whose consent is required before any thing required by a remediation notice may be done *shall grant, or join in granting*, such rights in relation to any of the relevant land or waters as will enable the appropriate person to comply with any requirements imposed by the remediation notice."[259]

In short, therefore, in common with other statutory remediation regimes,[260] this provision places the need to remediate contaminated land above the property rights of the individual. Such landowners are, however, entitled to be compensated by the appropriate person following the making of an application for compensation within the prescribed period.

The detail of the compensation provisions is to be found in Schedule 2 to the Contaminated Land (England) Regulations 2000. The period for making an application begins with the date on which the grant of rights in respect of which compensation is claimed took place. It ends on whichever is the latest of the following dates:

(i)   twelve months after the date of the grant of the rights;
(ii) where an appeal has been made in respect of a remediation notice, twelve months after the date on which the appeal is finally determined or abandoned; or
(iii) six months after the date on which the rights were first exercised.[261]

---

[257] Paragraph E45. For this purpose the enforcing authority is advised that it may obtain guidance from the way in which applications for housing renovation grants are means-tested, under the Housing Renewal Grants Regulations 1996 (SI 1996/2890, as amended). See Guidance, Chapter E, paras E47-49.
[258] Paragraph E46.
[259] Emphasis added.
[260] See, for example, s. 161B of the Water Resources Act 1991, discussed below at pp. 516-518.
[261] Regulation 2 of the Contaminated Land (England) Regulations 2000.

Applications for compensation must be made in writing and must be delivered or sent to the last known address for correspondence of the appropriate person to whom the rights were granted. Such applications must contain or be accompanied by the following information:

(i) a copy of the grant of rights in respect of which the grantor is applying for compensation, and of any plans attached to the grant;

(ii) a description of the exact nature of the interest in land in respect of which compensation is sought; and

(iii) a statement of the amount of compensation applied for, distinguishing between the amounts applied for under each of the various heads set out in the Schedule.

The loss and damage for which compensation is payable is as follows:

"(a) depreciation in the value of any relevant interest to which the grantor is entitled which results from the grant of the rights;

(b) depreciation in the value of any other interest in land to which the grantor is entitled which results from the exercise of the rights;

(c) loss or damage, in relation to any relevant interest to which the grantor is entitled, which –

    (i) is attributable to the grant of the rights or the exercise of them;

    (ii) does not consist of depreciation in the value of that interest; and

    (iii) is loss or damage for which he would have been entitled to compensation by way of compensation for disturbance, if that interest had been acquired compulsorily under the Acquisition of Land Act 1981 in pursuance of a notice to treat served on the date on which the rights were granted;

(d) damage to, or injurious affection of, any interest in land to which the grantor is entitled which is not a relevant interest, and which results from the grant of the rights or the exercise of them; and

(e) loss in respect of work carried out by or on behalf of the grantor which is rendered abortive by the grant of the rights or the exercise of them."[262]

Paragraph 5 of Schedule 2 to the 2000 Regulations sets out the basis on which compensation is assessed. The rules which apply in respect of the assessing of compensation for the compulsory acquisition of an interest in land[263] also apply in the present context, subject to any necessary modifications.

---

[262] Schedule 2, para. 4 of the Contaminated Land (England) Regulations 2000.

[263] See s. 5 of the Land Compensation Act 1961.

Where the loss suffered by the grantor falls within (e) above, in calculating that loss, account shall be taken of the expenditure incurred in the preparation of plans or other similar preparatory matters.[264] Schedule 2 further provides that compensation paid under section 78G shall include the grantor's reasonable valuation and legal expenses.[265]

Amounts of compensation determined under Schedule 2 may be paid either in a single payment or alternatively in instalments, as agreed by the parties. In any other case, subject to any direction of the Lands Tribunal or the court, compensation is to be paid as soon as reasonably practicable following the determination of the relevant sum.[266]

REGISTERS

By virtue of section 78R of the 1990 Act, enforcing authorities are under a duty to maintain registers of information relating to various aspects of the contaminated land regime.[267] The prescribed particulars which must be set out in the register are as follows:[268]

- remediation notices served by the enforcing authority;
- appeals against any such remediation notices;
- remediation statements or remediation declarations prepared and published under section 78H;
- appeals against charging notices served by the enforcing authority;
- notices issued by the enforcing authority under section 78C relating to the designation of land as a special site;
- notices issued by the Secretary of State under section 78D relating to the designation of land as a special site;
- notices given by/to the enforcing authority under section 78Q(4) terminating the designation of any land as a special site;
- notifications given to the enforcing authority by persons on whom a remediation notice has been served or who are or were required[269] to prepare and publish a remediation statement of what they claim has been done by them by way of remediation;
- notifications given to the enforcing authority by owners/occupiers of land in respect of which a remediation notice has been served or a remediation statement has been prepared and published, of what they claim has been done on the land in question by way of remediation.[270]

---

[264] Schedule 2, para. 5(4).

[265] Schedule 2, para. 5(6).

[266] Schedule 2, para. 6(2)(c).

[267] Section 78R(9) provides that these registers "may be kept in any form". Thus they may be kept in an electronic format.

[268] Section 78R(1)(a)-(l).

[269] By virtue of s. 78H(8)(a).

[270] The form and descriptions of information to be contained in this and the preceding notifications has been prescribed by the Secretary of State in the Contaminated Land (England) Regulations 2000 and by the Welsh Assembly in the Contaminated Land (Wales) Regulations 2001, SI 2001/2197 (W.157). Regulation 15(2) of the former Regulations prescribes the following descriptions of information: (a) the location and extent of the land sufficient to enable it to be

The duty under section 78R is, however, subject to the exceptions set out in sections 78S and 78T, respectively. These sections reflect a customary feature of public register regimes, namely that information which affects national security or which is of a commercially confidential nature may be excluded from the register kept by the enforcing authority.

The wording of sections 78S and 78T is broadly the same as that to be found in sections 21 and 22 of the 1990 Act which relate to registers of information in respect of the IPC regime. Whether or not information should be excluded from a Part IIA register on the grounds of national security is a matter to be determined by the Secretary of State. Exclusion on the grounds of commercial confidentiality is a matter determined by the enforcing authority or, on appeal, by the Secretary of State.[271] Information is to be regarded as being "commercially confidential" if "its being contained in the register would prejudice to an unreasonable degree the commercial interests" of an individual or person.[272] However, this definition is subject to a caveat: prejudice to the commercial interests of an individual or person is to be disregarded in so far as it relates to the value of the contaminated land or otherwise to the ownership/occupation of that land.[273] Thus in the words of the Circular:

> "... information cannot be excluded from the register solely on the basis that its inclusion might provide information to a prospective buyer of the land, thereby affecting the sale or the sale price."[274]

More detailed information in relation to Part IIA registers is to be found in the Contaminated Land (England) Regulations 2000.[275] Thus, for example, where a remediation notice has been served, the register must contain the following particulars:

(i)   the name and address of the person on whom the notice is served;

(ii) the location and extent of the contaminated land to which the notice relates sufficient to enable it to be identified by reference to a plan or otherwise;

---

identified; (b) the name and address of the person who it is claimed has done each of the things by way of remediation; (c) a description of any thing which it is claimed has been done by way of remediation; and (d) the period within which it is claimed each such thing was done. It should be noted, however, that no entry in connection with any notification under these provisions constitutes a representation by the body maintaining the register (or by any authority sending the particulars to that body) that what is stated in the entry to have been done has in fact been done or as to the manner in which it has been done: see s. 78R(3).

[271] Section 78T(1). Where information is excluded from the register on this basis, a statement must be entered in the register indicating the existence of commercially confidential information: see s. 78R(7).

[272] Section 78T(10).

[273] Section 78T(11).

[274] Circular, Annex 2, para. 17.11.

[275] SI No. 227.

(iii) the significant harm or pollution of controlled waters by reason of which the contaminated land in question is contaminated land;

(iv) the substances by reason of which the contaminated land in question is contaminated land and, if any of the substances have escaped from other land, the location of that other land;

(v) the current use of the contaminated land in question;

(vi) what each appropriate person is to do by way of remediation and the periods within which they are required to do each of the things; and

(vii) the date of the notice.

In the case of remediation declarations or statements, in addition to the declaration or statement itself, the register must contain the location and extent of the contaminated land sufficient to enable it to be identified as well as the particulars referred to in (iii)-(v) above.[276] Where a person has been convicted of an offence under section 78M in relation to a remediation notice, the register must contain the name of the offender, the date of the conviction, the penalty imposed and the name of the court.[277]

Enforcing authorities are under a duty to ensure that any Part IIA register which it maintains is available for inspection by the public at all reasonable times free of charge. Where the enforcing authority is the local authority, the register must be made available at its principal office. If the Environment Agency is the enforcing authority, the register must be made available at its office for the area in which the contaminated land in question is situated.[278] In either case, the enforcing authority must afford members of the public facilities for obtaining copies of entries on the register on payment of reasonable charges.[279]

INTER-RELATIONSHIP BETWEEN PART IIA OF THE 1990 ACT AND OTHER STATUTORY REMEDIATION REGIMES

Part IIA of the 1990 Act contains important provisions explaining when its provisions shall apply and when problems associated with contaminated land should be dealt with under other legal regimes: in particular the provisions relating to (i) integrated pollution control; (ii) waste management licensing, and the unlawful deposit of controlled waste; (iii) statutory nuisance; and (iv) radioactivity. Part IIA does not make explicit reference to the relationship between its own provisions and the works notice powers, contained within the Water Resources Act 1991, relating to the prevention of pollution of controlled waters and the cleanup of polluted waters. That matter will, notwithstanding the absence of clear statutory provision, nevertheless require discussion.

---

[276] Schedule 3, paras 4-7.
[277] Schedule 3, para. 12.
[278] Regulation 15(3)(a) and (b).
[279] Environmental Protection Act 1990, s. 78R(8).

Integrated pollution control[280]

Section 78YB(1) of the 1990 Act provides that no remediation notice may be served under Part IIA in any case where it appears to an enforcing authority that the IPC powers under section 27 are applicable to the significant harm or the pollution of controlled waters by reason of which the land in question is to be regarded as contaminated.

Section 27 of the 1990 Act applies where the commission of certain IPC offences[281] has caused harm which it is possible to remedy. In this situation the Environment Agency may:

"(a) arrange for any reasonable steps to be taken towards remedying the harm; and

(b) recover the cost of taking those steps from any person convicted of the offence."[282]

Section 78YB(1) therefore excludes the operation of the provisions of Part IIA where such an IPC offence has given rise to harm in the nature of land contamination which would otherwise have fallen within the new regime.

Since the Part IIA regime came into force, significant developments have occurred in the context of pollution control with the advent of the Integrated Pollution Prevention and Control Directive[283] and its national implementing measures, the Pollution Prevention and Control Act 1999 and the Pollution Prevention and Control (England and Wales) Regulations 2000.[284] As a consequence of the phased implementation of the Directive,[285] the IPC and IPPC regimes will co-exist for several years to come. It was stated prior to the making of the 2000 Regulations that the Secretary of State "may include" in those Regulations "provisions amending section 78YB(1) to refer to both section 27 of the 1990 Act and to any equivalent clean-up provision in the new PPC regime".[286] As it turned out, however, the Regulations opted for another way of dealing with this matter, as will become apparent below.

---

[280] The provisions to be described govern also the relationship between Part IIA and land contamination from processes falling within the local authority air pollution control regime (Part B processes under Part I of the 1990 Act).

[281] The offences under s. 23(1)(a) or (c). These comprise (i) operating an IPC prescribed process without, or other than in accordance with, an authorisation; and (ii) contravention of, or failure to comply with, any requirement of an enforcement or prohibition notice.

[282] Section 27(1). Note the requirements of approval from the Secretary of State; and, where the steps to be taken will be on, or will affect, land in the occupation of a person other than the person on whose land the prescribed (IPC) process is carried on, the permission of that occupier: see s. 27(2).

[283] 96/61/EC.

[284] SI 2000/1973. These Regulations were made pursuant to s. 2 of the Pollution Prevention and Control Act 1999. In effect, they rather than the Act are the means by which the terms of the Directive have been implemented in English law.

[285] The permit system which the Directive provides for must take effect for all plant previously authorised under the IPC/LAAPC regime by 2007.

[286] Circular 2/2000, Annex A, para. 7.8.

Integrated pollution prevention and control

The relationship between Part IIA and the IPPC regime is recognised by certain amendments which the 2000 Regulations have made to section 78YB. Thus Part IIA does not apply where the contamination of land is attributable to the final disposal by deposit in or on land of controlled waste, or some activity other than such a final disposal by deposit of controlled waste, and enforcement action may be taken in relation to the disposal or activity under the 2000 Regulations.[287] For the purpose of these provisions, "enforcement action" amounts to action under either regulation 24[288] or regulation 26(2)[289] of the 2000 Regulations. In effect, therefore, these provisions have been added to reflect the fact that landfill sites[290] which are now regulated under the IPPC regime may be the cause of land contamination, as indeed may other activities which also fall within the scope of IPPC.

Waste management licensing

Section 78YB(2) of the 1990 Act provides that Part IIA shall not apply in relation to any land in respect of which there is in force a waste management licence,[291] except to the extent that any significant harm or pollution of controlled waters is attributable to causes other than:

> "(a) breach of the conditions of the licence; or
> (b)   the carrying on, in accordance with the conditions of the licence, of an activity authorised by the licence."

The exception provided for here does not, therefore, rule out the possibility that the provisions in Part IIA will be activated where the land in question has been contaminated by historical activities on the site. However, since the exception relates to activities carried out under the authority of a waste management licence, it should be remembered that this will also create an exception in respect of licences originally issued under Part I of the Control of Pollution Act 1974. Such licences have been converted into waste management licences by section 77 of the 1990 Act.

Unlawful deposit of controlled waste

Section 78YB(3) deals with the relationship between Part IIA and the powers within section 59 of the 1990 Act to require the removal of waste unlawfully deposited. It provides that where land appears to be contaminated land by reference to the deposit of controlled waste in

---

[287] Section 78YB(2A) and (2B) as inserted by the Pollution Prevention and Control (England and Wales) Regulations 2000, Sched. 10, para. 6.

[288] This empowers a regulator to serve an enforcement notice where the view is taken that an operator has contravened, is contravening or is likely to contravene any condition of his permit.

[289] This enables the regulator to take steps to remedy the effects of any pollution caused in contravention of either regulation 32(1)(a), or (b) or (d).

[290] For the details of the permit regime which applies to landfills, see the Landfill (England and Wales) Regulations 2002, SI 2002/1559.

[291] Issued under Part II of the 1990 Act.

circumstances which appear to make applicable the powers under section 59, then a remediation notice under Part IIA may not be served.

The powers under section 59 may be summarised in the following way. Subsection (1) empowers the Environment Agency (or waste disposal authority) to serve a notice requiring an occupier to do certain things where:

> "any controlled waste [has been] deposited in or on any land ... in contravention of sections 33(1) ..."[292]

In such circumstances the things which may be ordered comprise one or both of the following:

> "(a) to remove the waste from the land within a specified period not less than a period of twenty-one days beginning with the service of the notice;
> (b) to take within such a period specified steps with a view to eliminating or reducing the consequences of the deposit of the waste."[293]

Failure, without reasonable excuse, to comply with the requirements imposed in such a notice involves the commission of a summary offence.[294]

This potential administrative and criminal liability on the part of occupiers is tempered however by the terms of subsections (2) and (3). Subsection (2) provides that a person served with such a notice under subsection (1) may, within 21 days, appeal to the magistrates's court.[295] Subsection (3) requires that that court shall quash the notice if it is satisfied that:

> "(a) the appellant neither deposited nor knowingly caused nor knowingly permitted the deposit of the waste; or
> (b) there is a material defect in the notice."

In any other case the court shall either modify the requirements of the notice or dismiss the appeal.

Section 59 includes also default and costs recovery powers. Subsection (6) states:

> "Where a person on whom a requirement has been imposed under subsection (1) above by an authority fails to comply with the requirement the authority may do what that person was required to do

---

[292] For s. 33(1), see above, pp. 372-385.

[293] Section 59(1)(a) and (b).

[294] Section 59(5). Provision is made for a fine not exceeding level 5 on the standard scale "and to a further fine of an amount equal to one-tenth of level 5 ... for each day on which the failure continues after conviction of the offence and before the authority has begun to exercise its powers under subsection (6) ...".

[295] The requirements of a notice are of no effect once an appeal has been lodged, pending determination of the appeal: subs. (4).

and may recover from him any expenses reasonably incurred by the authority in so doing it."

This default powers/cost recovery provision is conditioned on there having been some failure to have complied with the terms of a subsection (1) notice. In addition there should be noted the powers conferred upon the Agency and waste collection authorities, by subsections (7) and (8), to take action to remove waste from land and recover their reasonable costs in doing so.

Subsection (7) is applicable in any case where it may appear to such an authority that waste has been deposited in or on any land in contravention of section 33(1) of the 1990 Act, and that:

> "(a) in order to remove or prevent pollution of land, water or air or harm to human health it is necessary that the waste be forthwith removed or other steps taken to eliminate or reduce the consequences of the deposit or both; or
> (b) there is no occupier of the land; or
> (c) the occupier neither made nor knowingly permitted the deposit of the waste."

In such circumstances the authority in question:

> "may remove the waste from the land or take other steps to eliminate or reduce the consequences of the deposit or, as the case may require, to remove the waste and take those steps."

In terms of cost recovery for such action, subsection (8) provides that where action has been taken under subsection (7) the authority in question:

> "shall be entitled to recover the cost incurred by it in removing the waste or taking the steps or both and in disposing of the waste."

Where the action was taken under subsection (7)(a) the costs recovery is:

> "... from the occupier of the land, unless he proves that he neither made nor knowingly caused nor knowingly permitted the deposit of the waste."[296]

Where the action was taken other than under subsection (7)(a) the costs recovery power is exercisable against:

> "any person who deposited or knowingly caused or knowingly permitted the deposit of any of the waste."[297]

Cost recovery is limited by reference to what was "necessary".

---

[296] Section 59(8)(a).
[297] Section 59(8)(b).

Statutory nuisances

In some circumstances contaminated land problems, prior to the introduction of the new regime under Part IIA, might have fallen within the scope of the powers relating to statutory nuisances within section 79 of the 1990 Act. In order to avoid duplication of controls the 1995 Act has modified the definition of statutory nuisance by the introduction into section 79 of new subsections (1A) and (1B).

Subsection (1A) states that:

> "No matter shall constitute a statutory nuisance to the extent that it consists of, or is caused by, any land being in a contaminated state."

The expression "contaminated state" is defined by subsection (1B):

> "Land is in a 'contaminated state' for the purposes of subsection (1A) ... if, and only if, it is in such condition, by reason of substances in, on or under the land that:
> (a)   harm is being caused or there is a possibility of harm being caused; or
> (b)   pollution of controlled waters is being, or is likely to be, caused;
> ..."

It is the case, therefore, that the definition of what constitutes a "contaminated state" for these purposes has deliberately been set on a broader basis than the definition of "contaminated land" for the purposes of the Part IIA regime. The "contaminated state" definition refers merely to "harm" and the "possibility" of harm being caused, whereas the definition of "contaminated land" uses the concepts, "significant harm" and "significant possibility" of such harm being caused.[298]

The Circular explains:

> "Parliament considers that the Part IIA regime, as explained in the statutory guidance, sets out the right level of protection for human health and the environment from the effects of land contamination. It has therefore judged it inappropriate to leave in place the possibility of using another, less precisely defined, system which could lead to the imposition of regulatory requirements on a different basis."[299]

It should be noted, however, that:

> "...the statutory nuisance regime will continue to apply for land contamination issues in any case where an abatement notice under section 80(1), or an order of the court under section 82(2)(a), has already been issued and is still in force."[300]

---

[298] See above, pp. 543-544.
[299] Circular, para. 60.
[300] Paragraph 62.

Patently, therefore, enforcement action which has already been taken under the statutory nuisance regime is able to continue despite the coming into force of the Part IIA regime. Moreover, the Circular further notes that:

> "... the statutory nuisance regime will continue to apply to the effects of deposits of substances on land which give rise to such offence to human senses (such as stenches) as to constitute a nuisance, since the exclusion of the statutory nuisance regime applies only to harm (as defined in section 78A(4)) and the pollution of controlled waters."[301]

Radioactivity

Part IIA does not apply to harm or pollution of controlled waters in so far as this is attributable to radioactivity possessed by any substance.[302] It is, however, provided that the Secretary of State may make regulations applying the Part IIA regime in this situation; and the regulations may provide for the regime to take effect subject to such modifications as are thought appropriate.[303] In February 1998 the DETR (as it then was) submitted possible approaches to the application of the Part IIA to initial consultation. Further development of those proposals was expected in the light of that consultation exercise,[304] although at the time of writing, there are no further developments to report.

Works notices and cost recoupment under the Water Resources Act 1991 (sections 161 to 161D)

We describe elsewhere[305] the powers of the Environment Agency to take action to prevent or to deal with the pollution of controlled waters (and thereafter seek to recoup its costs);[306] and also how quite recently these powers of direct action and cost recoupment have been supplemented by the "works notice" procedure, under which the prevention/cleanup obligations fall not on the Agency but on the "polluter".[307]

Unlike the situations considered earlier in this discussion of the relationship between Part IIA and other cleanup/remediation regimes there is no clear statutory demarcation of the respective scopes of Part IIA and the provisions of the Water Resources Act 1991. Indeed, no such formal demarcation in this context exists. The Circular on Contaminated Land acknowledges this fact:

> "There is an obvious potential for overlap between these powers and the Part IIA regime in circumstances where substances in, on or under land are likely to enter controlled waters."

---

[301] Paragraph 63.

[302] Section 78YC.

[303] Section 78YC(a).

[304] Circular, para. 70.

[305] See Chapter 13.

[306] Water Resources Act 1991, s. 161.

[307] Sections 161A-D, added by the Environment Act 1995 (Sched. 22, para. 162).

Moreover:

> "The decision as to which regime is used in any case may have important implications, as there are differences between the two enforcement mechanisms."[308]

Rather than impose a legal demarcation between the boundaries of operation of each regime the approach in this context has been for problems to be averted by a process of informal consultation and co-operation between local authorities and the Agency. The Environment Agency's document *Policy and Guidance on the Use of the Anti-Pollution Works Notices* has been described, more generally, earlier.[309] Its present significance is that it presents the following guidelines, agreed by the DETR, in order to avoid potential overlap problems. To begin with, local authorities are expected to consult the Agency in any case where it may seem that land may be contaminated by reference to the "pollution of controlled waters" limb of the definition of that concept.[310] Once the Agency is aware of such a situation it may issue what is called "site-specific guidance" to the local authority with respect to the manner of performance of the latter's powers and duties under Part IIA.[311] In a case where it is the Agency, rather than a local authority, which first identifies land as actually or potentially giving rise to pollution of controlled waters, the Agency should notify the local authority so that the local authority may proceed to identify the land formally as contaminated.

These arrangements are designed to avoid action being taken under both regimes in relation to a single problem. The issue then arises, which of the two regimes should be favoured once the potential applicability of each is appreciated. The *Policy and Guidance* document, referred to above, expresses the view that where land is properly to be characterised as contaminated the provisions of Part IIA should be applied notwithstanding the potential applicability of the water pollution works notice procedures.[312]

THE EXPERIENCE TO DATE

It will have become apparent from the foregoing discussion that the new contaminated land regime under Part IIA of the Environmental Protection Act 1990 seeks "to place the burden of remediation on those responsible for the problem".[313] In other words, therefore, it can be said to reflect the application of the "polluter pays" principle. To date, the regime is still very much in its infancy both in terms of the time that it has actually existed and

---

[308] Circular, para. 63. In addition there may be a problem if a local authority were to purport to exercise powers under Part IIA and the Agency to exercise powers under the 1991 Act with a result that an individual might be served contemporaneously with two different and mutually incompatible notices.

[309] See above, pp. 521-524.

[310] See above, pp. 522-523.

[311] Guidance issued under s. 78V, which the local authority must "have regard to".

[312] See Circular, para. 64(d).

[313] Lawrence and Lee, (2003) 66 MLR 261 at p. 261.

the speed with which the regulatory bodies are performing their obligations and duties under the legislation. The general consensus seems to be that progress has been relatively slow, particularly with regard to initial matters, such as the drafting of inspection strategies by local authorities. Despite the fact that the Government made additional funds available to local authorities to implement the regime,[314] these new monies were not ring-fenced. Accordingly, it is entirely possible that some of the money was diverted to meet the costs of other priorities and responsibilities which arise at the local level.[315]

Originally it was predicted that the complex nature of the new regime would result in much litigation. However, to date the rather slow pace of implementation[316] has ensured there has been little in the way of formal regulatory action to give rise to dispute. However, it appears that this situation may before very long be likely to change.[317] Potential areas for public law challenge include the identification of "appropriate persons" who will be liable to pay for remediation work under the regime, the extent of the remediation which will be required either under a voluntary remediation statement or a more formal remediation notice, and the exercise by enforcing authorities of their obligations to exclude certain "appropriate persons" from liability groups and to apportion liabilities within such groups. Moreover, given the extensive procedural rule requiring consultation of potentially liable parties, and the emphasis on consensual rather than imposed solutions,[318] there will be much scope for legal arguments as to the proper interpretation and application of the primary and secondary legislation and the detailed statutory guidance to contribute constructively to the practical decisions reached by enforcing authorities. Given the level of costs associated with land remediation, even when cleanup is by reference to the "suitable for use" approach, it is inevitable that those who come under the regulatory gaze in terms of being "appropriate persons" may seek to ensure that the complex regime described in this chapter is being properly applied.

---

[314] In the comprehensive spending review for 2000, the Government allocated an additional £50 million over three years: see (2001) ENDS Report 322 at p. 19.

[315] This is a view shared by, amongst others, Hobley and McCann: see "Contaminated land in the UK – the current position" ELM 15 [2003] 79 at p. 84.

[316] Hobley and McCann suggest that "we are unlikely to see the bulk of initial determinations until well into 2005 and possibly 2006": *ibid.*

[317] See (2003) ENDS Report 341 at p. 27.

[318] See above, pp. 564-565.

Chapter 15

TOWARDS AN EU FRAMEWORK DIRECTIVE ON ENVIRONMENTAL LIABILITY

INTRODUCTION

On 23rd January 2002, following a decade or more of discussion and debate, the European Commission finally adopted a formal proposal for a Directive on liability for environmental damage.[1]

At the time of writing (late September 2003) the proposal is currently in the process of being steered through the complex EU legislative mechanisms – involving some quite substantial interplay between the European Commission, the elected European Parliament and the Council of Ministers. It is not possible to be sure whether, and if so when, agreement to a final text will be reached. Nor, accordingly, is it possible to know, as and when such final agreement may be reached, what will be the precise details of the legislative text.

It will be evident from the discussion which follows of the recent historical background to the European Commission's proposals that this has proven to be a complex subject upon which there has been ongoing difficulty in securing agreement, whether between Member States, or between stakeholders, on matters both of general scheme and of detail.

For a substantial period during the past 15 years it seemed that little progress was capable of being made towards agreement. Matters do seem now, however, to be moving forward, and with a fair momentum: albeit perhaps to a compromise achievement which may satisfy few proponents of EU action in this matter. Through much of 2002 and into 2003 there has appeared to be a firm desire between Member States that the long debate on the nature and scope of an EU environmental liability Directive should be brought at last to fruition; and sufficient progress has been made in discussions in the Parliament and in the Council for there to be good reason to think that before very long, and probably during 2004, the EU legislative process will come to conclusion and a Directive on this subject be adopted.

By late September 2003 the stage reached in the EU legislative process is that the Commission's proposals have been considered formally by the

---

[1] COM (2002) 17 final (OJ. C151/132): The full title of the proposed Directive is "Proposal for a Directive of the European Parliament and of the Council on environmental liability with regard to the prevention and remedying of environmental damage." See further on the Commission's proposal: Hatton (2002) 10 Environmental Liability 3; Brans (2002) 10 Environmental Liability 135; Jones (2002) Environmental Law and Management 5; and Thornton [2003] JPL 272.

European Parliament at First Reading[2] and the Parliament's many proposed amendments have been considered by the Council of Ministers. The Council has adopted by qualified majority[3] a Common Position,[4] in which its detailed position is evidenced as regards both the proposals initiated by the Commission and the amendments proposed by the Parliament.[5]

The next stage, in December 2003, will be the Second Reading by the Parliament (see update on p. xxii). At that stage the Parliament may propose no further amendments, in which case the measure will be adopted as a Directive in the form in which it exists in the Council's published Common Position. Alternatively, the Parliament may propose further amendments, in which case a process of co-decision "conciliation" within a committee of the Council and the Parliament will be triggered: a process designed to work out what compromise package may prove ultimately acceptable to both constituencies.

It is presently unclear whether or not Second Reading amendments will be voted by the Parliament. In all likelihood the Parliament will not choose simply to align itself in full with the Council's Common Position. It is to be anticipated that there will be support within the Parliament for the reinstatement of a substantial number of those amendments which the Council was unwilling to accept when reaching its Common Position. However, it may be significant that some of those amendments were voted through at First Reading with quite narrow majorities of members then present. At Second Reading it is necessary for amendments to be voted by an absolute majority of the whole Parliament (and not just of members present). It is therefore by no means certain how many of the amendments previously proposed to the Council may become reinstated if and when the matter may be put to a vote.

To sum up, we presently do not know whether or when a Directive will finally be agreed. However, given that the Parliament may not relish a return to "square one" following the Parliamentary elections in May 2004,

---

[2] 14th May 2003. The plenary session of the Parliament reviewed Reports from the Economic and Social Committee and also the Legal Affairs Committee of the Parliament. Following some substantial uncertainty the latter Committee was afforded jurisdiction in respect of this proposal, rather than the Parliament's Environment Committee. It appears that the Legal Affairs Committee is more sceptical of the merits of a "strong" EU liability measure than the Environment Committee would likely have been. Indeed the Legal Affairs Committee would appear to prefer a narrower and weaker liability measure than is acceptable to the Parliament in plenary session.

[3] Germany, Austria and the Republic of Ireland did not support the Common Position.

[4] Agreement was reached on core issues on 13th June 2003. The full text of the Common Position was released on 2nd September 2003.

[5] The Council's task in seeking to progress this measure has some added urgency in the light of the fact that a new Parliament will be elected in May 2004, and from this date the Parliament and the Council will contain members from the ten accession countries. Should the present proposal for a Directive not reach a certain stage of advancement in its legislative progress by May 2004 it will lapse and have to be reintroduced by the Commission. The Council deliberations of June 2003 made better progress in securing Member State agreement than had been anticipated; albeit that it did so by a combination of (i) amending a number of provisions proposed by the Commission, and (ii) refusing to accept the vast majority of the amendments proposed at First Reading by the Parliament.

there seems to be some good reason to believe that final agreement will be reached before very long. Should the Parliament vote no amendments at Second Reading that final agreement may come earlier still.

In these circumstances it would be inappropriate for this chapter to present a detailed review of the Commission's *original* proposals. It is evident that any final agreement which may be reached will be to a measure which will be different in a number of rather important respects from that originally proposed. Nor, given that matters will have moved on by the time this chapter sees light of day, does it seem valuable to describe and discuss comprehensively the large number of amendments which have been put forward by the European Parliament, but which have not – at least to date – found favour with the Council. Some of those amendments may well eventually find there way into any final text adopted, but it is certain that a good many will not.

In these circumstances this chapter will comprise:

- a brief summary of the policy development background to the Commission's present proposal, indicating how far the Commission's thinking on this "liability" issue has changed over the past decade or so;

- a summary of the proposal for a Directive as it presently exists in the Council's Common Position; and

- a quite selective and non-comprehensive discussion of certain matters upon which there appear to remain substantial differences between the Council and the Parliament.

The treatment, overall, will be rather less detailed than has been afforded the subject-matter of earlier chapters of this book. In addition to not wanting to describe in detail "shifting sands", this brevity of treatment is justified on a number of further grounds which warrant early mention because they help to put the EU proposals in proper context and perspective.

To begin with it should be emphasised that the Directive, if and when agreed, will not supercede *en bloc* the many and various liability rules which have been described so far in this book. The Commission's proposal, and the Council's Common Position, are clear on two important matters. First, the Directive does not lay down a template to which Member States' laws must match precisely. Rather, it provides that as a minimum certain liabilities must be secured within the laws of each Member State, but leaves much discretion to each Member State as regards how this may be achieved. As such, the EU Directive will not replace the laws which have so far been described. Those laws will remain, albeit that they may require modification in certain, quite slight, respects. Second, the Commission's proposal and the Council's Common Position make clear that the Directive describes a minimum liability regime which must be reflected within the laws of Member States. It does not, however, prevent Member States from maintaining in place (or subsequently enacting) liability laws which may be of broader import or which may be more stringent in nature.

The reference to "quite slight" in the previous paragraph needs explanation. As and when final agreement may be achieved and the proposed Directive adopted there will be a need for Member States to review their present laws on environmental liability in order to assess what changes may be necessary in order to achieve formal compliance with the Directive. It will become clear to many of the Member States, as they embark on this process, that a good many of the obligations under the Directive are already secured under their domestic law. This is not to underestimate the size of the task which will be presented to Environment Ministries in reviewing existing laws to assess where changes may be necessary; it is simply to warn against any initial assumption that the liability obligations provided for in the Directive will involve, in many Member States, enactment of very substantial new obligations over and above those which may currently exist. Indeed it might be naïve to think that it was not realisation of this fact that has allowed progress towards ultimate agreement to have moved forward quite substantially over the past 18 months. The message is that, whatever may in detail be agreed at EU level, a very substantial part of the rules described in earlier chapters of this book will remain intact.[6]

A further justification for the brevity of the discussion which follows is this: the liability proposals under review will, after adoption, apply with prospective effect only. This reduces quite substantially the practical importance to lawyers of monitoring minutely the deliberations of the Parliament and the Council. A contrast may be noted here with the keen interest which lawyers in the United Kingdom felt obliged to display towards both the pre-legislative policy development process and also the more formal legislative procedures connected with the contaminated land liability provisions (enacted in the Environment Act 1995, and brought into force in April 2000).[7] From at least the 1994 draft Bill stage in relation to what became the 1995 Act, and probably from an earlier date, it was evident that as and when these proposals might come into operation they would do so with retroactive effect – creating liabilities to fund the remediation of contaminated sites which would flow from historic connections with contaminated sites, and which would not depend on the

---

[6] In this chapter we deliberately refrain from seeking so early to make any detailed assessment of what changes may be needed to English law in order to meet the proposed Directive's minimum liability requirements. As will be apparent from earlier chapters in this Part of this book there exist already under English law a number of significant administrative powers under which competent authorities may impose cleanup or cost recoupment burdens on, amongst others, those who have caused harm to the environment. Indeed an assessment undertaken in mid-2002 by DEFRA indicated its provisional view that most of the provisions to be found within the Commission's proposals were more or less satisfied by existing United Kingdom environmental liability laws. And perhaps this is *a fortiori* the case as regards the provisions as they are contained within the Common Position (as described below).

[7] For a detailed discussion of the contaminated land regime, see above, Chapter 14.

actions of liable persons having been unlawful at the time those actions took place. Accordingly, the rules then under discussion had of necessity to be taken into account, even prior to enactment, in advising clients and in the drafting of transactional documents which would seek to make provision as between the parties for the allocation of environmental risk.

In contrast, the "prospective-only" nature of the EU obligations to be discussed in this chapter means that this impending liability regime will have application only in relation to conduct which will occur some years ahead. Even were final agreement very soon to be reached to the text of the Directive, and the Directive be adopted and come into force by publication in the Official Journal in 2004, it is anticipated that Member States will be afforded three years[8] during which to amend their domestic laws so as to make provision for the Directive's liability requirements. In other words the matter under discussion in this chapter is a liability regime which may, even with a fair head of wind, begin to apply only in relation to harm which is caused not before some date in 2007.

POLICY BACKGROUND TO THE PRESENT PROPOSALS

From civil liability to administrative liability: shifts in the Commission's thinking

An understanding of the proposals which were put forward by the Commission in early 2002 and which form the back-bone of the Council's Common Position described in this chapter, is assisted by some awareness of how the former body's thinking on the matter of environmental liability has developed over the past decade or so.

The development of some form of broad-based environmental liability Directive has been on the Commission's working agenda for more than a decade. However, the developments which have led to the present formal proposal may be regarded as dating principally from the Commission's experiences in seeking between 1989 and 1991 to make progress as regards a "strict" civil liability regime tailored to harm caused by "waste". Its controversial draft Directive proposals of 1989 were significantly recast in 1991, but in the face of continuing strong opposition from several quarters it agreed shortly after not to progress further those proposals.

This climb-down was, however, expressly stated to be "temporary only": the Commission promising to bring forward proposals for a *more broad-based civil liability regime*, a regime not tied only to harm caused by waste.

The European Commission's Green Paper (1993)

In 1993 the Commission issued an intriguing, but evidently rather hastily prepared, Green Paper, *Remedying Environmental Damage*,[9] indicating in

---

[8] A longer period than the more usual two years.
[9] COM 93 (47) final.

general terms its thinking as regards the possible shape of such a broad-based regime of strict civil liability for "environmental damage"[10] – a concept of damage which was defined within the Green Paper in a quite limited sense, as relating to the kinds of harm ordinarily compensable within national legal systems (i.e. personal injury, illness, property damage) but in situations where that harm has been caused by pollution.

Consultation on the Green Paper produced reaction not characterised by strong support. Some doubted the very need for such a measure at EU level (citing the principle of "subsidiarity" and calling into question any "level playing field" need for harmonisation of such civil liability laws).[11] Some felt that the measures would impact unduly severely on business, whilst others viewed the proposals as too modest, not covering "environmental damage *per se*" and not therefore giving sufficiently broad effect to the "polluter pays principle".

A further objection – and one which may insidiously have had some influence with the Commission – was that the case for establishing regimes of strict liability (in relation to traditionally compensable kinds of damage when caused by "pollution") within the ambit of Member State civil liability regimes more generally founded on notions of fault-based liability had not been adequately made. What, it was asked, was so special about harm caused by "pollution" that justified such very substantial differentiation between the treatment of claimants harmed in this way as compared with those harmed, for example, by more traditional accidents (where proof of fault is generally required)?[12]

The European Commission's White Paper – spring 2000

In the face of such a spectrum of opposition the Commission quite understandably took comfort in commissioning several research studies,[13]

---

[10] It should be recalled that the Green Paper regarded civil liability as just one limb of an integrated two-part policy approach to achieving remediation of environmental damage. The other aspect was to establish joint compensation funds into which contributions would be paid by those categories of operators whose actions had potential to do certain kinds of harm, and out of which funds would flow to pay for environmental remediation projects. This latter strand of policy appeared to one of the present authors to have more potential for securing environmental benefit than did the proposals for civil liability (see Jones, (1994) 8 TMA/ Environmental Liability Law Review 1). Nevertheless, following less than enthusiastic economic studies from consultants, allied also to concerns that such funding arrangements were too little targeted at actual individual polluters, this aspect of the Green Paper has received disappointingly little further attention. Note, however, the valuable review and discussion of such mechanisms by Hawke and Hargreaves (2003) 11 Environmental Liability 39.

[11] An argument which appears ultimately to have been won: see further below, p. 635.

[12] At the time such questions were greeted not by reasoned answer but rather by incredulity. See further, Chapter 1 above; and one of the present authors in Peter Wetterstein (ed.) *Harm to the Environment: the Right to Compensation and the Assessment of Damages* (OUP, 1996) Chapter 1.

[13] Principally a legal study of the then current environmental liability rules within and beyond the EU Member States, and a study of economic issues. The legal study was updated, and developed, quite recently by Chris Clarke – bringing his considerable expertise to this task. Document available on the European Commission website.

before coming forward in the spring of 2000 with a White Paper.[14] This Paper reflected, albeit covertly rather than overtly – and thereby causing much misunderstanding and confusion – something of a move strongly away from the Green Paper's earlier focus on *civil liability*, and towards Member State responsibility for ensuring, principally through the operation of *public law* systems of administrative direction and administrative cost recoupment, that those who threaten or cause environmental damage should bear the burden of preventing or repairing that damage.

The European Commission's Working Paper – summer 2001

This shift by stealth from notions of *civil liability* to an emphasis on effective systems of *administrative direction and/or administrative cost recovery* was taken a step further in July 2001 when the European Commission's Environment Directorate issued for consultation a quite brief Working Paper.[15]

Indeed, although again without making the matter explicit, this Working Paper produced pretty much a full "squaring of the liability circle". Whereas some had objected to the especially favoured civil liability status, bestowed by the 1993 Green Paper's proposals, upon those who had suffered illness or personal injury by "environmental" means (as compared with those who might have suffered such harm by other more conventional means), the Working Paper of 2001 indicated that the Commission was now minded to come forward with a proposal which would serve to maintain the internal rational coherence of systems of civil liability within Member States by *excluding entirely* such "environmental" personal injury-illness civil liability claims from it provisions.[16]

"Civil liability": a misnomer

This brief history may serve to explain a degree of linguistic confusion which has at times bedevilled, and may continue to bedevil, discussion of the various Commission proposals. The original proposals on waste (1989, revised in 1991) and the 1993 Green Paper were each quite properly described as proposals for harmonisation of Member States' rules on civil liability for "environmental damage" (albeit that the concept of "environmental damage" was defined in the unexcitingly limited way described above). Notwithstanding that the Commission's proposals have subsequently moved far away from civil liability for environmental damage, that label – "civil liability for environmental damage" – seems to remain engrafted within many minds, with a continuing power to mislead.

---

[14] For discussions, see Rehbinder (2000) 8 Environmental Liability 85; Faure (2001) 9 Environmental Liability 188; Bergkamp (2001) 9 Environmental Liability 251.

[15] Discussed by Bergkamp (2001) 9 Environmental Liability 207; and Faure and de Smedt (2001) 9 Environmental Liability 217.

[16] The Council's Common Position, discussed further below, states in Recital (14) that "[T]his Directive does not apply to cases of personal injury, to damage to private property or to any economic loss and does not affect any right regarding these types of damage."

The significance of these changes in Commission approach may be explained by indicating that had the Commission's present proposals followed the tenor of the 1993 Green Paper this chapter would fall not here but within Part 1 of this book. Given that, in contrast, the current proposals are founded on Member State obligations to secure remediation/liability burdens by imposing public law liabilities by the exercise of public law powers, this chapter is instead located here, within Part III, dealing with liabilities to *administrative direction* or to *administrative cost recoupment*.[17]

THE PRESENT PROPOSAL FOR A DIRECTIVE: THE COUNCIL'S COMMON POSITION

Introduction

A key overall objective of the proposed Directive may be seen in Common Position Recital (2), which explains, in language a little stronger than that used by the Commission itself in its original proposal, the link envisaged between liability rules and precautionary and preventive action on the part of those conducting activities which present risks to the environment:

> "The fundamental principle of this Directive should therefore be that an operator whose activity has caused the environmental damage or the imminent threat of environmental damage is to be held financially liable, in order to induce operators to adopt measures and develop practices to minimise the risks of environmental damage so that their exposure to financial liabilities is reduced."

Nevertheless, an inherent limitation as regards the practical utility of liability rules for achieving environmental ends is also noted. Recital (13) explains that:

> "Not all forms of environmental damage can be remedied by means of the liability mechanism. For the latter to be effective, there will need to be one or more identifiable polluters, the damage should be concrete and quantifiable, and a causal link should be established between the damage and the identified polluter(s). Liability is therefore not a suitable instrument for dealing with pollution of a widespread, diffuse character, where it is impossible to link the negative environmental effects with acts or failure to act of certain individual actors."

Not preclusive of more stringent national provisions

The Common Position makes clear in Recital (29) that:

---

[17] The exclusively "public law" nature of the present proposals is evident from Art. 3(3) of the Council's Common Position: "Without prejudice to relevant national legislation, this Directive shall not give private parties a right of compensation as a consequence of environmental damage or of an imminent threat of such damage." See also Common Position, Recital (14).

"This Directive should not prevent Member States from maintaining or enacting more stringent provisions in relation to the prevention and remedying of environmental damage ..."

Two points deserve mention here. First, we may note just how far justifications for this Directive have moved over the past decade. No longer is reliance placed on the "single-market" argument that harmonised EU liability rules are necessary in order to prevent businesses from seeking competitive advantage by shifting operations to Member States where the liability rules may be the least onerous. This argument, for which empirical support was never much apparent, seems now to have been discarded. The present proposal has as its legal base the "environmental protection" law-making powers of the European Union, and is not promoted as a "single-market" measure. Accordingly no problem, it appears, is now seen in Member States having between themselves significantly differing stringencies of environmental liability rules, so long as those which are the least stringent meet the minimum requirements laid down in the proposed Directive.

Secondly, the power to retain or enact more stringent rules than those to be found within the proposed Directive will make formal legal implementation of the Directive a rather different task than had the Directive proposed a fully harmonised community liability regime. Member States need focus, in that exercise, only on those aspects of their present liability rules which may seem to be less stringent than those provided for, as the Community minimum, by the Directive.

Strict liability for "environmental damage": fault-based liability for "harm to protected species and natural habitats"[18]

The main thrust of the Commission's proposal was that certain defined categories of operators,[19] whose occupational activities[20] present particular risks to the environment, should bear strict liability as regards being required to take action to prevent or to restore "environmental damage".[21]

---

[18] As will be explained below the adjective "protected" relates here both to the notions of "species" and "natural habitats". In other words, to be quite unambiguous the concept should be read as "protected species and protected natural habitats".

[19] The Common Position defines "operator" quite broadly so as to refer to "any natural or legal, private or public person who operates or controls the occupational activity or, where this is provided for in national legislation, to whom decisive economic power over the technical functioning of such an activity has been delegated, including the holder of a permit or authorisation for such an activity or the person registered or notifying such an activity" (Art. 2(6)). The Commission's original proposal was arguably narrower, focusing on the person who "directs the operation" of an activity covered by the Directive. The Common Position will, it seems, allow Member States a slightly wider margin of discretion as regards the persons upon whom liabilities are cast.

[20] Defined within the Common Position as "any activity carried out in the course of an economic activity, a business or an undertaking, irrespective of its private or public, profit or non-profit character" (Art. 2(7)).

[21] The meaning of this important concept is considered below.

In other words the proposed strict liability regime would not apply to all persons whose activities might cause environmental damage, but only to those categories of operators prescribed as bearing such liability within the Directive.[22]

However, although the provisions on "strict liability for environmental damage" are limited to such operators, the proposals apply more broadly, so as to cover *all categories of operations*, in so far as the harm threatened or harm done is to "protected species and protected natural habitats".[23] In the case of operators who fall within the categories bearing strict liability for environmental damage such liability in relation to protected species and habitats will also be strict.[24] For other operators such liability will be triggered only where the harm is a consequence of some fault or negligence.[25]

Prospective effect only

The Common Position, following the Commission's lead, contains provisions designed to secure that the Directive imposes liabilities prospectively and not retrospectively.[26] The key date in relation to such liabilities is the date three years after the Directive comes into force (by publication in the Official Journal). That "three years on" date is unlikely to be much before the beginning of 2008.

The Common Position states that the Directive shall not apply to:

- damage caused by an emission, event or incident that takes place before that date; or

---

[22] The operators so prescribed are listed by categories in what in the Council's Common Position is now Annex III.

[23] The Commission's original proposal labelled this category of harm "bio-diversity damage".

[24] This is because, as we shall see below, "damage to protected species and habitats" is one of three sub-categories within the general definition of "environmental damage" for which such Annex III operators bear strict liability.

[25] Note that the Parliament proposed an amendment under which, after five years operation, the Directive's liability provisions would apply so as to render *all* operators of *all* occupational activities (and not just those within Annex III) subject to strict liability in relation to all forms of environmental damage (i.e. damage to water, land and to protected species and habitats). This amendment was not adopted in the Council's Common Position.

[26] Remember that nothing in the Directive prevents Member States retaining/enacting more stringent measures: see, for example, the retrospective nature of the liabilities imposed in the UK as regards remediation of contaminated land, above at p. 540. In this context, note should also be taken of the provisions of the Wildlife and Countryside Act 1981 as amended by the Countryside and Rights of Way Act 2000. Under s. 28P of the 1981 Act (as inserted by the Countryside and Rights of Way Act 2000, s. 75(1) and Sched. 9, para. 1), various offences may be committed where a person has carried out an operation on a site of special scientific interest which damages any of the flora, fauna or geological or physiographical features of the land by reason of which the land was designated as an SSSI. In addition to being convicted of an offence, a defendant may also be served with an order by the court which convicts him requiring him (within a specified period of time) to carry out such operations for *restoring* the land to its former condition as may be specified in the order (s. 31(1) of the 1981 Act). A failure, without reasonable excuse, to comply with a s. 31 order amounts to a further criminal offence (s. 31(5)).

- damage caused by an emission, event or incident which takes place subsequent to that date, where that emission (etc.) derives from a specific activity which took place and finished before that date.[27]

This is followed, somewhat illogically perhaps, by a provision providing, in relation to such prospective liability, a 30-year period of limitation. Accordingly, where damage occurs more than 30 years after the occurrence of emissions (etc.), which themselves must have occurred after the Directive's liability start-date (see above), no liability will attach under the Directive.

The Common Position omits certain provisions contained within the Commission's original proposal which were designed to deal with issues of evidential uncertainty as regards when activities which may have caused particular damage occurred. In this connection two matters of some substantial practical significance are: (i) on whom may lie the burden of proof as regards when actions or their consequences occurred; and (ii) the weight evidentially of that burden. The principle proposed by the Commission in its original proposal was that where the competent authority can establish "with sufficient plausibility and probability" (something less, one assumes, than strict legal "proof") that the activity causing the damage occurred *after* the Directive's commencement date, the Directive shall apply unless this can be satisfactorily disproved by the operator.

The Commission's approach may be regarded as serving somewhat to have undermined the "headline" guarantee that the proposed Directive would not apply retrospectively. Under the Commission's proposal the position would, in fact, have been that the Directive would have applied to harm which could "plausibly" be argued to have been caused by activities after the commencement in any case where the defendant could not then prove that the activities in question actually occurred earlier. Such a rebuttable presumption might weigh heavily on an operator whose general activity presents a risk of the very kind of damage which has in a particular instance occurred. This kind of evidential principle is sometimes supported on the basis that it may provide a fair, evidential burden, response to the likely imbalance of knowledge, as between (i) competent public authorities and (ii) operators, in relation to the dates of past actions and precise historical activities of those operators. It appears not, on this occasion, to have met with approval on the part of the Council.[28]

---

[27] Common Position Art 17.

[28] Note also, that the Commission had proposed something of a make-weight within its original proposal. It proposed that if within one year of the commencement of the Directive's liability provisions, the operator lodged with the competent public authority an environmental impact statement of "reliable quality and veracity" evidencing "environmental damage which may have been caused by its activities", the shift in the evidential burden described above would not apply. This mechanism, by which operators would have been encouraged to "come clean" about the environmental harm they may have caused through their activities prior to commencement would have given rise to some significant tactical questions for operators. An important question in each case would have been to ask how far the information provided might serve as an admission of

Companies within Annex III: bearing strict liability for environmental damage

As indicated above, companies whose presumptively environmentally "risky" operations bring them within the categories of activities listed in Annex III to the Directive will under the proposals be required to bear the costs (either through their own actions or through reimbursement of public sector costs) of taking action to prevent or to clean up such "environmental damage" as they may imminently threaten or which they may have caused.[29] This obligation will take the form of a strict liability. It will exist regardless of fault being demonstrable or not on the part of the company in question.

There will be required within each Member State in this context a regime of strict liability as regards:

(a) liability to administrative direction requiring, as the case may be, the prevention or the remediation of environmental damage; and

(b) liability to reimburse the costs incurred by a public body in instances where such preventive or remedial action has been taken by such a body.[30]

The ambit of Annex III is clearly of importance. In the Common Position text it comprises some 12 paragraphs, each describing categories of activity by reference to particular schemes of control or regulation within existing EU environmental law Directives. The basic idea, albeit not carried to full logical conclusion, is that activities which, on account of environmental risk, have been singled out under EU law as requiring a regime of regulatory control, should for that same reason be appropriate candidates for strict liability obligations under this proposed Directive. Accordingly, the coverage of the Annex in the Common Position[31] extends to such matters as:

- the operation of installations subject to permit in pursuance of Council Directive 96/61/EEC concerning integrated pollution prevention and control;[32]

- waste management operations;[33]

---

liability in relation to national liability rules themselves applicable to actions and occurrences prior to the start-date for the Directive.

[29] See Common Position Articles 5 (Preventive action) and 6 (Remedial action).

[30] See further, Common Position Art. 8(1): "The operator shall bear the costs for the preventive and remedial actions taken pursuant to the Directive".

[31] The Annex in the Common Position largely comprises the same categories as in the Commission's original proposal. The main difference is in the sequence and arrangement of the categories.

[32] The Common Position excludes from this category "installations or parts of installations used for research, development and testing of new products".

[33] Such operations are specifically stated to include a number of more specific waste operations, but the Common Position adds to the Commission's original proposal the statement that "Member

- all discharges into inland surface water which require prior authorisation under Directive 76/464/EEC on pollution caused by certain dangerous substances; all discharges into groundwater which require prior authorisation under Directive 80/68/EEC on the protection of groundwater against pollution caused by dangerous substances; and the discharge or injection of pollutants into surface or groundwater which require a permit, authorisation or registration in pursuance of Directive 2000/60 establishing a framework for Community action in the field of water policy;

- water abstraction and impoundment of water subject to prior authorisation in pursuance of Directive 2000/60 (the Water Framework Directive);

- the manufacture, use, storage, processing, filling, release into the environment and onsite transport of dangerous substances, dangerous preparations, plant protection products, and biocidal products as each defined in existing EU regulatory Directives (e.g. Art. 2(2) of Directive 67/548 on the approximation of laws relating to the classification, packaging and labelling of dangerous substances);

- transport by road, rail, inland waterways, sea or air of dangerous goods or polluting goods;[34]

- the operation, in relation to releases into the air of polluting substances, of installations subject to authorisation under Directive 84/360 on the combating of air pollution from industrial plants;

- any contained use (including transport) involving genetically modified micro-organisms as defined in Directive 90/219;

- any deliberate release into the environment, transport and placing on the market of genetically modified organisms as defined in Directive 2002/12;[35]

States may decide that those operations shall not include spreading of sewage sludge from urban waste water treatment plants, treated to an approved standard, for agricultural purposes."

[34] As defined in Directives 94/55, 96/49 and 93/74 (transport by road, rail and sea respectively).

[35] The Parliament has called for a separate liability measure tailored to the specific risks presented by genetically modified organisms. See, for example, proposed First Reading Amendment 18a: calling for an article in the presently proposed Directive to call upon the Commission to present a proposal on liability for damage caused by GMOs, to supplement the present GMO regulatory framework. That proposal should, in particular, "address damage caused by the presence of GMOs in products, the producers of which did not make use of such organisms". The Council's Common Position has not adopted this proposed amendment, and has retained activities under the umbrellas of the "contained use" and "deliberate release" Directives as operations to which the strict liability provisions of the Directive shall apply. However, the limitation of the Directive to instances of "environmental damage" (as defined below), and the exclusion of any civil action under the Directive for damages, may render the proposed Directive a rather inadequate "liability-regime" response to this particular category of risk. In relation to GMOs it may be noted that the concerns as regards harm to species and/or habitats are by no means focused on the kinds of species and/or habitats which may have secured EU (or national) protection. Nor may there be likely to be pollution of water; nor harm to land which creates a "significant risk of human health

- transboundary shipment of waste, within, into or out of the EU, requiring an authorisation or prohibited under or by Regulation 259/93.

Mechanism for enforcement of liabilities: broad duties on Member State competent authorities

The mechanism proposed by the Commission for the enforcement of the preventive and remedial obligations referred to above is principally by way of the imposition of broad duties on the competent public authorities of Member States either to require liable operators to take necessary preventive or restorative action, or for the competent authorities to take such preventive or restorative action themselves and then to recover those costs from the liable operator.

This approach is followed in the Council's Common Position. However, the Council has re-drafted the Commission's proposals so as to require the imposition upon operators of a duty to act so as to prevent, or to minimise or begin to remediate damage, even in advance of any direction or action on the part of a competent authority.

The Common Position provides, for example, that where environmental damage has not yet occurred, but there is an imminent threat of such damage occurring, the operator shall without delay "take the necessary preventive measures". In other words this obligation to act arises independently of any direction from any competent authority.

This duty is supported by broad powers and duties in competent authorities within the Member State "at any time":

- to require the operator to provide information on such imminent threats or suspected imminent threats;

- to require the operator to take the necessary measures;

- itself to take those necessary measures.[36]

The Common Position continues:

> "The competent authority shall require that the preventive measures are taken by the operator".

What, one may ask, is the position if such an operator should fail to comply with the preventive obligations described above?

---

being adversely affected" (see the definition in the Common Position, Art. 2(1)(1)(c)). In so far as many of the concerns relate to (i) harm to bio-diversity within non-protected areas and harm to non-protected species, and/or (ii) economic loss to businesses following loss of 'organic' status following GMO contamination, the present proposals may seem rather inapposite to the task in hand. For a discussion of issues in this context, see Thornton (2001) 9 Environmental Liability 267.

[36] Common Position, Art. 5(3). Recovery of costs is authorised under Common Position, Art. 8, and "costs" is widely defined in Art. 2(6) to include, for example, administrative and legal costs.

There is here a key difference between the wording of the Commission's proposal and the wording of the Council's Common Position. The Commission's proposal stated:

"If the operator fails to comply ... the competent authority SHALL take the necessary measures."[37]

In contrast, the Common Position states:

"If the operator fails to comply ... the competent authority MAY take these measures itself."[38]

The implications of this change, from the Commission's contingent duty into the Council's contingent discretionary power, will be evident. Moreover, if we turn to the provisions of the proposed Directive on obligations in situations where harm has actually occurred and requires remediation we find a similar situation.

The Common Position text provides, again, that operators shall take the necessary remedial measures (as prescribed by the Directive).

The competent authority has power, at any time, inter alia:

- to require operators to take all the necessary remedial measures; and
- itself, in certain circumstances, to take such necessary measures.

This is backed by a provision that "[t]he competent authority shall require that the remedial measures are taken by the operator".[39]

However, as with preventive action, the Common Position states that:

"If the operator fails to comply ... the competent authority may take these measures itself."[40]

In contrast, the Commission's original proposal stated:

"If the operator fails to comply ... the competent authority shall take such measures."[41]

Determination of remedial measures

The Common Position provides that operators shall identify potential remedial measures in accordance with Annex II to the Directive, and shall

---

[37] Article 4(4) (emphasis added).

[38] Article 5(4) (emphasis added).

[39] Article 6(3).

[40] Article 6(3).

[41] Article 5(2). Note also the absence in the Common Position of any provision equivalent to the Commission's original Art. 6: This begins – "Member States shall ensure that the necessary preventive or restorative measures are taken: where it is not possible to identify the operator who caused the damage or the imminent threat ...; where the operator can be identified but has insufficient financial means ...".

submit them to the competent authority for approval.[42] Before coming to its decision as regards such approval the competent authority is required to invite certain categories of interested parties[43] to submit observations.

Annex II sets out what is described as a common framework to be followed in choosing the most appropriate measures as regards the remedying of environmental damage. It is in two parts: Part 1 dealing with remediation of damage to water, protected species and natural habitats; and Part 2 dealing with remediation of damage to land.

Remediation of damage to water, protected species and natural habitats: Part 1 of Annex II distinguishes between what it calls "primary", "complementary" and "compensatory" remediation. Primary remediation is remediation which returns the damaged resource to its baseline condition. Complementary remediation is any measure required to compensate for the fact that primary remediation to baseline level may not be possible. Compensatory remediation is designed to compensate for the losses to natural resources during the period between the occurrence of the original damage and effective remediation to base-line conditions (so-called "interim losses").

The basic principle governing remediation requirements is stated as follows:

> "Where primary remediation does not result in the restoration of the environment to its baseline condition, then complementary remediation will be undertaken. In addition, compensatory remediation will be undertaken to compensate for interim losses."[44]

In order to be clear that the concept of "interim losses" relates to loss of the services of natural resources *as benefits to and within the natural environment*, and does not include "losses" to *people* of the benefit of those natural resources, the Common Position states that such losses do "not consist of financial compensation to members of the public". Rather, remediation in relation to "interim losses" will consist of *additional* improvements to protected habitats and species or water at either the damaged site or another site, over and above that required for primary and complementary remediation.[45]

The guidance in Annex II indicates a range of criteria through the application of which the competent authority should select the appropriate remedial option.[46] In this context it may be noted that the discretion of competent authorities is such as to allow it to take into account costs of remediation and balance these against environmental benefits. So, for example, there is within Annex II a power to accept a lower level of

---

[42] Common Position, Art. 7.

[43] As defined in Common Position, Art. 12(1).

[44] Common Position, Annex II, para. 1(d).

[45] *ibid*, para. 1.1.3.

[46] *ibid*, para. 1.3.1.

primary remediation than is practically possible, in circumstances where this deficit is outweighed by the benefits of complementary or compensatory action elsewhere (and at lower cost).[47] There is also a power to "decide that no further remedial measures should be taken if … the cost of the remedial measures … would be disproportionate to the environmental benefits to be obtained."[48]

Remediation of land damage: Part 2 of Annex II begins with the following words:[49]

> "The necessary measures shall be taken to ensure, as a minimum, that the relevant contaminants are removed, controlled, contained or diminished so that the contaminated land, taking account of its current use or approved future use at the time of the damage, no longer poses any significant risk of adversely affecting human health … If the use of the land is changed, all necessary measures shall be taken to prevent adverse effects on human health."

It is also stated expressly that "a natural recovery option, that is to say an option in which no direct human intervention in the recovery process would be taken, shall be considered."[50]

Meaning of (i) "environmental damage" and (ii) "damage to protected species and natural habitats"

It will be evident that the meaning of these two concepts will be critical to an understanding of the scope of the broad obligations summarised above.

It is important to note at the outset, however, that the two concepts overlap. This is because the latter is a subspecies of the former: one limb of "environmental damage" is "damage to protected species and natural habitats". It is for this reason that Annex III operators will bear strict liability, rather than liability only in the event of fault or negligence, as regards such "damage to protected species and natural habitats". However, the concept of "damage to protected species and natural habitats" has also, it will be recalled, a significance of its own: in terms of the fault-based liability for "damage to protected species and natural habitats", to be imposed on operators of activities outside the ambit of Annex III.

"Environmental Damage" may come in any of three guises.

---

[47] *ibid*, para. 1.3.2.

[48] *ibid*, para. 1.3.3 (b).

[49] Words which might readily have flown from the pen of the draftsman of the UK contaminated land primary legislation and statutory guidance. Note also, the Common Position, Recitals (1): "Local conditions should be taken into account when deciding how to remedy damage"; and (7) "For the purposes of assessing damage to land … the use of risk assessment procedures to determine to what extent human health is likely to be adversely affected is desirable."

[50] Common Position, Annex II, para. 2.

Category 1: Damage to protected species and natural habitats

The *species* which are protected by the proposed Directive's liability provisions are those which are mentioned in Article 4(2) of, or Annex 1 to, Directive 79/409 on Wild Birds; and those within Annexes II and IV to Directive 92/43 on the protection of Habitats.

The *natural habitats* which are so protected are those mentioned in Article 4(2) of, or Annex 1 to, the Birds Directive; those within Annex II to the Habitats Directive, and also the breeding sites or resting places of the species listed in Annex IV to the Habitats Directive.[51]

In addition, the concept of "protected species and natural habitats" includes, *where a Member State so determines*, any habitat or species not so listed which the Member State "designates for equivalent purposes as those laid down" in the Birds and Habitats Directives. In other words it is optional for Member States how far the proposed Directive shall apply to species and habitats with national, but not also EU, protection.[52]

In relation to protected species and natural habitats the concept of "damage" is stated to comprise any damage that has "significant adverse effects on reaching or maintaining the "favourable conservation status"[53] of such habitats or species". Whether or not any such effect on reaching or maintaining favourable conservation status is to be regarded as a "significant adverse effect" is to be assessed by reference to a set of criteria for determining such "significance". This criteria is set out in Annex I to the Common Position.

Category 2: Damage to water

This comprises damage which significantly adversely affects the ecological, chemical and/or quantitive status and/or its ecological potential of the water as defined in the Water Framework Directive (Directive 2000/60).

Category 3: Damage to land

This is any land contamination which creates a significant risk of human health being adversely affected as a result of the direct or indirect introduction in, on or under land, of substances, preparations, organisms, or micro-organisms.

---

[51] These provisions in the Common Position go a little beyond the EU species and habitats designated within the Commission's original proposal. In particular, the reference to Art. 4(2) of the Birds Directive adds protection to migratory birds.

[52] Common Position, Art. 2(1)(3)(c). Contrast the mandatory application of the measure to such nationally protected species and habitats under the Commission's original proposal: see Commission proposal, Art. 2(2).

[53] This concept is itself elaborated at Common Position, Art. 2(4), defining such status separately as regards the favourable conservation of status of habitats, and of species.

Requirement as to causality

The proposals seek to provide some reassurance to industry that for the liability provisions to apply there will need to be found a clear link between the environmental harm in question and the specific activities of a particular operator.

The Common Position contains a number of statements and provisions which seem to be aimed at easing industry's general worries about "assumed guilt by association", of operators being rendered liable for damage simply because the harm is a kind of harm which a particular operator's activities might well have caused. A Recital to the Common Position declares that:

> "Not all forms of environmental damage can be remedied by means of a liability mechanism. For the latter to be effective ... a causal link should be established between the damage and the identified polluter(s). Liability is ... not a suitable instrument for dealing with pollution of a widespread, diffuse character where it is impossible to link the negative environmental effects with acts or failure to act of certain individual actors."[54]

Furthermore, within the substantive text of the proposed Directive itself it is provided, within an Article labelled "Exceptions", that the Directive:

> "... shall only apply to environmental damage or to imminent threat of such damage caused by pollution of a diffuse character, where it is possible to establish a causal link between the damage and the activities of individual operators."[55]

That such a causal link must be demonstrable may well provide operators with only a limited degree of reassurance. This is because certain key further questions are not addressed by the Directive. For example, such questions as:

- What will constitute a sufficient causal link for responsibility to attach?
- On whom will the evidential burden attach as regards proof of such causality? and
- How may that burden shift from one party to the other as evidence comes to be presented to the court?

The present proposal for a Directive appears quite content to leave these questions as matters to be left to the discretion of Member States. This makes some good sense. Decisions taken by each Member State on these matters are likely very largely to reflect that Member State's own particular rules on (i) the degree of proof required for success in civil claims (the argument for special rules on burden of proof in order to assist claimants being rather stronger where, for success, proof is required beyond a mere

---

[54] Common Position, Recital 13.
[55] Common Position, Art. 4(5).

"balance of probabilities"), and (b) compulsory disclosure by defendants of evidence relevant to the claimant's case (the case for a shift in the evidential burden being stronger where claimants may have difficulty obtaining such evidence).

In England where there is a system of (a) civil proof on a mere balance of probability, and (b) compulsory document disclosure, there would seem to be little head of steam developing for substantial change to rules of civil proof and evidence in the context of environmental claims.

Multiple causation

In cases where it may appear that the harm in question was caused by the combined activities of each of several operators, the Common Position provides that its provisions are without prejudice to any national provisions concerning cost allocation in cases of multiple party causation.[56]

In this matter the Common Position seems to confer on Member States a rather broader range of options than did the Commission's original proposal.[57]

Within the Commission's original proposal there was a provision which was evidently designed to provide a limit to the breadth of Member State discretion in this matter. That discretion, about how liability should be divided between multiple-causation parties, would have been subject to the following limitation:

> "Operators who are able to establish the extent to which the damage results from their activities shall be required to bear only such costs as relate to that part of the damage."[58]

This provision does not appear in the Common Position. The implications of this omission are not, perhaps, entirely clear.

On the one hand it may be argued that it will be permissible for each Member State to decide whether or not such an operator (who can establish the extent to which the damage is a result of his activities) may avoid the operation of whatever rules that Member State may generally apply as regards the division of burdens as between multiple causers of harm. This would, arguably, be in keeping with the apparent breadth of Member State discretion intended by Common Position, Article 9.

---

[56] Common Position, Art. 9.

[57] The Commission's original proposal for the Directive contained a provision under which where the competent public authority was able to establish with "a sufficient degree of plausibility and probability" that the same damage had been caused by the actions or omissions of several operators, Member States should be permitted to choose between two options: they might either provide that the relevant operators should be held jointly or severally liable for that damage; or they might provide that the competent authority should apportion the share of costs to be borne by each operator on a "fair and reasonable" basis. These options, and presumably others, remain open to Member States under the terms of the Common Position.

[58] Article 11(2).

Against such a conclusion, however, it may be argued that the scope of Member State discretion in cases of multiple party causation should be limited to cases where it is not possible to demonstrate what particular harm[59] was caused by any of several parties. It is in such circumstances, where proof of individual responsibility is lacking, that a solution by rule of law rather than measurement of responsibility by evidence is needed. In other words, the situation referred to (where an operator *can* establish the extent to which harm has resulted from his own activities) is one in which there is simply no call for the application of provisions of national law about how to divide liability as between those who have caused the harm in question but *cannot* establish by evidence the extent of their own contribution to that harm. On this view, which is suggested to be the better view, the position would remain as described in the Commission's proposed formula, notwithstanding that that phrase does not appear in the Common Position.

EXCEPTIONS, EXEMPTIONS AND DEFENCES

Exceptions and exemptions

The proposed Directive seeks to create some substantial "clear water" between its own environmental liability proposals and those liability regimes which apply to particular sectors of business activity which operate under established international agreements.

Therefore, for example, in the context of oil pollution the Common Position makes clear that it shall not apply in relation to actual or imminently threatened environmental damage which arises from an incident where liability is regulated by the Convention on Civil Liability for Oil Pollution Damage 1992 and the associated Compensation Fund Convention; Civil Liability for Bunker Fuel Convention 2001; Convention on Liability and Compensation for Damage in Connection with the Carriage of Hazardous and Noxious Substances by Sea 1996; and Convention on Civil Liability for Damage Caused by Carriage of Dangerous Goods by Road, Rail and Inland Navigation Vessels 1989.[60]

In the nuclear context the Directive will not apply to damage or risks from nuclear activities covered by the Treaty establishing the Atomic Energy European Community; nor will it apply to any incident or activity in respect of which liability or compensation is governed by the Paris Convention 1960, the Vienna Conventions 1963 and 1997, the Joint Protocol 1988 relating to the application of the Paris and Vienna

---

[59] Or, perhaps, to show by evidence what level of contribution was made by any such party to a general level of harm done.

[60] Common Position, Art. 4(2) and Annex IV. The Common Position goes beyond Commission proposals in requiring, in relation to these Conventions, that the exception is limited to cases where these Conventions are "in force in the Member State concerned".

Conventions, the Brussels Convention 1971 or the Convention on Supplementary Compensation 1997.[61]

More generally, and unsurprisingly, the proposals do not apply to "activities the main purpose of which is to serve national defence or international security, nor to activities the sole purpose of which is to protect from natural disasters".[62]

Similarly proposals will not apply to environmental damage or imminent threats of such damage where the damage is caused by:

- acts of armed conflict, hostilities, civil war or insurrection; or
- a natural phenomenon of exceptional, inevitable and irresistible character.[63]

Defences

Article 8, paragraphs 3 and 4, of the Common Position contains important and controversial provisions, which it may be helpful to set out in full.

Under paragraph 3:

> "An operator shall not be required to bear the cost of preventive or remedial actions taken pursuant to this Directive when he can prove that the environmental damage or imminent threat of such damage:
>
> (a) was caused by a third party and occurred despite the fact that appropriate safety measures were in place; or
>
> (b) resulted from compliance with a compulsory order or instruction from a public authority other than an order or instruction consequent upon an emission or incident caused by the operator's own activities."

Under paragraph 4:

> "The Member States may allow the operator not to bear the cost of remedial actions taken pursuant to this Directive where he demonstrates that he was not at fault or negligent and that the environmental damage was caused by:
>
> (a) an emission or event expressly authorised by, and fully in accordance with the conditions of, an authorisation conferred by or given under applicable national laws and regulations which implement those legislative measures adopted by the Community specified in Annex III, as applied at the date of the emission or event;

---

[61] *ibid*, Art. 4(4) and Annex V.

[62] Common Position, Art. 4(6), extending the scope of the exemption within Commission proposal Art. 3(7).

[63] Common Position, Art. 4(1).

(b) an emission or activity or any manner if using a product in the
course of an activity which the operator demonstrates was not
considered likely to cause environmental damage according to
the state of scientific and technical knowledge at the time when
the emission was released or the activity took place."

The "defences" under paragraph 4, both applicable only where no fault or
negligence in the operator is demonstrable, crept into the Commission's
proposals at a late stage in its deliberations. They are generally thought not
to have been part of the package put together within the Environment
Directorate, but to have been included as the "price" which that
Directorate had to pay to have the proposal adopted collectively by the
College of Commissioners. They are matters upon which a good deal of
impassioned discussion has already occurred – within, for example, the
European Parliament and its several committees. Indeed, for much of the
first part of 2002 there was good reason to believe that Member States – in
discussions within the Council of Ministers – were agreed that the
"compliance with permits" defence should be removed from the proposal.
Later in the year there came indications that a significant number of
Member States were rethinking their positions on this matter, as seems
evident from the above Common Position.

A good deal of uncertainty surrounds the precise scope of paragraph 4. To
begin with it is not clear whether or not the two clauses, (a) and (b), should
be divided by a missing word "or", thereby providing two separate
"defences". In support of such a contention is the fact that in the
Commission's original proposal these matters were treated as providing
quite different and discrete reasons for exemption from liability.[64] It may
not, however, be assumed that there has been a typographical omission in
the present Common Position. In the published minutes of the
Environment Council of 13th June 2003 (2517th Council Meeting) it is
stated to be a "mitigating factor" for an operator who has not been at fault
or negligent to demonstrate also that the emission or activity in question
was expressly authorised by the competent national authority *and* that the
emission (etc.) was not considered likely to cause damage, in the light of
the state of scientific and technical knowledge at the time of the event. The
inclusion here of the word "and", rather than "or", suggests quite strongly
that these two matters have deliberately been combined within the
Common Position into a two-requirement single ground for "mitigation" of
liability. As such "state of the art" becomes not a defence in its own right,
but a means of showing absence of fault where this is necessary in order to
benefit from an initially quite different defence, that of compliance with a
regulatory permit. In one remarkable stroke the Common Position may
have denied "state of the art" a discrete existence as a defence, and
narrowed substantially the ambit of the permit-compliance defence.

A second uncertainty as regards the scope of paragraph 4 of Common
Position Article 8 relates to the initial words: "The Member States may

---

[64] The Commission may want, in effect, to put its "or" in again.

allow the operator not to bear the cost ...". It is unclear whether this phrase means (i) "may prescribe laws under which in the circumstances described below a complete defence may be raised to liability to bear costs ... etc."; or (ii) "may in its discretion and on a case by case basis excuse an otherwise liable operator from liability to bear costs ...". If the latter is the better interpretation it would seem inappropriate to refer to this paragraph as providing a "defence": rather, it may do no more than to suggest grounds upon which an operator may be permitted by a Member State to make a "plea for mercy".

Role of individuals and NGOs within the proposed liability framework

Over the past decade there has been much debate about the position of adversely affected individuals and environmental NGOs within any proposed scheme of environmental liability.

Under the proposals as set out in the Council's Common Position such persons are afforded no special standing to take action *directly* to seek to render operators "liable".[65]

Instead, such persons are afforded rights –

- to submit to the competent authority any observations relating to such damage or imminent damage;

- to request the competent authority to take action under the Directive, such request being accompanied by the relevant information and data[66] supporting the observations submitted.

Where the request for such action and the accompanying observations show in plausible manner that environmental damage exists, the competent authority is required "to consider such observations and requests for action".[67]

The competent authority shall then, as soon as possible, inform those who have requested action of its decision to accede to or to refuse that request, and shall provide reasons for that decision.[68]

Following such a reasoned decision the affected party or interest group is required by the proposed Directive to:

---

[65] The Parliament proposed an amendment which would have conferred such right to take direct legal action against an operator in situations where there is an imminent threat of damage to the environment. The Common Position does not adopt this amendment.

[66] The Commission's proposal required that the "citizen" or NGO might be required to provide "all" relevant information. This obligation seems to have been moderated in the Common Position, so that it will suffice to provide sufficient data to make the contentions being made "plausible".

[67] Common Position, Art. 12(3).

[68] *ibid*, Art. 12(4).

"have access to a court or other independent or impartial public body competent to review the procedural and substantive legality of the decisions, acts or failure to act of the competent authority."[69]

Financial security

The proposal does not require compulsory insurance or other financial security.

The Commission's original proposal required Member States to "encourage" the use by operators of any appropriate insurance or other forms of financial security.

The Parliament proposed an amendment which would have required Member States to "ensure that operators use appropriate insurance or other forms of financial security to cover their responsibilities" under the Directive. The obligation would not, however, apply across the board immediately upon the liability provisions taking effect, but would operate from differing dates depending on whether the operation in question fell within the Integrated Pollution Prevention and Control regime.

The Common Position does not adopt this proposed amendment. Instead it modifies slightly the Commission's "encouragement" approach. The Common Position does not relate such encouragement specifically to "insurance", but provides more generally that Member States shall "take measures to encourage the development of financial security instruments and markets by the appropriate economic and financial operators" with the aim of "enabling operators to use financial guarantees to cover their responsibilities under the Directive".[70]

The language in which these requirements are couched clearly leaves much discretion to individual Member States. They may seem to require little of Member States. Such significance as they may have perhaps lies mainly in the reporting requirements of the Directive, under which each Member State will be required to send to the Commission information about its actions in relation to the various articles of the Directive, including the ways in which it may claim to have honoured these particular exhortations.[71]

---

[69] *ibid,* Art. 13(1).

[70] Common Position, Art. 14(1). Under Art. 14(2) the Commission must report, *inter alia*, on the availability of insurance and other financial instruments. However, this report is not due until eight years after the Directive comes into force.

[71] See Common Position, Art. 18.

INDEX

P

Q

R

S